THE LIBRARY
ST. MARY'S COLLEGE OF MARYLAND
ST. MARY'S CITY, MARYLAND 20686

W9-BKW-586

HABSBURG AND BOURBON EUROPE

1470–1720

HABSBURG AND BOURBON EUROPE

1470–1720

Roger Lockyer

LONGMAN

Longman
1724-1974

LONGMAN GROUP LIMITED
London
*Associated companies, branches and representatives
throughout the world*

© Roger Lockyer 1974

*All rights reserved. No part of this publication may be
reproduced, stored in a retrieval system or transmitted in
any form or by any means—electronic, mechanical,
photocopying, recording or otherwise—without the prior
permission of the copyright owner*

First published 1974

ISBN 0 582 35038 7

Distributed in the United States of America by
Longman Inc., New York, N.Y.

*Printed in Great Britain by
Western Printing Services Ltd, Bristol*

Contents

PART ONE

Habsburg and Bourbon Europe

ONE

Europe in the Late-medieval, Early-modern Period

Some fifty million people—less than the population of presentday Britain—were spread out over the continent of Europe at the close of the Middle Ages. They lived mainly in villages or isolated farmsteads, and were primarily engaged in agriculture and associated crafts. Industry was on a small scale, except in areas such as south-east Germany, where mining and metallurgy were major operations; Holland, which specialised in shipbuilding and fish-processing; and Flanders and northern Italy, where cloth manufacture was organised on highly intensive capitalist lines. In Europe as a whole, towns were the exception rather than the rule, and by twentieth-century standards they were very small. 'Big' towns were those which had twenty thousand inhabitants, and even in these the citizens were constantly aware of the fields and woods which surrounded them and of the country-dwellers who swarmed in on market and feast days to sell their produce and buy those articles which they could not make themselves. The rhythm of daily life was that of the seasons, and since good quality candles were a luxury most people got up at dawn and went to bed at sunset. Hours of work were long; holidays—other than saints' days and holy days— were virtually unknown; and long-distance travel was confined to the rich, to soldiers, pilgrims and beggars, or to those who were driven on by emotional or economic necessity. The fastest speed at which a man could travel was that of a galloping horse, and although princes and great merchants had their own postal services there was no regular system of communication for ordinary persons. The major concern of men and women throughout Europe was getting enough to eat, since for most of the people most of the time there was only a narrow gap between subsistence and starvation. Townsfolk as well as peasants prayed for good weather, and at harvest time many city streets were deserted while the inhabitants worked in the nearby fields to gather in the precious crops.

Some regions of Europe were more densely populated than others. In the Netherlands, for instance, the establishment of the cloth industry had led to the growth of an urban proletariat in towns such as Ghent and Bruges, while shipbuilding, fishing and ancillary services had caused the expansion of Amsterdam and Antwerp. In north-west Germany the Hansa towns, of which the most important were Lubeck and Hamburg, had swollen in size and importance as a result of their dominant position in overseas trade (though their supremacy was now coming to an end) and it was trade once again, though this time with Italy, that had promoted the expansion of cities like Nuremberg and Augsburg. France had only one really big city, Paris, but this was the greatest metropolis in western Europe, with a population estimated at 200,000. There was nothing to compare with it north of the Alps, but in Italy big towns were relatively common. Even in the pastoral south Naples had some 100,000 inhabitants, while in the urbanised north Venice and Milan had 100,000 each, and Florence and Rome were not far behind. In the general European context, however, large cities were untypical. For the majority of people a town was a place to be visited only occasionally, not to be lived in, and power and wealth were derived from landowning rather than commerce or industry.

The average expectation of life in late-medieval, early-modern Europe was low, and more babies died in childbirth than survived. This was true on both sides of the line which divided the rulers—those of 'gentle' birth who scorned manual labour and were usually wealthy enough to devote their lives, if they so wished, to the pursuit of pleasure —from the ruled. Because of the high rate of infant mortality, women were valued chiefly as child-bearers, tended to marry early, and were soon worn out by repeated pregnancies. Medicine was primitive and only the rich could afford to consult a doctor—not that this was to their advantage, since they were more likely to die from the remedies he prescribed than from the illness itself. Pain and physical deformity were accepted as part of the human condition, to be stoically endured, and plagues and pestilences were interpreted as God's punishment on wayward sinners. As most people lived in hovels that were cramped, insanitary and overcrowded, they could put up little effective resistance to disease, nor did their diet help. Meat was in short supply during the winter months, as were fruit and green vegetables, and vitamin deficiency must have been a common condition, though not recognised as such.

In the mid-fourteenth century western Europe had been decimated by the Black Death. Its incidence varied from place to place, but in many areas—central Germany, for instance—it wiped out between a third and a half of the population. The effect was dramatic. In towns and villages houses were left empty and rotting, while in the countryside fields that had long been cultivated reverted to scrubland. A smaller population meant a smaller demand for food and manufactures, and the Black Death was therefore followed by a prolonged slump. Manmade disasters worsened matters. For over a hundred years, from 1337 to 1453, England and France were at war, and although fighting was not continuous throughout this period, when it did take place it was destructive not only of people, buildings and crops, but also of the framework of law and custom on which an ordered society had gradually been constructed. Much the same was true of the Hussite wars in Bohemia in the early fifteenth century, and indeed there were few parts of Europe that were not ravaged by fighting at one time or another during the period 1350-1450. With the reduction of the human population by pestilence and war, wolves returned to claim their inheritance. They were to be seen and heard in the outskirts of Paris, in the hills of Rome, and in many other places from which they had much earlier been driven out. Human wolves also increased in number, for many men, particularly ex-soldiers, found it easier to make a living by forming robber bands than by pursuing more peaceful and legitimate pursuits. It is hardly surprising that the art of this period shows an obsession with death and decay, and the Dutch historian, J. H. Huizinga, in a justly famous book, describes the introspection, the lack of confidence, and the endemic violence that characterised what he called The Waning of the Middle Ages.

The situation was not, however, uniformly bad. Conditions varied sharply between one locality and another, and what was true of this year might not be so of next. In Europe as a whole, recovery was setting in by about 1470. The main reason for this seems to have been first the stabilisation and subsequently the growth of population as the effect of the Black Death at last wore off. The timing and pace of recovery varied, but as numbers increased so land was taken back into cultivation, houses were rebuilt, and the demand for food and goods increased. There was no sudden switch from slump to boom, from decay to regeneration, nor did plague and war come to an end. But it was largely out of the experience of the terrible century from 1350 to 1450 that the attitudes of early modern Europe were formed. The spiritual hunger created and unsatisfied during those years when death was ever-present undermined the authority of the Catholic Church and prepared the ground for the Reformation and Counter-Reformation; while the overriding need for order, even at the cost of liberty, led to the emergence of the Renaissance monarchies, in which power was focused on the centre and the will of the king was made the final arbiter.

The Holy Roman Empire

Among the states of western Europe the greatest in theory was one which, in practice, hardly existed at all, namely the Holy Roman Empire. This began its history on Christmas Day 800, when Charlemagne, apparently against his will, was crowned and hailed as Emperor by Pope Leo III at Rome. Leo planned to extend the authority of the see of Rome, and assumed that by his action he had made the Emperor into the secular arm of the papacy. But once the Holy Roman Empire had been created it acquired a reality of its own, and the wearers of the imperial crown became as much the rivals as the servants of the papacy. This rivalry led, in the eleventh century, to the struggle known as the Investiture Contest, in which both Popes and Emperors tried to assert their supremacy. It was the Emperors who were ultimately defeated, and the effective end of the medieval Empire came with the death of the Emperor Frederick II in 1250. The title survived, but it was now simply one of the dignities assumed by the ruler of Germany. Rudolph of Habsburg, who became German king in 1273, recognised this by abandoning any claim to central and southern Italy, though he retained his nominal sovereignty over the northern part. Some eighty years later Charles IV renounced even this shadowy authority, and when Frederick III was crowned Emperor in 1452 he was formally described as ruler over the 'Holy Roman Empire of the German Nation'.

This Empire straddled a large part of central Europe, stretching from the Alps in the south to the Baltic in the north, and from France in the west to Hungary and Poland in the east. Although the Emperor was nominal ruler over this vast area and its twenty million inhabitants, real power lay with some fifty ecclesiastical and thirty secular princes, of whom the most important were the seven Electors—the Duke of

Saxony, the Margrave of Brandenburg, the King of Bohemia, the Count-Palatine of the Rhine, and the Archbishops of Mainz, Cologne and Trier. These had the sole right to elect the Emperor, and they also formed the first Estate of the imperial Diet (*Reichstag*). There were, in addition, many smaller rulers—over a hundred counts, for instance; some seventy prelates; and about two thousand 'Imperial Knights', mainly concentrated in south-west Germany, who clung to their independence despite unfavourable social and economic conditions and owed allegiance solely to the Emperor. There were also some eighty imperial free cities which constituted the third Estate in the Diet (the second being composed of the non-electoral princes).

The consolidation and centralisation of authority which became characteristic of western Europe in the sixteenth century was to be found in Germany at the princely rather than the imperial level. The more important princes, as well as some of the lesser ones, usually had a privy council and financial chamber, and employed as administrators men who had been trained in Roman Law, which put the emphasis upon the authority of the ruler rather than the rights of the ruled. This does not mean that the princes were absolute within their own dominions. They were limited, in theory at any rate, by their allegiance to the Emperor, and in practice by the existence of representative assemblies of Estates, which had come into existence during the Middle Ages. The nobles were usually predominant in such assemblies, with the towns as the other main element: the peasants were rarely represented. Generally speaking the Estates had the sole right to vote taxes and were often invited to take part in legislation, since their consent made the task of law-enforcement easier. The strength of the Estates varied from one principality to another, but the history of the subsequent two hundred years was to show that a determined and able ruler could go a long way towards subduing and even eliminating them. While the princes were not absolute, then, they had powerful instruments at their disposal, if they were willing and able to use them, and could assert their independence of the Emperor at the same time as they eroded the political liberties of their own subjects.

Imperial administration was nothing like so centralised as that of the principalities. This was not for want of trying on the part of individual Emperors, who were only too conscious of the fact that they were in danger of becoming 'but perfect shadows in a sunshine day'. It might have been to their advantage to strengthen the institutions of the Empire, but unfortunately for them they were split personalities, part

German Emperors, part territorial magnates in their own right. As head of the house of Habsburg, the Emperor had interests which extended beyond the bounds of the Empire and might well run counter to its needs. This was particularly the case after 1477, when Maximilian I, son and heir to the Emperor Frederick III, married Mary of Burgundy and thereby acquired the greater part of the Burgundian inheritance. The fact that the concerns of the Habsburg Emperor were not necessarily identical with the advantage of Germany as a whole meant that the movement to regenerate the Empire and its administration grew up in opposition to the Emperors rather than in support of them, and centralised institutions which might have strengthened imperial power were in fact conceived as checks upon it. Maximilian, who was elected Emperor following the death of his father in 1493, therefore concentrated on developing family interests and his hereditary estates rather than the imperial authority, and much the same was true of his successor, Charles V.

With the collapse of the reform movement in the sixteenth century the Holy Roman Empire lost its last chance of survival as a political heavyweight. It was now the Habsburgs who gave prestige and authority to the Empire rather than the Empire to the Habsburgs, and although the formal recognition of this fact was delayed until 1806 (when Napoleon officially decreed the death of the Holy Roman Empire) it was already becoming apparent by 1500. When Charles V informed the Diet in 1521 that 'the Empire from of old had not many masters, but one, and it is our intention to be that one', he was a bad historian and a false prophet. The Empire had long had many masters, namely the princes, and even Charles, with his apparently limitless resources in men and money and the prestige that accrued to him as ruler over so large a part of the known world, could not turn back the tide.

Burgundy

To the west of the Empire were the duchy of Burgundy (part of which, in theory at any rate, fell within the imperial borders) and the kingdom of France. The heartland of Burgundy had originally been in France, in the area around Dijon where wine of that name is still grown. This territory had been handed over by the kings of France to a junior branch of the Valois house, and although it reverted to the crown in 1361 it was shortly afterwards granted to Philip the Bold, fourth son of

John II of France. Philip married Mary of Flanders, who brought with her by way of dowry not only Franche-Comté, to the east of France, but also Artois and Flanders, on the north-western border. During the first half of the fifteenth century Hainault, Brabant and Luxembourg were also added to the duke's dominions, and by the time Philip's son, Charles the Bold, became ruler in 1467, Burgundy was already an important state and looked as though it might eventually stretch unbroken from the North Sea to the Alps. The acquisition of the Low Countries, which were wealthy and densely populated—especially when compared with the old duchy lands around Dijon—shifted the centre of gravity of the Burgundian state towards the north-west, and Brussels became the ducal capital.

Charles the Bold's two great ambitions were to turn Burgundy into an independent kingdom, and to consolidate his possessions by taking control of the various territories which separated the Low Countries from Franche-Comté. He came within an ace of achieving his first ambition, but the Emperor Frederick III, alarmed by the rapid increase of Burgundian power, changed his mind at the last moment and refused to confer the royal title. As for the second, Charles acquired a complex of rights in Alsace but was foiled in his attempt to gain possession of Lorraine. His enemies, led by Louis XI of France, leagued against him, and in 1477 Charles was killed in battle. Charles's heir was his twenty-year-old daughter Mary, and Louis XI promptly invaded the ducal territories in order—so he declared—to protect Mary's inheritance. His real aim, of course, was to recover Burgundy for France, and he may have planned to effect this by marrying Mary. The young duchess, however, had her own views and was already engaged to Maximilian, the future Emperor. Faced with the French invasion she took her stand as the champion of Burgundian independence and won over the representatives of the cities and provinces of the Netherlands by summoning the Estates General to Ghent, where she granted them the 'Grand Privilege', formally confirming their separate customs, laws and 'liberties'.

Mary's action, and the subsequent charters in which she confirmed these 'liberties', undid much of the work of centralising ducal authority and creating effective institutions of government which had been one of the major achievements of her father's short but fruitful reign. This, however, was the price she had to pay for survival. Louis XI was a ruthless and remorseless foe, and unless Mary had checked him by force she would have had no duchy to rule over. With popular backing and military assistance from her husband, Maximilian, she fought off the French challenge, and although she died in 1482 she bequeathed a substantial inheritance to her son, Philip. In that same year Louis XI, recognising that he would be unable to extend French rule to the north-west except at too great a cost, signed the Treaty of Arras with Maximilian. By this he agreed to renounce his claims to the Netherlands in return for Maximilian's acknowledgement of the fact that the old duchy lands around Dijon were to be and remain an integral part of the kingdom of France.

Mary had apparently succeeded in preserving Burgundy as a separate political entity, but this was really an illusion. True she had saved it from absorption into France, but by her marriage she had linked its fortunes inextricably with those of the house of Habsburg to which her husband belonged. Squeezed between the Empire on one side and France on the other, Burgundy was too small and too fragmented to preserve more than a nominal independence. Its rulers, although they were proud to bear the style of Duke of Burgundy, acquired greater titles and more extensive responsibilities. Duke Philip, for instance, became King of Spain by right of marriage, and his son, Charles, was elected Emperor. Burgundy could bask in the reflected glory of its dukes, but it became little more than a pawn in the dynastic power game.

France

France, with a population of some fifteen millions, was one of the major states in western Europe, but the long struggle with England had sapped the strength and authority of her kings. Charles VII ascended the throne in 1422, but the English occupied the greater part of his kingdom and he needed all the help he could get, especially that of Joan of Arc, to drive them out. By 1436, however, he was master of Paris, and for the next twenty-five years he was free to concentrate on the task of restoring the prestige and power of his crown. Victory made all things possible. An army had been raised to defeat the enemy, and regular grants of money had been voted from 1440 onwards. With these resources Charles was able to impose his will not only on the English but also on his more recalcitrant subjects. The great magnates were brought to heel, as was the Church, and by the time Charles VII died in 1461 the authority of the crown was more firmly based than it had been for over a century.

Louis XI continued this process. Magnates who dared to challenge him were executed or imprisoned, and some of the great fiefs, such as the Duchy of Anjou and the County of Provence, were incorporated into the crown. Taxation was increased, as was the standing army which it helped to maintain, and although Louis was faced with a number of magnate revolts he managed to suppress them by a combination of luck and judgment. Abroad he was less successful. He failed in his takeover bid for all the Burgundian lands, and he was unable to bring off his scheme for a marriage alliance between the French and Spanish royal houses. Nevertheless he made tangible gains, not simply recovering the old duchy of Burgundy for France but also snatching from Spain the Pyrenean territories of Roussillon and Cerdagne. Louis XI's achievement, in short, was considerable. He encouraged the economic revival of France after the devastation of the Hundred Years War, he restored the authority of the crown, and he undermined magnate power by resuming some of the lands and jurisdictions which earlier kings had parted with. These policies were continued and elaborated by his successors.

Louis's intervention in Burgundy had not been due simply to a desire to regain for the French crown what had earlier belonged to it. He dreaded the emergence of a major state on France's eastern border, and he was already aware of the menace of expanding Habsburg power. Unfortunately his attempt to protect the long-term interests of his country and dynasty boomeranged. Instead of uniting Burgundy to France he drove Mary, politically as well as personally, into the arms of Maximilian, thereby considerably augmenting the strength of his rivals and potential enemies. And by failing to secure a Spanish marriage alliance he left the way open to Maximilian, who, whatever his failures as a politician, was a superb matchmaker. By the time Louis died, therefore, it was already becoming clear that France, having saved herself from English domination, would now have to struggle to avoid absorption into a Habsburg family empire. In this respect, as in those already mentioned, Louis's reign sets the pattern of French royal policy for the next hundred years.

Spain

To the south of France, beyond the Pyrenees, a new state was slowly being born. The old Visigothic kingdom of Spain had collapsed under the repeated assaults of Arab invaders (the Moors) in the eighth century, and for a time it looked as though they would take over the entire peninsula. Christian resistance continued in the north, however, and this provided the nucleus from which the kingdom of Leon emerged. At a later stage Castile split off from Leon and became a separate kingdom. There were also other regions which had managed to preserve their independence; among them Portugal (which became an independent kingdom in the twelfth century), the Basque kingdom of Navarre, and Catalonia (later part of the kingdom of Aragon). Until the early years of the eleventh century it was still not certain that any of these Christian states would survive, but by that date the impetus of the Arab invasions had been lost and the slow process of reconquest (the *Reconquista*) began with the capture of Moorish Toledo in 1085.

On a number of different occasions the Christian kingdoms (with the exception of Portugal) were united by brute force or marriage alliances, but in the absence of any system of primogeniture this precarious unity was invariably fragmented on the death of a ruler, since his sons shared out the various territories among themselves. In the early thirteenth century, however, Leon was finally incorporated into Castile, and the *Reconquista* got under way again with the capture of Valencia. But there it stopped, for the enlarged kingdom of Castile was convulsed by internal struggles between the magnates and the crown, and during the fourteenth century the other peninsular states, as well as foreign ones, were all drawn in to what had become a permanent civil war. Meanwhile the kingdom of Aragon, with the powerful support of Catalonian industry, had expanded into the western Mediterranean and taken over Sardinia, Sicily and southern Italy, incorporating them into an Aragonese trade zone. But this obsession with Italy weakened the position of the Aragonese rulers at home, and they, like their Castilian counterparts, were faced with repeated revolts by the magnates. This was the situation when, in 1469, Isabella, sister of the King of Castile, married Ferdinand, heir to the King of Aragon. Ten years later, in 1479, Ferdinand became king himself, and Isabella, whose brother had died some years earlier, at last forced the dissident Castilian magnates to acknowledge her right to the throne. With the union of the two crowns a united Spanish state now became a possibility.

Of the constituent kingdoms Castile, with its six million inhabitants, was by far the largest and most important, three times as big as Aragon and with a population six times as great. Its economy was based on pasture-farming, and every year some two and a half million sheep made the long journey from their summer pastures in the north to their winter grazing grounds in the south, under the control of the *Mesta*, the powerful trade union of sheep owners (see p. 61). Medina del Campo, the centre of the wool trade, was a flourishing town, and among the ports Seville was already predominant. Yet trade and agriculture were not held in great respect. The prolonged struggle against the Moors had led to glorification of the military virtues, particularly as epitomised in the three religious orders of Calatrava, Alcantara and Santiago, and the concept of the *Hidalgo*, the knight who lived for war and glory and despised all other forms of work, was widely accepted as the ideal to be aimed at.

Castile had a representative assembly, or *Cortes*, but its membership and the frequency of its meetings were both dependent on the crown. The situation was very different in Aragon, where all three constituent kingdoms had their own *Cortes*, which were genuinely independent. The consent of these *Cortes* was needed for all new taxes and new laws, and even when the main body was not in session standing committees acted as guardians of the constitution. In Aragon there was an additional safeguard in the Justiciar, a hereditary officer whose function was to uphold the law and the legitimate interests of the subject against the encroachments of royal government. The attitude of the Aragonese nobility towards their king was reflected in the notorious oath of allegiance which they swore: 'We who are as good as you swear to you who are no better than us to accept you as our king and sovereign lord provided you observe all our liberties and laws. But if not, not.' Yet although the nobles of Aragon were as proud as those of Castile they were poorer and less powerful politically. Merchants and townspeople played a far more important role in Aragon than in Castile, but their prosperity, based upon the commercial empire which Catalonia had built up in the western Mediterranean, was being eroded by the expansion of the Genoese. Economically as well as politically, therefore, Aragon was very much the junior partner in the federation with Castile.

When Ferdinand married Isabella he promised to live in his wife's kingdom, and he ruled Aragon through a council which was itself resident in Castile. Isabella was an extremely devout woman. One observer told how 'she used to leave secret alms in suitable places; she honoured houses of prayer; she would visit monasteries and houses of religion, particularly those which to her knowledge lived an honest life; and she endowed them generously'. Her greatest ambition was to carry to completion the gradual reconquest of the peninsula from the Moors, and to purify her peoples from all taint of unorthodoxy or heresy. As for Ferdinand, he was cunning, devious and unscrupulous, determined to consolidate the power of the crown at home and to add to his territories by timely intervention in European affairs.

Although the crowns of Aragon and Castile had been united, there was no union of states or peoples. Customs barriers still separated the two kingdoms and each kept its own laws, language and customs. While royal authority was extended and deepened in Castile it remained strictly limited in Aragon; only in foreign relations is it really accurate to talk of 'Spanish' policy as something which existed apart from the particular interests of the constituent kingdoms.

Portugal did not form part of the Spanish state at this period, although its kings had originally been drawn from the royal house of Leon. In 1385 the throne passed to an illegitimate branch of the family, and the new king, John I, had to fight hard to preserve the independence of his state against the Castilians, who were trying to take it over. He was successful, however, and under John and his descendants Portugal pursued its separate course and, in the fifteenth century, began the exploration of Africa—the first stage on the sea route to India which was to lead Portugal to greatness.

Italy

Although Germany, France and Spain were different in their languages, customs and political institutions, they were all essentially agrarian societies in which wealth and power came from the ownership of land and in which trade, however widespread and important, was a secondary activity, not suited to a gentleman. Northern Italy was different, since in this region the towns dominated the countryside and an urban civilisation had developed. Commerce and manufacture here were primary occupations, for Italy stood midway on the major European trade route from the Levant, where the riches of the Orient became available, to the markets of Spain, France, Germany and England. It was through acting as entrepreneurs that Italian businessmen developed not only commerce but also the associated activities of industry and finance and so became the first capitalists in Europe.

Northern Italy was dominated by Venice, Milan and Florence. These were not simply cities. The need for food and security had driven them to extend their control far into the surrounding countryside (the *contado*) and they had thereby become city-states, unlike any-thing else in Europe. Authority within these states lay either in the hands of the merchant oligarchs (Venice and Florence) or in those of a despot (Milan). Only in the south did a feudal society exist, in the kingdom of Naples.

The most renowned of all the city-states was Venice, sitting astride the commercial axis of Europe, which extended from the Levant, up the Adriatic, across the Alps and down the Rhine into the heart of the continent. Venetian merchants traded cotton and spices from the Levant for metals, especially copper, from central Europe, and the Venetian galley fleet, owned by the state, made regular journeys through the Straits of Gibraltar to England and the Netherlands. Venice could not possibly feed her large population from her own resources, even though she controlled considerable areas on the main-land. She was dependent for food, as well as trade, on regions which were dominated by the enemies of Christendom, the Ottoman Turks, and her diplomacy had to maintain a delicate balance between her western Christian commitments and the need to keep her Turkish lifelines open. Control of the Venetian state was in the hands of an oligarchy of merchant families, who dominated the Senate and ap-pointed the doge as nominal ruler. The only aristocracy was one of trade, and although merchants might buy land in the *contado*, the centre of their life, as well as the source of their wealth, was the city.

To the west of Venice lay the city-state of Milan, where political development had taken a very different course. The prosperity of Milan was based not only on trade but also on the manufacture of weapons and armour, and class conflict had broken out between the merchants and the artisans. Order had only been restored through a dictatorship imposed by the Visconti family, who in 1395 bought the title of 'Duke of Milan' from the Holy Roman Emperor. The Viscontis built up a mercenary army instead of a citizen one (which might have been less reliable), and to pay for this they created an efficient adminis-tration and an elaborate fiscal system. The brilliance of the Visconti court far outshone that of the monarchy of Naples, and Milanese despotism seemed to offer a glittering alternative to the republican governments of Venice and Florence. In fact, on the death of the last Visconti in 1447 a republic was declared, but fear of Venice drove the republican leaders to hire a mercenary captain, Francesco Sforza. Not for the first time the servant of the state turned into its master. Sforza, with an army behind him, took over the government and with it the title of Duke of Milan. To make his despotism acceptable to the citizens he built on a princely scale and gave lavish entertainments. The Visconti tradition was revived and Milan remained a brilliant, and menacing, exemplar of despotism.

Between Milan and Naples came Florence and the central belt of the Papal States. Although the papacy had been victorious in its struggle against the Emperors it had been humiliated by the newly emergent national monarchies in the late-thirteenth and early-fourteenth centuries, and its defeat at the hands of the French king was symbolised by the long period of papal residence at Avignon during the years 1308–78. During this 'Babylonish Captivity' the Popes had been unable to exercise any effective rule in their Italian possessions, but after their return to Rome they set about restoring their authority and by the middle of the fifteenth century were well on the way to establishing a despotism on the Milanese model. Of the remaining states of northern Italy, apart from Florence, Genoa was a republic, rich in trade but suffering from unstable government, and Savoy was an Alpine duchy rather remote from the affairs of its Italian counterparts and more or less under the influence of France.

Florence, which had despotic regimes to north and south and the Venetian republic on its eastern frontier, ultimately combined the elements of both systems. Florentine government had been in the grip of a merchant oligarchy, but this was resented by the artisans, who periodically broke into rebellion. From this unstable situation Florence was rescued not by a mercenary captain but by one of its own leading citizens, the banker Cosimo de' Medici. By 1434 Cosimo was virtual ruler of Florence. He held no formal office, and the only title that was ever given him was the popular one of *Pater Patriae*, 'Father of the Country'. Nevertheless he established his dynasty. It was his grandson, Lorenzo de' Medici, who became one of the greatest patrons of the Renaissance and made himself and his city celebrated throughout Europe. Lorenzo, like his grandfather, maintained a façade of republican government, but on the council which nominally ruled the state his supporters were assured of a permanent majority. Not surprisingly Lorenzo was succeeded in due course by his son, Piero.

In 1455 the major Italian states—Milan, Venice, Florence, the Papacy and Naples—made a formal league among themselves, the object of which was to preserve the balance of power in the peninsula and maintain Italian independence. The League itself did not last long but the equilibrium did, for in the north Venice and Milan effectively balanced each other, while in the south Naples and the Papal States did the same. Florence usually allied with Milan and Naples, and the Florentine–Naples axis, which linked the two major power groupings of the peninsula, was a very important element in stabilising Italian politics. Whenever this axis was broken, peace was threatened. This happened after Lorenzo the Magnificent became virtual ruler of Florence in 1469. He was threatened by the expansionist ambitions of Pope Sixtus IV, who succeeded in detaching Naples from her traditional alliance and persuading her to join in war against Florence. Peace and stability were only restored when Lorenzo, after careful diplomatic preparation, made a dramatic journey to Naples and convinced the king that his own best interests, as well as those of Italy, demanded a return to the Florentine alliance.

A much greater threat to this power balance came in the 1490s, and the source of the trouble was Milan. Following the assassination of Galeazzo Sforza (son of Francesco) in 1476, his young son, Gian Galeazzo, became duke. But effective authority was exercised by Gian's uncle, Ludovico, known on account of his saturnine complexion as *Il Moro*, 'the Moor'. Ludovico established a brilliant court in Milan, and under him the city flourished, but he had his enemies in the supporters of the young duke and they looked to Naples for assistance, since Gian Galeazzo had taken a Neapolitan princess for his wife. Ludovico became aware that his position was being threatened. Normally he could have hoped for support from Florence, and Lorenzo de' Medici in fact did his utmost to reconcile Milan and Naples. Unfortunately for Italy he died in 1492 and was succeeded by his son, Piero, whose own inclinations and those of his wife drew him much more towards Naples.

Ludovico saw himself being isolated, and to redress the balance in his favour he called on France for support. At the time this seemed to be a masterstroke, for Naples would hardly dare challenge so great a power as France. Also, by calling in the French as his allies, Ludovico had neatly obscured the fact that the Valois kings had quite a good claim to Milan itself. In the long run, however, Ludovico's action was disastrous, not simply from his own point of view but for Italy and the cause of Italian independence. The French were only too glad of the opportunity to break through the tightening ring of Habsburg power by expanding across the Alps, but by invading Italy they merely extended Valois–Habsburg rivalry into a hitherto peaceful region. Where France had led the Habsburgs soon followed, and whoever was successful in the long struggle that ensued, the independent states of Italy were bound to be the losers.

Scandinavia

At the northern end of Europe two of the bigger states, Sweden and Denmark (including Norway) had been linked by acceptance of the same ruler in 1389. This union was confirmed at Kalmar eight years later, but it became increasingly unpopular in Sweden, since it seemed to have opened the way to absolute royal rule of a sort that had long been anathema to the Swedish nobility. Their aristocratic nationalism was personified in Sten Sture, himself a nobleman, who became virtual dictator of Sweden from 1470 until his death in 1503, and was succeeded by other members of the Sture family. In Denmark, also, the nobles were politically a force to be reckoned with. They insisted on their right to elect the Danish sovereign, and tried to bind the kings they chose by making their election dependent on acceptance of a charter confirming aristocratic privileges. But kings, like lesser mortals, conveniently forgot their promises once they had come to power, and Christian II (1513–23) tried to prepare the ground for absolutism at home by winning prestige abroad. He revived the old idea of Scandinavian union and asserted his right to the crown of Sweden. In 1520 he defeated Sten Sture the Younger and consolidated his victory by the 'Stockholm blood bath' in which most of the Sture party were killed.

Not all, however. Gustavus Vasa, a distant relative of the Stures, who had lost his father and two uncles in the 'blood bath', made himself the leader of a resistance movement and, with the help of Lubeck, drove out Christian and the Danes. This marked the end of Scandinavian union. The ideal survived but it never again became a political reality. Nationalist sentiment proved too strong, and relations between the two Scandinavian powers grew rapidly worse. Their bitter rivalry and bloody wars were to be one of the key elements in the politics of northern Europe during the next two centuries.

Poland

The largest state in eastern Europe was the federal kingdom of Poland–Lithuania. Poland had been created by the coming together of various Slav tribes in the early Middle Ages, but, as with Spain, the unity of the state was constantly threatened by the scramble for lands that took place between a ruler's sons immediately following his death. This practice was not ended until the early fourteenth century, but when at last the territorial integrity of Poland was assured it made possible the emergence of a splendid and outwardly powerful monarchy. Under the cultured and immensely capable Casimir the Great, who ruled from 1333 to 1370, Poland enjoyed a long period of tranquillity and prosperity. Unfortunately for the dynasty Casimir had no male heirs, nor did his successor, Louis I of Hungary. In 1382, therefore, the Poles accepted Louis's daughter as their queen and arranged for her to marry Grand Prince Jagiello of Lithuania. In this way the federation of the two states was brought about.

The principality of Lithuania covered a vast area to the east of Poland, including a great deal of presentday Russia. The tribes inhabiting this region were pagan and were threatened by the crusading activities of the knights of the Teutonic Order, who had their bases in Prussia and Estonia. It was fear of the knights that drove Grand Prince Jagiello into a close alliance with Poland, and this was cemented not simply by marriage but also by his acceptance of the Roman Catholic faith.

The newly federated state stretched from the Baltic almost to the Black Sea, and during the reign of the ambitious Casimir IV (1447–92) the Jagiellos seemed set to become the major dynasty in northern Europe. It was in pursuit of this objective that Casimir secured the election of his eldest son, Ladislaw, as King of Bohemia in 1471, but his concern for the advancement of his family weakened his hold on his own state, and in particular on the Lithuanians, who had long felt that they were very much the junior partners in the federation. These strains came into the open on Casimir's death, since the Poles chose one of his sons to be their king while the Lithuanians elected another as their grand prince. For nine years the two countries pursued their separate ways, but in 1501 the Grand Prince of Lithuania was elected to the Polish throne and the federated state of Poland–Lithuania resumed its chequered existence.

The apparent greatness of the Polish kingdom was in some ways misleading. Behind the façade of royal government the internal administration was feeble and the crown's financial resources inadequate; and although Poland–Lithuania covered a vast area, her long frontiers were a source of weakness rather than strength. If this had not become obvious by 1500 it was because Poland's neighbours were as yet in no position to overthrow her. The break-up of the Scandinavian union, the restrictions on imperial power in Germany, and above all the fact that a consolidated Russian state was only in the early stages of its formation, were the conditions that made Polish 'greatness' possible. None of these was to be permanent.

Russia

Russia, as a political entity, did not exist. At the opening of the four-teenth century the Principality of Moscow was only one of a number of Russian states, and not necessarily the most important. Moreover the Grand Prince of Moscow was not even master of his own dominions, for he had to pay tribute to the Golden Horde, the inheritors of the Mongol empire of Genghis Khan, who had settled in the region around the Caucasus and the northern shores of the Caspian Sea. The rise of Moscow began with the accession of Ivan III ('the Great') in 1462. He was determined to shake off the chains of the Golden Horde, extend his rule to all the Russian peoples, and push his frontier westward into the Russian-speaking areas of Lithuania. The first of these aims was accomplished with relative ease. Ivan stopped paying tribute to the Horde, repulsed a Mongol thrust towards Moscow, and by 1480 was to all intents and purposes an independent sovereign.

The conquest or acquisition of other Russian-speaking areas was a much longer process, though Ivan made his intentions clear by assum-ing the title of Tsar of All Russia in 1493. His major achievement was the annexation of Novgorod. The city itself was taken in 1478, and by 1489 the whole area formerly under its sway had passed into Muscovite hands. To make sure that Novgorod would never again challenge Moscow, Ivan sacked it, transported its inhabitants, and closed the office of the Hanse, thereby cutting the town's links with the west. Other states, such as Yaroslavl and Rostov, were acquired by treaty, and at Ivan's death only Pskov and Ryazan remained nominally independent.

The claim to sovereignty over all the Russian peoples brought Ivan up against Lithuania, which had incorporated Smolensk, Kiev, and other formerly Russian areas. From 1490 onwards Ivan was engaged in a running battle with Lithuania, and although he did not succeed in capturing the town of Smolensk he pushed the Russian frontier steadily westwards.

The belief that Moscow had a destiny to reunite the Russian peoples under its banner and lead them to greatness was already widely established, and Ivan the Great consciously promoted it. In 1472 he married Sophie Paleologue, niece of the last Byzantine emperor, and from then on began to use the imperial double-headed eagle in his own seal and adopted much of the elaborate ceremonial of the Byzantine court. He also encouraged the Russian church in its claim that Moscow was the third Rome, now that classical Rome and its Byzantine successor had both fallen. Ivan the Great could not, in the course of only one life-time, transform his backward country into a modern, centralised state, but in both domestic and foreign policy he laid the foundations on which his successors were to build, and his reign marks the emergence of Russia as a major element in the power pattern of eastern Europe.

Bohemia and Hungary

On the south-western borders of Poland were the kingdoms of Bohemia and Hungary. Bohemia had become dependent on the German kings and emperors early on in its history, and it was as a reward for loyal service that the then prince of Bohemia was awarded a royal crown and title by the Emperor Frederick Barbarossa in 1158. The link between Bohemia and the Empire became even stronger in the fourteenth century, when the Bohemian king was elected Emperor as Charles IV. He was a powerful and effective ruler and a man of considerable culture. He took up residence in Prague, transformed it architecturally, and founded a university there. The long period of prosperity for Bohemia, inaugurated by his reign, only came to an end in the early fifteenth century with the appearance of John Hus, the religious reformer whose ideas were very close to those of John Wyclif and the Lollards.

Hus, a forerunner of the Protestant Reformation, was burnt at the stake as a heretic, but not before his religious beliefs had become widely accepted in Bohemia. The country was torn apart by civil war, and even when this came to an end in the late-1430s it was followed by struggles over the succession to the throne. Catholics favoured the preservation of the close link with the Holy Roman Empire, but nationalists, and particularly Utraquists,[1] wanted one of their own number as a ruler. They rallied round a Czech nobleman and Utraquist,

---

[1] So called because they insisted on their right to take communion 'in each kind' (*utraque* = each). It was the practice in the Roman Catholic Church for laity to receive only the bread. Utraquists, following Hus, demanded that all participants in the communion service, lay as well as clerical, should receive both the bread and the wine.

George Podiebrad, who was elected king in 1458, but he was denounced and formally deposed by the Pope and attacked by the Emperor Frederick III. Fighting continued until George's death in 1471, when the Bohemian Estates chose Ladislaw Jagiello, son of Casimir IV of Poland, to succeed him. There was a prolonged struggle over the succession, in which Ladislaw needed all the help his father could give him, but by 1478 he was firmly established.

Although he was now undisputed King of Bohemia, Ladislaw's authority was strictly limited. Bohemia was in effect an aristocratic oligarchy. The nobles dominated rural society and had reduced the peasantry to serfdom. They had also curbed the privileges of the towns and asserted their supremacy over the lesser nobility or gentry. In the Bohemian Estates the nobles formed a separate house, and although the other two houses, of gentry and burgesses, were of theoretically equal status when it came to law-making or voting supply, they usually followed the nobles' lead.

The Habsburgs had not abandoned their claim to Bohemia, and in 1494 they persuaded Ladislaw, who had just added to his dignities by being elected to the Hungarian throne, to agree that in the event of his having no children he would promote the Habsburg succession. This promise was reinforced by a double marriage of 1506. Maximilia n I's granddaughter Mary, sister of the future Charles V, was to marry Ladislaw's son, Louis; Maximilian's grandson Ferdinand, who in due course succeeded Charles V as Emperor, was to marry Ladislaw's daughter, Anna. Dynastic marriages of this sort were greatly to the liking of Maximilian, since they held out the prospect of expanding Habsburg influence at minimum cost, but these would not necessarily have produced the desired result unaided. It needed the intervention of the Ottoman Turks to make Habsburg claims a reality.

Hungary was largely a creation of the Magyar tribes who settled in the Balkan region round about A.D. 900, and a Christian state was established under St Stephen I, who was crowned in the year 1000. Hungary, like Bohemia, came under the powerful influence of its neighbour, the German Empire, and Sigismund, who was King of Hungary from 1395 to 1437, was also elected Emperor.

Unfortunately for Hungary she had another powerful ne ighbour, this time to the south. The Ottoman Turks were steadily advancing into the Balkans, and Hungary was a buffer state between them and the heartland of Christian Europe. Sigismund had been heavily defeated by the Turks at Nicopol in 1396 and thereafter pursued a defensive policy based on a line of specially constructed fortresses. But although the struggle against the Turks varied in intensity there could be no relaxation on the Christian side and one of the most famous Hungarian heroes of the time was Janos Hunyadi, who personified resistance to the Muslim invader. When Hunyadi, who had been the Emperor's regent in Hungary, died in 1456, the Hungarian Estates elected his son, Matthias Corvinus, as king. Matthias Corvinus was one of the most enlightened rulers of his day, a Renaissance prince who patronised scholars, built up a fine private library, and established the first printing-press in Hungary. Although hemmed in by powerful and aggressive neighbours he was determined to keep his country independent and make it a major state in south-eastern Europe. He almost succeeded in achieving his ambition. Taking advantage of a revolt of the Austrian nobility in 1485 he led an army across the border, occupied Vienna, and made himself master of Styria, Carniola and Carinthia. At the same time he pushed back the Turks in the Balkans and spoke of driving them out of Europe altogether.

The high hopes of Matthias Corvinus came to an end with his sudden death in 1490. He left no heir, and the Archduke Maximilian, the future Emperor, claimed the throne for the Habsburgs. The Hungarian Estates, however, elected Ladislaw Jagiello, who was already King of Bohemia. Ladislaw had first to expel the mercenary troops who had invaded Hungary in support of the Habsburg claimant, but this he succeeded in doing, and by the Treaty of Pressburg in November 1491 Maximilian agreed to renounce his pretensions to the throne on condition that if Ladislaw had no direct heir it should revert to the Habsburgs.

The Hungarian nobles had chosen Ladislaw in preference to Maximilian because they thought he would offer less of a threat to their own domination of Hungarian society, and in this assumption they were correct. Ladislaw, who was a lavish spender, needed the nobles more than they needed him, and he had to pay for their support. In Hungary, as in Bohemia, the power of the crown was weakened as that of the aristocracy increased. In 1507, for example, Ladislaw accepted the nobles' demand that no royal decree should be valid unless it was confirmed by the council, on which they were predominant; and in 1514, following the suppression of a peasant revolt, he allowed the entire rural population to be reduced to serfdom. He could not even persuade the nobles to contribute adequately to their own defence, and although the consequences of this did not become apparent during his own lifetime, they were made all too plain in 1526, when the Turks renewed their offensive.

The Ottoman Turks

Traditionally speaking, the fall of Constantinople—capital of the Christian Byzantine state which traced its descent unbroken from Justinian and the Roman Empire—in 1453 marks the beginning of Turkish penetration into Europe. But for more than a century before this date the Ottoman Turks had been pushing into the Balkans and probing the southern frontiers of Poland and the Holy Roman Empire. Constantinople, however, had been a symbol of Christian resistance, and its fall was a warning to European states that a new phase had opened in the struggle between the Christian and Muslim worlds. The victor of Constantinople was the Sultan Mohamed II, a great warrior and patron of scholars, who rebuilt the captured city and made it the capital of the Ottoman empire. From there he set out to consolidate Turkish rule over most of the area which had formerly belonged to the Byzantine emperors. Athens and much of the Morea were annexed, Serbia was occupied, and by 1464 Bosnia had also been taken over. Most of the Balkan peninsula was now Turkish, except for the strip of Dalmatian coast north of Albania which still belonged to Venice. The Turks also pressed into Wallachia, which became a client state, but there they halted, for they came up against determined resistance. They therefore turned south and west. The island of Rhodes, held by the military order of the Knights of St John, was attacked, and at the same time Italy was invaded and Otranto besieged. It was at this critical moment, with two major campaigns under way, that Mohamed II died in 1481.

The sudden death of Mohamed meant a breathing-space for Europe, since Turkish energies were consumed in a succession struggle. Italy was abandoned, as was the attack on Rhodes, until such time as a new sultan should be firmly established on his throne. It was a weakness of Ottoman rule that there was no clear line of succession. If a Sultan had a number of sons they would fight for the right to succeed him, and the throne would go to the one who reached the capital first and managed to capture (and preferably kill) his brothers. The first of Mohamed's sons to secure the throne was Bayezid II, but he could not prevent his brother, Jem, from fleeing to Rhodes, where the Knights of St John welcomed him and assured him of their protection. A

Turkish pretender was a valuable asset, and Bayezid recognised this by promising not to attack Rhodes and to pay the Knights an annual indemnity as long as they kept Jem in the west. Jem remained a valuable pawn in Christian hands, taken over first by the Pope and then, in 1495, by Charles VIII of France, who hoped to use him as a pawn in his projected crusade. Fortunately for Bayezid Jem died shortly afterwards, and the Sultan was at last free, if he so wished, to pursue a more aggressive policy towards western Europe.

In the Balkans Bayezid had carried out a holding operation, consolidating Turkish power in recently conquered areas and making raids into Habsburg territories to secure his frontiers. In the early 1490s he beat back a Polish invasion of Moldavia, and in 1498 sent his army into Polish Galicia. This counter-invasion was brought to a halt by bitter winter weather, but although Bayezid agreed to a truce he had made it abundantly clear that the Turks were not going to relinquish their hold on south-east Europe. Bayezid's forces also attacked that part of the Morea which was under the rule of Venice. The Venetian fleet was defeated, and the republic had to sue for peace in 1503. The commercial privileges of the Venetians within the Ottoman empire were confirmed, but Venice had to abandon the Morean ports, among them Lepanto. The Turks were now emerging as a strong naval power in the eastern Mediterranean.

Bayezid was less successful in dealing with the Mamelukes of Egypt, who resented the expansion of Ottoman influence into what they regarded as their preserve, and a six-year war, from 1485 to 1491, settled nothing. Bayezid left the Mameluke problem to be solved by his successor, and to remove all doubt about who this successor should be, he abdicated in favour of his youngest son, Selim, in April 1512, shortly before his death.

Selim, after securing himself on the throne in the traditional manner by executing his brothers, took up the struggle against the Mamelukes and carried it through to a triumphant conclusion. But first he dealt with the Persians, who controlled the area to the south and west of the Caspian and were the major contenders with the Ottoman Turks for domination of the Middle East. In August 1514 Selim heavily defeated the army of the Shah of Persia, thereby ensuring that the Persians would not be able to go to the support of their Mameluke allies. Now it was the turn of the Mamelukes to feel the full shock of the Ottoman attack, and under it their empire crumbled away. Their army was crushed at a battle fought near Aleppo in 1516, Syria was occupied,

and in January 1517 Selim entered Cairo in triumph. By the middle of
the following year he was back in Constantinople, having annexed the
entire Mameluke empire.

While Selim had been occupied in the east the European powers had
been given time to unite in their own defence. But they had signally
failed to do so. France and Spain were engaged in a bitter struggle for
control of the Italian peninsula, and although lip-service was paid to
the idea of a crusade nothing effective was done to bring it about.
Even the Popes who preached it were ambivalent in their attitude
towards the great enemy of Christendom. Innocent VIII received a
pension from Bayezid in return for keeping Jem prisoner, and as for
Alexander VI, far from aiding Charles VIII of France in his crusading
venture he asked for Turkish money to defend Naples against him.
The Turks, in fact, were coming to be regarded as elements in the
western European power pattern, as Charles V found to his cost.
Charles, elected Emperor in 1519, was bound to be aware of the
Turkish threat, since his hereditary lands of Styria, Carniola and
Carinthia were subjected to frequent raids. He also had a genuine wish
to unite Christendom against the Muslim invader, but as luck would
have it he had to face the disruptive forces unleashed by Luther. All
this meant that at the death of Selim in September 1520 Europe was in
no better condition to resist a renewed Turkish attack than it had been
forty years earlier.

The Idea of Europe

The failure of the European powers to combine in face of the Ottoman
threat is but one indication of the fact that 'Europe', politically speaking, was little more than a figment of the imagination. In the Middle
Ages there had been some sense of unity among the Christian peoples,
expressed in the term 'Christendom', but this had waned, along with
the Empire and Papacy—those two embodiments of the supranational
ideal—and feelings of loyalty were increasingly focused on national
rulers. This was not, of course, universally true. Germany, for instance,
never achieved nationhood during the Habsburg and Bourbon period,
and there is little evidence that states such as Saxony, Bavaria or
Cologne provided an outlet for nationalist sentiment in the way that
the monarchies of France, England and later Spain did. It is also the
case that the greatest figure in the sixteenth century was the Emperor
Charles V, whose authority straddled frontiers and, indeed, oceans;

and that the Papacy, after reeling under the initial shock of the protestant Reformation, recovered and reasserted itself as a spiritual power on a worldwide scale.

Yet although Roman Catholics throughout Europe were aware of their duty towards the Holy See, there was an increasing tendency to define catholicism in national terms, whether in Philip II's Spain or Elizabeth I's England. As for protestants, they were divided even among themselves, and while they longed for unity they had to operate, in practice, within fairly narrow secular frontiers. Habsburg and Bourbon Europe, then, was a collection of separate units having only a very hazy sense of some overriding Christian commitment.

It is sometimes assumed that Europeans acquired an awareness of their corporate identity as they expanded beyond their own continent, but there is little evidence of this. Professor Elliott has shown how long it took for the implications of the discovery of the New World to sink into the general consciousness,[1] and in any case as Europe expanded so also did the area of conflict between the individual European states. The Spanish, Dutch, English, French and Portuguese now fought out their battles in America, Asia and India as well as at home, and separate identities were merely intensified by transportation over many thousands of miles. It may be that inhabitants of other continents thought in terms of 'Europe', but very few Europeans did so. Even the political frontiers of the continent were uncertain. Was Russia part of it, particularly before Peter the Great? Were the Turks? To this and similar questions there were no clear answers because Europe itself, throughout the Habsburg and Bourbon period, remained elusive and undefined. In a loose sense it was the sum of its parts, but in practice the parts were far more meaningful and effective than the whole.

[1] J. H. Elliott, *The Old World and the New*, *1492-1650*, Cambridge University Press, 1970.

TWO

The Expansion of Europe in the Sixteenth Century

Knowledge of the World

Europe was not a closed economy in the fifteenth century. It was largely self-sufficient in staple foodstuffs and minerals, but it was short of gold and it relied on Asia not only for luxuries like silk but also for the spices which, in an age that knew nothing of refrigeration, cloaked the unpleasant flavour of rotting meat. These goods were bought by Venetian and Genoese merchants in Cairo, Damascus and other eastern Mediterranean markets and transported, either by sea or over-land, to western and northern Europe. Little was known about the areas which actually produced the highly valued spices, but it was generally assumed that since these were shipped to the Arab world from ports on the west coast of India, the sources must be somewhere on the mainland of that distant continent. China, which supplied silk, was even more distant, but in many ways it was better known in the west than India. For a century after 1250 the Tatar Khans controlled the greater part of central Asia, and it was possible for travellers to make the long journey by land from Europe to China. A number of people did so, most famous of them the Venetian merchant Marco Polo, whose account of his travels was widely read.

By the middle of the fourteenth century the situation was changing. The Tatar empire broke up and long-distance travel was no longer possible. In China the newly established Ming rulers began sealing off their country from all contacts with outsiders. Meanwhile the Otto-man Turks were pushing into Europe and blocking the old trade routes. Europe became like a beleaguered fortress, and traders and crusaders had a common interest in searching for new routes, not only to the silks and spices of the east but also to other Christian communities which were believed to exist there and which might be called in to redress the balance now tipping dangerously in favour of the Muslims.

There was general agreement among traders, seamen and educated men that the world was round and that Asia could therefore be reached by sailing either east or west. Little was known, however, about the distances involved or the extent of the major continents. Many people believed that Africa eventually merged into a great southern land mass that completely enclosed the Indian Ocean, thereby blocking access by sea, although a Venetian world map of 1459 showed it as circumnavigable. The westward route looked more hopeful, especially since it was assumed that Asia stretched a long way east and that only a relatively short gap of water separated it from Europe. This view was put forward by Cardinal d'Ailly in his *Imago Mundi*, written about 1410 and circulated in manuscript for some seventy years before it was printed at Louvain. D'Ailly was a typical late-medieval scholar, larding his work with quotations from Aristotle and the Bible and paying little attention to travellers' reports, but his book was widely read, and among those who studied it was Columbus, whose annotated copy survives to this day. Columbus also had a printed copy of Marco Polo's *Travels*, and was no doubt influenced by Polo's erroneous assertion that Cipangu (Japan) lay some fifteen hundred miles off the east coast of Cathay (China). Had this been the case, a brief Atlantic crossing should have brought the intrepid sailor to its shores.

The same false estimate of the breadth of Asia was made by Ptolemy, probably the most important single influence on geographical thinking in the late fifteenth century. Ptolemy was a hellenised Egyptian of the second century A.D., whose *Astronomy*, translated into Latin in the Middle Ages, had spread the belief that the earth was round. He had also written the *Geography*, a sort of gazetteer of the world, but this was unknown in the west until 1406, when it was translated into Latin from a Greek manuscript preserved in Constantinople. In 1475 came the first printed edition, and from then on the *Geography* was in constant demand. Later editions were embellished with maps which summarised available knowledge and did much to supplement Ptolemy's own conclusions. Columbus apparently had no direct knowledge of Ptolemy's work, but he was familiar with it at second-hand and could use it to buttress his argument that Asia lay within easy sailing distance of western Europe.

Another geographical tradition was that of the *mappae mundi*, which were mainly theological in purpose and showed Jerusalem as the centre of the world. However, the makers of these maps were often aware of current discoveries, and the *Planisphere* of Fra Mauro, drawn in 1459, showed western Europe and north Africa with considerable accuracy. But more important than these world maps, from the point of view of the explorers, were detailed charts based on the observations of countless numbers of ordinary seamen. These *portolani*, as they were called, were Mediterranean in origin, but the Genoese, who made great use of them, took them to Lisbon and Seville in the course of their normal trading ventures and thereby transmitted them to the west. Northern Europe had its own tradition of *rutters*—detailed gazetteers of coasts and harbours, with sailing instructions. When the *portolani* and the *rutters* were combined, they provided charts that were highly accurate, though restricted in range, and could be amended as new information came in. Spain and Portugal both saw the value of these, and at the *Casa de Contratacion*, in Seville, the Spaniards had a master-map, the *Padron Real*, first drawn in 1508 and kept constantly up to date.

Technical Advances

A similar fusion of Mediterranean and northern European traditions produced ships that were well adapted to oceanic exploration. The rough seas of the north and west had encouraged the building of sturdy vessels, short and squat, with high castles at both ends. They were fairly easy to navigate, had small crews, and usually operated with a single mast and a square sail. The Mediterranean countries, however, had developed galleys, which were longer and lighter in construction and carried large numbers of oarsmen for use in calm weather and for entering and leaving harbour. This made them speedy and reliable— Venetian galleys, for instance, made regular voyages to England and Flanders until well into the sixteenth century—but the space taken up by a large crew and the provisions necessary to sustain it meant that there was little room left for cargo. For bulk goods, therefore, the Mediterranean countries adopted the capacious north-European type of ship, but modified it by adding another mast or masts and combining the square sail with the lateen or triangular one of the Arab dhows. This marriage of the two traditions had taken place by the middle of the fifteenth century, and its progeny, the 'barque', was the ancestor of the ships that led the expansion of Europe. The Portuguese version of the barque was the 'caravel', a small ship of some sixty to seventy tons, and from this was developed the 'carrack', of anything up to a thousand tons. For exploration the smaller ships were preferable, since they could sail close to the shore and make landfall in shallow bays; but once a route was established bigger ships were needed to carry not only cargoes but also soldiers, administrators and settlers.

The techniques of sixteenth-century seamen showed little advance on those of their predecessors. For direction-finding the compass was in general use, but determination of latitude was something of a problem. In 1484 the King of Portugal appointed a commission of expert mathematicians to work out how to fix latitude accurately by means of sun-sights, and this subsequently produced the first European almanac designed especially for nautical purposes. But the existence of such aids to navigation did not mean that all explorers were familiar with them. There is no evidence that Columbus knew how to take sun-sights or even understood the principle behind them, and although schools of navigation were established by both Portuguese and Spaniards many of the sailors who took their small ships across the oceans relied on little more than the compass and their own acute observation of winds, tides and currents.

Despite the fact that the expansion of Europe coincided with the Renaissance there is little direct connection between the two. The recovery and translation of Ptolemy's work was certainly one important contribution to exploration made by Renaissance scholars, although in some ways this held back the advance of knowledge, since the Renaissance veneration for classical authors meant that even Ptolemy's errors were accepted as truths. In general Renaissance humanists[1] were concerned with old worlds rather than new ones, and scholars like d'Ailly are more important in the history of discovery than their humanist critics. Not until the major developments in science and astronomy in the late sixteenth and seventeenth centuries did the New Learning really begin to affect navigation, and by that time most of the major discoveries had already been made.

Overseas exploration's indebtedness to the Middle Ages was marked not simply in the field of learning but also in that of experience. Voyages of discovery did not suddenly begin in the 1490s, and the achievements of Columbus and da Gama would have been impossible without the groundwork laid by many hundreds of unknown men as well as a few whose names have survived. The fourteenth and fifteenth centuries, for instance, had seen the discovery and settlement of the Canaries, the Azores, the Madeira group and the Cape Verde islands,

---

[1] The meaning of this term is considered on p. 84.

which were stepping stones to America, and many of the techniques pioneered in these ventures were later applied to the New World. Even the impetus behind the great voyages of discovery was 'medieval', at least in part. The Portuguese were searching for spices and gold, but they were also inspired by the desire to search out hitherto unknown Christian communities, and to assert the superiority of the Christian religion over pagan Africans and Muslim Arabs. As for the Spaniards, they were passionate crusaders, and the faith which had swept them through to the conquest of Granada and the final defeat of the Moors carried them beyond, into North Africa and then across the Atlantic.

Spain and Portugal had other advantages as well as that which came from a fervent belief in the righteousness of their own cause. They were well placed at the junction of the Atlantic and the Mediterranean, and in the course of voyages eastward and westward their seamen acquired an invaluable knowledge of the techniques and traditions of both areas. They were also relatively barren countries, which could not easily support their populations and therefore had a surplus available for emigration. Both societies put great emphasis on the virtues of the warrior, provided his motives were pure, while their rigid social structure meant that anyone from the lower levels who wished to make a name and fortune for himself had to look across the seas.

Although the lead in exploration was taken by the Spaniards and Portuguese it would be wrong to assume that other Europeans were merely passive onlookers. Money was needed, as well as men and ships, and this was provided in great part by Italian and German finance houses. Florentine bankers established in Lisbon invested heavily in the Portuguese voyages to India, and so, later on, did the Germans. Genoese bankers, resident in Seville, put their money into Columbus's first and second voyages, and it was the knowledge of their support that persuaded the Spanish court to reconsider its initially negative attitude. Magellan, who led the first voyage of circumnavigation, was provided with trading goods by German financiers, the Fuggers; and Amerigo Vespucci, who gave his name to the new continent discovered by Columbus (himself a Genoese by birth) was a Florentine businessman who went to Spain as agent of the Medicis. Exploratory voyages were usually carried out by two or three small ships and did not demand a great deal of capital, but the exploitation of newly discovered trade routes and the despatch of settlers, soldiers and supplies required money on a vast scale. The Portuguese kings, in particular, whose revenue was relatively small, were heavily dependent on loans from the European money market to finance the development of the Cape route to the Indies. In an economic context, therefore, the expansion of Europe was the concern of the whole continent and not simply of the Iberian peninsula.

Portugal and the Cape Route

In 1415 the Portuguese captured the Moorish stronghold of Ceuta, opposite Gibraltar. This was the first success obtained by a European power against the Muslims in North Africa, and the relative ease with which it was accomplished raised hopes—false, as it turned out—that Portuguese and Christian rule might be established throughout this whole area. Ceuta was the terminus for the traders who came from the south across the Sahara, and from them the Portuguese heard of the gold mines of Guinea, and of ivory and slaves to be bought in that region. Portuguese fishermen were familiar with the waters off the north-west coast of Africa, and Prince Henry, younger son of John I of Portugal, had directed the settlement of the Madeira group of islands from 1418 onwards. In 1419 he was appointed governor of the Algarve, and established his headquarters on the coast, at Sagres, whence he could organise and despatch expeditions to explore the coast of Africa. Prince Henry, an ascetic, devoutly Christian man, was in no sense a Renaissance figure. His commitment to exploration came not from any desire to extend the frontiers of human knowledge but from his determination to carry the Christian banner into the Muslim world and, if possible, link up with Prester John, the mythical Christian ruler who was supposed to reign somewhere in the heart of the African continent.

Exploration of the African coast would no doubt have taken place whether or not Prince Henry had interested himself in it, because the lure of gold, ivory and slaves was too strong to resist. But Henry gave the movement coherence and put his own resources in men, money and spiritual commitment behind it. When he moved to Sagres the limit of exploration was Cape Nun, some five hundred miles south, but by 1434 Portuguese seamen had reached Cape Bojador and established that the African coast still stretched beyond it in a south-westerly direction. In 1436 Cape Blanco was rounded and nine years later Cape Verde was passed and the first slaves brought back. Henry (known in English as 'the Navigator') was head of the military Order of Christ, and as the fame of his achievements spread the King of Portugal gave him a monopoly of West African trade, while the Pope made his order solely responsible for missionary work in the newly discovered regions.

Henry died in 1460, by which time the seamen acting under his direction had reached Sierra Leone. There is no evidence that Henry was thinking in terms of a maritime route to India. The general opinion was that Africa merged into a southern continent and could not therefore be rounded, and in any case the exploration of the African coast was a sufficient incentive and achievement in itself. Without Henry to direct it, there was some slackening in the pace of exploration, particularly as the crown was short of money and became involved, in the 1470s, in a succession war with Castile. The monopoly of exploration was therefore leased out to a Lisbon merchant on condition that every year his ships should penetrate a hundred leagues further south. This condition was fulfilled, and Portuguese merchants and businessmen showed increasing interest in a venture that was now beginning to pay off. Exploration of the Ivory Coast was followed by that of the Gold Coast—names that vividly recall the major sources of wealth revealed by the explorers. Further west, the Grain Coast produced coarse but valuable pepper, while off the coast of Mauretania were rich seal fisheries.

In 1481 a worthy successor to Henry the Navigator appeared in the person of King John II. He organised exploration in the same methodical way, founding a navigation school and picking able and daring men to be his captains. John was determined to profit from the considerable trade being opened up by exploration of the African coast, and he also had high hopes of finding a passage to India. He painstakingly prepared an expedition for a long voyage, chose Bartholomew Diaz to command it, and sent him off from Lisbon in August 1487. Diaz was driven far out to sea by violent storms off the coast of Africa, beat his way back east, failed to find land, and then discovered that he was in the Indian Ocean. Without being aware of it he had rounded Africa.

Late in 1488 Diaz returned in triumph to Lisbon, having navigated his way back into the Atlantic past what he called the 'Cape of Storms', a name which John promptly, and significantly, changed to 'Cape of Good Hope'. John now ordered a full-scale expedition to India to be prepared, and at the same time he sent two agents out to the Middle East with orders to report on the Arab spice trade up the Red Sea and the prospects of navigation across the Indian Ocean. In spite of these preparations, however, nearly nine years passed before the expedition at last sailed, and while John was waiting there came, in 1492, the shattering news that Columbus had discovered what was apparently a much shorter, western route to the Indies. John died three years later, but by that time it was already becoming clear that whatever Columbus had discovered, it was not a short sea route to India. The new king, Manoel, took up the task that John had left unfinished, and Diaz was called in to supervise the planning of an expedition to be commanded by a former member of John's household, Vasco da Gama. In July 1497 da Gama set out from Lisbon with two well armed ships, the *St Gabriel* and the *St Raphael*, each of 100–120 tons; a much smaller and faster vessel, to be used for scouting; and a storeship. In November 1497 he rounded the Cape of Good Hope and celebrated Christmas off a part of the east African coast that he christened, appropriately, Natal. From there he sailed for India and in May 1498 reached Calicut. His epoch-making voyage had taken him ten months.

Vasco da Gama did not arrive, like Columbus, in an unknown world peopled by primitive savages. He found rich principalities, accustomed to trading with Arab and Persian merchants, and he had to use diplomacy, and occasionally force, to thread his way through the maze of fear, jealousy and curiosity that confronted him. Despite the difficulties put in his way by established traders—who suspected, with good reason, that his tiny fleet heralded a Portuguese challenge to their monopoly of the commerce of the Indian Ocean—da Gama managed to load a cargo of spices and precious stones and return with it to Lisbon, which he reached in July 1499. He had lost half his fleet and half his men, but he had demonstrated beyond any possibility of doubt that a sea route to the Indies existed and could be profitably exploited. King Manoel was making no empty boast when he assumed the title of 'Lord of the Conquest, Navigation and Commerce of Ethiopia, Arabia, Persia and India'.

Since the crown had established a monopoly over exploration it could now look forward to reaping some profits. Less than twelve months after da Gama's return, Pedro Alvares Cabral left with thirteen heavily armed ships and 1,500 men to establish Portugal as a major trading power in the Indian Ocean. On his way through the south Atlantic he sailed too far west—possibly by design—and landed on the coast of Brazil, which he claimed for his royal master. From there he continued his way east, and in September 1500 arrived in Calicut, where he established a 'factory' (trading post) and settled down to do business. Arab merchants were hostile, however, and engineered a riot in which the factory was burnt down and a number of Portuguese killed. Cabral therefore abandoned Calicut for its rival, Cochin. There he established another factory, loaded a cargo of ginger and pepper, and set out on the return voyage to Portugal, which he reached in July 1501.

Cabral's expedition had shown that the Portuguese would not be quietly allowed to insinuate themselves into the valuable traffic between India and western Europe. The hostility of Arab merchants would have to be contended with, and there would be no help from any native Christian princes, since these—contrary to all hopes and expectations—did not exist. In 1502, therefore, da Gama was sent out with a fleet of twenty-one heavily armed ships and orders to establish the Portuguese right to trade, if necessary by force. When he arrived in India he attacked and defeated a hostile Muslim fleet and bombarded Calicut as a demonstration of Portuguese power. Da Gama died before he could systematise the administration and development of the Indian trade, but in 1505 this task was begun by the first viceroy, Francisco d'Almeida. He saw the need to secure bases for the operation of Portuguese ships, and therefore ordered forts to be constructed on the east African coast and, on the other side of the Indian Ocean, at Cochin and Cannanore (north of Calicut). King Manoel had also commanded him to block the entrance to the Red Sea, 'so that no more spices can pass to the land of Soldam [Egypt] and all those of India may lose the notion of being able to trade with anyone but us'. It was to execute this order that in 1506 Almeida despatched a fleet to the Red Sea, captured the barren island of Socotra off its mouth, and forced Ormuz, in the Persian Gulf, to acknowledge Portuguese supremacy. This threat to Arab trade led to the formation of a native fleet, which in 1508 defeated a Portuguese squadron, but in the following year Almeida reasserted Portuguese command of the sea by a decisive victory at Diu.

Although Almeida appreciated the need for a few strategically placed strongholds to facilitate Portuguese trade in the east, he was opposed to the concept of a land-based empire, on the grounds that it would eat up men and money. As he told King Manoel, 'the greater the number of fortresses you hold, the weaker will be your power. Let all your force be on the sea, for if we should not be powerful at sea everything will at once be against us.' But Portuguese ships were operating in a hostile environment, at a great distance from their home base, and needed secure harbours for shifting cargo and refitting. This was recognised by Alfonso d'Albuquerque, who succeeded Almeida as viceroy in 1509. He was convinced that the Portuguese should have an eastern headquarters under their direct control, and picked on the island city and harbour of Goa, halfway up the west coast of India. In 1510 Goa was taken by storm, and for the next 450 years it remained the capital of the Portuguese empire. From Goa Portuguese naval squadrons could not merely protect their own ships but could also prey on native commerce in the Indian Ocean.

Albuquerque, however, was not content simply to control the spice trade from India. He wanted to penetrate to the areas from which the spices originated and to assert Portuguese mastery over the sources of supply. Cinnamon was grown near at hand in Ceylon, to which Almeida had sent an expedition in 1506, but pepper came from Java and Sumatra, nutmeg and mace were the products of Borneo and the Celebes, while cloves, the most highly prized of all spices, were cultivated in the Moluccas. From the East Indies these spices were brought to India by sea, through the narrow strait that separates the Malayan peninsula from Sumatra, and the key to this was Malacca. In 1511 Albuquerque took a big gamble by denuding Goa of ships and soldiers in order to assault Malacca. The gamble paid off, and Malacca became Portuguese. From this new base expeditions were sent to the spice islands themselves, and in 1513 a factory was set up in Ternate, one of the few islands that actually produced cloves.

Portugal now dominated the main spice-producing region of the world and was well placed to regulate the spice trade both to and beyond India. In 1515 Albuquerque sent an expedition to capture Ormuz and firmly establish Portuguese power in the Persian Gulf. His aim was to restrict and tax the movement of spices by Arab traders, so that they would be forced to put up their selling price to Venetian middlemen. This would work to the advantage of the Portuguese, who shipped their spices direct to Lisbon. Yet although it was the avowed intent of Portuguese policy to cripple Venice and take over her commercial supremacy, there were limits to its effectiveness. For one thing the task of policing the approaches to the Red Sea and Persian Gulf was beyond Portugal's limited resources; for another, Portuguese officials were increasingly inclined to turn a blind eye to native trade as long as they were given a share of its profits. Portuguese viceroys did not tamely accept the failure of their policy, and in the 1520s and 1530s they sent fleets at frequent intervals to cruise off the mouth of the Red Sea. By the middle of the sixteenth century, however, decline had set in; the volume of spices going to Venice by way of the Levant was as great as ever, and equal in quantity to the amount shipped by the Portuguese round the Cape of Good Hope.

The Portuguese in the Far East

From their base at Malacca the Portuguese could at last make contact with China and Japan, the Cathay and Cipangu which had for so long haunted the European imagination. China was reached in 1514, and the Portuguese traded at Canton until 1521, when the Emperor ordered them to leave. When, in the following year, the Portuguese attempted to assert their trading rights by force they were driven off by a Chinese fleet, and from then until 1554 trade with China had to be conducted by smuggling. In 1555 the imperial ban was lifted and the Portuguese became permanently established at Macao. As for Japan, the Portuguese first arrived there about 1543, and soon built up a flourishing trade. They were helped by the fact that the Ming Emperors of China, determined to isolate their realm as far as possible from undesirable foreign contacts, had forbidden their subjects to leave the country and closed their ports to the Japanese. Trade between the two states was promptly taken over by the Portuguese, who sold spices to the Chinese in return for silk and porcelain which they then shipped to Japan. The Japanese paid for these goods in silver, which was highly valued in China, where the Portuguese exchanged it for gold and further supplies of silk and porcelain. In this way the far eastern trade became self-financing, although goods were still shipped to Goa and thence to Europe.

Vasco da Gama was reported to have said that he made his voyage of exploration to India in search of Christians and spices. The Portuguees were disappointed in their hope of finding Christian rulers in the east, but they soon set about converting the natives, and the decline in the quality of Portuguese administration was to some extent offset by a spiritual revival. The Franciscans were first in the field, thereby demonstrating that the older religious orders were not so moribund as their detractors claimed. They were followed by the Jesuits, and missionary activity really gathered way after the arrival of Francis Xavier in India in 1542. Goa, which had been a bishopric since 1534, was elevated into an archbishopric in 1557, and a suffragan was appointed to Cochin. The missionaries were very successful in southern India, and in 1579 the Jesuits went to the Mogul court, at the invitation of the Emperor Akbar. They had high hopes of converting him and making Christianity the official religion of the entire subcontinent, but although they were again invited to the imperial court in the 1590s they never over-

came Muslim opposition. In Ceylon, however, the king was won over
to Christianity in 1557, and for the rest of the century missionary
activity went hand in hand with the gradual extension of Portuguese
control throughout the entire island.

The Portuguese who found their way to Japan spoke with enthusiasm
of the friendliness and courtesy of the native inhabitants. This encouraged the missionaries to extend their field of endeavour, and in
1549 Francis Xavier himself went to Japan, where he stayed for two
years. He was delighted with the Japanese. 'They are people of very
good will', he assured his fellow Jesuits at Goa, 'very sociable and very
desirous of knowledge. They are very desirous of hearing about things
of God.' In fact the obstacles to missionary activity were greater than
Xavier at first realised, yet the work went ahead and in 1559 a Jesuit
mission was welcomed to the imperial capital at Kyoto. Five years later
the Emperor ordered the expulsion of the Jesuits, but he was overthrown by a pretender whom they supported, and after that their
position seemed secure. In 1569 a Christian convert gave the Jesuits
the town of Nagasaki, which became their major base, and by the
end of the century there were said to be over 300,000 Christians in
Japan.

Francis Xavier also hoped to reach China, but all his attempts to
gain entry were frustrated and he had got no further than Macao by
the time he died in 1552. The Jesuits never gave up hope, however.
One of their number, Father Ruggiero, taught himself to read, write
and speak Mandarin, and cultivated good relations with the Chinese
officials of the province in which Macao was situated. In 1582 the
Jesuits were at last allowed to enter China, but for some time they were
confined to the provincial capital. They were famed not so much for
their missionary endeavours as for their scientific knowledge, and it
was largely for this reason that, at the very end of the century, they
were given permission to set up a house in Peking.

The Portuguese Commercial Empire

While the Portuguese government fostered and encouraged missionary
activity, the main interest of the crown was, of course, in the income
that accrued to it from the spice trade. In theory all this trade was the
king's, and the men who carried it on were simply his agents. The
spices sent back from the Malabar coast and Goa were shipped from
Lisbon to Antwerp, where they were sold to south German and other

merchants for distribution all over Europe. The major cargo was pepper, and it was on this insubstantial foundation that the power and prestige of the Portuguese crown were raised. As the empire expanded and became increasingly land-based it consumed more and more of the wealth it generated, and the king suffered from this. He was responsible for paying the soldiers and administrators, customs officials and accountants, who staffed the Portuguese bases, and the cost was considerable. In an effort to economise, salaries were kept at a low level, but this merely encouraged Portuguese officials to engage in black market deals and connive at smuggling in order to line their own pockets. After the early idealistic days, personal enrichment became the principal objective of those who ran the empire, and the crown could not effectively impose its authority on underpaid officials scattered over half the world. Although trade expanded, it was private individuals who profited rather than the state. King Sebastian recognised this when he abandoned the royal monopoly in 1570 and threw the spice trade open to all his subjects, on condition that they brought their goods to Lisbon and paid duty on them. This amounted to a confession of near-bankruptcy by the man who was generally assumed to be the richest royal merchant in Europe.

Despite the difficulty of maintaining garrisons and fleets thousands of miles from their home base, and the losses attendant on long trading voyages, Portuguese predominance in India and the East Indies was not seriously challenged by any other power in the sixteenth century. The reason for this was simple: the Portuguese were in command of the sea, and as long as they ruled the waves they could hold their empire. Sea power had never been used in this way before, and the Portuguese were the first to show that large armies and abundant natural resources were not essential to a nation's greatness. What nature had omitted to supply at home could be taken from foreign parts, and oceanic trade routes, unlike land frontiers, could be policed by relatively small forces. This lesson was eventually learnt by the inhabitants of other small seaboard states, notably the Dutch and the English. Direct trade between the United Provinces and the orient began only in 1595, but between 1598 and 1602 more than fifty Dutch ships were engaged in this lucrative commerce. Although the Dutch avoided India they soon made their presence felt in the spice islands, and by the beginning of the seventeenth century they were grasping the initiative in trade and settlement. The King of Portugal's reign as unchallenged lord of the commerce of the far east lasted for only a century.

Columbus

Christopher Columbus was not the first European to discover America. In the tenth century the Norsemen, pushing out from Greenland, had explored Labrador and the coast of 'Vinland' (New England); it is also possible that English fishermen from west country ports, sailing off Newfoundland in the fifteenth century, may have sighted land. But to Columbus belongs the credit for inaugurating the exploration and settlement of a new continent, despite the fact that he maintained until his dying day that he had discovered no such thing but simply the easternmost outposts of an old one.

Columbus sailed under the banner of Ferdinand and Isabella, the 'Catholic Kings' of Spain, but he was not a Spaniard. He had been born in Genoa in the middle of the sixteenth century, the son of a weaver and textile merchant. As a young man he travelled in the Mediterranean, and possibly further afield, and in 1476 was living in Lisbon, where his brother Bartholomew earned a living as a cartographer and bookseller. Columbus married the daughter of a man who owned one of the islands in the Madeira group and had built up a collection of maps and writings about the Atlantic. It was in his father-in-law's library that Columbus found much of the evidence to foster and support his belief that Asia could be reached by sailing westwards, and in 1484 he appealed to John II of Portugal to give him royal backing for a voyage of exploration. John and his advisers carefully considered the request and may even have put Columbus's claim to a practical test by sending out a reconnaissance themselves, but in the end they decided against him. They were too committed to the African route, and they thought, rightly, that Columbus exaggerated the breadth of Asia. Disappointed in his hopes of Portugal, Columbus turned to Spain. Isabella and Ferdinand were not at first disposed to support this Genoese adventurer, being fully committed to the struggle against the Moors in Spain. But as it became clear that this was in its closing stages—in Europe at any rate—and that Genoese financiers in Seville were prepared to support their fellow countryman with hard cash, they changed their minds.

Columbus could, of course, have set out with commercial backing only, without waiting for the approval of any crowned head, but such a proceeding had its risks. He was fully convinced that on the far side of the Atlantic he would eventually find the rulers of Cathay and Cipangu, and he would only carry weight with such potentates if he came as the accredited representative of a sovereign. He was also anxious to profit not simply in riches but also in honour from the fruits of his persistence and audacity. This was the significance of the letters patent issued to him by Ferdinand and Isabella, in which he was give the high-sounding titles of 'Admiral and Viceroy and Governor' of all the territories he should discover and also authorised to call himself 'Don Christopher Columbus. And so may your sons and successors . . . for ever and always.'

Columbus's first voyage was intended as a reconnaissance, and his fleet was therefore small. It consisted only of his flagship, the *Santa Maria*, of about 120 tons, and two sixty tonners, the *Nina* and *Pinta*. With these three ships Columbus set sail from Spain in August 1492. Two months later on 12 October, he sighted land in the Bahamas. Clumbus described what followed in his *Journal*. 'Immediately they saw naked people, and the admiral [Columbus himself] went ashore in the armed boat . . . The admiral brought out the royal standard, and the captains went with two banners of the green cross, which the admiral flew on all the ships as a flag, with an F and a Y,[1] and over each letter their crown, one being on one side of the cross and the other on the other. When they had landed they saw very green trees and much water and fruit of various kinds. The admiral called the two captains and others who had landed . . . and said that they should bear witness and testimony how he, before them all, took possession of the island, as in fact he did, for the king and queen, his sovereigns.'

Columbus had not sailed across the Atlantic simply to prove the truth of his theory that by so doing he could reach Asia. He was also hoping to find gold and other precious metals with which to enrich himself and reward and encourage his backers and crew. Noticing that some of the natives wore a small piece of gold 'hanging from a hole which they have in the nose' he was able to understand that further south 'there was a king who had large vessels of it and possessed much gold. . . . So I resolved to go to the south-west, to seek the gold and precious stones.' Making his way south he reached Cuba, which he declared to be the mainland of Cathay, and satisfied that he had proved all his major points he sailed for home, taking natives and gold samples with him. Early in March 1493 Columbus arrived in Lisbon, where John II received him with all the outward signs of honour, despite his chagrin at having thrown away the opportunity to be the explorer's

---

[1] The initials of King Ferdinand and Queen Isabella (Ysabel).

patron. From Lisbon Columbus went on to Spain, where he was given a triumphal welcome.

Ferdinand and Isabella were understandably impressed by the result of Columbus's expedition and prepared to subsidise a second voyage. But they had first to clear up the problem of what parts of the world had been pre-empted by Portugal. They therefore appealed to Pope Alexander VI, who in 1493 issued the bull *Inter Caetera Divina*, in which he drew an imaginary line from north to south 100 leagues west of the Azores. Portugal was to have the monopoly of all exploration east of this line, while Spain had the exclusive right to operate in the western section. John II of Portugal accepted the principle of division but asked for the line to be moved farther west. This was done by the Treaty of Tordesillas in June 1494, thereby confirming Portugal's sole right to the Cape route to India and also leaving the way open for her to claim Brazil.

When Columbus set out on his second voyage, in September 1493, he took with him seventeen ships and over a thousand men. The primary object of this expedition was to settle some of the newly discovered islands and use them as a base for further exploration of the area. The main settlement was made in Hispaniola, but Columbus chose a bad site and the settlers not only quarrelled among themselves but also roused the hostility of the natives. In 1496 Columbus returned to Spain, having accomplished little in the way of effective settlement. Two years later he set out again, this time exploring the north coast of South America, from where he made his way back to Hispaniola. Whatever his qualities as a seaman and explorer, Columbus was not a good administrator, and the settlers' complaints against him led the crown to appoint Francisco de Bobadilla to carry out an enquiry. Bobadilla supported the settlers and sent Columbus home in chains. Ferdinand and Isabella freed him and restored his titles and property, but although they allowed him to make his fourth, and last, voyage in 1502, they never again employed him in the government of the territories which he had acquired for them. Bobadilla, a harsh, ruthless and determined man, was far more effective, and it was he who turned the early settlements into reasonably ordered communities based on pasture-farming and panning for gold.

Columbus publicly asserted his conviction that all he had discovered was a western sea route to Cathay, although when he saw the volume of fresh water in the Orinoco delta, and realised that it was far too much to come from an island source, he confided to his *Journal* 'I believe that this is a very great continent, which until today has been unknown'. Others were already coming to the same conclusion. As early as 1493 Peter Martyr wrote that Columbus had found 'indications of a hitherto unknown continent', and in 1507 a German cosmographer published a map in which, for the first time, America was shown as a separate land mass. He named this 'America', after Amerigo Vespucci, whose account of his journeys, published in 1507, gave general currency to the belief that a new continent had been discovered. Vespucci was a Florentine businessman who went to Spain as an agent of the Medici banking house, studied geography and navigation as a hobby, and in 1499 made his first voyage, under the Spanish flag. He then switched his allegiance to Portugal, explored Brazil, and followed the coastline for many miles southwards. It was this long reconnaissance that convinced him that Columbus had inadvertently revealed a new world.

The Conquistadores

After Columbus had shown the way, the rate of exploration rapidly accelerated. By 1500 all the major islands of the Antilles had been discovered and about a thousand miles of the south American coastline reconnoitred. By 1512 four major settlements had been established in the West Indies, on Hispaniola, Cuba, Jamaica and Puerto Rico, and large land grants (*encomiendas*) had been made to private individuals. The new owners were in theory responsible for the wellbeing of the natives, who paid tribute and labour services to them, but in many cases the desire for profit took precedence over humanitarian considerations, and the natives were forced to work beyond the limits of their endurance.

A large number of the settlers who went out to the West Indies were restless men, often ex-soldiers searching for a swift way to wealth and fame. They were always eager to move on to a new place, and in particular to escape from the restricted confines of the islands to the limitless possibilities of the mainland. Such a man was Vasco de Balboa, who came from a minor gentry family and began his career in the New World as a planter in Hispaniola. In 1510 he joined an expedition to the mainland, and survived the horrors of famine, disease and attacks from the natives. In such conditions violence was the order of the day, and Balboa, after leading a revolt against the governor of the new settlement that had been established, took some of the more adventurous spirits with him, moved further up the coast and landed at Darien. From there he marched across the Isthmus, which at this point was at its narrowest, and in 1513 sighted the Pacific. A contemporary recorded the occasion:

'On Tuesday the twenty-fifth of September of the year 1513, at ten o'clock in the morning, Captain Vasco Nuñez, having gone ahead of his company, climbed a hill with a bare summit, and from the top of this hill saw the South Sea. Of all the Christians in his company, he was the first to see it. He turned back toward his people full of joy, lifting his hands and his eyes to heaven, praising Jesus Christ and his glorious mother, the Virgin, Our Lady. Then he fell upon his knees on the ground and gave great thanks to God for the mercy He had shown him in allowing him to discover that sea and thereby to render so great a service to God and to the most serene Catholic Kings of Castile, our sovereigns.'

Another footloose adventurer was Hernando Cortes, who also came from a gentry family and had the rare qualification among the early explorers and *Conquistadores* (conquerors) of a university education, at Salamanca. Cortes had first gone to Hispaniola, but finding the island already settled he joined the force which conquered and occupied Cuba. From there he was sent by the governor to explore the coast of the mainland. The governor was probably thinking in terms of a raiding expedition and reconnaissance, but Cortes had heard stories of a rich and mighty kingdom and was determined to search for it. When he came across a suitable site on the mainland he founded the settlement of Vera Cruz (True Cross), surrendered his commission to the magistrates he appointed, and received from them in return a new commission authorising him, in the name of the Catholic Kings, to continue searching on his own account. With these formalities over—and they showed the respect of the *Conquistadores* for the distant crown of Castile—he set out for the interior. But first of all he ordered all those who were afraid to come with him to return to Cuba, and provided a boat for the purpose. The other boats he burnt.

When Cortes left Vera Cruz in August 1519 his army consisted of less than six hundred men, with sixteen horses, ten small guns and thirteen muskets. With this he proposed to attack and overthrow the great Aztec empire, whose authority extended over most of modern Mexico. He had the invaluable assistance of the subject peoples conquered by the Aztecs; he also had the self-confidence and foolhardiness that came from knowing that the only alternative to victory was death. By November 1519 Cortes had fought his way through to the Aztec capital, Tenochtitlan, a city of some 300,000 inhabitants (larger than any town in Spain). There he was welcomed by the Aztec emperor, Montezuma, who had decided to use diplomacy instead of force, and heaped gifts on the *Conquistador* and his followers. But Cortes was distrustful of this generosity and ordered the seizure of the emperor. A riot broke out in which Montezuma, trying to calm his subjects, was struck by a stone and killed. The furious natives then set upon the invaders and drove them from the city. Cortes did not despair. He reorganised his little army, called for assistance from his native allies, and laid siege to Tenochtitlan. After eighty days it surrendered, and by the end of 1521 Cortes was master of Mexico.

The achievement of Cortes in taking over an entire empire was matched, if not excelled, by Francisco Pizarro, the illegitimate son of an army officer and prostitute, who had been abandoned as a child and earned his living looking after pigs. Pizarro fought as a soldier in the Italian wars and then joined the crew of one of the ships that Columbus took on his second voyage. His restless spirit led him first into the company of Balboa, whom he followed across the Isthmus of Panama to the Pacific coast, and then persuaded him to form a syndicate with some other adventurers to look for a fabulously wealthy kingdom that was reputed to exist somewhere in the south. After four years of searching Pizarro had accumulated sufficient evidence to convince him that this kingdom really did exist, and in 1528 he returned to Spain to ask Charles V for a formal grant of the lands he proposed to conquer. Pizarro arrived at Charles's court at the same time as Cortes, who was distantly related to him, and the climate of opinion was highly favourable to the *Conquistadores*. Pizarro was promised the governorship of all the territories he could acquire, and returned to the New World to make his fortune.

In 1523 Pizarro landed on the north-west coast of South America with 180 men and twenty-seven horses. The Inca empire, which he had come to subdue, stretched south for some two thousand miles and had a population of more than eight million people. It was a highly organised society, ruled over by an emperor who was worshipped as the living embodiment of the sun. Pizarro arrived at an opportune moment, for there was civil war in this vast region between the two heirs of the previous ruler, and the Spanish invasion was already under way before one of the heirs, Atahualpa, was able to defeat his rival and assume the imperial dignity.

The Incas, like the Aztecs before them, were stunned by the speed and audacity of the Spanish advance. The emperor himself was anxious to meet these white gods whose arrival had been foretold by certain prophecies, and accepted Pizarro's invitation to a rendezvous. Pizarro prepared an ambush, and at a given signal Atahualpa was seized and several thousand of his followers massacred. The emperor was the nerve centre of the entire Inca empire, and without him resistance was paralysed. Realising that the Spaniards were greedy for gold, Atahualpa promised to pay a ransom of a room full of it, and ordered precious objects to be sent from all quarters of his realm. Pizarro kept the gold but killed Atahualpa and planned to take over this vast empire for himself. However he had first to defeat his partner, Amalgro, who had explored the southern part of the Inca territories and claimed a larger share of the conquered lands than Pizarro was prepared to allow him. In 1538 civil war broke out among the *Conquistadores*, and although Pizarro was at first successful, and had Amalgro tried and executed, he was himself assassinated by Amalgro's supporters in 1541.

The Administration of the Spanish Empire

The age of the *Conquistadores*, which opened in 1519 when Cortes set out for Mexico, had come to an end by the middle of the century. The vast territories that they had added to the dominions of the crown of Castile needed ruling in an orderly fashion, and Charles V was determined that the *Conquistadores* should not get out of hand. In 1513 he appointed a royal governor, Pedro Arias de Avila, known as Pedrarias, to take over Panama from Balboa. Pedrarias was a man of iron, and when Balboa challenged his authority he had him arrested, tried on a charge of treason, and executed. In 1527 Charles V established an *Audiencia*, or court of appeal, for 'New Spain'—as the Spanish territories other than Peru were now called—and later gave it responsibility for the entire civil administration of the province. But the lawyers and civil servants of the *Audiencia* were simply not strong enough, in these early years of settlement, to deal with the sort of men who had come to seek their fortunes in America. A powerful royal deputy was needed, and in 1535 Charles appointed a soldier-diplomat, Antonio de Mendoza, as the first viceroy of New Spain. Four years later Cortes left America, never to return. He was now a marquis, and as rich as he was famous, but although he joined Charles V in the expedition against Algiers in 1541 he was never given any major military or administrative post. Charles V was understandably niggardly when it came to allowing his subjects a share of greatness, for he knew that if they rose too high their shadow might fall across his own throne.

Although the viceroys appointed to govern New Spain, and later Peru, were given large salaries and treated with great deference, their powers were limited, and patronage remained in the hands of the king. At the end of his term of office every viceroy had to submit to a judicial investigation into his rule, to see whether he had been guilty of misgovernment or speculation. This was carried out by the judges of the *Audiencias*, who gradually succeeded in establishing their authority and became the main agents of royal government in the New World. By 1600 ten of these courts had been created and they were directly responsible to the council of the Indies, set up by Charles V in 1524.

One of the major responsibilities of the *Audiencias* was the protection of native rights, and it was over this question that the crown and the settlers came into open disagreement. The method of colonisation on the mainland was similar to that pioneered in the Caribbean islands, and every settler was granted an *encomienda* of Indian households, who provided him with money and labour in return for protection and moral guidance. Some of these *encomiendas* were enormous—Cortes, for instance, allocated himself more than 20,000 Indian households— and the Catholic Kings were alive to the danger that feudalism, which they had effectively curbed in the old world, might establish itself, to the detriment of their own authority, in the New. This was a development which they were determined to prevent.

Their desire to control and eventually abolish the system of *encomiendas* was not prompted solely by secular motives. The assumption behind *encomiendas* was that the Indians, though admittedly inferior beings whose task was to work for their Spanish masters, should be well treated. In practice, however, there was a great deal of exploitation and brutality, and in many places the natives were no better than slaves. They found a champion in the friars, who displayed in America a social commitment and high idealism that had all too frequently been lacking among their brothers in Europe. The first friars to reach the American mainland were the famous 'Twelve', a group of hand-picked Franciscans sent out in response to a request from Cortes. They were followed a few years later by the Dominicans, and it was a member of this order, Bartolomeo de Las Casas, who became the embodiment of the Spanish conscience and the most famous church-man in the New World. Las Casas and his fellow friars had a great deal of sympathy for the Indians, whose customs they studied and whose languages they learned. It was as a direct consequence of the pressure kept up both in Spain and America by Las Casas and his supporters that in 1542 Charles V issued 'the New Laws of the Indies', declaring that all *encomiendas* should revert to the crown on the death of the existing beneficiary, and that the Indians should be returned to their villages. This meant that the settlers would be left with their land but without forced labour to cultivate it, a prospect which drove them to revolt. In New Spain Mendoza secured the suspension of the New Laws before they came into effect, while in Peru there was open resistance. But although the Spanish government was prepared to take its time, it did not waver in its ultimate aim. By the end of the sixteenth century the *encomiendas* had been eliminated, and royal *Corregidors* had established the crown's authority over the settler-barons.

In their concern for the welfare of the Indians the friars established colonies of their own, each concentrated round a newly built church, in which the traditional native way of life could be combined with instruction in the Christian faith. This practice was enormously ex-tended by the Jesuits, whose reservations in Paraguay, known as *reductions*, were virtually separate states. The effect of this policy was to divorce the life of the Indians from that of the Spanish settlers, and it might ultimately have led to the creation not simply of a self-governing Indian community but also of an Indian church directed by native bishops. But the ecclesiastical authorities in the New World were increasingly suspicious of the radicalism of the religious orders and resented their freedom from episcopal control. The first Bishop of Mexico had been appointed in 1527, and by the end of the century there were close on twenty dioceses in Spanish America. In 1565 and 1585 Mexican church councils ordered that the Trent decrees requiring all clerics to submit to episcopal control should be enforced in New Spain, and the authority of the ecclesiastical hierarchy was steadily expanded, to the detriment of the religious orders.

In Mexico, the Indians had been more or less forcibly integrated into the life of the settler community, and even after the reduction of the *encomiendas* they were subject to forced labour (*repartimiento*), which brought them under the supervision of Spanish ranchers or the Spanish managers of silver mines. In Peru the situation was basically different.

The Inca capital had been in the mountains, but Pizarro built a new one at Lima, in the coastal plain. The division between plain and high-lands, Spanish and native, remained a feature of Peruvian life, and there was nothing like the assimilation of the two cultures that took place in Mexico.

Indians who found their traditional pattern of agriculture disrupted, or who were forced to work in the mines, were often unable to adapt to the abrupt change in their way of life. They were also highly susceptible to diseases brought in by the conquerors. As a result the death rate went up, and the population of central Mexico shrank from about eleven million at the time of Cortes's arrival to some two and a half million by 1590. The same decline occurred in the Caribbean islands which were the first places to be settled in the New World. When Columbus discovered Hispaniola in 1492 it had a Carib popu-lation of about 300,000, but some fifty years later there were only five hundred Caribs left. Land was useless without labour, and since the Spanish settlers were not ready to do the work of cultivation them-selves, they needed another source of manpower. This was found in Africa. The first official record of Negro slaves in the New World dates from 1505, but it seems likely that they arrived soon after settle-ment began. Spanish merchants alone could not supply enough slaves, and the gap was filled by the Portuguese, who were already well established in the slave trade from west Africa to Europe. As Spanish occupation expanded so did slavery, and the demand for slaves was so high that it could not be satisfied. By the middle of the century the Portuguese were shipping about 13,000 slaves a year to the Spanish colonies, but there was room for many more, as Hawkins discovered when he tried to break into this monopoly in the 1560s.

Spanish Trade with the New World

Although the Portuguese traded with the Spanish colonies in the New World, they did so, nominally at least, only as the agents of the Spanish holders of licences (*asientos*). In theory trade with the Indies was reserved for Castilians—even Aragonese were barred from it—and it was channelled through the *Casa de Contratacion* (House of Trade) set up in Seville in 1503. Seville seemed the obvious place, for the countryside around it produced the grain, olive oil and wine needed by the early settlers. But as the colonies expanded and de-veloped they demanded a greater variety of goods, which Seville alone could not supply. Other parts of Spain were called on to redress the balance, and this at first stimulated Spanish industry to increase its production of arms and cutlery, leather, silk and fine cloths. But the demand was so great and growing at such a rapid rate that the resources of Germany and the Netherlands had to be tapped, and Seville became an entrepot for goods from all over Europe.

In the first half of the sixteenth century ships could leave Seville as and when they wished, provided they had paid the necessary dues, but in 1542 a convoy system was set up to meet the threat from French privateers, and in the 1560s, when the seas became infested with hostile ships, it was made permanent. Two fleets sailed from Seville every year. The first, for New Spain, left in May, with Vera Cruz as its destination, while the Peru fleet left for Nombre de Dios in August. The fleets wintered in the New World and then reassembled at Havana for the return journey.

The major cargo carried by the returning ships was silver. Some of this came from New Spain, but the principal source was the mountain of silver discovered at Potosi (in modern Bolivia). One-fifth (*quinto*) of all precious metals mined went to the crown, and American silver became a substantial item in the revenue of the kings of Spain. By 1580 it accounted for 10 per cent of the royal income, and as production mounted in the years that followed, this proportion rose to 25 per cent. The annual silver fleet was a great temptation for privateers, but the convoy system worked well, and although an occasional straggler might be lost the majority of ships reached Spain in safety.

American trade was not confined to Spain. After the Spanish occupation of the Philippines in the late 1560s, silk and other goods from China were shipped from Manila to Acapulco in Mexico. These imports had to be paid for in silver, and since Mexico's own silver supplies were fully consumed by domestic needs and royal taxation, part of the Manila cargoes were reshipped to Peru, which was rich in silver but poor in manufactured articles. This triangular trade between the two viceroyalties and the Philippines was not entirely to the liking of the Spanish government, since it meant that Peruvian silver was being diverted from Spain itself, but the volume of traffic was limited by the hazardous nature of the long sea voyage, and not until the seventeenth century did the Spanish crown formally prohibit all direct trade between Peru and New Spain.

America and Europe

The Spaniards were not the only Europeans in the New World. Brazil had been claimed by Portugal, and small-scale settlement took place. The region produced the highly prized red dye wood after which it was named, and the soil and climate were also well suited to the cultivation of sugar. For many years the Portuguese were too taken up with their eastern route to the Indies to pay much attention to this western outpost, and much of the territory was occupied by French settlers. In 1549, however, the first Portuguese captain-general was sent out, the French were gradually expelled, and new settlements were founded, among them Rio de Janeiro in 1567.

The northern part of the American continent was also left open by the Spaniards to foreign penetration. They simply did not have the resources to occupy this enormous area at a time when they were already fully extended in the centre and south; and expeditions sent out in the 1530s and 1540s found no trace of the precious metals which were the main incentive to colonisation. The French, however, were active in the exploration of the north American coast. Jacques Cartier made three voyages between 1534 and 1542, in the course of which he sailed up the St Lawrence, discovering that it was only a river and not the longed-for north-west passage to Asia, and formally took possession of the land of 'Canada' for the French crown. Some attempts at settlement were made, but they were not successful, and the exploitation of Cartier's discoveries had to wait until the next century. The same is true of the English, who had staked a claim to the north-west by sending out John Cabot in 1496. Cabot discovered Newfoundland, and Henry VII was sufficiently encouraged by the results of this expedition to send him off again. From this second voyage, however, he never returned, and although royal patronage was extended to his son, Sebastian, who may have explored the Hudson Bay region in 1508–09, English interest lapsed with the accession of Henry VIII. Not until Elizabeth's reign was an attempt made to establish a settlement, in Virginia, but this was not a success. The English and the French, in fact, found illegal trade with the Spanish empire and attacks on Spanish shipping more immediately rewarding than colonisation. They were content to leave the hard work and expense of founding viable settlements to the Spaniards, and then cream off the profits.

For Europeans the New World was primarily a source of precious metals. But there were other products, whose effect on the old world was to be of longer duration. When Columbus returned to Spain from his first voyages, he brought with him 'Indian corn', or maize, which rapidly became a staple item in the diet of southern Europe. Cartier was probably responsible for the introduction of beans to France, whence they spread to England ('French beans'). Tobacco seed was shipped from Florida to France in 1561, and snuff-taking and later smoking, introduced to the west by Sir Walter Ralegh, began their pernicious spread among the peoples of Europe. Potatoes and tomatoes were brought in to vary the somewhat dreary standard diet, and the Spaniards introduced turkeys to the western world, thereby displacing roast beef as the popular Christmas dish. They also brought back from Mexico the fruit of the cacao tree, which Cortes had found the natives using as a bitter porridge, but which, when mixed with sugar and milk, produced a delicious drink called cocoa. Not all the products of the New World were as welcome as these, and it seems likely that among the less desirable importations into Europe was venereal disease. But for better or worse the economy of the old world was firmly linked with that of America, the Far East and Africa, and the way was opened to the phenomenal expansion of western European power and trade which was to be so marked a feature of the ensuing centuries.

THREE

The European Economy in the Sixteenth and Seventeenth Centuries

Population and the Price Rise

Two major influences, an increase in population and a sharp rise in prices, affected the European economy in the sixteenth century. Accurate figures in either case are impossible to come by, but it seems likely that in the hundred and fifty years after 1450 the European population recovered from the sharp decline caused by the Black Death and repeated attacks of plague. One estimate is that in 1450 Europe had a population of between 40 and 50 million, while in 1600 the corresponding figure was 80 or 85 million—in other words an increase of at least 60 per cent. There are no very obvious reasons for this reversal of the previous downward trend. Presumably the survivors of plague attacks gradually built up an immunity to infection, and at the same time the brown rat was driving out the black rat—the main plague carrier. European states were also making public provision against famine, and the growth of an international grain market helped alleviate shortages in particular areas. Standards of living for the general population remained very low, and poor sanitation and inadequate medical knowledge left men and women at the mercy of disease, but it seems likely that the death rate was declining and that more babies were surviving to reach maturity.

The symptoms of an increased population became everywhere apparent. In the countryside pressure on available land led to an extension of the area under cultivation, as 'waste' was turned into pasture or arable. But more land, much of it of inferior quality, could not of itself provide an outlet for surplus population, nor could holdings be indefinitely partitioned and repartitioned among more and more children. Many people had to leave the land and either go to the ever-swelling towns or join the bands of 'vagabonds' who roamed the countryside, pillaging and terrorising the inhabitants. As for the towns, they were often unable to cope with increased numbers, particularly as there was only a limited expansion of industrial production and therefore little extra work available for the hundreds of people who needed it. The problem of poverty became acute in every country, and when in 1526 the Spanish humanist Juan Luis Vives produced his book *De Subventione Pauperum*, putting forward proposals for poor relief, it was swiftly translated into all the main European languages.

Europe remained predominantly rural, but urbanisation was increasing in pace. In 1500 there were probably only five cities with a population of more than 100,000—Constantinople, Naples, Venice, Milan and Paris. These continued to grow, but they were joined during the course of the sixteenth century, by seven or eight newcomers, among them Rome, Palermo, Seville, London, Antwerp and Amsterdam. Smaller towns were also increasing in size, and throughout Europe they acted as magnets, drawing towards them the surplus population from the surrounding countryside. For many men, however, the town was only a temporary resting place. The need to live drove them to join the professional armies which the rulers of Europe were creating during this period, or to cross the Atlantic and undertake the hazardous business of colonisation.

Increasing pressure of population on limited resources was one of the causes of the price rise which marked the period after 1450. There was no uniformity about this, and the intensity of inflation varied not only from decade to decade but also from one country to another. Galloping inflation did not come until after 1560, but in the period 1450–1500 there was a slow but steady rise of about one per cent per annum. Among the causes of the price rise was the increasing quantity of gold and silver entering the European monetary system. The principal source of gold was Africa. It came at first by mule train across the Sahara to the Mediterranean, but as Portuguese exploration of that continent advanced, more and more gold was brought by sea to Lisbon.

Silver was found nearer home, in eastern Europe, but the cost of mining it was high and capital was needed. In 1451 the Duke of Saxony authorised the use of lead to extract the silver from the ore, and gradually German production increased. By the 1540s, however, its relative importance declined as more and more bullion was shipped into Europe from Spanish America. The big change came after 1545 when a mountain of silver was discovered at Potosi (in presentday Bolivia). By 1560 European silver production had reached 65,000 kilograms a year (two-thirds of it German), but the American mines were producing 200,000 kilograms annually, and by 1581 this figure had jumped to 300,000.

The influx of silver at such a rate unbalanced the entire European financial system. Gold was virtually driven out of circulation, and, as agricultural and industrial production did not increase at anything like the same rate as the amount of money, prices soared. Spain felt the impact first, since she had the monopoly of bullion imports from the New World, but Philip II's constant involvement in European politics meant that silver, and with it inflation, was exported from Spain to other European countries. By 1600 Spanish prices were four times as high as they had been a century earlier. No other country suffered quite so badly as this—in France, for instance, prices rose two and half times during the course of the century—but inflation became a European phenomenon.

The price rise was not an unmitigated evil. The disparity in the level of prices between one part of Europe and another was a stimulus to trade, and merchants and agricultural producers on long leases at low rents could make their fortunes. People on fixed incomes, on the other hand, suffered great hardship; nor were wage-earners much better off, for although wages went up prices increased far more rapidly. The standard of living of the greater part of the European population therefore declined, at the very moment and for the same reason that huge fortunes were being made by entrepreneurs and financiers. The widening gap between wages and prices was at the root of a great deal of sixteenth century disorder—the Anabaptist rising in Munster in 1534, for instance—and patterns of life which had been based on the assumption of price stability were rudely shaken. As one French landowner commented in 1560: 'In my father's time there was meat every day, food was plentiful, men drank wine as though it was water. But all that has quite changed today. Everything is dear . . . the food of the most prosperous peasants is much poorer than the food which servants used to eat.'

Finance

The discovery of America and of a sea route to India slowly shifted the centre of gravity of the European commercial system from the Mediterranean to the Atlantic, and turned Antwerp into the financial capital of the continent. A milestone in its development came in 1499 when the King of Portugal's factor established himself in the city and made it the centre of distribution for the spices brought by Portuguese ships from the far east. In 1501 the first consignment of pepper from Lisbon was sold in Antwerp, and three years later a thousand tons of precious spices were brought up the Scheldt. Since the spice trade was so important to Europe, Antwerp became a magnet for merchants from all over the continent, and this in turn encouraged the development of banking and ancillary services. At first two fairs were held every year, but this number was later doubled, and the Antwerp fairs became in effect European markets in which the goods of several continents were bought and bartered.

Credit was common in these transactions, as was demonstrated in 1531 by the construction of a new Exchange, open to traders of all nations. For richer merchants, exchange operations gradually became more important than commerce, and by making loans at a high rate of interest they found a lucrative outlet for their capital. Antwerp's importance as a financial centre was enormously increased by its political connection with the Habsburg dynasty. In 1511 the city made its first public loan to the Netherlands government, and from then onwards such transactions were frequent. Interest rates fluctuated around 15 per cent, and there was no shortage of capital. As the Habsburgs became more and more involved in European war and diplomacy so the scale of their borrowing increased, and they were not alone in their demands. Henry VIII of England, for instance, raised a million pounds in loans on the Antwerp market during the closing years of his reign.

Although credit transactions were increasingly important they were not the only basis of Antwerp's wealth. The city was geographically well placed for trade with western Europe, and it also became a major centre for the cloth industry of the surrounding countryside. Trade, industry and finance were all inextricably involved in the prosperity of Antwerp, and for more than half a century the city's predominance in European economic life was unchallenged. By 1550, however, its great days were drawing to a close. The Portuguese factor had left in 1549, since the spice trade was now being handled direct from Lisbon, while the revival of the Levant route restored Venice to much of her former importance. German silver had been priced out of the market by American, which went direct to Spain, and the English cloth trade—

one of the foundations of the Antwerp market—was badly hit by over-production in the early 1550s. On top of these changes in the pattern of European commerce came the financial crises caused by the French and Spanish bankruptcies in 1557, the disruption that resulted from the outbreak of the revolt against Spanish rule, and finally the closing of the Scheldt by the Dutch. By the end of the century Antwerp was no longer the commercial and financial capital of Europe. Its place had been taken by Amsterdam.

Although Antwerp had been a major financial centre it was not the only one in Europe. In France the city of Lyons was well placed for merchants from Italy, Germany and Switzerland, and at its four annual fairs credit transactions became the rule. Just as the expansion of Habsburg power had stimulated the development of Antwerp, so Lyons profited from the wars and diplomacy of the Valois kings of France. It was to Lyons that Francis I turned for money to pay his armies and supply the German Lutheran princes, and in 1542 the governor of the city, Cardinal de Tournon, pioneered a new way of raising loans. There were many small investors who usually lent their capital to banks in return for an assured income at an average rate of 5 to 8 per cent. The cardinal, with the advice of Italian financiers, now offered a minimum of 10 per cent, guaranteed by the municipality itself. These *Tournons*, as they were quickly called, were extremely successful in tapping the considerable reserves of wealth distributed among the merchants, lawyers and richer artisans and farmers. Such people were more concerned with an assured income than repayment of capital, and the gilt-edged security of the city of Lyons suited their purposes ideally. The only danger to the long-term success of the scheme came from the fact that the royal revenue was not expanding at a sufficient rate to make possible the redemption of these loans, or even to maintain interest payments. By the time Francis I died in 1547 the debt to Lyons far exceeded the amount of money in the royal treasury, and the renewal of the Habsburg–Valois struggle under Henry II meant further appeals for loans. In 1555 Tournon revived his original plan but this time on a far bigger scale. He persuaded a consortium of bankers to advance two and a half million crowns to the royal government—a sum sufficient to wipe out the entire debt—and invited contributions direct from private persons instead of, as before, using the city of Lyons as an intermediary. The result was a sort of South Sea Bubble, as people rushed to lend money and assure themselves of a high rate of interest, but the large sums that were raised were dissipated in war. In August 1557 the French army was defeated at St Quentin, and in the following month the royal council announced that interest payments on the *Tournons* could not be met in full. Further suspensions followed, and the paper value of the *Tournons* dropped to 40 per cent.

Much the same happened in Spain. Although the crown's revenue was constantly increasing, due to the influx of bullion from the New World, it could not keep pace with expenditure, which went up and up. New devices were used to raise revenue, among them the vending of patents of nobility and the creation and sale of new offices, but these were not of themselves sufficient. The crown therefore made available *Juros*, which were, like the French *Tournons*, annuities on state revenues, sold for ten to fifteen times their yearly value. This national debt grew steadily, under the inexorable pressure of Habsburg involvement in European affairs, and on a number of occasions Charles V had to suspend interest payments. Nevertheless the debt mounted, and revenues were mortgaged far ahead. In 1554 Philip wrote in despair to his father, telling him that 'we do not know where or how these sums can be found, since the revenue from the Indies, with the charges assigned on them, cannot be disposed of for several years'. When Philip consulted the theologians they told him that as usury was against the laws of the Church he was not bound to pay interest, but he appreciated that if the crown repudiated its debts it would be unable to raise loans in future. In 1557, therefore, by the decree of Valladolid, he ordered that all interest payments should be suspended, that assignments on future revenues should be cancelled, and that *Juros* should be consolidated at a rate of 5 per cent. This amounted to a declaration of state bankruptcy, and coming as it did at the same time as the French government found itself unable to meet its commitments, it led to the severe financial crisis of 1557. The credit mechanism of the Antwerp fairs was upset, settlements of accounts were postponed, and a number of the south German banking houses went into liquidation.

Among those who suffered very heavy losses by lending to governments were the Fuggers of Augsburg—the Rothschilds of the sixteenth century. Fugger capital had expanded from a mere 200,000 florins in 1510 to over 5 million by the middle of the century, but the family lost more than 9 million florins on loans to the Habsburgs, and the rate of return on their capital showed a sharp decline. In the 1520s it was as high as 50 per cent, but by the 1550s it was down to 5½ per cent. Even this was rosy compared with what followed, for in the 1560s the

Fuggers made a net loss. Their days as the greatest bankers of the western world were over, and their place was taken first by the Genoese and then by the Dutch, who had the security of their enormous and increasing commercial wealth.

Financial operations could be extremely risky, yet they were essential to the political as well as the economic life of Europe, and by the end of the sixteenth century the methods originally pioneered by the Italians in the late Middle Ages had been widely adapted. An international credit system, whatever its imperfections, now existed; bills of exchange reduced the need for actual transfers of bullion; and banking was being increasingly recognised as a legitimate and desirable form of economic activity. Much of the old prejudice against the taking of interest ('usury') remained, but it had to come to terms with the facts of financial life—prominent among them the unwillingness of people to lend money unless they were repaid more than their original investment. A public bank was established in Venice in 1587, and although attempts to do the same in France and Spain in the first decade of the seventeenth century met with failure, the Dutch successfully launched the Bank of Amsterdam in 1609.

Industry

The capital which made possible the development of a credit system came from industry and commerce. The Fuggers, for instance, began as small traders in cloth, invested in copper mining, and in return for loans to the Habsburgs were given monopoly rights over the copper and silver mines first of the Tyrol and later Hungary and Silesia. The Fuggers came from Augsburg, which shared with Nuremberg the reputation of producing the finest gold and silver plate in Europe. It was not by coincidence that these cities of central and southern Germany gave birth to the first major European bankers outside Italy. They were astride the commercial land route from the Mediterranean to the north and west; they were within easy access of the mines and metallurgical industries of eastern Europe; they had trading connections all over the continent; and their close relationship with the Habsburg rulers impelled them into financial operations that transcended national frontiers.

The mining and extraction of precious metals demanded machinery, such as hydraulic hammers and ore-crushers, which was beyond the pocket of the ordinary artisan. Medieval industry had, generally

speaking, been a small-scale affair, in which the family was the basic
unit, but now there was an ever-widening gap between the capitalist
who owned the raw material and the workmen who processed it. This
applied to other industries as well as mining and metallurgy. Cloth
manufacture, for example, which involved more people than any other
occupation except agriculture, showed the same features. To escape the
restrictive regulations of urban gilds, capitalist clothiers would 'put
out' the raw wool to inhabitants of the surrounding countryside and
collect the finished product which they then sold. The cottager who
spun or wove the cloth had no share in its ownership, and was dependent for employment and payment upon the merchant who supplied
her.

Even in a new and relatively small-scale industry, such as printing,
there was a big gap between the workman who had nothing to offer
but his labour, and the person or persons who owned the press itself,
the founts, the stocks of paper and the other essential articles. The raw
material and the machinery were pieces of property, not belonging to
those who used them, and could be bought and sold, bequeathed or
given away, just like any other article. The profits of such industrial
operations went not to the workmen but to the owner, and the capital
which he thereby accumulated made possible the extension of his
influence. He could either spend it on more material and more
machinery, or invest it in loans. This nascent capitalism could be seen
in operation in a number of European centres, and it was no coincidence
that a place like Lyons, which was a centre of the silk industry and by
1515 had over a hundred printing presses, should have developed into
a major financial centre.

Although many industrial activities kept their family character, the
larger ones were based on a distinction between master and men.
Entry into the ranks of the masters became increasingly difficult. Long
apprenticeships were demanded, or substantial fees, with the result that
only those whose parents were already masters or who had money of
their own could hope to enter. The rest were 'journeymen'—men who
worked and were paid by the day (*journée*)—and since wages were
falling behind prices their economic as well as their social status
declined. They were increasingly excluded not simply from any control
over the industry in which they worked but also from any share in the
government of the cities where they lived. They became an urban
proletariat, living on or near the poverty line, and struggling to get
enough to eat. Since they had little or no hope of improving their

condition, except by destroying the social system which imprisoned them, their feelings were easily aroused by radical preachers, whether these spoke the language of politics or religion. This urban proletariat, then, was a seething cauldron of discontent, which at times bubbled over. There was a major revolt in Lyons in 1529, when the poor took over the government of the town; while in the Netherlands discontent which had its roots in economic and social conditions found expression in the Iconoclastic Riots (see p. 239). There was, in this sense, a close connection between religious and social radicalism.

Agriculture

Although towns were expanding and becoming increasingly important in the life of Europe, the majority of the population lived and worked on the land, and their condition varied from place to place. This was particularly marked in Germany. In the north-west, serfdom had generally speaking given way to leasehold tenure, but in the south-west, where the Church held a great deal of property, serfdom was slow to disappear and labour services and dues were strictly enforced— hence the widespread hatred of the Catholic Church. The biggest difference of all, however, was between western and eastern Germany. In the west villeinage had gone or was going, and as agrarian prices at last began to rise, in the second half of the sixteenth century, the position of the peasant improved. But east of the Elbe (with the exception of Electoral Saxony) it was the landlords who determined the nature of social and economic change. They had big estates, where grain could be grown in large quantities to supply the western European market, and easy access to lakes and rivers to transport it. They therefore created vast plantations, on which the peasants were not simply bound to the soil but subject also to their lords' jurisdiction. While villeinage was dying out in the west, then, it was being revived in the east.

The unfortunate peasant could not even escape into industry since this scarcely existed. Any articles which could not be produced locally were imported from the west, and there was consequently no incentive to establish native industries. Nor indeed would there have been any market for their products since the majority of people lived at such a low level that they had little or nothing to spare for manufactured goods. Even in the west industry never managed to break through to the mass market, but it could take advantage of the demand that came from urban populations. In eastern Germany there was little demand for anything other than luxury items for the landowners. Economically speaking, then, Europe was split down the middle, and the eastern part was not much more than a reservoir on which the inhabitants of the richer and more advanced western area could draw at will.

In France the Hundred Years War had caused widespread depopulation, and in many places cultivated land had reverted to waste. Recovery set in about 1480, and landlords were so anxious to restore production on their estates that they made agreements which were often highly favourable to the peasants. Long, or even perpetual, leases were granted in return for small money payments, and as inflation set in the value of these payments declined to such a point that many landowners faced bankruptcy. The peasants were also successful in throwing off their servile status, and in 1544 Francis I formally abolished villeinage on all crown properties. The peasants suffered, however, from a shortage of capital, because their holdings were divided and subdivided to meet the demands of an increasing population, and productivity was therefore limited. There was plenty of spare capital in France, but it went into unproductive investment rather than agriculture. Some peasants did well enough to buy up estates and become landlords themselves, but the majority produced only enough to live on and to pay the very heavy taxes to which they were subject. Even so their position was often better than that of the smaller nobles, who were not supposed to sully their hands with manual labour and were therefore dependent on the royal court or the army for additional income. In France, as in Germany, religious bitterness fed on this economic and social discontent.

Spain in some ways resembled eastern Germany, in that it had vast estates worked by a subordinate peasant population and not a great deal of industry. Although grain was produced in Old Castile, and the vine and olive were cultivated in the south, large parts of Spain were unsuitable for anything but sheep, and pasture farming was carried out on a very big scale. Every year some two or three million sheep would be shifted from their summer pastures in the north to their winter feeding four hundred miles south. They moved along traditional routes, consuming everything as they went, and were regarded by local farmers as little better than a plague of locusts. There was nothing these farmers could do, however, for the sheep owners had organised themselves into a powerful organisation called the *Mesta*, which, in return for loans to the crown, was given the perpetual right to use, at a fixed rent, any land through which its routes customarily passed.

Agriculture suffered from this, but the crown was more interested in the revenue it could secure from the *Mesta* than in maintaining a balanced economy. Other interests were also involved, for wool was the major product of Spain and, prior to the exploitation of the mineral resources of the New World, her main source of prosperity. Wool from all over Spain was collected at Medina del Campo and Burgos, and from there taken by mule train to Bilbao for shipment to Flanders. In the early sixteenth century a great deal had also been sent to the factories of Florence and Milan, but as the supply of English wool dried up, with the development of a native cloth industry in England, the demand for Spanish wool in western Europe showed a marked increase. The only limiting factor was the price, and Spanish wool-growers and merchants suffered from the fact that the Spanish price rise was always ahead of that in other countries. By 1550 Spanish wool was so expensive that sales slackened off, and the following decade saw a reduction of 20 per cent in the size of flocks.

The concentration on exports of raw wool prevented the textile industries of Barcelona, Valencia and other towns from attaining the size and level of activity that was reached in Italy and England. So too did the general prejudice against trade and industry. The rulers of Spain, like those of eastern Germany, preferred to import manufactured articles rather than encourage industrial production at home. This created an imbalance in Spanish trade, since the price of imported manufactures was higher than that of the exported raw materials. The gap was filled by bullion, but this meant that the prosperity of Spain became dangerously dependent on silver, and therefore on the lifeline that stretched from Seville across the Atlantic.

In Italy there was a sharp division, economically speaking, between the north and the south. The north was dominated by the great city-states, which drew their wealth mainly from trade, imported grain to feed their large populations, and looked to the small farmers of the surrounding countryside to supply them with olives, wine and meat. In the south there were many large estates, and Sicily was one of the major exporters of grain to southern Europe. Mediterranean trade had developed around the transport of corn from the Levant and Sicily to the cities of Italy and eastern Spain, and the merchants and shipbuilders of Venice and Genoa throve on this traffic.

Commerce

The other major source of Venetian wealth had been the spices which were brought overland from the east to the ports of the Levant, taken from there by Venetian ships, and distributed throughout the whole of Europe. The Portuguese discovery of a sea route to India and the far east disrupted this trade, not simply because spices were now being shipped direct from the East Indies to Lisbon, but even more because the Portuguese, in their attempt to establish a monopoly of this lucrative commerce, tried to close up the older routes through the Persian Gulf. In this, however, they were ultimately unsuccessful, and after a period in which it seemed as though the old spice routes and Venice would decline together, trade picked up, until by the middle of the century the volume of spices reaching Venice was as great as it had ever been.

In the late Middle Ages Venetian galleys had made regular annual voyages to Flanders and England, thereby linking the Mediterranean and the Atlantic trade zones. The two economies dovetailed nicely, since the south provided wine, olives and olive oil, fish and dried fruit, cottons and silks, while the north was rich in the necessities of life, such as grain, fish, timber and wool. Trade between the two areas increased during the sixteenth century, though it probably never equalled in volume the interchange of goods within each zone, but the initiative gradually passed from the Mediterranean to the Atlantic countries.

One reason for this was the expansion of western European commerce along the north–south axis from the Baltic to Spain. The Baltic area was naturally rich in timber, tar and other commodities that Spain needed for her merchant and fighting fleets. The Spanish mercantile marine was second in size only to the Dutch, and Bilbao was a major centre for shipbuilding. The quality of Spanish ships was demonstrated by the regularity with which they made the Atlantic crossing, but the demands of the shipyards depleted the not very abundant timber resources of the Iberian peninsula and Spain became increasingly dependent on supplies from the Baltic. As the sixteenth century advanced Spain also needed grain imports—since her own agriculture was dominated by pasture-farming—and these, once again, came from the Baltic.

Danzig was the major port for timber exports and even more so for grain, since the produce of Poland and east Germany could be easily transported to her along the Vistula. Danzig was nominally associated with Lubeck, the other major port of north-east Europe, in the Hanseatic League, but the interests of the two were beginning to diverge. Only a narrow neck of land separated Lubeck on the Baltic, from Hamburg on the North Sea, and in the late Middle Ages ships preferred to load and unload their goods at Hamburg rather than risk the long journey around the tip of Denmark into the Sound. Lubeck therefore became the major entrepot in the Baltic, and as capital of the Hanseatic League she was a power in her own right. The Dutch, however, pioneered the sea route into the Sound, and the number of ships using this increased very markedly during the sixteenth century. In 1500, for instance, only about 1,300 vessels passed into the Sound, but by 1600 the figure had risen to 5,000, of which the great majority were Dutch. Lubeck resented this Dutch 'invasion', which threatened her commercial supremacy, but despite her efforts to close the Sound to Dutch shipping by intervening in Scandinavian politics she could not maintain her dominant position.

The Dutch had moved into the North Sea in search of herring, and built a special type of ship, the 'buss', on which they could clean, salt and barrel the fish. In catholic Europe, with its regular weekly fast days, fish was an essential commodity, and it was also in demand during the winter, when meat was not easily obtainable. With the wealth and the experience obtained from herring-fishing the Dutch extended their activities into the carrying trade and by the end of the sixteenth century they had come to dominate this. It was Dutch ships which carried timber and grain from the Baltic to the Netherlands and Spain, and it was Dutch ships again which carried Spanish wool, wine and olives, as well as salt from Portugal, to the countries of northern Europe.

Until the 1530s the initiative in trade between the Atlantic and Mediterranean regions still lay with Venice, but she was hit by the Portuguese attack on her traditional sources of supply and was also finding it increasingly difficult to man the old-fashioned galleys which made the annual voyages to Europe. The last galley fleet to Flanders sailed in 1532, and after that date the Venetians ceased to have a major direct influence on the economic life of western Europe. Their mantle had fallen on the Dutch, and in the second half of the sixteenth century the Dutch were penetrating into the Mediterranean. They were drawn there by famine, for the Mediterranean had ceased to be self-sufficient in grain. The population of the Levant and Balkan area under Turkish rule was increasing and therefore consuming more and more of the corn it produced, while Sicily, that other major supplier of grain, was hit by bad harvests and also had to supply cities like Palermo which were rapidly growing. In 1575–77 there was famine in Sicily, and the effect of diminishing grain supplies was also felt in Naples. The gap between supply and demand was filled by the Dutch, who were used to carrying large quantities of grain from the Baltic and could ship it as easily to Italy as to the Netherlands and Spain. They also took salted cod, since Mediterranean fish supplies were insufficient, and pushed further and further east until by the 1590s they had reached the Levant, traditionally the preserve of Venice.

The Dutch were not alone in their penetration of the Mediterranean. English, and, to a lesser extent, German ships also took part in this, despite the risk of attacks from the pirates of the Barbary coast of North Africa. The presence of Atlantic ships in the Mediterranean symbolised the shift that had taken place in the power structure of Europe. In 1500 Mediterranean countries like Italy and Spain had been in the van of economic and intellectual life, and Europe had looked south for leadership and inspiration. By 1600 this was no longer so. The great days of the Mediterranean states were over, and the predominance of Spain did not long survive the death of Philip II. The Atlantic, which had previously been the frontier of the known world, was now becoming its centre.

Dutch Commercial Supremacy

There was no sudden or dramatic change in the European economy as the sixteenth century gave way to the seventeenth, but frequent slumps soon made it apparent that the rate of growth was slowing down. The buoyancy of the sixteenth-century economy had been due in large part to population expansion and inflation, but these two stimulants ceased to operate from the 1620s onwards. By 1650 at the latest prices had passed their peak and from then on remained stationary or began to fall. Much the same was true of population, though in some places decline had already set in by 1600. Repeated harvest failures led not only to deaths through starvation but also to a general lowering of the level of resistance to infectious diseases. Plague, which had always been endemic, became once again a major killer, and the outbreak of 1630 carried off some million and a half people in the Italian peninsula alone.

Crowded and insanitary cities were an obvious target, but plague and famine struck in the countryside as well and made the problem of rural depopulation acute in areas such as Valencia. The Mediterranean countries suffered most, and these natural disasters accelerated and confirmed the transference of economic and political power to northern and western Europe. While London, Amsterdam and Vienna were steadily increasing in size and numbers, Palermo, Messina and Seville were in decline. The population of Spain shrank from 8 million at the beginning of the seventeenth century to $7\frac{1}{4}$ million at the end, while Italy suffered an even more marked reduction from 13 to $11\frac{1}{4}$ million.

Northern Europe was not, of course, immune to plague and famine, and in many areas the operation of natural forces was intensified by manmade catastrophes. In Germany, for example, repeated invasions and devastations led to a fall in numbers from 20 million to just over 15 million during the course of the seventeenth century, and Poland and Hungary are two more instances of regions in which prolonged warfare caused a marked decline in the population. But although plague hit northern and western Europe in the second half of the seventeenth century it did not check the economic advance of seaboard states such as Holland, England and France. The herring industry remained the basis of Dutch prosperity, though as the century wore on there was increasing competition from the fisheries of New England and Newfoundland. Dutch merchants were also firmly ensconced in the extremely lucrative north–south trade between the Baltic and the Mediterranean, and even as late as 1720 more than 40 per cent of the ships on this route came from the United Provinces. The Dutch had constructed a bulk carrier, the *fluyt*, for the shipment of grain, timber and other commodities, and their freight rates were some 30 per cent lower than those of other countries. If international trade had been a free-for-all the Dutch would no doubt have continued to dominate it; but other states, envious of the prosperity of the United Provinces, used the instruments of government to foster their own trade and industry at the same time as they discriminated against those of others. The English Navigation Acts and Colbert's restrictive tariffs were examples of this mercantilist policy at work, for the prevailing assumption was that trade meant power and that the commercial expansion of one country must necessarily be at the expense of its rivals. It is not possible to say for certain how effective government measures were in altering patterns of commerce, but by 1700 the Dutch were no longer unchallenged as the leading merchants of the western world. The English and the French were close on their heels.

In their heyday, during the first half of the seventeenth century, the Dutch had given a lead to the rest of Europe not only in trade but in finance and industry as well. In 1609 they set up an Exchange in Amsterdam, which rapidly became a meeting-place for merchants and financiers from all over the continent, and four years later they established a loan bank to provide capital for mercantile ventures. Money was also invested in the manufacture of textiles, particularly the 'New Draperies'—lightweight cloths which had a big sale in the Mediterranean and other temperate regions. Dutch entrepreneurs were to be found all over Europe. Louis de Geer, to take but one example, virtually ran the Swedish mining and metallurgical industries, and other Dutchmen filled important positions in the economic life of Denmark, Poland and Russia. Dutch artisans moved across the entire continent, draining marshes, building canals and clearing forests. Despite Louis XIV's war against the United Provinces and his detestation of republicans, Dutch technicians were invited by Colbert to settle in France; and even the Italian marble which testified to the Sun King's glory in the palace of Versailles had to be bought by him from a Dutch contractor.

In the far east the Dutch forced their way into the territories which Portugal could no longer hold, and made themselves masters of the spice trade. They became the major suppliers of pepper to western Europe, they asserted their control over the production and sale of nutmeg, mace and cinnamon, and by 1663 they had imposed their rule on the main clove-growing regions as well. The Dutch East India Company established itself in Batavia, captured Malacca from the Portuguese in 1641, and also systematically drove them out of Ceylon. The English, after a fruitless attempt to challenge Dutch domination of the East Indies in the early part of the century, concentrated on India instead, as did the French. The consequence of this rivalry between the major trading powers was a big increase in the total volume of Asiatic goods reaching Europe. Tea became increasingly popular from the 1690s onwards, as did fine porcelain (china) and lacquer ware. Bengal silk was highly prized, but the biggest demand of all was for Indian cottons (calicoes), which became the rage from the 1680s onwards, despite the attempt of many European governments to restrict imports in the interest of home-based industries.

Other regions also made their contributions to changes in the pattern of European consumption. In the early years of the eighteenth century English and Dutch ships opened up direct trade with the Red Sea port of Mocha, where they purchased the coffee beans grown in the Yemen, and as the price of coffee fell it became, like tea, an article of mass consumption. So did tobacco and sugar, which came mainly from the New World. The West Indian colonies were the principal suppliers of sugar, and the demand for slaves to work the plantations was met by Portuguese, Dutch, French and English contractors. Tobacco came from the New England colonies of Virginia and Maryland, and also from Brazil. Much of it found its way to Amsterdam, where it was processed and distributed on an ever-increasing scale throughout Europe.

The enormous expansion of European trade created its own problems. Tobacco and sugar could be paid for in slaves and cloth, but there was no market for these in the far east. Commerce with that region depended on bullion, and as the inflow of silver from America gradually dried up, the silver surplus of the sixteenth century gave way to the bullion scarcity of the seventeenth. By the 1640s, the amount of gold imported into Europe was a mere 8 per cent of what it had been in the 1590s, while silver imports had dropped to under 40 per cent. A number of states—Spain and Sweden, for example—tried to conserve silver by minting a copper currency, but shortage of bullion remained a major problem, and the far eastern trades were looked on with some disfavour by governments which saw them as consuming large quantities of precious metals in return for luxury articles that were not really needed. But public demand for Asiatic products was so great, and the profits to be made were so enormous, that the East India trade could not be effectively curbed. Fortunately for the Old World the New came to its rescue, since the discovery and exploitation of gold in Brazil in the second half of the seventeenth century eased the shortage of precious metals and made it possible to stabilise European currencies as well as finance trade with the far east.

Religion and Capitalism

The rise to commercial predominance first of the United Provinces and then of England has sometimes been interpreted as evidence that protestantism and capitalism were natural allies. There is, in fact, little justification for such a view. Luther and Calvin were uncompromising in their condemnation of usury, while the canon law of the Roman

Catholic Church left far more loopholes for capitalist activity than did protestant theologians. The first European capitalists were to be found, at the beginning of this period, in catholic Italy, and two hundred years later capitalist activity was as marked a feature of catholic France as of protestant Holland and England. Scotland was one of the most committedly Calvinist countries in Europe, but capitalism did not thrive there; and in the United Provinces it was the religiously liberal regents rather than the hard-line Calvinists who were the leading financiers and entrepreneurs.

The accumulation and profitable employment of capital requires a degree of devotion to money-making that would seem, on the face of it, to be incompatible with spiritual values, either catholic or protestant, and although there may be connections between religious attitudes and commercial success they are not simple ones of cause and effect. Professor Trevor-Roper, for instance, has pointed to the key role of religious exiles in the economic life of western Europe at this period— whether they were Flemings who had abandoned the southern Netherlands rather than endure the restrictiveness of Counter-Reformation catholicism, or Jews expelled from Lisbon and Seville. These refugees came from the long-established trading centres of the medieval world and took with them into their adopted countries the accumulated expertise of many generations. This medieval inheritance, and the stimulus of exile, were at least as important as religious attitudes in making them the leading entrepreneurs of seventeenth century Europe.[1]

[1] H. R. Trevor-Roper, *Religion, the Reformation and Social Change*, Macmillan, 1967.

PART TWO

The Reformation of the Church

FOUR

Reformation and Counter-Reformation

When Luther nailed his theses to the door of Wittenberg church in
1517, he was announcing—albeit unknowingly—the end of medieval
Christendom. Not that there was anything particularly novel about
his action. For a professor of theology to publish theses as a basis for
disputation was a long-accepted practice, and in this case, as on former
occasions, the disputation duly took place. What gave the event its
retrospective significance was the speed with which Luther's ideas were
disseminated all over Germany and the western world, and the
ferment they aroused. It was as if the tinder had long been piled around
the catholic Church and was only waiting for a spark to ignite it.
Luther struck the match.

Looking back on it, the Reformation seems inevitable. The Roman
Church was sunk in corruption and worldliness and was out of touch
with an increasingly anticlerical society. It failed to revive itself in time
and was therefore destroyed. Yet this is too simplified a picture. For
one thing the catholic Church was no more worldly and corrupt in
1500 than it had been in, say, 1400; and, for another, it had already met
and contained major challenges from Wyclif and Hus. Nor was the
Church totally unregenerate. Movements such as that of the Brethren
of the Common Life and the Observant Franciscans had shown that
the impetus to reform was still alive, and given time and some encouragement from the top the Church might have purified itself before
it was overthrown.

The Church was not given time, however, for the Christian world
as a whole was no longer content to tolerate abuses which had earlier
been accepted with a wry shrug. This was in large part due to the
growth of an educated laity, which was not prepared to follow blindly

where the priest led. The late Middle Ages had seen a big increase in the number of lawyers, for example, whose main concern was the secular one of protecting property-rights, and who saw little difference between the Church and any other corporation. Lawyers, of course, formed only a small part of the population, though their influence was far-ranging; but many more people were directly affected by the invention of printing, which—coinciding, as it did, with the Renaissance —made possible the distribution not simply of classical texts but of Christian ones as well, on a scale hitherto undreamed-of. Men and women throughout Europe were now provided with open access to the Bible and could compare its message with that of the Church which was supposed to embody its values. The contrast was painfully obvious, and the cry for reform became increasingly insistent.

Christian Humanists showed how the New Learning could be used to purify the established Church without destroying it, but their methods of mockery and gentle persuasion were too slow for all those people who wanted rapid, fundamental and, if necessary, convulsive change. In the sixteenth (as in the twentieth) century the loudest voices made the greatest impact, and Christian Humanism was swamped by the tidal wave set off by Luther. From that moment onwards the unity of Christendom was shattered, and protestant churches were formed in bitter and often violent opposition to Roman Catholic ones.

This was indeed fratricidal conflict, for catholics and protestants came from the same spiritual stock and were driven on by the identical desire for regeneration. The origins of both the Reformation and Counter-Reformation went back through the Renaissance to the mystical and devotional movements of the late Middle Ages. Their common ancestry is indicated by the fact that such archetypal opponents as Luther and Loyola acknowledged their debt to Thomas à Kempis's noble work, *The Imitation of Christ*, which was written in the early fifteenth century. So, for that matter, did the Anabaptists, who were detested and condemned by catholics and protestants alike.

It is just conceivable that some sort of reconciliation might eventually have taken place between Lutherans and catholics. Luther himself had no desire to found a separate church, and would have been quite happy with the existing one if only it had satisfied his and his followers' spiritual needs. This was not the case, however, with the second generation of protestant reformers, of whom the most famous were Zwingli and Calvin. For them the Roman Church was essentially anti-Christian in that it was the work of man and not of God. They deduced from the Bible a ground-plan of ecclesiastical organisation radically different from the traditional one, and although they would, of course, have welcomed the reunification of Christendom, this would only have been acceptable to them on their terms. Far from regretting the gap that separated them from Rome they gloried in it, convinced that the distinctive characteristics of the churches they set up were soundly based on biblical precedents and represented a reversion to the practices of the early Christians.

As the protestants' position became more rigid, so did that of the catholics. There were in the papal court men like Cardinal Contarini who were ready to go a long way towards the protestants for the sake of reunification, but after the discussions at Regensburg in 1541, at which they seemed to be on the point of success, the initiative passed to the hard-liners. When the Council of Trent set about the task of redefining catholic doctrines, it did so in such a way as to emphasise the differences between these and protestant ones, and despite its avowed concern for reconciliation it was, in practice, committed to repudiation. The same hardness of spirit entered into the Papacy itself, as was demonstrated by the setting-up of the Index and Inquisition.

It may be that the Roman Catholic Church could not have survived and recovered, as it eventually did, without embracing the military virtues of conformity, unquestioning obedience, and strict discipline. It is certainly the case that, among the protestants, it was the Calvinists, with their tight-knit organisation and uncompromising attitudes, who were the most effective rebels and missionaries. Those who suffered were the moderates and original thinkers on both sides, who found it impossible to give their wholehearted consent to any of the prevailing orthodoxies, and thereby provoked the suspicion and sometimes the open hostility of the uncritical and committed majority. Philosophers and scientists, in particular, had to tread very carefully to avoid meeting the fate of Giordano Bruno, burnt by the Roman Inquisition in 1600 for daring to assert that the universe was infinite and that God had created more than one world.

Nevertheless the 'liberal' spirit survived among both protestants and catholics. The 'liberals' drew much of their strength from the anti-clericalism which had been so marked a characteristic of late-medieval Europe, and they objected to clerical arrogance whether it came from 'old priests' or 'new presbyters'. They did not accept that the Church, whatever its doctrinal hue, should be above criticism, for such immunity would encourage the smug self-satisfaction which was, in their eyes, the first symptom of decay. These critical attitudes did not find their fullest expression until the Enlightenment of the eighteenth century, but they were present, and often influential, in early-modern Europe. There was one big difference, however, between the earlier and later versions of anticlericalism. In general the 'enlightened' of the eighteenth century were atheists or deists, but in the sixteenth and seventeenth centuries there were few professing non-believers. Many anticlericals were wordly, complacent and lacking in spiritual awareness, but many more had a deep commitment to the Christian way of life. It was this that made them such perceptive and persistent critics of the established Church, whether protestant or catholic.

There was a paradox at the heart of the sixteenth century reform movement, in that it was designed to purge the church of worldliness, but often left it even more firmly embedded in lay society. If Christian Humanism had been successful in persuading the Church to renew itself, or if the Papacy had given a lead much earlier, then the intervention of the 'godly prince' might have been averted. But the dynastic rulers of early-modern Europe were in any case suspicious of men whose loyalties, by virtue of the fact that they were clergy, transcended secular boundaries, for as Henry VIII declared in shocked surprise, 'they be but half our subjects'. The princes were determined to concentrate all authority in their own hands, and to resume the 'franchises'—those immunities from the state's jurisdiction which had been granted away by their predecessors. The Church, of course, was the largest of all franchises, and its very existence was a challenge to princely pretensions.

The spiritual upheaval of the early sixteenth century gave the lay rulers the opportunity they wanted to attack and overthrow the Church, and it made little difference whether they were protestant or catholic. In Saxony, Denmark and Sweden, for example, the rulers embraced Lutheranism and consciously organised the new church on national lines. The kings of France and Spain, on the other hand, retained their formal commitment to the catholic faith, but they insisted on a degree of control of the Church within their dominions that was not far removed from that of the protestant monarchs. The Spanish kings, for instance, eventually acquired the right to appoint to all bishoprics and abbacies, and so did Francis I of France as a result of the Concordat of Bologna in 1516. The Pope remained the spiritual head of the Roman Catholic Church, but the enforcement of his nominal supremacy was everywhere dependent upon the consent and co-operation of the lay catholic sovereigns.

As a result of the reform movement of the sixteenth century, the Church throughout Europe as a whole shed a great deal of its worldliness and corruption. This was partly because it was plundered on a massive scale and stripped of much of its land; but it also attracted in increasing numbers men who had a genuine commitment to spiritual causes. Yet regeneration could not be taken for granted, and as time passed many of the earlier bad habits returned. In the early eighteenth, as in the early sixteenth, century there were widespread complaints about the ignorance and sloth of the clergy. Viewed from this angle, there is much to be said for regarding the protestant and catholic Reformations not as cut-and-dried events but as stages in the perpetual struggle which all institutions (and above all spiritual ones) must wage to keep alight the flame of their original inspiration.

FIVE

The Italian Renaissance

The Idea of a 'Renaissance'

A little over a hundred years ago, in 1860, the Swiss historian Jacob Burckhardt published a book that rapidly became established as a classic, and has remained in print until the present day. It was called *The Civilisation of the Renaissance in Italy*, and it did more than any other single work to propagate the idea that the Renaissance was a watershed in human history, marking the beginning of the modern world. Burckhardt's treatment of his themes displays his major conclusions: the first part, entitled 'The State as a Work of Art', is followed by sections on 'The Development of the Individual', 'The Revival of Antiquity', 'The Discovery of the World and of Man', and 'Morality and Religion'. Burckhardt believed that during the Middle Ages 'both sides of human consciousness—that which was turned within as that which was turned without—lay dreaming or half-awake beneath a common veil'. Not until the Renaissance pierced through the medieval mist to recover the art and literature of the classical world could mankind develop its 'modern' characteristics of self-conscious awareness, cultivation of individual personality, and morality without religion.

Burckhardt's interpretation of the Renaissance received rapid and widespread acceptance because it seemed to be demonstrably true in the visual arts. The sculptures and paintings of Michelangelo and the architecture of Brunelleschi and Bramante display a mastery of classical form and a sheer bravura that apparently spring direct from ancient Rome and Greece. The notebooks of the great artist Leonardo da Vinci, with their precise anatomical drawings, their detailed studies of natural phenomena, and their carefully worked-out designs for a whole variety of machines, including flying ones, show a human mind taking all knowledge as its sphere and probing the mysteries of the physical world in a way that medieval thinkers (or so it was assumed) never did; while the autobiography of the famous goldsmith Benvenuto Cellini reveals a self-awareness, a passionate concern for the individual, that had no obvious precedent. Medieval goldsmiths did not feel called upon to write their autobiographies, and even if they had done so it is unlikely that they would have begun, as Cellini did, with so magnificently self-confident a statement of intention: 'It is a duty', he wrote, 'incumbent on upright and credible men of all ranks, who have performed anything noble or praiseworthy, to record, in their own writing, the events of their lives.'

Burckhardt, then, appeared to be stating the obvious—or, rather, making clear what ought to have been obvious. But the intensive study of the Renaissance, which his work inaugurated, has led to substantial modifications of his interpretation. In particular it has been shown that the Middle Ages were neither so static nor so dream-shrouded as he— and, for that matter, many of the leading figures of the Renaissance— assumed. Dante, who lived from 1265 to 1321, could hardly be described as lacking in personality, as any reader of the *Inferno* will know; nor, for that matter, could Marsilio of Padua who, in 1324, completed his blistering attack on the pretensions of the medieval papacy, the *Defensor Pacis*. The mere citing of names, of course, proves nothing, but there are many other considerations to be taken into account. Classical studies, for instance, had not completely died out during the Middle Ages, nor is it the case that medieval scholars and artists were uninterested in the world around them. To take just one example, the painting of Jan Arnolfini and his wife[1] by the Flemish artist, Jan van Eyck, who died in 1441, shows a capacity for detailed observation, an awareness of form, and a sensuous feeling for colour—qualities which are often held to be 'typically Renaissance'.

In the non-visual field the link between medieval and modern is even more marked. Prominent among the early physicists, for example, were Roger Bacon (d. 1294) and Thomas Bradwardine (d. 1349), whose work provided a basis for the scientific advances of the seventeenth century. Indeed, from the point of view of the natural sciences, the Renaissance, with its emphasis on the arts and humanities, was a period of regression, interrupting the development of experimental techniques and disrupting the process of accumulating knowledge about the nature of the physical world.

[1] In the National Gallery, London

Much of the difficulty and confusion that arises from attempts to analyse the Renaissance as a historical phenomenon is caused by the overlapping meanings of the word itself. In its simplest sense it indicates the revival of interest in classical antiquity that took place in Italy in the late fifteenth and sixteenth centuries; in a more complex manner it refers to the impact of this revival on the visual arts of the western world; and, most complicated of all, it suggests a reawakening of the human spirit after a long period of hibernation. To try and limit the area of confusion the treatment of the Renaissance in this chapter will concentrate on the first of these meanings, and in particular upon the recovery of Roman and Greek literature, since this 'literary Renaissance' was to have so powerful an impact upon the society, the religion and the politics of sixteenth century Europe.[1]

City-states and Culture

The background to the Renaissance in Italy was the transformation that was taking place in the urban economies. Italy suffered during the fourteenth and fifteenth centuries from plague, trade depressions, economic uncertainty and political unrest, just like the rest of Europe, and much of her population lived near or below the poverty line. Yet at the same time the leading merchant entrepreneurs were building up fortunes on a princely scale, and reinvesting much of this capital in their various business activities. Capital came from the profits of trade: Florentine fortunes, for instance, were made from buying English wool for the north Italian weaving industry. The demands of international trade led to the development of more sophisticated methods of managing money. So did the demands of international taxation, for the Florentine merchants acquired the monopoly of collecting papal taxes from all over Europe. The techniques of banking were elaborated and refined, letters of credit came into use, insurance was developed, and accounting was made more accurate through the invention and increasing application of double-entry book-keeping. In short, the

---

[1] This is not in any way to denigrate the visual arts, but they cannot be dealt with adequately in a small space, and lists of names and styles are, in themselves, meaningless. For a fuller treatment of this aspect of the Renaissance the reader is referred to the works listed in the Bibliography under the heading *The Arts* (p. 573). Considerations of space have also led to the exclusion of another major topic which demands detailed treatment, namely the Scientific Revolution; a bibliography for this will be found on pp. 572–3.

profits of finance were added to those of trade, and the entrepreneurs who were the principal beneficiaries of this process were also among the major patrons of Renaissance scholars and artists.

Capitalism alone, however, would not explain the appearance of the Renaissance in Italy and economic factors have to be set in the social and political context of the city-state. These were comparatively small units in constant competition with their neighbours. This encouraged a great sense of civic pride, and when relations degenerated into war civic pride was elevated into patriotism. It was, for example, the Florentines' fear of Milan that made them aware how highly they valued the institutions of their state—the lineal descendant, so they claimed, of the ancient Roman Republic—and the virtues of civic life. They demonstrated their awareness by supporting and encouraging artists and men of letters, as if to show the world that only in a climate of republican liberty could intellectual and artistic creation flourish. The despots, on the other hand, sought to prove that when it came to patronage they were the true heirs of classical greatness, and the Viscontis and the Sforzas, to take the two obvious examples, spent on a lavish scale. It was very important for the development of the Renaissance in Italy that whether rulers were princely despots or republican merchants they shared the same values in arts and letters. There was no reason, on the face of it, why merchants should not have been content simply to accumulate wealth while despots built up their armies and civil services: the fact that they chose to compete in patronage meant that the riches obtained by both trade and power were at the service of the Renaissance in Italy.

Big cities, and even, in a limited sense, city-states, also existed in Europe north of the Alps—in south Germany, in the Netherlands and on the southern shores of the Baltic—and were not lacking in private wealth and civic pride. These were, in fact, the first areas outside Italy to feel the full impact of the Renaissance, but although they stamped it with characteristics different from those which had been most marked south of the Alps, they were nevertheless dependent in the first instance on Italian inspiration. Their society and economy were prepared for the Renaissance, but the spark had to come from Italy. One of the main reasons for this was that these northern cities were islands of urbanism in a great sea of feudal agrarian society, in which the tone was set by landowners and clerics and the prevailing literary forms were still knightly romances and devotional works.

Italy was remarkably self-contained, protected by the sea on two sides and the Alps in the north, and it was the feudal south rather than the urban north which seemed to be out of the main stream of life. Also the influence of the Church was far feebler in Italy than it was elsewhere. The Avignon captivity had removed the papal court from Rome, and even after the Popes returned in 1378 they behaved much like other secular princes where the government of their states and relations with their neighbours were concerned. In the spiritual sphere, however, as distinct from the temporal, the papacy shared the weakness of the Church as a whole. North Italian culture was largely lay, and in Italian universities the faculties of theology, which elsewhere were the real power centres, had only limited influence. The citystates themselves were not, of course, irreligious, but it was obvious that control over them belonged to lay merchants or despots and not to bishops and clergy. Mercantile wealth had created in these cities a leisured class outside the Church-university nexus, and the individual, provided he was rich or talented enough, was free to develop as he thought fit.

The Classical Revival and Humanism

There is one other important reason for the appearance of the Renaissance in Italy rather than elsewhere. The presence of the classical world was felt not only through its physical remains—though these were a constant reminder and stimulus—but also through the living tradition of Roman law. Italian jurists were more familiar with the Digest and Code of Justinian than with any other works, and as the administration of city-states, whether republican or despotic, expanded and became more complex, lawyers played an increasingly important and influential role in society.

Leading Italian humanists[1] of the fifteenth century believed they were reviving classical civilisation and discounted the idea that they derived anything from the Middle Ages, whose culture they despised. They would acknowledge their debt to two great pioneers of the early fourteenth century, Petrarch and Boccaccio, but farther back than that they would not go. This cavalier attitude towards the origins of the Renaissance needs some modification, however, as has already been indicated. In the first place, even allowing for the fact that in Italy the medieval world disappeared earlier than it did in the rest of Europe, the early fourteenth century was still 'medieval'. And secondly,

---

[1] The meaning of this term is considered on p. 84.

Petrarch and Boccaccio did not suddenly emerge out of nothing. They also had their precursors, and it is among these that the Renaissance originated.

The earliest signs are to be found, during the closing decades of the thirteenth century, in a number of north Italian cities, as well as in Naples. In Padua a group of lawyers alternated their legal duties with the study of classical literature. Latin poetry was their favourite recreation, and in 1314 one of their number, Albertino Mussato, took Seneca as a model for the first secular tragedy to appear since classical times. The delighted citizens of Padua showed their appreciation by reviving a custom of antiquity unknown to the Middle Ages by crowning him with laurel. At Verona humanist pursuits were encouraged by the magnificent collection of texts gathered together from the ninth century onwards in the chapter library, where Petrarch himself later studied. It was a scholar of Verona who first applied humanist critical attitudes to the study of classical literature and proved that there had been two Plinys, the elder and the younger, and not one, as had been assumed up to that time. Humanist studies flourished in Dante's Florence, and also in Sicily, where the early Angevin kings had created a fine royal library, including many Greek texts. Greek was still a living language in Calabria and Sicily, and in the early fourteenth century Robert I set scholars to work translating Greek texts into Latin, and invited leading Byzantine scholars to his court.

The significance of this early humanism is that it was not the result of any conscious dissatisfaction with medieval philosophical attitudes or of a deliberate desire to revive the culture of antiquity. It developed out of the pattern of classical studies as it already existed in the Middle Ages. In its later stages the Renaissance became self-conscious and repudiated its medieval ancestry, but in fact it was not a clearcut break with the past. This early humanism also shows that so far as intellectual stimulus was concerned there was nothing inevitable about the later predominance of the northern cities. The kingdom of Sicily would have seemed to be the obvious starting point for any revival, since it was so close to the Greek world not only of antiquity but also of Byzantium; but its culture was virtually confined to the court circle, and this provided too narrow a base. Civic pride, particularly when it was spurred on by the emulation of neighbours, proved to be a more fruitful soil in the long run. This may also be the reason for the failure of the Renaissance to establish itself outside Italy until the late fifteenth century. In France, for instance, during the closing decades of the fourteenth century, the clerks of the royal chancery were writing letters and poems on classical models and transcribing classical manuscripts. There were links between this incipient humanism and the Italian Renaissance, but the French revival never took off in the way that the Italian did. Older cultural patterns, rooted in theological treatises and knightly romances, presumably proved too strong for it.

The major achievement of the early humanists was to demonstrate that classical Latin could be a flexible as well as an elegant instrument, and that classical literature could provide a complete education for the whole man. Medieval interpretations of the classics had become stereotyped, like schoolbooks which give extracts from major writers and a selection of 'authoritative' comments. Petrarch and his fellow humanists looked at ancient writers with fresh eyes, and asked questions of them which were different from the accepted ones. Petrarch, in particular, saw that behind the corpus of Latin thought and literature stood that of Greece, and therefore that Greek—which he vainly tried to master—would be of the greatest value to future humanists.

Florence responded warmly to the writings of Petrarch, who was himself the son of a city merchant, but even more so to those of Petrarch's friend Boccaccio (1313–75). From this moment onwards the revival of classical arts and letters flourished in Florence. Greek and Latin manuscripts were hunted down in monastic libraries and other places where they had lain unnoticed and unread for centuries, and hitherto unknown works—those of Tacitus, for example, and Cicero's letters—were discovered. The Florentine Niccolo de Niccoli bankrupted himself in building up a magnificent library of eight hundred books, and a contemporary describes how 'if he heard of any book in Greek or Latin not to be had in Florence, he spared no cost in getting it; the number of Latin books which Florence owes entirely to his generosity cannot be reckoned. . . . Strangers who came to Florence at that time, if they missed the opportunity of seeing him at home, thought they had not been in Florence.'

By 1500 the word 'humanist' was being increasingly used as a description of Renaissance scholars. Strictly speaking it meant a person who taught the *studia humanitatis*, that is to say a grammarian (and no doubt, quite often, a pedant). But in current usage the term acquired a much broader meaning. A humanist was a man who ostentatiously rejected the medieval inheritance, cultivated style and rhetoric, and fashioned his thoughts and actions as closely as possible on classical models. Some humanists, Petrarch among them, never reconciled their own high valuation of contemplation and meditation with the political commitment which they found in writers such as Cicero. But for the majority the ancient world, as revealed through a study of classical literature, was the ideal preparation for an active public life, and made possible the fullest development of the human personality.

The first stage of the Renaissance, in which there were great figures like Petrarch and Boccaccio but not really a general movement, lasted until about 1370. By that time the Renaissance had captured Florence, and Florence, as a consequence, captured the imagination first of other Italian cities and then of the whole western world. Humanists came to play a major part not only in the creative life of Florence but also in the administration of the city-state. This example appealed to other cities, and enthusiasm for classical arts and letters spread rapidly, particularly after the formation of the Italian League in the mid-fifteenth century, which kept peace in the peninsula by establishing a balance of power.

The initiative in forming this League was taken by Cosimo de' Medici, and it is perhaps significant that as the Florentine Renaissance was being taken up by other Italian states Florence itself was ceasing to be a republic in all but name. The Renaissance had derived much of its early vigour from Florentine republicanism: now it was to be bent to the service of despotism. Princely courts, with their elaborate bureaucracies, needed trained humanist administrators just as much as merchant republics, and despots were quick to see that one result of encouraging humanists would be the glorification of themselves, their principalities and their dynasties.

The Ideal of the Gentleman

Lesser states, which could not possibly compete in political power with the major ones, could yet hope to equal them in scholarship and the arts. This was why some of the smallest principalities, Urbino, Mantua and Ferrara among them, became of great importance in the development of the Renaissance. One effect of court patronage was to revive the 'knightly epic' in a new Renaissance dress: it was at the princely court of the Estes in Ferrara, during the fifteenth century, that Boiardo wrote his epic poem, *Orlando Innamorato*, which is set in the days of Charlemagne and tells of the love of Orlando (more commonly known as Roland) for the king of Carthage's daughter, Angelica. Boiardo left his romance unfinished, but the theme was taken up by Ariosto (1474–1533), who used it to glorify the house of Este. In his *Orlando Furioso* Ariosto describes how Orlando, the model of a perfect knight, is driven mad(*furioso*) by his unrequited love for Angelica and is involved in a whole series of fantastic adventures, including the recovery of his lost wits from the moon by a fabulous beast called a hippogriff.

Orlando Furioso became a best-seller throughout Europe, and carried the fame of the ducal house of Este wherever it went. There was one book, however, which had more influence than any other in spreading Renaissance ideals beyond the Italian peninsula. This was *The Courtier*, by Balthasar Castiglione,[1] and it was based not on one of the great courts such as Milan, but on the miniature one of Urbino. In the late fifteenth century the Duke of Urbino had built up a magnificent library, and his librarian proudly recalled that 'In no respect did he look to expense. Whenever he learned of the existence of any desirable book in Italy or abroad he sent for it without heeding the cost. It is now above fourteen years since he began to make this collection, and he has ever since maintained at Urbino, Florence, and elsewhere, thirty-four transcribers, and has resorted to every means requisite for amassing a famous and excellent library—which it now is.'

With such an inspiration the court at Urbino developed into a model of what a Renaissance court should be: learned, cultured, civilised and urbane. Castiglione spent twelve years there and was so impressed that he conceived the idea of writing a number of conversation pieces in which various friends of his, chief among them the Duchess of Urbino, discuss the qualities required in a perfect courtier. Such an ideal figure did not, of course, exist, but Castiglione defended his work, and showed its classical inspiration, by declaring that 'I shall be quite content to have erred in the company of Plato, Xenophon and Cicero. For . . . just as, according to them, there exists the Idea of the perfect Republic, of the perfect King and the perfect Orator, so there exists that of the perfect Courtier.' The qualities demanded of a gentleman were good manners, discretion, a proper sense of his social rank, and an unostentatious cultivation of his own best interests. The ideal, which has been enormously influential since the time of the Renaissance, is fast losing its appeal today, but in the sixteenth century *The Courtier* was

[1] This is available as *The Book of the Courtier* (ed. G. Bull, Penguin Classic. 1967).

required reading in every court, large and small. Castiglione himself became a figure of European reputation, not simply as the author of this handbook of gentlemanly behaviour but as the supposed embodiment of the qualities it advocated. When the news of his death reached the imperial court no less a person than Charles V himself declared that Castiglione had been 'uno de los mejores caballeros del mundo' ('one of the finest gentlemen in the world').

The Significance of Printing

Among the medium-sized states which took up the Renaissance was the Papacy. Humanist scholars were employed in increasing numbers from the mid-fifteenth century onwards, and Nicholas V in particular was a great patron. He brought scholars and artists to Rome, he encouraged the translation of Greek texts into Latin, and he established in the Vatican what was to become one of the most famous libraries in the world. His attitude towards the Middle Ages was demonstrated by the decision he took to demolish old St Peter's, even though it was built round the original church of Constantine, and to create something more magnificent in the classical manner. He could boast, with justification, that 'in all things I have been liberal: in building, in the purchase of books, in the constant transcription of Greek and Latin manuscripts, and in the rewarding of learned men'. In Lord Acton's famous phrase 'on that day [when Nicholas V was elected] the new learning took possession of the Holy See, and Rome began to be considered the capital of the Renaissance'.

Although the Renaissance was always primarily a revival of classical Latin, scholars from Petrarch onwards had seen the necessity for Greek, and the study of this language began in earnest in the early fifteenth century. Greek authors had been known to the Middle Ages, but mainly through translations into Latin, and a great deal of Greek literature, as distinct from philosophical works, was untranslated and therefore unknown. If Greek were now to be revived, teachers would be needed, and the obvious source of these was Byzantium, since in Constantinople Greek was still a living language. As early as 1397 the Byzantine Manuel Chrysoloras had been appointed to a chair in the university of Florence, and his fame attracted students from all over northern Italy. Contacts between Italian and Byzantine scholars were further strengthened by the ecumenical councils held at Ferrara and Florence in 1438–39, and the process of transmitting Greek learning to the west was accelerated by the fall of Constantinople in 1453, since scholars who fled from the Turks took their most valuable manuscripts with them.

The problem of copying and disseminating classical texts was transformed by the invention of printing. This took place in Germany in the mid-fifteenth century, but whereas in northern Europe the printing press was used mainly for 'established' literature such as Bibles, manuals of devotion and medieval romances, Italian printers concentrated on classical texts. Their workshops became in effect academies where scholars congregated. Among the most famous of these humanist printers was Aldus Manutius, who in the late fifteenth century founded the Aldine Press at Venice, and by the time he died every major Greek author was in print, thanks largely to his efforts. It was the invention of printing which made sure that the Renaissance (unlike its Carolingian and twelfth-century predecessors) would be more than a flash in the pan, for the printed book transcended geographical limitations and transmitted to the entire western world the achievements of a handful of scholars.

The recovery of Greek was accompanied by a renewal of interest in Hebrew studies. Hebrew texts, like Greek ones, had been known to the Middle Ages, but there had been little incentive to study them. This was now provided by the desire to remove medieval accretions and get back to the original sources. If real understanding of Latin literature depended on some knowledge of Greek, then it was equally the case that real understanding of the Bible depended on some knowledge of Hebrew. Rome under Nicholas V became one of the main centres of Hebrew studies. Another was Spain, which, until the expulsion of 1492, had a large and flourishing Jewish community. The leading Christian scholar in the field of Jewish studies was Pico della Mirandola who did the greater part of his work in fifteenth century Florence. His most celebrated pupil and successor was Johann Reuchlin, who published the first Christian-Hebrew grammar in 1506 and became the greatest Hebraist of his day.

The Renaissance and Christian Morality

Pico della Mirandola had not been inspired simply by an abstract love of learning. He had a mystical belief in the fundamental harmony of all created things and he hoped to find in Hebrew writings the keys to the understanding of the universe. In this he was the heir of the Renaissance's rediscovery of Plato. The centre of Platonic studies was Florence, where the Medicis patronised the young scholar Marsilio Ficino, giving him a house, a library and an income in return for a lifelong devotion to the study of Plato. By 1468 Ficino had translated the Platonic *Dialogues* into Latin, and a group of friends and scholars, the Platonists, gathered round him to join in the exposition of the master's ideals.

One big problem confronting all humanist scholars was the inadequacy of the texts they had to use. Since they were convinced that classical studies were the only possible basis for a worthwhile life, they saw how important it was that their sources should be pure. This involved comparing texts and relating them to their historical context. In this way the new science of critical philology was born, and it was applied not only to classical texts, but also to the Bible, the early Christian fathers and the history of the Church. The *Annotationes* of Lorenzo Valla was one of the earliest examples of biblical criticism, pointing out the places in which the Vulgate (the only authorised Latin version of the Bible) contained mistranslations from the Greek. Valla was employed by Pope Nicholas V, but papal patronage did not restrict the range of his critical enquiries. He treated Christianity in a comparative fashion, comparing it with other moral systems such as Stoicism and Epicureanism; he questioned the assumption that the Apostles actually wrote the Apostles' Creed; and he demonstrated conclusively that the so-called Donation of Constantine, on which papal claims to a territorial state in Italy were based, was an early-medieval forgery.

It might seem from the example of Valla that the Renaissance was anti-Christian and sceptical to the point of atheism, and it has often been assumed that the revival of the ancient world meant the revival of paganism. But such an impression is a long way from the truth. Critical methods were valued not because they would undermine the foundations of Christianity but because they would reveal them in all their original strength. One of the reasons why the humanists were so insistent that they had broken with the Middle Ages was their conviction that medieval scholars had scrambled together a hotchpotch of knowledge from various sources in a totally indiscriminate manner. They were determined to separate the grain from the chaff, on the assumption that Christianity, since it was undoubtedly true, had nothing to fear from the removal of erroneous practices and doctrines, however hallowed these were by time. Similarly the Platonists were trying not to bypass Christianity but to integrate it, in a discriminating and accurate manner, with other sources of knowledge. Even Renaissance pride in the individual had its religious significance, since it encouraged the belief that man was not so corrupt in his nature as to be unable to attain an intuitive knowledge of God.

On the other hand, in so far as humanists were increasingly employed in the service of the state their main interests were secular, and they could consider problems of human conduct and morality—as, for example, Seneca had done—without necessarily putting them into a religious context. Therefore, while the Renaissance could and did deepen religious knowledge and understanding, it could also encourage a secular attitude which left little room for religion. The clearest example of this is to be found in the writings of the Florentine Niccolo Macchiavelli (1469-1527), for whom ancient Rome was the model to be emulated, and who produced in *The Prince* a manual of statecraft based on an unblinkered analysis of human weaknesses, which ran counter to all accepted codes of morality.

In *The Prince* Macchiavelli considered such questions as 'Whether it is better to be loved or feared?', and came to the conclusion that 'it is much safer to be feared than loved . . . for love is held by a chain of obligation which, men being selfish, is broken whenever it serves their purpose; but fear is maintained by a dread of punishment which never fails'. Machiavelli was concerned not with the moral obligations of rulers but with the most effective methods by which they could secure their ends, 'for how we live is so far removed from how we ought to live, that he who abandons what is done for what ought to be done, will rather learn to bring about his own ruin than his preservation. . . . Therefore it is necessary for a prince who wishes to maintain himself, to learn how not to be good.' Macchiavelli's contemporaries were shocked by such cynical realism, but in fact he had only analysed the political practices (as distinct from theories) of his own day, and many rulers, both at the time and later, studied his precepts and took them to heart.

Medieval or Modern

The Renaissance had its limitations, of course. It spread among the rich and educated, and to some extent among the bourgeoisie (where this existed), but it made little direct impact on the mass of the people. It was also, as had been indicated, much stronger on the arts than the sciences. Philology was, it is true, a science of a sort, and Renaissance architects and artists made big advances in understanding and applying the principles of perspective. But in spurning the medieval intellectual inheritance Renaissance humanists rejected a great deal of valuable work in physics and mechanics, and although they translated Greek and Hellenistic scientific texts they never related these either to medieval treatises or to the actual technology of their own day. Instead they bred a 'gentlemanly' distaste for manual labour which precluded experiment. Even in their major achievement, the recovery of classical Latin, they did not always avoid sterility. For instance their emphasis on Cicero as the only possible model for a fine prose style could result in a manner of writing so highly rhetorical that it concealed the meaning rather than revealing it. There is, sadly, some truth in the accusation made by their critics that they turned Latin from a living language into a dead one.

The question remains, was the Renaissance 'medieval' or did it really usher in the 'modern' world? This would perhaps have been easier to answer a hundred years ago, when most western countries were still ruled by a wealthy élite, educated in the classics, steeped in Christian values, and imbued with the ideal of the gentleman. All this has now changed. Western civilisation in the second half of the twentieth century is based on science and technology, mass culture, and the practice of some form or other of democracy—characteristics which owe little or nothing to the Renaissance. Yet if the Renaissance was not 'modern', by our standards, neither was it 'medieval'. Although its roots went back in Italy to the thirteenth century, and it was nourished on classical texts that had been copied by medieval scribes and preserved in medieval libraries, it was out of sympathy with the arts and philosophy of the Middle Ages, and looked back to Rome and Greece as a golden age.

The Renaissance was, in fact, very much a product of its own day, 'late-medieval' in some ways, 'early-modern' in others. This was because the medieval world itself was changing fundamentally, with the growth of nationalism, the breakdown of the feudal order, the expansion of trade and towns, the decline in the authority of the Church and Empire, and the emergence of an educated laity. Attitudes and assumptions which had been taken for granted in, say, 1350 were unacceptable in 1450, and it was because Renaissance scholars and artists provided an alternative set of values that they made such an impact. Classical arts and literature of themselves would never have set

Europe alight, had it not been for the increasing awareness that existing knowledge and ways of thought were inadequate. Just as the great explorers, looking for new routes to the old world of Cathay, stumbled on a hitherto unknown continent, so the humanist scholars, looking over their shoulders at the glowing vision of classical antiquity, moved forward into a world which they helped to make very different from anything that had been known before.

SIX

Erasmus and Christian Humanism

Germany and the Netherlands

In the cities of the Netherlands, at the western end of the trade axis that joined Italy to southern Germany, a capitalist economy was coming into existence in the late Middle Ages. This was based on the weaving industry, which was organised on a massive scale, but although cloth was the major source of wealth it was not the only one. Metallurgy was another, and Liège had become one of the principal centres of the iron industry, producing firearms that were exported all over Europe. Liège was also an important link in the mesh of international finance, as was Antwerp, which controlled the Flemish weaving industry. The leading merchants of these two cities became the Florentines of the west, expanding their commercial activities into the fields of banking, insurance and financial speculation.

Rich merchant oligarchies and proud quasi-independent cities: these were sufficiently close to the Italian pattern to suggest that the social and economic conditions for a 'native' Renaissance had been created. Much of the wealth of these Netherlands cities was in fact used for the encouragement of arts and letters, and by the late fifteenth century artists such as Albrecht Durer (1471–1528) were following the trade routes to Italy and back. There was, however, one major difference between the Italian city-states and the Netherlands communities. In the Netherlands cultural life was dominated by the dazzling Burgundian court, which was still rooted in the chivalric tradition of the Middle Ages, and, through its elaborate pageants and ceremonial, preserved the myth of medieval 'courtliness' long after it had ceased to have any reality. The nobility of the Netherlands drew its wealth from land, not trade, and the gulf between the two cultures—one which looked to the court, and one which looked to the cities—could not easily be bridged.

This was why the Netherlands Renaissance was slow in coming to fruition.

Midway between the Netherlands and Italy stood the south German cities, which were entering upon one of their greatest periods of prosperity. The merchants of Augsburg, Nuremberg and other towns were the men who exchanged the minerals and textiles of the west for the spices and silks bought by the Venetians in the Levant, and the profits of this traffic were enormous. They also had at hand another source of wealth. The general economic recovery of the fifteenth century stimulated the production of metals and minerals, and the major European deposits of these were to be found in south and east Germany, the Tyrol, Bohemia and Hungary. Improved techniques meant that mines could be dug to a greater depth, and machinery, powered by water, was used on a large scale. All this demanded capital, and the merchants of the south German cities were ideally placed, both geographically and financially, to provide it. These cities therefore became centres of capitalism, where huge fortunes were accumulated. The Medicis of Germany were the Fuggers, who started in a small way as weavers and extended their activities into international trade, particularly with Venice. In the third generation Jacob Fugger (1459–1525) invested in mining and was granted enormous mineral concessions in return for loans to hard-up princes. With capital provided by trade and invested in industry the Fuggers rapidly became the biggest bankers of the western world and numbered the house of Habsburg among their clients.

The Fuggers were given titles of nobility, but they never became independent princes like the Medicis. This was because the south German cities, though rich and proud, could not stand alone. They were dependent on the support of the Emperor for the preservation of their privileged trading position, and they were physically part of a society that was rural and feudal rather than urban. Yet the links with Italy were so close that there was a constant interchange of artists and scholars between the two areas, and Augsburg and Nuremberg became the first major centres of the Renaissance outside Italy itself. Students from these cities, and particularly those studying law and medicine, regularly went to the great Italian centres at Bologna and Padua, while tourists were drawn, then as now, by the magnet of Rome. More important even than the sum of these individual first-hand encounters was the influence of printing. By 1500 there were fifty presses in Germany (compared with more than seventy in Italy) and the works of the Italian humanists were translated into German long before they appeared in French or English.

If Germany had been without any native cultural traditions she would presumably have duplicated the development of the Renaissance in Italy. But in fact she had a great deal of her own to contribute, including much that seemed at first to be incompatible with humanism on the Italian model. In Germany, more perhaps than in any other country, there was evidence of a spiritual hunger that was not being satisfied. The majority of people were outwardly orthodox in their belief and practices—the Hussite heresy, for instance, had not made much progress outside Bohemia—but all too often religion consisted of stale rituals devoid of any spiritual content. The Church was too rich and too worldly to be able to fulfil its essential function of guiding and satisfying spiritual aspirations. Pluralism and non-residence were widespread, and even where priests were in residence they were often so poor and ignorant that it was a case of the halt leading the blind.

This state of affairs would have been intolerable even in a stable and tranquil society, but Germany in the late Middle Ages had been torn by plague and war and disrupted by economic and social change. People were only too aware of the instability and transitoriness of mortal life, but when they looked to the Church for help they found little or none. Not surprisingly they slipped into superstition, and used such things as relics, images and pilgrimages, which were meant to be aids to true religion, as substitutes for it. The Church, like any institution, had always been faced with the problem of renewing itself in order to meet the challenges of a changing society, and so far it had always done so. But the last movement of renewal, that of the friars in the thirteenth century, had lost its initial impetus and degenerated into complacency or frustrated radicalism. As for the monasteries, which were meant to be reservoirs of spirituality from which the whole of the Christian community could be refreshed, their general condition (despite honourable exceptions) was deplorable. They had become burdens on a society from which they took a heavy toll in money and manpower, and to which they contributed nothing. In short, the spiritual hunger of the laity in Germany was not being satisfied by those who claimed the sole right to do so. The hungry sheep looked up but were not fed.

The failure of the Church over Europe as a whole had already led to violently anticlerical movements, which in some places had crossed the doctrinal frontier into heresy. In early fifteenth-century Bohemia, for example, John Hus had led a revolt against the established church whose wealth and corruption he despised. Hus had been burnt at Constance despite a safe-conduct from the Emperor, but heresy survived in Bohemia and elsewhere, and dissatisfaction was rife. Heresy, however, was not the only reaction. More typical, in Germany at any rate, was the growth of movements of lay spirituality which stayed within the framework of the catholic church while to some extent bypassing its main institutions and dogmas. Germany had a strong mystical tradition, and among the most influential mystics was Master Eckhardt (?1260–?1328) who preached and wrote in the vernacular and taught that man could attain direct communion with God. His followers formed themselves into groups called 'The Friends of God', and produced a considerable volume of devotional literature with a wide circulation. A collection of these works, the *Theologia Germanica*, was to be a major influence on Luther.

The Brethren of the Common Life

The mystical movement had lost much of its vigour in Germany by about 1400, but it was going from strength to strength in the Netherlands, where its teachings were spread in the late fifteenth century by Gerard Groote. He journeyed all over the Netherlands, preaching spiritual communion with God, and some years before his death he formed a community devoted to education and the care of the poor, whose members called themselves 'The Brethren of the Common Life'. There were two branches of this movement. One went in the direction of regular monasticism, and led to the founding of a community of canons at Windesheim, which became a major centre of the reform movement in the Netherlands and Germany. It was a monk of this community, Thomas à Kempis, who, in the early fifteenth century, wrote *The Imitation of Christ*, which rapidly became a sort of spiritual handbook for men and women all over Europe. Thomas expressed, very simply and beautifully, the ideal of the Brethren that a Christian's life should be modelled as closely as possible on that of Jesus. While there was no question, of course, of rejecting the Church, since salvation was to be found only through the sacraments which the Church administered, the whole emphasis of the *Imitation* is on the personal responsibility of the individual to lay himself open to the love of God. 'Would that I might obtain this favour, Lord to find Thee alone and by Thyself, to open unto Thee my whole heart, and to enjoy Thee even as my soul desireth; and that henceforth none may look upon me, nor have regard to me; but that Thou alone mayest speak unto me, and I to Thee.'

The other branch of the movement developed into lay monasticism. The Brethren committed themselves to a strict way of life, but they remained in the world instead of cutting themselves off from it. They, like Thomas à Kempis, were concerned above all with the quality of life of individual Christians, and they saw in the direct inspiration of the Bible, rather than in the forms and ceremonies of the established Church, the swiftest and surest way to men's hearts. The Brethren wanted to bring the world closer to God, and believed that the best method for doing this was education. If children were taught at an early age to read and study the Bible and to take Christ as their model, they would become an enormously powerful and influential spiritual force, working towards the transformation of society.

On the face of it there would seem to be little identity of interests between the Brethren of the Common Life and the Italian humanists, whose passion was the recovery and study of classical, pagan texts. But many humanists, in fact, were concerned as much with Christian as with classical antiquity, and even those, such as the Platonists, who appeared to be most deeply involved in pagan thought, were searching for moral and spiritual guidance. The classical renaissance, in short, had become a Christian renaissance, and it was the shared concern for regeneration through education that linked the Brethren with the humanists. The German scholar Rudolf Husmann, who studied in Italy and was so ardent an advocate of Latin studies that he changed his barbarous 'Gothic' name to the more classical one of 'Agricola', spent some time in the Netherlands persuading the Brethren of the relevance of humanist activities to their own aims. So successful was he that when the Brethren decided to appoint a headmaster for the school they established at Deventer in Holland, they chose one of Agricola's pupils, Alexander Hegius. In his curriculum Hegius blended the humanist emphasis on the classics with the religious ideals of the Brethren, and Deventer rapidly acquired a reputation as one of the finest schools in Europe. It was therefore entirely appropriate that it should have counted among its graduates the man who became the key figure in the Renaissance north of the Alps and the living embodiment of the two traditions, Desiderius Erasmus.

Erasmus

Erasmus, born at Rotterdam between 1466 and 1469, was the illegitimate son of a priest. Like many an able boy from a poor background
he found an opening for his talents in the Church and therefore
entered the Augustinian order of canons regular, though he had no
real vocation for the monastic life. He was lucky in that his order was
not so decayed as many, and he was given the time and the opportunity to study the classics and to make acquaintance with the work of
the Italian humanists. After six years he was granted leave to continue
his studies at the Sorbonne, in Paris, the intellectual capital of medieval
Europe, and in 1499 he went to England, where he made the acquaintance of John Colet and Thomas More. These two English humanists
encouraged Erasmus to pursue his career in 'sacred letters', but he soon
realised that before he could make any real progress in this direction he
would have to deepen his knowledge of Greek. As he wrote in 1501,
'I have already tasted of Greek literature in the past, but merely (as the
saying is) sipped at it; however, having lately gone a little deeper into
it, I perceive—as one has often read in the best authorities—that Latin
learning, rich as it is, is defective and incomplete without Greek; for
we have but a few streams and muddy puddles, whilst they have pure
springs and rivers rolling gold.'

Erasmus made his way to Venice, where he became a member of
the informal academy surrounding the printer Aldus Manutius and
deepened his knowledge of classical literature, both Greek and Latin.
Books such as the *Adages* (a collection of several thousand pithy sayings
drawn from the classics) and *In Praise of Folly* (an entertaining satire on
the affectations and vices of contemporary society) gave him a European reputation. His first major work appeared in 1516, with the
publication of his edition of the Greek New Testament accompanied
by his own elegant Latin translation. This was a landmark in biblical
studies, because it gave scholars for the first time the original text of
the fundamental document of the Christian Church, the fount of
theology and morality. Not everybody was pleased with Erasmus's
achievement. Those scholars who had been brought up in the older
medieval tradition and had studied the Bible only at secondhand,
through the medium of the various commentaries and glossaries of
theologians, in which they were expert, regarded Erasmus and his new
methods as a challenge to their intellectual supremacy. They were right

to do so for, in the preface to the second edition of his New Testament in 1519, Erasmus openly attacked these 'schoolmen' and their sterile 'scholasticism'. Following the example of Renaissance humanists, and in particular that of Valla, whom he much admired, he called on scholars to employ the new techniques of critical philology to obtain a really profound understanding of the Bible and the early Fathers.

Erasmus was still theoretically a monk, but he refused to go back to the cloister and instead earned his living, and his reputation, as a free-lance writer. He was the first major European figure whose fame and influence were based on the printed book. Without the enormous readership created by the printing press this delicate and sensitive valetudinarian would have been known only to his circle of personal acquaintances and those who had access to his manuscripts. Instead he was read and admired throughout the Christian world. The sheer volume of his writings was proof not only of his industry but also of his appeal; and although he began with no consciously worked-out reform programme, one gradually emerged from his books. He saw Church and society in decay all around him and believed that the only remedy lay in a return to the scriptures. The Italian humanists had shown the importance of a moral education founded on knowledge of classical literature, but they had not given this a specifically Christian bias. They were inclined to keep their religion and their learning in separate compartments, but Erasmus fused the two into the synthesis of Christian Humanism. Because the clergy, who ought to have given the lead in spiritual matters, were conspicuously failing to do so, he appealed over their heads to that relatively new phenomenon, the educated lay community. It was among this section of society that discontent with the clergy was particularly acute, and lay critics cared so much about religion that rather than leave it in the hands of a corrupt and worldly clergy they would take up the urgent task of reform themselves.

Erasmus's major weapon was ridicule. He laughed to scorn all those aspects of society which he despised, particularly those formal observances of the religious life which had lost any real spiritual meaning: ceremonies, pilgrimages, veneration of saints and images, and relic worship. He also condemned the monastic vocation on the grounds that all forms of human activity were 'callings' as long as they were carried out in a Christian spirit. Human life itself was a vocation, and all men and women should concentrate on following as closely as possible the example of Christ, as recorded in the Bible, in whatever sphere of activity it pleased God to place them. For Erasmus the message of the Bible was essentially simple. This was why he was angry with the 'scholastics' who, with their logic-chopping, had turned it into an involved puzzle to which they alone had the key. By so doing they had barred ordinary men and women from the direct inspiration of the scriptures. Erasmus wanted to have the Bible translated into the vernacular so that every literate human being could have immediate and personal access to it. Improvements in education would, he assumed, increase the number of those who were literate, until at last the goal of a truly Christian community would be achieved. This was the meaning of Erasmus's comment, in the preface to his New Testament, that he longed for the day when every farmer's boy would whistle the psalms as he ploughed his furrow.

This transformation was to be accomplished by a massive programme of education. What the Brethren of the Common Life had done on a small scale must now be extended to the entire Christian world. New schools would have to be founded, and the curricula of existing ones remodelled along Christian Humanist lines. New textbooks would also have to be written, so that education could be firmly based on the twin foundations of biblical study and classical learning. Since Latin was the key to knowledge, an understanding of its structure was essential: hence the importance of grammar, and therefore of grammar schools. Seen in the light of this exalted view of education, schoolmasters and scholars were at the very centre of the life of the community, fulfilling God's purpose by transforming it through the workings of Christian morality.

The sheer scope of this programme gives some idea of the range of Erasmus's vision. A big problem, of course, was expense, since schools could not be built and schoolmasters paid without money. But the Church was rich, and much of its wealth was consumed unprofitably. If monasteries were dissolved and the endowments of bishoprics reduced, large sums of money could be released for education. Clerical vested interests might prove resistant, but they could be brought to heel by the representatives of the lay community which had such a vital interest in the creation of a healthy, moral and Christian society. Erasmus therefore appealed to the princes of Europe to take the lead in reforming the Church where the Church itself was unable or unwilling to do so. He also urged them to keep out of wars, since these not only encouraged unchristian attitudes, such as anger and cruelty, but also consumed vast sums of money that could be more profitably spent on education.

The implications of Erasmianism, where dogma and Church organisation were concerned, were little short of revolutionary, even though Erasmus himself was careful not to make these explicit. His Christianity, like that of the Brethren from whom he had imbibed it, was essentially a system of morality: it left little room for mystical exaltation, except in its concentration on the figure of Christ. Although it accepted the fall of man it took an optimistic view of human potentialities, since by the use of reason (as long as it was accompanied with humility and devotion) man could hope to attain knowledge and understanding of God, Erasmus believed that theological speculation was a waste of time, and assumed that catholic dogma, as expounded by the Church, provided a satisfactory framework within which every individual could work out his own salvation. As far as this salvation was concerned, only a few beliefs were essential—trust in God's grace, for instance, and in the redemptive power of His son. The rest, including the entire structure of the Church, were inessential in the sense that they could vary from place to place and from time to time.

France

The astonishing thing about the 'Erasmian programme' is that so much of it was put into effect, not only through the direct influence of Erasmus himself but also through that of reformers who had arrived independently at similar conclusions. In France, where early humanism had made little progress outside the court, Renaissance influence was limited until the impact of Christian Humanism. The Sorbonne was still firmly rooted in late-medieval scholasticism, and the first person successfully to challenge this and to show that humanist studies, far from being irrelevant to theology, were essential to it, was Jacques Lefèvre d'Etaples. He studied in Florence and Padua, acquiring an extensive knowledge of the philosophy of Plato and Aristotle, and was also well read in the late-medieval mystics. On his return from Italy in the 1490s he lectured on Aristotle and soon became the leader of the humanists in the university of Paris. He concentrated on making Aristotle available to French scholars through Latin translations, and he also translated the works of the Florentine Platonists.

There was no specifically religious cast to Lefèvre's studies at this time, but in 1505 he underwent a profound spiritual experience, and as a result determined to devote his life to work on the Bible. In 1509 he produced the Quintuplex Psalter, in which five versions of the psalms were placed side by side for comparison; and he followed this up in 1512 with an edition of St Paul's Epistles in which the standard Vulgate text was printed alongside his own translation, which he had corrected by reference to the Greek original. In 1523 came his major work, a translation into French of the New Testament, which he later extended to the Old Testament as well. Like Erasmus, Lefèvre insisted that 'good works'—in the sense of formal actions like reciting a fixed number of prayers or going on a pilgrimage—were valueless without inward spiritual regeneration, and that the Bible contained all that was necessary for salvation. This led him into asserting that men are saved by faith alone, a belief which was not unknown to the catholic Church but, unfortunately for Lefèvre, had become the rallying-cry of Luther. Lefèvre came under suspicion of heresy and therefore retired from Paris to Meaux, where he was protected by his former pupil, Bishop Briçonnet.

Briçonnet, a humanist and ardent reformer who had already set about improving the quality of life of the clergy in his diocese, welcomed his old friend and master. He also gave his approval to Lefèvre's simplified form of worship, which left out invocations to the Virgin and saints, forbade genuflections and the use of lighted candles, and made some substitution of French for Latin. By this time, however, Lutheranism was spreading into France, and the conservatives in Church and state were increasingly alarmed. Francis I held them in check, but in 1525 he was taken prisoner and sent captive to Spain. During his absence the defenders of orthodoxy rallied and Briçonnet was summoned before the *Parlement* of Paris to answer charges of heresy. The Meaux group was broken up, even though Briçonnet was acquitted, and Lefèvre eventually made his home in the court of Francis I's sister Margaret, Queen of Navarre, who shared his mysticism and his belief that the scriptures were the only secure foundation for a Christian life.

Lefèvre was an example of Erasmianism without Erasmus. He had a great admiration for the Dutch scholar but had arrived at his own conclusions independently and was concerned not so much with their international application as with their effectiveness within France. He worked to reform the Church from inside, but—like Erasmus—he was overtaken by events. By about 1530 Lutheranism had spread so widely that all reform was suspect, and Lefèvre had to choose between accepting orthodoxy or being accused of heresy. Although he shared

Luther's belief in redemption through faith alone he would not follow him into breaking with the established Church. Such a break would, he thought, destroy any hope of fundamental reform and turn the energies that ought to be devoted to the task of spiritual regeneration into the sterile channels of partisan controversy. In this pessimistic assumption he turned out to be only too correct.

Spain and Italy

Another important centre of an autonomous Erasmian reform movement was Spain. Because of its later identification with Roman Catholicism in its most rigid and uncompromising form, and the fact that the Inquisition was more effective there than in any other country, it is often assumed that Spain was impeccably orthodox and hostile on principle to the idea of reform. This was certainly not the case in the late fifteenth century. In the words of a French historian[1] 'In no European country was Erasmus read, revealed, translated more freely. No government so actively encouraged the diffusion of his work.' The background to this reform movement, and indeed one of the main causes for it, was the deplorable state of the Spanish church—for in this respect Spain was no different from the rest of Europe. Bishops were almost always recruited from among the nobility and were as much secular as spiritual in their interests, while the religious orders were in general worldly and lax in discipline. As for parish priests, the great majority were ignorant and uneducated. But religious enthusiasm was strong in Spain, and had been made more fervent by the *Reconquista*, the long struggle against the Moors. Already it seemed to many Spaniards that God had chosen them to be the leaders of a revived Christianity. Reformers were therefore welcomed as men who would prepare both Church and state in Spain for the high demands that were to be made upon them.

The leader of the reformers was Cardinal Ximenes de Cisneros, confessor to Queen Isabella of Castile. He had studied law and theology at the University of Salamanca, and after serving for some years in Rome seemed all set for a career in the ecclesiastical hierarchy. A sudden spiritual conversion persuaded him instead to embrace the religious life, and he joined the Observant Franciscans. He might never have returned to public affairs had it not been for Isabella, who knew

[1] Henri Hauser, *Les Débuts de l'Age Moderne*, Paris, 1956. p. 270.

of his reputation and persuaded him to undertake the task of reform. By 1495 Ximenes was Archbishop of Toledo and primate of Spain; in effect he was chief minister in both Church and state. He immediately began reforming the religious orders, of which he had had personal experience, and during his years in power he succeeded in imposing the high standards of the Observants on all the Franciscan houses.

Ximenes realised that no reform movement could achieve any lasting result unless it was accompanied by fundamental changes in the pattern of education. He therefore founded a new university at Alcala, in 1508, in which specific provision was made for the teaching of Greek and oriental languages. Alcala rapidly became a major centre of humanist studies, and scholars from the university produced an edition of the Greek New Testament which was in print (though not published until later) in 1514, two years before the appearance of Erasmus's edition. The greatest achievement of Alcala, however, was the Complutensian Polyglot Bible, which was inspired and carried through to completion largely by Ximenes. In this great work the authorised Vulgate version was printed in parallel with the original texts, so that cross-references could easily be made and difficulties in interpretation clarified. Ximenes was also behind the project to publish all the writings of Aristotle in both the original Greek and a Latin translation, though this ambitious scheme was halted by his death.

Ximenes saw no reason for the Catholic Church to be suspicious of humanist reformers. His own orthodoxy was impeccable, as was proved by his appointment as Chief Inquisitor, and the result of his work was that the Church in Spain, far from being torn apart by internal criticism, was united and revivified. Lutheranism and other heresies, which spread so rapidly throughout the rest of Europe, made virtually no headway in Spain. The success of Ximenes would, of course, have been far less easy of attainment had it not been for the unswerving support of the Queen. This was an illustration of Erasmus's contention that Christian princes ought to take the lead in reforming the Church. But it also demonstrated a weakness in Erasmus's reasoning, for the authority of princes did not extend beyond the frontiers of their realm, whereas the Church was universal. A national reformed church was in a sense a contradiction in terms, and exaltation of the authority of the prince could lead to the break-up of that Christian unity which Erasmus, like other humanist reformers, wished to preserve. But the Christian Humanists were prisoners of their own times. Only the papacy could undertake the reform of the whole Church, and so far it had shown itself unwilling, as well as unfitted, to grapple with so prodigious a problem.

Erasmianism in Spain did not die with Ximenes, because it was strongly rooted not only among the clergy but in the laity as well. The influence of the humanists at the court of Charles V was so considerable that the more conservative churchmen were not listened to. Charles, in any case, valued the support which Erasmian scholars gave him in his struggle to persuade the papacy to take up the challenge of ecclesiastical reform. Not until about 1530 did the climate of opinion begin to change in favour of the conservatives. By that time the Pope and the Emperor had come to terms, and the rapid spread of Lutheranism in Europe made all reformers increasingly suspect. In 1537 the Inquisition forbade the reading of Spanish translations of Erasmus's works and ordered the expurgation of the Latin originals. The Erasmian reform group was broken up and its adherents were faced, here as elsewhere, with the unpalatable choice between increasingly reactionary orthodoxy or heresy.

Italy, the birthplace of Renaissance humanism, produced a most uncharacteristic reformer—the Dominican monk Savonarola. He made his name as a preacher, prophesying doom for a corrupt and worldly society, and Lorenzo de' Medici invited him to Florence. There, after the French invasion and the expulsion of the Medicis had apparently confirmed his gloomy predictions, he became the virtual ruler of the city, proclaimed the kingdom of Christ, and set out a programme for radical reform of the Church, including that of the papacy and papal household (the 'Curia'). His spectacular career lasted only four years and ended at the stake, but he had shown that even in the birthplace of the Renaissance there were destructive emotional forces waiting to be unleashed. Savonarola's mystical fervour and his demand that the Church should be reformed had obvious affinities with the Christian Humanist attitude, but he was hardly a Renaissance figure, for he included in his denunciation much of the New Learning and the society to which it had given birth.

In Germany, humanism had to overcome the opposition of the scholastics, who were strongly entrenched and far more vigorous in their intellectual life than was the case elsewhere in Europe. Humanist influence gradually increased, however, and found particularly fertile soil in incipient German nationalism. Since Germany did not exist as a political entity, and the Emperor proved to be an inadequate focus for patriotic sentiment, German nationalism found its outlet in hatred of the papacy—which was accused of using Germany simply as a milch cow—and of the corrupt and wealthy Church which the papacy upheld. Humanists, with their critical attitude towards clerical wealth and their demand for radical reform, made an immediate appeal to German national feeling, and this was reinforced by the humanist study of the German past, particularly through the recovery of Tacitus. It was the identification of humanism with nationalism that led many scholars to welcome Luther's challenge to Church and papacy, and to place German humanism at the service of the protestant Reformation.

The Achievement of the Christian Humanists

By the second decade of the sixteenth century Christian Humanism was both a programme and a force, and it seemed as though, by sheer pressure of opinion, it would bring about the reformation it so fervently desired. Under its impact schools and universities were founded, such as the Trilingual College at Louvain—so called because its curriculum was based on the study of Latin, Greek and Hebrew—and the Collège de France, set up by Francis I. Older institutions and traditions did not, however, disappear overnight. Medieval curricula survived alongside humanist courses, and in many cases the initial impetus of humanism on the universities was followed by a period of reaction.

As for the reform of Church and society in general, this was inevitably a slow process, but the volume of informed criticism was building up to a point at which major changes might well have been brought about. At this particular moment, however, Luther appeared, and very rapidly the quiet (though insistent) voice of Erasmus was drowned by the thunder of Wittenberg. Under the pressure of attack and counter-attack positions rapidly hardened, and not only the international Church but also the international community of scholars was fragmented. Erasmians were everywhere forced to commit themselves and take sides. Some saw in protestant reformers and lay princes the best hope of achieving their aims. Others, like Erasmus himself, believed that unity was essential, and therefore rallied to the defence of the catholic Church.

It may seem, on the face of it, that Erasmianism was a failure, since it was overtaken by events before its proposals were put into full effect. But once the smoke of battle had drifted away it became apparent that many of the main features of the Erasmian reform programme had in fact come into existence. The Counter-Reformation produced a revivified catholic Church in which the education of priests and reform of the religious orders were given high priority, and the Jesuits, through their schools and universities, became transmitters of the Erasmian inheritance. The protestant churches, also, concentrated on reform of the clergy and a higher standard of education, and catholics and protestants alike were working towards an improvement in the general moral standards of European society. Melancthon and Calvin, just as much as the Jesuits, were the heirs of Erasmus, and the Academy which Calvin founded at Geneva built up its great reputation on a basis of classical learning as a preparation for study of the scriptures. Europe in 1600 was far from the purified and united community that Erasmus had worked for, but across the barriers of fanaticism and intolerance the exchange of ideas continued, and more of the principles of Christian Humanism survived than had seemed possible half a century earlier.

SEVEN

Luther

The Papacy and Germany

In the late Middle Ages the prestige of the papacy suffered a sharp decline. For nearly sixty years the Popes were 'exiles' in Avignon, and although they returned to Rome in 1378 a disputed election led to the Great Schism, when there were at least two and sometimes three Popes, each claiming to be the only true one and declaring his rivals deposed and excommunicate. Not until 1417, with the election of Martin V, did the catholic Church once again have a single, unchallenged head, and for a long time afterwards the effects of more than a century of papal weakness were making themselves felt. The authority of the Popes had been eroded not simply in Christendom but more immediately within the Papal States in Italy. Martin and his successors set about regaining these temporal possessions, and at the same time they reformed papal administration, bringing it more in line with that of the secular states. The central government of the Church undoubtedly grew more efficient as a result, but one effect of this was a substantial increase in papal revenue. With their newfound wealth the Popes were able to patronise artists and scholars on a lavish scale, and they made Rome the capital of the Renaissance. But the glories of Rome, and the smooth efficiency of the papal tax-gathering machine, did nothing to make the Church more spiritual; nor did the recovery of the Papal States, since the Popes behaved exactly like their fellow rulers, displaying the same concern for territorial aggrandisement and the establishment of their own dynasties.

Since the cardinals were chosen mainly from among the leading Italian familes it is not surprising that the papacy was similarly restricted. Sixtus IV, who became Pope in 1471, was a member of the Rovere family, and used the patronage of the Church for the benefit of his relatives. Five of his nephews and one grand nephew were appointed cardinals, among them Giuliano della Rovere, the future Julius II, while another nephew was married into a princely Italian house. Innocent III, who succeeded Sixtus in 1484, was also an Italian aristocrat, and his rapacity was epitomised by his own vice-chamberlain's comment that 'the Lord desireth not the death of a sinner but rather that he may live and pay'. Innocent was followed by the Borgia Alexander VI, who was a gifted and intelligent man but quite unscrupulous when it came to the advancement of his family and in particular of his son Cesare Borgia. The Ferrarese envoy gave his opinion that 'ten papacies would not suffice to satisfy this brood', and from Florence Savonarola denounced the corruption of the papal court and the wickedness of its head. Julius II, who was Pope from 1503 to 1513, was a fire-eater, who became the object of an oblique but scathing attack by Erasmus. He was succeeded by the Medici Leo X, a cultured, peace-loving man whose great ambition was to complete the rebuilding of St Peter's and who issued an indulgence for this purpose in 1513.

When Leo had first gone to Rome, as a young man, his father, Lorenzo the Magnificent, had warned him: 'Take care. You are going into the sink of iniquity.' There was all too much truth in this observation. The eternal city was being transformed by the genius of artists of genius, such as Michelangelo, Raphael and Bramante—all of whom worked for Julius II—but the money needed to sustain all this brilliance corrupted everything with which it came into contact. At a time when Europe was showing unmistakable evidence of great spiritual hunger the Church stood in urgent need of reformation from within. If the papacy failed to give a lead the initiative would pass either to lay rulers or to individual reformers. In either case the unity of Christendom would be threatened.

Savonarola, who bitterly attacked the Pope for neglecting his spiritual duties, had called on the King of France to undertake the great task of reform, and it was in fact Louis XII who inadvertently made the first move in this direction. Louis was so angry at what he regarded as Julius II's 'betrayal' of him, in forming the Holy League,[1] that he deliberately revived the conciliar ideal. On the face of it there was nothing particularly alarming in his proposal that a general council of the Church should be summoned to initiate reform, but this was to

[1] See below, p. 212.

ignore the fact that the Conciliar Movement of the late Middle Ages had been a serious challenge to papal power, and Martin V and his successors had done their utmost to ensure that no general council should meet again.

For political reasons, therefore, Louis XII summoned a general council of the Church to meet at Pisa in May 1511. Such an action amounted to very little, especially since the French armies were shortly afterwards driven out of Italy, but the threat of a French-dominated council prompted Julius to summon one of his own, to the Lateran, in April 1512. This was not a representative body, since the Italian wars prevented the attendance of delegates from France, England and Germany. Nor was the climate of opinion at Rome and within the upper levels of the ecclesiastical hierarchy conducive to reform. Inertia and vested interests were still formidable obstacles to change, yet there were some signs of movement, of which the Lateran Council itself was one. In its recommendations, given effect by a papal bull of 1514, it concentrated upon two major abuses. The first was pluralism, which gravely weakened the impact of the Church at parish level, but the council's proposals amounted to little more than pious exhortation. The second was monastic indiscipline, and here the council took a step in the right direction by requiring that all members of religious orders should be under episcopal authority when working outside the confines of their own house. The Lateran Council, in short, marks the beginning of the long process of catholic reform, but its actual achievements were minimal. The corruption of the papacy, the worldliness of the Church as a whole, and the subordination of spiritual to financial considerations, were virtually untouched by it.

The financial pressures of the Church were particularly burdensome in Germany, where there was no national monarchy to stand between the people and the demands made upon them by Rome. Unlike the parish priests, who were often very poor, the prince-bishops lived in luxury and were all too frequently preoccupied with secular matters. The more important bishoprics were generally regarded as preserves of the aristocracy, and there was therefore nothing exceptional in the fact that when the Archibishopric of Mainz fell vacant in 1514 the candidate put forward to fill it was Prince Albert of Hohenzollern, younger brother of the Elector of Brandenburg. Since he was already the possessor of two bishoprics he needed a dispensation to add a third to his collection, and this could only be obtained from Rome by the payment of a large sum of money. The Hohenzollern family, which welcomed this opportunity to extend its influence, was prepared to advance the necessary cash, which it borrowed from the Fuggers. Albert planned to find the money to repay his family by sharing with the Pope the profits from the preaching of an indulgence for the rebuilding of St Peter's.

An indulgence was based on the belief that over the years the Church had built up 'a surplus of merits' which it could sell to those who were truly contrite, in order to release them from part of the penance which they were bound to carry out as a visible sign of their inward repentance. In 1476 Pope Sixtus IV had extended the operation of indulgences to souls in purgatory, where the dead had to do penance for all the sins for which they had not given satisfaction during their lifetimes. The danger of indulgences was that those who bought them would assume that they were buying not simply remission of penance but absolution from the sin itself. Archibishop Albert tried to insist that anyone buying an indulgence should first confess and give some evidence of contrition, but Tetzel, a Dominican friar who had been entrusted with preaching the indulgence in Germany, went beyond his brief and allowed it to be assumed that, in the words of a popular jingle:

As soon as the coin in the coffer rings,
The soul from Purgatory springs.

Frederick the Wise, Elector of Saxony, would not allow Tetzel to enter his territories. He had no objection to indulgences in principle, but he had created at Wittenberg a collection of some five thousand relics—including hay and straw from the manger at Bethlehem, and parts of the original cradle—which drew pilgrims from all over Germany, not least because they could thereby benefit from an indulgence granted by a previous Pope. Frederick did not want a rival attraction, and the inhabitants of Wittenberg had to travel some miles to the frontiers of Saxony if they wished to purchase an indulgence from Tetzel. Many of them did so, however, and returned to the city convinced that they had bought absolution for themselves or those they had loved.

Martin Luther

The realisation that a papal agent was taking advantage of the credulity of the masses, and deliberately obscuring spiritual truths for financial gain, deeply shocked many people, among them Martin Luther. Luther had been born in 1483 in a small Saxon town where his father, a hard-headed copper miner, was gradually working his way up in the world and moving from poverty to relative affluence— though during Martin's childhood money was always short. In 1497 the young Luther was sent to Magdeburg, where he attended a school run by the Brethren of the Common Life, and in 1501 he went on to university at Erfurt, where by 1505 he had become a Master of Arts. Erfurt university was a great stronghold of the 'schoolmen' whom Erasmus and the Christian Humanists so despised, and particularly of those called 'nomalists' who emphasised the gap between reason and revelation and insisted that man's limited and finite intelligence could never understand the divine. Knowledge of God was to be obtained only by revelation, and the main source of this was the Bible.

This insistence on the apartness of God and the enormous gap between Him and man struck an immediate response in Luther, who was obsessively aware of his own state of sinfulness. His search for God led him at first into the monastic life, and in July 1505 he entered the house of the Augustinian Friars at Erfurt. This was an Observant order, which kept to the strict discipline of the original foundation, yet even among dedicated men Luther was distinguished by the extreme asceticism which he practised. As he later said of himself: 'If ever a man could have got to heaven through monkery I would have done so.' Yet rigorous discipline and frequent confession conferred no peace of heart on Luther. He had been brought up to believe—as the Church taught—that man could gradually make himself acceptable to God, with the aid of the sacraments and through the performance of good works. Yet Luther was convinced that God could not possibly love so sin-ridden a creature as himself, and he came to hate this Father who demanded love from his children but made it impossible for them to approach him with any feelings other than awe and fear. Like the Elizabethan poet Fulke Greville he despaired of the

> . . . wearisome condition of humanity;
> Born under one law: to another bound.
> Vainly begot, and yet forbidden vanity;
> Created sick, commanded to be sound.

With anguish in his soul Luther pursued his monastic vocation, and in 1508 he was sent to the Augustinian house at Wittenberg to strengthen the teaching at the university recently founded there. In 1509 he was back at Erfurt, because of widespread opposition among his brethren to a proposal to unite all the Augustinian houses in Germany. They feared that such a union might lead to the softening of the strictness of their Observant rule, and therefore decided to appeal to the head of their order in Rome. For this mission they selected Luther, and in 1510 he arrived in the capital of the Christian world. There, if anywhere, he could hope to find peace of heart, but although he climbed the Scala Santa on his knees and did everything else that a good pilgrim should, he returned to Wittenberg in 1511 with his fears and doubts still tormenting him.

In the six years that followed, Luther lectured on the Psalms and St Paul's Epistles to the Romans, and it was during the course of his preparation for these that he found what he had always been seeking. Man, he realised, could not possibly draw near to God of his own free will, since his nature had been so corrupted by original sin that everything he did drove him towards evil. A human being trying to attain salvation through his own efforts was like a badly made clay model trying to reshape itself. The potter—in this case God—must intervene. Man could do nothing but wait for the divine spark, to set him alight and burn out the sin from him. He could not *force* God to intervene: he could only rest assured in the faith that since God had sent Christ into the world, there was hope for all sinners. Faith was essential, and through faith alone would ultimately come salvation.

There was nothing particularly new about this insistence on the power of faith. St Paul had emphasised it, and so had St Augustine, one of the early Christian fathers, in whose writings Luther discovered it with great joy. Luther now became certain that awareness of sin was a sure sign that the Holy Spirit was at work, and it was borne in on him with the force of revelation that the self-loathing which had driven him to despair was in fact the first stage in the process of regeneration.

The implications of this 'revelation' were far-reaching, and Luther had not even begun to work them out when, in 1517, he was caught up in the controversy over indulgences. Luther was appalled at the realisation that a papal agent was persuading credulous men and women to believe that by purchasing an indulgence they could buy pardon from sin. The self-disgust and revulsion that should precede and accompany true repentance were an essential part of the process of spiritual regeneration, and there could be no short cuts. By selling indulgences the Church was denying the whole purpose of its existence, for God could not be fooled and the last judgment could not be averted by waving a piece of paper sealed with the papal arms. The credulous who bought indulgences were in fact being left to wallow in sin by the very institution that had been created to lead them from it. Luther decided to formulate his views and make them public. Wittenberg was full of pilgrims who had come to venerate the Elector's collection of relics, and in October 1517 Luther made a bid for their attention by pinning up ninety-five Latin theses on the notice-board of the town church. In these he made his opinions clear, although he was careful to avoid any direct attack on papal authority. Instead he put all the blame upon Tetzel by observing that if the Pope came to know of the tricks being used to sell indulgences he would let St Peter's fall to the ground rather than build it with such contaminated money.

The ninety-five theses were swiftly translated, printed and disseminated throughout Germany. Nothing like it had been seen before, and but for the printing press Luther's protest might have been made unheeded. Probably no one was more surprised than Luther himself at the storm created by his words. He tried to withdraw his theses, but they were already public property, and the Archbishop of Mainz, in whose diocese Wittenberg lay, sent them to Rome with a request that Luther should be inhibited from any further exposition of his dangerous opinions.

When Pope Leo X first heard the news from Wittenberg he assumed that the whole thing was simply another monkish quarrel, but after reading the theses he realised his mistake and cited Luther to appear at Rome to answer charges of heresy and rebellion against ecclesiastical authority. The citation was forwarded to Cardinal Cajetan, the papal legate in Germany, who had gone to Augsburg for a meeting of the imperial Diet. Cajetan hoped for the Emperor's co-operation in bringing Luther to trial, but Maximilian was busy making arrangements to have his grandson, Charles, crowned King of the Romans,[1] and for this he needed the support of the Electors, among them Frederick the Wise of Saxony. Frederick, who probably never met Luther and can hardly have approved of his views on relics and indulgences, nevertheless insisted that the rebellious monk—who was, after all, one of his own subjects—should not be handed over until he had been given a chance

---

[1] This title was usually given to the Emperor's eldest son, and implied a right of succession to the imperial throne.

to defend himself. In October 1518, therefore, Luther went to Augsburg, not simply to ask for pardon from the legate but to argue his case. Cajetan, a man of great learning and integrity, insisted on the need for obedience to the catholic Church, which, by virtue of its divine institution, had access to truths other than those contained in the Bible and had been entrusted with the guidance of the Christian world. But Luther, in three days of disputation, took his stand firmly on the scriptures and would not budge. The argument merely revealed the wide gap between the two men, and Luther left Augsburg hurriedly for fear that sterner action might be taken against him.

In the following month Luther appealed from the authority of the Pope to that of a general council of the Church. He was still anxious to avoid an open break with Rome, but he was carried along by the force of his own arguments and the torrent of emotion released by his actions. He was fortunate that, at this crucial juncture, imperial authority was so weak. In January 1519 Maximilian died, and for the next six months, until the election of Charles V in June, Luther's protector, the Elector Frederick, was a much courted man. By the end of this period Luther had become a national hero and it would have been extremely difficult for any German ruler to execute judgment against him. In July 1519 the reformer went to Leipzig, for a disputation with a distinguished German theologian, John Eck. During the course of this formal argument Eck accused Luther of being a Hussite. Luther replied that although he hated heresy the doctrines of Hus (with which he was, in fact, unfamiliar) had contained some truth and the Council of Constance had been wrong to condemn him. The significance of the disputation with Eck is that Luther, in defending his views, went well beyond his original position. He denied the authority of both Popes and councils, and appealed to the Bible, as interpreted by private judgment based on faith.

The Development of Luther's Ideas

Luther was by now increasingly aware of the fact that the implementation of his beliefs would entail fundamental reform of both church and society, and in the following year, 1520, he developed his programme in a number of pamphlets, written in a vigorous polemical style, which became best sellers. In the *Sermon on the Mass*, Luther insisted that Christ's sacrifice on the cross had been made once and for all. There could be no question of re-enacting it, as the priest claimed to do in the mass. Priests were said to 'offer' this sacrifice, but how could a mere man offer God anything except himself? Priests made their communion with God by bread and wine, while the laity were restricted to bread alone, but Luther declared that anyone who had faith was a priest and therefore entitled to take the sacrament 'in both kinds'. Some of these themes were developed in *An Appeal to the German Nation*, published in the summer of 1520. This was a clarion call to national and anticlerical feeling. If, as Luther claimed, the Church was the community of all believers and not simply the minority who were ordained, the secular ruler of this community had a duty to intervene and redress abuses if the ecclesiastical authorities failed to take action. There was no need to acknowledge papal authority or to pay taxes to Rome, since the Bible made no mention of the Pope or his supposed supremacy. The Bible did, however, show secular rulers organising the Church within their own dominions, and this should therefore be part of their functions. As for practices such as clerical celibacy, for which there was no scriptural basis, they should be forbidden, and monks and nuns should be expelled from their monasteries, since the whole world was God's cloister. There should also be an end to pilgrimages and similar 'good works' that had no truly spiritual content, and rites and ceremonies should be simplified in order to avoid superstition.

Education needed reforming if society was to be freed from the grip of papalism and a corrupt Church. To promote true learning every town should establish schools (for girls as well as boys) in which Bible study should be the basis of the curriculum. Luther's aim in all these reforms was to return to the fundamental Christian truth that salvation depends on faith, and that knowledge of the scriptures, by which faith is transmitted and reinforced, should be available to all men and women.

In October 1520 appeared the pamphlet *Concerning the Babylonish Captivity*, written in Latin and aimed at ecclesiastics. In this Luther struck at the roots of 'priestcraft' by reducing the number of sacraments from seven to three—the eucharist, baptism and confession. He also reiterated his denial of transubstantiation. This was the belief, officially adopted by the Roman Catholic Church in the early Middle Ages, that in the sacrament of the eucharist the 'elements'—that is the bread and the wine—were transformed into the body and blood of Christ. This doctrine was more complex than appears at first sight, since it depended on the distinction drawn by medieval schoolmen (who derived their approach from Aristotle) between the 'substance' of anything, which is its true nature, and the 'accidents', which are its physical components. A chair and table, for instance, would share the same 'accidents', both being made of wood and glue, but they are 'substantially' different. In the sacrament of the eucharist there was no question of a change in the 'accidents'. To all outward appearances the bread remained bread, the wine wine; but the 'substance' had been miraculously transformed.

This doctrine was unacceptable to Luther because it implied that God operated only in the spiritual world of 'substances' and not in the physical one of 'accidents'. It also made the presence of God in the sacrament depend on the initiative of the priest in celebrating the eucharist. This was to put limits upon the freedom of action of God, and to subordinate Him to the will of mere man—a reversal of the true order of things. Luther was convinced that God pervaded the entire physical world, and that his real presence was to be found in the bread and wine regardless of whether or not they had been consecrated by a priest. This was why, in his proposals for educational reform, he declared that Aristotle and those medieval philosophers who derived their concepts from him should no longer be studied. Their distinction between 'substances' and 'accidents' was, for him, mere mumbo-jumbo, and, like indulgences, it persuaded the credulous that there was a short cut to God. The whole point of Luther's beliefs and teachings was that there were no such short cuts. The Christian must not look to the Church or the priest to win salvation for him, since there was no intermediary between God and man other than Jesus Christ. God would 'save' whom He wished when He wished, and no thought or action of mortal men and secular institutions could influence the divine will. Every human being must be his own priest, and all that was required of the Christian was patience and confidence in the justice and mercy of a loving God. Faith was essential: everything else was secondary or irrelevant.

The last of Luther's major writings in 1520 was entitled *The Freedom of a Christian Man*. Luther was concerned here primarily with spiritual freedom, his theme being that by voluntarily submitting to the will of God the Christian frees himself from subjection to any earthly authority. He should obey the 'powers that be', since these are ordained by God, but he should never act against his own conscience. The only real bondage is that of sin, and the only hope of release consists in opening the entire inward being to God's grace. Not everybody, of course, could be assured of salvation. God had predestined some to be saved and 'reprobated' others to damnation, but however unjust this might seem to human reasoning it must be freely accepted as part of the divine plan. The Christian, however, must always hope, and constantly bear in mind the redemptive power of Christ and His sacrifice on the cross. It followed from Luther's argument that 'good works' in the conventional sense (pilgrimages, public acts of contrition, etc.) could not possibly affect a man's chances of salvation. 'Good works', he wrote 'do not make a good man, but a good man does good works; evil works do not make a wicked man, but a wicked man does evil works.' The daily routine of living—the sweeping of a floor, the cooking of a meal—could be truly good works if they were done out of the love of God. Luther denied the distinction between the sacred and the secular, upon which, for instance, the monastic ideal had been based. Since there was no possibility of attaining perfection in this world there could be no grades of goodness, and a monk was no nearer heaven than a ploughboy or housewife. Any task could be sanctified by faith, and any place was holy if God chose it for His purposes.

In his insistence that religion concerned man's inmost being and that externals were irrelevant, Luther obviously had much in common with the Christian Humanists. This seemed so clear to the Dominican Martin Bucer, sent as formal observer to a convention of the Augustinians in 1518, that he was immediately converted to Luther's views, commenting that 'what Erasmus insinuates, he speaks openly and freely'. Erasmus did not disapprove of what Luther was doing. He wrote to Frederick of Saxony, urging him not to listen to those who wished to silence Luther, and he also appealed to Leo X to withdraw his decree condemning Luther's works and to appoint an international commission to consider the proposals made in them. Yet there was no real meeting of minds between Luther and Erasmus. Luther was indebted to the Christian Humanists in that he used the works of Erasmus, Lefèvre and Reuchlin to arrive at the deepest possible understanding of the Bible, but classical culture meant little to him, and far from taking a basically optimistic view of human nature he saw it as being sunk so deep in sin that only God could pull it free; hence his comment that 'Erasmus does not take grace into sufficient account'.

Many humanists supported Luther, particularly in the early days when he appeared to be the champion of enlightenment against medieval obscurantism. Among them was Philip Melancthon, whose life's work was to express Luther's ideas in a systematic fashion and to reconcile them, as far as possible, with the Christian Humanism of Erasmus. But other humanists came to realise that Luther's intellectual inheritance was more medieval than classical, and they were repelled by his manner. Erasmus and the majority of the Christian Humanists spoke with a quiet, albeit insistent, voice and relied on reason and intelligence to do their work. Luther, on the contrary, had an earthy, rumbustious approach and expressed his views so vehemently that he forced the Christian world to take notice of him. The advent of Luther signalled the eclipse of the Erasmians' hope of gradual and peaceful change, for he spoke the language of religious revolution.

The Break with Rome

In June 1520 Leo X had issued the bull *Exsurge Domine*. 'Arise O Lord!' it began, 'and judge Thy cause. A wild boar has invaded Thy vineyard' (an appropriate metaphor for a great huntsman like Leo). It went on to condemn a number of Luther's beliefs, to order the public burning of his books, and to threaten him with excommunication if he did not recant. Luther's reply was to light his own bonfire at Wittenberg and to burn on it not only the papal bull but the books of canon law as well. In January 1521, therefore, the Pope formally pronounced sentence of excommunication against Luther, and called on the Emperor to take the necessary enforcing action. Charles V was a devout and orthodox catholic, who would have been only too glad to put an end to Luther. But he did not wish to antagonise his newly acquired German subjects, especially the princes, and he was aware of the enormous popular support for Luther. Charles therefore issued a proclamation condemning Luther's heresies and forbidding the printing or publication of his works, but he also granted the reformer a safe conduct to Worms so that he could defend his case publicly before the Diet due to assemble there.

Luther knew that if he went to Worms his life might be in danger, for an imperial safe-conduct had not prevented the Council of Constance from burning John Hus. Nevertheless he decided to go, and set out from Wittenberg in April 1521 on a journey that turned into a triumphal progress. An observer described him about this time as 'Of middle height, emaciated from care and study so that you can almost count his bones through his skin. . . . He is affable and friendly, in no sense dour or arrogant. . . . In company he is vivacious, jocose, always cheerful and gay no matter how hard his adversaries press him. Everyone chides him for the fault of being a little too insolent in his reproaches and more caustic than is prudent for an innovator in religion or becoming to a theologian.' When Luther first appeared before the Emperor and the assembled Estates at Worms he seems to have been ill at ease and made a poor impression. But on the following day he recovered his confidence and spoke firmly and well. He refused to retract anything he had said unless it could be clearly demonstrated from the Bible that he had erred. 'Unless I am convinced by the testimony of scripture or by evident reasoning—for I trust neither in Popes nor in councils alone, since it is obvious that they have often erred and contradicted themselves—I cannot and will not recant.'

The Emperor and the legate had hoped that Luther would either submit to the impressive display of authority assembled at Worms or react so violently that he would turn opinion against him. In fact his measured and temperate reply, with its appeal to conscience, made a deep impression, and any attempt to execute sentence against him would almost certainly have been resisted. On the following day Charles V made a declaration which, in its own way, was equally impressive. 'It is certain that a single friar must err if he stands against the opinion of all Christendom. Otherwise Christendom itself would have erred for more than a thousand years. Therefore I am determined to set my kingdoms and dominions, my friends, my body, my blood, my life, my soul upon it. For it were great shame to us . . . if in our time, through our negligence, we were to let even the appearance of heresy and denigration of true religion enter the hearts of man.'

Luther did not linger at Worms, where the Emperor was preparing an edict to outlaw him by placing him under the 'ban of Empire' and to restrict the circulation of his writings. Before the end of April he was on his way back to Wittenberg, but he never reached there. In the early stages of his journey he was 'kidnapped' by officers of the Elector of Saxony and spirited away to the castle of the Wartburg, near Eisenach. Frederick had taken this extraordinary course of action in order to free himself from the embarrassment of openly defying the Emperor. He could now counter any demand to hand over Luther by disclaiming all knowledge of his whereabouts.

Luther made the most of his involuntary retreat from the world by setting to work on a translation of the Bible into German. Meanwhile, in Wittenberg, the transformation of religious life had already started.

The lead in this was taken by Andreas Carlstadt, a professor at the university there, whose studies in St Augustine had brought him to a belief in salvation through faith alone, very similar to that of Luther. Now, in Luther's absence, Carlstadt pressed ahead with the reformation in Wittenberg, and on Christmas Day 1521 celebrated a mass in which no vestments were worn and no elevation of the sacraments took place, while both bread and wine were administered to the congregation. Early in 1522 monks and nuns were encouraged to leave the cloister, and priests started taking wives for themselves. Much, though not all, of this was in accordance with Luther's own attitudes, but Carlstadt went significantly beyond these in encouraging the destruction of images and the abolition of vestments. He also interpreted Luther's doctrine of the priesthood of all believers in a way that implied social equality, and it began to seem as if the reformation in Wittenberg might move at so rapid a pace that it would spark off revolution and thereby alienate the leading members of the community, who had so far been sympathetic to Luther's ideas.

The town council of Wittenberg appealed to Luther—whose whereabouts had become known—to go back and stop the rot. Now that the Emperor had left Germany, in order to attend to the problems of his many other dominions, there was no longer any reason for Luther to remain in the Wartburg. In March 1522, therefore, he returned to Wittenberg after nearly a year's absence. He accepted many of Carlstadt's changes—the opening of monasteries, for example, and the encouragement of clerical marriage—but he restored altars, candles and ornaments to churches, since such things were, he believed, aids to devotion if used in the right way, and were also visible signs of the respect due by man to the majesty of the Almighty. While the use of German instead of Latin in the mass was retained, as was the administration of communion in both kinds, Luther did not share Carlstadt's distrust of vestments and images. He wanted to turn the Church back to what it had been, not to create something entirely new. Carlstadt was forbidden to preach, and left Wittenberg. In his subsequent writings he went on to deny the real presence of God in the sacraments. This was too much for Luther, who summoned him to Wittenberg, deprived him of his ministry, and in September 1524 procured an order from the Elector expelling him from Saxony.

Another radical, Thomas Muntzer, was also expelled. Muntzer had started his career in the textile centre of Zwickau, in south-east Saxony, where he had found a receptive audience among the weavers. He was a visionary, very much in the tradition of late-medieval German mysticism, who believed that the second coming was fast approaching and that God had already chosen the 'saints' who were to survive. The Rule of the Saints was to be brought about on earth, as a prelude to the last judgment, and Muntzer regarded it as his divinely ordained duty to destroy the existing social order, based as it was upon the rule of the ungodly, and replace it with an egalitarian one. This attitude appealed to the artisans, apprentices and peasants who formed the bulk of Muntzer's followers, but it made no sense to Luther. For him the world was of secondary importance, and he had no wish to become identified with social radicalism since this would merely make it more difficult to gain acceptance for what he was convinced were profound and essential religious truths.

Lutheranism and Society

Luther was right to be alarmed at the spread of radical doctrines, since Germany in fact was on the brink of social upheaval. His ideas had spread like wildfire not simply because they contained a religious message that satisfied spiritual hunger but also because they challenged the existing order of things. The Reformation in Germany came at a time when population growth was increasing the pressure on land and sending up prices, a process that was accelerated by the inflationary effect of expanding silver production from the German mines. Landlords, determined to compensate for the impact of the price rise on their own incomes, attempted to impose or reimpose labour services, while princes, particularly the smaller ones, levied new taxes and swept aside local and customary restraints upon their freedom of action by invoking Roman law. In south-west Germany, which was politically very fragmented, peasant resistance to this pressure had taken the form of the *Bundshuh* movement, which aimed at the overthrow of the established economic and social order. The preaching of Muntzer and other radicals was of immediate relevance to this. While the peasants wanted equality for economic reasons, Muntzer saw it as the will of God; the upshot was that peasant dissenters increasingly used the language of religious radicalism. Discontent was not confined to the peasantry. The religious and social influence of the towns was considerable, and urban artisans and small traders were ready to join in the struggle in order to preserve their rights.

In June 1525 a major revolt erupted in the Black Forest region and spread rapidly throughout southern Germany. There was no co-ordinated rebellion, but the separate outbreaks quickly established links, and to a certain extent there was a common programme. Among many statements of the rebels' aims, one that attained sufficient fame to elicit a reply from Luther was the *Twelve Articles*. These contained a mixture of religious and social demands. The first article insisted that ministers should be elected by the entire congregation and should teach 'the holy gospel pure and simple, without any human addition', while subsequent ones called for the abolition of tithes, the end of serfdom, fair rents, and a return to old laws and customs. These were moderate demands, and indeed in many places the leaders of the peasant revolt were themselves men of substance who did not share the egalitarian fervour of the radicals.

Luther had some sympathy with the peasants, as he made clear in his *Friendly Admonition to Peace, concerning the Twelve Articles of the Swabian Peasants*, published in April 1525. In this he blamed the 'princes and lords, and especially you blind bishops and mad priests and monks [who] do nothing but flay and rob your subjects in order that you may lead a life of splendour and pride, until the poor common people can bear it no longer'. At the same time he insisted that the rebels were wrong to use force: 'The fact that the rulers are wicked and unjust does not excuse tumult and rebellion, for to punish wickedness does not belong to everybody, but to the wordly rulers who bear the sword.'

The peasants had claimed, in their third article, that since Christ had died for all men, great and small, there should be an end of serfdom and inequality. Though this was an obvious echo of Luther's views in *The Freedom of a Christian Man*, the reformer reacted strongly against the implication that he had been thinking in worldly terms. 'This article', he complained, 'would make all men equal, and turn the spiritual kingdom of Christ into a wordly, external kingdom; and that is impossible. For a wordly kingdom cannot stand unless there is in it an inequality of persons, so that some are free, some imprisoned, some lords, some subjects. . . . A slave can be a Christian and have Christian liberty.' Whatever the rebels may have thought of Luther's distinction between carnal and spiritual liberty they were not to be held back at this late stage, and by the spring of 1525 over a quarter of a million 'peasants' were up in arms. North-west and north-east Germany were not affected, nor was Bavaria, but in southern Germany revolt was widespread.

With the rebellion at its height, Luther penned one of his most notorious pamphlets, *Against the Murderous, Pillaging Hordes of Peasants.* In this he came out in defence of the secular authorities and called on them to show no mercy to the rebels, who had taken up the sword without divine authority. 'Therefore they may be treated like mad dogs. Strike, throttle, stab secretly or openly, whoever can, and remember that there is nothing more poisonous, more hurtful, more devilish, than a rebellious man.' Carlstadt had been appalled at the effects of his teachings, and had been reconciled with Luther, but Muntzer led the peasants against the army raised by the Swabian League. In May 1525 his followers were slaughtered in battle with the Landgrave Philip of Hesse, and Muntzer himself was captured, tortured and executed. By the time Luther's pamphlet actually appeared the revolt was all but over, and the defeated peasants were being treated with a savage ferocity that far excelled anything they had done themselves. The princes had no need of Luther's exhortation to be merciless, and some hundred thousand peasants were put to death in the process of 'restoring order'.

It is unlikely that Luther's writings on the Peasants' Revolt had more than a marginal effect. The peasants would have revolted anyway, and the lords would have repressed them savagely whatever Luther had said. Nevertheless the protagonists of religious reformation now had to take account of the situation created by the defeat of the rebellion, and in particular of the consolidation of princely authority. Throughout large areas of Germany Church organisation was breaking down. In Saxony, to take but one example, there was considerable confusion. The bishops, who remained loyal to orthodox catholicism, could hardly give a lead in carrying through the Lutheran reformation. At the parish level there was great variety in forms of worship, and diversity of religious beliefs easily merged into agrarian and sectarian unrest. The preservation of order in both Church and state demanded uniformity, and only the secular power could enforce this. In 1526, therefore, the Elector of Saxony made the use of the Lutheran litany obligatory throughout his territories, and in the following year he ordered a general visitation of the Saxon church.

Luther may have assumed that the role of the state in religious affairs would be merely temporary, but he had no effective alternative to offer. He did not really care a great deal about the formal structure of the church provided it taught the gospel: he would have been happy to see the Roman Catholic Church preserved if only it had been prepared to meet this essential condition. Except in a formal sense,

Lutheranism had not been imposed from above; on the contrary, it was the support of the masses that enabled it to challenge and destroy the established Church. But after Luther's disavowal of the peasants its future came to depend increasingly on the attitude of the lay princes, and his triumph was also theirs.

EIGHT

The Reformation in Germany and Switzerland

Germany

The majority of the German princes in the 1520s were opposed to Lutheranism, but they were also deeply critical of the papacy. In 1522–23 the Diet of Nuremberg therefore refused to support the demand of Pope Adrian VI for the execution of the Edict of Worms but insisted that a free general council of the Church should be summoned to meet on German soil within twelve months. In 1524 another Diet agreed to enforce the Edict so far as this was possible, but Charles V's brother Ferdinand, who acted as regent during the Emperor's long absences from Germany, had already privately admitted that 'Luther's doctrine has taken such deep root that among a thousand persons there is not one who is not to some extent touched by it'. Charles—who had other urgent problems to deal with, such as the Turkish menace and the hostility of France—shared the desire for a general council and believed, with some reason, that if only the Pope would agree to summon such a body the problem of Lutheranism in Germany might solve itself. While the Pope delayed, however, both catholics and protestants were preparing to defend themselves, and Elector John of Saxony (who succeeded his brother Frederick in 1525) formed the League of Torgau with another Lutheran convert, Landgrave Philip of Hesse.

The success of their initiative was shown at the Diet of Speyer in 1526, when it was provisionally agreed that individual rulers should be allowed to decide the nature of the religious settlement within their states. In return for this concession the Lutheran princes were prepared to provide money and men for the Emperor's wars, and it was Lutheran troops in the service of Charles V who shocked catholic Europe by sacking Rome in 1527. By 1529, when the Diet again assembled at Speyer, Charles had been successful in Italy while Ferdinand had stabilised the position on the eastern frontier of the Empire. The need for the support of the Lutheran princes was not, therefore, so great. Ferdinand, presiding as usual in the absence of his brother, consequently took a far more intransigent attitude and persuaded the majority of the Diet to accept his demand that there should be toleration for Roman Catholics throughout the Empire and no further innovation in religion nor secularisation of Church property. This led to a formal protest signed by Elector John, Landgrave Philip, and the representatives of all the major towns except Augsburg, declaring that 'In matters touching God's honour and the salvation of our souls each man has the right to stand alone and present his true account before God. On the last day no man will be able to take shelter behind the power of another, be it small or great.' With this high-sounding declaration of fundamental principles protestantism was formally born.

While Lutheranism had been the only species of religious protest, unity among the dissenters could be taken for granted. But as the reformation spread into south Germany and Switzerland it took on different forms. It seemed obvious to Landgrave Philip that such differences weakened the reformers' cause, and in September 1529 he invited Luther and Melanchthon to meet Zwingli, Oecolampadius and Bucer in his castle at Marburg. He hoped that in the ensuing colloquy certain basic points of agreement would be formulated, but his hopes were not entirely fulfilled. The main point of disagreement among the reformers was over the nature of the sacraments, and Luther began the public debate with an uncompromising gesture when he chalked the words *Hoc est Corpus Meum* on the table in front of him. In fact there was a considerable measure of agreement on everything except the nature of the sacraments, and although at one stage in the proceedings Luther angrily told Bucer 'You are of another spirit from us', in October he was referring to 'our friendly talks' and to 'agreement on almost every point'. Nevertheless the Marburg Colloquy did not produce any statement of faith upon which the reformed churches could unite, and to this extent it was a failure.

When another Diet assembled at Augsburg in June 1530 Charles V himself was present, for the first time since his condemnation of Luther at Worms. He had at last secured the Pope's agreement in principle to summon a general council, but the Pope had insisted that first of all the Lutherans should be reconciled, and this was Charles's aim at Augsburg. At the invitation of the Emperor, Melanchthon, Zwingli and Bucer were present to see if they could come to terms with the Catholics; Luther was not included in the invitation since he was still under the ban of Empire. Melanchthon had prepared a confession of faith, in which he put the emphasis on those points on which Lutherans and catholics were in agreement—such as belief in the real presence of God in the sacrament of the eucharist. He was prepared to go some way beyond this for the sake of unity, and in the course of negotiations agreed to accept episcopal authority and auricular confession,[1] and only insisted on communion in both kinds until such time as a general Church council should decide on this question. The south German towns drew up their own confession of faith—a sign of protestant disunity—while Zwingli made it clear that he stood by the truth of his beliefs and would accept no compromise. The Roman Catholic representatives assumed that Melanchthon's obvious desire for reconciliation was a reflection of protestant weakness, and they therefore took a hard line, insisting on the acceptance of clerical celibacy, transubstantiation, the redemptive power of 'good works' as well as faith, and the spiritual supremacy of the Pope. There could be no agreement on these conditions, and in fact this Diet marks the end of any real hope of reconcilation among the various Christian groups, although efforts to restore unity continued. The Confession of Augsburg, which Melanchthon had drawn up in the expectation that it would prove a basis for unity, became instead the foundation charter of a separate Lutheran church.

Even if Melanchthon had succeeded in reaching agreement with the Roman Catholics it is doubtful whether his compromise would have been acceptable even to his fellow Lutherans. Luther himself was already losing patience with attempts at reconciliation, and John of Saxony and Philip of Hesse declared that they would not be bound by anything that Melanchthon said or did. The Diet, recognising that there was no point in prolonging negotiations, formally announced that the protestant princes were to be given seven months in which to return to communion with Rome, an ultimatum to which the protestant princes replied by withdrawing from the Diet. In November 1530 the Emperor, who was more than ever convinced that some decisive action must be taken before the situation passed the point of no return, ordered that traditional doctrines and practices should be observed throughout the Empire and that the property and goods of the Church should everywhere be restored.

This seemed tantamount to a declaration of war, and the protestant

---

[1] Confession to a priest (literally 'to the ear of' the priest).

princes and towns came together at Schmalkalden, where they formed a league for mutual defence. The aims of this league were security for all protestants, including the Evangelicals (as the followers of Zwingli and later Calvin were called), and the settlement of religious disputes by a general Church council which should meet in Germany, outside the range of papal control. In defence of these aims the Schmalkaldic League was prepared to fight, and although Luther was opposed to the whole idea of resistance to the secular authority he was eventually persuaded that imperial law itself permitted resistance in cases of extreme injustice.

It may be that the show of resistance by the protestant princes served its purpose in that it persuaded Charles not to try force at this stage. As always, he had commitments outside the Empire which drained his resources in men and money, and the catholic German princes were more liberal in protestations of support than in material assistance. Religious divisions did not, after all, entirely obliterate other differences, and suspicion of the Emperor remained a powerful negative force even among catholic rulers: the Wittelsbach Dukes of Bavaria, for instance, were ardently catholic, but they were also deeply distrustful of Habsburg aims. Charles V, recognising that he was in no position to undertake a religious war in Germany, therefore agreed to the Peace of Nuremberg in June 1532. In return for assistance against the Turks the protestants were now to be left in peace until such time as a general council of the Church could assemble.

Charles's conciliatory policy gave the protestants time to extend the reformation in Germany and consolidate their position. In the spring of 1534, for instance, the Schmalkaldic League used its troops to restore the Duke of Wurttemberg to the territories from which he had been expelled by the Swabian League some fifteen years earlier. Philip of Hesse also opened negotiations with Francis I of France, who was always ready to subsidise the enemies of the Habsburgs. But while the protestants were successful in consolidating their political power, religious unity still eluded them. In 1536 Luther and Bucer, meeting at Wittenberg, agreed on the Wittenberg Concord, drawn up by Melanchthon, which affirmed the real presence while denying transubstantiation. The south German towns also accepted this, but the Swiss could not bring themselves to do so and the protestant churches therefore remained divided.

Melanchthon was still hopeful that unity might be achieved not simply among the protestants but within the Christian Church as a whole.

Francis I was prepared to encourage such hopes, since they gave him the opportunity to undermine the Emperor's role as self-appointed arbiter of Christendom, and Bucer, as well as Melanchthon, put forward proposals which he hoped might be the basis for an acceptable compromise. But the Swiss denounced the duplicity of the French king, who claimed to be the champion of Christendom at the same time as he secretly negotiated with Christendom's greatest enemies, the Ottoman Turks (see p. 313). Bullinger declared that Francis I was 'an irreligious and ambitious libertine, caring neither for Christ nor for Germany', and although Melancthon was prepared to go to Paris and test the French king's sincerity, the Elector of Saxony, with Luther's support, forbade him to do so. The outlook for the advocates of Christian reunion was, however, brighter than it had been for many a year, since Paul III, who ascended the papal throne in 1534, really wanted reconciliation, and at last summoned a general council of the Church to meet at Mantua in May 1537.

The protestant princes were deeply suspicious of the papal initiative. Although they paid lip-service to the ideal of reunion they had no intention of giving way on what they regarded as essentials, and they were afraid that if they accepted an invitation to the council they would be committing themselves to accept its decisions. They had long been advocates of a council meeting in Germany under the headship of someone other than the Pope, but a solution which might have satisfied the German protestant princes would not have been acceptable to Christendom as a whole. Charles refused to summon a council to meet in Germany, and insisted that the decisions of the papal council should be accepted within the Empire. However, when the protestant princes made clear their determination to fight rather than submit to such terms, the Emperor once again drew back. Ferdinand was in dire need of money for the defence of the Empire against the Turks, and Charles, as well as being heavily committed elsewhere, did not want to stifle all hope of eventual reunion by taking violent action. In April 1539, therefore, the 'Interim of Frankfurt' was issued, guaranteeing that the protestant princes would be free from attack for at least fifteen months, as long as the spread of protestantism and the further secularisation of Church land were halted.

Since Francis I, who was antipathetic to general councils unless summoned as a result of his own prompting, had also announced that he would not support the papal initiative and would forbid French bishops to go to Mantua, Paul III postponed the council *sine die*. This was a blow to the advocates of reconciliation, but it did not mean the end of all their efforts. The key to success seemed still to be in Germany, and the protestant leaders were therefore invited to attend the Diet at Regensburg in 1541. Bucer, Melanchthon and later Calvin were all present on this occasion, and the leader of the papal delegation was Cardinal Contarini, whose learning, integrity and deep desire for reconciliation could not be doubted. Regensburg was the last occasion on which representatives of the catholic and protestant Churches sat round a table together and tried to heal the breach between them. They came closer to agreement than had ever seemed possible, and Contarini consented to allow communion in both kinds if congregations showed a desire for this; to permit (though not encourage) the marriage of priests; and to reject the doctrine that salvation could be achieved through 'good works' alone. The points of agreement were summarised in the Articles of Regensburg, but the negotiators, carried away by their own enthusiasm, had gone beyond what general opinion on both sides was willing to accept. Luther, when he studied the Articles of Regensburg, openly denounced them. The Pope similarly rejected the concessions made by Contarini, and it became clear, even to Charles V, that reconciliation was a mirage.

It may have been as a consequence of his disappointment and disillusion after the failure of the Regensburg negotiations that Charles began seriously to consider the prospect of imposing a settlement by force of arms. He would first have to neutralise Francis I, but by 1544 this had been achieved. Francis, after suffering heavy defeats at the hands of the coalition which Charles had built up against him, agreed to the Peace of Crépy, by which he bound himself to give no further assistance to the German protestants and to remove his opposition to a general council of the Church. With this major obstacle out of the way the long postponed council could now go ahead, and the Pope convoked it to Trent for May 1545.

Charles was therefore free to deal with the German protestant princes. In 1545 the Pope offered him substantial financial assistance for operations against the heretics, and in the following year, at another meeting of the Diet at Regensburg, the protestant princes repeated their refusal to accept the decisions of any general Church council under papal leadership. Charles was aware that the longer he delayed the more dangerous the situation would become, because protestantism was still spreading. By 1545 all north-east and north-west Germany had become Lutheran, and so had large parts of the south-west. The only exceptions were Bavaria, Augsburg, and the bishoprics along the Main. Among the princes who had declared in favour of Luther were the Elector of Saxony and the Elector of Brandenburg. In January 1546 the Elector Palatine also received the sacrament in both kinds and agreed to follow the lead of the Schmalkaldic League. There now seemed to be a distinct possibility that the electoral college might acquire a protestant majority; and the prospect of a Lutheran Emperor was more than Charles could stomach.

If Charles had openly declared that he intended to wage war on the Lutherans he would have united the protestant princes against him. Instead he emphasised his intention to restore order within the Empire, and called on all those who had respect for his authority to co-operate in this task. He did not, of course, anticipate any sudden collapse on the part of his opponents, but he wanted to provide a face-saving excuse for any of the princes who were prepared to abandon the cause of protestant unity for the sake of their own interests. The opportunity was grasped by Maurice, Duke of Saxony, who was the head of the Albertine branch of the Saxon house and coveted the electoral lands and dignity which belonged to the Ernestines. He agreed to assist the Emperor in restoring imperial authority—which meant, in effect, bringing the protestant princes to heel—and in return was promised the electoral title once the incumbent Elector, John Frederick, had been defeated.

Luther did not live to see the outbreak of religious war. He died in February 1546, but Charles's preparations were not completed until the following June. In that month the Emperor wrote to his sister Mary to tell her what he proposed to do. 'Unless we take immediate action, all the states of Germany may lose their faith and the Netherlands may follow. After fully considering all these points I decided to begin by levying war on Hesse and Saxony as disturbers of the peace. . . . This pretext will not long conceal the true purpose of this war of religion, but it will serve to divide the protestants.' In July 1546 the ban of Empire was formally pronounced against John Frederick and Philip of Hesse, and military operations began. The protestants were in a strong strategic position, since they could block the passes through the Tyrol on which Charles was dependent for reinforcements from Spain and Italy; on the other hand they were suspicious of each other and lacking in effective leadership. Although the war went badly for Charles at first, he managed to get troops from both Italy and the Netherlands and, by the end of 1546, he had secured his base in southern Germany.

In spring of the following year he launched an attack on John Frederick, caught up with him at Muhlberg, and defeated and captured him. In May Wittenberg fell and in the following month Philip of Hesse made his submission to the Emperor.

Although the protestants held out in north Germany, the south and much of the centre was now at last under Charles's control. He therefore summoned the Diet to Augsburg in 1547 to decide on a religious settlement for Germany. The outcome of these deliberations was the 'Declaration of how things are to be managed in the Holy Roman Empire, touching the question of religion, until the general council can be held'—usually referred to as the 'Interim' of Augsburg. In the Interim minor concessions were made to the protestants, such as clerical marriage and communion in both kinds, but otherwise conformity to catholic doctrine was insisted upon. In fact the Interim could not be enforced everywhere. Many protestant princes were extremely reluctant to co-operate, and the degree of popular resistance showed just how deeply Luther's ideas had penetrated into German society. Smaller units, like the imperial free cities, were forced to obey and Bucer and a number of other reformers fled to safety in England and elsewhere. But German protestantism could not be wiped out by the issuing of a decree, and although in many places the catholics began to recover the initiative, the work of counter-reformation would have demanded the concentration of all Charles's resources, and even then would have been a slow process.

Charles's triumph was self-defeating to the extent that it demonstrated how great a menace imperial authority could be to princely liberty. The Elector of Saxony was formally tried and sentenced to death, and although the sentence was committed to one of imprisonment the greater part of his lands was taken away and given, along with the electoral dignity, to Maurice. Philip of Hesse was kept in prison, and however justified this treatment might have seemed to Charles it created deep resentment among the other princes. Maurice of Saxony, in particular, now that he had become Elector, recognised that the revival of imperial power threatened his own independence and ambitions, and he gradually built up a defensive league among the protestant princes. In October 1551 this league came to terms with the new King of France, by which Henry II bound himself to supply large sums of money in return for the cession of three bishoprics near the French frontier. This agreement was formally ratified by the Treaty of Chambord, signed in January 1552, and in the following April the protestant forces took the field. Augsburg was captured and Charles had to flee first to Innsbruck, where he was very nearly trapped by Maurice, and thence south, over the Brenner Pass. The catholic princes, prominent among them the Duke of Bavaria, did not lift a finger to help him. They, like Maurice, had learnt the lesson that religious uniformity could be bought at too high a price if it entailed the erosion of princely independence.

Since the Emperor had been chased out of Germany it was left to Ferdinand to come to terms with the victorious Maurice, and this he did in the Treaty of Passau, concluded in August 1552. John Frederick of Saxony had already been released from prison, but Maurice insisted on the freeing of Philip of Hesse and on the suspension of the Interim until the summoning of a new Diet: in return for these concessions he agreed to support Ferdinand against the Turks in Hungary. Later that year, however, Charles reappeared in southern Germany, where he turned for help to the Margrave of Bayreuth, an unscrupulous and brutal adventurer who, in the name of protestantism, had laid waste great tracts of catholic territory. This alliance between the catholic Emperor, who was supposed to be the guardian of the Empire, and a protestant robber prince, confirmed the worst suspicions of the German rulers, and they came together, irrespective of religion, to suppress the Margrave and restore at least a semblance of order. In January 1553 Charles left Germany, never to return, and in the following year he authorised Ferdinand to preside at the forthcoming Diet, and to make whatever concessions he considered necessary.

The Diet opened at Augsburg in February 1555, and agreed on the terms of a 'Religious Peace'. This officially recognised the existence of Lutherans—though not of Zwinglians, Calvinists or Anabaptists—and left the ruler of every state free to decide which of the two forms of Christian faith he would adopt for his dominions. Any subject who could not accept the decision of his prince was to be allowed to emigrate, after selling his property at a reasonable price. As for the free cities, where the catholics had made some recovery during the time of Charles's ascendancy and the enforcement of the Interim, it was decided that they should treat both protestants and catholics equally.

The problem of the ecclesiastical principalities was not so easily settled. Ferdinand was afraid that if the prince-bishops who ruled these territories were allowed to adopt protestantism and establish their dynasties on confiscated Church property, the temptation to do so would be too great. He did not wish to see a majority of protestant princes within the Empire, and in particular he was determined that the electoral bishoprics of Mainz, Cologne and Trier should not slip into protestant hands. He therefore insisted that any ecclesiastical ruler who changed his faith should automatically lose his office, and that a Roman Catholic should be elected to take his place. The protestant princes refused to accept this 'Ecclesiastical Reservation', but when it became clear that Ferdinand would not agree to peace unless he was satisfied on this point they gave way. The Reservation was not included in the formal agreement in which the terms of the Religious Peace were embodied, but it was issued, with the princes' reluctant consent, as an imperial edict.

The Religious Peace of Augsburg did not mean the end of religious wars in Germany, but it symbolised the failure of Charles V's attempt to keep the Empire united and catholic. Charles himself, worn out by the long struggle, formally renounced the imperial crown in September 1556 and abdicated in favour of his brother Ferdinand. Yet although Ferdinand was widely respected and was relatively free from the dynastic responsibilities that had dissipated Charles's energies and resources, he did not attempt to take up the struggle again. He had the imperial title and the Habsburg lands in Germany and eastern Europe, and these were enough. He knew from experience that power lay with the rulers of the separate states and that his own authority was dependent upon recognition of this fact. The German princes were the real victors at Augsburg, and their rights were defined in the legal maxim *cuius regio, eius religio*—he who rules a territory shall determine its religion. Whether protestant or catholic the princes were agreed on one thing—that the maintenance of their own independence was to take priority over all other considerations.

Zwingli and Zurich

Although Luther was the first in time of the protestant reformers he was not the only one. Resentment of the obvious abuses of the catholic Church, and the widespread desire for a purification of faith and worship, found expression also in the towns of south Germany and Switzerland. These were, in general, prosperous communities, nominally part of the Empire but enjoying a considerable measure of autonomy. They benefited from their position astride one of the major trade routes of the western world, and the interchange of goods was accompanied by an interchange of ideas. South Germany and Switzerland had been strongly influenced by the Christian Humanist movement, and the ground had thereby been prepared for reformation.

Ulrich Zwingli was Swiss by birth, and had attended university in the humanist centres of Basle and Vienna before being appointed people's priest in the principal church in Zurich. He was a man of considerable learning, familiar with the works of Plato, Seneca and Cicero, and a great admirer of Erasmus, from whom he acquired his belief that the Bible and the early Christian fathers were the foundations upon which the true faith should be built. The Church, of course, claimed to be the guardian of faith, but Zwingli was not impressed by the catholic clergy he encountered. At Zurich they spent their time in gaming and eating, and their reading was virtually confined to secular books. The Renaissance had passed them by, and such study as they engaged in was restricted to scholastic theology and canon law.

Zwingli was convinced that faith demanded an active commitment, and before ever he heard of Luther's protest he had come to see his main task as preaching and teaching the pure gospel. He approved, of course, of Luther's stand against indulgences, since in 1518 he had persuaded the magistrates of Zurich to refuse admission to Tetzel's counterpart. Subsequently he studied the writings of both Luther and Hus, but it seems likely that even if Luther had never appeared, Zwingli would have set on foot the work of reform at Zurich. He began by attacking all those practices of the Roman Catholic Church for which there was no authorisation in the Bible, and in 1523 published articles condemning transubstantiation, fasts, pilgrimages and papal supremacy. The councillors of Zurich were impressed by Zwingli's arguments, and ordered a public disputation between him and a catholic representative. Zwingli was adjudged the victor in this contest, and as a consequence the council introduced public Bible-reading and vernacular prayers in January 1524, and also denounced clerical celibacy. Early in 1525 religious houses were dissolved, and in April of that year the mass was formally abolished. It was replaced with a simple communion service in which preaching and prayers played the major part.

Because Zwingli found no justification in the Bible for a great deal of catholic ritual and for images, he wanted these swept away. In this he differed from Luther and was perhaps nearer to the position of Carlstadt, who visited him in Zurich. Zwingli would not accept

Luther's view that the physical and the spiritual were simply two aspects of the same divine nature, and in his *Commentary on the True and False Religion* he expounded his own position. 'Body and spirit are such essentially different things', he wrote ,'that whichever one you take, it cannot be the other'. For this reason he denied that there could be any trace of the real presence of God in the consecrated sacraments. For him the service of communion was simply an act of commemoration, and any assertion of the real presence, whether it came from the catholics or from Luther, was mere superstition.

Zwingli did not deny the need for divine grace, but he put much greater emphasis on the *law* of God, as revealed in the Bible, which Christ gave man the will to obey. It followed from this that a truly Christian community must follow as closely as possible the biblical pattern, and that the state, no less than the Church, must create the conditions necessary for the Christian life. In fact Zwingli virtually merged the Church with the state, for, as he wrote, 'a church without the magistrate is mutilated and incomplete'. The magistrates' task was not simply to keep order and preserve property. They were also the guardians of public conduct, and at Zurich they set up a court of morals to supervise the conduct of citizens and punish any backsliding. This evangelical reform of the lives of individual men and women, carried out through the agency of the civil government, was one of Zwingli's major contributions to the protestant Reformation. Nothing like it was attempted by Luther, partly, at least, because the conditions of life in Saxony were so different from those in the towns of Switzerland.

In 1529 the five Swiss cantons which had remained catholic formed a coalition and determined to use arms to bring the protestants to heel. Zwingli had no hesitation about countering force with force. As a young priest he had accompanied the Swiss mercenaries into Italy, and had been present at the battles of Novara and Marignano (see p. 212); now he went as chaplain with the protestant army raised to defend the city he loved. In fact the war was ended almost before it began, through the mediation of Berne. But two years later fighting broke out in earnest, and in October 1531 Zwingli was wounded, taken prisoner, and executed.

Zwingli was not a major reformer in the sense that Luther and later Calvin were. Zurich was too small a world to have much influence outside, and the fusion of Church and state which worked so well there had only limited relevance to other countries. But Calvin, for instance, learnt much from Zwingli's example, and despite the defeat and death of the reformer Zurich remained a protestant city. Zwingli's place was taken by his son-in-law, Henry Bullinger, a fine scholar and teacher who kept in touch with reformers all over Europe. Bullinger carefully avoided the involvement in Swiss political life which had led to the destruction of Zwingli. Instead he concentrated, like Melancthon, on unifying the protestant churches, and the first Helvetic Confession of Faith, produced in 1536, was largely his achievement.

Basle and Strasburg

The reformation came to Basle with John Oecolampadius, who was born in Germany in 1482. He was educated in the humanist centres of Heidelberg and Bologna, acquired a good knowledge of Latin and Greek, and studied Hebrew under Reuchlin. Not surprisingly Oecolampadius had a great respect for Erasmus, and in 1515 collaborated with him on his edition of the New Testament. In 1520 he was offered a post as preacher in Augsburg and he arrived in that city just as the impact of Luther's protest was beginning to be felt. The division of opinion within Augsburg was reflected in Oecolampadius himself, and in an attempt to find certainty and peace of mind he entered a monastery. When he found, as Luther had done, that the monastic life provided no solution for his particular spiritual problems, he left the cloister, in 1522, and broke with the catholic Church. In the following year he began teaching theology in the University of Basle, and in public debates he urged that the example of Zurich should be followed.

The magistrates of Basle had reservations. They were alarmed by the spread of Muntzer's radical doctrines and were afraid that any change in the religious establishment might open the way to revolution. They therefore asked the advice of Erasmus, who was at that time living in their city. Erasmus advocated moderation, as always, and opposed any break with the catholic Church. His influence, however, was rapidly declining. In 1524 he and Luther had publicly quarrelled after an exchange of pamphlets on the subject of free will, and Luther accused him of seeing the Bible only as a guide to moral conduct and of ignoring the mystical elements in the Christian faith. At the same time as Erasmus came under attack from the leading protestant reformer, he was also increasingly criticised by the catholics, who regarded him (in the words of Bishop Fisher) as having laid the egg that Luther hatched. In the noise of battle Erasmus's voice was drowned, and the magistrates of Basle came over to the opinion of Oecolampadius, that the Church in their city should be thoroughly reformed. In 1529, therefore, after a popular rising against the catholics, they abolished the mass and ordered the removal of images from churches.

In Basle, as in Zurich, religious and civic life became virtually one. Oecolampadius advocated the reintroduction of excommunication as a weapon for purifying the Church in Basle, and proposed that the imposition of this penalty should be the responsibility of elders elected by the congregations. But excommunication, given the close relationship between Church and state, would almost inevitably involve exile as well, and the magistrates were not prepared to leave such a formidable weapon in the hands of persons over whom they had no control. Overriding the objections of Oecolampadius, they insisted that the power of excommunication belonged to them alone. By so doing they made sure that the government of the Church, as of the city, of Basle would remain in the hands of the lay magistrates.

Strasburg was an imperial free city, which suffered from absentee bishops and the poor quality of the resident clergy. It was also a major centre of the book trade, and therefore particularly susceptible to the influence of the printed word. The works of Luther and Melanchthon were widely circulated, and the ground was thereby prepared for reformation. As early as 1521 Matthew Zell, one of the few priests to show evidence of passionate commitment to the spiritual welfare of his flock, was 'preaching the pure gospel', and in 1523 he welcomed to the city Martin Bucer, the former Dominican who had been converted by Luther. Under Bucer's influence the town council ordered the abolition of images and in 1529 formally suppressed the mass. Bucer introduced a simplified service which clearly showed the influence of Luther. His emphasis was on preaching and the exposition of the Bible, but he also encouraged the congregation to take part, as in Lutheran services, by communal hymn singing.

Bucer was more 'puritan' than Luther in his attitude to images and ceremonies, and he also differed from both him and Zwingli in believing that Church and state should be entirely separate, though parallel, bodies. But, like Oecolampadius, Bucer had to face opposition from the lay magistrates, who refused to allow anyone other than themselves to exercise the power of excommunication. Bucer therefore never completely achieved his ambition of creating an autonomous reformed church in Strasburg, but he remained a much-loved and respected figure, and only left the city after the victory of Charles V and the imposition of the Interim of Augsburg. He died in England in 1551.

The Anabaptists

Anabaptism as an organised movement had its origins in Zurich in the circle of Zwingli's friends. Conrad Grebel was prominent among those who wanted a far more radical reformation than anything Zwingli had in mind, and his ideas spread rapidly, first among his fellow intellectuals and then into the countryside outside Zurich, where the peasants were smarting under the twin evils of heavy tithe payments and increasing rents demanded by non-resident urban landlords. Grebel and his followers rejected Luther and Zwingli alike. They acknowledged no authority other than that of the Bible and they believed that the true Church consisted only of the 'saints', who could be identified by the fact that they had undergone spiritual conversion. As a consequence of this conversion they were freed from sin, and then—and only then—could they be truly baptised. Adult baptism therefore became a distinctive feature of this sect, and gave its adherents their name, but it was only one indication of their detachment from the world around them. Anabaptists believed that the 'saints', far from attempting to remodel the secular community, must withdraw from it, since it was the fruit of sin. They must refuse to take part in government, reject all oath-taking, never resort to law (which was man-made, and therefore evil) and never engage in war. In some Anabaptist communities property also was regarded as a pernicious human invention, and the holding of lands and goods in common was practised.

With their tendency towards communism and their denunciation of the existing social and religious order, the Anabaptists obviously had much in common with the earlier radicalism of Carlstadt and Muntzer. Grebel, in fact, was in touch with Muntzer in 1524, and welcomed him as one who shared some, but not all, of the Anabaptist attitudes. A surviving letter from Grebel to Muntzer not only summarises Anabaptist beliefs, but also shows an awareness of the suffering that such beliefs would inevitably entail. 'True Christian believers', wrote Grebel, 'are sheep among wolves, sheep for the slaughter. They must be baptised in anguish and affliction, tribulation, persecution, suffering and death. They must be tried with fire, and must reach the fatherland of eternal rest not by killing their bodily enemies but by mortifying their spiritual ones.'

The Anabaptists did not have to wait long for the days of tribulation to arrive. Although they offered no physical threat to society, their insistence on withdrawing from it was an affront to established authorities, who feared that if their example was widely copied it would undermine the entire social order. Rulers were also suspicious of the association between Anabaptism and political radicalism, particularly after Muntzer's involvement in the Peasants' War in Germany. Hostility towards Anabaptists was common to Roman Catholics and protestants alike. Luther, for instance, who had appealed to conscience in his struggle against the Pope, had come to appreciate that if every man acted according to his own conscience there would be an end of order and government. Zwingli was equally anxious to demonstrate that the religious reform which he was advocating had no undertones of radicalism, since such links would have alienated the ruling oligarchy on whom he depended for the accomplishment of his aims.

The established authorities in Church and state used all the power at their disposal to put down what they regarded as a dangerously radical movement. In 1526 the magistrates of Zurich ordered that all infants were to be baptised, and that any Anabaptist caught in the city should be put to death by drowning. Driven out of Switzerland, the Anabaptists spread into north Italy and the Tyrol and settled in considerable numbers in Moravia. Others took refuge in Strasburg, and it was estimated that there were some two thousand of them in the city by 1534, when the magistrates decided to compel infant baptism and expel all those who would not agree to it. In 1529, at the Diet of Speyer, catholics and Lutherans agreed that Anabaptism should be a capital offence, and hundreds of men and women were put to death by authorities whom they did not acknowledge for breaking a law which they regarded as contrary to God's explicit commandment.

One result of this savage and prolonged persecution was to wipe out the moderate leadership among the Anabaptists and leave the way open for more violent men to take over. The effect of this was seen in the dramatic happenings at Munster in 1534. In the previous year the city of Munster had revolted against its bishop and opened its churches to reformers, among them Anabaptists. The two most prominent Anabaptists were a Dutch baker, John Mathys, and a tailor, John of Leyden, who were strongly under the influence of Muntzer's writings.

In February 1534 these two took power in the city and inaugurated the 'rule of the saints'. Property was abolished, adult baptism was made compulsory, and all opponents of the new regime were expelled forthwith. As the news of these events spread, it created alarm and consternation among all those who upheld the existing order of society. Their worst fears seemed to be confirmed when, following the death of Mathys in a sortie, John of Leyden became sole governor and announced that all goods, including wives, would in future be held in common. A number of princes had already combined their resources and raised an army to put an end to such wickedness. In 1535 the Munster experiment came to a bloody end when the town was taken by storm, and John of Leyden, who by this time had accumulated sixteen wives, was tortured to death.

Anabaptism did not die out as a result of Munster. Menno Simmons —a Roman Catholic priest who was converted to Anabaptism shortly after the collapse of the Munster experiment—led the Netherlands' communities away from the excesses associated with John of Leyden, and organised them into 'Congregations of Christ'. The 'Mennonite Movement' as it became known, gradually increased its influence in Holland, until in 1577 William of Orange officially granted its members freedom of worship. The Mennonites also spread into north Germany, while another Anabaptist group, the Hutterites, was active in Moravia. Some Anabaptist communities also survived in south Germany and Switzerland, but they were never a major influence there.

This radical reformation, which challenged the protestant Reformation from the left, obviously owed much of its inspiration to late medieval mystical movements, which had also influenced Carlstadt, Muntzer and others. It stood apart from the main streams of Lutheranism and Calvinism, and it combined religious and political discontent in a way that challenged the fundamental assumptions of society. It is easy to see in the Anabaptists the protagonists of religious liberty, or communists born before their time, In fact, of course, the Anabaptists did not believe in religious liberty, and their courage derived from a deep but narrow conviction of their own righteousness and of the sinfulness of others. Nor were they committed to class warfare, or indeed to any sort of warfare. But their stoicism under dreadful persecution cannot but arouse admiration, and the astonishing fact is that, despite the determination of established Churches and states to root them out, they survived.

Calvin and Geneva

John Calvin was born at Noyon, north-east of Paris, in 1509. His father was a lawyer who looked after the affairs of the local bishop; his mother a very devout woman who took her son to pray before the statues of the saints. Calvin's parents had already decided that he should enter the priesthood, since, with their connection with the bishop, they could hope to provide more than adequately for him; the boy in fact received his first benefice at the age of twelve. In 1523 he was sent to school in Paris, where he attended the College of Montaigu. This had been founded by John Standonck, one of the Brethren of the Common Life, at the turn of the century, and although it was now perhaps better known for its rigid discipline than its devotion to classical studies it gave Calvin a good grounding in Latin literature. His humanist leanings were also encouraged by frequent visits to the house of Guillaume Budé, who was renowned for his knowledge and love of Greek literature. From Paris Calvin went to Orleans and thence to Bourges, in order to fulfil his father's wishes by studying law. By 1532 he was a qualified lawyer, but in that year he underwent a profound spiritual experience which left him irrevocably committed to the religious life. Two years later he returned to Noyon, where he formally renounced his benefices. France was at this time, however, a dangerous place for critics of the established Church, and Calvin decided to go on his travels. He went first to Strasburg and finally to Basle, where he found a form of worship and a religious and moral atmosphere that suited him.

While at Basle Calvin set to work on the writing of a catechism which should help French reformers in their task of propagating their beliefs and also serve to rebut the charge of Anabaptism which had been levelled against them by Francis I. This catechism, which was published at Basle, in Latin, in 1536, was the first draft of Calvin's great work, *The Institutes of the Christian Religion*. Later editions of the *Institutes* put much more emphasis on the organisation of the Church, but in this early version Calvin was mainly concerned with defining his theological position. His approach was in many ways similar to that of Luther. He declared that the scriptures were the sole source of guidance on matters of faith, and that errors remained errors no matter how long a tradition they had behind them. Salvation came through faith alone, but since faith was a gift from God it followed that it was not given to all and sundry but only to those whom God had pre-destined for eternal life. 'God hath once for all determined both whom He would admit to salvation and whom He would condemn to destruc-tion. We affirm that this counsel, as far as concerns the elect,[1] is founded on His gratuitous mercy, totally irrespective of human merit, but that to those whom He devotes to condemnation the gate of life is closed by a just and irreprehensible and incomprehensible judgment.'

No Christian, of course, could hope to carry out God's will without constant reassurance of divine guidance, and this came via the sacra-ments. Calvin would admit only two sacraments, baptism and eucharist, since these alone were to be found in the Bible. He rejected the doctrine of transubstantiation, yet believed that just as Christ had once descended to man, so the communicant was lifted up by the Holy Spirit into the presence of the Lord, there to taste, albeit briefly, the delights of eternal salvation that were one day to be his. This accept-ance of some sort of 'real presence' was obviously closer to Luther than to Zwingli, and in this Calvin demonstrated that his lawyer's precision and humanist learning were not incompatible with mystical reverence for the divine. In general, however, Calvin's legal training was clearly apparent in the methodical arrangement of the *Institutes* and the con-cern with God the law-giver, whose commands have been made known and are to be obeyed. Chaos and anarchy were the work of the devil. The task of the Christian, in this world, was to impose the order of God, to create a society as coherent and disciplined as the Republic of Plato, yet based on divine revelation rather than fallible human reason.

There was little apparent prospect of turning the France of Calvin's day into a spiritual community on the lines he advocated—though this, of course, was his great hope and long-term ambition. Calvin found his opportunity in Geneva, a virtually independent city whose in-habitants elected their own officers and màde their own laws. In 1535 the mass had been formally suppressed in Geneva, and in the following year the reformed religion had been adopted. But this was reformation in appearance only. Many citizens, possibly a majority, remained luke-warm about the changes, and the work of spiritual transformation had barely begun when Calvin arrived in July 1536.

Calvin was on his way from Basle to Strasburg when chance—or God—brought him to Geneva. His name was already known in

---

[1] Those whom God has chosen for salvation and thereby 'elected' to eternal life.

reformed circles, and the advocates of religious change appealed to him to stay and complete the process of spiritual regeneration that they had set on foot. Calvin could not resist such a call, especially as he would be able to put into practice at Geneva the theories on church organisation which he had already begun to formulate. He did not believe, like Luther, that the task of maintaining order in the world could be left to the existing secular authorities. Nor did he agree with Zwingli that Church and state were really one. Calvin was convinced that while all government, secular as well as spiritual, should conform to the will of God, the control of the spiritual life of a community should be in the hands of the Church alone. The bourgeoisie of Geneva, however, who were rich and cultured and had come under the influence of Erasmus, were not enthusiastic about the proposed diminution of their power, and would have preferred something closer to the pattern of Zurich. Their suspicion showed itself in the elections of February 1537, when a majority was returned which was unfavourable to Calvin, and in April the magistrates of Geneva ordered him to leave the city.

Calvin went first to Basle and thence to join Bucer at Strasburg. There he spent several years as priest in charge of the French refugee church, and married a widow whom he converted from Anabaptism. Calvin obviously learnt much about ecclesiastical organisation during his 'exile' in Strasburg. He agreed with Bucer on the need to separate Church and state, and he studied at first hand the problems arising from a close relationship between the two. This proved invaluable to him when in 1540 the reform party, which had been restored to power at Geneva, begged him to go back to the city. He agreed to do so only after an assurance that this time there would be no hindrance to the carrying-out of his programme, and in September 1541 he returned in triumph to Geneva, never again to leave it.

Calvin held no official position at Geneva other than that of preacher and professor of theology, but he was without doubt its leading citizen. Not long after his return he drew up, in collaboration with the city magistrates, the *Ecclesiastical Ordinances*, in which he elaborated his ideas on Church government. He divided the officers of the Church into four main groups: ministers (or pastors), teachers, deacons and elders. Ministers were to be responsible for preaching and administering the sacraments; teachers were to carry out the vital task of Christian education; and deacons were to look after the poor and sick. As for elders, 'their office is to keep watch over the lives of everyone—to admonish in love those whom they see in error and leading disorderly lives. Whenever necessary they shall make a report concerning these to the pastors, who will be designated to make brotherly corrections.' This was to be the Genevan version of the Zurich court of morals, with the important difference that control over it was to be vested in the Church and not the magistrates.

Candidates for the ministry were to be screened by a committee of existing ministers before being presented first to the town council and then to the people. The congregation retained the right of veto, but could not put forward its own nominee: if this was 'democracy' it was carefully limited and guided. Ministers were to hold weekly meetings to expound points of scripture, and every month a synod was to be convened at which the weaknesses of all the members of the Church were to be publicly denounced. The last word in matters of discipline was to rest with the consistory, an elected body of ministers and elders, which was given authority to impose penalties ranging from admonition to exclusion from the sacraments. Calvin also wanted the consistory to have the sole right to pronounce sentence of excommunication, but in Geneva, as at Strasburg, the magistrates struggled hard to prevent this. Calvin, however, was relentless in the pursuit of what he conceived to be the only true solution, and in 1555 the council conceded that the right to excommunicate should be vested in the consistory. Now at last the Church was master in its own house.

Although Calvin, like Luther, claimed freedom from the Church of Rome, he was in no sense an advocate of toleration in religion. His attitude towards what he regarded as heresy was demonstrated in 1553, when Servetus arrived in Geneva. Servetus denied the divinity of Jesus, much to the horror of Calvin, who believed that Christ's dual nature provided the connection between the world of man and the infinite universe of God. He therefore refused Servetus admission to the sacraments, and denounced him before the council. Calvin's enemies rallied to the defence of Servetus, and to some extent the conflict over the fate of this unfortunate man became a struggle for power between Calvin and those who believed that his reformation had gone too far. In the event, Calvin's mastery of the city was asserted in a most striking manner. The council, with Calvin's full approval, sentenced Servetus to be burnt at the stake. Calvin had not only demonstrated his authority: he had also given warning that the Calvinist church would be ruthless in the defence of its own orthodoxy.

By 1555 Calvin had established his supremacy over Geneva. The influx of religious refugees and the expulsion of opponents meant that it became a 'holy city' in which the 'elect' formed virtually the whole community. John Knox, who was himself an exile in Geneva in 1556, expressed a view of Calvin's achievement that was widely shared among reformers, when he wrote that Geneva 'is the most perfect school of Christ that ever was in the earth since the days of the Apostles'. The influence of Geneva increased even more after Calvin founded the Academy in 1559. The main purpose of this institution was to prepare men for the Calvinist ministry, and the curriculum was based on Latin, Greek and Hebrew as essential tools for the study and interpretation of the scriptures. At the time of Calvin's death there were some 1,200 pupils in the lower, or 'school', section of the Academy, and about 300 'undergraduates', among them many foreigners. Beza, who succeeded Calvin as spiritual leader of Geneva, was the first rector, and the Academy became famous throughout Europe for the quality of its scholarship. It showed how the revival of learning which was one aspect of the Renaissance could be harnessed to the cause of the reformed faith, and it became one of the channels through which the inheritance of Erasmus was transmitted to the protestant world.

In 1559 Calvin published the final Latin version of his *Institutes*, and a year later he produced the definitive French text. When Calvin's disciples carried copies of the *Institutes* into France, the Netherlands, Scotland, England and elsewhere, they took the seeds of revolution with them. For Calvin was a revolutionary. He contrasted the world as it ought to be with the world as it was, and he convinced the 'elect' that their mission was to impose the ideal upon the imperfect. The ecclesiastical organisation which he had minutely described and which could be seen in operation at Geneva, could be applied to any country. Since the Calvinist church was autonomous it was not necessarily dependent upon the co-operation of the lay prince or magistrates. It could function effectively underground; and its missionaries, most of whom had been trained in the Genevan Academy, were prepared to face persecution and death. By the time Calvin died in 1564 the revolutionary impact of his doctrines was making itself felt throughout large parts of Europe.

NINE

The Reformation outside Germany and Switzerland

Denmark

Scandinavia was out of the main stream of European culture in the late Middle Ages, largely for geographical reasons. It was too far removed from the major centres of activity in Italy, France and elsewhere, and its climate was not such as to tempt artists and men of letters away from more temperate zones. The New Learning of the Renaissance made little impression on these remote northern parts, and Copenhagen, for instance, did not even have a university until 1478. But the influence of Christian Humanism had been felt, and a Carmelite friar, Paulus Helie, had led an Erasmian-style reform movement in the Danish church. He took his stand on the Bible as interpreted by the early fathers, and at first he welcomed Luther's protest as another step towards the regeneration of catholicism. Only after he realised that Luther was prepared to split the Church rather than compromise did Helie come out against him, but by that time, in Denmark as elsewhere, the opportunity for self-regeneration had gone. The future of the Danish church was now to depend on the lay prince.

Since 1513 the ruler of Denmark and Sweden had been Christian II, an advocate of catholic reform and an admirer of Erasmus, whom he met at Bruges in 1521. But Christian recognised the advantages—particularly the financial advantages—which accrued to any ruler who embraced Lutheranism, and he was therefore tolerant of Lutheran ideas and of those who advocated them. He might indeed have openly committed himself to Lutheranism but for the fact that a nationalist revolt broke out in Sweden, and in order to suppress it he needed the help of his brother-in-law, the catholic Emperor Charles V. As it happened, Christian was not able to put down the Swedish revolt because of a challenge to his rule at home. He had tried to build up an alliance between the crown, the townsmen and the peasants, whom he released from serfdom, but the absolutist implications of this policy were all too obvious to the Danish clergy and nobility, who joined forces and rebelled against him. Christian was forced to flee, and in March 1523 the Danish magnates offered the throne to the Duke of Schleswig-Holstein, who took the title of Frederick I. Frederick could hardly afford to alienate the higher clergy who had helped him win the crown, and he therefore publicly committed himself to uphold the rights of the established Church. Yet at the same time he chose Hans Tausen, the 'Danish Luther', as his chaplain, and declared his willingness to tolerate any doctrine based on the Bible until such time as a general council of the Church should decide on disputed issues. Denmark had trading links with north Germany, where the Reformation was rapidly establishing itself, and also with the Netherlands, a major centre for the printing and distribution of heretical books. Lutheranism came into Denmark along these international trade routes and spread rapidly throughout the country.

The fate of the Reformation depended to a great extent on the nobles. If they opposed it and clung to their alliance with the clergy there would be little hope of the formal adoption of Lutheranism. Such an alliance, however, was no longer so obviously necessary, since Frederick had abandoned his predecessor's attempt to build a power base on the peasants and townspeople. The nobles were also aware that the creation of a state church might give them the opportunity to acquire ecclesiastical lands. They were not motivated solely by self-interest, of course. Lutheran ideas had spread among them as among the rest of the population, but the fact that there was no obvious clash between their economic interests and the adoption of the reformed religion made it easier for them to support proposals for a state church.

Frederick had to tread carefully. The course of events in Germany was obviously of direct relevance to Denmark, and he had the additional problem of being a usurper who needed the maximum possible support. In 1526 a Diet at Odense decided that bishops should in future be consecrated by the archbishop instead of the Pope and that fees previously paid to Rome should go instead to the king. In the following year another Diet decided that Lutheranism should be tolerated, pending a final decision by a general Church council. Meanwhile the insistence on clerical celibacy was relaxed and monks were allowed to leave the cloister. When the Diet again met, at Copenhagen, in 1530, it was widely assumed that some sort of religious settlement would be made, and the protestant representatives came prepared with a Confession of Faith. Frederick, however, had to deal with a revolt led by the exiled Christian, and needed money from the Church. He would therefore not agree to any fundamental changes, and the Diet broke up with nothing settled.

In the three years that remained of Frederick's reign the Reformation gathered great strength, though its formal triumph was not assured until Frederick's son, Duke Christian, firmly planted himself on the Danish throne. This was no easy task. The prelates were opposed to him, since he was known to be a reformer, and the nobles, who had profited from generous grants of land which Frederick had made them in return for their support, were struggling to retain their power. The towns rose against the nobles, and in many places the peasants rose as well. The various rebellions were aided and abetted by Lubeck, leader of the Hanseatic League, which hoped to regain its dominant place in the economy of the Baltic states, and for some years there was anarchy in Denmark.

By 1536, however, Christian III was master of his kingdom. He defeated Lubeck and forced her to accept terms which signalled the eclipse of the Hanseatic League; he solved the problem of Sweden by renouncing any claim to that kingdom; he put down a revolt in Norway, which he declared to be a Danish dependency; and in order to recover the vast sums he had spent on securing the Danish throne he confiscated all the property of the Danish church. Bishops were henceforth to be salaried servants of a state church, under the supreme headship of the king. The triumph of the Lutherans was assured by the appointment of Peter Palladius as Bishop of Zeeland. He had studied at Wittenberg and was strongly recommended by Luther and Melanchthon, who approved not only of his doctrines but also of his administrative ability. Through constant preaching and frequent visitations Palladius thoroughly reformed the Danish church, and he raised the standard of the episcopate by the appointment of men such as Tausen, who was made a bishop in 1541. In Denmark, as in Saxony and elsewhere, protestant opinion surging up from below had been moulded by the ruler into a state church that apparently satisfied the spiritual aspirations of the majority of his people at the same time as it substantially reinforced his own authority.

Christian III's victory over Norway, which had been left 'unattached' after the break-up of the Scandinavian union, meant the adoption of the Reformation in that country as well. In Norway,

however, there was very little popular support for Lutheranism, and
the state church was imposed by the will of the ruler. The ordinances
already drawn up for the Danish church were applied to Norway by
the Diets of Oslo and Bergen in 1539, and the crown took over all
ecclesiastical property.

Sweden

In Sweden the fate of the Church was bound up with the movement
for national independence. The Swedish bishops were enormously
rich, and saw no reason to break with the Danish king who upheld
their privileged position. The 'patriots', therefore, under the leadership
of Gustavus Vasa, looked for support to the advocates of religious
reform. In 1523 Gustavus Vasa was proclaimed King of Sweden, after
a war of independence that lasted several years and cost a great deal of
money. He proposed to recoup his losses at the expense of the Church,
but could not count on popular enthusiasm for this, since Lutheranism
had made little headway in Sweden and the people in general remained
loyal to the traditional forms of worship. At the Diet of Vasteras, in
1527, the bishops rejected a suggestion that they should engage in a
public disputation with the advocates of reform, and their action
rallied the conservative elements. Gustavus only won the day by
threatening to abdicate. The appalling prospect of renewed civil war,
anarchy and the possible reimposition of Danish rule persuaded the
Diet to accept the king's proposals. It therefore agreed that the 'surplus
wealth' of the Church should be handed over to the crown, and that no
restriction should be placed on the preaching of 'the word of God'.

It was now up to the reformers to implant the Reformation in the
hearts and minds of the Swedish people. The two key figures in this
movement were Olaf Petri and his brother Laurentius. They had both
studied at Wittenberg, where they had come strongly under the
influence of Luther and Melanchthon, and in 1526 Olaf had produced a
translation of the New Testament into Swedish, with which to begin
the process of Christian education on the reformed model. In 1531
Laurentius was appointed archbishop, and five years later, in a synod
held at Uppsala, it was decided that the Latin mass should be replaced
with a vernacular communion service drawn up by Olaf; that clerical
celibacy should be abolished; and that all ministers should preach 'the
word of God'.

By 1539 a Lutheran state church was firmly established in Sweden and was beginning to take root among the people as a whole. But the Petri brothers had not fought for freedom from Rome only to accept enslavement to the crown, and the struggle to preserve a degree of independence for the church brought them into open conflict with Gustavus Vasa. In this struggle they were defeated, for Gustavus was a national hero, the living embodiment of Swedish independence. In 1539 he had Olaf Petri arrested on a charge of treason and sentenced to death. Though Petri was not executed, the trial achieved its intended purpose of stamping out opposition to the king's will. Gustavus now appointed a German Lutheran, George Norman, as 'superintendent', with authority to bring the Swedish church under state control, as had been done in Saxony. This 'German period' lasted until 1544, when the Diet, again meeting at Vasteras, formally adopted the Reformation on behalf of the Swedish nation. At the same time it replaced the elective monarchy by a hereditary one, vested in the House of Vasa.

Although Gustavus was now unchallenged ruler of Sweden he continued to keep a close watch over the Church in his dominions. But by the time he died, in 1560, the Reformation had become a popular movement, stimulated by the Swedish Bible which the Petri brothers had produced in 1541. Olaf Petri died in 1552, but his brother lived on for another twenty years and after Gustavus's death became the acknowledged leader of the protestant church in Sweden. He was largely responsible for the Church Ordinance of 1571, by which many traditional ceremonies were retained. The Church remained largely self-governing, and although the king was responsible for appointing bishops his choice was limited to those who had been pre-selected by representatives of the clergy and laity. As for doctrine, no formal confession of faith was adopted and the only explicit commitment was to 'the pure word of God' as revealed in the scriptures. The Reformation in Scandinavia clearly owed much to the example and writings of Luther and Melanchthon, but it was less concerned with theological definitions and disputes, and in Sweden at any rate the protestant church was not so dependent on the lay ruler as was its German counterpart.

The Netherlands

Although the cities of the Netherlands were formally part of the Duchy of Burgundy they preserved a considerable degree of independence, and the Renaissance and Christian Humanism had both found a warm welcome from the educated bourgeoisie whose intellectual range, like that of their trade, extended over the whole of Europe. Erasmus himself was resident at Louvain for a time, and his criticism of the wealth, the corruption and the lack of true spirituality of the Roman Catholic Church found ready hearers. Luther's writings also circulated widely, since Antwerp had very close trading links with Germany, but Charles V was determined that heresy should not be allowed to take hold of his native land. In January 1521, following the excommunication of Luther, an edict was issued ordering the confiscation of all Lutheran books in the Netherlands, and later on the Edict of Worms, with its restrictions on freedom of publication, was enforced. The tolerant climate in which Erasmus had flourished was rapidly changing to one of repression, and in September 1521 the great Christian Humanist left for Basle.

Charles would have liked to introduce the Spanish Inquisition into the Netherlands, but there was considerable opposition to this proposal from representatives of the educated and ruling groups. He therefore abandoned the idea, but there was nothing to prevent him from reviving the local inquisition, and this he did in 1522. His first appointment as Inquisitor-General for the Netherlands was a layman, and Charles did not bother to consult the Pope—a sure sign that he intended to keep religious policy under his personal control. In the following year, however, Pope Adrian, who was himself a Burgundian, appointed the same man as papal Inquisitor, thereby asserting that ultimate responsibility for the spiritual welfare of the Netherlands rested in Rome. In fact the Inquisition in the Netherlands was never as independent as that in Spain, nor could it be used in the same way as an instrument of royal policy, though Charles insisted that the approval of his council should be sought before any sentences were passed.

In July 1523 the first protestant martyrs—two former Augustinians —were burned at Brussels, and in 1529 and 1531 edicts were issued proclaiming death for Lutherans, for those who sheltered them or failed to report them, for those who spread their writings, and even for those who publicly discussed matters of faith. This repressive legislation did not, of course, eradicate protestantism from the Netherlands. City magistrates were often sympathetic to the critics of the Church, and it was not until after 1550 that Charles transferred jurisdiction in heresy cases from city councils to provincial tribunals which were more susceptible to his pressure. By 1530 it was estimated that about a quarter of the population of Antwerp was Lutheran, and the influx of foreign merchants into that town made it extremely difficult for the government to prevent the dissemination of protestant opinions and literature.

The policy of repression was successful in that it checked the spread of protestantism and drove it underground. But while the faint-hearted could be coerced into conformity, those who were really committed looked for something even more radical. They found it in Anabaptism, and in the 1540s and 1550s the Mennonites spread rapidly, not only in Holland but in the southern Netherlands as well. Most of the 'protestant' martyrs of this period were in fact Anabaptists, and there were Mennonite communities in Amsterdam, Leyden, Haarlem and elsewhere. Yet although the Anabaptists were regarded as a threat to society and were therefore mercilessly persecuted, they were actually preoccupied with spiritual regeneration, which implied withdrawal from the world around them. As for the Lutherans they had no pattern of church government other than that which involved the state, and since the secular ruler in the Netherlands was hostile, Lutheranism, like Anabaptism, tended to be a matter of individual protest rather than an organised challenge. In the 1550s, however, Calvinism began penetrating into the Netherlands from Geneva, and in the next decade from France as well. The Calvinists had the fanaticism of the other heretics, but in addition they had a pattern of organisation which could be applied regardless of the lay ruler. Fortunately for Charles V he abdicated before Calvinism had really gained a hold in his Netherlands territories. It was left to his son to confront and try to overcome a major challenge to princely authority.

France

In France, as in a number of other western European countries, Christian Humanism was working towards a purification of the catholic church from within when it was swamped by the onrush of Lutheranism. The forces of conservative orthodoxy were particularly strong in Paris. In 1521 the Sorbonne formally condemned the works of Luther, and in the same year the *Parlement* put the Edict of Worms into effect by forbidding the publication of any religious work without the prior approval of a faculty of theology. Two years later the first Lutheran martyr, a former monk, was burnt at the stake.

It was not possible, however, to prevent the infiltration of Lutheran ideas into France. For one thing there were very close trading and intellectual links between France and Germany, and Lutheran writings, smuggled in by merchants coming to the great fairs at Lyons, could be distributed from there all over the kingdom. Lyons was a long way from Paris, it had no powerful faculty of theology such as the Sorbonne to contend with, and its population included an industrial proletariat ready to welcome any radical ideas. But Lutheranism did not simply follow the trade routes. It sprang up of its own accord in many different places, and it appealed not only to the socially deprived but also, for example, to many humanists who saw in Luther an ardent spokesman of the reform policies they themselves had been advocating.

In a strong monarchy like France the fate of the Church depended to a large extent on the king. Francis I seems to have been conventionally devout, and did not forget that he had sworn at his coronation to protect the catholic faith. But it was not at all easy in the early 1520s to draw a dividing line between catholicism and heresy. Was Lefèvre, for instance, a heretic? And what about the humanist scholar Louis de Berquin, who in 1521 translated Luther's pamphlet against the bull of Leo X and proclaimed his acceptance of the principle of redemption through faith alone? The Sorbonne had no doubts, nor did the majority of the judges of the *Parlement* of Paris. In 1522 the king had to intervene to prevent the Sorbonne from condemning Lefèvre, and in 1523 he saved Berquin from almost certain condemnation by the *Parlement* by ordering his case to be transferred to the *Grand Conseil*, which acquitted him. The fact that the most ardent champions of orthodox catholicism were not only opponents of the New Learning but also defenders of local and individual liberties against the encroachments of royal power encouraged Francis I to be discriminating in his attitude towards religious unorthodoxy and not to indulge in blanket condemnation.

In Germany, Scandinavia, and later in England, one of the attractions of protestantism to secular rulers was that it brought the Church under their control. In France the crown was already exercising a *de facto* right of appointment to abbacies and bishoprics even before this was formally conceded by Pope Leo X in the Concordat signed at Bologna in 1516. In future the king was to nominate and the Pope would issue the necessary bulls. Certain minimum conditions of age and learning were laid down for candidates for high ecclesiastical office, but no provision was made for enforcing these against the will of the king, and they remained virtually a dead letter. The Concordat was, in fact, a political bargain made at the expense of the French church, and although it did not give Francis the supreme authority in ecclesiastical matters that, for instance, Henry VIII was later to assume in England, it put the crown in a commanding position without incurring the risk of civil war or other disturbances.

The *Parlement* deeply resented the way in which Francis had bartered away the liberties of the Church in France without so much as a pretence at consultation, and therefore refused to register the Concordat. It was encouraged in its resistance by the Sorbonne, which had hitherto supplied many of the candidates for ecclesiastical benefices and believed that the French church should in practice rule itself. Not until 1518 did the *Parlement* reluctantly give way. The Sorbonne held out for some time longer, and was only cowed by the arrest of some of its leading members and threats of sterner measures.

In February 1525, however, Francis was defeated at Pavia and taken prisoner by the Emperor (see p. 224). For more than a year the king was away from his kingdom, and the forces of reaction, led by the *Parlement* and the Sorbonne, took advantage of this heaven-sent opportunity to undertake the extirpation of heresy. In March 1525 special commissions were appointed, consisting of two judges of the *Parlement* and two doctors of theology, to deal with heresy cases, and the regent was persuaded to accept the principle that the *Parlement* should be the final court of appeal in such matters. In May 1525 the Sorbonne formally condemned a number of Erasmus's works, Briçonnet was summoned to appear before the *Parlement*, and the Meaux group was broken up. The fate in store for reformers was indicated when Berquin, arrested for the second time, was found guilty of heresy and handed over to the *Parlement* to be sentenced. Early in 1526 the *Parlement* issued a decree forbidding all discussion of religious questions unless these were authorised by the Church and in conformity with its teachings, and it also prohibited the use of French translations of the Bible.

This period of conservative reaction was brought to an end by the return of Francis I. He ordered the *Parlement* to drop the case against Berquin, who was thereby saved once again from the flames, and he took the members of the Meaux group under his protection. But there was no general toleration. Francis needed the money which the Church in France could provide, and he was also allied with the Pope in the League of Cognac. He recognised that much of the support for heterodox attitudes within France would be removed if only the Church would reform itself, and he therefore encouraged his chancellor, Antoine Duprat, to take the lead in this. In 1528 provincial church councils were held at Sens and Bourges, and the more obvious abuses were denounced. But nothing positive was accomplished. Duprat, although he was an archbishop and an abbot, owed his promotion to service to the crown rather than any spiritual qualities, and the Church showed itself more concerned with the defence of its own privileges than with fundamental reform.

Sporadic arrests and occasional executions of heretics continued, and in 1529 the *Parlement* took advantage of the absence of Francis from Paris to arrest Berquin for the third time and have him burnt at the stake. Francis realised that his negotiations with the German protestants would be endangered if he allowed the persecution of Lutherans to continue within France itself. But it was by no means clear that heresy in France was predominantly Lutheran. The influence of Zwingli was already beginning to make itself felt, and an outburst of image-breaking at Lyons in 1529 suggested a puritan attitude far more in tune with Zurich than with Wittenberg. Another sign of Zwinglian influence came in the 'Affair of the Placards' in October 1534. Placards, or posters, violently attacking the mass, were stuck up in Paris and a number of Loire towns, and one was even pinned to the door of the king's bedchamber in the château of Amboise. These posters were as offensive to Lutherans as to catholics, and the king's fury is to be explained not only by his sense of shock and personal affront but by his realisation that protestantism in France had entered a more violent and uncompromising stage. It was hardly surprising that Francis moved much closer to the conservatives, and in early 1535 he banned the publication of any new books until further notice.

From 1535 onwards the French government was committed to the destruction of heresy within the kingdom, even though the intensity of persecution varied with the fluctuations in French foreign policy. The advocates of orthodox catholicism were in favour of peace with Charles V, since this would put an end to negotiations with the German protestants, and they were delighted when, in 1538, Francis I met the Emperor at Aigues-Mortes and agreed to unite with him in suppressing heresy. An edict was issued ordering the French courts to take action against suspected heretics, and two years later the responsibility for carrying out this policy was formally vested in the *Parlement*. In 1542 the Sorbonne established its own Index of prohibited literature, and in the following year it drew up twenty-four articles of the catholic faith to which suspected persons could be required to give their assent. Whatever hopes the protestants might have had of a more tolerant attitude diminished with the failure of Francis I's foreign policy; and at the Peace of Crépy, in 1544, the king renewed his commitment to the extirpation of heresy.

While Francis I had been an unenthusiastic persecutor, his son, Henry II, who succeeded him in 1547, was a determined champion of the orthodox faith, resolved to rid his kingdom of heretical infection. Persecution of protestants was stepped up, and in 1548 a special court, the *Chambre Ardente*, was created within the *Parlement* of Paris, to specialise in religious cases. Henry also issued letters patent to the Jesuits in 1551, authorising them to establish a college in Paris, though in this he offended the *Parlement* and the Sorbonne, which, as champions of a national 'Gallican' church, resented the 'invasion' of an order which was identified with supranationalist attitudes.

A new situation was created by the arrival of Calvinist missionaries from Geneva. The first of these reached France in 1553, and over the next ten years Geneva supplied nearly ninety pastors for the Huguenots (as the French Calvinists were known). Huguenot services were at first held in secret, but in May 1558 several thousand protestants publicly worshipped in Paris, under the protection of armed sympathisers. Calvinism spread with a speed that amazed even Calvin himself, but its centre of gravity shifted away from the north and east of France— which came increasingly under the control of catholic families, particularly the Guises—towards the maritime areas of the west and southeast. Lutheranism had found the bulk of its adherents among the artisans and bourgeoisie of the towns, but Calvinism spread rapidly upwards into the highest social groups. In 1555, for instance, Anthony of Bourbon, head of the house of Vendôme and king-consort of Navarre, was converted, and among many other Huguenots of high birth was Gaspard de Coligny, Admiral of France.

The king had to tread carefully when he was dealing with nobles such as these. Henry was also restrained by the fact that his energies and resources were concentrated on the continuing war with Charles V. The Guises, who were by now the leaders of the catholic aristocracy in France, were particularly anxious for a peaceful conclusion to the Habsburg–Valois struggle, so that the whole weight of the crown's authority and resources could be turned against the Huguenots. Their wish was fulfilled when, in April 1559, Henry made peace at Cateau-Cambrésis and immediately ordered the rigid enforcement of the laws against heresy. When some of the more liberal lawyers of the *Parlement* of Paris protested against this and asked for the abolition of the death penalty in religious matters, Henry promptly ordered their arrest. It seemed as though French protestantism was about to face a life-and-death struggle, but in July 1559 Henry was killed in a tournament and the day of reckoning was postponed.

Spain

The close links between Spain and the Netherlands after the accession of Charles to the Spanish throne facilitated the inflow of heretical books from Antwerp, and some of Luther's writings, translated into Castilian, appeared in Spain as early as 1521. Their impact, however, was very muted, particularly when compared with the rest of Europe. The 'holy war' against the Moors had given the Spaniards a crusading zest for the catholic faith; the reforms of Cardinal Ximenes had removed many of the most obvious abuses; and the widespread acceptance of Erasmian ideals encouraged the assumption that the Church would purify itself. In fact in the early sixteenth century 'Illuminism' seemed to be a greater danger to orthodoxy than any more obviously heretical movement. Illuminists believed that through the cultivation of mystical ecstasy they could attain direct communion with God, and that they were thereafter free from sin. 'Good works' were obviously of no relevance in an Illuminist context, and to this extent its practitioners prepared the way for Luther. It was for this reason that Illuminism was formally condemned by the Inquisition in 1525.

The Inquisition continued to ferret out 'Lutheran' groups, but in the period up to 1558 it dealt with little more than a hundred cases, half of which concerned foreigners. Lutheranism was clearly not a major challenge to the catholic faith in Spain, but by the time Philip II succeeded his father the lines of religious division in Europe had hardened and Spain had appointed herself the guardian of orthodoxy. In 1558 the Inquisition uncovered protestant cells in Seville, and in the following year an *Auto de Fé*, of which the climax was the burning of heretics, took place at Valladolid in the presence of Philip II. Others followed, and the Inquisition, in its determination to preserve the purity of the catholic faith, cut off Spain from the intellectual life of the rest of Europe. In 1558 it banned the import of books and ordered that all those which were printed in Spain should receive the prior approval of the Council of Castile. In 1559 Spanish students were forbidden to study outside the kingdom, and in the same year a new version of the Spanish Index of forbidden works, first issued in 1545, was published and strictly enforced. Some cultural links with the Netherlands and Italy survived, but Spain, which in the early sixteenth century had been among the leaders of the intellectual life of Christendom, turned in on itself. The price of maintaining orthodoxy was sterility.

Italy

In Italy one of the centres of the reform movement, at Naples, was the creation of Juan de Valdes, brother of Charles V's secretary. He was an Erasmian humanist, but also a mystic in the Illuminist tradition, who fled to Italy in 1529 after the Spanish Inquisition had begun investigating his activities. He saw in Luther's doctrine of salvation through faith alone a recognition of the possibility of direct communication between the individual and God, but although this brought him near to Luther's position he did not approve of the German reformer and never broke with the catholic Church. After his death his followers moved much closer towards Lutheranism, partly because the pressure of events was making it increasingly impossible to maintain a midway position.

The influence of Valdes was not confined to Naples. Among those who were affected by his teaching was Bernard Ochino of Siena, the head of the Capuchin order, who fled from Italy in 1542 rather than face the Inquisition and died in exile among the Anabaptists in Moravia. Peter Martyr, a friend of Ochino, was also influenced by Valdes, and openly committed himself to the protestant faith. Among those on whom the impact of Lutheranism was more direct was Peter Paul Vergerio, who had been sent as papal nuncio to the Diet of Augsburg in 1530, and took part in the negotiations between German protestant leaders and catholic representatives in 1541. During the course of preparing a major work designed to show up the errors of the reformers, Vergerio became convinced that truth in fact was on their side. In 1549, therefore, he fled from Italy and assumed the leadership of the small band of Italian Lutherans who settled in Germany.

Another centre of the reform movement in Italy was Ferrara. Hercule d'Este ruled this small state with its brilliant court, and his wife was a French princess, Renée, daughter of Louis XII. Renée had come under the influence of Margaret of Navarre, and she made Ferrara a haven for French protestant refugees. Calvin visited her there in 1536 and remained her spiritual adviser for the rest of his life. Smaller protestant communities were to be found in Lucca, Siena and a number of other northern cities, where the papacy was very unpopular. The turning-point came with the establishment of the papal Inquisition in 1542. From then onwards pressure mounted against the reformers, and rulers who refused to conform found themselves threatened by hostile combinations. Hercule d'Este, for instance, fearing the loss of his duchy, expelled protestant refugees from his dominions and sent his wife back to France. The last survivors of the Valdes congregation were pushed out of Naples, and all over the peninsula the advocates of reform found themselves faced with the choice of returning to orthodoxy or going into exile. By 1560 at the latest all Italy except Venice (where religious liberty survived) had been won back to the Roman Catholic Church.

TEN

The Reformation of the Roman Catholic Church

Sources of Inspiration

The widespread desire for spiritual regeneration that was one of the characteristics of late fifteenth and early sixteenth century Europe led eventually to the reform of the catholic Church. This process is often called the Counter-Reformation, because it acquired definition in the 1540s and 1550s by consciously setting itself against protestant doctrines and practices. But there was far more to the catholic reformation than mere reaction against protestantism, and the impulse towards purification and renovation had been evident for at least half a century before it transformed the papacy and thereby made possible the codification of doctrine and discipline by the Council of Trent.

Erasmus and his fellow Christian Humanists were catholic reformers, who hoped to harness the New Learning of the Renaissance in such a way that it would enable the Church to meet the demands made on it by a rapidly changing society. There were also adherents of older traditions working creatively within more conventional frameworks to ensure that the inheritance of many centuries of catholic faith and practice should make a living contribution to the contemporary world. It has already been pointed out that classical studies did not suddenly *begin* with the Renaissance. The works of Aristotle had become available, through Latin translations, in the early thirteenth century, and one of the greatest achievements of the Middle Ages in the realm of thought had been the fusion of Christian beliefs with Aristotelian philosophy accomplished by St Thomas Aquinas (1225-74) in his *Summa Theologica*. St Thomas saw man as essentially a rational being, able to distinguish right from wrong and thereby steer his own course towards salvation. He needed guidance, of course, but this was available not merely from the Church but also from the state: 'For men associate for this purpose, that together they may live well, which each living singly could not do. But to live well is to live according to virtue. Hence a life according to virtue is the end of human association. ... But since man is, by a life according to virtue, destined for the attainment of a further end, which consists ... in the enjoyment of God, human society also must have the same end as the individual man. It is not, therefore, the final end of a society to live according to virtue, but by means of a virtuous life to attain to the enjoyment of God.'

St Thomas's view of human nature was basically optimistic. In this he stood at the opposite pole from his great predecessor, St Augustine (354–430), who in his *City of God* made clear his belief that man, since his eating of the fruit of the tree of knowledge and his consequent expulsion from the garden of Eden, was a fallen creature, unable to lift a finger to help himself. While St Thomas regarded Church and state as integral parts of a system designed to lead all Christians towards salvation, Augustine declared that the state, being the work of un-regenerate man, was fallible and corrupt, and that there could be no gradual and general progress towards salvation since eternal blessedness was reserved only for those on whom God had chosen to cast his grace. 'Many reprobate live among the elect: both come into the gospel's net, and both swim at random in the sea of mortality, until the fishers draw them to the shore. And then the bad are thrown from the good.'

Thomism—that is, the philosophy of St Thomas Aquinas—had remained a powerful influence throughout the Middle Ages, and was by no means moribund in the sixteenth century. For example, Luther's opponent, the Dominican Cardinal Cajetan, produced a commentary on the *Summa* which showed that the relevance of Aquinas's teachings had not been diminished by the passage of time, and this revived Thomism made a powerful contribution to the catholic reformation. Yet Augustinianism also was a living force (as was demonstrated most dramatically by Luther), and the pure and austere Augustinian tradition was kept alive in catholic centres such as the University of Louvain, from where it was eventually transmitted to the Jansenists.

As well as Thomists and Augustinians there were also a number of catholic theologians attempting to bridge the gap between the two Christian traditions by reconciling the omnipotence of an almighty God with man's freedom of choice. Among the most distinguished of such scholars were two Jesuits, Francisco de Suarez (1548–1617) and

Luis de Molina (1535–1600), and although their work aroused intense passions and often hostility, this in itself was proof that the medieval inheritance was still relevant.

The catholic reformation also drew inspiration from late medieval mysticism. The writings of the German mystics (see p. 96) had an influence that extended far beyond their own country. They were widely read in the Netherlands; they were well known in France, where Lefèvre d'Etaples published translations of a number of them; they were also one of the sources of the Spanish mystical movement of the early sixteenth century. If Luther obviously owed a great deal to the German mystics, so also did the Jesuit Peter Canisius, who recaptured much of Germany for the catholic faith.

The spirit of renewal was to be seen at work not only in new communities, such as the Brethren of the Common Life, but in some of the older ones as well. While the religious orders had lost much of their original quality, the picture was not entirely black. The Carthusians, for instance, maintained high standards of discipline and learning, and the Charterhouse at Cologne was one of the major centres of the spiritual revival in northern Europe. As for the friars, whose role was crucial since they brought the Christian message into the fields and market-places of the workaday world, they were coming strongly under the influence of the Observants, so called because they insisted on observing the original strictness and poverty of the Franciscan and Dominican rules. The Observants had to struggle against the Conventuals, who preferred to leave things much as they were, but they showed that the old orders were not so sunk in worldliness as to be beyond hope of recovery.

The reformation of the catholic Church would have been an even slower and more hesitant process than was in fact the case had it not been for the influence and example of certain individuals. Ximenes was one, though he thought and acted within a narrowly Spanish context; John Eck, the opponent of Luther and a formidable controversialist, was another, since he showed that scholarship and orthodoxy were not incompatible and that the reception of the New Learning did not necessitate the abandonment of the old. Even the papal court had its reformers. Matteo Giberti (1495–1543), for instance, was secretary to Clement VII and encouraged him to pursue an anti-imperial policy that might leave the papacy both politically and spiritually free: he was also an early member of the Oratory of Divine Love—a group of clerics and laymen who united in the search for a deeper spirituality, and put their Christian faith into practice through works of charity—and when in 1528, after the traumatic experience of the sack of Rome, he retired to his diocese of Verona, he became a model bishop and a great source of inspiration. The Englishman Reginald Pole, the Venetian Gasparo Contarini and the Neapolitan Gian Pietro Caraffa were other examples of men of great learning and ability who never wavered in their adherence to the catholic Church.

Both the catholic and the protestant Reformations derived from the same widespread hunger for a more spiritual, a more relevant and a less worldly religion, and for at least a couple of decades, in the 1520s and 1530s, it was not by any means certain that these two aspects of the same reform movement would necessarily diverge. By the 1550s, however, this was all too clear, and as the gap widened the attitude of each side grew more rigid. With more or less open war between the two Reformations the differences were emphasised while the areas of common ground were ignored. Not only this. When it came to defining doctrine the Council of Trent set out to make the break between catholic and protestant as clear as possible, and in so doing it emphasised certain parts of the catholic inheritance at the expense of others—Augustinianism, for instance, which could claim the support not only of Augustine but of St Paul himself, came under suspicion as a 'protestant' doctrine and was virtually rejected. Many beliefs and attitudes which had been acceptable before the 1550s were not tolerated after that date, and whereas the catholic Reformation had appealed to the Christian community at large, the Counter-Reformation—which covered, roughly speaking, the century from 1550 to 1650—put orthodoxy above universality. It may well be that without paying this high price the catholic Church would not have survived. But the fragmentation of the Christian community at a time when the rate of change in the political, economic, social and intellectual spheres was increasing so violently, was in many respects a tragedy.

New Orders

In Italy, as in Germany and the Netherlands, one way in which individuals could satisfy their spiritual needs was by meeting regularly, praying together, and carrying out works of charity among the poor and sick. These 'Oratories', as they were called, sprang up spontaneously in a number of centres; that at Rome, for instance, made its appearance in 1516 at a time when the hopes of the reformers had been roused by the Lateran Council. The Roman Oratory was broken up when the city was sacked in 1527, but some of its members had already founded a new order, the Theatines. This was a community of priests, living together in poverty, chastity and obedience, and at the same time working in the world around them. Their aim was to show what the priestly life really entailed, and they set an example of good learning combined with pastoral care that was to be characteristic of the catholic Reformation. The Theatines were few in number and drawn largely from the aristocracy, so the extent of their influence was limited; but the fact that a new order had actually been founded and had received papal approval (in 1524) was a sign of vitality in a type of institution that many people regarded as moribund.

Another group which owed its origins to the influence of an oratory, this time one at Brescia, was the Ursulines, an order for women which was founded in 1535. Its members worked at first among the poor and the rejected: only later in the century did they establish a school and thereby begin their transformation into a major teaching order.

Two other new orders were the Somaschi, founded about 1530 by a Venetian nobleman and recognised by the Pope in 1540, and the Barnabites, founded in Milan in the early 1530s and given papal recognition shortly afterwards. The Somaschi were particularly concerned with the poor and destitute, and made the establishment and maintenance of orphanages their principal task. The Barnabites concentrated on pastoral work, and held evangelical meetings in the open air. These two orders were in part a response to the appalling suffering caused by the constant wars that devastated northern Italy, but they were also an attempt to rediscover the original spirit of the friars and the evangelising fervour which had taken them into the sprawling towns of western Europe.

This spirit was by no means dead in the older orders. The Franciscans for instance, were among the earliest missionaries in the New World, and it was from the Observant Franciscans that the order of the Capuchins emerged. The Capuchins, given official recognition in 1528, chose secluded places in which to establish their communities, but they carried out their work in towns and villages, preaching and caring for the sick, particularly the lepers. The Capuchins came dangerously near suppression in 1542, after the head of their order, Bernard Ochino, defected to the protestants, but by the 1570s they had fully recovered and were rapidly expanding.

The new orders of the sixteenth century were closer in spirit to the friars than to the monks. They did not reject the contemplative ideal embodied in the monastic orders; their spirituality took a more active form. This was clearly demonstrated in what was to become the most famous of the new orders, the Society of Jesus, founded by Ignatius Loyola.

Loyola, born in 1491, came from a gentry family which lived in the Basque country of northern Spain. Brought up to the profession of arms, he fought against the French invaders at Pampluna in 1521 and was badly wounded in the leg. For many months he was an invalid, confined to bed, and during this time he reflected on the course of his life and became aware of its purposelessness. He began reading translations of German mystical writings, and in 1522 lived as a hermit in a cave outside Manresa, where he underwent a profound mystical experience. After Manresa he was totally committed to the service of God and in 1523 he set off on a pilgrimage to Jerusalem. He had at this stage no clear purpose, other than to visit the holiest Christian site, but he was conscious of his need to communicate his love and knowledge of God and to give others the chance of sharing his experience.

Before Loyola could teach he had first to educate himself. He therefore became a student at the university which Ximenes had founded at Alcala. There he met a number of fellow students who shared his desire for devotion to God's service, and they formed a community among themselves. It was to aid them in practising the techniques of meditation that Loyola wrote the first draft of his *Spiritual Exercises*, based on his own experience. The Inquisition came to hear of this and feared that the Illuminist heresy might be at work. In 1527, therefore the Holy Office formally ordered Loyola not to undertake any teaching until he had completed four years' study of theology.

Loyola moved to Paris, where he became a student for a time at the College of Montaigu, and once again he attracted to himself a number of individuals who wished, like him, to combine the contemplative ideal with active pastoral work. In 1534 this band of disciples took a vow at Montmartre to live in poverty and chastity in the service of God and to go on pilgrimage to the Holy Land. In fact they got no farther than Venice, because of Turkish military operations in the eastern Mediterranean, and there they stayed for some time, working in hospitals and caring for the sick. During this period of waiting, Loyola made contact with some of the leading figures in the catholic reform movement. By the middle of 1537 it was clear that the idea of a pilgrimage to Jerusalem would have to be abandoned, and the members of the small band now implemented the decision to place their lives at the disposal of the papacy. Loyola, who had been ordained priest in June of that year, therefore led his companions to Rome, where their contacts ensured them a welcome from Pope Paul III. They had first to be cleared of lingering suspicions of heresy, however; yet even after thorough investigation had confirmed their orthodoxy it was not certain that they would be allowed to found a new order. Caraffa urged them to become Theatines, but Loyola was convinced that he and his companions had something to offer which could not be expressed within any of the existing orders. He used all his qualities of persistence, diplomacy and sheer strength of character to persuade other people that the Society of Jesus, which he proposed to form, really was necessary. His success was confirmed in September 1540 when the Society was officially inaugurated by the papal bull *Regimini Militantis Ecclesiae*.

Loyola himself was the first General of the Jesuits, and held this office until his death in 1556. He was a man who impressed all those who came into contact with him. One of his followers reported that 'his soul was invariably of an even temper . . . it made no difference whether he was on his way from mass or had had dinner, or whether he had just got out of bed, or had been at prayer, whether he had received good news or bad, whether things were quiet or the world upside down . . . for he was always in a state of self-mastery'. The quasi-military ordering of the Jesuits obviously owed something to Loyola's early years as a soldier, and there may have been more than a touch of Spanish fanaticism about his total commitment. But Loyola cannot be summed up in simple terms. Although he was born a Spaniard and trained as a soldier, he acquired a mastery of the mystical techniques of the German and Netherlands tradition. Although he put a high value upon contemplation and practised it constantly, he was also an active and extremely able organiser. And although he had received only a sketchy education before his conversion and could never at any time be called an intellectual, he saw the need to attract men of learning into the Society and to give novices a firm grounding in the classics as well as theology.

The Jesuits were far from being just another religious order. Their Church was the whole world, and the evidence of their commitment to God was to be seen not in any formal ceremonies but in their un-remitting pastoral care. To sustain this activity faith alone was not enough. Jesuits were given a long training, designed to fit them for the life they had chosen. They were set to work at first in hospitals, and sent on pilgrimages barefoot with nothing but alms to support them. Then they were educated in the classics, philosophy and theology, and taught to preach. After this they were given instruction in the techniques of meditation, based on Loyola's *Spiritual Exercises*. Only after they had successfully completed all these stages were they allowed to become full members of the Society of Jesus.

Not all aspirants were able to meet the demands made on them by this formidable course of training, but they were not therefore rejected. Membership of the Society was in three grades, and those who could not complete the course remained in the third of these. The second was reserved for those who, having passed through all stages, took the three vows of poverty, chastity and obedience. The first grade was confined to those who took a further oath of direct obedience to the Pope if he sent them on foreign missions. Although the General was in theory responsible to the Society which elected him, he was to all intents and purposes a monarch, acknowledging no earthly superior other than the Pope. It could be said of the Society of Jesus, as of the secular kingdoms of western Europe, that it met the challenge of a changing world by elevating the authority of the ruler and moving in the direction of absolutism.

Loyola had envisaged the Jesuits as missionaries, carrying the Christian faith to the new worlds being opened up across the seas, and by the time he died the Society was at work in India, Japan, Africa and America. He had not thought of Europe as a mission field, but his order appeared at a critical moment, when the catholic Church, having reeled under the shock of the protestant challenge, was at last recovering its strength for a counter-attack. It was Paul III who charged the Jesuits with the task of combating heresy inside Christendom, especially in Germany, where those princes who had remained faithful to Roman Catholicism were in need of preachers and teachers of the highest quality. Members of the Society were accordingly sent to Germany in the 1540s, settling first at Cologne and later at Ingoldstadt. It was at the latter town, in 1549, that the Dutch Jesuit, Peter Canisius, began the work that was to make him famous. He founded colleges and schools in Ingoldstadt, Prague, Cologne, Innsbruck and a number of other important centres, and from his headquarters at Vienna he travelled widely, preaching wherever he went. He did more than any other single person to turn back the tide of protestantism in the area where it had first started flowing, and by the end of the century there were over a thousand Jesuits at work in Germany.

Loyola had not intended the Society of Jesus to be a teaching order. When he founded the Jesuit college at Rome in 1550 it was as a seminary for the training of novices, but he was later persuaded that non-Jesuit pupils should be admitted. This was the first step in making the Jesuits the schoolmasters of catholic Europe. Their success was rapid and remarkable. Colleges and schools were founded in Italy, in Spain and in France. Sometimes the Jesuits were welcomed, and found rich and powerful patrons who made the accomplishment of their task relatively easy. In other places they were regarded as interlopers or worse. In Spain, for instance, the crown and the hierarchy of the Spanish church thought of them as papal agents, while the Dominicans, who were strongly entrenched in the Inquisition and the various faculties of theology, regarded them as rivals. In France also there was opposition from those bodies, such as the Sorbonne and the *Parlement*, which wanted the Church to be French first and catholic second.

The Jesuits would never have made headway had it not been for their outstanding ability, since success fed upon success. In France, for example, they established the College of Clermont in 1550 and built up its reputation to such an extent that by the early 1570s it had some 3,000 pupils and was famous all over Europe. Jesuit schools and colleges attracted in particular the children of the rich and influential, and in this way the Society acquired a hold on the upper classes of catholic Europe that made it admired, feared, and later resented. Jesuits shared many of the qualities of Calvinists—the sense of commitment, the capacity for organisation, and the high intellectual level—and like the Calvinists they helped to preserve and to transmit much of the New Learning of the Renaissance. In this, as in so many other ways, the catholic and protestant Reformations showed their common ancestry.

The Awakening of the Papacy

The reformation of the catholic Church depended ultimately on a change of heart at Rome, since only the papacy could give the necessary leadership. In 1512 Julius II had summoned the Lateran Council, which, if it accomplished relatively little, at least pinpointed one major source of weakness—the indiscipline of the religious orders—and began the essential task of restoring episcopal control. In January 1522 it seemed as though the reforming spirit had at last entered Rome when the Netherlander Adrian of Utrecht was elected Pope, as Adrian VI. He was a man of integrity, a long way removed in spirit from the Italian princelings who had used the papacy for their own purposes, and he turned his attention towards the reform of the papal adminis-tration. The members of the Curia, however, and in particular the cardinals, resented this attempt by a man whom they regarded as an uncultivated outsider to impose discipline on them, and they did their best to frustrate Adrian's intentions. In any case he was not given time to carry them out, for he died in September 1523 and was replaced by an Italian aristocrat, the Medici Clement VII.

Clement was a Christian Humanist and a peacemaker, who saw it as his main task to prevent the papacy from becoming subordinate to either of the two great powers who were fighting for supremacy in Italy and the western world. He was particularly suspicious of Charles V's insistence on the need to summon a general council of the Church, for fear that this would merely rubber-stamp Habsburg plans and reduce the Pope to the status of imperial chaplain. His attitude was therefore that which one of his legates advised: 'Never offer a council. Never refuse it directly. On the contrary, show that you are willing to comply with the request, but stress the difficulties in the way. Thus you will be able to ward it off.' No doubt there was something ignoble about this policy, yet Clement's fears were not without justification, for Charles V, although a devout catholic, showed a tendency—which was to be even more marked in his son—to identify the interests of catholicism with those of the house of Habsburg.

Although Clement made some attempt to remedy the more obvious abuses in the organisation of the catholic Church, the reformation of the papacy did not really get under way until the pontificate of Paul III, 1534-49. The new Pope was a member of the Farnese family and devoted to its interests; he was also a humanist and art-lover. Yet if in some ways he was simply one more Italian aristocrat wearing the papal tiara, in others he was a genuine reformer. He reduced the number of officials in the papal Curia, he improved the standards of administration, and two years after his election to the papacy he appointed a commission to study the whole question of Church reform. The commissioners included the leaders of the catholic reform movement, most prominent among them Caraffa, Contarini, and the Englishman Reginald Pole, and their report did not mince words. They laid the blame for corruption squarely on the avarice of the papacy, since it was this that led to the sale of spiritual offices. They also gave their opinion that no fundmental reform would be possible until the quality of the clergy was improved. In order to achieve this they recommended that much greater care should be exercised in the selection of candidates for the ministry; that all priests, including bishops, should be resident; and that benefices should be awarded solely on grounds of merit. When they turned their attention to monasticism their attitude reflected that of Erasmus, as was shown by their recommendation that the enclosed contemplative orders should be abolished. Yet at the same time they were critical of the Erasmian approach of publicly exposing abuses and pouring ridicule on institutions, and proposed that all publishing should be brought under the control of ecclesiastical censors.

Although Paul III gave general approval to the report of the commission he did little about it, other than order the eighty or so absentee bishops in Rome to return to their dioceses. He was aware that pressures within the catholic reform movement were pushing in different directions. On the one hand there were liberals, like Contarini, who were prepared to go a long way towards the Lutheran position on discipline and dogma. On the other hand there were hard-liners, like Caraffa, who were persuaded that the catholic Church must stand firm on its established beliefs and practices and refuse to compromise. Paul favoured the liberals, and in 1541 he sent Contarini to represent him at the discussions with protestant leaders at Regensburg. But the liberals on both sides were now being disowned by those in whose name they spoke, and the concessions which Contarini made for the sake of Christian unity were repudiated by the Church as a whole. He returned to Italy a disappointed man, and remained without influence and under suspicion of heresy until his death shortly afterwards.

From about 1540 the catholic reform movement steadily contracted into the Counter-Reformation, and Caraffa became its driving force. He had formerly been nuncio in Spain, where he admired the work of the Inquisition, and it was at his insistence that Paul III reluctantly agreed to set up a similar body at Rome. In July 1542 six cardinals, including Caraffa, were appointed Inquisitors-General, with authority over all catholics and power to examine suspected heretics, arrest, imprison and, if necessary, execute them. Caraffa regarded every liberal as a potential heretic, and his point seemed to be proved when Bernard Ochino and Peter Martyr, two of the leading liberals, went into exile rather than face an Inquisitorial investigation, and later announced their conversion to protestantism.

The establishment of the Holy Office at Rome marks the moment at which the catholic Church rallied its defenders and, like Luther at Worms, refused to budge. The Inquisition's regulations, drafted by Caraffa, were quite uncompromising. 'First, in matters of faith, no time must be lost; where there is the least ground for suspicion, vigorous action must at once be taken. Secondly, there must be no question of lenience for a prince or a prelate, however exalted his station. Thirdly, most rigorous action must be taken against those who seek to escape by placing themselves under the protection of a powerful person: but the man who admits his error must be treated leniently and with fatherly mercy. Fourthly, we must not stoop to any kind of toleration for the heretics.'

The power of the Inquisitors was obviously limited by secular considerations. Where the ruler of a state refused to allow the Holy Office to operate they could do little, but they were helped by the changing climate of opinion. While a big state, like Venice, could maintain a *de facto* tolerance, smaller principalities—Ferrara, for example, where Renée of France had provided a haven for protestant refugees—were frightened into submission.

The Council of Trent

Until the 1540s the line between orthodoxy and heresy had not been easy to draw. Adherents of redemption by faith alone, for instance, could appeal to the authority of Augustine; while those who advocated the administration of the communion in both kinds could point to the fact that this had been the practice in the early Church. Some authoritative definition of doctrine was needed, and this would only be acceptable if it came from a general council of the Church. Paul III was prepared to take the fateful step of summoning such a body, but not until (in the words of one of his legates) 'it is agreed that the Pope is absolute master of the council'. It was on this understanding that in 1536 he announced his intention of convoking a council to Mantua. But international complications—and in particular Charles V's reviving hope of restoring religious unity by means of the colloquies being held between catholics and protestants in Germany—led to postponement. Not until 1542 was Paul at last able to convene the council, this time to Trent. It was in the cathedral of this small imperial city, deep in the southern Alps, that some thirty bishops and fifty theologians assembled for the opening ceremony in December 1545. By the time the council completed its work, eighteen years later, about 270 prelates had taken part in its deliberations. The great majority of these came from Italy. Spain contributed just over thirty, France just under, and Germany a mere two. It was ironic, and not without significance, that a council summoned to deal with problems that had arisen in their most acute form in northern Europe should have been composed over-whelmingly of representatives of the Mediterranean world.

Although the Pope took no formal part in the Council of Trent his legates made sure that his views were fully represented, and it was the papal secretariat which provided the essential element of continuity. In this way the danger of a revival of conciliarism (the assertion that councils are superior to Popes) was avoided, and papal supremacy was confirmed by the decision that the resolutions of the council were not to be binding until the Pope had formally promulgated them. At the very beginning of the council a dispute arose between those members (a majority) who wished to deal first with questions of discipline, and the papalists, who wanted matters of doctrine to take precedence. This was not simply a procedural dispute. The advocates of disciplinary reform hoped, like Charles V, that if the Church removed some of its most glaring abuses the protestants might agree to return to it, so that in due course decisions on doctrine could be made by a reunited Christian community. They feared that if doctrine was defined first then the alienation of the protestants would be confirmed. The papalists, on the other hand, were not interested in reconciliation with the protestants if this entailed compromises on matters of doctrine which they regarded as fundamental.

To reconcile these opposing viewpoints it was eventually decided that doctrine and discipline should be considered simultaneously. In fact, however, the first session of the council concentrated mainly on doctrine. It took the Augsburg Confession of Faith, accepted by the Lutherans, as its point of departure, and formulated its own articles of faith in contradistinction to it. Such a procedure by its very nature emphasised the differences between protestants and catholics rather than the common ground they shared, and signalled the defeat of the liberals. It was decided, for example, that the Vulgate was the only authorised version of the Bible; that priests were the only persons who had the right to expound and interpret the scriptures; and that the traditions of the Church were of equal value with the revelations of God's will contained in the Old and New Testaments. On the disputed question of salvation, it was decreed that God had given His grace to all men through the mediation of Jesus Christ, and that faith need activating by 'good works'. Even without faith the redeeming power of God could operate through the seven sacraments. As for communion in both kinds, this was forbidden except in special circumstances and by express permission of the Pope.

The council was not allowed to continue its deliberations at Trent undisturbed. In early 1547 Charles V began his victorious campaign against the Schmalkaldic League, and it seemed that he would soon be in a position to dictate his terms not simply to the protestants but to the catholics as well. Such terms were not likely to be acceptable to the advocates of papal authority, and they therefore proposed that the council should be removed from imperial territory to a safer refuge at Bologna. This decision was taken in March 1547, shortly before the Emperor's triumph at Muhlberg, and Charles reacted strongly against it. He forbade any of the Spanish bishops to attend, and when the imperial Diet met at Augsburg in 1548 it refused to recognise the assembly at Bologna or be bound by any decrees it might issue. The Pope therefore suspended the council.

It was March 1551 before the delegates again assembled at Trent for a brief session. Protestant theologians, who had been invited to attend the council, arrived in January 1552, but it soon became clear that each side had gone too far in defining its position for any agreement to be reached. This reinforced the belief of the hard-liners that the catholic Church should concentrate on putting its own house in order, and not be any longer distracted by the will-of-the-wisp of reconciliation. The council had already affirmed the doctrines of the real presence and transubstantiation, and had asserted the validity of the veneration of saints. No doubt there would have been further progress on these lines but for the fact that the sudden collapse of the imperial position in Germany, and the menacing advance of Maurice of Saxony, caused the council once again to suspend its sessions, in April 1552.

The final session of the Council of Trent took place in 1562–63, and its main achievement was the promulgation of decrees requiring bishops to be resident, to preach regularly, to conduct annual visitations of their dioceses and to supervise works of charity. They were also required to establish seminaries in every diocese for the education of candidates for the ministry, to ensure that only those who were suitable were allowed to proceed to ordination, to watch over the moral life of their clergy, and to take disciplinary action where necessary. This emphasis on the quality of the clergy and the role of the bishops was one of the characteristics of the Counter-Reformation. The protestants, with their belief in the priesthood of all believers, downgraded the role of the clergy and either did away with bishops altogether or severely curtailed their functions. The Counter-Reformation took the contrary attitude and strengthened the authority of bishops and parish priests alike, so that they might give the necessary lead to the catholic laity. This was more than a question of emphasis. There was a profound difference of belief between those who put individual conscience and the Bible first, and those who insisted that conscience and the scriptures must be interpreted by the Church in the light of its own traditions and understanding.

The decrees of the Council of Trent did not transform the catholic Church overnight. While they were swiftly accepted in Italy and in many of the catholic states of Germany, the rulers of France and Spain put difficulties in the way. The Tridentine decrees were never formally confirmed by the French crown, though they were accepted by a number of provincial church councils in 1580–84 and eventually ratified by an assembly of the French clergy in 1615. In Spain the decrees were valid only in so far as they did not conflict with the rights of the crown. The papacy could not do much to improve the standard of the episcopate in either France or Spain while appointments in both countries were in the hands of the monarch, and throughout the whole of the catholic world the Church was so deeply enmeshed in the complex structure of lay society that spiritual considerations could not always triumph over secular ones. Even where the Church was free to act, it was not always ready or able to do so. Decrees alone could not make a lazy bishop into a hard-working one, and if prelates chose to be absent from their sees there was little that could be done to recall them.

Despite these reservations, the Council of Trent did mark a turning-point in the history of the catholic Church. Taken in conjunction with the foundation of the new religious orders, the establishment of the Roman Inquisition, and above all the spiritual regeneration of the papacy, it gave catholics a certainty about their own beliefs and practices that had previously been lacking. In the first shock of the protestant Reformation the weakness of the Church had been all too apparent, and it had seemed as though the ramshackle structure might not be able to survive. Now the foundations had been strengthened, to give a firm base on which the spiritual life of the catholic world could be reconstructed.

The Reformed Papacy

While a weak or corrupt papacy was a grave impediment to the catholic Church, a powerful and purified one was a priceless asset. In 1555 the champion of the hard-liners, Pietro Caraffa himself, was elected to the papal throne as Paul IV. He was a disciplinarian, and one of his first actions was to order the bishops at the papal court to return to their sees. He had no time for liberalism, and it was during his pontificate that the first papal Index of prohibited books—including all the works of Erasmus—was published. Although Paul IV was seventy-nine at the time of his election, he was overflowing with energy and struck fear into his subordinates. But he was by birth a Neapolitan, convinced that the Church could never be free while the Habsburgs dominated Italy, and he wasted many of his assets on an anti-Spanish crusade which, in the nature of things, could accomplish little.

Paul died in 1559, and Pius IV was elected to take his place. Pius was very much a Medici, as he showed by creating members of his own family cardinals while they were still under age, but during his pontificate the reform of the papal Curia went ahead and Pius set an example to other bishops by opening a seminary for the diocese of Rome. His successor, the saintly and ascetic Pius V, elected in 1566, was a stern disciplinarian who aimed to achieve for Rome what Calvin had done for Geneva. He ordered the enforcement of clerical residence and monastic discipline, he issued edicts against simony and immorality, and he put new life into the Inquisition. Pius V was not content simply with negative measures. A new catechism was issued in 1566, and he followed this up with a new breviary in 1568 and a revised missal two years later. In 1568 he also appointed two Congregations of cardinals to supervise the work of conversion in Europe and the world beyond. In financial affairs Pius V concentrated on reducing the expenses of the papal court and administration, and he demonstrated his sense of priorities by abolishing annates and forbidding the preaching of indulgences. In future the revenue of the papacy was not to be based on either the exploitation of the Church's bishops or the perversion of its doctrines.

Gregory XIII, who succeeded Pius V in 1572 and occupied the papal throne until 1585, was also a determined reformer, but a much gentler character. He longed to see Europe recovered for the catholic faith, and to this end he supported the Catholic League in France and the seminary priests in England. Gregory recognised that the papacy must work with the established powers in catholic Europe rather than against them, and so he developed and perfected the system of papal ambassadors ('nuncios'). The duty of these resident papal viceroys was not simply to negotiate with secular rulers but also to intervene directly in the religious life of the country to which they were accredited. They were responsible for keeping up pressure on the bishops to ensure that the decrees of the Council of Trent were enforced. They were also useful in countering the centrifugal tendencies inevitably present in an international Church by insisting on the reality of papal supremacy.

Another of Gregory XIII's achievements was the revival of the link between the papacy and scholarship. In 1580 he gave his approval to a revised text of canon law; he ordered a printing-press to be set up for the express purpose of publishing major works of eastern literatures; and in 1582 he suppressed the old Julian calendar, which was ten days out in its alignment, and proclaimed his own more accurate one, the Gregorian.

Under Sixtus V (1585–90) the reformed papacy was at the height of its prestige, actively promoting the interests of the catholic Church throughout the world. The atmosphere at Rome had changed out of all recognition, and there was a sense of commitment to spiritual causes that had been almost totally lacking in the early sixteenth century. Sixtus limited the number of cardinals to seventy, and in 1587 he divided them among fifteen Congregations. Some of these were concerned with mundane matters like the organisation of the food supply and transport systems for the city of Rome—which Sixtus rebuilt on a magnificent scale—but others were responsible for major sections of the work of the Church, and provided the direction and co-ordination that had so often been lacking. In this way the cardinals were transformed from over-mighty aristocrats into hardworking bureaucrats, and the papacy, like the secular monarchies, reasserted its authority over all its subjects.

The Achievement of the Catholic Reformers

The transformation of catholicism was a gradual process, involving hundreds of people whose names have not been recorded. But there were some key figures who set an example and encouraged others to follow it. Such a man was Charles Borromeo, Archbishop of Milan from 1560 to 1584. As the nephew of Pius IV he had been made a titular abbot when he was only twelve, and cardinal at the age of twenty-one, even though he had not taken holy orders. He was, in fact, a product of the old, unreformed Rome, but his life was changed by a sudden spiritual conversion of the sort which many other reformers, catholic and protestant, experienced. From that moment onwards he was totally committed to the service of God and the catholic Church. He played a big part in the closing session of the Council of Trent, and helped draft the revised catechism which was designed primarily for the instruction of parish clergy. In 1566 he retired to his diocese—the first Archbishop of Milan to be resident for nearly eighty years—and immediately set about raising the standards of his clergy. He held regular synods, visited all the parishes in his see, established three seminaries in the city of Milan and another three outside, and founded the Confraternity of Christian Doctrine from which the Sunday School movement was to develop. Borromeo was a hard, austere man, easier to admire than to love, but he became a model of what a post-Tridentine bishop ought to be, and his influence extended far beyond the diocese of Milan.

At the opposite pole from Borromeo, whose spirituality found expression in the active life, came the Spanish mystics Teresa of Avila (1515–82) and John of the Cross (1542–91). St Teresa was a Carmelite, whose spiritual autobiography has become a classic of its type. Although a mystic she was also a good administrator, and helped found seventeen new houses for her order. St John was directly influenced by Teresa, whom he met in 1567, and it was under her guidance that he founded the first house of discalced (barefoot) Carmelites. Although the writings of the two saints show the influence of the German mystical tradition they were essentially originals, and the flowering of their spirituality is a reminder that the catholic Reformation was not simply a matter of decrees and administrative reorganisation: it drew its strength from deep spiritual wells, and embraced the contemplative as well as the active life.

Yet while Saints Teresa and John of the Cross were just as much products of the catholic revival as, for instance, Borromeo, their particular type of contemplative spirituality was not characteristic. Generally speaking the spirituality of the catholic reformation was active and committed, finding expression in good works among the poor and sick. Although the older enclosed orders survived, the new ones operated within the world rather than outside it, and the emphasis at all levels, from the Pope down to the humblest parish priest, was on the spiritual commitment which transforms even the most ordinary task. It is sometimes suggested that only the protestants sanctified humdrum daily existence, but in fact this applies equally to regenerated Roman Catholicism: in this respect, as in so many others, both catholics and protestants were heirs to the demand which expressed itself so strongly in the closing Middle Ages for a religion that should connect with everyday life, for an uncloistered spirituality.

The spiritual aspect of the catholic reformation was also apparent in the practice of frequent communion, which became one of the features of the Roman Catholic Church from the mid-sixteenth century onwards. For priests, daily celebration of the mass became increasingly common, while the laity were encouraged to communicate at least once a month, although for the bulk of the population annual communion at Easter was usually regarded as an acceptable minimum.

The puritan distrust of the arts, which was to be seen most markedly in Calvinism, did not affect the catholic Church, except in so far as it encouraged a reaction in their favour. Art for art's sake was regarded with suspicion, and the glorification of the human body was frowned on—as Paul IV demonstrated by ordering an artist to clothe some of Michelangelo's nudes in the Sistine Chapel. But art in the service of God was highly valued, and catholic churches of this period came more and more to resemble ornate threatres, lavishly and often dramatically decorated, where the ceremonies of the catholic faith were celebrated with all the compelling ritual of robes, incense, and chanted Latin. In this sense the age of the catholic reformation is the age of the Baroque.

The impetus of the Counter-Reformation endured for about a century, but by 1650 it was at a low ebb. This did not mean that the Church had everywhere returned to the state of corruption in which it had been sunk at the time of Luther, nor that devout and committed men had ceased to find in it the opportunity to express their Christian belief; in 1650, for instance, St Vincent de Paul and his followers, the Lazarists, were working among the poor and suffering in the slums of France, bringing faith and hope to those whom society had rejected or simply forgotten about. Yet the very success of the Counter-Reformation in defeating the protestant challenge bred a measure of complacency, and the emphasis which was placed on the formal structure of the Church tended to stifle initiative and adaptation.

The decline in impetus must not, however, be exaggerated, and in any case much of the work of the Counter-Reformation was to endure. Protestantism had been checked and, in some places, swept back; an enormous missionary effort had been mounted in America, India, and the far east; the papacy had been restored to its spiritual leadership; and, most important of all, the Roman Catholic Church had demonstrated that it was capable of renewal even when it was so sunk in corruption and worldliness that it seemed as if God must have abandoned it.

PART THREE

Habsburg Europe

ELEVEN

Freedom and 'Liberties'

The desire for freedom, by which is meant the right to control one's own destiny, was to be found at all levels in sixteenth-century Europe. This was not so, however, with the desire to preserve 'liberties', for these were time-honoured privileges and traditional ways of doing things which served to protect the interests only of the wealthier sections of society. The mass of the people, having nothing to lose, had no need of such safeguards, and only rarely did their struggle for a greater degree of freedom merge with the property-owners' defence of their own 'liberties'. When this did happen, however, it created a highly volatile and dangerous situation.

The freedom of Christian Europe as a whole was threatened by the advance of the Ottoman Turks, who had taken over much of the Balkans and were pushing up against the eastern frontiers of the Holy Roman Empire. The burden of defending Christendom fell on the shoulders of the Emperor, and Charles V and his successors took their responsibility seriously and spent much of their time and a great deal of their money in campaigns to hold back the infidel. They were not prompted solely by altruism, since the hereditary lands of the Habsburg family were directly menaced by the Turkish armies. Yet they were guarding far more than their own self-interest, for if the Turks had in fact broken through the Habsburg defences the whole of central and eastern Europe would have been imperilled.

Charles V was bitter at the knowledge that while he was fighting to preserve the freedom of Christendom, the ruler of one of the greatest Christian states, the kingdom of France, was actively intriguing against him, even to the extent of allying with the Turkish invader. On the face of it this was treachery to the Christian cause, but Francis I of

France was not simply an unprincipled adventurer, though this was the impression often given by his actions. He also was engaged in a struggle for freedom, but in his case the immediate threat came not from the distant Turk but from the Habsburg Emperor himself.

Sixteenth-century Europe was Habsburg Europe. This remarkable family had, over the course of several hundred years, built up its territorial base in Austria and from there had expanded westwards by virtually appropriating the Holy Roman Empire. The next big leap forward came under Maximilian I, of whom it was said: 'Bella gerant alii. Tu, felix Austria, nube!'[1] By taking Mary of Burgundy as his wife, Maximilian brought the Low Countries and Franche-Comté under Habsburg sway; and by arranging the marriage of his son, Duke Philip of Burgundy, to Joanna of Spain, he opened the way to a further extension of Habsburg power, this time into the Iberian peninsula. All this immense agglomeration of territories was concentrated, by hereditary descent, in the person of Maximilian's grandson, the Emperor Charles V, and given the fact that he was also presented with the New World discovered on the far side of the Atlantic, there seemed no reason why Habsburg power should not continue to expand until it embraced the whole of Christendom within its orbit.

The one country which, above all others, was determined to prevent this, was France. The rulers of this rich kingdom, which had only recently emerged victorious from the Hundred Years' War with England, were only too conscious of the fact that they had Habsburgs to north, east and south of them. Francis I and his successors felt the noose being drawn tighter and tighter about them, and were determined to break out of this stranglehold before it was too late. It was to preserve their own freedom, therefore, that the French monarchs fought the Habsburgs in Italy, intrigued against them in Germany, and joined hands with their Turkish enemies. As it happens, there is no evidence that Charles V, as distinct from some of his chief advisers, was in fact aiming at a world empire. Nevertheless, France's fears were justified, for it is in the nature of power to go on expanding, and if the French kings had not fought for their freedom they might well have become Habsburg puppets.

There were many elements in this epic struggle, which the great Belgian historian, Henri Pirenne, described as 'un conflit d'entre une maison et une nation'.[2] It was in one sense a tug-of-war between the

[1] Let others make war. You, fortunate Austria, marry!'
[2] 'A conflict between a dynasty (*lit.* a house) and a nation',

past and the future, with Charles personifying the medieval concept or supranational authority while Francis embodied the modern nation state that acknowledges no superior. It was Christian morality versus Macchiavellian realism. It was the broad view as opposed to the narrow. But as well as being all these it was also a straightforward struggle for power between two dynasties, the Habsburg and the Valois, in which the odds were heavily in favour of the Habsburgs. If Charles could have delivered a knock-out blow he would have been unchallenged master of the western world. Francis was concerned primarily with survival as a free, sovereign ruler.

Where the internal history of sixteenth-century states was concerned, 'liberties' were more important than freedom. In the Middle Ages power had been diffused and the ruler's authority had been held in check by such things as customary law, private and corporate franchises, representative assemblies, and a socially dominant aristocracy. These limitations did not disappear overnight at the beginning of the sixteenth century, but in states as far removed as Spain and Russia, France and Sweden, the central government began steadily strengthening its authority. Customary law was modified or superseded by Roman law, with its emphasis on the rights of the ruler. Private and corporate franchises were resumed by the crown, and representative assemblies were bypassed or dispensed with. Most important of all, the nobles were edged out of government and replaced by 'new men', educated at the universities, trained in law, and totally committed to the royal service. Throughout Europe the 'Rule of the Secretaries' marked the emergence of powerful monarchies determined to assert their authority over all their subjects. This was not the result of any abstract or theoretical belief in the virtues of absolutism. It was the only practicable alternative to the aristocratic factionalism that had brought about the collapse of so many governments in the late Middle Ages.

The 'old' nobles, of course, resented their exclusion from power, and struggled either to avoid it or to restore the former state of affairs. In Poland they were all too successful and turned factionalism into a constitution; in Sweden they forced the monarchy to compromise, for a time at least; in Russia they were eventually overwhelmed. Generally speaking, in western Europe, they were fighting a losing battle, but by their very existence they offered an alternative focus of loyalty to that provided by the crown, and were a visible reminder of an older and more traditional order of things. When the old nobles called on the

crown to respect their 'liberties' they were in fact insisting on their
exclusive right to a share in government, but as champions of traditional attitudes their appeal went far beyond the narrow limits of their
own class. In the Netherlands, for instance, they had the support of
many of the merchant oligarchs who ruled the towns and were themselves ardent defenders of urban 'liberties'; while in late-sixteenth-
century France they were followed by thousands of ordinary people
whose primary concern was religious freedom or the preservation of
long established and accepted forms of government.

The rulers of early-modern Europe found 'liberties', of whatever
variety, an impediment to their freedom of action, and above all a
limitation on their power to raise money. This was a particularly
sensitive point, since the strength of a monarchy was directly related to
the amount of money it could command, and rulers needed larger and
larger sums not simply to pay for their expanding administrations but
also to meet the costs of more or less perpetual war. Where representative assemblies existed—such as the *Cortes* of Castile—they might be
persuaded to vote additional supply, but they did so with extreme
reluctance, and the sums raised were never sufficient. The general
assumption was that the ruler should live off his own resources, including those which, by 'age-old' custom, were provided for him by his
people. Anything novel smacked of despotism and was resisted.

Where princes persisted in their demands, and resorted to unfamiliar
methods of money-raising, they aroused resentment among their richer
subjects. Sometimes this could lead to open rebellion, as happened in
the Netherlands when Philip II ordered the imposition of the 'Tenth
Penny'. More usually it built up anger against the government and
placed an increasingly heavy responsibility on the person of the king.
As long as he was a grown man, strong-minded and capable of enforcing obedience, the government would continue to function. But when
—as in France after 1559—the throne passed to a minor, the accumulated resentments burst their bounds, and in the absence of a strong
king the crown alone was not a potent enough symbol to hold faction
in check.

The most dangerous moment for all sixteenth-century governments
came when the privileged classes' defence of their 'liberties' fused with
the struggle for a greater degree of freedom by those at the bottom of
the social pyramid. There seemed, on the face of it, little chance of such
a fusion. The masses were oppressed just as much by the rich and noble

as by the crown, and would have had more reason to join the king than his opponents. Conversely, the upper classes had everything to fear from radicalism surging up from below. Yet there were a number of occasions on which the basic differences were submerged, for a time at least, in a common cause, and these were the moments of acute crisis in a state.

Before considering these occasions something must be said about the causes of radicalism among the masses. This was primarily an urban phenomenon—though not exclusively so, as was shown by the so-called Peasants' War in Germany in the 1520s[1]—and had its roots in economic distress. It was not just a question of the contrast between the squalid poverty of the masses and the ostentatious luxury of the privileged minority, though this was an ever-present source of bitterness. Radicalism was to be found most frequently in towns, such as those of the Netherlands, where the population was dependent on one major industry for its livelihood and suffered severely from fluctuations in international trade. Yet even towns that were not primarily industrial were affected by these fluctuations, for with the growth of population in the sixteenth century many parts of Europe ceased to be self-sufficient in foodstuffs and came to depend on imports. Generally speaking, southern and western Europe consumed the grain produced by the north and east, and any dislocation of the trade routes, whether through natural causes such as bad weather or manmade ones such as war, could lead to hunger and starvation among the urban proletariat. Even where food was available it was not always adequately distributed, for early-modern governments, however powerful they seemed to be by comparision with their immediate predecessors, were ill-equipped for major administrative tasks. They were handicapped by inadequate statistics—no sixteenth-century ruler knew for certain how many subjects he had, for example—and dependent on 'civil servants' who were thin on the ground, lacking in effective authority, and open to bribery.

It was because the urban masses were always hovering on the border-line between poverty and starvation that they embraced radical ideas, whether these were couched in a political or a religious form. The Anabaptists, who rejected established society as the work of unregenerate man, made a strong appeal, as was shown by their takeover of the town of Munster in 1534, and this was one of the reasons why

---

[1] 'So-called' because the revolt was not confined to peasants but included urban artisans as well as disaffected elements from all levels of society.

secular authorities of all religious denominations persecuted them without mercy. Calvinism and catholicism could be equally radical in their impact when operating at the lowest social level. In the late 1570s, for example, Calvinists took the lead in setting up the revolutionary 'Council of Eighteen' in Brussels, while ten years later radical catholics established the 'Council of Sixteen' which imposed a reign of terror upon the city of Paris.

Because such movements of mass protest invariably failed in the long run, it is tempting to dismiss them as essentially negative and destructive. This is in one sense what they were, since their immediate objective was to destroy an unjust social order. It is also true that the passion for secular change was inextricably entangled with religious and mystical beliefs in the imminence of the second coming and the end of all earthly society. At the same time they were the expression of something more positive—namely an egalitarian and democratic political philosophy which had its roots deep in the Middle Ages and had shown a remarkable capacity for survival among the uneducated and the illiterate. This philosophy ran counter to prevailing assumptions about the privileges attaching to ownership, the deference due to rank, and the obedience owed to the 'powers-that-be', yet it was as much part of the European consciousness as the more formal and elaborate expositions of Machiavelli, Jean Bodin,[1] or, at a later stage, John Locke.

The two major occasions, during the sixteenth century, on which the radicalism of the masses was welded with the privileged classes' defence of their own 'liberties' were the Revolt of the Netherlands and the French Wars of Religion. In both the solder was a common religious faith. This was not at first apparent in the Netherlands, for although revolt there was sparked off by the magnates, acting in defence of their traditional right to participate in government, they drew back, horrified, when the Iconoclastic Riots showed them what depths they had opened up. But one or two of the magnates—most notably, of course, William of Orange—and, more important, a substantial section of the lesser aristocracy, saw the need to join forces with the radicals if the revolt was to have any chance of success. William of Orange eventually

---

[1] The Frenchman Jean Bodin (1530–96), one of the leading political theorists of his day, published his *Six Books concerning the State* in 1576. In this work he analysed the concept of 'Sovereignty', which he defined as 'the absolute and perpetual power of commanding in a state', and declared that 'there is nothing on earth greater than a sovereign prince.'

adopted the Calvinist faith in a deliberate move to broaden the base of his support, and as for the lesser nobles, the most committed and successful among them were the Sea Beggars, who embraced a fanatical Calvinism which made a direct appeal to the urban proletariat. Without this powerful bond the Sea Beggars might never have gained entry into the towns of Holland and Zeeland, and Philip II would have remained ruler of a united Netherlands.

In France, during the Wars of Religion, the various factions among the aristocracy similarly gave themselves a mass following—with all that this entailed in the way of political influence—by using the language of religious commitment, whether or not they really believed it. Their success is pinpointed by two contemporary quotations. The Venetian ambassador, who saw one side of the coin, informed his government that 'these wars are born of the wish of the Cardinal of Lorraine to have no equal, and the Admiral and the house of Montmorency to have no superior'. But a French protestant saw only the reverse side, and declared that 'this war is not like other wars, for even the very poorest man has an interest in it'. Both were correct, for religion—in France as elsewhere—blurred the distinction between idealism and self-interest, and led men to support causes of which, in different circumstances, they would have disapproved.

Fortunately for sixteenth-century rulers, the alliance between upper class discontent and lower class radicalism was usually shortlived. The privileged minority might genuinely feel that the demands of government threatened their 'liberties', but when they saw the violence of the radical protest they had unleashed, they usually retreated into conformity. In Castile, for example, in the 1520s, the nobles' fear of being ousted from power by Charles V's 'Burgundians' led them to challenge royal authority in the 'Revolt of the *Comuneros*'. But they were alarmed and alienated by the increasing radicalism of their urban supporters, and so soon as Charles accepted their (very moderate) demands they joined him in suppressing the rebellion. By so doing they demonstrated a fundamental truth about resistance to government in the early-modern period, namely that the defence of their 'liberties' by the privileged sections of a community was essentially conservative. Even if they rebelled, it was not to change the existing order of things but to stop it from changing to their disadvantage. The masses, on the other hand, wanted root-and-branch reform, a fundamental transformation of a society which offered them nothing.

The rulers of Habsburg Europe had therefore to steer a careful course. To hold their states together and make their government effective they had to reduce the area of private and corporate 'liberties'. But they must not go so far, or so fast, as to drive the privileged minority into alliance with the propertyless and radical majority. Given a steady hand at the helm and reasonable weather, their chances of survival were high.

TWELVE

Western Europe and the Italian Wars 1494–1516

Maximilian I and the Movement for Imperial Reform

In 1493 the German Electors, meeting in solemn conclave following the death of the Emperor Frederick III, offered the imperial crown to his son, Maximilian, who had held the title of 'King of the Romans' since 1486. Maximilian I, aged thirty-four, was the very embodiment of a perfect knight—handsome, with a commanding presence; a warrior, scholar, poet and patron of the arts. Unfortunately he did not supplement these virtues with any marked degree of political realism, and although he was full of grandiose schemes he was seldom able to translate them into solid achievements. As Emperor, Maximilian's main aims were to get a sufficient revenue and also an army with which to pursue his dynastic interests. Opposition to this came from the reforming party among the princes, which was determined to create central institutions strong enough to restore internal peace to the Empire—which was sadly in need of it—and to preserve order. If money and troops were to be raised, then the reformers wanted them to be used for Germany and not simply placed at the disposal of the Emperor. They did not share Maximilian's assumption that anything that was good for the Habsburgs was automatically good for the Empire.

In 1495 Maximilian summoned a Diet to meet at Worms, in the hope that the assembled Estates would provide money and troops sufficient for him to make a formal progress into Italy, where he would be crowned by the Pope. By the time the Diet opened, however, the European state system had been convulsed by the French invasion of Italy, and Maximilian was determined to fish in these troubled waters. Germany, of course, stood to gain nothing from such an adventurous foreign policy, and hard bargaining therefore took place between

Maximilian and the reform party. The reformers were, on the face of it, remarkably successful. They persuaded Maximilian to issue a proclamation of 'Eternal Peace', banning private war within the Empire, and also to set up a supreme court, the *Reichskammergericht*. The chief justice of this new court was to be appointed by the Emperor, but most of the other judges were to be chosen by the German states. In theory the *Reichskammergericht* was to be financed by a poll tax, the 'Common Penny', but under the terms of the agreement between Maximilian and the princes part of the proceeds of this tax was to be used to provide an army for the Emperor. Many princes therefore refused to allow the Common Penny to be collected in their states, for fear of subsidising imperial absolutism, but in doing this they starved the *Reichskammergericht* and thereby undermined the effectiveness of their own reform programme.

Maximilian used his share of the revenue raised by the Common Penny, as well as the money which he made by selling a monopoly of Tyrol silver-mining to the Fuggers, to raise an army which he led into northern Italy. In his military (as distinct from his matrimonial) ventures Maximilian was never lucky, and after a number of humiliating reverses his money ran out and he had to return home, a laughing-stock. His lowered prestige, as well as his desperate need for hard cash, meant that he could not hold out against the reformers' demand for the further implementation of their programme.

The triumph of the reformers was signalled at the Diet of Augsburg in 1500, when Maximilian agreed to the establishment of an imperial governing council, or *Reichsregiment*, made up of twenty-one Electors, princes, and other representatives of the Empire. The reformers hoped that the *Reichsregiment* would become the real governing body of the Empire, and had this come to pass Maximilian would have been little more than a constitutional monarch, the formal head of a federation of principalities. But in fact the *Reichsregiment* was stillborn. It had inadequate financial resources and no bureaucracy to enforce its will; it had no control over the Emperor's foreign policy; and, most serious of all, it lacked the wholehearted support of the Electors, who were more concerned to uphold their own independence than to strengthen imperial institutions. As a consequence the *Reichsregiment* was dissolved in 1502 and the reform movement petered out.

Maximilian made further, and futile, attempts to intervene in the Italian peninsula, but he accomplished nothing, and in the closing years of his life he concentrated increasingly on the affairs of his own family.

In particular he wanted to secure the imperial crown for his grandson, Charles, by having him elected King of the Romans, an honorary title which implied a right of succession. The Electors were open to persuasion, and Maximilian borrowed money from every conceivable source in order to woo them. But even in this project he was doomed to failure, for he died in 1519, before his preparations were complete, and Charles had to begin the enormously expensive process all over again.

As Emperor, Maximilian was a failure, for imperial power was no more of a reality at the end of his reign than it had been at the beginning. But as head of the house of Habsburg he was remarkably successful. He secured recognition of the Habsburg claim to Hungary and Bohemia, he consolidated Habsburg authority in Austria, and he recovered part at least of his wife's inheritance and added Franche-Comté and the Netherlands to his family's already vast possessions. In the long run his most spectacular achievement was to extend Habsburg rule to Spain and its dependencies, through the marriage of his son. Such an outcome could hardly have seemed likely at the time, since it was made possible only by a number of unexpected deaths, but in dynastic, as opposed to imperial, policies Maximilian had luck on his side.

Although Maximilian's grandson, Charles, was a strong candidate for the imperial crown in 1519, the election was by no means a foregone conclusion. The Pope, in particular, was working against his candidature, for fear that the increasing extent of Habsburg power should turn the dream of world empire into a reality and leave the papacy as simply one among a number of Italian principalities. The Pope would have preferred Francis I of France, who not only put himself forward as a candidate but also spent vast sums of money to secure his election. The German princes, however, were aware of Francis' ambitious nature, and had at least as much to fear from Valois dynastic entanglements as from Habsburg ones.

In the end Charles seemed to be the candidate who aroused the least amount of opposition, but his election was not secured until he had agreed to certain capitulations. By accepting these he bound himself to rule the Empire in accordance with existing laws and customs; to take no major political decision without consulting the imperial Diet; to refrain from using foreign troops or foreign statesmen in Germany; and to set up a new *Reichsregiment* to rule the Empire when he was absent from it. In fact for nine years after the Diet of Worms, in 1521, Charles was away from Germany, and in 1522 he formally appointed his brother, Ferdinand, as head of the *Reichsregiment*, transferring to him the Habsburg duchies of Austria, Carinthia, Carniola, Styria and the Tyrol. Ferdinand, however, was frequently engaged in the defence of the eastern borders of the Empire against the Turks, and so the *Reichsregiment* was left to its own devices in trying to preserve peace and internal order.

The weakness of the new *Reichsregiment*, as of the old, was that it lacked sufficient support from the Electors. Much more effective were the associations of princes and towns, of which the most politically significant was the Swabian League. This demonstrated its power in 1519 when it turned its forces against the Duke of Wurttemberg, who had been levying private war against one of the imperial free cities, and expelled him from his duchy. Some years later, in 1523, it suppressed a revolt by the Imperial Knights. The effectiveness of the action taken by the Swabian League was in sharp contrast to the limited achievements of the imperial institutions. These might have become more powerful if the Empire itself had grown together, but the reverse was the case. When religious differences were added to personal and political ones, there was no longer any hope of imperial unity. Protestant princes refused to accept the rulings of the *Reichskammergericht*, which had a majority of catholic judges; they boycotted the imperial Diet; and, like their catholic counterparts, they ignored the *Reichsregiment's* attempts to maintain internal peace. Neither Charles V nor the German reformers were able, therefore, to transform the shadowy existence of the Empire into a solid political reality.

Burgundy

The nominal ruler of what remained of Burgundy (namely the Netherlands and Franche-Comté) was Duke Philip, the baby son of Maximilian and Mary. Maximilian claimed the right to act as regent, but many towns were suspicious of him and feared that he intended to erode their traditional 'liberties'. Maximilian seemed to be confronted in the Netherlands with the same centrifugal tendencies that were to cripple him in the Empire, and the collapse of his authority was so complete that when he took up residence in Bruges early in 1488, to await the assembly of the Estates General which he had summoned to meet him there, the citizens closed the gates and held him virtual prisoner. His father, the Emperor Frederick III, had to raise an army and march on the rebellious city before its inhabitants lost their nerve and allowed Maximilian to leave.

From this moment onwards Maximilian's fortunes improved and Habsburg rule became increasingly acceptable in the Netherlands especially after 1493 when, on the election of Maximilian as Emperor, his son Philip, now fifteen, took over the government of the duchy. Three years later, in October 1496, Philip married Joanna, second daughter of Ferdinand of Aragon and Isabella of Castile, and in February 1500 a son was born to them, whom they named Charles, in memory of the last great Duke of Burgundy. There seemed little likelihood at the time of Philip's marriage that his wife would one day inherit Castile, but the death of her brother and elder sister meant that when Isabella died in 1504 Joanna became Queen of Castile, and Philip took the title of king.

Philip went some way towards achieving his grandfather's aim of centralising the administration of his disparate territories. There was already in existence a Chamber to supervise the ducal revenues, and in 1504 a high court was established, with jurisdiction over all the duchy lands. For the formulation of policy and for administration Philip relied mainly on his Privy Council, in which the leading aristocratic families were well represented, but he also kept on good terms with Estates General, thereby securing for himself a steady inflow of public money.

The success of Philip's policy was shown by the absence of any anti-governmental reaction following his sudden death in September 1506. The nobility were content with the considerable degree of influence they already held, and as for the towns, they were too jealous of their individual privileges to form a united front except for a short time and for the remedy of specific grievances. The new duke, Charles, was only six years of age, and the real ruler of Burgundy was Philip's sister Margaret, widow of the Duke of Savoy, an educated and cultured woman who welcomed artists and men of letters to the ducal court. In 1515, however, Charles was declared of age and took over the government of his duchy. He had been born at Ghent, had spent all his life in the Netherlands, and was a much loved and popular figure. His chief adviser was Guillaume de Croy, lord of Chièvres, whose policy was one of alliance with the ruling oligarchs in the towns. These oligarchs were alarmed by the widespread unrest among the urban proletariat consequent upon the economic dislocation caused by the movement of the cloth industry out of the towns into the countryside, and they saw strong ducal government as the best guarantee of their own privileged position. They showed their loyalty at a meeting of the Estates General at Ghent in 1517, when Charles was about to set out for Spain, following the death of his grandfather Ferdinand; and again in 1519, when they welcomed the news of Charles's election as Emperor.

The Netherlands in fact had to pay a high price for their share in Charles's glory, and were to be heavily taxed for the mounting of military campaigns that were of little relevance or benefit to them. But Charles never exhausted the fund of affection that he had acquired through his birth and upbringing, and although he became more drawn towards Spain as he grew older, and chose a Spanish monastery in which to end his days, he was proud of his Burgundian ancestry and never forgot that, as he told the Estates in 1520, 'son coeur avait toujours été par deça'.[1]

The 'Catholic Kings'

In Spain, as in the rest of Europe, the close of the Middle Ages had been a period of instability in which aristocratic factions had engaged in private warfare and flouted the rule of law or the dictates of any central authority. Isabella was determined to put an end to this situation in Castile, and for this purpose she and Ferdinand used a medieval institution, the *Hermandad*, or brotherhood. This was a sort of urban police force, and in 1476 Ferdinand and Isabella reorganised it as the *Santa Hermandad*, under the control of a royal council directly responsible to themselves. The men for this force were provided by the towns and villages on a fixed quota basis, and as nobles were excluded from membership it was highly successful in putting down aristocratic factionalism and disorder, using savage punishments as its main deterrent. The initiative in all this came from the crown, but the *Cortes* of 1480 showed its approval by forbidding the building of new castles and outlawing private war.

Although Ferdinand was determined to put down overmighty subjects, he was not opposed to aristocrats as such. Apart from an 'Act of Resumption' of 1480, restoring to the crown much of the land that the nobles had taken from it during the period of weak royal rule, he

---

[1] 'His heart had always been among them' (literally 'on this side').

made no attempt to undermine their wealth or privileges, and they remained, as they always had been, the leaders of society. They also continued to fill the great offices of state, but increasingly the actual business of government was carried out by men of lower (though rarely low) birth who had been trained in the law. One of the functions of these *letrados* was to keep the towns in order, and in 1480 officials called *Corregidors* were appointed to all the major cities in Castile, to act as the king's representatives. As for the *Hermandad*, the central organisation was wound up in 1498, by which time its task had been completed, though the crown kept on local bodies as a useful police force and reservoir of troops.

Ferdinand recognised the need to make the crown rich if it was to be efficient. Among the wealthiest institutions in Spain were the military orders, and as the masterships of these fell vacant Ferdinand had himself appointed, thereby acquiring for the crown not only the enormous revenues of the orders but also their considerable patronage. Another source of patronage was the Church, and here Isabella was determined to win back for the crown the rights of appointment which had lapsed during the time of troubles. This, however, was a slow process. In 1486 the Pope agreed that in return for Spanish support of his policy in Italy he would allow the crown to appoint to all major benefices in Granada. In 1508 this privilege was extended to America, and in practice was gradually stretched to cover all appointments to major clerical offices in Spain as well. Not until 1523, however, was Charles V formally granted the right of presentation to all the Spanish bishoprics. The religious orders were also brought under royal control after 1494, when Pope Alexandra VI, who had bestowed on Ferdinand and Isabella and their heirs the title of 'the Catholic Kings', also gave them authority to reform the religious houses within their dominions—a task they entrusted to Cardinal Ximenes, who performed it admirably.

Probably the most famous, or most notorious, example of the extension of royal power into the spiritual sphere was the Inquisition. This had been established in Castile by papal bull in 1478, but appointments to it were in the hands of the crown. The Inquisition's primary task was to deal with converted Jews and make sure they did not relapse into un-Christian practices. It was the product of considerable antisemitism, prompted partly by crusading zeal, partly by jealousy of Jewish enterprise in commerce, finance and administration. As many *conversos* panicked and took flight, the Pope tried to reassert his ultimate authority by insisting on a right of appeal to Rome, but he was in no position to quarrel with the Catholic Kings because he desperately needed their support against the French in Italy.

The Inquisition remained, therefore, the servant of the crown. It had jurisdiction over all Christians, lay and clerical (with the exception of bishops), in matters of heresy, and there was no appeal from its verdicts. Those found guilty of heresy were fined, imprisoned, or burnt at public ceremonies (*Autos de Fé*). Ferdinand deliberately extended the operation of the Inquisition to Aragon, despite opposition, particularly from the towns, whose economic life was badly disrupted through the flight of Jews and *conversos*. There is no reason to doubt Ferdinand's zeal for the catholic faith, but the Inquisition also had the major political advantage of being the only royal institution that operated throughout Spain as a whole. There was a further incentive to the encouragement of its work from the fact that property confiscated by the Inquisition passed into the hands of the crown. The culmination of the Inquisition's pressure came in 1492, when Ferdinand and Isabella ordered all Jews to be converted or go into exile. The majority chose exile, and Spanish economic life never really recovered from this exodus of so many enterprising people. The Catholic Kings, although they were warned of the effects, regarded damage to the economy as a price worth paying to rid their kingdom of religious impurity.

The significance of the Inquisition and of the long struggle with the Pope to win control over ecclesiastical appointments is that the Spanish monarchy, from the moment of its foundation, identified itself in a particular way with the Spanish church. The rulers of Spain in the sixteenth century were, on the whole, discriminate in their use of ecclesiastical patronage—though Ferdinand was not above occasional acts of nepotism—but to all intents and purposes they were as powerful in ecclesiastical matters as the kings of France, even though they had no formal Concordat with the Pope. Catholicism and national interests were so closely interwoven in Spain that it soon became all but impossible to distinguish one from the other. The Pope might be head of the Church, but he ruled in Spain only by permission of the crown.

The year 1492 also saw the triumphant conclusion of the long process of reconquest, when Granada was captured and the last Moorish kingdom in the peninsula came under Christian control. The Moors were given generous terms. They were allowed to keep their own laws, customs and religion, in much the same way as the other constituent kingdoms of the Spanish monarchy, and the first Archbishop of Granada was a scholar with a genuine interest in Arabic culture, who believed in a gradual process of conversion and absorption of the Moors.

Isabella, however, was impatient, and turned to Ximenes, who used swifter methods of forcible conversions and mass baptisms. This sudden change of treatment, especially when it involved an attack on their entire way of life, goaded the Moors into rebellion in 1499. The revolt was put down and the Moors, like the Jews before them, were given the choice of conversion or exile. The choice was merely theoretical for the majority of Moors, since they were too rooted in Granada, and usually too poor, to contemplate exile. They became reluctant Christians, and were thereby brought within the competence of the Inquisition. Yet the Moors remained an unassimilated element in Spanish society, despite attempts to incorporate them. In 1508, for instance, they were forbidden to wear their traditional dress and use their time-honoured customs, but such a decree could not be enforced in the face of widespread and stubborn passive resistance. The problem of the Moors was not solved during the lifetimes of Ferdinand and Isabella.

Cardinal Ximenes carried the crusade against the Moors into the enemy's home territory by mounting a major campaign in North Africa—for which the Pope had granted a special tax, the *Cruzada*, some years earlier. In 1505 Mers el Kebir was captured, and in 1509 Oran fell to the Spaniards. It is conceivable that a Christian kingdom might have been established in North Africa, but the money and troops required for such an enterprise were more urgently needed elsewhere. A number of Spanish garrisons were left on the North African coast, but the opportunity to give Spain a firm base on the opposite side of the Mediterranean, which would have been of enormous value to her later in the century, was lost.

North Africa had to be abandoned because Ferdinand put Europe first. His main objective in foreign policy during the early years of his reign was to recover the Catalan counties of Cerdagne and Roussillon which had been lost to France in 1462. To this end he made alliances with France's neighbours. That with England was cemented by the marriage of his daughter Catherine to the heir of Henry VII, while the Emperor Maximilian was won over by the offer of another daughter, Joanna, as a bride for his son, Duke Philip of Burgundy. In fact Ferdinand secured the return of the two counties by diplomacy in 1493, as part of the price paid by Charles VIII of France for peace at home while he was away on his Italian expedition. But Ferdinand, as

King of Aragon, was also ruler of Sicily, and had a claim to the king-dom of Naples, which had at one time belonged to the Aragonese ruling house. This brought him up against French ambitions in Italy, and eventually involved him in war (see p. 209).

Isabella died in November 1504. Despite her deep love for her far-from-faithful husband, she had never acknowledged any obligation to bequeath her throne to him, and she showed how little she appreciated the concept of Spanish unity by leaving Castile to her daughter Joanna, Duchess of Burgundy. The kingdom of Spain was preserved by chance. Joanna's husband, Philip, who had assumed the title of King of Castile, died suddenly in September 1506, and Joanna herself, overcome by grief and despair, sank into madness. In 1509 she retired to the castle of Tordesillas, and in the following year the *Cortes* of Castile recognised Ferdinand as governor of the kingdom. This meant that when Ferdi-nand died, in January 1516, he left not only Aragon but also Castile to his grandson, Charles.

The achievement of Ferdinand and Isabella was considerable. They created what was in effect a national Spanish Catholic Church under royal control; they stamped out disorder and reduced the dangerous political power of the aristocracy; they brought the towns as well as the nobility under their sway; and they extended their dominions not only in Spain itself and in Italy but also in the New World which Columbus discovered for them in 1492. They did not, of course, complete everything they started, nor did they work miracles. Spain remained at Ferdinand's death a federation of kingdoms rather than a unitary state; the nobility were still restless; and royal government, although stronger and more efficient than it had been at their accession, needed further remodelling in order to cope with the increasing demands made upon it. Yet, as Macchiavelli wrote of Ferdinand, 'he may almost be termed a new prince, because from a weak king he has become for fame and glory the first king in Christendom'.

Charles I of Spain

The new ruler of Spain, Charles I, did not speak Spanish and had never visited the peninsula. In the eighteen months which passed between his accession and his arrival in Spain, Cardinal Ximenes, now an old man of eighty, continued governing in the tradition of Ferdinand. He lived long enough to be dismissed by Charles but not to meet him nor to see the unfavourable impression made by the new king. Charles was surrounded by his Burgundian advisers, prominent among them Chièvres, and seemed to think that the best thing for Spain was to be placed under Burgundian administrators. The archbishopric of Toledo, left vacant by the death of Ximenes, was given to Chièvres' nephew: another bishopric went to the king's Burgundian tutor, Adrian of Utrecht; while a Fleming was appointed to preside over the meeting of the Castilian *Cortes*. These and similar appointments created widespread discontent among the native Spaniards. The Castilian *Cortes* which met at Valladolid in February 1518 called on Charles to respect the laws of Castile, while the *Cortes* of Aragon refused to recognise him as king until 1519 when they acknowledged him only as joint sovereign with his mother, Joanna the Mad.

Charles's bid for the imperial crown was far from acceptable to his Spanish subjects, who assumed, not without reason, that Spanish interests would be sacrificed to Habsburg ones. By 1520 Charles was impatient to leave for Germany, and summoned the Castilian *Cortes* to meet at Corunna, where his spokesman made a long speech defending the king's acceptance of the imperial crown on the grounds that it would enable him to take the lead in defending the catholic faith which the Spaniards held so dear. Considerable pressure was also put on delegates to vote supply, which they eventually did (though it was never collected). But anger mounted, particularly when Charles sailed from Spain in May 1520, leaving Adrian of Utrecht to act as regent.

The Castilian towns had long resented the erosion of their liberties by pressure from the crown. They disliked the *Corregidors* and they particularly objected to the requirement that their deputies to the *Cortes* should have full and irrevocable authority to vote taxes. They would have preferred a system closer to that which prevailed in the Netherlands, where the towns preserved the right to withhold ratification from any agreement made by their representatives. All this smouldering discontent flared into open rebellion—the Revolt of the *Comuneros*—and delegates from the various communes, meeting at Avila, declared that they would not recognise Adrian as regent. Yet this was not at first a radical movement. The leaders of the revolt usually came from noble families, and the demands of the *Comuneros* were moderate. They wanted the removal of Burgundian councillors, regular meetings of the *Cortes*, and a limit to taxation. Later, they demanded that the *Cortes* should have the right to assemble at will and discuss matters of general interest. There was no question of renouncing their allegiance to Charles: it was his presence in Spain that they wanted more than anything else.

When he heard of the revolt, Charles made it known that the subsidy was not to be collected and that he would not employ foreigners to govern Spain. As proof of his good intentions he appointed two distinguished Spanish aristocrats to act as co-regents with Adrian. By this time the rebels were becoming divided among themselves. The nobles were alarmed by the increasing radicalism of the movement, fearing for their own safety and the preservation of their privileged position if the revolt continued. Since Charles had accepted their demands, they now rallied to the support of the regents, and in April 1521 helped the royal army defeat the rebels at Villalar. In the following October Toledo capitulated, and by the spring of 1522 the Revolt of the *Comuneros* was virtually over.

Meanwhile, in 1519 another revolt, that of the *Germania*, had taken place in Valencia. The *Germania* were gilds of artisans, and although their ostensible aim was independent republican government for Valencia they were in fact engaged in a class struggle against the nobility. Not surprisingly the nobles gave their support to the viceroy of Aragon, who crushed the rebellion in 1521, although it was some years before order was finally restored and a general pardon issued.

Charles returned to Spain in July 1522. Now that he was actually Emperor his prestige had increased, especially after his championship of orthodox catholicism against Luther at the Diet of Worms. He had made some effort to learn Spanish and he had also replaced the unpopular Chièvres by his mother's trusted counsellor, Mercurino Gattinara. In 1523 Charles summoned the Castilian *Cortes* and demanded a vote of supply to cover the expenses of his journey to the Empire. The *Cortes* tried to insist that grievances should first be remedied, but Charles would not hear of this. There was no question now of revolt, and the subsidy was granted. Royal authority in Spain was never again challenged in Charles's reign, and the Emperor himself became increasingly popular as he showed his growing affection for his Spanish kingdom. Charles had been born a Burgundian but he became a Spaniard by choice, and this, more than any formal act of policy, made him loved and respected by his Spanish subjects.

The French Monarchy under Charles VIII and Louis XII

In 1483, when Louis XI's son ascended the throne as Charles VIII, the French monarchy was basking in the prestige that came from its identification with victory over the English in the Hundred Years War. Powerful magnates still presented a challenge to royal authority, but the crown was well placed to meet this threat. The main organ of government was the royal council, and although membership fluctuated according to the wishes of the king, this body included not only the great aristocrats, who held the major offices of state, but also 'experts' of lower birth (but often better education), prominent among them men who had been trained in the law. The supreme court of justice was the *Parlement* of Paris—an offshoot of the medieval royal council and still claiming, by virtue of its ancestry, some say in the formulation of policy—but the king could, if he so wished, remove cases from the *Parlement*, either by transferring them to a tribunal called the *Grand Conseil*, which was more amenable to royal pressure, or by appointing special commissioners.

This overlapping of institutions was typical of sixteenth-century France, since administrative reform was usually carried out by creating new offices while leaving the old ones intact. The financial organisation was particularly complex, since although France was nominally one kingdom, the various provinces clung to their traditional rights and privileges. The major tax was the *Taille*, levied annually—though not from the Church, the nobles, and those members of the Third Estate (roughly speaking, the prosperous but non-noble sections of society) who had bought exemption from it. In theory the *Taille* was voted by the Estates General, and when this representative body assembled in 1484, to make provision for the reign of the new king, it duly voted supply. But in practice the level of the *Taille* was fixed by the royal council and divided out among the various regions. The only check on royal capacity—though an effective one—was that demands for money must not be so great as to arouse serious opposition. Other taxes were the *Aides*, levied on the sale of specified articles; the *Gabelle*, levied on salt; and Customs, which were charged not only at the ports but also at some provincial boundaries. Lack of coherence and uniformity was a feature of all these taxes.

The French monarchy was to become the epitome of absolutism in the late seventeenth century, but this was far from being the case in the early years of the sixteenth. It is true that the Estates General did not

meet for a long period after 1484, but many provinces had their own
Estates (and were called, for this reason, *Pays d'Etats*). Some of these
provincial Estates retained control over taxation, and the financial
needs of the crown, particularly after the Italian wars broke out, make
frequent meetings necessary. It is also true that the French kings
possessed the largest standing army in western Europe, but while this
was an invaluable instrument of foreign policy it could not be used
with any real effectiveness to enforce the king's will at home. It consisted mainly of cavalry, and was recruited from the French nobility,
who would hardly have agreed to act against their own interests. For
infantry the king had to rely on Swiss and German mercenaries, and
the cost of these was so considerable that even the great wealth of the
French monarchy could not sustain it for more than a few years at a
time. Like Spain, the Empire and Italy, France was a jigsaw of local
and personal privileges and immunities, enshrined in laws which the
king generally observed, although in matters that closely concerned
the crown he would sometimes override them.

Charles VIII was only thirteen when he became king in 1483, and
the government was in the hands of a regent, his sister, Anne of
Beaujeu. After the strong rule of Louis XI the magnates were in a
restive mood, and Anne had to face an aristocratic rebellion led by the
Duke of Brittany and supported by foreign powers. She managed to
suppress this, but was faced with an even more serious challenge in
1488 when, on the death of the Duke of Brittany, his daughter and
heir, also called Anne, accepted an offer of marriage from Maximilian,
King of the Romans. Since Maximilian already controlled the Netherlands, and was almost certain to become Emperor himself in due course,
the addition of Brittany to his territories would leave France dangerously hemmed in. The regent therefore invaded Brittany and forced
the duchess to take Charles VIII as her husband. By this bold but
successful stroke the great duchy of Brittany was ultimately incorporated into the possessions of the crown of France.

By the time Charles VIII came of age, order had been restored to his
kingdom, the nobles had been pacified—for a time, at least—and he
could therefore afford to indulge his private dreams. Charles was an
extraordinary creature. The Venetian ambassador described him as
'small and ill-formed in person, with an ugly face, large lustreless eyes
which seem to be short-sighted, an enormous aquiline nose and thick
lips which are continually open. He stutters, and has a nervous twitching of the hands which is unpleasant to watch.' Charles was an avid

reader of chivalric romances and saw himself as the last crusader, whose duty it was to drive the Turks out of Christendom and be crowned king in Jerusalem. He had some claim to the former crusader kingdom of Jerusalem, through his descent from the house of Anjou. More immediately he had a claim to Naples, since the Aragonese dynasty which ruled there had only come to power in 1442 by driving out the Angevin rulers, who were of French origin. Naples could be a useful base for the descent on the Turks, and Charles determined to assert his remote claim to it, particularly when an invitation to do so came to him from the ruler of Milan. This combination of crusading idealism, desire for glory, and childish fantasy, was the origin of the Italian wars which were to destroy the independence of Italy and involve France and Spain in a struggle that lasted for a century and a half.

Charles was succeeded by his cousin, Louis XII, who had been among the leaders of the aristocratic revolt during Charles's minority, but had later joined the king in his Italian campaign. Louis had good bourgeois qualities. He was economical, he kept the *Taille* at a standard rate in order to ease the burden on the poor, he improved the administration of justice and encouraged the process of codifying the various provincial laws. Louis's moderation won for him the popular title of 'Father of his People', and foreign observers commented on the ready obedience his subjects yielded him. Yet it was during Louis's reign that the practice of levying the *Taille* without even the formality of consultation became established, and although he kept taxes low he did so only by raising loans and mortgaging the royal domain to an extent which seriously burdened his successors. Louis's need for money arose from his determination to renew the war in Italy, and he was abetted in this by his chief adviser Georges d'Amboise, Archbishop of Rouen. Amboise was a French Wolsey, and had similar ambitions—among them, possibly, the papal tiara itself.

Louis's Italian involvement led to nothing but expense and frustration, and while he was fully occupied south of the Alps his enemies attacked him at home. Henry VIII struck into north-west France from the English stronghold of Calais, while Spanish troops occupied the southern part of Navarre, the Pyrenean kingdom which was ruled over by a junior branch of the French royal house. Louis was saved not by his own exertions but by dissension among his enemies. It was Anglo-Spanish disagreements that made it possible for him to reach an 'honourable' peace, even though he had to leave Ferdinand in possession of southern Navarre. Louis died in 1515, having accomplished remarkably little, yet the monarchy was still popular, and the nobles, now that they had an outlet for their ambitions and energies in the Italian peninsula, were generally quiescent. This, then, was the situation which the new king, Francis I, found awaiting him.

Francis, aged twenty-one, was the *beau idéal* of a Renaissance prince: handsome, a lover of learning, a great patron of the arts, a builder on a magnificent scale, and a devotee of his own glory. It was in pursuit of glory that Francis set out for Italy in August 1515, with the flower of the French nobility in his army. Unlike his predecessors he was victorious and established French mastery over the northern part of the peninsula. Spain was in no position to challenge French supremacy, for in 1516 Ferdinand died and his successor, Charles, needed a period of peace in which to establish his authority. Italy was therefore given a breathing space, and the conflict between France and Spain shifted to Germany, where a new Emperor was to be elected in 1519. Francis made it known that he was a candidate, and bribed on a lavish scale. But Charles could count not only on sentiment but also—and far more important—on the Fuggers, the greatest banking house in Europe. It was Charles, therefore, and not Francis, who was elected to the imperial throne. The Franco-Spanish rivalry had now become merged into a dynastic struggle between Valois and Habsburg, in which the cards seemed to be heavily stacked in favour of Charles V.

The Struggle for Italy

When Ludovico, *Il Moro*, called on France for assistance against Naples in 1494 he may have been thinking in terms of diplomatic support, no doubt accompanied by threats of intervention. What he sparked off, however, was intervention itself, for Charles VIII was only waiting for a suitable opportunity to seize Naples as a base for his projected crusade. In 1494, therefore, Charles set out for Italy at the head of a magnificent army of some 30,000 men. At this critical moment the Italian states were crippled by disunity. Venice, for instance, refused to join Naples in fighting the invader, and although Piero de' Medici offered help from Florence, the citizens drove him out and called on Savonarola to save them. Savonarola, who had foretold the coming of Charles VIII as a man sent by God to cleanse the Roman Church of its foul corruption, went out to welcome the 'liberator'; but it was not long before the licentiousness and brutality of the French soldiers had made them so unpopular with the Florentines that Savonarola had to beg Charles to continue his journey.

Charles did so, and on the last day of December 1494, he arrived in Rome, where his army took two hours to pass in procession and finished by torchlight. There was some talk among the French cardinals of fulfilling Savonarola's vision by deposing the simonaical Pope (Alexander VI, Borgia), but Charles was primarily concerned with securing a safe passage to Naples, and therefore accepted the Pope's protestations of friendship. The journey southwards from Rome was a promenade. As the great French army moved ever closer to his dominions King Alfonso abdicated in favour of his young son Ferrandino, and in February 1495 Charles entered Naples unopposed.

At first the French were welcomed, but the honeymoon period was of short duration. Neapolitan nobles resented the way in which Charles appointed Frenchmen to high offices, while the people as a whole were embittered at the heavy taxation which they had to pay to maintain an army of occupation whose licentiousness, arrogance and brutality made it unbearable. Young King Ferrandino was in exile in Sicily, where he was supported by Spanish money and Spanish troops commanded by Gonzalo de Cordoba, who had led the Christian forces in the final and victorious stage of their struggle against the Moors in Granada. Ferdinand of Spain also built up the League of Venice against France. Among its adherents were the Emperor Maximilian (who had some claim to be overlord of Milan): Venice (now awake to the fact that France offered a real threat to her own independence); and the Pope. Milan also joined the League, since Ludovico had become duke himself, following the death of his nephew, and felt his security endangered by the continuing French presence in the peninsula.

Charles realised that if he lingered in Naples he would be trapped. He therefore set out for France, leaving an occupation force behind him, and had entered the southern part of the duchy of Milan before he found his way blocked by League forces at Fornovo. Here, in 1495, a short but savage fight took place in which the French suffered heavy losses but broke through to the mountain passes and safety. The French garrison left behind in Naples did not last long. The troops were decimated by a new scourge, syphilis, and under constant Spanish attack. By the spring of 1496 they had capitulated, and Ferrandino was back in his kingdom (where he died shortly afterwards).

This first French invasion of Italy was a comparatively brief affair, but it was of considerable significance. It showed that the rich and artistic city states of the peninsula were ripe peaches ready for picking. It marked the virtual end of Italian liberty, since France could only be expelled by calling in another outside power, Spain. And, most far-reaching of all, it brought into the open the latent opposition of interests between France and Spain that was to be the dominant theme of a great part of the history of Europe in the ensuing two centuries.

Without the French to protect them the Florentines were at the mercy of the League of Venice, and the Pope thundered excommunications against Savonarola—who continued to denounce the profligacy and luxury of the papal court. A number of leading citizens were alarmed by the evidence of Florence's isolation, and after news came of the death of Charles VIII they seized Savonarola and handed him over to papal commissioners for trial and subsequent execution.

Farther north, Ludovico seemed well entrenched after the death of Gian Galeazzo in October 1494. The Emperor Maximilian, short of money as always, sold him the ducal title and sent ambassadors formally to invest him with the duchy. Under Ludovico the Milanese court became one of the most brilliant in Italy, and among the many artists summoned to work there was Leonardo da Vinci. But Ludovico's position weakened after the accession to the French throne of Louis XII, for Louis's grandmother had been a Visconti, and he therefore had some claim to Milan itself. The renewal of French interest in the peninsula was welcomed by Pope Alexander VI, for purely personal reasons. His great ambition was to establish his son, Cesare, as temporal ruler in the Papal States, thereby giving the Borgias a base from which they could eventually establish themselves as independent princes. The fact that the territories which Cesare was reconquering in the Romagna belonged of right to the papacy and not to the family of the Pope did not unduly burden the conscience of Alexander. He looked to France for help, and Louis's chief minister, Amboise, was only too willing to offer assistance, in return for a cardinal's hat. A bargain was struck, and Amboise became a cardinal, while Louis had his marriage annulled so that he could take as his second wife the widowed Anne of Brittany, thereby preserving her duchy for France. In return for these concessions Cesare Borgia—the model for Machiavelli's 'Prince'—was made a French duke and married to a French princess. When Louis XII set out for Italy, in 1499, Cesare went with him.

The Italian states showed their lack of unity for the second time. Venice was bought off by Louis's promise that he would extend her

western frontier with territory taken from Milan. Florence welcomed
an end to her isolation. As for Naples, the new king, Federigo, was
duped by Louis's assurance that he had no designs on anywhere other
than Milan. The League of Venice, formed to protect Italian liberty
against 'barbarian' invaders, had collapsed, and the inability of the city
states to unite in defence of their own essential interests had been
strikingly demonstrated.

In October 1499 French troops entered Milan, from which Ludovico
had already fled. The exiled duke's appeal to the Emperor Maximilian
produced little more than expressions of sympathy, but Ludovico
managed to raise an army of Swiss mercenaries—reputed to be the
finest soldiers of their day—and returned in triumph to Milan, where
the citizens were chafing under heavy taxation and the forcible
transfer of some of their territory to Venice. From Milan, Ludovico
went on to seize Novara, but there, in 1500, the French besieged him,
and his Swiss mercenaries, rather than fight their fellow-countrymen
in French pay, deserted him. The Machiavellian methods which had
made *Il Moro's* career so strikingly successful,[1] had failed him at last,
and he spent the remaining years of his life in French captivity.

Louis XII was now Duke of Milan. But the taste of victory had
merely whetted his appetite, and he shifted his attention farther south,
to Naples. He had, however, learnt from his predecessor's mistakes,
and before attempting to intervene in Naples he came to terms with
Ferdinand of Aragon. By the Treaty of Granada, signed in 1500, the
two monarchs confirmed an earlier agreement that France and Spain
should split the Neapolitan kingdom between them. French troops
occupied the northern part, including the city of Naples, while the
Spaniards took possession of the south. It was not long before fighting
broke out over the division of the spoils. At first the French had things
all their own way, but Cordoba eventually overcame them and, at the
beginning of 1504, forced them to capitulate. Ferdinand now added
Naples to his dominions, and the 'Kingdom of the Two Sicilies' was
once again united under Aragonese rule.

Venice and the papacy had both profited from their alliance with
France, but in their private ambitions the Borgias were not so lucky.
With French help Cesare reconquered the Romagna, but on the day

---

[1] Burckhardt said of Ludovico: 'No one would probably have been more
astonished than himself to learn that for the choice of means as well as of ends a
human being is morally responsible.'

his father died, in August 1503, he was ill with malaria and in no position to defend his family interests. The papal tiara went to an enemy of the Borgias, Guiliano della Rovere, who took the title of Julius II, and the territories which Cesare had conquered for himself passed back into the hands of the papacy. Julius, who was a fiery warrior, used these lands as a base from which to extend papal temporal power, but his advance eventually brought him up against Venice. He therefore joined the League of Cambrai, which Louis XII and the Emperor Maximilian had formed for the express purpose of stripping Venice of her mainland possessions. In May 1509 a French army heavily defeated the Venetians at Agnadello, but Venice, with a persistence that was typical of her, refused to give up the struggle, and this gave Julius II time to appreciate that the real threat to papal independence came not from Venice but from France. In 1510, therefore, a *renversement des alliances* took place. Julius formed a Holy League to drive the French once again from the peninsula, and he was joined in this by Venice and also by the Swiss—who had been weaned away from their traditional French alliance by the prospect of becoming a papal militia. In April 1512 an army of the League was defeated in a hard-fought battle at Ravenna, but at this point Maximilian opened the Tyrol passes to the Swiss, who poured down towards Milan. The French, who had lost their commander at Ravenna, withdrew, and when, in the following year, Louis XII attempted to recover Milan his army was crushed by the Swiss at Novara.

The Holy League had apparently accomplished what it set out to do. The French invader had been expelled from the peninsula, and the Italian states had recovered their liberty—except for Naples, which was now firmly annexed to Spain. The restoration of the *status quo* was symbolised by the return of the Sforzas to Milan and the Medicis to Florence in 1512. In the following year another member of the Medici family ascended the papal throne as Leo X. Much of the brilliance of court life came back with the old dynasties, and for a time it seemed as though the period of foreign invasions had been but a brief and unhappy interlude in the brilliant history of Renaissance Italy. In fact it was the restoration of the *status quo* that turned out to be an interlude. The Holy League was no more successful than the League of Venice had been in keeping the Italian states united. In September 1515 Francis I crushed the Swiss infantry (and destroyed the myth of Swiss invincibility) at Marignano, and made himself Duke of Milan. The French were once again the paramount power in northern

Italy, and the Concordat signed shortly afterwards at Bologna implied papal recognition of this fact.

The only threat to French supremacy came from Spain, since Ferdinand was aware that the French claim to Naples could always be revived. But Ferdinand's death in 1516 removed this threat. His heir needed time to establish his position, first in Spain and subsequently in the Empire. Not until 1521 did Charles V take up the challenge which Francis I had thrown down at Marignano. When he did so, however, the liberty of the Italian states quickly disappeared, this time for good.

THIRTEEN

Charles V, Francis I, and the Habsburg–Valois struggle for supremacy

Charles V

The Emperor Charles V was not simply ruler of the Holy Roman Empire. As head of the house of Habsburg he owned great family estates in Austria; as Duke of Burgundy he ruled the Netherlands and Franche-Comté; as King of Spain he was master not only of Aragon and Castile but also of the Balearic Islands, Sardinia, Sicily and southern Italy; and as if this enormous agglomeration of territories was not enough, a number of his less reputable subjects presented him with the mastery of the New World across the Atlantic. It really seemed as though Dante's ideal of a universal monarchy was about to be realised, for as Charles's chief adviser, Gattinara, informed him in 1519, 'God has been merciful to you. He has raised you above all the kings and princes of Christendom to a power such as no sovereign has enjoyed since your ancestor, Charlemagne. He has set you on the path towards a world monarchy, towards uniting all Christendom under a single shepherd.'

Yet although domination of the western world seemed to lie within the bounds of possibility, there is no evidence that Charles was aiming at it. He did not even have any comprehensive policy towards the territories already under his rule. His counsellors might talk of imperial ideals, but Charles himself concentrated on dealing with problems as they arose. He tried to keep Germany united, to counter the spread of heresy, and to hold back the Turks. Meanwhile the empire which he had acquired largely by chance remained a collection of separate entities, each with its own marked identity, linked only by their common allegiance to Charles himself.

Charles was not an impressive figure. He had the typically long Habsburg jaw, he was not particularly intelligent, and he was addicted to heavy eating and drinking. A Venetian ambassador gave the following description of the Emperor in middle age: 'He is of moderate height and has a grave look. His forehead is broad, his eyes blue, with a look of energy, his nose aquiline and a little bent, his lower jaw long and projecting so that his teeth do not meet and one cannot hear the ends of his words distinctly. His front teeth are few and bad. He has a good colour, and a short beard, bristly and white, well-proportioned to his figure.' If Charles had not been born on the steps of a throne it is unlikely that he would ever have carved out an empire for himself. And having been given a great inheritance, he seemed, in practice, to have little idea what to do with it. Yet he cannot be dismissed as a failure. He made a great impression on his contemporaries, and while conscious of the dignity attending his unprecedented authority he also had the capacity to make himself loved. Although he could not keep Germany united or prevent the spread of heresy, he maintained relentless pressure on the papacy and thereby helped open the way to reform of the catholic Church. He did more than any other ruler to check the advance of the Turks, and he left the house of Habsburg in a position from which it was not to be dislodged for many centuries. If he did not transform his inheritance he at least preserved it.

Charles had a council of state with members from the various parts of his empire, but he did not use it for the formulation of policy, relying instead on a small circle of close advisers. Chièvres was among the most important of these until his death in 1521, and he, as befitted a Burgundian noble, was primarily concerned with the defence of the Netherlands by agreements with France and England. Chièvres realised that France, alarmed by the enormous expansion of Habsburg power, would not be content unless she herself were allowed to expand into northern Italy, and it was his agreement to French control of Milan that kept the peace during the period immediately preceding and following the election of Charles as Holy Roman Emperor.

Chièvres' place in Charles's circle of advisers was taken by the Piedmontese, Mercurino Gattinara, who really had an imperial vision and hoped to use the council of state and an imperial treasury as the tools with which to weld Charles's dominions into a unified whole. Far from wishing to compensate France, Gattinara longed to eliminate this dangerous rival, and he was convinced that the key to domination of Christendom lay in Italy, and in particular in Rome. Gattinara was

behind the secret agreement with Pope Leo X in May 1521, as a consequence of which the French were driven out of Milan, and it seemed
as though his ideal of a union between the secular and the spiritual
heads of Christendom was about to be fulfilled in January 1522 when
Charles's former tutor, Adrian of Utrecht, became Pope. Unfortunately Adrian died in 1523 and was succeeded by the Medici Clement
VII, who was more inclined towards France. Seven years of diplomacy
and warfare were needed before Clement finally came to terms with
Charles V and crowned him Emperor, and the year of the coronation
was also the year of Gattinara's death. The idea of a Habsburg empire,
controlling the whole of Christendom, died with him.

There was no imperial chancellor after Gattinara. Charles relied
instead on his secretaries. The French secretariat, responsible for the
northern part of Charles's dominions, was headed by a Burgundian,
Nicholas Perrenot, Lord of Granvelle, and was primarily concerned
with foreign and imperial affairs. The southern area fell within the
domain of Francisco de los Cobos, the Spanish secretary. Cobos came
from a minor gentry family and had worked his way up in the Spanish
secretariat until, under Charles, he became the leading figure in it.
During the Emperor's long absences from Spain, Cobos was the
effective ruler of the kingdom. Yet Charles never became the prisoner
of his ministers, and kept the ultimate responsibility for policy decisions
firmly in his own hands. It was Charles's personal determination to win
back from France the old duchy lands of Burgundy (around Dijon)
that led to the inclusion of a restoration clause in the Treaty of Madrid,
imposed upon Francis I in January 1526 as the price of his freedom.
Even as late as 1548, in the Political Testament which he drew up for
the guidance of his son, Charles urged Philip never to abandon the
claim to 'our country'. It is not without significance that while Gattinara was talking of a world empire, Charles was dreaming of lying
at rest beside his ancestors in the cathedral at Dijon.

For the government of the separate states which constituted his
empire Charles depended on members of his own family, except for
the Italian possessions, which were generally under Spanish viceroys.
In Germany, for instance, his brother Ferdinand was made King of the
Romans and given the hereditary Habsburg possessions; in Spain he
made his son, Philip, regent as soon as the boy came of age; and in the
Netherlands he appointed as his deputy first his aunt, Margaret of
Savoy, and then his sister, Mary of Hungary. These distinguished
figures were the visible embodiments of Habsburg rule, but their power

derived from the Emperor and Charles reserved all major decisions as well as control over appointments for himself. One of the reasons for the absence of any effective imperial administrative institutions in Charles's empire was that he himself was the active head, constantly travelling from one territory to another, receiving reports, issuing orders, and allocating resources. While he lived, his empire was a reality because he made it so, but even before his abdication he had come to recognise that the maintenance of unity between such disparate states was a task beyond the capacity of any one man.

The Netherlands

Among the richest of Charles's dominions were the Netherlands, and after the death of Chièvres in 1521 Charles reverted to the traditional ducal policy of strengthening the organs of central government. In 1531 he set up three councils to aid the regent. The council of state, consisting mainly of nobles, was to advise her on policy, while the council of finance and the secret council (or council of justice), both of them staffed mainly by lawyers, were to supervise the administration of the revenue and the law. While this conciliar organisation was undoubtedly a big step forward in the direction of centralisation, the defenders of local autonomy could look to the Estates General and the provincial Estates. The Estates General as a body had no right to commit the towns and provinces it represented. It listened to the demands of the government, formulated its own grievances, and then reported back to its constituent communities. Not until all these had approved of a tax could it come into effect, and the towns in particular were very reluctant to pay for Charles's policy if they saw no advantage in it for themselves. When, in 1534–35, the regent proposed to the Estates General that there should be a closer federation of the provinces and a fixed scale of contributions to a common fund in case of war, Holland made only a conditional acceptance, while Flanders rejected the scheme altogether.

The more broad-based the government of a town, the more opposed it was to any increase in taxation. Charles realised this, and therefore pursued a deliberate policy of narrowing the franchise. At Tournai, for instance, a charter of 1522 excluded the gilds from any share in the administration, and the same procedure was repeated at Brussels in 1528. Ghent was a more difficult problem to deal with, since social and economic unrest, caused by declining industry and unemployment, found a focus in opposition to taxation. In 1538 Ghent openly rebelled against the demand that it should contribute towards the cost of defending the Netherlands, and the regent appealed to her brother for support. Charles assembled an army, occupied Ghent in February 1539, and put down the revolt with great severity. The privileges of the town were annulled, and government was restricted to an oligarchy.

Generally speaking the Burgundian nobles were contented with Charles's rule. The most important of them were made Stadtholders, or governors, of the separate provinces, and Charles was also liberal in appointments of nobles to the highly prized Order of the Golden Fleece. The nobility also approved of the fact that the vast extent of Charles's empire opened to them possibilities of employment far beyond the narrow confines of the Netherlands; the only aristocratic opposition came from the Duke of Guelders, whose territories strad- dled the frontier between the Netherlands and Germany. With the assistance of French money, and in the name of provincial inde- pendence, Charles of Egmont, Duke of Guelders, terrorised the northern Netherlands. He died undefeated in 1538, but when his successor, Duke William, tried to continue the same policy, Charles was at last goaded into action. In 1543 he took over the duchy by force and annexed Guelderland as the seventeenth province of the Nether- lands.

The long delay before any effective action was taken against the Duke of Guelders was just one example of the ways in which the Netherlands suffered from having a ruler who was not only ane absente but also had other and more pressing commitments. In many respects the aims of Charles and of his Burgundian subjects ran counter to each other. The Netherlands had, for some years at any rate, to bear the main financial burden of Charles's commitment to defend Christen- dom against the Turks and the heretics, and of his antagonism towards France. There was a great deal of truth in the comment made by a Venetian in 1559 that the Netherlands were 'the treasures of the king of Spain—these his mines, these his Indies, which have sustained all the Emperor's enterprises'.

The towns and provinces of the Netherlands would have been prosperous even without an Emperor as their ruler, and sometimes the diplomatic entanglements of Charles's policy operated against their economic interests. To take one example, his support of his brother- in-law, the exiled Christian II of Denmark, led the Danes, in retaliation, to close the Sound to Dutch shipping—much to the advantage of

Lubeck and the Hansa towns which were the commercial rivals of the Netherlanders. Yet although, for the majority of the inhabitants of the Low Countries, Charles's government simply meant heavy taxation, he remained a popular figure. When in October 1555, he appeared before the Estates General at Brussels to announce his abdication, leaning on the shoulder of William of Orange and surrounded by the Knights of the Golden Fleece, the deputies felt not only grief but also a sense of loss. However burdensome Charles's rule had been to his Netherlands' subjects, he could tap deep springs of affection and pride. Only after his abdication, with the accession of the unsympathetic Philip, did the burden come to seem unnecessary and intolerable.

Spain

The most important of all the constituent states of Charles V's empire was undoubtedly Spain, which eventually provided not only most of the troops but also most of the money with which he pursued his aims. He was King of Spain for forty years, although for the greater part of that time he was away from his kingdom. Nevertheless he kept a close watch on Spanish affairs, and throughout his peregrinations he was accompanied by the councils which ruled the constituent kingdoms. The most important of these was the council of Castile, composed mainly of lesser nobles and lawyers, which acted both as a court of law and an administrative body. Aragon had its own council, consisting of native Aragonese (with the exception of the treasurer, who was usually a Castilian). The council of Aragon was also responsible for the government of Habsburg possessions in Italy until the formation of a separate council of Italy in 1555. With the exception of Castile, which was ruled by a regent, the councils transmitted their orders to the viceroys who were the Emperor's personal representatives in the various kingdoms. Within Spain itself there were the viceroys of Aragon, Catalonia, Valencia and Spanish Navarre; in Italy and the Mediterranean there were viceroys in Sicily, Naples and Sardinia; while the Spanish possessions in the New World were divided between the viceroys of New Spain and Peru.

Charles had at his disposal in Spain a number of other councils whose competence was not confined to a particular area. The most senior of these was the council of state, consisting of great magnates and officials, but its functions were mainly honorific and he rarely consulted it. Closely linked with the council of state was the council of war, remodelled in 1522; but perhaps the most important was the council of finance, established in 1523. There was also the council of the Inquisition, and the council which controlled the considerable property and wealth of the three military orders. The existence of so many councils inevitably entailed a great deal of overlapping and caused confusion and delays. There would have been even more confusion had it not been for Charles's secretaries, who acted as links between him and the councils and kept the complex system running reasonably smoothly. In the process certain secretaries increased enormously in importance, becoming, in effect, secretaries of state. Cobos, for instance, was one of the principal members of the council of finance and was also appointed to most of the other councils. He was therefore well placed to co-ordinate their activities, and in the course of doing so he cemented his own power and made himself virtually indispensable to his imperial master.

After the suppression of the Revolt of the *Comuneros* Charles had little trouble with the *Cortes*, and the principle was established that the voting of supply must precede redress of grievances. With the money produced by taxation Charles raised a national army, particularly strong in infantry, whose organisation and tactics were worked out by Cordoba. Yet although Spain provided many thousands of soldiers for the Emperor she could not satisfy his insatiable demands. Mercenary troops had therefore to be hired in Germany and the Netherlands, and money was essential if these men were to be kept reasonably loyal and disciplined. The consequence for Spain, as for the Netherlands, was increasing taxation, but the *Cortes* of Castile was far weaker than the Burgundian Estates General and could make no more than a token resistance to the unceasing demands for money. Not until the very end of Charles's reign did the inflow of silver from the New World ease the pressure; during the 1530s and 1540s it was Castile which bore the main burden of financing his operations, taking over the responsibility from the Netherlands, where the limits of taxative capacity had already been reached.

The major source of revenue from Castile was the *Alcabala*, nominally a sales tax, although it had in fact been turned into a lump sum payment to which every town and village contributed a fixed quota. There were, in addition, subsidies voted by the *Cortes*, whom Charles summoned on at least fifteen occasions, and the revenue from the military orders. The total income of the government from Castile increased by 50 per cent during Charles's reign, and it was mainly the poorer classes who paid. In 1538 he summoned the Castilian *Cortes* to Toledo and asked the nobles to agree to a new tax, on foodstuffs, which should apply to all sections of the population. But the nobles refused, and simply advised him to modify his foreign policy in such a way as to reduce his need for money. The advice was no doubt sound, but in practice it meant that the Spanish nobles, despite their enormous wealth, were refusing to make any contribution towards the costs of government. Charles was forced to rely on occasional benevolences from his richer subjects, and from the sale of *Juros*—interest-bearing loans which had first call on future revenues and therefore solved the crown's immediate financial problems at the expense of its future financial stability. Meanwhile, as Philip told his father in 1545, 'the common people who have to pay the subsidies are reduced to such distress and misery that many of them walk naked'.

Francis I

The major obstacle to the establishment of a Habsburg hegemony over Europe was Francis I, King of France, who was determined not simply to defend his inheritance but also to strengthen and extend it. His major achievement at home was to bring the Church, the *Parlement*, and the great feudatories under royal control, at the same time as he elevated the dignity of the crown. The title of 'Majesty', previously reserved for the Emperor, was applied by Francis I to himself, and he was the centre of a brilliant court, which was constantly on the move— from Paris to Fontainebleau, for instance, or to one of the châteaux he built along the river Loire. The reinforcement of royal authority at home would have been of little value, however, if it had been accompanied by a diminution of France's status abroad, and Francis was acutely conscious of the threat of encirclement by Habsburg power in Spain, the Netherlands and Italy. If he was unscrupulous in the means he used to oppose this, allying at one moment with the Pope, at another with the German protestants, and at all times with the Ottoman Turks, this was because he desperately needed assistance. It seemed on occasions as though only the determination of the French king stood between Charles and the attainment of that world monarchy which Gattinara had proclaimed.

Francis I was determined to assert the principle that all secular power within France derived ultimately from the king. He had therefore to overcome the opposition of the *Parlement*, which stood for the preservation of established laws and customs and was unwilling to concede the king in practice the unlimited authority that was his in theory. A major clash came over the registration of the Concordat of Bologna, since the *Parlement* claimed that the king had no right to part with the liberties of the French church. Francis' anger burst out in 1518 when he told a delegation from the *Parlement* 'that there was only one king in France, and that he would take good care that there should never arise a Venetian senate within his kingdom'. His defeat and capture at Pavia meant a set-back to the gradual advance of royal power, since the *Parlement* took advantage of his absence to reassert its ancient right to advise on policy. But when he returned from captivity in 1526 he took up the struggle once again. The *Parlement* did not give way easily. As its president informed Francis in 1527, 'we know well that you are above the laws and that neither laws nor ordinances can constrain you. Yet, you . . . should not wish to do everything that lies within your power, but only that which is good and just'. Francis replied with an edict forbidding the *Parlement* to interfere in matters of state or to modify royal decrees, and requiring it in future to petition the crown every year for confirmation of its authority. The *Parlement* had therefore failed in its bid to play a political role, but although Francis held it in check for the rest of his reign it still occupied an honoured place among French institutions and had not abandoned its high claims.

The great fiefs were a more difficult problem to deal with, since these were states within states. Among the greatest of them was the vast territory in central France which belonged to Charles, Duke of Bourbon. The duke, who was head of the junior branch of the house of Bourbon, had married the heiress of the elder branch, but when she died without issue in 1521 Francis claimed that her lands escheated to the crown. Bourbon, highly embittered by what seemed to him to be naked robbery, opened secret negotiations with the Emperor and agreed to lead a rebellion against Francis I. The plot miscarried, Bourbon had to flee, and his estates were confiscated by the crown. Francis was forced to return these by the terms of the Treaty of Madrid, but in 1527 Bourbon was killed leading the assault of the imperial army upon Rome, and the Bourbon inheritance was finally incorporated into the domain of the French royal house. In 1525 the crown also absorbed the fief of Alençon, while two years later a royal marriage prepared the way for the incorporation of the Albret property. The lands of the Duke of Brittany had already been added to those of France by marriage, but not until 1532 was the duchy of Brittany formally and irrevocably united to the crown of France.

France, like the dominions of Charles V, had to bear the cost of prolonged war, and found this increasingly exhausting. Francis was reluctant to increase the *Taille*, since this might lead to rebellion, but he had many other means of raising revenue at his disposal. He sold off some of the lands belonging to the crown; he collected clerical tenths with such frequency that they became a regular part of the royal income; he sold titles and offices; and he borrowed huge sums both from his own subjects and foreign bankers. All these expedients, however, served only to conceal the fact that the revenue of the French crown was not equal to the enormous and increasing demands made upon it. Francis and his kingdom both needed peace, but in fact they were committed to an exhausting struggle against Habsburg power.

The Italian Wars, 1516–30

When, in 1516, Charles became King of Spain, he needed time in which to visit his new kingdom and freedom from diplomatic entanglements. He therefore came to terms with Francis I and, by the Treaty of Noyon, bound himself not only to restore southern Navarre (which his grandfather, Ferdinand, had seized) but also to marry the French king's infant daughter. Charles may have intended to honour his commitments, but once in Spain he realised that the restoration of Navarre would cause deep resentment and he therefore took refuge in procrastination. By the time the Revolt of the *Comuneros* broke out, in 1521, Navarre had still not been restored, so Francis decided to capitalise on Charles's domestic difficulties by sending French troops across the Pyrenees. These captured Pampluna—after a siege in which Ignatius Loyola, helping to defend the city, was wounded—but in June were driven back into France.

This campaign, which confirmed Spain in her possession of the greater part of Navarre, marked the reopening of Habsburg–Valois conflict after several years of peace. Even without the dispute over Navarre there was little chance of avoiding war. Apart from the natural rivalry between two young, proud and ambitious monarchs, there were other problems to which force seemed the only answer. Francis, encircled by Habsburg territory, was determined to maintain his bridgehead in Milan: Charles, on the other hand, needed to secure the vital link between his southern and northern dominions, which ran through Italy into Germany and also, via Franche-Comté, to the Netherlands. Milan, which dominated the entry to the Alpine passes, was the key which could open this route to Charles, and he resolved to wrest it from France. In May 1521 he came to a secret agreement with Pope Leo X, who promised to support his policy and crown him Holy Roman Emperor in return for imperial protection for the papacy and the Medici family. The agreement was to be sealed by a joint attack upon Milan, and in November 1521 imperial troops occupied the city and drove out the French defenders. Early the following year, Lautrec, the French commander, tried to recover the initiative. He struck down towards Milan from the north-east, but the Swiss mercenaries on whom he depended were short of money and eager for a swift conclusion to the campaign. They pushed Lautrec into attacking a strong imperial position at Bicocca, near Monza, and thereby precipitated their own defeat. Lautrec had to retreat into France, leaving Milan in the hands of the Emperor.

The grand coalition (including England) which Charles V had built up against France received an unexpected access of strength in late 1522 when the Duke of Bourbon opened secret negotiations with the Emperor. Plans were drawn up for joint operations against France, and were put into effect during the summer of 1523. Bourbon made a thrust into eastern France aiming at Dijon; Spanish troops struck into southern France across the Pyrenees; while an English army, breaking out from Calais, advanced swiftly towards Paris. For a moment it looked as though this triple blow might be too much for the French king. But winter, mutual distrust, and the lack of any effective co-ordination blunted the allied effort, and the armies returned to their bases. The following year saw Bourbon launch an invasion of Provence which at first made rapid progress but then bogged down in the siege of Marseilles. The city could not be completely cut off because Genoese ships, under the command of Andrea Doria, held the sea routes open for their French ally. Bourbon had therefore to raise the siege and beat a long retreat into Italy. The French army, following him up, appeared once again before Milan.

This challenge to imperial domination of northern Italy was short-lived. On 24 February 1525, which happened to be Charles's birthday, the French army was crushingly defeated at Pavia, due south of Milan, and Francis himself was taken prisoner. The victory was so complete that Charles could dictate the terms of a settlement. If Francis agreed to accept these, thereby acknowledging Habsburg supremacy in Europe, he would be restored to his kingdom. If not, he would remain a prisoner in Spain. Francis understood the position perfectly. Having made a private protestation that promises extorted under duress were of no validity, he signed the Treaty of Madrid, which was the price of his freedom. In this he promised to restore the old duchy of Burgundy (around Dijon) to Charles, to renounce all French ambitions in Italy and to abandon his inherited claim to suzerainty over Flanders, Artois and Tournai. He also agreed to restore the Duke of Bourbon to all his French lands, and to join with the Emperor in a crusade against the Turks. Having committed himself to these terms, which he had no intention of observing, Francis was released and returned to his kingdom, leaving his children behind him as hostages.

In the Treaty of Madrid Charles displayed his power rather than his generosity, and all those who feared Habsburg domination promptly allied with Francis. In the years that followed, Charles frequently showed his bitterness against the French king who had broken solemn promises and continued to thwart imperial plans for the protection and peace of Christendom. But the power structure of Europe was not to be determined by the outcome of a single battle, and Francis' continued opposition to Habsburg plans sprang from more than personal pride and love of mischief-making. For Charles and his advisers Habsburg predominance in the western world seemed to be one of the basic facts of life. Francis was chief among those who, by refusing to accept this, showed that it was not a fact but simply a situation that could be altered.

Even before Francis returned to his kingdom the enemies of the Emperor were drawing together, and in May 1526 the League of Cognac was formed, with the Pope, France, Venice, Florence and Milan as members. Clement VII owed his election to Charles, but he had no wish, at this stage, to become an imperial chaplain, and he resented the pressure which Charles was putting on him to summon a general council of the Church. Clement believed that general councils were a threat to papal authority; he was also a Medici prince, who wished to preserve as much as possible of the independence of Italy.

Charles appealed to his brother Ferdinand and the Diet for assistance against his enemies, and the German princes, anxious to demonstrate that differences over religion had not undermined their attachment to the Emperor, raised an army and sent it south, across the Alps, in 1527. Among the soldiers were many Lutherans, who openly boasted that they came with hempen halters to hang the cardinals and a silken one for the Pope himself. As if religious bigotry were not enough, the troops were also unpaid and mutinous as they advanced on Rome. In May the eternal city was taken by storm and the imperial troops sacked, raped, plundered and pillaged for a whole week. The Pope only escaped by fleeing to the castle of San Angelo, where in June, after some semblance of order had been restored, he surrendered to the imperial commander.

The news that the troops of the Holy Roman Emperor were sacking the capital of the Christian world caused a revulsion of which Charles's enemies were swift to take advantage, and early in 1528 France and England formally declared war on him. Once again a French army appeared in the plains of Lombardy, but having failed to capture Milan it turned south to reassert the old Angevin claim to Naples. For a time it looked as though the military parade of Charles VIII was about to repeat itself. The French reached Naples, laid siege to the city, and waited for it to capitulate. They were confident that no supplies could reach it by sea because Doria was blocking the approaches. But Doria was short of money and dissatisfied with French promises. Charles offered not only to subsidise him but also to recognise Genoese independence, and Doria therefore took his ships, and with them command of the sea, over to the Emperor's side. This transformed the situation, since imperial reinforcements could now be sent in from Sicily and Spain. The French had to raise their siege and retreat the whole length of the peninsula, fighting as they went. In June 1529 they were defeated at Landriano, not far from the scene of Francis I's victory at Marignano, and the Emperor was once again master of Italy.

It was time for a European settlement, for the Turks were almost at the gates of Vienna and heresy was spreading beyond the frontiers of Germany. Francis was far from reconciled to defeat, but the events of the two years since his return to France had served merely to confirm the verdict of Pavia, and he was now ready to negotiate. In August 1529 the Peace of Cambrai was signed between the two enemies. This time Charles formally renounced any claim to the old duchy lands of Burgundy, and in return Francis abandoned any pretensions to French suzerainty over Flanders and Artois and also any further French interest in Italy. The intention behind the treaty was that Habsburg–Valois relations should in future be based on friendship rather than fear, and the reconciliation was symbolised by a marriage between Francis and Charles's sister Eleanor, which took place in the following year.

Shortly before the Peace of Cambrai the Emperor and the Pope had come to terms in the Treaty of Barcelona, signed in June 1529. Clement VII accepted the new power pattern in Italy and declared that he had decided 'to become an imperialist and to live and die as such'. The treaty contained the usual commitment to a crusade against the Turk, now more than ever necessary, but said nothing about summoning a general council of the Church, since Clement could still not reconcile himself to so distasteful a prospect. The Pope's family interests were secured by Charles's promise to restore the Medicis to Florence and give them a ducal title.

In August 1529 Charles at last appeared in Italy, arriving by sea at Genoa, and prepared for his coronation. Rome was the obvious place for this, but the situation on the eastern frontiers of the Empire was so serious that Charles could not afford to wait for the necessary preparations to be made. In February 1530, therefore, he was crowned by the Pope in the cathedral at Bologna. This ceremony marked the union of the temporal and spiritual heads of Christendom which was so dear to Charles's heart. It was also—though Charles, of course, was not to know this—the last occasion on which the Holy Roman Emperor would be crowned by the Pope.

The Italian Wars, 1530–59

Charles assumed that having made peace with France and the Pope he could devote himself to those two major problems, heresy and the Turks. Yet neither of these could be solved at all easily, and as the years passed it became increasingly apparent that the treaties of Barcelona and Cambrai had settled nothing. Francis was still suspicious of Habsburg power and still intriguing with Charles's enemies. As for Clement VII, he avoided any openly anti-imperial commitment but made his pro-French sympathies clear by going to Marseilles in 1533 for the wedding of his niece, Catherine de Medici, to Francis' son Henry, Duke of Orleans (the future Henry II). When, in late 1535, the last Sforza claimant to Milan died, Charles formally took possession of the duchy, but Francis declared that this was an infringement of his own rights. To show that he would not simply be ignored, Francis sent his troops into the duchy of Savoy, which was an imperial satellite, occupied Turin, and prepared once again to strike down towards Milan. Charles riposted with an invasion of Provence, but this was no more successful than the earlier campaign—led by Bourbon—had been. Charles was understandably bitter at the way in which his plans were being constantly frustrated. He even challenged Francis to personal combat, in which Milan and the old duchy lands of Burgundy should be the prizes. But such gestures only served to show that a stalemate in fact existed and that there was nothing Charles could do to resolve the situation. In 1538, therefore, he met Francis I at Aigues-Mortes, just outside Nice, and agreed to a ten-year truce. Nothing specific was said about Milan, but the two rulers declared their intention to unite against the Turks and the protestants, those twin menaces to catholic Europe.

For some months the newfound friendship of Habsburg and Valois burgeoned, and when, in the winter of 1538–39, Charles needed to get from Spain to the Netherlands in order to put down the rebellion at Ghent, Francis I invited him to go via France, and fêted him *en route*. In 1540, however, Charles formally invested his son, Philip, with the duchy of Milan, and this roused the anger of Francis, who had not abandoned all hope of one day recovering it. A favourable opportunity seemed to present itself in 1542. Charles was still recovering from the failure of his expedition to Algiers in the previous year (see p. 312), and Francis therefore ordered his armies to take the offensive. The French were at first successful. In the south-east the town of Nice, one of the few possessions remaining to the Duke of Savoy, was taken, while on the Netherlands frontier the fortress of Luxembourg was captured in August 1542. Francis was thinking in terms of a grand alliance against the Emperor, in which the Lutherans, the Pope and the Turks should somehow all be linked, but the inherent contradictions of such a scheme stifled it at birth: the Pope, for instance, was as horrified as the German protestants at the news that Francis had invited the Turkish fleet to make its western headquarters in Toulon! Charles acted with uncharacteristic speed and determination, and in 1544 joined with Henry VIII in an invasion of France that carried him within striking distance of Paris. Francis' only consolation came from the fact that his troops had defeated an imperial army at Ceresole in Piedmont, but his resources were too strained for him to follow this up with an attack on Milan. Both sides were, in fact, close to exhaustion, and in September 1544 they concluded peace at Crépy. Francis once more renounced any claims to suzerainty over Flanders and Artois. He also promised to stop his aid to the German protestants and to support Charles in demanding that the Pope should summon a general council of the Church.

The fruits of this treaty were seen in Charles's campaign in Germany, which led to the defeat of the protestant princes at Muhlberg. The leaders of the Schmalkaldic League had appealed to France for help, but Francis died in March 1547, and the new king, Henry II, needed time to establish himself. By 1551, however, he was ready for action, and responded to the feelers put out by Maurice of Saxony. In January 1552 terms were formalised in the Treaty of Chambord. Henry, claiming to be the 'Defender of German Liberty', agreed to assist the princes in their campaign against the Emperor. In return he was to be given effective sovereignty over the three imperial bishoprics of Metz, Toul and Verdun.

Henry set out on his 'German journey' in the spring of 1552, but having occupied the three bishoprics he seemed reluctant to press on across the Rhine and therefore returned, somewhat ingloriously, to France. Before the end of the year Charles had laid siege to Metz, but the French garrison, led by Francis, Duke of Guise, fought a skilful defensive campaign which forced the Emperor to withdraw, without taking the town, in January 1553.

The shifting of the main area of Habsburg–Valois conflict from Italy to the Netherlands was a sign that the centre of gravity of European politics was moving westwards. By the 1550s Gattinara's old idea of a world empire under Habsburg rule was stone dead, and even the more limited vision of European hegemony had given way before the realities of power. Charles had found that the effort of keeping Spain, the Netherlands, Germany and Italy all under the same central government was too great; he had also come to realise that the southern and western sections of his empire had one set of interests and preoccupations, while Germany and the Habsburg lands in Austria had another. He therefore planned to leave Germany and eastern Europe to his brother's family, while his own son, Philip, should inherit Spain, Italy, the Netherlands and the New World. The chances of consolidating Habsburg power in western Europe became even more favourable when, in 1553, Mary Tudor ascended the throne of England. Her self-appointed task was to restore her kingdom to the catholic faith, and for this she needed the support of the greatest catholic family in Christendom. Negotiations were therefore opened for a marriage between Mary and Philip, and the wedding took place in July 1554. With English sea power to guard the Channel route, Spanish communications with the Netherlands would be assured, and France would be effectively encircled. Having apparently secured the future of his dynasty, Charles could now begin the long-drawn-out process of abdicating his many titles and dignities.

Henry II made one more attempt to re-establish French influence in Italy. In December 1555 the new Pope, Paul IV, who was fanatically anti-Spanish, opened secret negotiations with the French monarch and offered to transfer the kingdom of Naples to Henry's son. Once more a French army—this time commanded by Francis of Guise, the hero of Metz—crossed the Alps and advanced towards Naples. But Guise and his troops were not given time to complete their assignment. Philip II, the new Habsburg ruler in the west, was determined to use his concentration of power to cripple his family's old enemy. In June 1557 England declared war on France, and in the following August a Spanish army struck south from the Netherlands. Guise and his troops were hastily called back to meet this new threat, but they were too late to prevent disaster. The French army, under Constable Montmorency, was routed at the battle of Saint Quentin, and Montmorency himself was taken prisoner. The way to Paris was now open, and it seemed as though nothing could check the Spanish advance. Fortunately for Henry, however, the long strain of war had taken its toll, and Philip's resources were virtually exhausted. Spain simply could not afford another major campaign, and so the victory of Saint Quentin was not exploited. Guise even managed to recover prestige for France by capturing Calais from the English in January 1558, and he went on from there to the Netherlands frontier, where his successes made it possible for Henry to negotiate peace on terms of equality.

In April 1559 negotiations were at long last concluded at Cateau-Cambrésis. France kept Calais and the three imperial bishoprics of Metz, Toul and Verdun, but she gave up Savoy and Piedmont and finally abandoned any claim to a foothold in Italy. The bitter conflict, dragging on for nearly half a century, had done little more than confirm the *status quo*, yet in the process it had consumed the wealth of two of the richest monarchies in Europe. Spain was kept going only by the influx of precious metals from the New World. France had no such windfall, and the huge burden of public debt, as well as the strain of taxation, weakened the authority of the monarchy and prepared the ground for civil war. In Italy the prosperity and independence upon which the brilliant civilisation of the Renaissance had been based, had been brought to an abrupt end, and only Venice, now the home of the arts, remained unconquered. In south-eastern Europe the Turks had taken advantage of Christian disunity to strike into Hungary and

Austria; they had also extended their naval power into the western Mediterranean. As for the hope expressed by Erasmus and the Christian Humanists, that the resources and energies of the rulers of Christendom would be concentrated on the reform of the catholic Church, this had vanished in the smoke of the battlefields, and heresy, having taken a firm hold on Germany and northern Europe, was now spreading in its most virulent form into France and the Netherlands. This was the heavy toll levied by Habsburg and Valois conflict on the whole of Europe.

FOURTEEN

The Revolt of the Netherlands

Philip II and the Burgundian Magnates

The Netherlands were notoriously difficult to rule, since the population of about three million people was distributed among some three hundred cities, each of which was a focus of local patriotism. Charles V had tried to centralise the government of the Netherlands, but he had had to tread warily because he wished to retain his subjects' loyalty and persuade them to make a substantial contribution towards the financing of his foreign policy. In a country that was in some respects a federation of cities the personality of the ruler was of great significance, for it was virtually the only unifying force. Even in language the Netherlands were divided, since the ten northern provinces spoke Dutch while the six southern Walloon provinces were French-speaking; the remaining province, Flanders, was split between the two linguistic groups. Philip, unfortunately, could speak neither French nor Dutch, and since he was not by birth a Burgundian he could not appeal to the affections of his Netherlands' subjects as Charles had done. Nor did he go out of his way to win their trust and love. He had spent the four years prior to his father's abdication in the Netherlands, but he made little impression on the people, and his cold manner contrasted unfavourably with the warmth of Charles. In August 1559 Philip returned to Spain and never again set foot outside his kingdom. His Netherlands' subjects were aware of their ruler only through the orders that came from him, and they felt increasingly alienated from a distant government that offered them nothing but high taxation and religious persecution.

Although Philip obviously had little love either for the Low Countries or their inhabitants, he was determined to hold on to them. For one thing he regarded his inheritance as a trust from God, which must not be parted with; and, for another, the Low Countries were rich, and he needed all the money he could lay his hands on. Antwerp, in particular, was essential to the financial mechanism of the Habsburg dominions, for it was the centre from which the bullion of the New World was distributed throughout the old, and its financiers had acquired an expertise in raising loans and manipulating exchanges which Philip could not afford to dispense with.

In addition to the problems raised by intense local pride, linguistic differences, and fluctuations in the economy, there was the increasing danger of religious heterodoxy. Charles V had taken a firm stand against the spread of heretical doctrines into his Burgundian territories, and although the severity of his edicts had offended the nobles and bourgeoisie, whose attitude to religion was moderate and Erasmian, they had generally supported him against the Anabaptists, whose rejection of secular authority they abhorred. In the 1540s, however, Calvinism began infiltrating into the Low Countries from Geneva and Strasburg, and by the mid-1550s had reached Antwerp. With the coming of peace in 1559 the frontier between France and the Netherlands was opened, and Huguenot missionaries spread their faith not only along the lower classes but also, and more significantly, among the lesser nobles and urban oligarchs who were the virtual rulers of Netherlands' society. In 1561 the Walloon ministers of the Calvinist congregations drew up a confession of faith, modelled on that of the Huguenot church, and by 1566 Calvinist organisation, with its headquarters at Antwerp, embraced the whole of the southern Netherlands. It had mass support in the textile manufacturing areas—Ghent, for instance—and it operated simultaneously at all levels of society in a way that had not been true of Anabaptism or Lutheranism. While its impact was most marked on the southern provinces, the northern ones were affected by the community which John à Lasco had established at Emden, just outside the Netherlands' border. In short, despite the severe punishments prescribed for heresy and the campaign waged against it by the Netherlands' Inquisition, Calvinism was spreading rapidly.

Philip was determined to crush heresy, firstly because he detested it and secondly because it implied a challenge to royal power which he would not tolerate. He was also aware that by strengthening his authority in the sphere of religion he would reinforce it in secular matters, thereby taking a big step towards his goal, which was the transformation of the

Netherlands into a unified and centralised state under the direct control of the Spanish crown. At first he moved circumspectly and continued his father's policy of associating the Burgundian magnates with royal rule by appointing them as Stadtholders (provincial governors). Count Egmont, for instance, was made Stadtholder of Flanders and Artois, while William of Orange was appointed to govern Holland, Zeeland and Utrecht. Magnate influence could be of great value to the king in his dealings with the Estates General, as was shown in 1558. Philip had demanded a nine-year subsidy, but delegates were most unwilling to commit themselves to such a large amount and only did so, reluctantly, after Egmont and William had used all their powers of persuasion. Even then they made their grant conditional on Philip's readiness to receive a remonstrance setting out the liberties of the Netherlands. The king resented such bargaining, but he needed the money and therefore accepted these terms. He also agreed to the recall of the Spanish troops, after William and Egmont had persuaded him of the necessity of such a gesture, and by the beginning of 1561 this had been carried out.

When Philip quitted the Netherlands in August 1559, never to return, he left Margaret of Parma, the illegitimate daughter of Charles V, as regent. Margaret was advised by the council of state, on which the great magnates and leading officials were represented, but the reins of power were really in the hands of the council's president, Anthony Perrenot, lord of Granvelle. There was little to be said against Granvelle as a person. He was the son of Charles V's minister, a Burgundian by birth, and a charming, cultivated man of Erasmian tendencies in religion. But because he was Philip's mouthpiece he became identified with the programme of religious orthodoxy and political absolutism which Philip had decreed. The magnates, who realised that they were being bypassed, made Granvelle the focus of their anger and pressed for his dismissal.

The Burgundian magnates were in general men of great wealth, proud of their ancient lineage and inclined to regard the Spaniards as upstarts. They were often connected by blood or marriage with noble houses in Germany or France, and frequently held lands outside the frontiers of the Netherlands. Greatest of all the magnates was William of Orange. He owned vast estates in Brabant, Luxembourg, Flanders and Franche-Comté, and had also inherited the tiny principality of Orange, in France. He was therefore a sovereign ruler in his own right. William had been brought up at the ducal court in Brussels and was a favourite of both the Emperor Charles V and the regent, Mary of

Hungary. In his country house at Breda he lived in great magnificence, but although he thought of himself as a Burgundian he kept up his German connections, and in 1561 he took as his second wife—much to the disapproval of Philip II—the daughter of Maurice, the Lutheran Elector of Saxony who had chased Charles V out of Germany. Among William's friends in the Burgundian nobility was Count Egmont, a jovial soldier who had helped win the great victory at St Quentin and who believed, no less strongly than William, that the rule of the *parvenu* Granvelle should be brought to an end. This attitude was shared even by those who were not William's friends. Chief among these was the Duke of Aerschot, whose wealth was second only to William's and who regarded the magnificence of the Prince of Orange as an affront to his own dignity. The nobles, in short, even though they were not a homogeneous group, were determined to regain some of their former political power. There was nothing consciously revolutionary about their attitude, and they were socially conservative. But they regarded Philip as a dangerous innovator who was riding rough-shod over the 'liberties of the Netherlands' liberties which they identified with their own interests.

Hostility to Granvelle became more intense when a scheme was announced in 1559 to create three new archbishoprics and fourteen new bishoprics for the Netherlands. This would free the Low Countries from subordination to German sees, which had hitherto overlapped into the Netherlands, and would give them, for the first time, an autonomous ecclesiastical organisation. But however desirable this might appear, it could also be the prelude to the creation of a centra-lised secular administration. Such a prospect did not appeal to the Burgundian nobles, nor did they approve of the transfer of patronage over these new sees from cathedral chapters to the crown. Previously they had used the Church as a useful refuge for their younger sons, but this avenue would now be closed to them. Resentment extended out-side the gilded circle of the aristocracy. The bourgeoisie who con-trolled the towns saw the significance of the fact that these new bishops would strengthen royal power in the Estates General. As for the com-mon people, they feared an intensification of religious persecution and were easily persuaded that Philip was about to introduce the Spanish Inquisition. He had, in fact, no intention of doing so, if only for the reason that the Netherlands' Inquisition was in some ways more rigorous than its Spanish counterpart; but fear of the Spanish Inquisition was bound up with fear of Spain and its ruler. Popular opposition to the new bishops was so intense that they had to be given armed guards, and in the eastern part of the country they were unable to take possession of their sees.

Granvelle had not prompted the new scheme but he profited by it, since he was made a cardinal and became the first primate of the Netherlands. Margaret was alarmed by the news which reached her of widespread unrest and made a bid for magnate support by summoning an assembly of the Knights of the Golden Fleece. When this took place, in June 1562, the knights made full use of their right of free speech to criticise Granvelle's administration, and advised the regent to summon the Estates General. At the same time they sent one of their own number to Philip with a request that he would reconsider his policy.

Philip replied with kind words but gave no indication of a change of heart. William therefore decided to bring the challenge to Granvelle into the open. When the Estates General met he became the virtual leader of the opposition, and in March 1563 William, Egmont, and Count Horn—the crusty old Admiral of the Netherlands—formally demanded the dismissal of Granvelle. When this was not forthcoming they resigned from the council of state. This was a blow to the regent, for in the absence of Spanish troops she could not hope to maintain order without magnate support. Philip, who was heavily committed to a naval campaign in the Mediterranean, was anxious to avoid further trouble in the Netherlands. He therefore authorised Margaret to make concessions. She complied with the magnates' demands by dismissing Granvelle from office in 1564 and promising to rule with the council of state, on condition that William and his associates returned to it.

The 'Compromise' and the Calvinists

The magnates had gained nearly all they wanted, but the religious problem had not been solved. Most of the great nobles were conventional Roman Catholics of Erasmian inclination, who objected to religious persecution on the grounds that it created disorder and thereby threatened to shake the foundations of the society which they dominated. Among the lesser nobles, however, Calvinism had made considerable inroads, and their hatred of Roman Catholicism gave them the leadership of a patriotic resistance movement. This was all the more dangerous in that the early stages of the religious wars in France had shown how effective a challenge to royal government could be mounted by an aristocratic-Calvinist combination. The success of the Huguenots, however, owed much to the complacent lethargy of the established Church in France. Philip had no time for such lukewarm catholicism, and was determined to expose his Netherlands' territories to the intense fervour of the revivified Roman Church. He did this by encouraging the Jesuits to begin missionary work in the Low Countries, creating a catholic university at Douai, and issuing strict instructions that the decrees of the Council of Trent were to be put into full operation. This seemed like a return to the oppressive policy associated with Granvelle, and the magnates on the council of state particularly resented the fact that they had not been consulted. They felt it incumbent upon them to try once again to persuade Philip to reconsider his policy. As William declared in a discussion in the council of state towards the end of 1564, 'the king errs if he thinks the Netherlands, surrounded as they are by countries where religious freedom is permitted, can indefinitely support these sanguinary edicts. However strongly I am attached to the catholic religion I cannot approve of princes attempting to rule the consciences of their subjects and wanting to rob them of the liberty of faith.'

The council decided to send Egmont to Philip to state their case. Egmont was warmly received, but his pleasure at this turned to anger and disgust when he returned to the Netherlands, only to find that Philip had instructed the regent not to depart from the policy of repression. William, Egmont and Horn once again withdrew from the council of state, but it was not clear what further action they could take. Egmont and Horn were both loyal subjects of the king and anxious not to do anything that might be construed as treacherous. As for William, he felt that the time was not yet ripe for an open challenge, and he was out of sympathy with the more extreme elements among the lesser nobility. These were men who, unlike him, had little to lose from rebellion. They were mainly small landowners, hard hit by the price rise and unable to recoup their losses (as the magnates did) through service to the state. Religious radicalism came naturally to them, and they looked to William's brother, Louis of Nassau, for a lead.

While William and the other magnates were holding back, the initiative passed to these lesser nobles—not all of them Calvinist, by any means—who in 1565 formed a league called the 'Compromise'. The aim of the Compromise was to persuade Philip to abolish the Inquisition and relax or withdraw the edicts ordering the enforcement of the Trent decrees. Louis and his fellow noble, Count Brederode, were behind the plan to set out their demands in a petition to the regent. They appealed to the magnates for support, but while William was ready Egmont and Horn held back. In April 1566, therefore, Brederode formally presented the petition to Margaret. Less than half of the Compromise's four or five hundred members had ridden in to Brussels to support Brederode, and one of Margaret's advisers, contemptuous of such an undisciplined job, commented 'Quoi, madame! Peur de ces gueux!'[1] The name of 'gueux', or 'beggars', stuck, and the petitioners gloried in it. Brederode and his followers left Brussels with begging-bowls ostentatiously dangling from their necks, and rode in triumph to Antwerp, where unemployment had combined with religious dissent to create an explosive situation.

Margaret realised that unless she made some concessions to the Compromise she might be faced with a major rebellion. She therefore gave orders that the religious decrees should be interpreted in a moderate manner—which amounted, in fact, to virtual suspension. She also asked the magnates to return to the council of state. The situation was already getting out of hand. In many places the Calvinists had come into the open and were holding services under the protection of armed men—a state of affairs that had an ominous parallel in France. In July 1566 the radical wing of the Compromise agreed to co-operate with the Calvinists. Their basic interests were far from identical, since the lesser nobles—many of whom were still catholics —were primarily interested in recovering their social and economic status, whereas the Calvinists were determined to gain religious toleration as a prelude to the establishment of the Calvinist faith throughout the Netherlands. Nevertheless the short-term objective was the same— namely to put such pressure on Philip's government that its oppressive rule would be relaxed.

The magnates did not necessarily welcome such developments. When William went to Antwerp in July 1566, at the special request of the regent, he showed his displeasure at the rapturous reception given him by the discontented populace. He had no wish to fragment the Netherlands, to divide the rich from the poor or the protestants from the catholics, and he regarded the Calvinist leaders and their allies among the lesser nobles as dangerous hotheads who, by their lack of caution, would destroy the chances of increased political liberty. He

---

[1] 'What, madam! Afraid of these beggars!'

showed his own attitude by setting on foot a programme of public works to remove the economic causes of unrest and by ostentatiously going to mass, in an attempt to calm the fears of the catholics.

Economic unrest was not confined to Antwerp. War in the Baltic had interrupted the flow of grain from that area, and prices throughout the Netherlands were rapidly rising, particularly after the bad harvest of 1565. Near-starvation hit the urban proletariat hardest, and they were ready to vent their anger in any way that offered itself. They did not need the Calvinists to tell them that the Church was rich while they were desperately poor, and in August 1566 their rage boiled over in the 'Iconoclastic Riots'. An English resident of Antwerp told how the mobs poured into the streets and began ransacking churches, chapels and monasteries, smashing every image they could lay their hands on. 'Coming into our Lady Church it looked like hell: there were above 1,000 torches burning, and such a noise! as if Heaven and Earth had gone down together, with falling of images and beating down of costly works.' These iconoclastic riots spread to other towns, and it made no difference whether the Calvinist ministers joined the mobs or tried to restrain them—everywhere churches were stripped of their ornaments and images trampled into fragments. This was a revolt of the common people, and although it was concentrated on the churches it could easily turn against property in general. Not only the magnates but many of the lesser nobles as well were appalled by the fury they had unleashed, and rallied to the defence of the status quo.

Margaret hastily came to terms with the leaders of the Compromise, and in August 1566 they agreed to lay down their arms and not to interfere with catholic worship as long as protestant preachers were allowed to continue their work in those places where they had already established a foothold. This 'Accord' was duly enforced by the magnates in their capacity as Stadtholders, and at Antwerp, for instance, William drove out the Calvinists from the churches they had taken over and persuaded them to build their own conventicles. The outburst of violence was, in fact, shortlived, and order was quickly restored as grain prices fell. But it brought about a catholic-conservative reaction, especially in the Walloon provinces, and it made all property-owners think twice before allowing themselves to be drawn into movements of religious or political dissent.

Margaret took advantage of this swing in public opinion to try to restore the authority of her government. She had already written to Philip, asking him to send troops, and had also despatched agents to hire mercenaries in Germany. It soon became clear that she regarded the 'Accord' as an agreement extorted from her under duress and one that she was not bound to keep. The attitude of the magnates now became crucial. William was prepared to consider a national uprising, before it was too late, and he invited Egmont and Horn to a conference with him and his brother Louis. Egmont, however, believed in Philip's good faith, and all William's arguments could not shake him from this conviction. 'Alas, Count Egmont,' said the disappointed William, 'you and your like are building the bridge for the Spaniards to cross over into our country.'

William could easily have put himself at the head of a protestant revolt, but although he recognised that the Calvinists shared his passion for the independence of the Netherlands he realised that they were a divisive force. He was also aware of the fact that revolutions need money, arms and supplies, and that the Calvinist congregations, despite their assurances, were unable to provide these on the necessary scale. Across the border in Germany, however, were Lutheran princes who might well be willing to help a movement of revolt that had protestant undertones—as long as these were not Calvinist. In short, by uniting with the Calvinists William would have forfeited not only the support of the catholic majority in the Netherlands but also of his friends and relatives in Germany, and this was far too high a price to pay.

Failing William, the leadership of the Calvinist resistance passed to Brederode, who raised an army and marched into Zeeland in March 1567. Margaret, who was increasingly distrustful of the magnates, had demanded that they should take a new oath of loyalty to the king. Aerschot and the conservatives had done so without hesitation; Egmont pondered for some time, but eventually took the oath; William, however, refused. He did not trust Philip, and his sympathies were with those who opposed Spanish rule. Yet he would still not commit himself to the Calvinist rebels. Brederode and his followers, who had gathered in the open country outside Antwerp, were therefore left unsupported and were easily crushed by Margaret's army of mercenaries. Brederode himself fled to Germany. He was followed by William, who knew that his lack of open involvement would not save him from a revengeful government. Hundreds of lesser men also went into exile rather than face the days of repression which, they were convinced, were about to return.

If the magnates, the lesser nobility, the Calvinist congregations and the urban proletariat had all combined, Spanish rule might well have been overthrown, but the fundamental differences of aim and attitude between these groups could not simply be submerged in a national uprising. William was untypical in his willingness to subordinate all other considerations to the overriding principles of political liberty. By trying to keep the disparate elements of resistance united he had succeeded only in making himself universally distrusted.

William the Silent and the Sea Beggars

Had Spanish rule been marked, during William's exile, by moderation and tolerance of religious dissent, the embers of revolt might well have burnt out. But Philip had determined to assert his own authority in the most effective manner before it was too late. At his orders the Duke of Alva had assembled an army of some nine thousand men in Milan, and by August 1567 he was in the Netherlands, with secret orders to 'make all the states into one kingdom, with Brussels its capital'. The 'liberties' of the various towns and provinces were to be curtailed, religious uniformity was to be imposed, and the Netherlands were to be made to contribute a full share to the enormous cost of Philip's policies.

Alva began with a reign of terror. The magnates thought themselves safe because of their membership of the Order of the Golden Fleece, but no privileges were allowed to prevail against the royal will, and Egmont and Horn were committed to prison. All over the country the leaders or potential leaders of resistance were swept into the Spanish net. A special tribunal, the 'Council of Troubles', was set up to deal with cases of religious and political dissent, and soon acquired the appropriate nickname of the 'Council of Blood'. Most of the nobles were allowed to go free after they had signed their submission, but there was no mercy for the ruling oligarchs of the towns, and in January 1568 over eighty leading citizens were publicly executed in Brussels. In that same month Philip wrote to Alva: 'the towns must be punished for their rebelliousness with the loss of their privileges; a goodly sum must be squeezed out of private persons; a permanent tax obtained from the Estates of the country. It would therefore be unsuitable to proclaim a pardon at this juncture. Everyone must be made to live in constant fear.'

While Spanish troops held the Netherlands in their iron grip it seemed that the only hope of salvation must come from outside. In February 1568 Brederode had died, leaving William as the unchallenged leader of the resistance movement. Still hoping to play down religious differences and combine all opposition elements into one, William published his *Justification* in April 1568. In this he asserted his loyalty to Philip, heaped all the blame on evil counsellors, and called for a united front against Alva. To spur his fellow-countrymen into resistance he planned a three-pronged attack on Spanish forces, in which his brother Louis and the Huguenots were to take part. Louis had some success in the northern province of Groningen, but the other invasions collapsed before they had even got under way. Alva was therefore free to move north to deal with Louis, but before he did so he decided to give a warning to those who might be thinking of taking advantage of his absence. On Whitsunday 1568 Egmont and Horn were led out on to a scaffold in the market-place in Brussels and publicly executed. Alva had shown beyond any possibility of doubt that resistance to the royal will, even from men who had never wavered in their loyalty to the crown, would not be tolerated.

William's spring campaign had failed, and Louis, defeated by Alva, had to fall back into Germany. In October 1568 William himself led a force of mercenaries deep into Brabant and linked up with a small Huguenot detachment. But there was little popular support for him—a sign that Alva's policy of terror was beginning to pay dividends—and he had to make a humiliating retreat into France. Alva had good reason to write to Philip that 'we may regard the Prince of Orange as a dead man'.

Meanwhile the reign of terror continued in the Netherlands. Between 1567 and 1573 the Council of Blood condemned over 9,000 people, of whom more than a thousand suffered death or exile. The exodus of refugees was so great that it began to affect the economy of the country, but this did not alter Alva's determination to make the royal government financially secure. To do this he needed a source of income which should be outside the control of the Estates General, and he therefore summoned this body in March 1569 and demanded approval of a permanent ten per cent sales tax on the Spanish model. The Estates General was cowed into agreement, but in the country at large there was widespread opposition to this 'Tenth Penny'. The Estates of Utrecht refused to ratify the grant and were promptly summoned before the Council of Blood. There they were found guilty of neglecting their duties during the iconoclastic outbreak, and their privileges were annulled. Yet despite this calculated warning, opposition to the new tax continued to mount. Even Alva had to recognise that force alone could not ensure the smooth working of this complex fiscal measure, and he therefore postponed its introduction. It is doubtful, in fact, whether it ever came into operation.

William and Louis spent the greater part of 1569 fighting alongside the protestants in France and it was the Huguenot leader, Coligny, who suggested that William should take under his protection the refugees from the northern provinces of the Netherlands who had organised themselves into a pirate force under the name of the 'Sea Beggars'. As sovereign prince of Orange William issued letters of marque to the Beggars, authorising them to prey on Spanish shipping. In return he could hope for a share of the money they made from captured prizes. Until this time William's attention had been concentrated on the southern Netherlands, even though he was Stadtholder of Holland and Zeeland. Religious dissent was at its strongest in southern towns such as Antwerp, Ghent and Ypres, but the Spanish stranglehold was much tighter there than in the north, where the inlets and harbours of the coasts of Holland and Zeeland could not easily be policed. It was William's growing appreciation of this fact that persuaded him to ally with the Sea Beggars, and by so doing he began the gradual shift of emphasis from south to north that was to lead, not to independence for the Netherlands, but to the creation of a new state.

The Sea Beggars were accustomed to using the ports of south-east England as a refuge and springboard. In 1572, however, Elizabeth, afraid of being dragged into war with Spain, ordered them to leave her territory. The Beggar fleet of some twenty-five ships, with eight hundred fighting-men on board, put to sea, but was driven by a spring storm to take shelter in the port of Brill, in Holland. Their commander intended simply to plunder the town and sail away, but he found that the Spanish garrison had been sent to Utrecht, to suppress riots, and that Brill was undefended. He therefore took possession of the town in the name of the Prince of Orange, and sent word of his action to La Rochelle. When Louis, who was at La Rochelle, heard this news he immediately sailed with the rest of the Beggar fleet and seized the port of Flushing. Success proved infectious, and one after another the towns of the northern provinces opened their gates to the Beggars.

When William realised that the Beggars' action had set off a major revolt in the north, he made another attempt to raise rebellion in the south. While his brother Louis led a Huguenot force which occupied Mons, William struck into Brabant and Flanders. But there was still no sign of popular enthusiasm for his cause and once again he had to retreat across the frontier. It was at this moment of disillusion that he decided to disband his army and place himself at the head of the liberation movement in Holland and Zeeland.

William had no love for the Sea Beggars. They were mainly Calvinists and iconoclasts, fanatical in their faith and ruthless in propagating it. The urban oligarchs, or 'regents', who ruled the towns did not welcome these 'liberators' whose yoke threatened to be far more burdensome than that of the Spaniards; and where the magistrates were really determined—as in Middelburg and Amsterdam—they could fight off the Beggar threat, at least for a time. But oligarchic rule was not unchallenged. While the wealthier citizens and the catholic clergy feared the Beggars, there were many elements among the lower classes who had nothing to gain from the preservation of the existing social order and were more than ready for change. These elements by themselves would have been able to accomplish little or nothing, but when they linked up with the rebel forces outside the towns they could often overthrow the oligarchs, or at least force them to admit the Beggars.

Support for the rebels was not confined to religious and social radicals, however. Resentment against the Spaniards, and particularly against the proposed 'Tenth Penny', had increased to such a point that even good Roman Catholics were prepared to join the struggle for freedom. The Beggars played up to this patriotic sentiment, and often won over the catholic majority by promising to leave them free to worship as they wished. As the Beggars' hold became more secure, however, their policy became more ruthless. Churches were plundered, clergy slaughtered, and catholic magistrates expelled from office and replaced by Calvinist ones. As for freedom of worship, this was applied only to Calvinists; not simply catholics but Lutherans and Anabaptists also were forced to go underground. Calvinism, in short, far from being a natural growth in the northern provinces, was imposed on them by a ruthless and determined minority, and even as late as 1587 the Calvinists constituted a mere ten per cent of the population of Holland. What they lacked in numbers, however, they more than made up for by singleness of purpose and total commitment. William, still hoping for a united Netherlands whose freedom should be based on religious toleration, tried to restrain the Beggars, and in January 1573 dismissed their leader from his command. But he could not ignore the increasingly obvious fact that the Calvinists were the only successful revolutionaries. In April 1573, therefore, William took the politically significant step of joining the Calvinist church.

The Netherlands United and Divided

Spanish forces in the Netherlands had been held in check by Huguenot pressure on the southern frontiers. But the Huguenots were weakened and thrown into confusion by the Massacre of St Bartholomew in August 1572 and Alva was able to turn his attention towards the north. At the beginning of 1573 Spanish troops surrounded the town of Haarlem, in Holland, and the magistrates prepared to negotiate. But a popular uprising, under Beggar inspiration, led to the overthrow of the magistrates and the proclamation of a policy of 'No Surrender'. For seven long months the town held out, but although William realised that its loss would be a heavy blow to his own and the Beggars' prestige he could make no headway against the encircling Spanish troops. In July 1573 Haarlem fell, and it looked as though resistance in the northern provinces would collapse.

However, the situation was not so hopeless as it seemed. Philip II, caught up in a fierce struggle against the Turks in the Mediterranean, found the strain of simultaneous operations on two fronts more than his finances could bear. Spanish troops in the Netherlands were left without pay and promptly mutinied. They marched on Antwerp, pillaging as they went, and refused to fight until their arrears had been settled. This gave William's forces a valuable breathing-space, but by early 1574 Philip had somehow found money to pay his rebellious troops, who thereupon returned to Holland and laid siege to the important town of Leyden. William did not dare risk another Haarlem. Attempts to raise the siege by a diversionary attack from Germany led only to the death of his brother Louis, but William stood firm and when the magistrates of Leyden began to waver he ordered that they should be replaced by men of stronger fibre. He also persuaded the new leaders to agree to the cutting of the dykes. This was no easy decision, since it would mean letting the sea into the surrounding lowlands, which had been laboriously reclaimed, thereby destroying the livelihood of many peasant farmers. But a desperate situation demanded desperate remedies. The dykes were cut, the sea came flooding in, and the besieging Spanish troops began to sink into the mud. They panicked, raised the siege and beat a swift retreat. William's prestige soared, and popular opinion once again swung behind the resistance movement.

The strength of opposition to Spanish rule had already achieved one major triumph by persuading Philip to recall Alva in November 1573. The new governor-general of the Netherlands was Don Luis de Requesens, whose orders were to reverse Alva's policy of repression. Requesens issued a general pardon and announced the abandonment of the Tenth Penny. On the important question of religion, however, he had nothing to offer, for Philip had declared that he 'would rather lose the Low Countries than reign over them if they ceased to be catholic'. The Calvinists, whose hold on the northern provinces was daily becoming firmer, would not consider any settlement which did not give them at least freedom of worship. When Requesens realised that peace was not possible on terms that would be acceptable to his royal master he prepared to use force. But at this critical juncture, in September 1575, Philip was forced to postpone repayment of his debts. This amounted to a declaration of bankruptcy and it smashed the fragile mechanism of Habsburg credit. Money could not flow across the exchanges, and the Spanish army—which was composed mainly of German and Italian mercenaries who served only for pay—turned from fighting to pillage.

Requesens might have been able to restore order, but in March 1576 he died. Until such time as a new governor could be appointed from Spain, authority devolved on the council of state, which promptly purged itself of pro-Spanish members and summoned the Estates General, including representatives from the rebel provinces of Holland and Zeeland. The Estates decided to raise an army for self-defence, and appointed the Duke of Aerschot as commander. It looked as though unity among the magnates, which had been broken by the Iconoclastic Riots, was about to be restored.

A Netherlands' army was already in existence in the north, and William offered to place this at the disposal of the Estates General as long as satisfactory terms could be agreed. There was a big gap between the two sides. The resistance movement in the north was popular and Calvinist, with socially radical undertones. In the south, on the other hand, it was catholic, aristocratic and conservative. The gap might never have been bridged but for the Spanish army. In November 1576 the mutinous and unpaid soldiers vented their frustration on the city of Antwerp, pillaging and raping the inhabitants and burning down their houses. Some 7,000 citizens were killed and about a third of the town wiped out by troops who were nominally in the Netherlands to protect the inhabitants from rebellion. All hesitation on the part of the

Estates was swept aside by the news of this 'Spanish Fury', and the now united provinces came together in the Pacification of Ghent. The divisive religious issue was put into cold storage by a declaration that the heresy laws should everywhere be suspended until such time as an ecclesiastical settlement was agreed on by the Estates General.

When the new governor-general—Philip II's half-brother, Don John of Austria—arrived in the Netherlands early in 1577, he appreciated the need for conciliatory gestures. In February, therefore, he issued the 'Perpetual Edict', in which he declared his acceptance of the terms of the Pacification of Ghent, and agreed to withdraw Spanish troops from the Netherlands. So far as the aristocratic leaders of the revolt were concerned, this gave them all they wanted; but William did not trust the new governor, and was alarmed by the fact that the Perpetual Edict spoke of restoring the catholic faith throughout the entire country. Such a provision would be entirely unacceptable to Holland and Zeeland, and they determined therefore to keep up their fight against the Spaniards. The fragile union of the provinces might have been broken at this stage had it not been for the impatience of Don John, who suddenly took possession of the citadel of Namur, denounced William as a traitor, and called for a purge of the Estates General. This amounted to a repudiation of the Perpetual Edict and it drove the conservative aristocratic leaders of the south into renewed alliance with William.

This unity was shortlived, for a sudden outbreak of popular revolts in the southern towns revived all the fears of the property-owners. In Brussels a radical 'Council of Eighteen' took control of the city and called on William to assume command. William, when he arrived, was given a hero's welcome, but this merely increased the suspicion of Aerschot and the other conservative magnates. Aerschot withdrew to Ghent, where he rallied the catholic nobles—the 'Malcontents'—around him. Ghent, however, had a Calvinist consistory as well as a radical tradition, and with William's connivance Aerschot was arrested and packed off to exile in Germany. The Calvinists then took over the city and set up a radical council on the Brussels pattern.

It seemed as though the Calvinist takeover of the north was now to be repeated in the south, but if this was the price of independence the Walloon provinces were not prepared to pay it. In January 1579 Artois, Hainault and the Walloon-speaking part of Flanders signed the Union of Arras, by which they swore to uphold the Roman Catholic religion. The northern provinces of Holland, Zeeland, Utrecht and

Gelderland riposted with the Union of Utrecht. William was still hopeful of restoring unity on a *Politique* basis (see p. 267), by subordinating religious issues to political ones, but in fact there was little prospect of reconciling the two extremes.

While Don John was governor-general, suspicion of him acted as a unifying force, but he died in October 1578 and was replaced by Alexander Farnese, Duke of Parma. Parma, the illegitimate son of Margaret, former regent of the Netherlands, was a great soldier and a man of integrity, whose high birth and noble bearing made him acceptable to the conservative aristocrats of the southern provinces. He was also plentifully supplied with money, since Philip had decided, for a time at least, to give the reconquest of the Netherlands priority over all other matters. Parma made it clear that there would be no harsh treatment of any individuals or towns which returned to their allegiance, and in May 1579 he signed the Treaty of Arras with the Walloon provinces, agreeing to recognise and uphold their privileges and to withdraw Spanish troops in return for their acceptance of his authority. There seemed little likelihood of the nobles recovering political power —which had been their original aim—but at least under Parma they could hope to preserve their privileged position in society. William's resistance movement was far too involved with social radicalism to be acceptable to them.

William had still not given up hope of reuniting all the provinces in opposition to Spain, but he realised that he himself had become too committed to one faction to be an effective focus for patriotic feeling. What was needed was a man who could command the support of the catholic majority at the same time as he led an anti-Spanish crusade in which the vanguard would be made up of committed Calvinists. William thought he had found such a figurehead in the Duke of Anjou, brother to the King of France, and in 1581, at a meeting of the Estates General at the Hague, he persuaded thirteen out of the seventeen provinces to throw off their nominal allegiance to Philip and offer it instead to Anjou. But it soon became clear that Anjou—an arrogant and unprincipled adventurer—was a bad choice. He resented the fact that while he was the official embodiment of national, centralised authority all the important decisions were taken by the provincial Estates. It was in an attempt to remedy this and give himself a power base that he used his French troops in a surprise assault upon Antwerp in January 1583. The attack was beaten off and its only effect was to alienate opinion in the Netherlands. As William told Anjou 'the people are now so incensed against you that they openly say they would rather die at the hands of their enemies than be in hazard every day to such dangers as these'. Yet although William had no illusions about Anjou, he saw no substitute for him. He could not conceive of a successful rebellion against the enormous might of Spain without foreign aid, and Anjou still seemed to offer the best hope of this.

The problem of Anjou in fact solved itself, for the duke died suddenly in June 1584. The following month saw the assassination of William. He had been for so long the embodiment of resistance that his death was a heavy blow. As an English observer had written, he was 'a rare man, of great authority, universally beloved, very wise in resolution in all things and void of pretence; and that which is worthy of special praise in him, he is not dismayed with any loss or adversity'. In the early days of the revolt William's removal from the scene might well have proved crippling, but by working in close co-operation with the urban leaders and the provincial Estates he had taught them how to organise themselves. They were now equal to the task of continuing the struggle without him, but as Parma's inexorable advance continued, their need for support from abroad became ever greater. In August 1584 the Spaniards captured Ghent; in March 1585 Brussels surrendered; and in August came the biggest blow of all, the fall of Antwerp. Resistance was now virtually confined to Holland, Zeeland and part of Gelderland, and even these might eventually have succumbed but for the protection afforded them by the great rivers and their command of the sea. Shortly after the fall of Antwerp the rebel provinces came to terms with Elizabeth of England, who agreed to provide an army of 4,000 men under the command of her favourite, the Earl of Leicester, on condition that he was appointed governor-general of the provinces.

The Emergence of a New State

Leicester was no more successful than Anjou in resolving the intricate religious and constitutional problems of the rebel provinces. Many of the old ruling families in the towns had been swept out of office by the Sea Beggars and replaced by more committed men. But the new oligarchs, once they had tasted power, soon began to assert their authority and were unwilling to take orders from Calvinist ministers or congregations. The rebel movement was therefore split between the 'Libertinists', or moderate Calvinists, and the 'Precisians', or rigid ones. The

Precisians were socially radical, the Libertinists conservative, and the bitterness of the class struggle was only made more intense by being conceived in religious terms. It is doubtful whether Leicester understood the nature of the conflict, but he became increasingly identified with the Precisians, whose stronghold was Utrecht and who wanted a complete ban on trade with the Spanish enemy. Their motives were not simply patriotic. The carrying trade between the Baltic and Spain, which was dominated by Dutch ships, had continued throughout the years of rebellion, since it was essential to both sides. Amsterdam flourished on it, and the merchant oligarchy which ruled the town had become the great champion of Libertinist attitudes. Without the revenues that came from Dutch commerce it was not clear that the rebellion could be sustained, but the Precisians were untroubled by such mundane considerations, for they hated the Libertinists almost as much as they hated the Spaniards. In April 1586, therefore, they persuaded Leicester to issue a decree banning all trade with the enemy.

The Estates of Holland did not meekly submit to this decree. Since they controlled the purse strings they were in a very powerful position, and they found a spokesman in Jan van Oldenbarneveld, who held the office of Advocate. They could also count on the support of William's son, Maurice of Nassau, and most of the army. Leicester was caught in a web of conflicting interests which tied him hand and foot, and in November 1586 he returned to England. In the following year he made one more attempt to impose his authority as governor-general, but this was no more successful than the first. In 1588, therefore, he resigned his office and left the Dutch to their own devices. English troops remained, however, and Elizabeth continued her financial support.

If Parma could have kept up his military pressure at this particular juncture, when his opponents were so divided, he might have restored Spanish rule over the entire Netherlands. But Philip was planning a major campaign against England, and ordered Parma to keep his troops in readiness to cross the Channel once it had been swept clear by the Armada. The struggle in the Netherlands had by now become simply one part, and not necessarily the most important, in the jigsaw of Spanish policy, and although the Armada was defeated and Parma's troops never landed in England, they were soon called on to intervene in France. After the assassination of Henri III in 1589 Philip saw his chance to win the French throne for himself, or at the very least to establish the pro-catholic, pro-Spanish party in power. In 1590, therefore, Parma was ordered to invade France, in support of the Catholic League, and from then until his death in 1592 he was never able to concentrate his forces against the rebel provinces of the Netherlands.

Meanwhile Maurice reorganised the army of the United Provinces and took the offensive. In 1590 he captured Breda, and in the following year took Zutphen, Deventer and Nymegen. In the opening years of the seventeenth century he struck into Flanders, capturing Ostend and Sluys, and it looked for a time as though all the work of Parma might be undone. But the Spaniards discovered a very able general in the person of Ambrosio Spinola, who recaptured Ostend in 1604, after a long siege, and was shortly afterwards appointed to command all the Spanish forces in the Netherlands. The struggle might have gone on indefinitely had it not been for the financial exhaustion of Spain and the war-weariness on both sides. Yet peace was inconceivable until Spain gave at least *de facto* recognition to the independence of the north, and this she was very reluctant to do.

Such recognition was made easier, however, by the granting of 'home rule' to the southern Netherlands. In 1596 Philip II had appointed his nephew, the Archduke Albert of Austria, as governor-general of the Netherlands, and promised that if he were to marry Philip's daughter, the Infanta Isabella, they would be appointed joint sovereigns of the Low Countries. Philip fulfilled his promise in 1598, shortly before his death, and from then on the 'Archdukes', as they were called, were nominally independent rulers of a state consisting of the southern provinces. In practice they had to keep in line with Spanish policy, since Spanish troops remained in the Netherlands, and it was also agreed that if they were to die without issue their territories would revert to the Spanish crown—as happened in 1621.

The Archdukes became popular in the southern Netherlands, and they made a number of attempts at reconciliation with the united provinces of the north. Religion, however, remained a stumbling-block, since the Archdukes insisted on toleration for Roman Catholics throughout the entire Netherlands—a provision which was quite unacceptable to the Calvinist oligarchs of the north. The ideal of reunion survived, but in fact the Netherlands had split into two distinct states, and every year that passed drew them further and further apart from each other.

In 1606 the Archdukes at last declared their willingness to treat with the United Provinces as an independent state, and in February 1608 Dutch and Spanish delegates began negotiations. Spanish insistence on religious freedom for Roman Catholics in the United Provinces prevented the conclusion of a peace treaty, but in March 1609 the representatives of the two sides agreed to a twelve year truce, which from the point of view of the United Provinces was more significant for what it left out than what it put in. The Dutch were not barred from their lucrative trade with the Spanish empire; they were not obliged to raise their blockade of the Scheldt, the river on which the trade of Antwerp depended; nor were they required to guarantee freedom of worship for Roman Catholics. Whatever reservations the Spaniards might make in theory, in practice they had conceded that the United Provinces were an independent and sovereign state.

This was not what William of Orange had fought for, and indeed it ran counter to the original objective of the revolt, which had been to keep the Netherlands free but united. There was nothing inevitable about the division of the Low Countries and the emergence of a new state out of the northern provinces. Netherlands sentiment remained strong in the south, which would have welcomed reunion if only it could have been brought about on acceptable terms, and there was no great love for the Spaniards. The line of division between the United Provinces and the Spanish Netherlands was dictated as much by military and strategic considerations as political ones. If Spinola could have pushed further north or Maurice further south, the frontier would have reflected this. It did not mark the dividing line between French and Flemish speaking, since this ran much further south, nor did it in effect create modern Holland and Belgium, since a substantial part of the southern Netherlands was in due course to be incorporated into France. The Low Countries, in fact, might never have divided, and the northern provinces—which had the geographical advantage of being furthest removed from the physical presence of Spanish troops—might have kept alive the spirit of resistance in *all* the Netherlands, had it not been for the chance arrival of the Sea Beggars and the consequent imposition of fanatical Calvinist rule. Once the division was established, other considerations, of course, came into play. The merchants of Amsterdam were only too glad of the opportunity to assert their supremacy over Antwerp, while the urban oligarchs of Holland revelled in their freedom from aristocratic control. Also, as time went on, north and south gradually acquired separate identities and made these more pronounced by embracing opposed religious faiths. Yet to contemporaries there was nothing fore-ordained about the emergence of the United Provinces, nor did the new state seem likely to survive. Only time was to show that this unwanted offspring of the struggle for independence was to be a sturdy child, more than capable of holding his own.

FIFTEEN

The French Wars of Religion

The Crown and the Magnates

Henry II of France was in many ways the embodiment of the kingly ideal. Tall and well built, with dark expressive eyes and a noble brow, he restored dignity to a court that, under his father Francis I, had become increasingly notorious for its licentiousness and frivolity. But although Henry looked every inch a king he had acquired a habit of introspection that made him excessively reliant on his subordinates. He saw so clearly the different aspects of every problem that he was frequently unable to make up his mind what course to follow.

The French monarchy appeared to be powerful and deeply rooted, yet it suffered from fundamental weaknesses. Among the most important of these was the inadequate financial basis of the royal government. By English standards the king of France was rich—Henry's income, for instance, was about £1.25 million a year; some five times that of Elizabeth I—but the calculated 'policy of magnificence', which found expression in a luxurious court, lavish entertainments, expensive embassies, and above all in war, cost far more than the crown could raise from its own resources. The gap could not be filled by taxation, even though the *Taille* was regularly levied and its rate increased. The crown had therefore resorted to the sale of offices to those who were anxious to improve their social standing, and this device became so lucrative that in 1531 Francis I set up a special department to deal with it Many new judicial and financial offices were created solely for the purpose of selling them, and in 1568 Charles IX also imposed a tax on the transfer of offices from one person to another. The right to hold a given office thereby became a piece of property, protected by the law, and men who were in theory the king's servants were in practice outside the range of his effective control. This was the significance of Chancellor

L'Hôpital's observation that while the crown appeared to be absolute it was lacking in hands and feet.

Despite heavy direct and indirect taxation the crown could not meet its commitments without borrowing. Big loans were raised from the Customs farmers; the international money market which centred on Lyons was called on to contribute; and a new breed of financiers arose to handle these increasingly complex transactions. By the time Henry II died the crown was heavily in debt, and interest payments ate up a large part of the annual royal revenue. The problem of matching public expenditure to public income was not, of course, unique to France: even Philip II, with all the wealth of America at his disposal, could not avoid bankruptcy. But the poverty of the French crown weakened its effectiveness at the very moment when religious and social tensions were threatening the stability of the state.

Religious tension came from the spread of Calvinism at all levels in French society. By the 1560s about half the French aristocracy had embraced this form of protestantism, and Coligny estimated that there were well over two thousand Huguenot congregations scattered throughout France. In 1561 the Venetian ambassador reported that there was not one single province uncontaminated by heresy, and that if it were not checked it would challenge the established Church and split the state. One of the reasons for the advance of Calvinism was the poor condition of the established Church. Subordinated to the crown by the Concordat of 1516, its higher levels were reserved for the aristocracy, and pluralism, simony and worldliness were endemic. The Cardinal of Lorraine, for instance, who was a member of the powerful Guise family, was Archbishop of Rouen at the age of fourteen, and he later acquired the bishoprics of Metz and Verdun and eleven abbacies. At the other end of the social scale parish priests were often poor and politically radical, and when their discontent fused with that of the peasantry and urban proletariat it created an explosive situation.

The Huguenot church was organised on the lines laid down by Calvin, with ministers, elders and deacons elected by the various congregations. This ecclesiastical hierarchy would have been sufficient in normal circumstances, but the threat of persecution and the hostility of catholics forced the Huguenots to look to their own defence. A military organisation therefore grew up alongside the ecclesiastical, and as the situation became more and more threatening so the military aspect of Huguenotism became increasingly pronounced. From 1560 onwards Calvinist congregations began placing themselves under the protection of nobles who, while they professed the Calvinist faith, were often more concerned with their own factional struggles. The noble would usually be elected to the consistory as an elder of the church, and the minister, who was meant to guide him and the congregation as a whole, might well be a member of his household. Congregations could do little to control these powerful men, on whom their safety depended, and resolutions such as that passed by the synod of La Rochelle in 1581, recommending that 'princes and great lords shall be advised to observe the articles of our discipline' were little more than wishful thinking. Although the Huguenots were compelled, for the sake of survival, to subordinate themselves to aristocratic faction-leaders, they thereby became pawns in the nobles' struggle for political power.

While Henry II was alive the various factions among the nobility could be held in check. His chief adviser was Anne of Montmorency, Constable of France and head of the great house of Montmorency, which was very powerful in the centre and north of France. The Constable's supremacy was deeply resented by the catholic family of Guise, whose power base was in eastern France, and in particular by Francis, Duke of Guise, the conqueror of Calais. Violent quarrels took place between the two men, but Henry, by making clear his affection and trust for both of them, managed to contain their rivalry within the framework of royal government. He shared with Francis of Guise a passion for war and physical exercise, and another of his favourites was Marshal Saint-André, one of the finest soldiers in France.

Henry was only twenty-eight when he came to the throne in 1547, and being a robust man who kept himself very fit there was no reason to assume that his reign would be short. But Henry's passion for martial sports undid both him and his kingdom. In June 1559 he celebrated the signing of peace at Cateau–Cambrésis by holding a tournament in which he took part. During the course of this he received, in the words of an English eye-witness, 'such a counterbuff as drove a splint right over his eye on his right side'. The wound was at first thought to be slight, but Henry did not recover from it. In a few days he was dead. As one historian has commented, 'his life was like the sluice gates damming up a flood. By his death the waters were released.'[1]

[1] N. M. Sutherland, *The French Secretaries of State in the Age of Catherine de Medici*, Athlone Press, 1962, p. 94.

Henry left four sons, the eldest of whom—who now became king as Francis II—was only fifteen years of age. Montmorency's predominance ended with Henry's death, since the new king was married to Mary, Queen of Scots, who persuaded him to put his trust in the Guises, her mother's family. The Guises came from the junior branch of the ducal house of Lorraine and had only become prominent in French life in 1527, when Francis I made Claud of Lorraine a duke and peer of France—an honour hitherto reserved for princes of the blood. Claud's son, Francis, second Duke of Guise, developed into a brilliant soldier and was appointed Lieutenant-General of the kingdom by Henry II. He saw it as his duty to protect France not simply against outside enemies but also against those who were undermining it from within. He detested the Huguenots and in particular the House of Bourbon, which was closely linked with them.

The Bourbons, descended from Saint Louis, were the senior princes of the blood. Anthony of Bourbon, head of the house, was king-consort of Navarre, and had been converted to Calvinism by his wife, the reigning queen of this small state (part of which had been annexed by Spain in the time of Ferdinand). His younger brother, the hunchback Louis, Prince of Condé, was also a protestant, but although he had spent some time in Geneva and openly proclaimed his Calvinist convictions, political ambition rather than religion was his driving force. As a younger son, Condé was of no great significance; but with a Huguenot army behind him he would be a man to be reckoned with. This was the political significance of his claim to be 'Protector-General of the Churches of France'.

While the Guises were identified with Roman Catholicism, and the Bourbons with Calvinism, the Montmorencies were split. The Constable himself was a devout catholic, but his nephews were all Huguenots. Chief among them was Gaspard, Count of Coligny, who in 1552 had been appointed Admiral of France. He had been captured at St Quentin in 1557 and during his two years as a prisoner-of-war had become a convinced Calvinist. He was not personally ambitious, and recognised the need to uphold royal authority, but he was determined that his fellow Huguenots should at least be free to worship as they wished. More level-headed than Condé, Coligny hoped to arrive at a negotiated settlement, but he realised that this would hardly be possible while the king was under the control of the Guises. For this reason he was prepared to join Condé in challenging Guise power.

Catherine de Medici

While the three great noble families were jockeying for position, the defence of the interests of the crown rested largely with Henry II's widow, Catherine de Medici. This gifted and spirited woman was descended, through her father, from the Medici rulers of Florence, and, through her mother, from Saint Louis. During Henry II's lifetime she had kept very much in the background, but now, at the age of forty, she suddenly found herself plunged into the centre of a political whirlpool. She concentrated all her energies on defending the inheritance of her children and trying to restore peace and order. Her task was very difficult, since so much of the authority of the crown had gone with Henry II, but surrounded as she was by men whose loyalty could not be relied on, she showed courage and resourcefulness worthy of her Medici forebears. Yet the strain was enormous, for, as she wrote to her daughter, the Queen of Spain, after the death of Francis II, 'God ... has deprived me of your brother ... and left me with three small children, and in a kingdom utterly divided, in which there is not a soul in whom I can trust at all who has not got some private purpose of his own'.

Catherine had no wish to become the 'prisoner' of the Guises, but she had little choice, for they were the favourites of Francis II and his queen. Condé, however, with the support of the Huguenots, was prepared to challenge them, and he urged his brother, Anthony of Bourbon, to come to court and claim his rightful place as regent of France. Anthony did indeed come to court, but he was too feeble to assert himself and soon returned to Navarre. Condé therefore decided to appeal to force. In early 1560 a plan was drawn up—to which he was party, though he was not the actual author of it—to concentrate armed bands from all over France at the château of Amboise, where the king was resident. The king would be seized, and with him the Guises, who would be killed if they attempted to resist. At this juncture Condé would arrive at court, as if by chance, and on behalf of the entire nation demand the redress of grievances and in particular the expulsion of the Guises. Some Huguenot congregations were involved in the plot, and Condé tried to present himself as the advocate of religious liberty, but his principal aim was to force himself on the king.

By March 1560 the conspirators were ready, but so were their enemies. The armed bands were rounded up before they could strike a blow, and although some of their leaders eventually broke through to

Amboise it was only to be hanged from the battlements of the château or thrown into the Loire that flows beneath it. Nothing daunted, Condé planned another attempt on the same lines. But once again the Guises were forewarned, and they now persuaded the young king that he must take action against this dangerous subject. Francis ordered Anthony of Bourbon to bring his brother to court, and Anthony, as usual, obeyed. Condé was arrested, tried for treason and, in November 1560, sentenced to death. But in December, while Condé was waiting to be executed, Francis II died and the political situation was immediately transformed.

The new king, Charles IX, was a boy of nine, and this time there could be no doubt that a regent would have to be appointed. Anthony of Bourbon returned to court to claim this office, but Catherine put herself forward as a more acceptable alternative. She knew that the Guises would never agree to a Bourbon regency, and in any case, having been freed, as if by a miracle, from the Guise stranglehold, she had no wish to become a Bourbon puppet. She persuaded Anthony to renounce his claim in return for the title of Lieutenant-General of the kingdom and a promise that his brother, Condé, should be pardoned. She also summoned the Estates General to assemble at Orleans in December 1560—their first meeting since 1484. Her aim was a settlement of religious disputes before these erupted into civil war; she also hoped for a substantial subsidy to reduce the crown's debts and thereby strengthen its authority.

When the delegates assembled, however, the representatives of the Third Estate refused to vote any supply and indicated their own solution by pointing out that while the crown was poor, the Church was rich. They also called for *de facto* religious toleration until such time as a national council could decide on a final settlement. Such proposals were, of course, anathema to the French clergy, but Catherine was already thinking along similar lines. Like many Roman Catholics she believed that the Council of Trent, by its rigidity, had destroyed rather than improved the chances of reconciliation among the Christian churches, and she was prepared to consider a national solution, particularly in view of the fact that the Council of Trent was no longer in session. The Pope, of course, was far from welcoming such an initiative, and when he heard of Catherine's proposal he promptly announced that the Council of Trent would be reconvened. But Catherine was reluctant to abandon her idea altogether, and although she stopped talking of a national church council she nevertheless persuaded protestant and catholic representatives to come together at Poissy in September–October 1561 for what was officially described as a 'Colloquy'. She hoped for constructive discussion on details, on lines similar to the colloquies held in Germany under Charles V, but in this she was disappointed. Argument swiftly focused on fundamental questions such as the nature of the sacraments and the authority of the Church, and any prospect of a limited agreement was lost in the great gulf that opened up between the two sides.

Despite the failure of the Colloquy of Poissy, Catherine did not abandon all hope of reconciliation. Although a Roman Catholic herself, she was far from bigoted, was impressed by the advance of Calvinism in France, and recognised the need to come to terms with it. Her attitude was very similar to that later associated with the *Politiques* (see p. 267), in so far as she gave priority to political principles, especially the maintenance and strengthening of royal government. In any case she was tolerant by nature and appreciated the futility of persecution when dealing with persons whose faith went so deep that no amount of torture could possibly root it out. 'When I see these poor people burnt, beaten and tormented', she wrote about the persecution of the Huguenots, 'not for thieving or marauding, but simply for upholding their religious opinions; when I see some of them suffer cheerfully, with a glad heart, I am forced to believe that there is something in this which transcends human understanding.'

As part of her plan to reconcile catholics and protestants in France, Catherine had invited Theodore Beza, rector of the Geneva Academy, to attend the Colloquy of Poissy, and she held long discussions with him at court before the assembly opened. The catholic nobles were alarmed by what seemed to them to be Catherine's increasing commitment to the Huguenot cause, and they may genuinely have believed that she was in danger (from their point of view) of apostasy. Faced with this threat to the old faith, Guise and Montmorency dropped their differences and joined with Marshal Saint-André to form the 'Triumvirate', in the spring of 1561. Their aim was to preserve the established catholic Church, if need be against the crown, and they looked for support from Spain. It was not clear what the Triumvirs could do to enforce their policy, but at the end of the year, seeing that Beza was still enjoying Catherine's hospitality despite the failure of the Colloquy, they ostentatiously withdrew from court. They were joined by Anthony of Bourbon, who still hankered after the regency and was seduced by the Triumvirs' promise to support his wife's claims to

Spanish Navarre. The lines of religious division were already being blurred by aristocratic factionalism.

Catherine recognised that the withdrawal from court of the catholic nobility might well be the prelude to civil war. In a bid to avert this she summoned representatives from the various *Parlements* to join with members of the royal council in drawing up a formula for the peaceful settlement of religious disputes. This was then promulgated by the Edict of Saint Germain, issued in January 1562. By its terms, protestants were guaranteed freedom of conscience and of private worship. Public worship was forbidden them in town centres, where it was likely to provoke a violent catholic reaction, but it was permitted in the suburbs. Permission was also granted for the formation of Huguenot consistories and synods. The significance of the Edict of Saint Germain was that it gave formal recognition to the Huguenot church and provided for the coexistence of the two faiths while preserving the privileged position of the catholics. It was in fact the prototype of the Edict of Nantes that ultimately brought the religious wars to an end, but in 1562 it could not command general acceptance. The Huguenots were conscious that theirs was an expanding faith and they cherished hopes of making further inroads into the established Church. The catholics were fully aware of this, and regarded the Edict as the first step along a path that would lead to the destruction of all they held dear. Guise and the catholic nobility therefore denounced it and refused to accept its terms. By so doing they were resisting the royal authority and making any non-violent settlement virtually impossible, but this was a risk they were prepared to take. Catherine recognised that she must look to her own defence, and therefore asked Coligny and Beza to sound out the Huguenots. Coligny did so, and subsequently informed Catherine that there were 2,150 Huguenot congregations, all of which were prepared to offer men and money. Catherine had not openly committed herself to the protestant side, but she had certainly encouraged the protestants to feel that they had her approval.

The outbreak of civil war could not now be long delayed, and was sparked off by an incident that took place early in March 1562. The Duke of Guise came upon a protestant congregation worshipping publicly (and therefore illegally) in the town of Vassy, and ordered his men to break it up. The congregation resisted, and in the resulting fracas some thirty Huguenots were killed and three times that number wounded. As the news of the 'Massacre of Vassy' spread, protestants all over France took fright. Condé called on them to send him troops and concentrated his forces at Orleans. Catherine, still hoping to prevent war, summoned Guise to court, but instead he joined up with his fellow Triumvirs and marched on Paris. Catherine then appealed to Condé and Coligny to come to court and protect her and the young king, but they, in turn, refused. This left Catherine with no alternative but to throw in her lot with the Guises.

The Huguenots' Struggle for Survival

The first war of religion, which broke out shortly after the Massacre of Vassy, was an affair of skirmishes rather than major battles, but it removed many of the leading figures from the scene. Anthony of Bourbon died of wounds received at the siege of Rouen; Saint-André was killed fighting at Dreux in December 1562; and Francis of Guise was assassinated at Orleans in the following February. The protestants suffered the temporary loss of Condé, captured at Dreux, but effectively offset this by themselves capturing Constable Montmorency. Since the assassination of the Duke of Guise had freed Catherine from her 'captivity' she could now take the initiative in bringing about a reconcilation. Peace terms were negotiated by the two prisoners-of-war, Condé and Montmorency, and promulgated in the Edict of Pacification of Amboise in March 1563. This reaffirmed liberty of conscience but restricted freedom of worship to the nobility: those lower in the social scale were to be allowed to worship publicly in only one town in every district. Calvin and Coligny both blamed Condé for agreeing to terms which benefited his own class at the expense of the Huguenot church as a whole, but given the takeover of the protestant congregations by the lay nobility such an outcome was hardly surprising.

The war had shown that the Huguenots, though very strong in certain areas, were not a majority of the French population. Moreover their zeal had alienated many of those who might otherwise have been prepared to accept a tolerant settlement. Beza himself commented on this in a letter to Calvin in 1562. Referring to the Huguenots, he said 'Their violence in the destruction of altars is incredible, and we have been quite unable to prevent it here. In short, all things are suddenly changed, so that I am amazed at the spectacle; for the enemy in a hundred years, even if victorious, could not restore, in this city alone, what has been destroyed in the space of two hours.'

The best chance of preventing a renewal of violence still seemed to lie in strengthening the crown, and Catherine hoped that the Estates General, which she had summoned to meet at Pontoise in 1561, would assist this by dealing with the king's debts. The Third Estate, however, would only agree to vote supply if Catherine accepted a programme of retrenchment in the royal household that would have impaired rather than restored the king's authority. Catherine therefore decided to bring forward her young son in a bid to rally public opinion behind the crown. On the face of it Charles IX was hardly the ideal person for such a role. Although not without attractive characteristics—he wrote poetry and exchanged verses with the great Ronsard—he was only thirteen years old and suffered from ill health. But whatever his natural disadvantages he was the only king available, and Catherine therefore declared him of age and took him on an extended progress through his realm. Her aim was clear—to make the court once again the focus of French society and politics, and to keep the nobles employed in ceremonial functions there rather than leave them to squabble among themselves. This, in effect, was the programme which the *Politiques* were subsequently to adopt.

During the royal progress, which lasted from 1564 to 1566, Catherine and her son arrived at Bayonne, where they were met by Catherine's favourite daughter, Elizabeth, wife of Philip II of Spain. Also present was the Duke of Alva. No plots were hatched at this meeting, but rumour ran wild, and the Huguenots feared that Catherine and Alva between them had agreed on some master-stroke that in due course would crush the protestants. These forebodings seemed to be fulfilled when Alva took his army along the eastern border of France in the summer of 1567, *en route* from Milan to the Netherlands. Nobody could be sure of his intentions, and Huguenot leaders, fearing a surprise attack decided on a *coup d'état* to give them possession of the king. Charles IX and his mother were at Meaux when the protestants struck in September 1567, but the attempt failed and the king escaped to Paris. The catholics immediately took up arms, and the second of the religious wars broke out. Only one major engagement took place, in which Constable Montmorency, the last survivor of the Triumvirate, was mortally wounded. In March 1568 the Peace of Longjumeau restored the *status quo*, except for some tightening of the limitations on Huguenot public worship. It was a settlement that satisfied neither side.

Catherine had been deeply shocked by the 'Incident of Meaux'. The protection of her children and their inheritance mattered more to her than anything else, and she was convinced that the Huguenots were aiming at revolution. This led her to abandon the policy of moderation with which she had previously been identified, and to throw in her lot with the hard-line catholics. These now had the support of the king's younger brother, the Duke of Anjou (future Henry III), who persuaded Catherine to rescind the edicts giving Huguenots freedom of worship and to follow the example of Alva, whose strong-arm tactics in the Netherlands seemed to be paying good dividends. In December 1568, therefore, new edicts were issued, annulling all former grants of freedom of worship for Huguenots and ordering protestant ministers to leave the kingdom. Catherine planned to go further and seize the Huguenot leaders, Condé and Coligny, but the news leaked out and sparked off the third war.

Bitterness had by now reached such a point that in this war cruelties were common on both sides. As one Huguenot leader said, 'we fought the first war like angels, the second like men, and the third like devils'. Priests were killed, women and children put to the sword, and prisoners massacred—all in the name of God. Anjou defeated the Huguenots at Jarnac and Moncontour, and in the first of these battles Condé was taken prisoner and immediately executed. But Coligny, now sole commander of the Huguenot forces, re-formed his army and kept it intact by avoiding any pitched battle. His tactics paid off, for the crown's strained finances would not permit it to keep forces in the field for very long, and Catherine had therefore to reopen negotiations.

In August 1570 peace was concluded at Saint Germain on terms similar to those of the Edict of Amboise. Liberty of conscience and limited freedom of worship were restored to the Huguenots: in addition they were granted the right to garrison and hold four strongholds —La Rochelle, Montauban, La Charité and Cognac. This Peace of Saint Germain marked Catherine's return to her earlier policy of moderation. Now that the hot-headed Condé had been removed she had less cause to fear a protestant revolution and far more reason to be alarmed by the catholic Guises, with their Spanish contacts. She hoped to calm passions at home as well as tensions abroad by marriage alliances. Her first idea was that her daughter Margaret should marry Philip II (now a widower), but Philip rejected this—thereby confirming Catherine's distaste for all things Spanish—and Margaret instead was engaged to Henry of Navarre, son of Anthony of Bourbon. At the same time Anjou was put forward as a suitor for Elizabeth of England.

In the summer of 1571 Coligny returned to court and urged the carrying-out of the *Politique* policy of uniting protestants and catholics in a crusade against Spain. In this he had the full support of the young king, who came to love and admire the protestant leader and looked on him as a father. The change of policy was reflected in an approach to the leaders of the Netherlands' resistance movement, who had previously been regarded merely as rebels. Charles had two long interviews with Louis of Nassau, in which they discussed the possibility of French rule over the southern Netherlands in return for military assistance against Spain. So enthusiastic was the king that in August 1572 he informed William of Orange that he would shortly lead an army of 15,000 men against the common foe.

Catherine was not happy about all these developments. Although temperamentally a *Politique*, she resented Coligny's dominance over her son. She was also aware of the formidable strength of Spain, particularly after the resounding victory at Lepanto in October 1571 (see p. 283), and was afraid that Coligny might drag France into a war that could not possibly be won. Charles IX, however, was no longer listening to his mother. When Louis of Nassau seized Mons in May 1572, following the unexpected success of the Sea Beggars at Brill, Charles and Coligny agreed (without consulting Catherine) that a Huguenot army should march to Louis's aid. Six thousand troops were assembled and moved towards Mons, but they were defeated by a Spanish force from the Netherlands. It looked as though war with Spain could not now be averted, and Catherine, appalled by the prospect and bitter at the alienation of her son's affections, determined on a sudden and violent counterstroke.

Ever since the assassination of Francis, Duke of Guise, in February 1563, murder had been a political weapon. The Guises blamed Coligny for the assassination, and although Coligny had declared his innocence and had been formally exculpated by a royal edict in January 1566, neither he nor the Huguenots in general ever expressed regret for the deed. Francis' son, Henry, the new Duke of Guise, was determined to avenge his father's death, and Catherine, who was aware of this, decided to make use of him. She proposed, quite simply, that Coligny himself should be assassinated, thereby freeing the king (or so she fondly imagined) from an influence that had become too dominant. The Huguenot nobles were assembled in Paris in August 1572 for the wedding of Margaret and Henry of Navarre, and it was while he was returning one day from a visit to court that Coligny was shot.

Unfortunately for Catherine he was only wounded, not killed. The Huguenots, angry and alarmed, immediately demanded an inquiry, to which the king seemed likely to agree. Catherine feared that such an inquiry would expose her own complicity, and rather than risk this she now proposed a general massacre of all the protestant leaders—this, at least, is a possible explanation of the events that followed, although much is obscure and the degree of Catherine's involvement remains uncertain.

Catherine convinced her son that the Huguenots intended to overthrow the throne and that his life would be in danger unless he took immediate preventive action. Charles therefore gave his consent to the massacre, which took place in the early hours of 24 August 1572, Saint Bartholomew's Day. Catherine may have been thinking in terms of a limited operation, but she reckoned without the frenzy of the Paris mob, which had never wavered in its devotion to the old faith. Young Sully, the future minister of Henry IV, told how 'as I walked out into the street I was horrified. There were madmen running to and fro, smashing down doors and shouting "Kill! Kill! Massacre the Huguenots!" Blood spattered before my eyes and doubled my fear.' Some 3,000 Huguenots were slaughtered in Paris, and the orgy of killing that went on for several days extended to the provinces, where at least another 3,000 were massacred. Henry, Duke of Guise, personally supervised the killing of Coligny. As for Henry of Navarre, the young Huguenot bridegroom, and his namesake, the new Prince of Condé, they were held prisoner at court and forced to renounce their protestant faith.

The news of the Massacre of Saint Bartholomew reverberated throughout Europe. At Rome a solemn *Te Deum* was held in thanksgiving and the Pope ordered a commemorative medal to be struck. Philip II was equally delighted and told Catherine that the punishment meted out to Coligny 'and his sect was indeed of such value and prudence and of such a service, glory and honour to God and universal benefit to all Christendom, that to hear of it was for me the most cheerful news'. The joy of the catholics was only matched by the horror, anger and apprehension of the protestants. It was widely assumed, not least among the Huguenots, that the Massacre had been plotted by Catherine and Alva in their meeting at Bayonne and was part of a general plan to exterminate protestantism. If Catherine had hoped that the Huguenots, deprived of their leaders, would succumb, she was badly mistaken. Protestant ministers and rank-and-file Huguenots stood firm and filled the gap left by the removal of aristocratic leadership. In southern and western France the Huguenots threw off their allegiance to the crown and organised a state-within-a-state, defended by its own armed forces. At La Rochelle the royal governor was refused admission, and in the war that followed—the fourth—the town held out against the investing army of Anjou. Fighting went on until 1573 and was only ended when Anjou, having been elected to the Polish throne, left for his new kingdom. The peace terms were announced in the Edict of Boulogne, issued in July 1573. Liberty of conscience was confirmed and freedom of worship for protestants was authorised at La Rochelle, Nîmes, Montauban, and in the houses of certain great nobles. These terms were less generous than those of Saint Germain in 1562, but they marked the retreat of the catholics from the uncompromising position taken up in 1568.

The Triumph of the Politiques

Catherine's sudden abandonment of her policy of moderation, which led to the Massacre and the fourth war, had alienated not only the Huguenots but the Politiques as well. This term had been in use since about 1564 to describe those who put political before religious considerations, among them many devout Roman Catholics. The Politiques advocated a strong monarchy as the solution of France's ills, but their royalism had been badly shaken by Catherine's identification of the crown with catholicism at its most intolerant. They were also alarmed by the catholics' dependence on Spain, which threatened the very existence of France as a great power. They therefore linked up with the Huguenots, and the Politique governor of Languedoc, the Roman Catholic Henry of Montmorency-Damville (younger son of the former Constable) headed what was to all intents and purposes an independent state, committed to the principle of religious toleration. This state had its own 'capitals' at the Huguenot centres of Nîmes and Montauban, collected its own taxes (thereby further impoverishing the crown) and summoned its own meetings of Estates. Damville was the de facto ruler of all France south of the Loire.

The alliance between the Politiques and the Huguenots was in many ways a union of opposites, for following the Massacre the Huguenots had become increasingly critical of monarchical rule as it existed in France. In his Du Droit des Magistrats sur Leurs Sujets, published in France in 1574, Beza had declared that the people, under the leadership of the 'lesser magistrates', were justified in deposing a tyrant, and this right of resistance was reasserted and elaborated by Philip Duplessis-Mornay in his *Vindiciae contra Tyrannos* of 1579. The term 'lesser magistrates' was, of course, liable to several interpretations, but the Huguenot nobles assumed that it referred to themselves and justified their actions.

The *Politiques* had far more sympathy with the view put forward by Bodin in his *Republic* (1576) that peace could only be restored if the authority of the crown were elevated above all factions; but until such time as Charles IX broke free from the catholic-Guise net their natural loyalty could find no focus in the person of the king. They looked instead to the Duke of Alençon, Catherine's fourth and youngest son. This unstable and ambitious young man hated his brothers because they stood between him and the throne, and now that Anjou was out of the way in Poland, Alençon could concentrate his malevolent attentions on the king. A first attempt to seize Charles failed because of a last minute change of route, but Alençon then joined with Henry of Navarre in planning a *coup d'état* at the palace of Saint Germain. The plot miscarried and Catherine arrested the two princes and carried the king off to Vincennes. There, in May 1574, Charles IX died at the age of twenty-four.

By imprisoning Alençon Catherine had left the way open for the succession of Anjou, who, as soon as he heard the news of Charles's death, abandoned his Polish subjects and returned post-haste to his native land. In February 1575 he was crowned at Rheims as Henry III, and it looked as though France at last had a king who was worthy of the name. Henry was twenty-two, in good health, and intelligent. Catherine, after urging him to keep his court in good order and devote himself to the government of his kingdom, retired into the background. Alençon, on the other hand, escaped from imprisonment in September 1575 and placed himself under the protection of Damville, in Languedoc, where he was later joined by Henry of Navarre. The Huguenots, burning with desire to avenge the massacre and to ensure their future safety, gave him their support. So did the *Politiques*, who accepted the claim made by Henry of Navarre that they were not fighting against the crown but against the Guise faction which threatened to subordinate France to Spain. Although religion was still one of the major forces behind this fifth war, it was being increasingly used in the service of personal ambitions and factional intrigue.

The war was uneventful, but it convinced Catherine and the king that since they could not beat the Huguenot-*Politique* combination they must come to terms with it. Alençon (who had succeeded to his brother's title of Anjou when Henry became king) negotiated the Peace of Monsieur of May 1576, which marked the protestant triumph. Under its terms, which were promulgated by the Edict of Beaulieu, Huguenots were free to worship everywhere except in Paris and places of residence of the royal family. Mixed Roman Catholic and protestant tribunals were to be set up to judge cases in which persons of different faiths were involved, and the Huguenots were given eight fortified towns as guarantees of their security.

This 'protestant peace' produced a catholic reaction. From 1568 onwards regional catholic associations had come into being pledged to defend the principles of *Une foi, une loi, un roi*,[1] and these now coalesced into the 'Holy Christian Union', or 'Catholic League'. The leader of the League was Henry of Guise, the idol of the citizens of Paris, who was in close touch with Spain. On the face of it the League offered no threat to the king since it was committed to the cause of monarchy, but this was on the assumption that the king would not only be himself a catholic but would actively defend the established Church. Henry III, by coming to terms with the Huguenots, could be regarded as having betrayed this trust, and he was quick to see the danger of the crown once more being isolated. In a tactical move of some brilliance Henry III therefore announced that he would himself be the leader of the League and would permit only the catholic religion in his kingdom. The Huguenots immediately prepared for war, but this time they had to fight without the *Politiques*, since Henry III had won over Anjou and Damville. This sixth war was a scrappy and inconclusive affair, though on the whole the catholics had the better of the fighting, and it ended with the patched-up Peace of Bergerac in September 1577, which restored the *status quo*. In the following month, however, Henry III issued the Edict of Poitiers, in which he declared that all leagues were to be dissolved and that freedom of worship for Huguenots should be restricted to those towns which had enjoyed this right before the recent outbreak of hostilities. In other places public protestant worship was to be confined to the suburbs. The number of mixed tribunals was also cut down, and the Huguenots' tenure of their fortified towns was reduced to six years.

Henry III's aim was to show that liberty of conscience and limited

---

[1] 'One faith, one law, one king.'

freedom of worship would be guaranteed by a strong, catholic monarchy, but he had first to demonstrate that the monarchy was indeed
strong enough to impose its authority not simply on the Huguenots
but on the catholic factions as well. In this he failed, mainly because of
the defects in his own character. He suffered from the same inability as
his father to transform words into consistent policy, and he alternated
between bouts of frenetic activity and long periods of inertia. Henry
was deeply religious, but even in this sphere he oscillated between
extremes of asceticism and elaborate ritual. Surrounded by men he
could not trust he attempted to create a new nobility out of his favourites, but these were chosen for their charm rather than their abilities,
and they brought Henry's court into increasing disrepute. One contemporary described in July 1576 how 'there is beginning to be a lot of
conversation about the *mignons*, who are much hated and scorned by
the people, as much for their haughty manners as for their effeminate
and immodest appearance. . . . These *mignons* wear their hair long,
curled and re-curled artificially, on top of [which they wear] little
velvet bonnets like those of girls in the brothels. . . . Their occupations
are gambling, blaspheming, jumping, dancing, quarrelling, fornicating,
and following the king around.' With courtiers such as these Henry III
was unable to command sufficient respect, and he therefore failed in his
attempt to make the throne a firm foundation-stone around which
French society could be reconstructed.

In the late 1570s and early 1580s disorder seemed to have become
endemic in France. Anjou had gone off to seek his fortune in the
Netherlands and subsequently in England, but the Huguenots were
still in arms, under Henry of Navarre, and open war, the seventh,
broke out in 1580, although it lasted for only a few months. In 1581
Henry III fell seriously ill, and following his recovery his actions
became increasingly eccentric. Despite the huge debts of the crown he
spent lavishly on gifts and pensions and on court festivities; heaped
titles, offices and estates on favourites like Joyeuse and Epernon; and
spent more and more of his time on such matters as the founding of a
monastery at Vincennes and the creation of a new order of penitents.
This was the situation when, in June 1584, Anjou died. The heir to the
throne was now Henry of Navarre, whose title to it was incontro-
vertible since he was descended from a brother of Saint Louis, but who
was, of course, a protestant. Faced with the appalling prospect of a
Huguenot king the Catholic League reconstituted itself, and in December 1584 Henry of Guise signed the secret Treaty of Joinville with the

Spanish ambassador. This bound Philip II to subsidise Guise and the League in their struggle against the heretic; they, in their turn, promised to try and bring about the succession of Henry of Navarre's colourless uncle, the catholic Cardinal of Bourbon.

It seemed as though the crown was once again to be left isolated and impotent while catholics and protestants fought for power, but this was a situation which Henry III, like his mother, was determined to avoid. Since the crown was not strong enough to stand alone, and he could hardly commit himself to the heretic King of Navarre, Henry III decided to throw in his lot with the catholics. In July 1585, therefore, he cancelled all grants of freedom of worship to the Huguenots and gave them six months in which to be either reconciled to the Church of Rome or exiled from the kingdom.

If the Huguenots were to survive they would have to fight, and 1586 saw the opening of the eighth and last of the wars. Sometimes known as the War of the Three Henries—Henry III; Henry, Duke of Guise; and Henry of Navarre—it was a struggle for the succession in which religion played a subordinate role. As one of the royal secretaries, Villeroy, commented: 'le masque de la religion est levé. C'est l'ambition qui nous régente.'[1] Both sides were successful on the battlefield. Henry of Navarre showed considerable military ability by routing the royal army at Coutras, in October 1587, but Guise defeated the Huguenots' German allies at Vimory and again at Auneau. Henry III, meanwhile, was increasingly restless at the restraints imposed on him by the Guise alliance, and alarmed at the radicalism of Paris.

It was among the Paris bourgeoisie, notorious for their fanatical adherence to the catholic faith, that the revival of the Catholic League had begun, and the city had now become a virtual republic. Its rulers were the Council of Sixteen (so named after the sixteen districts of Paris; the membership was about fifty) and they encouraged the preaching of inflammatory sermons which turned popular feeling against the king. Henry was bitterly aware of the fact that in what was said to be his capital city he had no real authority, and he decided on a show of force to bring the inhabitants to heel. Early in 1588 he sent 4,000 Swiss mercenaries into Paris with orders to arrest the agitators. The League had long been prepared for such a coup, however, and had

[1] 'The mask of religion has been lifted. It is ambition which calls the tune.'

made its preparations accordingly. An appeal was sent to Guise, and the duke, ignoring the king's orders to the contrary, marched on the capital. In May 1588 Guise made a triumphal entry, and when Henry tried to assert his authority the smouldering hatred of the citizens flared into open rebellion. One eye-witness described how 'all took arms, went into the streets, took the chains and barricaded the corners and intersections. The artisan left his tools, the merchant his business, the student his books. . . . Everywhere were frightful cries and seditious words to arouse the people to white heat.' This 'Day of the Barricades' was a defeat for the king. His Swiss troops were penned in and forced to surrender, and Henry had to flee from the city.

Guise might at this stage have seized the throne for himself, but instead he restored order in Paris and encouraged Henry to come to terms. Once again the king had to bow to superior strength. In July 1588 he issued the Edict of Union, appointing Guise Lieutenant-General of the kingdom and leaving control of foreign and domestic policy effectively in the hands of the League. In the following October the Estates General met at Blois, but if the king had hoped to find support among the deputies he was swiftly disillusioned. Out of some five hundred delegates, nearly four hundred were members of the League, and they made it clear that they held Henry responsible for the collapse of the royal administration and the weakness of the crown's finances. Far from voting additional supply they called for reductions in the level of taxation, and Henry added this further humiliation to the countless others for which he blamed the Guises.

In December 1588, spurred on by hatred of the Guises and encouraged by the defeat of the Armada which their Spanish allies had sent against England, Henry took his revenge. He had invited the Duke of Guise to his château at Blois on the pretext of discussing urgent affairs of state, but as Guise arrived he was assassinated. On the following day his brother, the Cardinal of Guise, was also murdered. Henry went himself to tell the good news to his mother. 'I could endure [the duke's] insolence no longer' he declared. 'I mean now to be king and no longer a captive and a slave. . . . So, Madam, I am now sole King of France, without a partner.' Catherine had used the same methods herself, in the Massacre of Saint Bartholomew, but had lived to see how political assassinations rebounded on their perpetrators. By 1588, however, she was a tired and sick woman, and in January of the following year she died. Henry III was at last 'sole King of France, without a partner'.

Just as the Huguenots had renounced their allegiance after the Massacre of St Bartholomew, so now the catholics moved into open rebellion. The doctors of the Sorbonne formally absolved all Henry's subjects from their obligation to obey him, and by identifying itself with the cause of 'provincial liberties'—previously espoused by the Huguenots—the League turned itself for the first time into a popular revolutionary movement. Its programme appealed particularly to the younger members of the provincial bourgeoisie who were trying to carve out for themselves a career in local administration, since the opportunities for advancement at a national level had been substantially reduced by the crown's policy of permitting the inheritance of public offices. They gave the catholic cause a social and political programme as well as a cutting edge which it had previously lacked.

Henry IV and the Edict of Nantes

Since Henry III had been rejected by the catholics, he had little alternative to allying with the protestants, and in 1589 he was formally reconciled with Henry of Navarre. The two Henries combined their forces and moved against Paris in April of that year, but on the first day of August Henry III was assassinated by a young Dominican friar, who saw in him the enemy of God and the Church. The catholics' nightmare had at last come true, for the Huguenot Henry of Navarre was now King Henry IV of France.

On the face of it Henry's position was unenviable. The majority of Frenchmen were catholics and would be unlikely to support a protestant monarch; yet if he were to abandon his faith he would alienate and embitter the substantial minority of Huguenots. He was not even master of his own kingdom, and his opponents, led by Guise's brother, the Duke of Mayenne, had the support of Spain. Yet Henry had considerable advantages, even though these were not at first apparent. For one thing he was a grown man, of great charm and strength of character, with none of the neurotic tendencies of his predecessor. Also he could count on the support of the *Politiques* and of those moderate members of the Catholic League who were repelled by the prospect of subordination to Spain. This was particularly the case after the death of the Cardinal of Bourbon in 1590, since there was no obvious catholic candidate for the French throne, and Philip was known to be pressing the claims of his own daughter.

Henry also had the advantage of being a good soldier—as he showed in September 1589 by defeating a much larger force under Mayenne at the battle of Arques, near Rouen. In 1590 he besieged Paris, but was compelled to retreat when Parma struck down from the Netherlands with his highly trained army. In the following year Parma again invaded France, and was preparing for yet another intervention when he died in December 1592. Philip was anxious to have his daughter's claim to the French throne formally acknowledged, and it was at his insistence that Mayenne summoned the Estates General to Paris in 1593. When the representatives assembled, however, they showed themselves antagonistic to Spanish claims, particularly since Henry IV had transformed the situation by announcing, in July 1593, his conversion to the Roman Catholic faith. Against a King of France who was both French and catholic, Philip's daughter stood little chance, and although many French catholics had understandable doubts about the depths of Henry's new-found faith, his action had opened up the prospect of ending the religious wars which had plagued France for more than a quarter of a century.

Many of the catholic nobles who had hitherto given their support to Mayenne were now prepared to rally to Henry. He stood for the principle of legitimacy, of the hereditary right to property, upon which their own social predominance was based, and they were alarmed by the increasing radicalism of the League. This radicalism had been demonstrated in its most extreme form during Henry's siege of Paris in 1590. The city was starving, and even the bones of the dead were ground to powder to make bread, but the Committee of Sixteen kept resistance going by a reign of terror. They set up a Committee of Public Safety and showed their attitude towards established authorities by arresting the President of the *Parlement* of Paris and two of its judges and executing them on a charge of treason. This violence produced a reaction even within the city itself, and many merchants, financiers and office-holders came to see that their position, like that of the nobles, depended upon the restoration of royal authority. The change of attitude was so marked that when, in March 1594, Henry again appeared before the gates of Paris—this time as a catholic sovereign who had just been crowned at Chartres—there was virtually no resistance. The king was at last master of his own capital.

Henry symbolised the *Politique* belief that religion should be divorced from politics and that national interests should take precedence over all others. To make clear that, so far as he was concerned, the civil wars were now over and that the only major threat was from outside,

Henry issued a formal declaration of war against Spain in January 1595. Philip II was still a formidable opponent, as was shown when Spanish troops captured Calais in 1596 and Amiens in 1597. But these incursions served to prove the truth of Henry's claim that his enemies were the enemies of France. Gradually the League chiefs came to terms with him—helped by the fact that in 1595 Clement VIII formally received Henry into the Roman Catholic church—and in October of that year Mayenne laid down his arms.

Three years later, in May 1598, France and Spain made peace at Vervins. Both sides were heavily in debt, war-weariness was widespread, and France in particular needed a long period of peace in which to recover from the strain of civil as well as foreign war. Apart from recognising Henry as King of France the Peace of Vervins merely confirmed the settlement made at Cateau-Cambrésis in 1559. At the time this had been regarded as a defeat for France, since it marked the abandonment of French claims to Italy, but by 1598 the fact that France had not only survived but maintained her frontiers intact was taken as just cause for rejoicing.

In April 1598, shortly before the signing of peace with Spain, Henry issued the Edict of Nantes, designed to settle, for a time at least, the problems created by the existence within a France that was nominally united and catholic of a substantial and unreconciled protestant minority. The Edict guaranteed liberty of conscience to all Henry's subjects, but restricted freedom of worship for the Huguenots to those places where it was already established. Mixed tribunals were reconstituted for cases in which both catholics and protestants were involved, and the Huguenots were allowed to garrison about a hundred fortified places at the crown's expense. These terms obviously owed much to earlier edicts, starting with that of Saint Germain in 1562, and they reflected the weakness, not the strength, of the crown. The Edict of Nantes was in fact an admission that the King, however much he wished to guarantee the security of his Huguenot subjects, could not do so; he could only give them the means to defend themselves. There was opposition to the Edict from both protestants and catholics, but the inescapable fact was that neither side was strong enough to wipe out the other and that the only alternative to perpetual civil war was coexistence on agreed terms.

In 1560 there had been a real possibility that the Huguenots might take over France altogether and move it firmly into the protestant camp, but by the end of the sixteenth century they were clearly declining: there were, for example, only some 800 Huguenot congregations compared with more than 2,000 in 1562. Although the protestants were strong in the south and west they formed a mere ten per cent of the population as a whole, and while the Edict gave them a certain security it also created a defensive mentality which was a long way removed from the missionary enthusiasm of the first Calvinists. French protestantism survived, but only at the cost of virtual stagnation.

The triumph of the crown under Henry IV was a defeat for factionalism. First the protestants and then the catholics had identified themselves with the cause of provincial liberties and representative government, but the *Politique* belief that the solution to France's problems lay in a powerful monarchy had won general acceptance by 1598. This may have opened the way to eventual absolutism, but certainly not in the short run. There was nothing 'new' about Henry's rule except its effectiveness, and the basic strengths and weaknesses of the French crown remained much as they had been prior to 1559. Henry simply demonstrated what had long been the case, that an adult king, provided he was hard-working, determined and capable, stood a very good chance of getting his own way.

SIXTEEN

Spain under Philip II

Administration and Finance

On 16 January 1556 Charles V gave up his sovereignty over Castile, Aragon, Sicily and the Spanish possessions in the New World, in favour of his son, Philip II. The new king, even though he was to become the symbol and embodiment of all things Spanish, had the fair hair and bright blue eyes of his German forebears. He loved music, being himself an accomplished performer on the guitar, and he also had a passion for rare books and manuscripts. He built up a magnificent collection of pictures, particularly strong in the works of Titian and Tintoretto, and housed part of it in the Escorial, the great palace which he built for himself outside Madrid. The Escorial was a comment on the various aspects of Philip's character. Not only was it huge, impressive and dignified as a building, appropriate for a man who ruled over so much of the known world; it was also a mausoleum for his father, a symbol of Habsburg family pride, a monastery and a church. It was rich with the splendour of the transitory material world, but it also served as a constant reminder of that timeless spiritual existence of which Philip was always conscious.

Assured of the support of God, and confident in his own and his family's right to the high position they occupied, Philip ought to have been a strong king. Yet he mistrusted his own judgment and constantly sought the advice of others—even though he distrusted them as well. It was this lack of confidence which led to interminable delays, for Philip would gather conflicting opinions, weigh them in his own mind, and arrive at his decision only after a long process of evaluation. Although he stayed up far into the night reading and annotating reports and documents, he could never keep abreast of all the demands that were made on him. As his reign went on, the delays grew to be interminable, and Pius V was expressing a widely held view when he wrote that 'Your Majesty spends so long considering your undertakings that when the moment to perform them comes the occasion has passed and the money all been spent'. Yet Philip's methods had their advantages. A number of problems in fact solved themselves before he got round to dealing with them, and as for those which he did tackle, he was prepared to take a long-term view and not be put off by immediate reverses. This was shown most strikingly in 1588, when the Armada which he had sent against England suffered defeat and humiliation. A lesser man would have vented his rage upon the unfortunate commander, but Philip refused to blame the Duke of Medina-Sidonia for what was clearly a judgment of God. Nor did he see any reason to change his basic strategy. He had adopted his policy only after prolonged consideration, and had no reason to doubt that it was the correct one. More armadas must therefore be built and launched against the heretic until, in the fulness of time, God's purpose was accomplished.

Despite his Germanic appearance, Philip was a Spaniard at heart. As the Venetian ambassador commented in 1559, the king 'has no esteem for any nation except the Spanish; he consorts only with Spaniards and with these only he takes counsel and governs . . . he takes no notice of Italians and Flemings and least of all Germans'. In fact, Philip identified himself not so much with Spain as with Castile, and one of the most marked features of his reign was the way in which Spain and her great empire became a Castilian preserve. It was resentment towards the highly privileged Castilians, and towards the king who granted these privileges, that created much unrest in Aragon and led to rebellion there in the closing years of Philip's reign.

The administration of Spain and the Spanish empire under Philip II was very similar to what it had been under Charles V. The king was his own chief minister, but he made use of secretaries of state, the first of whom was Gonzalo Perez, a protégé of Los Cobos. After Gonzalo's death in 1566 his place was taken by Antonio, his illegitimate son. Antonio Perez was hardworking, ambitious and unscrupulous, and he identified himself with the aristocratic faction that centred round Philip's favourite, the Prince of Eboli, taking over its leadership after the prince's death in 1573. On the disputed question of how the Spanish empire should be organised, the Eboli faction advocated the federal solution of autonomous territories, each with its own customs, laws and privileges. It was opposed by the Alva faction, which pressed for hard-line measures to unify the disparate states and bring them under the close control of the crown. Philip at first inclined towards Alva, as was shown when he sent the duke to take command of operations in the Netherlands, but Alva's ultimate failure there led to his recall in 1573 and the eclipse of his faction. Philip turned instead to the Eboli group and it was at their suggestion that he appointed, as Alva's replacement, the soft-liner Requesens.

The triumph of the Eboli faction was, of course, a triumph for Antonio Perez, whose rapidly increasing influence was matched only by his ambition. For a time everything seemed to be going his way, but his fear of rivals led him, among other things, to the assassination of a political opponent. This apparently took place with Philip's approval, since Perez had convinced the king that the unfortunate victim was plotting against the state, but in reflecting upon these events Philip's suspicions were aroused. In 1579, therefore, he dismissed Perez from office and ordered his arrest—having already chosen Cardinal Granvelle, the son of Charles V's Burgundian secretary, to replace him. Perez, however, was not so easily disposed of. He fled to Aragon, where he appealed to the court of the Justiciar and invoked the liberties of that kingdom in his own defence. The final chapter in the history of Antonio Perez was not to be written until after the suppression of the revolt in Aragon.

Factionalism among the Castilian aristocracy could have been a danger to Philip, but in fact he kept it under control. The nobles were excluded from any direct part in the administration, except for those positions such as governor, viceroy and army or navy commander which required a man whose lineage and social status would automatically command respect. They were, it is true, encouraged to attend the council of state, which was supposed to advise the king on policy, but Philip never attended meetings himself and on all important matters consulted only with a smaller and more intimate group of advisers. The council of state, in short, was a successful device for giving the aristocracy the appearance of power, and encouraging them to work out their disagreements within a non-violent context, while effectively depriving them of any real part in the formulation of policy.

In contrast to the council of state, which was essentially an amateur body with little or no administrative machinery, there were the highly professional councils for the various kingdoms. The council of Castile was the most important of these, but by the time Philip died there were also councils for Aragon, Italy, Portugal, the Netherlands and the Indies. These councils were in permanent attendance on the king, and it was through them that he transmitted his commands to the various territories under his rule. They were staffed mainly by university-trained lawyers and administrators, devoted to the service of the crown and content to act as the executants of royal policy rather than the formulators of it. The councils, therefore, were the king's instruments, and he set the advice they gave him against the information he received from his regular, sometimes daily, correspondence with the viceroys and governors who actually administered the constituent states. In this way he kept the consideration of general questions to himself, and prevented the emergence of any institutional challenge to his own authority.

Philip was in receipt of a revenue larger than that of any other European sovereign, yet it was not enough for his purposes. American silver was a major source, but it needed supplementing. In 1554, for instance, it provided only 11 per cent of the total revenue, and although this figure had risen to 20 per cent by 1598 it was still less than the income from taxes levied in Castile and only about the same as the contribution made by the Spanish church. The greatest single source of revenue had been the *Alcabala*, or sales tax, but by the time Philip came to the throne this had been turned into a fixed sum and the *Cortes* of Castile had procured the promise that it would not be increased. Customs dues, at the internal frontiers as well as the ports, and a tax on the transit of sheep and cattle, also contributed to the royal finances, but for additional sums the king was dependent upon the assistance of the *Cortes*. Where (as in Castile) the *Cortes* were willing to co-operate by voting subsidies (*Servicios*), Philip was only too glad to summon them frequently; this was not the case in Aragon, however, and meetings of the Aragonese *Cortes* were therefore few and far between. The Church was taxed via the *Cruzada*, granted by the Pope for three years at a time and renewed, however reluctantly with comparative regularity. The Church also provided 'royal tithes'; a tax called a 'subsidy'; the revenue from vacant sees and the military orders; and, from 1567 onwards, the *Excusado*—a tax on parish property granted by Pius V to help pay for the war in Flanders.

Almost as important as raising money was making sure that it was available as and where required. For this the king was dependent on the Genoese bankers who operated the financial mechanism of western

Europe and were prepared to advance money to him on the security of certain specified sources of revenue. As the expenses of the Spanish crown increased, so did these loans, and by 1575 it was estimated that the total debt equalled five times the annual revenue and that the entire income for any year was consumed in payments of interest and repayments of capital. In 1575, therefore, Philip took the drastic step of cancelling all agreements made with the Genoese bankers. The result was a loss of confidence in Spanish credit and a breakdown of the system of transferring money, which led, among other things, to mutiny in the royal army in the Netherlands. The crisis was only ended when the council of finance came to an agreement with the Genoese bankers, restoring them to their privileged position, rephasing the repayment of capital, and consolidating all loans at an interest rate of five per cent. By 1596, however, shortage of money had once more become crippling, and the crown again suspended payments and announced that its debts would have to be rephased. This collapse of the royal finances goes far towards explaining the readiness with which Spain came to terms with France in 1598.

Philip II and the Church

Spanish blood and Spanish treasure were poured out in the defence of the catholic faith and Habsburg interests. Philip took it for granted that what was good for Spain was good for the Church, and although he acknowledged the Pope as spiritual head of the catholic community he did not regard himself as bound to accept the decisions of Rome where they conflicted with his own views. As he wrote to Sixtus V, 'God and the whole world know my love for the Holy See, and nothing will ever make me deviate from it. . . . But the greater my devotion the less I shall consent to your failing in your duty towards God and towards the Church . . . and at the risk of being importunate to Your Holiness and displeasing you, I shall insist on your setting to the task.' Philip, in other words, regarded himself as lay protector of the catholic Church, with the self-appointed duty not simply of fighting in its defence but also of ensuring its spiritual regeneration. When in, 1559, for example, the Council of Trent was at last reconvened and the Emperor Ferdinand and the French both put pressure on the Pope for a more accommodating attitude towards the protestants, it was the Spanish representatives who, on Philip's orders, insisted that there should be no compromise.

Philip, in general, approved of the principles behind the reforms decided on at Trent, but was determined to retain the initiative in his own hands. It was for this reason that while he encouraged the holding of provincial councils of the Church he insisted, in face of the Pope's disapproval, that his own representatives should be present. In 1582 Cardinal Quiroga, whom Philip had nominated as Primate of Spain, summoned a synod to Toledo, which drew up a reform programme. This owed much to the Trent decrees and was in sympathy with them, but there was not so much sense of urgency in Spain as elsewhere in catholic Europe. The fact that the Spanish church had been effectively purged by Cardinal Ximenes, and that it was under the ever-watchful eye of the most committed of catholic monarchs, made Trent less relevant to Spain than to other countries—or so at least it seemed to Philip and many Spanish clergy.

The ill-defined frontier between papal and royal authority led to a number of disagreements. The most striking of these concerned Achbishop Carranza of Toledo, Quiroga's predecessor as primate. Carranza had been one of the Spanish representatives at the Council of Trent and had also acted as confessor to Philip before he became king. However, he ran foul of the Spanish Inquisition and was incarcerated. The Pope insisted that the archbishop should be sent for trial to Rome, but Philip, whatever doubts he may have had about Carranza's guilt, was reluctant to accept the implied papal claim to sit in judgment on a Spanish bishop. For seven years Carranza languished in prison while the struggle between Philip and the Pope dragged on. Pius V refused to renew the grant of the *Cruzada* or to authorise the payment of the clerical subsidy, and in 1563 Philip riposted by withdrawing his ambassador from Rome. Eventually it was Philip who gave way by permitting the archbishop to go to Rome, where judgment was eventually given in his favour. But such conciliatory gestures were rare, and Philip, convinced of his own spiritual integrity and the innate superiority of all things Spanish, kept a firm hold on 'his' Church. All major ecclesiastical appointments were made by the crown; papal bulls were allowed to be published only after they had received royal approval; and although appeals to Rome were in theory permitted, in practice very few cases got beyond the council of Castile.

The Turkish Threat

During the first half of his reign, Philip's main concern was with the Mediterranean, where the Turkish advance was continuing. Algiers and Tripoli, both of them strongholds of corsairs who preyed on Christian shipping, were virtually satellite states of the Sultan. Philip could not ignore them because they could so easily cut the vital link between Barcelona and Genoa, through which men, money and supplies flowed to the Spanish forces in the Netherlands. At first he tried to copy the methods of his father (see p. 312), and early in 1560 a Spanish expeditionary force of some 18,000 men invaded the island of Djerba, to the west of Tripoli. When the Turkish fleet, stationed at Constantinople, heard of this, it moved with great speed and determination, routed the Spanish ships which were keeping the lines of communication open, and left Philip's army with no choice but surrender. Philip learnt the lesson of this bitter failure, and decided not to challenge the Turks again until he had first built up Spanish sea power. The results of this policy soon became apparent. In 1563 the Spaniards beat off a corsair attack on Oran, and by the following year they had a fleet of some hundred galleys operating in the western Mediterranean.

Although Philip had created a powerful fleet, he was reluctant to commit it to action for fear that its defeat would leave the coasts of Spain open to attack. This accounts for his reluctance to support the Knights of St John, when their island fortress of Malta was assaulted by the Turks in 1565. But the days of undisputed Turkish mastery of the central Mediterranean were passing—as was indicated by their repulse from Malta—and five years later came an opportunity to challenge them in their home waters. In 1570 the Venetians appealed to Spain and the Pope for aid in dealing with a Turkish invasion of the Venetian island of Cyprus. Pius V assured Philip that in return for the despatch of Spanish forces he would not simply renew the *Cruzada* but also grant a five-year clerical subsidy. Philip therefore agreed to commit himself, albeit reluctantly. The outbreak of the Morisco revolt in Granada (see p. 284) had aroused fears that the Turks might strike at Spain itself, and the situation in the Netherlands, where Alva appeared to be in control, allowed the diversion of resources elsewhere. The king appointed his half-brother, Don John, to command the Christian fleet, and in October 1571 this won a resounding victory over the Turks in the gulf of Lepanto. The Ottoman navy was virtually wiped out and some 30,000 of the enemy killed or captured.

Lepanto was a severe blow to Turkish prestige, but it did not mean the end of the Sultan's power at sea. With a determination that matched Philip's own, he ordered another fleet to be built and soon made up the losses suffered at Lepanto. The Christian allies—Spain, Venice and the papacy—could not agree on a joint strategy and were not even able to expel the Turks from Cyprus. Philip had no intention of spending Spanish money for the benefit of Venetian trade or the Pope's crusading ambitions, and therefore recalled his ships. If Lepanto had shown that the Turks were not invincible at sea, it had also demonstrated that they could not be driven out of the Mediterranean altogether. Realisation of this led both sides gradually to disengage, particularly after 1580, when the Sultan was increasingly occupied with Persia while Philip was concentrating his attention on northern Europe. The Spaniards were left in control of the western and central Mediterranean—subject, of course, to the depredations of the Barbary corsairs—while the Turks were unchallenged in the eastern part.

The long struggle against the Turks had its repercussions within Spain itself, where the Moriscos, the converted Moors, were still unassimilated. They were in touch with their brethren in north Africa, and it was assumed, often rightly, that corsair raids on the Spanish coast were planned with Morisco assistance. This situation, with resentment on one side and fear on the other, was explosive, and the actions of the Spanish government were the spark which set it off. In 1567 new laws were introduced giving the Moriscos three years in which to leave Spain. Those who stayed on were to renounce their separate identity and give up speaking Arabic, wearing Arab dress and using Arab customs. The choice between exile or conformity was a false one, since the Moriscos' home was Spain and they had neither the wish nor the means to go into exile. Assimilation might have been possible, given a big programme of education and a long-term view, but the government was thinking in terms of immediate results, and far from trying to absorb the Moriscos it excluded them from the armed services and the church. This negative attitude could produce nothing but hostility, and on Christmas Eve 1568 the Moriscos of Granada rose in revolt.

The War of Granada was a long-drawn-out affair, fought with great bitterness on both sides. The Spanish government was unprepared for the outbreak, and took time to assemble an army. In 1570, however, Don John launched a full-scale campaign against the rebels, and by the autumn of that year they had been crushed. The government decided on the drastic solution of moving the entire Morisco population of some 150,000 away from the coastal areas, where it seemed to present such a threat to Spanish security. About 30,000 died on the long march inland: the survivors were dispersed among scattered towns and villages in the hope that they would gradually merge into the population as a whole. But they remained in practice an unassimilable element, and the Spanish insistence on religious orthodoxy and purity of blood cut them off from the very society that they had been commanded to join.

Philip II and Western Europe

As the 1570s drew to a close, Philip's attention shifted away from the Mediterranean, where the Turkish threat had been contained if not destroyed, towards the states of the Atlantic seaboard. He had been involved in this area from the beginning of his reign, because of the troubles in the Netherlands, but the outbreak of religious war in France and the commitment of England to the protestant cause had created not only a major challenge to Spanish power but also an opportunity for Philip to defeat all his enemies together. In 1578, the year in which Parma began the reconquest of the Netherlands, the death of the King of Portugal opened up the possibility of uniting the Iberian peninsula under Spanish control. The king had been killed leading the flower of the Portuguese nobility in a chivalric but disastrous campaign against the Moors in Morocco. The new king, Cardinal Henry, was old and feeble and had no heir. Among those with a good claim to succeed him was Philip himself, whose mother, Isabella, had been the daughter of Manoel I of Portugal.

Philip prepared the ground carefully, by ransoming many of the nobles who had been captured in Morocco and distributing bribes on a lavish scale among members of the administration. He also emphasised the advantages of a Spanish takeover, particularly so far as the preservation and protection of the Portuguese empire were concerned. By the time King Henry died, in 1580, Philip was ready. In June his troops crossed the border and within four months had occupied the entire country. In April of the following year the Portugese *Cortes* formally recognised Philip as their king, and he in return guaranteed the preservation of Portuguese liberties.

The acquisition of Portugal gave Philip two great advantages, in the shape of a large fleet and Atlantic ports from which to operate. Taken in conjunction with a substantial increase in the flow of bullion from the New World this meant that Spain was now well placed for a major campaign against her enemies, and in particular against England. The need for some decisive action was all too apparent, for as Philip himself observed in 1587 'the intervention of the English in Holland and Zeeland, together with their infestation of the Indies and the Ocean, is of such a nature that defensive methods are not enough to cover everything. It forces us to apply the fire in their own homeland, and so fiercely that they will have to rush back and retire from elsewhere'. A big programme of shipbuilding was put under way, and the council of war was hived off from the council of state and given its own executive machinery. 1587 would have been a good year for the despatch of an armada, from Philip's viewpoint, since the Guises were in the ascendant in France, and Parma was advancing in the Netherlands. But the Spanish admiral, the Marquis of Santa Cruz, insisted on waiting until his fleet could be assured of a crushing superiority in numbers, and Drake's raid on Cadiz in the spring of 1587 set back the preparations already made.

The Armada eventually sailed in May 1588—some 130 ships bearing over 20,000 sailors and soldiers. Its commander was not Santa Cruz, who had waited so long that death overtook him, but the Duke of Medina Sidonia, a great aristocrat whose experience in naval administration and high social standing made him a plausible if not inspired choice. The Armada was not designed as an expeditionary force. Medina Sidonia's orders were to avoid battle with the English, to maintain a tight formation, and simply to sweep the Channel clear so that Parma's seasoned troops could cross over from the Netherlands. Medina Sidonia did what he was told, and by the time the Armada anchored off Calais in August 1588 it had lost only two ships. But although Philip had given detailed instructions to his naval commander, he had not solved the crucial problem of how and where Parma's troops were to be embarked. Parma assumed that the port of Dunkirk would be used, but this was too shallow for direct embarkation, while if the soldiers had been ferried out to the galleons they would have been exposed to attack from the English and Dutch ships. In fact the army never embarked. While the Armada was waiting, the English attacked with fireships, broke up the tight formation, and fought a running battle in which the Spanish galleons suffered heavy damage. Short of food and ammunition, Medina Sidonia did not dare face the return passage through the Channel. Instead he took his ships right round the north coast of Scotland and south past Ireland, through terrible seas which battered and destroyed them. Of the great fleet that had set out from Spain, only half eventually returned.

The effect of the defeat of the Armada on Spain was similar to that of Lepanto on the Turks. The material loss was quickly made good, but the blow to Spanish prestige was enormous. Philip did not accept the judgment of 1588 as final. The great strength of Spain was demonstrated by the fact that in 1596 a new armada, better equipped than the earlier one, was ready to sail, and this time the capture of Calais by the Spaniards gave them a deepwater port from which an invading force could be embarked. The only element of uncertainty came from the weather, but this proved decisive. Violent storms broke up the armada, destroying a third of its ships, and when it set out in the following year, with its losses made up, raging seas and violent winds again dispersed it. Philip did not live long enough to show his determination and assurance of ultimate victory by organising yet another armada.

Spanish policy towards France was no more successful. In 1589 Philip had ordered Parma to stay on the defensive in the Netherlands so that he could, at a moment's notice, lead his troops against the Huguenots. He thereby lost what might have been a good chance of reuniting all the provinces under Spanish rule. Parma's interventions in France were extremely effective, and forced Henry of Navarre to raise the siege of Paris, but in the long term the identification of the Catholic League with Spain worked in Henry's favour. Philip's assumption that what was good for Spain was good for the catholic Church had never found much acceptance outside his own kingdoms, and the confusion of religious and political issues, from which he had hoped to profit, was being resolved in a highly unfavourable manner by the revival of the French monarchy.

Revolt in Aragon

In the last decade of his reign Philip had to deal with a revolt at home, in his kingdom of Aragon. This was a long-term consequence of his 'Castilianisation' of government, which caused resentment among non-Castilians and sapped their loyalty to the monarchy. All this resentment was brought out into the open by the flight of Perez, who took refuge in Aragon and called on the Justiciar for protection. The office of Justiciar was hereditary in a noble Aragonese family, and the Justiciar's court had the customary right to deal with cases in which the liberties of Aragon were involved. Philip, whose respect for such traditional liberties was considerable, agreed to pursue his action against Perez in the Justiciar's court, but the case became a *cause célèbre*, and as it dragged on Perez's revelations became more and more indiscreet. Philip had no wish for the secrets of his government to be published to the world, and therefore arranged with the Justiciar that the charge against Perez should be changed to one of heresy and the case transferred to the Inquisition.

By this time, however, Perez had become a popular hero and was regarded as the champion of Aragonese liberties against an absolutist and encroaching Castilian crown. His supporters among the lesser nobility rescued him from the Inquisition and restored him to the custody of the Justiciar. Further attempts to transfer him were blocked by the same methods.[1] There was talk of setting up a separate republic and appealing to Henry of Navarre for assistance. Philip was confronted with a major revolt in the heartland of his empire, and he had to assemble a substantial army in order to suppress it. In fact there was no opposition to his troops as they moved into Aragon in the autumn of 1591. The pattern of the Revolt of the *Comuneros* repeated itself, with the nobles at first joining the rebels and then, alarmed by the increasing radicalism which threatened their own privileged position, turning against them. Deprived of aristocratic support, the revolt quickly collapsed.

Now that Philip had Aragon at his mercy he could have integrated it with Castile and created a unitary state in Spain. But nothing was further from his thoughts. He made no attempt to annul the 'liberties' of Aragon nor even drastically to remodel them. Apart from reasserting his right to appoint viceroys from outside Aragon (as Charles V had done), and to dismiss the Justiciar should circumstances demand it, Philip left Aragon with the traditional distinctive features of its separate identity. This was in accordance with his assumptions about the nature of monarchical rule. Philip insisted that all his subjects must obey him, but he accepted that the royal authority should operate within an intricate network of local and individual rights and privileges. If this was absolutism it ran through very narrow channels, and Spain under the Habsburgs remained a federation of kingdoms owing allegiance to a common head but protected against him by the force of immemorial custom.

In 1595 Philip became ill with an infection of the blood, and three

[1] Perez eventually escaped and entered the service of Henry IV of France.

years later he retired to the Escorial to spend the last days of his life. It was in this palace-monastery, which he had created out of nothing and which enshrined so much of his own personality, that he died in September 1598 at the age of seventy. Although he had spent the greater part of his reign at war, either with the Turks or his fellow Christians, he seemed to have accomplished very little. France remained independent and potentially hostile, England was undefeated, the Netherlands had not been recovered, and the Turks still controlled the eastern Mediterranean. To make matters worse, the cost of this negative achievement had been enormous. The wealth of the Indies had been consumed; Spain, and in particular Castile, had been crushed by the burden of taxation; and military virtues had been exalted to the detriment of economic ones.

There was, however, another side to the coin. Philip had united the Iberian peninsula under Spanish rule and had added the Portuguese overseas empire to the already vast territories belonging to the crown of Castile. He had contained Turkish sea power; he had stopped the southern Netherlands from succumbing to protestantism or becoming independent; and he had helped uphold the catholic cause in France. Many of these things might have happened anyway, but the fact that they happened when and as they did must be attributed largely to Philip. He inherited from his father a double responsibility: to defend the Roman Catholic faith and to preserve a family empire against which powerful enemies were leagued. He was committed, in other words, to the maintenance of the *status quo*, and on the whole he was successful in preserving it. Given the conditions of late sixteenth-century Europe this was a major and positive achievement.

SEVENTEEN

Poland, Russia and the Baltic States in the Sixteenth Century

Poland

Fear of the Teutonic Knights had led to the formation of the federal state of Poland–Lithuania in the late fourteenth century, and the threat from the north remained a major preoccupation of Polish rulers during the course of the next hundred years. Casimir the Great, after a long struggle, forced the knights to accept the Peace of Thorn (Torun) in 1466, by which they agreed to hand over western Prussia to him, including the port of Danzig, and to hold eastern Prussia as a fief of the Polish crown. After Casimir's death, however, the knights denounced the treaty and extended their rule throughout the whole of Prussia once again. The Polish kings were fully occupied elsewhere, and not until 1519 could Sigismund I at least turn his attention towards his northern borders. He sent his army against the Teutonic Knights and defeated them in a number of battles, but could not drive them out of Prussia altogether. At this point the situation was transformed by the decision of their grand master, Albert of Hohenzollern, to adopt the Lutheran faith and secularise the Prussian possessions of the order. Sigismund was prepared to accept this if it meant peace on his Baltic border. Western, or 'Royal' Prussia once again became Polish, but East Prussia was formed into a duchy, under the hereditary rule of the Hohenzollerns, who paid homage for it to the King of Poland. The domains of the Teutonic Knights were now confined to Livonia and Estonia.

On the eastern frontier of Poland–Lithuania a major threat was developing with the rise of the principality of Moscow. Ivan III had already raided Lithuania in the closing years of Casimir's reign, and after Casimir's death he promptly renewed his attacks. In 1494 the

Lithuanians were forced to concede substantial areas and to acknowledge Ivan's claim to be Tsar of all the Russians (including, by implication, the many Russian-speaking peoples who lived in southern and
eastern Lithuania). Sporadic fighting continued during the next
twenty years, and although Polish–Lithuanian forces heavily defeated
the Russians at the battle of Orsha in 1514 they lost control of the
region around Smolensk, which became part of the Tsar's dominions.
Generally speaking the Poles could not, at this stage, hold up the
Russian advance westwards. All they could hope to do was slow it
down.

Lithuania was under pressure not only in the east but also in the
south, where the Ottoman Turks, having established themselves on the
Black Sea coast, were pushing into Moldavia. In the 1490s a Polish
attempt to reassert sovereignty over this region was crushingly
defeated, and after Sigismund I came to the throne in 1506 he concentrated on defending the *de facto* frontier by building a line of forts. This
stopped the Turks from penetrating further into Polish–Lithuanian
territory, although occasional raiding continued.

The Polish kings were nominal masters of a great state, but in all really
important matters they were dependent on the nobility, which formed
some ten per cent of the total population. In the national Diet (*Sjem*)
the greater nobles dominated the Senate or Upper House, while the
lesser nobility, or gentry, were masters of the Lower House. On many
questions the rule of unanimity prevailed, which meant that a single
opposing voice could hold up the adoption of a measure. The king
had some area for manoeuvre between the magnates and the gentry,
but the landowners as a whole were united in the defence of their own
privileges and preferred weak government to strong.

In society as in politics the nobles *were* Poland, and at a time when
serfdom was rapidly disappearing from western Europe it was being
reimposed in the east. Peasants had no legal right to leave their masters'
estates, and their payments and labour dues were remorselessly increased while the amount of common land available to them was cut
down. On territory belonging to the crown they had a right of appeal
to royal judges, but on nobles' estates they were completely at the
mercy of the landowner, the judgment of whose courts was final. The
towns on the other hand retained a large measure of independence,
but only on condition that their inhabitants confined themselves to
trade. In 1496 it was made illegal for townsmen to hold property in a

rural area, and in this way the aristocratic dominance of landed society was written in to the constitution. Yet although the nobles were rich and powerful they showed remarkably little concern for the national interest. They seem to have assumed that the crown would protect them at its own cost, and when Sigismund I called on them to vote money for his programme of fortress-building on the south-eastern frontiers they came near to open revolt.

During the course of the sixteenth century, the Polish nobles' determination to defend their 'liberties' to the utmost was reinforced by the claim to freedom of conscience and worship in religion. Diversity of religious belief had long been a feature of the Polish scene, for the Greek Orthodox Church had many adherents in Galicia, while the Russian Orthodox Church was entrenched in Lithuania. In other parts of the country the population was mainly Roman Catholic, though there was a large Jewish minority. The Roman Catholic Church in Poland, as in much of the rest of Europe, was worldly and corrupt at the opening of the sixteenth century, and very much under the influence of the king—particularly after Casimir received from Rome the right to appoint to bishoprics. Lutheranism spread rapidly in German-speaking areas, and this was accelerated by the transformation of East Prussia into a Lutheran duchy in 1525. Sigismund I, although he was aware of the faults of the Roman Catholic Church, did not want to see it disappear from his dominions, and issued a number of decrees against heresy, but only the bishops showed any enthusiasm for enforcing these. As far as the secular authorities were concerned, Lutheranism was acceptable on condition that it did not lead to social discontent. When social and religious radicalism did coincide, then the authorities were swift to take action. In 1525, for instance, when the artisans of Danzig rose in revolt, seized church property in the name of Luther and threatened to establish a commune, Sigismund took the town by assault and restored the *status quo* at the sword's point.

Lutheranism did not make much appeal to the Polish nobility, who were put off by its markedly 'German' flavour and its insistence on the need for obedience to the ruling prince. By 1550, however, Calvinist beliefs were infiltrating into Poland, and the presbyterian mode of church government, in which the pastor was elected by the laity and watched over by lay elders, made an immediate appeal to the nobility. It seemed to sanctify their social position by giving them the same control over the spiritual life of the community that they already exercised over its material aspects. There was no need for missionaries from Geneva or elsewhere. Calvinist ideas spread rapidly, and the protestant nobles soon came to be in a majority in the Polish Diet. Sigismund II, who succeeded his father in 1548, did his best to stem the protestant tide. Personally speaking, he was in favour of a state church on Hussite or anglican lines, but he needed the support of the catholic bishops if he was not to become simply a puppet in the hands of the nobles, and the bishops demanded that in return for their loyalty he should enforce religious orthodoxy. This was easier said than done, for Poland had become a refuge for protestants of varying opinions from all over Europe. The Bohemian Brethren, for instance, who adhered strictly to the teachings of John Hus, arrived in 1548, having been driven out of their own country; Anabaptist refugees found a home on the estates of sympathetic nobles; while in 1569 a Unitarian community was established at Rakow. Decrees against heresy could not be put into operation against the will of the landowners, and these were in favour at least of toleration, if not of outright commitment to the protestant cause. When the catholic bishops attempted to carry out a programme of repression, the Diet of 1552 countered with a demand for communion in both kinds and a vernacular mass. The nobles also pressed for a national church council to decide on the religious future of Poland, but the king—under strong pressure from the bishops, who knew that this might well be the prelude to their own downfall—withheld his consent.

Protestantism continued to spread, however, and looked as if it would sweep everything before it; but by the 1560s the Counter-Reformation was already under way in Europe, and its effects were soon felt in Poland. In 1563 a papal nuncio arrived, bringing with him a copy of the Trent decrees. He failed to persuade the Diet to accept these, though the king agreed to do so, but he did receive royal permission for the Jesuits to enter Poland. They arrived in 1565, and in five years brought about a dramatic transformation of the religious scene. They established colleges which became nurseries of the revived catholic faith; they used their considerable powers of persuasion to win over many leading Polish families; and they seemed all set to turn Poland into a catholic state. The protestants, alarmed by these developments, decided to sink their differences, and in 1570 the Calvinists, Lutherans and Bohemian Brethren formed a federation by accepting the Consensus of Sendomir. Under the terms of this agreement, every church was to keep its own organisation and form of worship, but synods were to be held in common.

The hardening of the lines of division between protestants and catholics might well have led to civil war, but the nobles appreciated that religious toleration was so closely intertwined with the maintenance of their own liberties that one could not exist without the other. It was to guarantee the preservation of both that in 1573, during the interregnum between the death of Sigismund II and the accession of Henry of Valois, the nobles agreed on the Compact of Warsaw, which they vowed not only to observe themselves but also to impose on all future rulers. 'As there is great discord in this kingdom touching the Christian religion', it ran, 'we promise, in order to avoid sedition such as has come to other kingdoms . . . that all of us of differing religions will keep the peace between ourselves and shed no blood.'

Sigismund II might have taken a stronger stand against the protestant nobility had it not been for the fact that he desperately needed their assistance. In 1558 Ivan the Terrible of Russia launched an invasion of Livonia, where the Teutonic Knights were still clinging to power. Livonia had a common frontier with Lithuania, and if the knights were to be expelled it was obviously in Poland's interests that she rather than Russia should take their place. Polish involvement in the fate of Livonia increased in 1561, when the Teutonic Knights dissolved their order, and in November of that year Sigismund declared the incorporation of Livonia into Lithuania. In face of the Russian menace, there was an obvious need to strengthen the rather loose, federal link between Lithuania and Poland, particularly since there were some people in Lithuania—adherents of the Russian Orthodox Church, for instance, and certain of the nobility—who would have preferred to come to terms with Ivan. This strengthening was brought about at Lublin, in 1569, when the decision was taken to end the federation and to fuse Poland and Lithuania (including Livonia) into a single, unitary state.

The struggle for Livonia was still in progress when Sigismund II died in 1572. He left no heir, and with him the rule of the Jagiello dynasty in Poland came to an end. Since the nobles had always insisted on the elective character of the Polish monarchy, it was now up to them to find a successor. There was no shortage of candidates for the Polish throne, but neither was there any general agreement on who to elect. The Roman Catholics were in favour of a Habsburg, and if the Emperor Maximilian II had taken his chance he might have added Poland to the already considerable dominions ruled over by his family. The Lithuanians on the other hand, preferred Ivan the Terrible, as the best guarantee of peace along their border with Russia. This deadlock was resolved by the French ambassador, who put forward the name of Henry of Valois, Duke of Anjou. Henry was acceptable to all parties, but only on condition that he did not try to impose absolutism or religious uniformity. Therefore, before his formal election in 1573, the new king was invited to accept the Henrician Articles. By these he would have bound himself to summon the Diet every two years and to be advised by a council of senators in the intervals between one Diet and another. Not surprisingly, Henry found such terms extremely distasteful and refused to accept them. This caused considerable confusion, and before the situation could be clarified Henry received the news of his accession to the throne of France. In the summer of 1574, therefore, he abandoned his Polish subjects to their interminable wrangling and returned home. The throne of Poland was once again vacant.

This time the catholics seized their opportunity, and the Polish primate announced that the Emperor Maximilian II was the new king. The senate approved his nomination, but the gentry of the lower house declared the election of Stephen Bathory, Prince of Transylvania, on the assumption that he—unlike a Habsburg—would be clay in their hands. The senate acquiesced and Stephen Bathory was duly elected King of Poland. He proved to be an excellent choice, for although a committed Roman Catholic, who wanted to reform the Church along the lines laid down by the Council of Trent, he was also tolerant by nature and aware of the need to preserve religious peace in Poland. His assumptions were shared by his chancellor, John Zamoyski, and the two men managed to set a catholic reformation on foot in Poland without unduly straining the mutual toleration that existed between the various faiths.

Stephen saw the need to expel the Russians from Livonia and reassert Polish sovereignty in this economically important region. He rallied the peasants and townsmen, as well as the gentry, to this patriotic cause, and also formed an alliance with the Swedes. In a brilliant campaign, which lasted from 1579 to 1581, he swept the Russians out of the territory they had conquered and forced Ivan to accept the Treaty of Yam Zapolsky, renouncing all Russian claims to Livonia.

The need for Poland to cultivate good relations with Sweden as a counterweight to Russia was so obvious that after the death of Stephen Bathory, in 1586, the Diet elected Sigismund, son of John III of Sweden, as their new king. Sigismund III was a taciturn and melancholic man, whose major passion in life was the advancement of the

Roman Catholic faith to which he had been converted. He regarded Poland merely as a stepping-stone to Sweden, and in 1592, on the eve of his accession to the Swedish throne, was prepared to trade his Polish crown to the Habsburgs in return for their support in Scandinavia. Such an attitude hardly endeared him to the Polish nobles, who still felt sore at the cavalier manner in which they had been treated by Henry III; nor was his intolerant catholicism welcome in a country which had hitherto been remarkably free from religious fanaticism.

Sigismund might nevertheless have been acceptable if he had fulfilled the hopes pinned on him by uniting Poland and Sweden in a defensive alliance against Russia. Unfortunately he became a major obstacle to the achievement of this aim. Following the death of his father in 1592, the Swedes refused to recognise Sigismund as king until he promised to rule constitutionally and preserve the established protestant church; and when, four years later, he attempted to free himself from these restrictions by the use of Polish troops, they declared him deposed (see p. 304). Sigismund never returned to Sweden, but his refusal to abandon his claim to the Swedish throne led to war between the two countries.

It seemed at one time as though the struggle between the two branches of the Vasa family—the Swedish and the Polish—would be transferred to Russia, for Sigismund could not resist fishing in the disturbed waters of the 'Time of Troubles' (see p. 301). He hoped to secure the Russian throne for himself or his son, thereby blocking similar Swedish ambitions and also opening Russia to the missionary activities of the revived Roman Catholic Church. It was in pursuit of these ambitions—neither of them directly relevant to Poland—that Polish troops were sent into Russia. These were at first remarkably successful, and in 1610 captured Moscow. They held on to the city for a year before being driven out, and some time later, in 1618, they again laid siege to the Russian capital. But Polish intervention had led to the resurgence of Russian national pride, and Sigismund had eventually to withdraw his troops. He held on to Smolensk—lost to the Russians a century earlier—but although this was in some ways a strengthening of Poland's eastern border it was also a standing affront to Russian pride and a constant incitement to revenge.

Within Poland itself, Sigismund's principal aim was to strengthen the authority of the crown, and in theory there was much to be said for freeing royal government from the restrictions imposed upon it by aristocratic selfishness. But instead of emphasising the monarch's role as a symbol of unity and defender of national interests, Sigismund identified himself with religious intolerance, absolutist tendencies and dynasticism. This led to an armed revolt of the Polish nobles, supported by the protestants, in 1606, and order was only restored after Sigismund had accepted the principle that the sovereign might be deposed if he attempted to rule in an unconstitutional manner. In short, far from strengthening the Polish monarchy Sigismund had lowered its prestige and weakened its authority.

Russia

Ivan the Great died in 1505, and the throne passed to his son Basil (Vasili) II, who continued the policies of strengthening the Tsar's authority at home and expanding the frontiers of the Muscovite state. Renewed war against Lithuania resulted in the annexation of Smolensk, in 1514. Other additions to the Tsar's dominions included Ryazan, to the south of Moscow, and Pskov, to the north-west.

So far as administration was concerned, Basil virtually excluded the boyars (the hereditary aristocracy) from state affairs and replaced them by secretaries—a development very similar to that which was taking place in the monarchies of western Europe. The boyars were not, of course, reconciled to this cutting down of their power, but they could not effectively challenge Basil. Their opportunity came in 1533 when Basil died, leaving as heir a three-year-old son, Ivan. For over a decade competing boyar factions engaged in a ruthless power struggle, and Ivan had to learn at an early age the arts of subterfuge, deceit and violence. At times it seemed as though the state which his father and grandfather had skilfully pieced together would collapse like a house of cards, but their work had in fact been so well based that it endured even this major crisis. Ivan managed not only to survive but actually to manoeuvre himself into a position of such strength that by the time he was seventeen, in 1547, he was ready to assume power. He therefore declared his minority ended and had himself crowned 'Tsar and Grand Prince of all Russia'.

Ivan IV was a passionate man, given to outbursts of uncontrollable fury, and his childhood experiences left him with a deep hatred of the boyars. Yet at first—under the influence of his much-loved first wife Anastasia, who came from the boyar family of Romanov—he was determined to rule justly and moderate his absolute power. In 1549 he summoned the first *Zemski Sobor*, or national assembly, and in 1550 he issued a code of law which provided, among other things, that the normal method of legislation should be by decrees of the boyar council, or *Duma*, subject only to confirmation by the Tsar. Central administration was improved by the creation of departments, while the military needs of the state were met by the formation of a standing army (the *Streltsy*). Local administration was also transformed. First of all the powers of the provincial governors were reduced, and then in 1555 all districts were given permission to elect councils to take over the work of the governors.

These developments, had they continued, might have led to the growth of genuinely representative institutions, and set Russia on a different path from that of absolutism. But the failure of his foreign policy led Ivan to search for a scapegoat, and he soon convinced himself that the boyars, acting in treacherous collusion with his foreign enemies, were responsible for the humiliating reverses which Russian armies had suffered. Ivan determined to take his revenge. In 1564 he left Moscow and announced his decision to abdicate. But in a couple of letters to the merchants and people of the city he threw the blame for all the disorders and defeats that the country had undergone on the boyars. This gamble paid off, for the citizens invited him to come back on his own terms.

Ivan now set about breaking boyar power by striking at its economic foundations. Towns and districts from all over Russia, amounting in all to about half the country, were placed in a separate and special category of *Oprichnina* or crown land, and their boyar owners were replaced by men who owed everything to the Tsar. The *Duma* was allowed to control all land outside the *Oprichnina*, and individual boyars were permitted to retain their offices and dignities, but the Tsar was now owner of half the country and had created a new aristocracy to counter the old. The boyars did not give in without a struggle. Plots were frequent, but Ivan met them with merciless repression which earned him the name of 'the Terrible'. The reign of terror extended to the peasantry, who were forbidden to leave the *Oprichnina*, where they were virtually condemned to permanent servitude. Many, of course, did leave, and fled to the periphery of the Tsar's empire, beyond the effective range of his vengeance. But their flight caused an acute shortage of labour in many areas, making the lot of those who stayed behind even more miserable.

The military failures which led to Ivan's abandonment of his reforming policy came about as a result of his attempt to take over Livonia. Before this, however, he had been very successful in a number of campaigns against the Tatar khanates—the successor states of the Mongol empire. Kazan was taken by assault in 1552, and in 1556 the Khanate of Astrakhan was annexed, thereby securing Russian control over the river Volga and the trade route to the Caspian. Ivan's councillors urged him to follow up these successes by an attack on the Crimean Tatars, but he insisted on switching his attention to the north-west, where he intended to gain an exit to the Baltic. At first his campaign against Livonia went well. By 1558 much of eastern Estonia was in Russian hands and Ivan's troops had captured the port of Narva on the Gulf of Finland, thereby winning access to the Baltic and its valuable trade.

Ivan was helped by the fact that Poland was not ready for a major war, but this situation changed after the unification of Poland and Lithuania in 1569 and even more so after Stephen Bathory was elected King of Poland in 1575. Sweden, alarmed by the Russian advance in an area which she regarded as her own sphere of influence, took possession of Reval and laid claim to the whole of Estonia. Ivan was faced with growing opposition and at the same time he had to deal with a stab in the back from the Crimean Tatars, who captured Moscow in 1571 and burnt it to the ground (except for the Kremlin). By 1579 Stephen Bathory had defeated Ivan's armies and was carrying the war into Russia itself. In 1579 he besieged Pskov, while the Swedes were completing their conquest of Estonia with the capture of Narva. Ivan had to acknowledge defeat. In 1582 he agreed to the Treaty of Yam Zapolsky by which he made peace with Poland at the price of renouncing all Russian claims to Livonia, and in the following year he formally ceded Estonia to Sweden. The exclusion of Russia from access to the Baltic had been confirmed, and the long Russian struggle to take over part of the possessions of the Teutonic Order had ended in total failure. This was the situation when Ivan the Terrible died in 1584.

Ivan's legacy to Russia was a mixture of good and bad. His defeats in the north must be set against his considerable successes against the Tatars and his extension of Russian power towards the south and east. Similarly his failure to gain direct access to the trade of the Baltic was partly compensated for by the fact that English merchants, with Ivan's active encouragement, were opening up the direct route to

Russia, via the White Sea. By splitting Russia in half Ivan disrupted the economy, caused rural depopulation, and brought many parts of his dominions to the verge of chaos. Yet he succeeded in centralising the Russian state and in creating a class of landowners which owed everything to the crown and regarded loyalty to the Tsar as its own best security.

Ivan could not, of course, overcome the fundamental weakness of any absolutism—namely its dependence on the vagaries of hereditary succession. His son and successor, Theodore (Fedor) I, was, in Ivan's own words, more fitted to be a bell-ringer in a convent than Tsar of Russia, and was totally dependent on his brother-in-law, Boris Godunov. On Theodore's death, in 1598, Boris formally took possession of the throne, but in fact he had been ruler of Russia since at least 1585. Boris continued many of Ivan the Terrible's policies. He supported the crown nobility against the boyars, and tried to check rural depopulation by enforcing serfdom in its most rigid form. He encouraged English merchants to develop their trade through the White Sea; and after five years of hard fighting he forced the Swedes to hand back, in 1595, the Finnish territories which they had snatched from Ivan. Along the southern borders of Russia, he built a string of fortified towns, to hold the Tatars in check, and he offered subsidies to the Habsburg Emperor, Rudolf II, to help contain the growing menace of the Ottoman Turks.

While Boris lived, the Russian state and its imperial head were relatively strong, but after his death in 1605 the 'Time of Troubles' set in. Boris's son, Theodore (Fedor) II, died in the same year as his father; while Theodore I's heir, Dmitri, had died in 1591. But a pretender soon appeared and with boyar support took possession of Moscow in 1605 and declared himself to be Tsar Dmitri. The pseudo-Dmitri's wild life and catholic tendencies soon alienated him from his supporters, however, and in 1606 another revolt took place, led by a boyar, Basil Shuiski. This was successful, the pseudo-Dmitri was killed, and Basil Shuiski became Tsar. He paid his debt to the boyars by formally promising not to rule without their advice and not to take any action against them except by due process of law.

The support of the boyar landowners did not make Basil Shuiski any more acceptable to the peasantry, particularly those who had fled from the iron rule of Ivan the Terrible and set up a quasi-independent Cossack republic in southern Russia. They now rose in rebellion under a second pseudo-Dmitri. Basil appealed to Sweden for help, and in

Charles IX sent him a Swedish expeditionary force. But this action return for a formal renunciation of all Russian claims on Livonia only served to draw in Charles's enemy, Sigismund III of Poland. In 1609 Sigismund's troops laid siege to Smolensk, and in the following year another Polish army, moving towards Moscow, defeated a combined Russian-Swedish force at Klushino. In July 1610, therefore, the Moscow boyars, supported by the clergy, forced Basil Shuiski to abdicate and enter a monastery. The throne of the Tsars was now without a legitimate occupant, and the northern powers struggled for possession of it.

The boyars preferred Polish rule to that of Sweden and joined with the crown nobility in offering the throne to Sigismund's son, Ladislaw, on condition that he would accept the Orthodox faith. Sigismund, however, was determined to open up Russia to Roman Catholicism and refused to accept the proposed terms. This affront to Russian national and religious pride sparked off an uprising against the Polish troops—who had been allowed in to Moscow on the assumption that Ladislaw would accept the offer of the throne—and they had to take refuge in the Kremlin. Chaos was now general throughout Russia, and the 'Time of Troubles' only began to draw to a close when Michael Romanov—a member of the popular boyar family which had provided Ivan the Terrible with his first wife—managed to rally Russian nationalist feeling behind him. In 1612 the Polish troops in Moscow were compelled to capitulate, and in the following year a specially summoned *Zemski Sobor* chose Michael as Tsar. With his accession the long rule of the Romanovs began.

The fact that the Russian state had survived the 'Time of Troubles' demonstrated the strength of the foundations laid by Ivan the Great and Ivan the Terrible. They had created a new power in northern Europe and extended the rule of the Grand Prince of Moscow from the White Sea to the Caspian. In the west, Russia was pressing hard against the frontiers of Poland-Lithuania, while in the south and east the way had been opened to expansion at the expense of the Tatar khanates. At home a crown nobility had been created as a counterweight to the boyars, and the absolute authority of the Tsar had been asserted as the only viable alternative to aristocratic factionalism. The Tsar had become the focus not simply of national pride but also of religious sentiment. The belief in 'Holy Russia', in the Third Rome ruled over by the heirs of the Caesars, no doubt meant little to the peasants who had the strait-jacket of serfdom forced upon them, but

it was a political myth of great potency, and one that the states of
Europe had to reckon with.

Sweden

The main concern of Gustavus Vasa, who ascended the Swedish throne
in 1523 as Gustavus I, was to increase the authority of the crown at the
expense of the aristocracy. For nearly two hundred years the Swedish
nobility, through the council which they controlled, had taken a major
part in the government of the country, and the fact that the monarchy
was elective served to emphasise that the king was the servant and not
the master of his people. In Sweden, however, as in other European
states, the sixteenth century saw increasing emphasis on royal authority as the guarantor of order in a period of social and religious
revolution, and it was in the reign of Gustavus I that this concept
triumphed—for a time, at least—over the older 'constitutional' one.
Gustavus had all the advantages which came from subordinating the
Church and transferring its wealth to the crown, and he could call on
the support of the non-aristocratic elements who were represented in
the *Riksdag* (Diet). In 1544 he persuaded the *Riksdag* to accept the
Succession Pact, transforming Sweden from an elective into a hereditary monarchy. Previously the aristocracy had been able to demand a
quid pro quo, in the shape of confirmation of their own privileges,
before electing a new king, but in future they would be poorly placed
to bargain with a monarch who owed his throne not to them but to
God.

Gustavus I succeeded because he worked hard at the business of
government and kept out of expensive foreign adventures. Apart from
a brief war with Russia he remained at peace, but at the same time he
built up Swedish defences by expanding the navy and, in 1544,
founding a conscript army. His successor, Eric XIV, held a view of the
royal office which was even more exalted than that of Gustavus I, and
Eric, like his father, cultivated the *Riksdag* and the non-aristocratic
groups in Sweden. But he did not pursue his father's pacific policy.
The powers of northern Europe were already scrambling to take over
the possessions of the Teutonic Order, and Eric was determined that
Sweden should have a substantial share of the spoils. When, in 1561,
the port of Reval in Estonia appealed to Sweden for protection, Eric
sent an expeditionary force which gradually occupied the greater part
of Estonia and laid the foundations of a Swedish empire in the Baltic.

This led to hostilities with Denmark, which regarded the Baltic as a Danish preserve and was determined to maintain a monopoly of direct trade with the west.

The formal occasion for war was provided by Frederick II of Denmark, who wished to revive the Scandinavian union and ostentatiously displayed the Swedish arms as part of his own escutcheon. Eric took up the implied challenge to Swedish independence, and from 1563 to 1570 the two countries were locked in the bitter struggle known as the Seven Years War of the North. The strain of prolonged fighting upset the balance of Eric's unstable character. Relations between him and the Swedish aristocracy were already bad, since they resented his preference for 'new men'—the 'Rule of the Secretaries'—but Eric's mistrust and suspicion of the nobles now mounted to such a degree of intensity that in 1568 he stabbed one of their leaders to death. The nobles rose in self-defence, deposed and imprisoned Eric, and in 1569 transferred the crown to Eric's brother, who took the title of John III. One of John's earliest actions was to end the exhausting war with Denmark. By the Peace of Stettin in 1570 he promised that Sweden would give up her Estonian lands, but he always found excuses for not carrying out this solemn engagement, and Estonia in fact remained Swedish.

John III was an expert theologian who hoped to lead the way to reconciliation between the Roman Catholic and Lutheran churches. He combined the elements of Lutheran and catholic worship in a liturgy of his own devising—the 'Red Book'—and in 1577 ordered this to be used in the Swedish church. He also agreed to receive envoys from Rome, hoping that he would be able to persuade the Pope to make concessions, such as authorising clerical marriage and communion in both kinds. When he found that the Pope was not willing to compromise he broke off negotiations and in 1580 ordered the envoys—whose only significant achievement had been the conversion of his son, Sigismund—to leave the country. John did not withdraw the Red Book, and so long as he was king his supporters—the 'Liturgists'—could be assured of considerable influence in ecclesiastical affairs. But they had no real hold over the Swedish people, who had become deeply attached to their Lutheran church, and John's reforms, however well-intentioned, only served to sow distrust between him and his subjects.

In foreign affairs John continued the expansionist policy of his predecessor by strengthening the Swedish hold on the Gulf of Finland.

Kexholm was captured, the Russians were driven out of the whole of Estonia, and in September 1581 Narva was taken by storm. Two years later Ivan the Terrible agreed to a truce which left Sweden in possession of the territories she had occupied.

Much of Sweden's success had been due to an informal alliance with Poland, and the advantages of this were so obvious that on the death of Stephen Bathory in 1586 John proposed that his own son, Sigismund, should be elected king. The proposal was accepted, and in 1587 the prospect of an eventual union between Sweden and Poland was opened up by Sigismund's accession to the Polish throne. This prospect became a reality in 1592, when Sigismund succeeded his father as King of Sweden. But Sigismund soon aroused opposition to his rule. His committed Roman Catholicism evoked no favourable response from his Lutheran subjects, and the nobles, who found themselves once again excluded from government after a brief honeymoon period at the opening of John's reign, feared that Roman Catholicism would go hand-in-hand with royal absolutism. Aristocratic rebels found a leader in John's brother, Duke Charles, and Sigismund, after vainly trying to assert his authority with the aid of Polish troops, had finally to return to Poland in 1598. He left Sweden under the effective control of Charles and an aristocratic council.

The alliance between the nobles and the ambitious and unscrupulous Charles soon broke down, but Charles won the support of the *Riksdag*, which he summoned frequently, by posing as the guardian of popular 'liberties' against the threat of aristocratic oligarchy. In 1600 the *Riksdag* confirmed sentences of death on a number of Charles's leading opponents among the nobility, and from then on his rule was virtually unchallenged, even though he did not formally assume the crown (as Charles IX) until 1604. The council, which had formerly been the heart of the administration, declined with the aristocracy, and in 1602 the *Riksdag* formally resolved that 'henceforth the council shall give advice and not govern'.

The enmity between the Polish and Swedish branches of the house of Vasa made it essential for Sweden to come closer to Russia. Charles kept on good terms with Boris Godunov, and in 1609 he signed a treaty with Basil Shuiski by which he bound himself to send an expeditionary force to the Tsar's assistance in return for the abandonment of Russian claims on Livonia. This immediately brought Sweden into open conflict with Poland, who claimed Livonia for herself, and in 1610 Polish troops were instrumental in bringing about the deposi-

tion of Basil Shuisky. In the following year Denmark also joined in
the war against Sweden, and the 'Time of Troubles' that had begun in
Russia with the death of Boris Godunov spread throughout the entire
Baltic area. This was the position when, in October 1611, Charles IX
died, leaving as his heir and successor a sixteen-year-old boy named
Gustavus Adolphus.

With a new king in Sweden and, from the end of 1612, a new Tsar
in Russia, peace was gradually re-established in northern Europe. In
1613 Sweden and Denmark came to terms in the Treaty of Knared.
Sweden agreed to pay a large indemnity, and until it had been paid the
Danes were to hold on to Alvsborg, in south-west Sweden, which they
had captured during the war. On the other hand, Swedish ships were
to be free from all tolls as they passed through the Sound—the strip of
water which marked the entrance to the Baltic. The Swedish war
against Poland dragged on until the Truce of Tolsburg in 1618, but by
the time this was signed peace had already been concluded with
Russia by the Treaty of Stolbovo, in 1617. Under its provisions the
Tsar formally recognised Swedish sovereignty over Kexholm and
Ingria, thereby implicitly accepting Swedish control over Russian
trade passing through the Gulf of Finland. Sweden had now achieved
one of her major aims, and, as Gustavus Adolphus proudly informed
the *Riksdag*, 'the Russian . . . cannot now launch a single boat (let alone
a fleet) on the Baltic without our permission'.

Gustavus's pride was justified, for in the course of the sixteenth
century Sweden had begun to break through the Danish barrier which
cut her off from direct trade with the west; she had established, in
Estonia, the nucleus of a commercial empire in the southern Baltic;
and she had held back Russian westward expansion. At home the
dispute between the crown and the aristocracy, which had led to blood-
shed on more than one occasion, seemed to have been resolved. At his
accession Gustavus Adolphus accepted a charter which listed the abuses
committed by Charles IX and set up safeguards against any repetition
of them. The new king swore to uphold the Lutheran state church and
not to impose any new taxes without the consent of the council and
Riksdag. He promised that councillors should be free to offer their
advice without fear of royal anger, and that the noble holders of great
offices of state should be secure in their tenure as long as they fulfilled
their duties. The best assurance that the voice of the nobility would
once again be listened to came from the appointment of a great
aristocrat, Axel Oxenstierna, as chancellor and the king's obvious

readiness to be advised by him. It seemed as though aristocratic constitutionalism and royal absolutism might be able not merely to coexist but even to work together in harmony, thereby providing a secure political base from which Sweden could make a bid for predominance in northern Europe.

Denmark

Christian III had firmly established himself on the Danish throne by 1536, and his main concern thereafter was to hold on to it. To avoid undermining the financial strength of the crown he kept out of war and worked towards a settlement with the Emperor Charles V, who had still not reconciled himself to the exclusion of Christian II and his descendants from the Danish throne. Peace, amounting to confirmation of the *status quo*, was at last concluded at Speyer in 1544, and from then until the end of his reign, in 1559, Christian III was free from foreign entanglements. Peace soon gave way to war, however, when Frederick II, 'a brutal extravert',[1] succeeded to the Danish throne. Frederick hoped to revive the Scandinavian union under his own leadership and threw down a challenge to Eric XIV by quartering the Swedish arms with his own. The Seven Years War of the North which followed was, however, more than a personal squabble between two kings. Denmark was clinging to control of the Sound, since her wealth and her greatness derived from the tolls levied on the trade which flowed through this major artery. Sweden, on the other hand, was a rising power, impatient of the checks which history and geography had imposed upon her. These seven years of open warfare were the first round in the struggle not simply for control of the Baltic but, in the long run, for mastery in northern Europe. Both states were more or less evenly matched, and the war in fact decided nothing. But the financial strain had been very great on Denmark, and Frederick, his martial ardour assuaged, spent the rest of his reign in peace and used his revenues for more constructive purposes—such as subsidising the great Danish astronomer, Tycho Brahe.

The Treaty of Stettin, which brought the Seven Years War of the North to an end, provided for joint meetings of the Danish and Swedish councils to settle outstanding disputes. But this implied a degree of aristocratic influence which was unacceptable to Christian

---

[1] Michael Roberts, *The Early Vasas*, Cambridge University Press, 1968. p. 153.

IV, who ascended the Danish throne in 1588 at the age of eleven and took over the government in 1596. He was also resentful of the expansion of Swedish power into the Arctic regions over which Denmark claimed sovereignty, and after the failure of attempts at a negotiated settlement he prepared for war. His opportunity came when Sweden was embroiled with Russia in 1611. German mercenaries in Danish pay struck into south-east Sweden and captured Kalmar, while on the west coast Alvsborg, near Gothenburg, was occupied. By the Treaty of Knared, which brought the war to a close in 1613, Sweden agreed to pay Denmark a very large indemnity for the return of the occupied territory; but the Danes—mindful of the way in which the Swedes had broken their promise to withdraw from Estonia in 1570—insisted on holding on to Alvsborg until the last instalment of the indemnity had been handed over. For their part the Danes recognised the right of Swedish ships to pass through the Sound without paying toll. Denmark had not abandoned her traditional claim to control the entrance to the Baltic, but she had been forced to acknowledge the fact that other people, such as the Swedes and the Dutch, had a vital interest in Baltic commerce and could not be excluded merely at will. In short it was now the turn of Denmark, as it had earlier been that of Lubeck and the Hanseatic League, to adjust to a situation in which her financial and political strength was being gradually eroded by the emergence of new powers in northern Europe.

EIGHTEEN

The Ottoman Turks, and Central and Eastern Europe, in the Sixteenth Century

The Ottoman Turks

In contrast to the disunity of the Christian powers in the early sixteenth century, the Ottoman Turks were a united and formidable fighting force. Their major asset was an army which was regarded by its enemies with a justified mixture of awe and fear. This army was the fruit of Turkish tolerance towards the peoples they had conquered, for although the greater part of the population of the Ottoman empire was Jewish or Christian, the Turks were not interested in conversion. Christians were left in peace to practise their religion, on condition that they paid tribute money (which was used to finance the military campaigns of the Sultan) and accepted the obligations imposed by the system of *Devshirme*. This involved the conscription of male children from Christian families for the service of the Sultan. They were taken away from their parents, brought up as Muslims, sent to various parts of the empire to be trained, and then drafted into the army, either as Janissaries (infantry) or Sipahis of the Porte (household cavalry). There were some 30,000 men in all, divided equally between infantry and cavalry, and they formed the finest fighting force in Europe. There were in addition the ordinary Sipahis, or feudal levies, who provided the bulk of the cavalry.

Although the Turks seemed—and were—so formidable, they were not without their weaknesses. The fact that the state was geared to war meant that it had to keep on fighting. As long as the frontiers of the Ottoman empire were moving forward, the army was fully occupied and reasonably contented, but holding operations were not to its liking. The Turks were behind the west in artillery and military engineering, and as they struck deeper and deeper into Europe they came up against the limits imposed by contemporary means of communication. By the time the Sultan had left Constantinople and arrived in the Balkans to mount a major campaign he would have only a few weeks left before the onset of winter, and it was this factor, as much as the resistance of the western powers, that eventually limited the Ottoman advance. There was also the problem of fighting on two fronts. By 1520 the belligerence of Persia had been curbed, but this happy state of affairs would obviously not endure for ever, and on a number of occasions a successful Turkish offensive in the west had to be called off because of a renewed threat from the east.

Suleiman I, 'the Magnificent', who succeeded his father, Selim, in 1520, was one of the greatest of all sixteenth-century rulers; a warrior but also a cultured and learned man, a lover of the arts and a lawgiver. A Venetian observer described his appearance shortly after he ascended the throne. 'He is twenty-five years old, tall, but wiry, and of a delicate complexion. His neck is a little too long, his face thin and his nose aquiline. He has a faint moustache and a small beard: nevertheless his expression is pleasant, although his skin has rather a pallor. His reputation is that of a wise lord, he is said to be studious, and everybody hopes that his rule will be good.' Expectations were fulfilled, for under Sulieman the Ottoman empire reached the pinnacle of its power and prestige, while its ruler became renowned not only throughout the Muslim world but among his Christian enemies as well.

One of Suleiman's first actions was to demand tribute from young King Louis II, the ruler of Bohemia and Hungary. When this was refused, he invaded Hungary and, in August 1521, captured Belgrade. This marked the limit of Turkish advance for some years, because of the need to concentrate men and money on the campaign against Rhodes, but in 1526 Suleiman gave orders to renew the offensive. The Hungarians were divided among themselves, and when Louis took the decision to risk fighting, before all his forces had assembled, he was signing his own death warrant. In the battle that took place at Mohacs, north-west of Belgrade, in August 1526, the Hungarian army was totally destroyed, and Louis, fleeing from the disaster, was drowned. The Turks swept north, occupying Buda and Pest, until they came up against the frontiers of Austria. There they paused to consolidate their gains and prepare for an assault upon the Habsburg capital, Vienna. By 1529 Suleiman's plans were complete. In May he left Constantinople, in July he arrived at Belgrade, and in late September he appeared before Vienna. But already the winter was drawing on, and the campaigning season was virtually at a close. Suleiman tried to take the city by storm, but the defenders beat back the Turkish assailants, and he had to order a retreat. His troops suffered badly from the cold as they made the long march back to Belgrade in bitter weather, but at least they were free from any other enemy, since Ferdinand was in no position to follow up his victory.

Ferdinand, who had taken the title of King of Hungary after the death of his brother-in-law, Louis II, would have been willing to make terms with the Sultan, but Suleiman would not abandon John Zapolya, ruler of Transylvania, who also claimed the Hungarian throne (see p. 327). In 1532, therefore, fighting broke out again along the Danube, but Suleiman was held up for three vital weeks by the resistance of a key fortified position, and his projected attack on Vienna was turned instead into a foray in strength. The Turks suffered from the fact that they had no major base north of Belgrade, and this, as well as renewed trouble from Persia, persuaded Suleiman to agree to a truce with Ferdinand in 1533.

As long as Turkish possessions in the southern Balkans were protected by the buffer state of Transylvania, Suleiman had no compelling reason to intervene. But in 1540 John Zapolya died, leaving only an infant son to succeed him. Ferdinand promptly asserted his right to Transylvania (as a former part of the kingdom of Hungary) and sent his troops into Turkish Hungary to attack Buda. The Transylvanian nobles appealed to Suleiman for assistance, and in August 1541 the Sultan arrived in Transylvania and installed Zapolya's son, John Sigismund, as ruler. Two years later he renewed his Danube offensive and this time succeeded in capturing Gran, which gave him the base he needed. The Turks now controlled two-thirds of Hungary, including Transylvania, and in 1547 Ferdinand, unable to change this situation, accepted it by agreeing to pay tribute to the Sultan for the remaining third of Hungary, over which he actually ruled. Suleiman thereby achieved his principal objective of securing the Ottoman hold on the Balkan peninsula by a line of buffer states; he was now more concerned with consolidating what he already held than with pushing further into Europe.

Much the same considerations affected Suleiman's eastern policy. Further expansion, at the expense of the Persians, would help secure possession of the former Mameluke territories and enable them to be firmly incorporated within the Ottoman empire. Therefore, in the 1530s, Suleiman renewed the struggle against Persia. In 1533, pushing east towards the Caspian, the Turks captured Tabriz; in the following year, striking south-east along the Tigris, they took Baghdad and pressed on to the shores of the Persian Gulf. Ten years later, in 1548–49, the area around Lake Van was occupied, and by the time Suleiman died Ottoman territory extended unbroken from the Black Sea to the Persian Gulf. In the east as in the west the Turks had come up against the limits imposed by geography and communications, which prevented them from operating at full strength against major powers such as Persia and the Habsburgs. But the Ottoman empire was protected by a ring of dependent territories which guarded it against sudden attack and left it firmly embedded in south-eastern Europe and the Levant.

During Suleiman's reign the Turks also became a major naval power. Mohamed II had assaulted the island of Rhodes, held by the Knights of St John, who preyed on ships taking pilgrims to Mecca and threatened Turkish communications in the eastern Mediterranean. The attack had been brought to a premature halt by Mohamed's death, but by the time Suleiman came to the throne forty years later the acquisition of Egypt and Syria had made it even more essential to protect the sea route from Constantinople to Cairo, and this could not be done while the Knights were still ensconced in Rhodes. In June 1522, therefore, Suleiman ordered an all-out attack on the island, and by the end of the year it was his. For combined operations of this sort a navy was, of course, essential, but the idea of using it as a separate force to transform the balance of power in the Mediterranean was slow to develop. In 1532, however, the Genoese admiral Doria, who commanded the naval forces of Charles V, pounced on the port of Coron, in the Morea, and occupied it. This showed Suleiman the possibilities of sea power, and he was quick to learn the lesson. The Turks were lacking in experience at sea, but on the Barbary coast of North Africa lived Muslim corsairs who made fat profits from attacking and plundering Christian ships in the Mediterranean, and who were only too pleased to offer their services to the Sultan in return for subsidies. Greatest of all the corsairs was Khaireddin Barbarossa, and in 1534 the Sultan appointed him Admiral of the Turkish fleet. Barbarossa inaugurated his command by striking at Tunis, whose Moorish king was a Spanish puppet, and capturing it in August 1534. From there he could threaten Sicily and southern Italy, and even the vital imperial line of communications from Barcelona to Genoa.

Charles V decided on a major operation to cut out this cancer, and in June 1535 the imperial fleet under Doria carried the Emperor and a large army to the coast of North Africa. The citadel and town of Tunis were taken by storm and the greater part of Barbarossa's fleet was captured. It seemed for one euphoric moment as though Charles had finally solved the corsair problem, but Barbarossa himself escaped to Algiers with a number of ships, and from there he continued his raids. If Charles could have followed up his successful assault on Tunis with one on Algiers he might indeed have checked the growth of Turkish naval power in the central Mediterranean, but as always he had other commitments which prevented him from exploiting his victory.

Two years after his capture of Tunis, Charles was given the opportunity to challenge the Turks at sea in their own end of the Mediterranean. In 1537, as part of their campaign to take over the surviving outposts of the Venetian commercial empire, the Turks attacked Corfu. The Venetians appealed to the Emperor for support, and Charles ordered Doria to take command of the combined Christian fleets. The opposing navies clashed at Prevesa, south east of Corfu, in 1538, and the allies were heavily defeated. Turkish command of the eastern Mediterranean was now a fact of life, and remained so until Lepanto, over thirty years later. In the central Mediterranean Charles went on to the defensive, but he could not prevent the Turks, with French assistance, from penetrating into this area, nor could he crush the corsairs. In 1541 a combined operation against Algiers, designed to repeat the success of the Tunis expedition, was broken up by violent weather and accomplished nothing. Two years later the Turkish fleet openly co-operated with the French in the capture of Nice, and went on to spend the winter in Toulon, which became a Muslim enclave in the Christian world. This affront to the Christian conscience lasted only a few months, for Francis I, recognising the damage to his reputation caused by so open an alliance with the infidel, paid the Turks to return to Constantinople in 1544. They did so, pillaging Naples *en route* and leaving a trail of fear behind them.

Barbarossa died in 1546, but the Ottoman naval offensive continued. In 1551 the Sultan's navy captured Tripoli, and Philip II's attempt to retake it in 1560 met disaster at Djerba. Occasional mammoth campaigns against corsair bases were not an effective way of checking Turkish naval power, as Philip quickly came to realise. Instead he decided to challenge the Turks in what they had made their own element by building a big Spanish navy. He was still thinking primarily in terms of defence, but the situation was changing to his advantage. The Turkish repulse from Malta in 1565, and the Sultan's failure to support the Morisco revolt of 1569, showed that Ottoman sea power, like Ottoman land power, was up against the geographical limits of effective operation. In the eastern Mediterranean, however, the Turks were still predominant, and in 1570 began their assault on the Venetian-held island of Cyprus. Their action led directly to their total defeat at Lepanto in 1571, but the long-term consequences of this were, like those of Charles V's capture of Tunis, less significant than at first seemed likely. The Sultan ordered more ships to be built to replace those that had been lost, and soon the Turks were as formidable at sea as they had ever been. In 1574 they even expelled the Spaniards from Tunis and thereby added a third corsair state to the two—Algiers and Tripoli—already in existence.

By the closing decade of the sixteenth century, Spain and the Turks had come to accept the fact that they could neither of them dominate the entire Mediterranean. In fact the ultimate victors of their long struggle were the Dutch and the English, those Venetians of the north, who were used to long voyages and showed great daring, as well as great persistence, in exploiting the opportunities open to them. There was more than a touch of irony in the fact that Muslim Turks and catholic Spaniards had unwittingly combined to render up the Mediterranean to their common enemy, the protestant sea powers of northern Europe.

Under Suleiman's successor, Selim II (1566–74), there was no major change in the land frontiers of Turkey, but when Murad III came to the throne in 1574 he began preparations for a big campaign against the Persians, who had renewed their challenge to Ottoman power. The war opened in 1578, and went well for the Turks. By 1584 Murad had conquered Georgia, and in the course of the next three years he established Ottoman rule over the adjacent area of Azerbaijan. The Shah was forced to sue for peace, and in 1590 recognised Turkish possession of the occupied territories. With his eastern frontiers once more secure, Murad III took up afresh the struggle against the Habsburgs, which was continued by his successor, Mohamed III (1595–1603). The Turks were not at first successful. Sigismund Bathory, the ruler of Transylvania, joined the Emperor in resisting the Ottoman attack, and from 1601 to 1605 Transylvania, which had hitherto been a

Turkish satellite, came under imperial control. But the Emperor showed such a degree of insensitivity to the local inhabitants, affronting both their protestant religious beliefs and their local and class privileges, that he swung opinion back in favour of the Turks. Yet although, as a consequence, the Sultan was able to conclude peace on favourable terms, the Turks made no gains of any significance. By the treaty of Zsitva-Torok in November 1606 the Sultan agreed to accept the Emperor as an equal after one final payment of tribute money, and to accord him his full titles. As for frontiers, each side was to hold the territory it already occupied.

By the time peace was made a new Sultan was on the Ottoman throne. Ahmed I (1603–17) had the misfortune to coincide in time with Shah Abbas, one of the greatest of Persian rulers. Shah Abbas was determined to regain the territories snatched by Murad III at a time of acute internal dissension within Persia, and Ahmed was unable to stop him. The Turks were pushed out of the western Caspian area and in 1612 had to sue for peace. They agreed to cede all the lands they had acquired in 1590, and although war was renewed in 1615 the same terms were confirmed in the peace settlement of 1618.

The Turks in the early seventeenth century were undoubtedly a less formidable power than they had been a hundred years earlier. There is no simple explanation for their decline, though inflation, debasement, and corruption among officials were becoming endemic in the Ottoman state. With static frontiers, the army grew restive, and as the *Devshirme* system no longer produced enough recruits, Muslim children were admitted in increasing numbers to the regiments of Janissaries. The old *esprit de corps* declined and so did discipline. The Janissaries' main incentive now was pay, and when this was not forthcoming, as in 1589, they broke out in revolt. The period 1596–1610 also saw repeated outbreaks of rebellion among the Sipahis, partly as a consequence of resentment at inflationary pressures. In short, two of the foundations upon which Turkish power had been based—a flourishing economy and a highly disciplined army—were showing signs of weakness at the opening of the seventeenth century, and after a period of phenomenal expansion the Ottoman Turks were moving towards the first stages of their long retreat.

The Empire

When the Emperor Maximilian I died in January 1519 there was some suggestion that he should be replaced not by his eldest grandson, Charles, but by Charles's younger brother, Ferdinand. Charles, however, insisted on his prior right. He did so not simply out of pride but also on the grounds that if Ferdinand were elected he would not have possession of Spain or the Netherlands, since these had already passed to Charles by hereditary descent, and would therefore be unable to maintain the imperial dignity. There was much weight behind this argument, for the imperial revenues were totally inadequate for the tasks that devolved on the Emperor, particularly that of defending Christendom against the Turk. Yet in 1556, when Charles decided to abdicate, he split his dominions along the very lines which, some forty years earlier, he had found unacceptable. Ferdinand and his heirs retained the imperial title and the Habsburg hereditary lands in eastern Europe. The rest—Spain, Italy, the Netherlands and the New World— went to Philip and his descendants. This meant that the Emperors were left with the trappings of power but not much of the financial reality, nor could they any longer pretend to be 'universal' rulers. Ferdinand was crowned not in Rome but in Frankfurt, and the area over which he had been elected to rule was referred to with increasing frequency and accuracy as 'the Holy Roman Empire of the German Nation'.

Although Charles V retained control over imperial policy until his abdication, Ferdinand had for many years been in charge of the day-to-day administration of the Empire. As for the Habsburg estates in south-east Europe, these went first to Charles, as head of the family; but when, in 1521, Ferdinand announced his betrothal to the daughter of the King of Hungary, Charles handed them over to him. The formal transfer took place in February 1522, and Ferdinand now became ruler of the dukedoms of Upper and Lower Austria, Styria, Carinthia, and the greater part of Carniola. This immediately brought him up against the Turks, who were advancing into the Balkans. They invaded Austria in 1529, laying siege to Vienna, and attacked again in 1532 and 1541. Ferdinand appealed to his brother and the German princes for support against the infidel, but this was not always forthcoming. Charles had so many commitments that he could never give his undivided attention to any one of them, while the German princes were more afraid of a powerful Emperor than of the Turk. Ferdinand had to work out his own salvation, and had it not been for the fact that the Turks were operating over extended distances and had to take account of the Persian menace in their rear, the Habsburg lands might have gone the way of Bosnia and Serbia.

Apart from the Turks, the major problem with which Ferdinand was confronted was that of religious disunity. He was successful in negotiating the Religious Peace of Augsburg in 1555, but although the protestants agreed to this they were far from satisfied. For one thing the peace made no mention of Calvinists; and, for another, it forbade any change in the ecclesiastical principalities. As it happened, the only way in which protestantism could continue to expand after the mid-sixteenth century was by taking over these prince-bishoprics, since the major secular states had by now committed themselves to one side or the other. Enforcement of the 'Ecclesiastical Reservation' would therefore limit the continued progress of the Reformation and preserve a catholic majority among the Electors.

Protestants could take comfort from the fact that they outnumbered the catholics in the imperial Diet, but the sense of security which this gave them was undermined by the rapid progress of the Counter-Reformation. Ferdinand had given a great boost to this by inviting the Jesuits to Vienna in 1551 and subsequently to Prague. The Jesuits rallied the disheartened adherents of the old faith, clarified and emphasised the basic doctrines of the catholic Church, and began to make converts among politically important families. The catholics were no longer in retreat, and their newfound confidence was reflected in the changing composition of the second house of the Diet—that which was made up of the non-electoral princes. Until the mid-1570s the protestants were in the majority in this house, but after that date their numbers declined until they became a minority. In the upper house of Electors, only the Elector of the Palatinate put religious considerations before all others; the other two protestant rulers, the Electors of Saxony and Brandenburg, attached greater importance to preserving the unity of the Empire, even if this meant supporting the catholic Emperor. The more committed protestant princes, therefore, under the leadership of the Elector Palatine, began to challenge the principle of majority rule which they had hitherto accepted, and they also refused to regard the judgments of the *Reichskammergericht* as binding in religious matters, since it was bound to enforce the laws of the Empire, including the Ecclesiastical Reservation. Disputes over religion effectively immobilised much of the legislative, judicial and administrative machinery of the Empire, and made both sides think in terms of self-help.

In 1564 Ferdinand died and was succeeded by his eldest son, Maximilian II. The new Emperor, who was an Erasmian humanist by temperament, had inclined to Lutheranism at one time, and believed that Lutherans and catholics should practice mutual tolerance. He had to accept the fact that although he was committed by his office to the defence of the catholic Church, the majority of his subjects were protestant. This applied even to the Habsburg hereditary territories. In Austria, for instance, where the Roman Catholic church had been in poor shape, most of the nobles had defected to Lutheranism, carrying their peasants with them. Since the nobles dominated the Austrian Estates, they defended religious and constitutional 'liberties' simultaneously—thereby, of course, encouraging the contrary assumption, that catholicism must go hand in hand with absolutism. So far as Maximilian II was concerned they had little to fear. Even had he wished to become absolute he could not have done so, for he needed the support of the nobles against the Turks. As it was, he not only confirmed the privileges of the Austrian nobles, but in 1568 and 1571 formally recognised their right to freedom of worship within their own houses.

Maximilian's policy of peaceful coexistence between protestants and catholics died with him in 1576, for his eldest son, who became Emperor as Rudolf II, had been educated in Spain and was an uncompromising Roman Catholic. Rudolf encouraged the Jesuits and other religious orders to continue the work of counter-reformation within his dominions, and he took strong action against the protestants inside Austria. He could not, any more than his predecessor, afford to alienate the nobility, but he was determined to stamp out protestantism from the towns. Protestant ministers were expelled, as were those citizens who refused to conform to the established faith, and Roman Catholics were given a monopoly of municipal government. The opportunity to extend this policy to rural areas came with a peasant revolt in Upper Austria in 1594, sparked off by heavy taxation, consequent on the renewal of the Turkish offensive. After the revolt had been suppressed, in 1597, protestants were driven out of the countryside and Tridentine catholicism was enforced: even communion in both kinds, which the Pope had permitted in Habsburg hereditary territories at the insistence of Ferdinand I, was forbidden.

Much the same happened in Styria, Carniola and Carinthia, which

Ferdinand I had left to his second son, the Archduke Charles. The Turkish threat had made it essential for Charles to have the support of the Lutherans among the nobles and in the towns, and in the 1570s he granted them freedom of worship as well as the right to educate their children in the reformed faith. In the 1580s, however, Turkish pressure relaxed with the outbreak of war against Persia, and Charles gradually withdrew these concessions from the towns. He also founded a university at Graz, under Jesuit leadership, as a centre from which the Counter-Reformation could spread out. In 1590 Charles was succeeded by his son the Archduke Ferdinand, who stepped up the campaign against protestantism in the towns and encouraged heretics to emigrate from his territories.

In all the Habsburg hereditary estates the Lutheran nobility felt themselves increasingly isolated as catholic rulers went over to the offensive. They feared not only for their religion but also for their privileges, and this made them all the more determined to challenge the advance of catholic absolutism. Their moment came in the early years of the seventeenth century, when the Emperor Rudolf, who had long been a virtual recluse in his castle at Prague and suffered from intense morbid depression, showed obvious signs of mental derangement. He was unable to cope with a rebellion that broke out in Hungary in 1605 and threatened to infect Austria and Moravia. A Habsburg family council therefore assumed *de facto* authority and sent his brother Matthias to restore order. Matthias realised that the future of Habsburg rule in south-east Europe was at stake, and made substantial concessions. The Estates of Hungary, Austria and Moravia all had their 'liberties' confirmed and were given guarantees of freedom of worship. It seemed as though protestantism had triumphed at the very moment when it was threatened with extinction.

Matthias had hoped that Rudolf would abdicate in his favour, but Rudolf, although he reluctantly handed over most of his other dignities during the course of the next few years, was deeply resentful at what he regarded as the lack of loyalty shown by his own family, and refused to give up the imperial title. Not until Rudolf's death in 1612, therefore, did Matthias formally become Emperor. Despite the fact that he had earlier made concessions to the protestant Estates, he shared the same assumptions about religion as his brother, and encouraged the agents of counter-reformation to continue and expand their work in the Habsburg hereditary lands. Generally speaking, however, he was content to leave the making and enforcing of policy to others while he enjoyed the glittering ceremonial of court life, the magnificent art collection built up by Rudolf, and the charms of his pretty wife.

Religious and political affairs were mainly in the hands of the Bishop of Vienna, Melchior Klesl, who believed in conversion through persuasion rather than force. This brought him up against radical catholics, who admired the 'Spanish qualities' of commitment and inflexibility and wanted to apply to the whole Empire the hard-line policies that had been pioneered in Bavaria and tested out in Austria. They were in a strong position, since their leader was the Archduke Ferdinand of Styria, who had been chosen by the Habsburg family to succeed the childless Matthias. They showed their strength and their determination in 1618, when the Bohemian crisis came to a head (see p. 341). Klesl urged moderation and mutual concessions, but Ferdinand would have none of it. Ignoring Matthias, who was now old and feeble, he had Klesl arrested and took over the direction of policy himself. In March of the following year, 1619, Matthias died and Ferdinand became Emperor. The days of toleration and coexistence were over, and the Estates throughout the Habsburg lands now had to look to their own defence.

The German Princes

The Habsburg Emperors were not, of course, the only rulers in Germany. The Empire was a federation of states, large and small, and the princes who governed the larger ones were independent monarchs in all but name. The majority of them were protestant, but they were far from united. This lack of unity was partly a reflection of the internal disputes within the Lutheran church, following the death of Luther in 1546 and Charles V's enforcement of the 'Interim' after 1548. Luther's spiritual heir was his friend and close associate, Philip Melanchthon, who had been responsible for the Church Ordinance of 1528 on which the organisation of the reformed religion in Saxony was based. Melanchthon had never shared Luther's aggressively uncompromising attitudes, however, and rather than leave Wittenberg after the Emperor's triumph, he accepted the Interim. His assumption was that the ritual and ceremonial of the Roman Catholic Church were acceptable so long as they did not clash with the commands of scripture, and he still hoped for reunion between the protestant and catholic Churches. There could be no question of this, however, while the protestants themselves were divided, and Melanchthon was therefore concerned to emphasise the common ground they shared rather than the points of difference. On the key question of transubstantiation he moved appreciably nearer Zwingli's position of denying any real presence, and he already shared many of Calvin's beliefs about predestination. Such a conciliatory attitude was not supported by the more extreme Lutherans, however, who had fled from Wittenberg rather than accept the Interim. They attacked Melanchthon as the betrayer of Luther's ideals and insisted that there should be no compromise on the fundamental tenets of the Lutheran faith.

Melanchthon died in 1560, at a time when the prospect of protestant unity seemed more and more remote. In 1577 the hard-line Lutherans produced the 'Formula of Concord', which deliberately rejected the Zwinglian doctrine of the eucharist and the Calvinist doctrine of pre-destination. In the years that followed, most of the Lutheran states accepted the Formula and ordered its enforcement, but it remained unacceptable to the followers of Melanchthon—the 'Philippists'. These drew closer to the Calvinists, thereby preparing the way for the reception of Calvinism in areas of Germany that had hitherto been Lutheran. Most important of these were the Palatinate, Bremen, Anhalt and Hesse. In 1613 the Elector of Brandenburg was also con-verted from Lutheranism to Calvinism, but he could not persuade his subjects to follow suit and therefore allowed both protestant faiths to be practised within his territories.

Many Lutherans regarded the Calvinists as a greater threat than the catholics. This was the attitude, for instance, of the ruler of the most powerful of all Lutheran states, Electoral Saxony. From 1553 to 1586 the Elector of Saxony was Augustus I, a cool, calculating prince who lived frugally and left a fortune to his successor. Augustus was sympa-thetic to Philippist doctrines, which he introduced into his lands, but he became increasingly convinced that the advocates of Philippism were secretly working for a Calvinist takeover, and rather than risk this he reverted to orthodox Lutheranism. In 1580 he joined with the Electors of Brandenburg and the Palatinate (both of which states were at that time Lutheran) and a number of other princes and cities in accepting the Formula of Concord, and Philippism and Calvinism were henceforth excluded from Saxony. Augustus was succeeded by his son, Christian I, who favoured Philippist doctrines and believed that protestants of all kinds should unite in self-defence. In 1591 he brought about the 'Torgau alliance' of the protestant princes of the Empire, but in the same year he died, leaving only a minor to succeed him.

While the Elector of Saxony was generally acknowledged to be the doyen of the German protestant princes, his counterpart among the catholics was the Duke of Bavaria. Albert V (1550–79) and his successor William V (1579–97) were both committed catholics, determined to maintain the old faith in their territories. Albert had to tread carefully at first, since in the 1550s it still seemed as though protestantism was sweeping everything before it in Germany, and a number of Bavarian nobles had Lutheran sympathies. By the early 1560s, however, the revival of the catholic Church was under way, and Albert put the full force of his secular authority behind it. He welcomed the Jesuits, he encouraged the reform of the clergy, and in 1569 he established a censorship. The same policies were followed by William V and his successor Maximilian I. Bavarian subjects were given the choice of Roman Catholicism or exile. Attendance at church, the taking of the sacraments and the use of the confessional were made obligatory, and the duchy of Bavaria became the great stronghold of the Counter-Reformation in southern Germany. The exclusion of protestant nobles and towns from the Bavarian Estates considerably weakened this body, which became little more than a rubber stamp for approving the duke's financial proposals. The connection between revived catholicism and absolutism was nowhere more marked than in Bavaria, and it was this example which provided Rudolf II with a blueprint for the reconversion of his Austrian lands. It also inspired the radical catholics who came to power with the Emperor Ferdinand II.

The most committed and intransigent of all the protestant states was the Palatinate. This was made up of two separate units: the Lower Palatinate on the Rhine, with its capital at Heidelberg; and the Upper Palatinate, which stretched from Nuremberg to Bohemia. From 1559 to 1576 the Palatine Electorate was ruled over by Frederick III, whose deep piety had led him to examine all the main Christian faiths in order to find the best one. Brought up as a Roman Catholic, he had been converted to Lutheranism at the age of thirty-one, but he later became convinced that Calvinism accorded more closely with the Bible and natural reason, and proceeded to impose this faith on his subjects. Frederick was the first major German prince to accept Calvinism, and his conversion aroused the hostility not only of the Emperor but of the Lutheran princes as well. They welcomed the fact that under Frederick's successor, Ludwig, the Palatinate reverted to Lutheranism, but in 1584 Ludwig was succeeded by the Calvinist Frederick IV. Under his rule the Palatinate became a major centre of

Calvinism, and the university of Heidelberg assumed the same import-ance for German Calvinism that Wittenberg held for Lutheranism.

The Calvinists were, in general, more internationally minded than the Lutherans. The Palatine Electors, for instance, sent troops and money to help the Dutch in their struggle for independence, and they also provided assistance for the French Huguenots. This was very different from the attitude of Augustus I of Saxony, who regarded the Dutch and French Calvinists as heretics, and preferred to put his trust in the Emperor and the catholic princes. These diametrically opposed protestant approaches towards the major problems of the day were also to be seen in German affairs. Saxony, for example, was committed to the maintenance of imperial institutions and of the Religious Peace of Augsburg, which had legitimated Lutheranism. The Calvinists, on the other hand, had been excluded from the Religious Peace, and therefore had no interest in preserving it. Nor were they prepared loyally to accept the decisions of imperial institutions when these went against them. In 1601, for instance, the Palatinate rejected the juris-diction of the *Reichskammergericht* in religious disputes, and in 1603 it refused to bow to majority opinion within the Diet.

Disunity among the protestant princes had already led to a number of striking catholic successes. In the 1580s, when the Archbishop-Elector of Cologne announced his intention of turning Lutheran and secularising his principality, the Emperor, with the aid of Spanish troops, deposed him and installed a more fervent catholic in his place. Some years later, in 1608, the Duke of Bavaria, acting as the Emperor's agent, put down a protestant rising in the imperial city of Donauworth, north-west of Augsburg. When, in that same year, the imperial Diet assembled at Regensburg, the protestant Estates protested against this action as a breach of the Religious Peace of 1555, but they were met with a catholic demand that all ecclesiastical property which had been transferred to lay ownership since the Religious Peace should be restored. The catholics had in mind such examples as the secularisation of the bishoprics of Magdeburg and Halberstadt, carried through in the 1560s with the active encouragement of the Elector of Brandenburg, and since they were in a majority in the Diet they had good reason for believing that their demand would be met. But the Palatinate declared the Diet's proceedings invalid and refused to take any further part—an example that was followed by Brandenburg and most of the other protestant states. These now came together in a defensive alliance, the Protestant Union. Of the major protestant princes only the Lutheran

Elector of Saxony held aloof. He resented the Calvinist leadership of the Union and he personified the *Politique* attitude, that religious disputes should not be allowed to disrupt political life.

Maximilian I of Bavaria met the protestant challenge by forming the Catholic League in 1609, and it looked as though Germany was moving inexorably towards a renewal of religious war. A crisis arose over the principality of Julich-Cleve, which stretched along the Rhine and was intermingled with the territories of the see of Cologne. In 1609 the mad Duke of Julich-Cleve died, leaving as heirs his two sisters, who had both married Lutheran princes. Each of the two husbands—Wolfgang William of Neuburg and John Sigismund of Brandenburg—laid claim to the whole duchy but agreed to a joint occupation until the question of ownership should be settled by arbitration. Meanwhile the Emperor, who was under pressure from Spain as well as members of his own family, and was in any case appalled at the prospect of a protestant state in so strategically sensitive a position, sent his cousin to administer the territory.

The princes of the Protestant Union, convinced that the Emperor's action was simply the first step towards dispossessing the rightful heirs, promptly mobilised their troops. The Catholic League ordered a counter-mobilisation. Christian of Anhalt, chief minister of the Elector Palatine and the driving force behind the Union, appealed for assistance to Henry IV of France, who was only waiting for an opportunity to renew the traditional French policy of undermining Habsburg power in Germany by encouraging the protestant princes. The earlier pattern of religious war within Germany as part of an international conflict might well have repeated itself had it not been for the assassination of Henry IV. Following this the crisis was resolved without recourse to war, although the Protestant Union, with the assistance of Dutch troops, expelled the Emperor's administrator. By the Treaty of Xanten, signed in 1614, Wolfgang William (who had by now been converted to Roman Catholicism) received Julich and Berg as his share of the duchy lands. John–Sigismund, who had undergone a conversion in the opposite direction and announced that he was now a Calvinist, was given possession of Cleve and Mark.

War had been averted because neither side was ready for it, and for a time it seemed as though more pacific counsels might prevail. The accession of the moderate Matthias as Emperor, the truce between Spain and the United Provinces, and the abandonment by France of her forward policy following the death of Henry IV, all helped to produce a more relaxed atmosphere. So did the fact that the Elector of Saxony, whose influence on the German protestants was still consider-able, was committed to co-operation with the catholic princes and to preservation of the Empire's administrative structure. Nevertheless the fundamental inability of imperial institutions to hold the balance between catholics and protestants had been clearly demonstrated, and there were extremists on both sides—Christian of Anhalt, for instance, and the Archduke Ferdinand—who saw no virtue in compromise and were preparing for a future confrontation. They did not have long to wait, and it was the Palatinate, appropriately enough, which set in motion the train of events leading to war.

Bohemia

Ladislaw Jagiello, King of Hungary and Bohemia, died in 1516 and was succeeded by his young son, Louis II. Four years later Suleiman the Magnificent demanded the payment of tribute, and, when this was refused, decided to assert Ottoman supremacy by force of arms. In 1521 he took possession of Belgrade, and would no doubt have pressed deeper into Louis's dominions had it not been for the need to turn his attention elsewhere. In 1526, however, he renewed his offensive and shattered the Christian forces at the battle of Mohacs. Louis died while fleeing from the battlefield, and Charles V's brother, Ferdinand, now claimed the Bohemian throne. The Bohemian Estates rejected Ferdi-nand's assertion that the crown was his by hereditary right, but in due course they elected him as king. They insisted, however, that Ferdi-nand should respect their traditional 'liberties', including the right to worship as they pleased. There was considerable diversity of religious belief in Bohemia. The majority of the population adhered to the Utraquist church, which had preserved a number of Hussite practices—most notably communion in both kinds and vernacular services—but Lutheranism was also making itself felt, particularly in German-speaking areas. In the late 1520s Anabaptism was brought in by refugees who settled in Moravia, where their skill as craftsmen made them welcome to the landowners; and from the middle of the century, Calvinist doctrines were being widely and rapidly disseminated.

Ferdinand was careful not to alienate the Bohemian nobles, since he needed their financial support for the struggle against the Turks. The nobles, however, made the mistake of committing themselves to the wrong side when, in 1546, Charles V and his brother decided to move against the Elector of Saxony. Although they had not been officially convoked, the Bohemian Estates assembled and drew up a list of demands which would have given them virtual sovereignty within the kingdom. The nobles also began concentrating their forces in order to give active assistance to the Elector, but all these preparations were cut short by news of the Emperor's triumph at Muhlberg. The Bohemian Estates were now at the mercy of Ferdinand, who could dictate his own terms. He left the nobles untouched, except for a handful of individuals, and concentrated on the towns, which he regarded as nests of heresy. Municipal self-government was abolished, and elected magistrates were replaced by royal officials. This curbing of urban independence had considerable constitutional implications, for it meant that the third house of the Bohemian Estates, that of the burgesses, now consisted virtually of royal nominees. Ferdinand also insisted that the Estates should formally recognise that the crown of Bohemia was hereditary in the Habsburg family, and that his son Maximilian was therefore heir to the throne.

Ferdinand ordered the expulsion of the Anabaptists from his kingdom of Bohemia, and persecuted those who remained. He could hardly expel the Lutherans, however, since they were so numerous. Instead he concentrated on persuading the Pope to permit communion in both kinds within the Habsburg lands, hoping that this would reconcile the Utraquists to the Roman Catholic Church and check the further spread of heresy. He also encouraged the Jesuits to extend their activities in Bohemia, particularly among the greater nobles, many of whom had retained at least a nominal commitment to the old faith. Protestants were sufficiently alarmed by these manifestations of catholic revival to sink their differences, and in 1575 the Lutherans, Calvinists, Utraquists and Bohemian Brethren (Anabaptists) agreed on a single statement of belief, which they called the 'Bohemian Confession'. They wanted this to be made part of the law of the land through formal acceptance by the Bohemian Estates; but Ferdinand's successor, Maximilian, afraid of constitutional checks on his freedom of action, persuaded the protestants to be content with his royal promise to maintain religious liberty within Bohemia.

By the time Maximilian died in 1576 about two-thirds of the population of Bohemia was protestant and only about one-tenth Roman Catholic—though the proportion of catholics among the nobility was considerably higher. The new Habsburg ruler, Rudolf II, would have liked to eradicate protestantism from all his dominions, but he had to accept the fact that in Bohemia the protestants were so strongly entrenched that little short of a major upheaval would remove them. In the opening years of the seventeenth century he had the opportunity to put his ideals into practice in Transylvania, but the persecution of protestants, combined with an attack upon the liberties of the Estates, led to the outbreak of rebellion there (see p. 329). Rudolf needed all the support he could get, not least against his brother Matthias, who was seeking to replace him. The Bohemian Estates, unlike those of Austria, Hungary and Moravia, remained true to Rudolf, but they exacted a substantial price for their loyalty. By the 'Letter of Majesty' of July 1609 Rudolf formally granted freedom of conscience to all his Bohemian subjects, irrespective of their social standing, and liberty of worship to the nobles and those towns which belonged to the crown. He also gave the Estates control over ecclesiastical organisation within the kingdom.

The victory of the protestants in Bohemia was threatened in 1611 when, at Rudolf's invitation, his cousin, the Archduke Leopold, sent a force of mercenaries to attack Prague. Rudolf hoped by this *coup d'état* not only to restore his effective rule over Bohemia but also to assert his continuing right to the imperial throne. The Bohemian Estates promptly appealed to Matthias, who came to their assistance and drove out the invaders. The Estates thereupon elected Matthias as King of Bohemia, and for the next five years they were secure in the enjoyment of their religious and constitutional liberties. In 1617, however, they were faced with the prospect of a new ruler. The Austrian Habsburgs had agreed that the childless Matthias should be succeeded as Emperor by his cousin, the Archduke Ferdinand of Styria, and in order to strengthen Ferdinand's claim it was proposed that he should first be accepted as King of Bohemia and Hungary.

The Bohemian Estates, however, were not prepared to recognise that the crown was hereditary, nor were they persuaded that Ferdinand would be the best choice for election. His leadership of the extreme catholics made him unacceptable to the protestants, and there was widespread fear that he would try to impose absolutism at the expense of political and religious liberties. Unfortunately for the protestants, they could not agree on a suitable alternative candidate. The Lutherans favoured the Elector of Saxony, while the Calvinists wanted the Elector Palatine. Meanwhile Matthias was pressing for the recognition of Ferdinand, and in the end the Estates gave way on condition that the new ruler should guarantee the Letter of Majesty. This Ferdinand did— though he had no intention of being bound by the Letter—and in June

1617 he was formally 'accepted' as King of Bohemia. The days of religious and political freedom within this Habsburg kingdom were now numbered.

Hungary

Following the defeat of Hungarian forces at Mohacs, in 1526, and the death of King Louis II, Hungary was divided into three separate states, whose boundaries fluctuated with the fortunes of war. In the west, 'Royal Hungary' was claimed and occupied by Charles V's brother Ferdinand; in the centre, 'Turkish Hungary' was incorporated into the Ottoman empire; while in the east, Transylvania, at one time an independent principality, was left in the hands of John Zapolya, the former *Voivode* (governor). A group of Hungarian nobles declared their allegiance to Zapolya and 'elected' him king of all Hungary. Ferdinand would not, of course, accept this, and for over ten years Royal Hungary suffered the horrors of civil war between adherents of the two claimants in addition to the occasional eruptions of the Turks. Eventually, in 1538, Ferdinand and Zapolya came to terms, which were set out in a secret treaty. Zapolya recognised Ferdinand as *de facto* king of Royal Hungary, but Ferdinand acknowledged Zapolya not only as ruler of the rest but also as nominal king of all Hungary, on condition that after his death the throne should revert to the Habsburgs.

At this time Zapolya had no heir, but subsequently he remarried and had a son, John Sigismund. When Zapolya died in 1540 the Transylvanian Estates elected John Sigismund as prince, declared themselves to be vassals of the Sultan, and appealed to him for defence against Ferdinand, who had invaded Turkish Hungary in support of his own claim. Suleiman was only too glad to take John Sigismund under his patronage. Turkish troops drove Ferdinand away from Buda, which he was besieging, and pushed westwards. Ferdinand, faced with the prospect of being expelled from Hungary altogether, came to terms in 1547. He agreed to pay tribute to the Sultan for Royal Hungary, to acknowledge the Turkish right to hold central and southern Hungary, and to recognise Transylvania as a nominally independent state under Turkish 'protection'. Maximilian II confirmed these terms by the Treaty of Adrianople in 1568.

Ferdinand brought Royal Hungary under the supervision of the centralised institutions he had set up in Vienna to administer the

Habsburg lands. But in Hungary, as in Bohemia, he was faced with the problem of the spread of protestantism. The Roman Catholic Church in Hungary had been very much under the sway of the nobility, and had not been renowned for its spiral qualities. It was severely weakened by the fact that nearly half of its bishops were killed at Mohacs, and that both Ferdinand and Zapolya, in their desperate need for money, secularised a great deal of church property. It was hardly surprising in these circumstances that Lutheranism made rapid inroads, particularly among the German-speaking population. The Magyar nobles were more inclined to Calvinism, for they found—as did the Polish nobility—that lay control of a presbyterian church reinforced their dominant position in society. Ferdinand, however, put all his weight and influence behind Roman Catholicism, and as the Counter-Reformation gathered momentum in the Habsburg lands the Hungarian protestants felt themselves increasingly threatened.

Lutheranism, Calvinism, and also Unitarianism, spread into Transylvania, and the protestants came to be numbered among the most ardent of Transylvanian nationalists, for they believed—with good reason—that political and religious liberty went hand in hand, and that both would be menaced by a Habsburg takeover. In 1571 the Transylvanian Diet declared that there should be freedom of worship for catholics and protestants alike, and this was accepted by Stephen Bathory, who was elected sovereign prince in succession to John Sigismund in 1571.

Stephen Bathory, the son of a former *Voivode* of Transylvania, ruled his principality for only a few years. In 1575 he was elected to the throne of Poland, whereupon the Transylvanian Estates chose his brother, Sigismund Bathory, to be their prince. The Bathories had been brought up under Jesuit influence, and were both Roman Catholics, but whereas Stephen was tolerant by nature and preferred persuasion to coercion, Sigismund was determined to bring the Counter-Reformation to Transylvania. For the sake of religion he was even prepared to sacrifice his throne, and at the end of 1597 he suddenly announced his abdication in favour of the Emperor Rudolf II. This caused chaos, which lasted for several years while opposing forces struggled for possession of the principality. In 1601, however, imperial troops finally gained control, and Transylvania became a Habsburg possession.

Rudolf was determined, in Transylvania as in Royal Hungary, to break the power of the nobles and impose Roman Catholicism. In

Royal Hungary he might have succeeded, given time, but in Transylvania the only result of his policy was to drive his newly acquired subjects into rebellion, under the leadership of one of their own nobles, Stephen Bocskay, whom they elected as their prince. When the Estates of Royal Hungary heard the news, they promptly demanded guarantees of their own religious and political liberties, and the Estates of Austria did the same. It looked as though the Transylvanian uprising had set off a chain reaction which might end by destroying Habsburg power in eastern Europe, and the Habsburg family moved swiftly to avert this danger. Rudolf was elbowed aside by his brother Matthias, who recognised that he was negotiating from a position of weakness and therefore conceded all the major demands that were made upon him. By the Peace of Vienna of June 1606, Stephen Bocskay was formally recognised as Prince of Transylvania, while the inhabitants of Royal Hungary were guaranteed the enjoyment of their religious and political liberties.

To Stephen Bocskay, therefore, belongs the credit for preserving religious and political liberty not only in Transylvania but in Royal Hungary as well. He continued to rule his principality until his death in 1608, when he was succeeded by the tyrannical and unpopular Gabriel (Gabor) Bathory. Five years later Gabriel Bathory was assassinated, and the Transylvanian Estates elected in his place Gabriel Bethlen ('Bethlen Gabor'), a member of a leading protestant family, who had been driven out by Bathory and had taken refuge with the Turks. The Sultan had recognised him as Prince of Transylvania even before Bathory's death, and in 1615 Matthias also acknowledged him as rightful ruler. Matthias, to whom Rudolf had formally transferred the Hungarian crown in 1608, remained King of Hungary until 1618, when he abdicated in favour of his cousin Ferdinand, who was already King of Bohemia. This was the situation at the outbreak of the Thirty Years' War.

PART FOUR

Habsburg against Bourbon

NINETEEN

The Triumph of the Politiques

In sixteenth-century Europe religion was the language of politics, and political protest was therefore inextricably entangled with religious dissent. This could be a great source of strength to independence movements, as was shown in the Revolt of the Netherlands, but it could also be a weakness in that the re-establishment of religious orthodoxy was almost invariably accompanied by the suppression of political 'liberties'. The classic demonstration of this came in the early seventeenth century, when the Bohemian nobles, acting in defence of their traditional privileges, became for a brief moment the champions of protestant Europe. Their example inspired revolt in all the Habsburg hereditary lands, and everywhere the cause of the Estates was also that of religious liberty. The Habsburg Emperor, on the other hand, was the protagonist of catholic orthodoxy, and as he forcibly restored his authority over his family possessions he set in motion the counter-revolution in which the Roman Catholic faith and princely absolutism went hand-in-hand. The defeat of protestantism was therefore a defeat for the Bohemian Estates and their 'liberties'.

In Germany the first half of the seventeenth century saw the gradual disentanglement of religious and political dissent. Among the German princes the lead in this was given by the Elector of Saxony, who was bitterly attacked, both at the time and since, for his 'lukewarm' attitude towards the defence of the protestant faith, but who insisted that religious and political issues could and should be separated. He had no intention of abandoning his own Lutheran beliefs, which formed a strong bond between him and his subjects, but he saw no reason to change the existing situation within the Empire, since the weakness of the central imperial authority provided the best possible guarantee of princely 'liberties'. If the protestant challenge provoked a catholic reaction this would, he feared, upset the *status quo*—as indeed happened in 1629, when the Edict of Restitution led to the establishment of the Emperor's authority in parts of Germany from which it had long been absent. This drove the Elector into open opposition to his imperial overlord, but his basic attitude remained unaltered. His vindication came with the Peace of Westphalia, which brought the Thirty Years War to an end, for this was essentially a secular settlement, and so far as Germany was concerned it restored the *status quo*, based on the *Politique* principles of religious diversity and princely independence.

In France the opening decades of the seventeenth century saw the same intertwining of magnate factionalism and protestant dissent that had brought about the Wars of Religion. But the rise of Richelieu changed all this. He was a devoted catholic and a cardinal, but hew as also a *Politique*, who believed that the overriding need in France was for strong secular government. As long as the Huguenots accepted royal authority he was prepared to guarantee them freedom of conscience and limited freedom of worship, and this was the solution he eventually forced them to accept. The success of his policy was demonstrated after his death, for when the magnates and the officeholders joined hands in defence of their 'liberties' and plunged France into the period of acute instability and sporadic violence known as the *Frondes*, the Huguenots remained untypically quiescent. For the first time a political protest was taken out of its 'traditional' religious context and left to stand alone. It then became clear, as Richelieu had all along assumed, that the defence of 'liberties' by itself provided too narrow a base for a successful rebellion, and the collapse of the *Frondes* opened the way to royal absolutism.

Richelieu's self-appointed task of divorcing religious from political dissent was made easier by the fact that protestants could be clearly divided from Roman Catholics. In the United Provinces, however, the problem was more complicated, for there the underlying dispute was between two extremes of the same Calvinist faith. The religiously intolerant hard-line Calvinists stood for strong central government under the house of Orange: the moderates, on the other hand, stood for provincial 'liberties' and the rule of the merchant oligarchs—the 'regents'. Dutch history throughout this period showed a pendulum swing from one extreme to the other. The decentralised republicanism associated with Oldenbarneveld was replaced by the quasi-monarchic rule of Stadtholders Maurice and Frederick Henry. This, in turn, gave way to the regent regime of De Witt, which lasted until 1672, when it was overthrown by William III of Orange. William's victory was, on the face of it, a triumph for the hard-liners, yet in fact he showed himself to be as much of a *Politique* as Richelieu. He saw that the United Provinces could not afford the luxury of perpetual squabbles over religion if this resulted in political and military weakness, and once his own authority was firmly established he restrained the intolerance of the hard-liners, left the moderates alone, and showed a due respect for provincial 'liberties' where these did not impede the efficient functioning of the state.

The difficulties that faced central governments when they tried to crush political dissent were lessened if they could claim to be the champions of religious orthodoxy—as in France and the Habsburg hereditary lands. This was not the case, however, in Spain, where the catholic faith commanded universal adherence but where the kingdoms other than Castile clung tenaciously to their political 'liberties'. Spain had always been a federation of states rather than a unitary one, but the relentless pressure of war made it necessary to harness the financial and military strength of *all* the constituent kingdoms. This was the aim of the Count-Duke of Olivares, who virtually ruled Spain from 1621 to 1643, but in trying to achieve it he brought his country to the brink of total disintegration. Catholicism alone, in the absence of any internal religious challenge, was not a strong enough bond to hold all Spaniards together, and although the idea of loyalty to the nation and its royal master had come to be accepted in some parts of Spain—notably Castile—there were other parts, such as Catalonia, where men were still prepared to fight in defence of their local 'liberties'. Olivares's appeal to what he called the 'supreme law' of national preservation therefore fell on deaf ears, and his attempt to integrate and unify the states of the peninsula was frustrated by the strength of centrifugal forces. Spain remained a federation of separate communities, and its nominal unity was only preserved, after Olivares's fall, by royal confirmation of the 'liberties' of the constituent kingdoms.

This failure to establish effective central government in Spain, as a prelude to modernising the antiquated and administrative machinery of the state, was partly responsible for the erosion of Spanish power and the eventual victory of France in the long struggle for supremacy. Conversely, countries which did strengthen their central authority thereby increased their efficiency and their capacity for endurance. In Sweden and Denmark effective government came in with the establishment of absolute royal rule and the subordination of the old nobility. Brandenburg became a major state as and when the Great Elector succeeded in imposing his will upon the aristocracy; and the recovery of Russia from the 'Time of Troubles' started with the restoration of Tsarist authority by Michael Romanov. Even the Dutch, those champions of provincial 'liberties', accepted the need for stronger central control at times of crisis—and these were frequent in the seventeenth century.

France was more like Spain, in that the theoretically unlimited sovereignty of the crown was restricted in practice by the existence of 'liberties' which it could not easily evade or abolish. These could delay the execution of the royal will, but they could not hold it up indefinitely so long as the king and his ministers were unwavering in their purpose. The crown was probably not strong enough at this stage to undertake fundamental reform of the governmental structure, but Richelieu showed that the existing system, with all its deficiencies, could be made to yield enough money to meet the demands of policy. This was not the case in Spain, especially as the revenue from the New World decreased. Fundamental reform really was necessary here, but only the crown could carry it out, and the crown—as Olivares discovered to his cost—was too weak.

Throughout Europe as a whole existing political, administrative and social structures were under strain, because of the movement away from the feudal-agrarian pattern of the Middle Ages towards a capitalist society in which commerce and industry played an ever larger role. It has been argued that the tension caused by the rise of capitalism in societies that were structurally unprepared for it, brought about a 'crisis of government' in the mid-seventeenth century, leading to rebellions in England, France, Spain and elsewhere.[1] The difficulty about such an interpretation is that there is no definitive way of either proving or disproving it. Nor is it certain that the major states of western Europe were any nearer to breakdown in the 1640s than they had been in, for example, the 1560s.[2] Even if they were, it was not necessarily for the same reasons. Nationalist sentiment, for instance, played a crucial part in the Portuguese revolt but none at all in the French *Frondes* and the English civil war. Also, if capitalism was a force

---

[1] Cf. the first four essays in *Crisis in Europe*, ed. Trevor Aston, Routledge, 1965.

[2] Cf. J. H. Elliott, 'Revolt and continuity in early-modern Europe', *Past & Present* 42 (1969).

of change it is difficult to see how it can have inspired the uprisings in England, France and Catalonia, since in every case these were sparked off by the determination of the upper sections of society to preserve the *status quo* in face of governmental attempts to alter it. This is not to say that the growth of capitalism had no effect on the political history of mid-seventeenth century states, but economic forces operated in a diffuse and complex way, and their political significance depended on the extent to which they became involved with social and religious discontent. Where they did become so involved, they made yet more acute the stresses already existing within states that were, throughout this period, struggling to maintain a balance between the old world of provincial and sectional 'liberties' on the one hand and the new world of national, centralised control on the other.

The difficulty of tracing the relationship between the growth of capitalism and political change becomes even more marked when it is attempted on an international scale. Increasing tensions generated within the existing state structure of Europe by differing rates of economic change may have been among the causes of the Thirty Years War, but there is no clear way of showing this. Of those causes which can be clearly traced, religious liberty and political 'liberties' were the most important. They were also the most obvious, but there was a third cause, less apparent but no less significant—namely, commercial gain. The Dutch, for example, were fighting for the right not simply to determine their own religious and political future but also to replace Portugal as the paramount commercial power in the Far East and Brazil. In the same way Gustavus Adolphus, when he marched into Germany to defend the protestant cause and protect his own country from possible invasion, was simultaneously carving out a Swedish trading empire in the Baltic.

Most of the major issues were clarified or resolved by the peace settlement of 1648. So far as religious liberty was concerned, the right to freedom of conscience was recognised within the Empire, though not in the Habsburg family possessions. There was no provision for freedom of worship, but any subject who could not accept the religion established by his ruler was to be free to emigrate, and Germany had such a profusion of principalities that the choice was wide open. As for 'liberties', where these had been identified with the defence of 'national' interests against an outside force, as in the United Provinces and certain German states, they survived; but where they had been associated with the struggle of Estates to preserve sectional privileges against the encroachment of central government, as in the Habsburg hereditary lands, they were destroyed. Nothing specific was said about the commercial issue, but the Dutch were left free to exploit their supremacy, and Sweden was confirmed in possession of the Baltic regions that gave her a stranglehold on north German and Russian trade.

There was no mention of feudalism or capitalism in the Westphalia treaties, yet the settlement of 1648 was not without its significance in this respect. The Habsburgs remained predominant in eastern Europe, but they were simply the apex of a pyramid that was based on a mainly servile peasantry. The real victors in this part of the world were the landowners. Such a statement may sound paradoxical in view of the fact that aristocratic landowners had been identified with the unsuccessful challenge to Habsburg rule by the various Estates. But once the Habsburgs had overcome this political threat they were quite content to reinforce the existing social structure, since they themselves were part of it. The old aristocracy might, in some places, be expelled and replaced by a new one, as happened in Bohemia, but so far as the peasants were concerned there was little to choose between the old and the new. The landlords, whoever they were, remained a heavy burden on society in eastern Europe, but because they had the support of the state behind them they could rivet their chains ever more firmly on the unfortunate peasantry.

The situation was different in northern and western Europe. Landowners were important figures there as elsewhere, but serfdom had virtually disappeared, industry was expanding, towns were swelling in size and population, and commerce was beginning to rival agriculture not simply as a source of wealth but even as a way of life. The centre of gravity of the European economy was shifting from the Levant and Mediterranean towards the Atlantic and the Baltic. This was a process that had started long before 1618 and was to continue long after 1648, but the Thirty Years War was not simply an irrelevant interlude somewhere in the middle of it. This can best be demonstrated in a negative fashion. If the Habsburgs had been successful in the war, Europe would have developed in a very different way. With Ferdinand II unchallenged in Germany, a joint Habsburg attack might well have crushed the United Provinces, the Dévots (see p. 386) would have come to power in France, and western Europe would have been reclaimed for absolutism and the Counter-Reformation, with all that this implied in the way of orthodoxy, respect for traditional values, and suspicion of innovation. In the long run this could hardly have held back the creation of a capitalist economy, but it would almost certainly have slowed down the rate of change. In fact, of course, the Habsburgs were defeated, and the Thirty Years War therefore marked the triumph of the new world over the old, at the same time as it confirmed the division of Europe into an economically advanced west and a backward and often poverty-stricken south·and east.

TWENTY

The Thirty Years War

The Bohemian Crisis

Bohemia in the early seventeenth century was that rarest of all things in Europe, a religiously tolerant society. The Hussite wars of the 1420s had provided a terrible example of the destructive effects of intolerance, and since that time Roman Catholics, Utraquists, Calvinists, Lutherans and Anabaptists ('Bohemian Brethren') had lived side by side in relative peace, if not harmony. There were, of course, hard-liners among both catholics and protestants, but until 1617 they were not able to make much headway. In June of that year, however, the election of the Archduke Ferdinand of Styria to the Bohemian throne marked the end of compromise, for he was the embodiment of Counter-Reformation catholicism in its most unbending form. From the very beginning of his reign he showed his intention of weakening the protestants' position in Bohemia, for of the ten Deputies he appointed to rule his kingdom, seven were Roman Catholics. The Bohemian protestants recognised the danger signals, and tenaciously clung to their rights as set out in the Letter of Majesty (see p. 326). A dispute soon arose over two churches which were being built by the protestants. They claimed to be acting lawfully, on the grounds that the Letter of Majesty specifically authorised the exercise of the protestant faith on royal land. But the government asserted that the land in question was no longer royal, having been handed over to the Roman Catholic Church. When the protestant leaders refused to accept this judgment, the Deputies ordered their arrest.

A section of the nobility, under the leadership of Count Thurn, claimed that the Letter of Majesty was being infringed, and called on the 'Defensors'—whose appointment had been provided for in the Letter—to summon a national assembly. This they did, and when the assembly met in May 1618 the anger of the delegates focused on two of the catholic Deputies who had earlier called on Ferdinand not to confirm the Letter. The protestant nobles led a march on the royal palace, and in the brawl that ensued, the two Deputies and their secretary were thrown out of a window. As a means of execution this was a failure, since the intended victims landed, unharmed, on a rubbish heap in the courtyard. But 'Defenestration' was as much a symbol as an act. First used in the Hussite rising, it had become the accepted manner of asserting Bohemian independence against an occupying power. The Defenestration of Prague, in short, was a deliberate challenge to Ferdinand.

The protestant nobles now took over the administration of Bohemia, and, with the approval of the Estates, appointed thirty-six 'Directors' to run the country. It was also decided to raise a national militia, under Thurn's command. The new government protested its loyalty to Ferdinand, and blamed Jesuits and 'evil counsellors' for blinding him to the true interests of his subjects, but there was no doubt about the revolutionary implications of their actions. The Directors knew that the rebellion had little chance of success so long as Bohemia stood alone. They therefore called on the Estates of all Habsburg lands, whose privileges were threatened by the advance of catholic absolutism, to join them in defence of religious toleration and political 'liberties'. In particular they hoped for support from Moravia, but their call fell on deaf ears. For twelve long months the Bohemians had to maintain their struggle unaided, against the foremost monarchy in the Christian world, and this was a great drain not simply on available supplies of men and money but also on morale.

Religion might have provided unity and strength, but in fact the various protestant denominations, although they practised coexistence, were deeply suspicious of each other, above all the Lutherans and Calvinists. Apart from religion there was little basis for a genuinely popular movement of revolt. The greater part of the population consisted of peasants who were exploited by those very 'liberties' which the nobles were so anxious to preserve, and although a skilful propaganda campaign might have persuaded them to unite with the greater landowners in a patriotic and religious crusade, no attempt was made to launch one. The Bohemian nobles, in fact, were just as apprehensive about a peasant rising as they were of strong Habsburg rule, and by trying to confine their protests within the limits of the ex-isting social order they deprived it of what little chance it had of success.

The national militia was of limited value as a fighting force, since the recruits, though often enthusiastic, were poorly equipped and lacking in military training and experience. If the rebellion was to prosper it would have to be nourished by foreign powers, and the Directors therefore despatched envoys to all the protestant states of Europe. The Dutch promised material assistance, but the greatest encouragement came from the Palatinate, which offered to subsidise a mercenary army under the command of a professional soldier, Ernest von Mansfeld, the illegitimate offspring of a noble German family. Mansfeld signalled his arrival on the Bohemian scene by capturing the catholic city of Pilsen in November 1618 and checking the advance of an imperial army which had already been despatched from Vienna.

Christian of Anhalt believed that the moment of decision had now come, and at his prompting the Elector Palatine summoned a meeting of the Protestant Union. Everyone present, with the exception of the youthful Elector himself, realised that Christian's aim was to secure for his master (and also, of course, for protestantism) the crown of Bohemia, and there was considerable doubt about the wisdom of affronting the Habsburgs in this way. In the end the delegates refused to provide either men or money for the Bohemian rebels, and instead gave their backing to the Elector of Saxony's suggestion that all the parties to the dispute should get together to resolve their differences peacefully. A conference was arranged for April 1619, but before it could take place the situation was completely altered by the death of the Emperor Matthias in March. His successor would have to be formally elected, but there could be little doubt that the successful candidate would be Ferdinand, King of Bohemia and Hungary, who had made himself the champion of the hard-line catholics.

There was little to be said against Ferdinand as a person. He was a cheerful and friendly man of forty, somewhat lacking in a sense of his own dignity and warm-hearted and generous to his family and friends. Yet outward appearances were deceptive in so far as they implied a lack of resolution, for Ferdinand was totally committed to the catholic cause, which he identified with that of the house of Habsburg. He was not a man for compromise, and this was well known in Prague. Therefore, although he offered to pardon the rebels if they laid down their arms and returned to their obedience, the Bohemian Estates preferred to put their trust in the sword. Their defiant example was now, at last, followed in Moravia and Austria, and it looked as though the simmering discontent within the hereditary

Habsburg lands was about to boil over into rebellion, as it had done in 1606. Thurn hoped to bring this about by a dramatic gesture, and in the spring of 1619 he led his army in a march on Vienna. By June he had reached the suburbs of the Habsburg capital, but before he could press home his attack he received news that Mansfeld had been defeated. Afraid that the Bohemian Estates might panic and abandon the struggle, Thurn beat a hasty retreat to Prague.

As a result of Ferdinand's accession to power (although he had not, as yet, been formally elected Emperor) the lines of division rapidly hardened. In June 1619 the princes of the Protestant Union, meeting at Heilbronn, agreed to send money to the Bohemian rebels, raise an army for their own defence, and maintain the *status quo* in Germany. In the following month all four constituent territories of the Bohemian crown (Bohemia, Lusatia, Moravia and Silesia) agreed on mutual aid against the common foe, and were joined, in August, by the Estates of Austria.

The Directors of the Bohemian revolt were not figures of sufficient standing to capture the imagination of protestant Europe, and now that Ferdinand had been deposed, a new king was needed. There was no agreement, however, on who this new ruler might be. Since the majority of the Bohemian Estates were Lutheran they would have preferred the Elector of Saxony, but John George detested rebels, even when they were protestant, and took the *Politique* view that the maintenance of his own position depended upon respect for the Emperor and acceptance of the authority of imperial institutions. He would not challenge Ferdinand's right to the Bohemian throne, since the election had been carried out in a perfectly legitimate manner, and although he hoped to avoid committing himself in any struggle, he was more likely to support the Emperor than oppose him.

Failing John George, the obvious choice was Frederick V, Elector Palatine and nominal president of the Protestant Union. He was a young man in his early twenties and had the disadvantage—from the Bohemian point of view—of being a Calvinist. He was also gentle-natured, rather naïve, and totally lacking in the qualities required of a revolutionary leader. But he was the senior protestant prince in Germany, his grandfather had been William the Silent, and his father-in-law was James I of England, ruler of one of the major protestant powers. If Frederick were elected to the Bohemian throne the rest of Europe would be involved, whether willingly or otherwise—or so, at least, Christian of Anhalt argued. Everything depended on the Bohemian Estates, and on 26 August 1619 they declared the throne to be vacant and offered the crown to Frederick. Two days later another election took place, at Frankfurt-on-Main. There could be little doubt about the outcome. Of the seven princes who traditionally had the right of choosing a new Emperor, the three ecclesiastical ones were bound to support Ferdinand. Saxony took the same line, though for different reasons, and Brandenburg followed suit. Of the remaining two Electors, the King of Bohemia was Ferdinand himself—since news of his 'deposition' had not yet reached Frankfurt and would, in any case, have been treated with derision. This left only the Palatinate, which, after a belated and vain attempt to split the catholic ranks by putting forward Maximilian of Bavaria as a candidate, bowed to the will of the majority. By a unanimous decision, therefore, Ferdinand was elected to the imperial throne.

Without support from England and other protestant powers, the Bohemian venture was likely to be a hazardous one for Elector Frederick, but after some initial hesitation he took his decision without waiting for any assurance of outside help. He was swayed by Christian of Anhalt's belief that once the die was cast the protestant powers would have to rally to his cause and by his own conviction of the rightness of his action. 'It is a divine summons which I must not disobey,' he bravely declared. He also added, in a phrase whose irony only became apparent in the subsequent years of terrible suffering, that if he rejected this summons 'the effusion of much blood and the wasting of many lands' would be laid to his account.

In October 1619 the new King of Bohemia arrived in his capital, accompanied by his charming wife, Elizabeth. In the same month Maximilian of Bavaria offered an army to the Emperor Ferdinand. Maximilian was a small, pale-faced man with a high-pitched voice, but however unimpressive in appearance he was by far the most intelligent, as well as the richest, of the German princes. Although he appointed himself the champion of the catholic cause, Maximilian was fully aware that Habsburg interests did not always coincide with German ones. When he had formed the Catholic League, at the time of the Cleves-Julich crisis (see p. 323) he deliberately excluded the Emperor; and in 1617, when the League was re-formed, the Habsburgs were again kept out. It was this revived League which now offered to raise an army of 24,000 men, under Maximilian's command, and place it at the Emperor's disposition. Ferdinand was to pay all expenses, and

Maximilian was to hold any Habsburg lands he regained as a pledge of reimbursement. Maximilian's motives were not, of course, entirely altruistic. He hoped that by offering the Emperor an army he would make it unnecessary for Ferdinand to call on Spanish aid. He had also received a secret promise that the electoral title would be taken from the Palatinate and granted to Bavaria. In this way the junior branch of the Wittelsbach family, to which he belonged, would assert its supremacy over the senior branch headed by Frederick.

In one important respect Maximilian's calculations were based on a faulty premiss. He hoped to avert Spanish intervention, but this was already inevitable. Spain's major concern for the last half century and more had been the maintenance of her rule in the Netherlands and the winning back of the rebel provinces. She had no land connections with the Netherlands, however, and had to send troops and money by sea. This route became increasingly dangerous with the advance of protestant sea power in the Channel, and a safer alternative was provided by Spanish control of Milan and alliance with Genoa. Troops landed at Genoa made their way north through Milan and into the Valtelline, a narrow pass that ran some sixty miles due east through part of Switzerland. From this they emerged into the Tyrol, and marched west and then north through Alsace and along the Rhine, until they reached the Netherlands. There were certain sensitive areas along this route. One of them was the Valtelline and the adjacent territories of northern Italy. Another was the Lower Palatinate, which straddled the Rhine. If the Elector Frederick were to call for support from the Dutch—as seemed not unlikely—the passage of Spanish forces and supplies along the land route from Italy would become infinitely more difficult. Time was running short for the Spaniards, since the twelve-year truce with the Dutch was due to expire in April 1621 and they would have to secure their position on the Rhine well before that date. In July 1620, therefore, Spinola moved his army from Flanders into the Palatinate, and by late August he had taken over Frederick's possessions on the left bank of the Rhine.

In that same month the army of the Catholic League, some 30,000 strong, crossed into Austria. It was under the command of Maximilian's general, Count von Tilly, a brilliant soldier whose devotion to the catholic cause (he was a pupil of the Jesuits) and ascetic mode of life had earned him the nickname of 'the monk in armour'. Tilly forced the Austrian Estates to abandon their alliance with the Bohemian rebels and then took over the government in the name of Maximilian.

From Austria he pressed forward into Bohemia, linking up with imperial forces already fighting there, and marched towards Prague. Frederick's army, under Christian of Anhalt and Thurn, was in no state to offer effective resistance. The commanders were divided among themselves, the troops were unpaid and mutinous, and the inhabitants of Prague and the surrounding countryside showed little enthusiasm for 'their' cause. Frederick had been elected on the assumption that he would bring with him support from the whole of protestant Europe. But the only protestant prince to march was John George of Saxony, and he was in alliance with the Emperor. His troops followed those of Tilly and occupied Lusatia, which had been promised him by Ferdinand as a reward for his loyalty. Frederick's soldiers were therefore left to face the enemy alone, and they took up a defensive position on the White Mountain, immediately to the west of Prague. There, in November 1620, Tilly defeated them in a battle that lasted little more than an hour. After one brief year the 'Winter King' was an exile, and never saw his kingdom again.

Ferdinand was determined to make such an example of the Bohemian rebels that he would have no further trouble. In June 1621 twenty-seven nobles, accused of leading the rebellion, were executed. Others had their property taken from them. Eventually about half the land of Bohemia was forcibly transferred into new ownership, and the main beneficiaries were army officers and officials who had remained true to the Emperor. In 1621 all protestant ministers were compelled to leave the country, and six years later Ferdinand ordered all his Bohemian subjects to make a choice between catholicism or exile. Some 30,000 families chose exile, mainly in Saxony. The rest adjusted their consciences and stayed put. Decrees of 1627 and 1628 ended the elective monarchy and declared Bohemia and Moravia to be hereditary possessions of the house of Habsburg. Protestants in Austria were given the same hard choice. Only those who had the good fortune to live in Lusatia, now under the rule of the Lutheran Elector of Saxony, could freely practise their faith. As the Bohemian rebels had feared, the link between protestantism and the 'liberties' of the Estates in the Habsburg lands led to the extermination of both.

The Triumph of Ferdinand II

In January 1621 Ferdinand imposed the ban of Empire on Frederick, now a refugee in the Hague. This carried with it the loss of all the

Elector's territories, and was a warning to other princes as well as a punishment for the unfortunate Frederick. When the German princes and cities belonging to the Protestant Union met at Heilbronn in the following month they protested against this arbitrary action, which threatened the rights of all German rulers; but Ferdinand disregarded their complaints and ordered them to disband their army. Divided among themselves and lacking any effective leader, the states gave in. The Union had ceased to have any relevance, and in May it was formally dissolved. As for the troops which had been raised—but never used—for the defence of 'German liberties', they were taken over by Mansfeld, who had been promised subsidies by the Dutch.

In the winter of 1620 Mansfeld had led his troops into the Lower Palatinate, where they linked up with a small force of English volunteers. Tilly followed him in and chased him out into Alsace. The army of the Catholic League now occupied the electoral territories on the right bank of the Rhine, leaving the left bank in Spanish hands. Only the English garrisons held out, but with no hope of reinforcements their surrender was a matter of time. In September 1622 Heidelberg capitulated, to be followed in November by Mannheim. The last English garrison, at Frankenthal, surrendered in April 1623. Maximilian took over the government of the conquered territories, re-imposed catholic worship, expelled Calvinist ministers, and presented the magnificent library of the protestant university of Heidelberg to the Pope as a thank-offering. In February 1623 the Emperor formally transferred the electoral title to Maximilian. The grant was of a provisional nature in that it was to be for life only, but Ferdinand had clearly asserted his right to dispose of the lands and titles of German princes as he thought fit. Maximilian might profit from this in the short run, but in the long term it was an action that threatened all rulers, catholic and protestant alike.

Ferdinand assumed that what was good for the house of Habsburg was good for the catholic Church, but this view was not shared by the rulers of another great catholic state. The French had never accepted as final their expulsion from Italy during the long struggle against Habsburg power in the sixteenth century, and although they were not yet ready to send an army into the peninsula they were anxious to weaken the Spanish hold on the Valtelline. Until 1622 the French government was preoccupied with the Huguenots (see p. 384), but following the Peace of Montpellier in October of that year it was free to concentrate on Italy, and made an alliance with Venice and Savoy to expel the Spaniards from the Valtelline. The Spaniards promptly asked for the Pope's protection, and admitted papal troops into their fortresses. This effectively countered the French initiative, but only for a time. In 1624 Richelieu returned to power and with him came a new vigour and ruthlessness. He had been associated with the *Dévots*, who favoured a Spanish alliance, but he came to recognise that his twin objectives of restoring royal authority at home and making the name of France great abroad could not be achieved without confronting the Habsburgs. In early 1625, therefore, he gave French support to an operation in which Swiss troops from protestant cantons —the Grisons—drove out the papal garrisons and closed the Valtelline to the Spaniards. The *Dévots* were appalled by the sight of a French cardinal condoning military operations against the spiritual head of the Catholic Church, and turned against their former protégé. When Spanish troops from Milan reoccupied the Valtelline, Richelieu did not dare risk open war, particularly as the Huguenots were once again giving trouble. He therefore reluctantly accepted the Treaty of Monzon, in March 1626, which restored the *status quo*. Richelieu's first tentative intervention in European affairs had been ineffective, but he had shown the direction in which French policy was moving, and as his position at home became increasingly secure so his initiatives abroad acquired a keener cutting edge.

Another power, this time a protestant one, was also moving away from its neutral position. After the breakdown of negotiations for a marriage between the Prince of Wales and the Spanish Infanta in late 1623, England became increasingly hostile towards Spain. James I did his best to restrain the bellicosity of his subjects, but following his death in March 1625 England became openly committed to the struggle against the Habsburgs. There was little hope at this stage of effective support from France—although plans were far advanced for a marriage between the new king, Charles I, and a French princess— and English diplomacy therefore concentrated on the protestant states of Scandinavia, which were threatened by the advance of imperial forces into northern Germany. The King of Sweden, Gustavus Adolphus, was willing to lead a protestant crusade, but he demanded subsidies on a scale sufficient for a major campaign, and insisted that there should be no restrictions on his freedom of operation. The English government, perennially short of money, took the cheaper course of allying with Christian IV of Denmark. He was an older and more experienced king than Gustavus, was connected by marriage with the Stuarts, and had something of a military reputation. Christian held lands in Holstein, which formed part of the Lower Saxon Circle (one of the administrative regions into which the Holy Roman Empire was divided), and he also hoped to add the bishopric of Osnabruck to the possessions of the Danish crown. The chances of doing this had, however, diminished with the advance of Tilly's army in 1623. Tilly established himself in the Lower Saxon Circle, and his presence there was not only a barrier to Danish expansion but also a threat to the protestant princes of the region. In May 1625, therefore, Christian persuaded the states of the Lower Saxon Circle to elect him as their president and agree to the raising of an army to defend their 'liberties'. He had assurances of support from the Dutch as well as the English, but these turned out to be largely illusory. The attitude of the English Parliament prevented Charles I from carrying out his commitments, while the Dutch had to find money first for their own defence. There could be no question of help from France, since Richelieu was fully occupied with the Huguenot revolt which was brewing throughout 1625 and came to a head in the early part of 1626.

The Emperor had not sat idly by while his enemies gathered their strength. In late 1624 he authorised one of his own subjects to raise an army which—unlike that of Tilly, who was responsible to Maximilian of Bavaria and the Catholic League—should be wholly at his disposal. The subject in question was Albert von Waldstein, better known as Wallenstein. He was born in 1583 of a noble but impoverished protestant Bohemian family, became a Roman Catholic during his travels in Italy, and attached himself to the service of Ferdinand, who at that time was still only an archduke. Marriage to a wealthy widow gave Wallenstein the money with which to speculate, and he did very well out of lands confiscated from the Bohemian rebels. By 1623 he owned about a quarter of Bohemia, and had been appointed military governor of Prague. He was a complex individual, clearheaded and ruthless in some respects, but liable to fits of depressive inertia. He was also a firm believer in astrology, and one of his horoscopes was cast by no less an authority than the great Kepler. Wallenstein was a man whose ambitions knew no bounds but who had no clear principles or objectives other than his own advancement. His opportunity came when he offered to raise twenty thousand men at his own expense and command them in the Emperor's service. Ferdinand accepted this offer, and

Wallenstein, who showed superb administrative ability in the way in which he both raised an army and made provision for its payment and supply, took his men off to Germany to link up with Tilly. In April 1625 he was formally appointed commander-in-chief of the imperial army and shortly afterwards created Duke of Friedland.

For the campaigning season of 1626 the protestant allies planned a double thrust: one by Mansfeld into Bohemia, and the other by Christian IV of Denmark into central and southern Germany. Mansfeld hoped to slip round Wallenstein, who was quartered in Magdeburg, but Wallenstein was ready for him and, in a sharp engagement at Dessau in April 1626, beat back his attempt to cross the Elbe. Mansfeld had to retreat into Brandenburg (nominally neutral), where he regrouped his forces and took the circuitous northern route through Brandenburg territory into Silesia. Meanwhile Christian struck south between the two main catholic armies. Tilly guessed his plans and called for reinforcements from Wallenstein, who sent several thousand men. Christian realised that his enemies were too strong for him and began to withdraw, but in August 1626 Tilly caught up with him at Lutter, south of Brunswick, and wiped out half his army. There was no longer any question of a protestant offensive. By late 1627 Christian had been driven back into Denmark, and Holstein, Schleswig and Jutland were all occupied by Tilly's troops. Meanwhile Mansfeld had reached Silesia but was too late to link up with Bethlen Gabor (see p. 532), who had already come to terms with the Emperor. With his troops unpaid and deserting him, Mansfeld wandered aimlessly down into the Balkans and reached Sarajevo, where he died in November 1626.

The triumphant Ferdinand was now master of the greater part of Germany. He had also established his authority in the Habsburg possessions after putting down a peasant revolt in Austria (in 1626) sparked off by his anti-protestant measures. It was in 1627 and 1628 that Ferdinand also completed the process of welding Bohemia into the Habsburg hereditary lands. Meanwhile Wallenstein, continuing his victorious progress, occupied Mecklenburg by the end of 1628, expelling the reigning dukes who had fought against the Emperor. Ferdinand showed his gratitude by transferring to Wallenstein not only their lands but the ducal title as well.

The conquest of Mecklenburg brought Wallenstein (and imperial power) to the shores of the Baltic, and gave him possession of the important ports of Wismar and Rostock. He was now in a position to put into execution a plan which Olivares had long been nurturing. As early as 1624 the Spanish minister had contemplated forming a company which should unite the trading towns of Flanders and the Hanse in an attempt to take over the carrying trade between the Baltic and southern Europe upon which the wealth and therefore the strength of Spain's enemy, the United Provinces, was based. Spanish ships could hardly enter the Sound, since this was dominated by Denmark; but if a port could be found in northern Germany the Hansa towns might be prevailed upon to provide a navy. Wallenstein was obviously a key figure in the fulfilment of this ambitious plan, since he alone had possession of the ports and the Emperor had appointed him 'General of the whole Imperial Fleet and Lord of the Atlantic and Baltic'.

But Wallenstein was, as always, difficult to tie down. He had a number of good excuses for not acting, among them the fact that Lubeck and Danzig, two of the most important Hansa towns, were suspicious of Spanish intentions and refused to co-operate. There were, however, weightier arguments in favour of delay. For one thing Wallenstein was no great lover of the Spaniards and did not wish to see their influence extended into northern Germany, where it might challenge his own. And, for another, he realised that the building of a Habsburg fleet in the Baltic might antagonise not only Denmark but also Sweden, and bring Gustavus into Germany. In any case he needed a bigger port than Wismar or Rostock, and for this reason he besieged Stralsund in July 1628. But the town refused to capitulate, and called for assistance from the Danes and Swedes, who sank their differences and co-operated in its defence. Without a navy Wallenstein could not hope to take Stralsund, and he therefore abandoned the siege. But when Christian IV attempted to follow up this success by landing troops on the Pomeranian coast, Wallenstein wiped them out. Christian was in no state to continue the struggle against such formidable opposition, and Wallenstein, aware of the growing threat from Sweden, persuaded the Emperor to offer him generous peace terms. By the Treaty of Lübeck of June 1629 Christian was allowed to keep his Danish possessions and Holstein, but had to abandon his claims on the north German bishoprics, give up his leadership of the Lower Saxon Circle, and, of course, withdraw from the war.

Now that the Emperor was at last the master of Germany he felt free to impose his will. In March 1629, therefore, he issued the Edict of Restitution, ordering that all lands which had been taken from the catholic Church since 1555 should be restored to it. This affected two secularised archbishoprics (Bremen and Magdeburg), twelve bishoprics, and over a hundred religious houses, as well as a number of towns: in Augsburg, for instance, which was almost entirely protestant, the practice of the Lutheran faith was banned and ministers were exiled. The dislocation entailed in this forcible redistribution of German territory was enormous, and thousands of protestants had to choose between expulsion or conversion. The significance of the Edict was not confined to the sphere of religion. Most of the secularised bishoprics were in north-west Germany, where the Emperor's power had been at its weakest. Now, by appointing imperial administrators to take them over, he established his authority in the heartland of German protestantism.

The manner in which the Edict had been issued, without consultation with the princes or approval by the Diet, was an affront to all German rulers, whatever their religion. If the Emperor could redistribute lands in this way, no prince could sleep securely. Yet there was little that could be done to oppose the imperial will as long as Ferdinand had Wallenstein and an army at his command. The princes hated this upstart adventurer who had proudly declared that 'he would teach the Electors manners. They must be dependent on the Emperor, not the Emperor on them.' Under the leadership of Maximilian of Bavaria they now united to secure his dismissal.

The Emperor had summoned the Electors to meet at Regensburg in the summer of 1630. The protestant Electors of Saxony and Brandenburg showed their resentment at the Edict by staying away, while the catholic Electors, although they attended, were in no conciliatory mood. The Emperor's bargaining power was weakened by the fact that he needed their agreement to two major proposals. The first was the election of his son as King of the Romans. The second was military assistance against the Dutch. These two proposals were both to the benefit of the imperial family rather than the Empire, for the Emperor's son, the Archduke Ferdinand, had married the Spanish Infanta— thereby cementing the alliance between the two branches of the house of Habsburg—and the war against the Dutch was entirely a Spanish affair.

Hitherto it had been the Emperor who looked for aid from Spain rather than vice versa, but the long strain of war was beginning to tell on Spain, and in 1628 she had suffered the grievous loss of her treasure fleet. The Spaniards assumed that since they had come to the aid of the

Empire at the time of the Bohemian crisis,[1] they should now receive assistance in return. But the German Electors were of the opinion that Spanish actions had been prompted by self-interest, and that Germany had nothing to gain from joining in the war against the United Provinces. Their opposition to the Emperor's proposals was stiffened by French envoys, who were present at Regensburg, hoping to detach Bavaria from the Habsburg cause and make Maximilian the lynchpin of a middle party or 'third force'. The Emperor, who knew that Maximilian's loyalty to him was provisional, acted with extreme caution and played his hand badly. If he had agreed to some of the Electors' demands they might have been prepared to meet him half way, but he was afraid to budge, and in the end got nothing. He had to promise to part with Wallenstein, who resigned in August 1630. He had also to accept that there should be no German participation in the war against the Dutch, and that his son should not, at this stage, be elected King of the Romans. Regensburg, then, was a triumph for the Electors and for French diplomacy.

At the same meeting, however, France suffered a diplomatic defeat, over the Mantuan question. In December 1627 the last Gonzaga heir to the duchy of Mantua had died, and the French claimant, the Duke of Nevers, took possession of part of his territories. Mantua, however, was in law an imperial fief, and Ferdinand had long ago agreed that any fiefs falling vacant in northern Italy should go to Spain. He therefore refused to invest Nevers. Montferrat, which also formed part of the ducal territories, could pass through the female line and was claimed by Spain and Savoy who agreed to divide it between themselves. But the fortress of Casale (in Montferrat), which dominated the route from Genoa to Milan, refused to open its gates, and was therefore besieged by the Spaniards. This was a golden opportunity for France to assert her continuing interest in Italy, and following the fall of La Rochelle, the last major Huguenot stronghold, in October 1628, Richelieu was free to act. In March 1629, therefore, Louis XIII in person led his troops across the Alps and forced the Spaniards to raise the siege of Casale. All this was done without any formal declaration of war, but France had clearly committed herself to the anti-Habsburg cause. In the summer of 1629, following the return of Louis XIII, imperial troops, detached from Wallenstein's army, marched through

---

[1] Spain had provided subsidies for the imperial armies, and a token Spanish contingent fought alongside the Emperor's troops in Bohemia in 1619–20.

the Valtelline to take possession of Mantua, which the Emperor had declared sequestrated, and the Spaniards again besieged Casale. This time Richelieu took command of a French relieving force. Early in 1630 he occupied Savoy and captured the fortress of Pignerol, the gateway to Italy. He could not prevent the fall of Mantua, which the imperial army entered in July 1630, but Casale still held out, encouraged by the death of the great Spinola, who had been in charge of the siege.

At Regensburg, however, the French envoys assumed that the fall of Mantua would be followed by the loss of Casale. They therefore grasped at the Emperor's suggestion of a treaty by which he would recognise Nevers as Duke of Mantua in return for the cession of Casale and Pignerol to Spain and a French promise not to intervene in the internal disputes of the Empire. Richelieu was furious when he heard of these concessions, and persuaded Louis XIII to repudiate the treaty, on the grounds that his ambassadors had exceeded their instructions. For Richelieu a bridgehead into Italy and involvement in the affairs of the Empire were essential, since without them he would be unable to fulfil his aims. His obduracy was rewarded, for the situation in Germany, until now so favourable to the Habsburgs, suddenly turned against them, and he was able to exort terms that were more to his liking. By the Treaty of Cherasco, in April 1631, the Emperor agreed to recognise Nevers as Duke of Mantua without any restrictive reciprocal commitments on the part of France. It was further agreed that all troops should be withdrawn from northern Italy, but Richelieu held on to Pignerol and had French possession of this key fortress confirmed by agreements with Savoy in 1631–32.

By clinging to Pignerol, France signalled her commitment to a forward policy. In northern Europe the same was true of Sweden and Stralsund, for although the Danes had done most to help Stralsund fight off Wallenstein, it was Sweden who profited from the victory. Gustavus Adolphus persuaded Christian of Denmark to withdraw his troops, and at the same time convinced the magistrates of Stralsund that they needed the protection of a sizable Swedish garrison. This gave Sweden a foothold from which she could strike into Germany. Gustavus Adolphus had long been considering the possibility of intervention, for, as he said in 1627, 'as one wave follows another in the sea, so the papal deluge is approaching our shores'. The establishment of Swedish power on the southern side of the Baltic would obviously

bring with it considerable economic advantages, but such considerations were secondary to Gustavus. He believed that German protestantism and Swedish security were two sides of the same coin, and
although he appeared to be the aggressor when he intervened in Germany, he thought of himself as waging an essentially defensive war. It
was only after his military triumph had opened the way to unthought-
of possibilities that he began to expand his ambitions.

Gustavus Adolphus and Wallenstein

Gustavus Adolphus, 'the Lion of the North', was a tall, fair-haired man
of thirty-five with a commanding presence. Generous and impulsive
by nature, he had taught himself the art of war by careful study, and
was already one of the best soldiers in Europe. In June 1630 he landed
in Pomerania with an expeditionary force of some 4,000 men, reviving
protestant hopes and challenging imperial domination of Germany at
the very moment when it seemed to have been established beyond
question. By the capture of Stettin and the occupation of much of the
surrounding area, he gained control of Pomerania, whose duke became
his first major German ally. Command of the south Baltic coast secured
his supply lines to Sweden, and he was now ready to push south-west
into Germany. His task was made easier by the Treaty of Barwalde
concluded with the French in January 1631, for this provided subsidies
to keep his armies paid and provisioned. Richelieu was quite happy to
subsidise somebody else to fight France's battles, and the Swedish
military presence was sufficiently remote for him to assume that it
offered no threat to French interests. In return for the subsidies,
Gustavus Adolphus promised to tolerate Roman Catholic worship in
any lands he should occupy. He also agreed to respect the territories of
the Duke of Bavaria, since Richelieu was still optimistic about his
chances of building a 'middle party' or 'third force' based on Maximilian.

Gustavus Adolphus hoped to unite the German protestant princes
under his leadership. But John George of Saxony saw the Swedish
presence as a threat to German freedom (as well as to the 'liberties' of
the princes), and he persuaded an assembly of protestant German
states which met at Leipzig in February 1631 to make provision for the
raising of an independent army. This was soon set on foot, and the
command of the new force was given to Hans George von Arnim,
who had formerly served under Wallenstein but had left imperial

service out of disgust at the Edict of Restitution. The German protestants at last had an army of their own to match that of the Catholic League, and if they chose to co-operate with the King of Sweden it would be on terms of equality and not as subordinates.

While Gustavus Adolphus was waiting to see whether or not Saxony and Brandenburg would join him, Tilly besieged the city of Magdeburg. This was one of the great centres of protestantism in northern Germany, and had a symbolic as well as a strategic significance. Gustavus had assured it of his support, but he could only get to it across Brandenburg territory and the Elector was a skilled procrastinator. By May 1631 the city could hold out no longer. Tilly's troops poured in and set to work to plunder it. By chance or design some buildings were set on fire, and soon the whole place was in flames. Magdeburg was destroyed and twenty thousand of its inhabitants perished with it. This disaster stirred up protestant feeling throughout Europe. The United Provinces made a treaty with Sweden, agreeing to provide subsidies, while Gustavus himself marched on Berlin and forced the Elector of Brandenburg to accept a Swedish garrison and provide money for the protestant cause. He then completed the occupation of Pomerania and also conquered Mecklenburg, which he restored to the dukes whom Wallenstein had expelled and replaced. Gustavus needed to act swiftly in order to restore protestant confidence after the loss of Magdeburg and if possible to engage Tilly before reinforcements arrived from Italy (where peace had just been concluded at Cherasco).

Tilly was in an awkward position, for in May 1631 his master, Maximilian of Bavaria, had made a secret agreement with Richelieu by which, in return for French recognition of his electoral title, he promised not to aid the enemies of France or to attack her friends. Since Gustavus Adolphus had been acknowledged in the Treaty of Barwalde—which he had insisted on making public—as the ally of France, Maximilian could hardly permit Tilly to attack him. Yet Tilly was also, in a sense, the Emperor's general, and now that Wallenstein was no longer present with an army the defence of northern Germany rested on him alone. His troops were in any case short of food, for Wallenstein—in whose duchy of Friedland they were quartered— witheld supplies, in the hope that Tilly's failure would open the way to his own return to power. Tilly had therefore to move his men, and since he could not openly attack the Swedes he turned instead against John George of Saxony, whose lands were generously provided with food and other supplies, whose refusal to enforce the Edict had been an affront to the Emperor, and who was, in any case, defying imperial commands by raising an army. In September Tilly's forces crossed the Saxon border and occupied Leipzig, the electoral capital. John George now had no choice but to call for aid from Gustavus, yet even so he insisted on an equal partnership. Gustavus did not stop to quibble over terms but took his army, now some twenty-four thousand strong, to link up with the eighteen thousand Saxon troops. Against this formidable combination Tilly opposed some thirty-five thousand men and his own untarnished reputation. In September 1631 battle was joined at Breitenfeld, just north of Leipzig. In a savage fight the Saxons were driven from the field, but the Swedes stood firm, and one of Gustavus's generals, Count Horn, led a counter-attack which carried the day. Tilly lost half his army as well as all his artillery, and had to retreat towards Bavaria.

In one battle Gustavus had transformed the military and political situation. There was virtually no other army in the field against him, and Germany lay open to his advancing troops. Leaving the Saxons to hold East Germany, he moved south-west along 'Priests' Alley', through the rich lands of the bishopric of Wurzburg. In November he entered Frankfurt-on-Main—the first foreign conqueror ever to ride in triumph through the administrative capital of the Holy Roman Empire. Despite opposition from Spanish troops, he crossed the Rhine and in December 1631 occupied Mainz. Meanwhile the Saxons, not content with a simple holding operation, had struck through Silesia into Bohemia, where they captured Prague in November.

Richelieu was alarmed by the unexpected speed and depth of the Swedish advance. He had assumed that Gustavus would hold the Emperor in check in northern Germany while French diplomats built up the Bavarian-based 'third force' in the south. Now, to his consternation, Gustavus was on the Rhine. In December 1631, therefore, Richelieu took the Archbishop-Elector of Trier under his protection and sent French troops to occupy the Rhine fortress of Philippsburg. But he could not alter the fact that Gustavus was now master of Germany and that his headquarters at Mainz had become a *de facto* capital. The next moves depended on Sweden, not on France. As for the Emperor, he had momentarily panicked after the news of Breitenfeld, and even considered withdrawing the Edict of Restitution and fleeing to Italy. But on second thoughts he took the more characteristic course of continuing the struggle, and in December 1631 he recalled

Wallenstein. This time Wallenstein dictated his own terms. He was to be confirmed in his dukedom of Mecklenburg, he was to have the possession and the revenues of all imperial territories that he liberated, he was to have full authority in military matters and was to be free to undertake negotiations with the Saxons. What he was proposing, in fact, was an alliance, as between equals, but the Emperor was in no position to stand on his dignity. He desperately needed the thousands of armed men that Wallenstein alone could supply and lead.

In April 1632 Gustavus began his advance into Bavaria, which had so far been free from the horrors of war. Tilly attempted to hold up the Swedish crossing of the Danube at Donauworth, but failed to do so and received a wound from which he shortly afterwards died. Gustavus captured Augsburg, and in May he entered Munich, the Bavarian capital. Riding at his side in this moment of triumph was the half-forgotten Frederick V, who had unwittingly set all these events in train. It was one of the few bright moments in a life that had been clouded by defeat and disappointment, and that was to come to an early end in the following year.

As the Swedes advanced they systematically devastated the rich Bavarian countryside, partly as a punishment on Maximilian, partly as a warning to all those who dared support the imperial and catholic cause. Yet Gustavus's progress was in some ways deceptively successful. Ingoldstadt and Regensburg held out against him, and by failing even to attack them he left the initiative in the hands of his enemies. For Wallenstein had already reappeared on the scene, capturing Prague in May 1632 and driving von Arnim out of Bohemia. He was now engaged in secret negotiations with the Saxons, who had appealed to Gustavus for assistance. Gustavus knew that John George was untrustworthy and did not dare abandon him for fear of driving him into Wallenstein's arms. Had Gustavus besieged Regensburg he might have forced Wallenstein to come to its relief. As it was, he had to call off his advance towards Vienna and move north towards the retreating Saxons.

By this time Gustavus had recognised the implications of his unexpected but unparalleled success and was formulating proposals for a settlement of the German question on the basis of twin protestant leagues. One of these, a *Corpus Bellicum*, was to be responsible for military affairs, including the maintenance of a standing army under one supreme commander—probably, though not necessarily, himself. The other, a *Corpus Evangelicorum*, would take over civil administration.

Gustavus did not intend these bodies to be an alternative to the existing Empire—since this would have been unacceptable to Saxony and Brandenburg, the leading protestant states—nor did he seriously envisage claiming the imperial crown for himself. His purpose at this stage was the preservation of the existing structure of the states and Empire and the confirmation of security for the protestants. As for territorial gains, he was clearly thinking in terms of holding on to part at least of the south Baltic coast. This was necessary for the security of Sweden; also the profits that would accrue from port revenues and the expansion of Swedish trade would be some recompense for the heavy cost of saving German protestantism.

Whatever Gustavus's long-term aspirations he had no time to develop them, for John George's appeals for assistance were becoming more and more urgent, and Wallenstein himself was ensconced in a strong fortified position—the *Alte Feste*—to the west of Nuremberg. In September 1632 Gustavus launched a frontal attack on the *Alte Feste* but was beaten off—his first repulse, and one that lowered his prestige and caused substantial desertions among the thousands of mercenaries serving in the Swedish army. Gustavus had to pull back from Nuremberg and regroup his forces before he could take up his pursuit of Wallenstein, who had resumed his advance northwards, towards Saxony. In October 1632 Wallenstein captured Leipzig and was preparing winter quarters at Lutzen, to the south-west, when Gustavus caught up with him. Gustavus planned a surprise attack, but a contingent of Wallenstein's army stumbled on the Swedes and gave the game away. On the morning of 16 November 1632 battle was joined at Lutzen and the heavy fighting lasted until nightfall. Wallenstein had to abandon the field and retreat into Bohemia, but the Swedes had little cause to celebrate their victory, for among their dead was numbered Gustavus Adolphus. The astonishing career of the man who had come to personify the protestant cause had abruptly ended.

Although the Swedes had lost their king they did not abandon his policies. The Swedish forces found new leaders in Horn and Bernard of Weimar, while the civil administration was taken over by Gustavus's chancellor and close friend, Axel Oxenstierna. In the spring of 1633 Oxenstierna called representatives of the four Circles under Swedish occupation—Swabia, Upper and Lower Rhine, and Franconia—to a conference at Heilbronn, where he persuaded them to set up a defensive league. Saxony refused to join the League of Heilbronn, since John George was determined to make his peace with the Emperor, but a protestant coalition, similar to that envisaged by Gustavus, had at last come into being. Richelieu would still have preferred a 'third force', built round a Bavarian–Saxon axis, but since neither of the parties would agree to this he had to make the best of a bad job and accept the League of Heilbronn. The death of Gustavus Adolphus opened the way to French supremacy in Europe, and the changing balance of power was reflected in the fact that France and Sweden were to be joint and co-equal 'protectors' of the new League.

The protestant allies won their first major victory in November 1633, when Bernard of Weimar invaded Bavaria and captured Regensburg. Meanwhile Wallenstein brooded in Bohemia, spinning a web of intrigue by secret negotiations in which everything was possible and nothing certain. The Emperor became increasingly suspicious of the ambitions of his overmighty subject, particularly when he heard that Wallenstein had demanded an exclusive oath of loyalty from his officers. Secret orders were despatched from Vienna to Ottavio Piccolomini, Wallenstein's principal lieutenant, instructing him to capture his commander-in-chief, alive or dead. Wallenstein was physically ill, and had to be carried on a litter, while his men were deserting him. He appealed to the Saxons for support, and was on his way to the Saxon border when he was assassinated by a group of his own officers—Scots, Irish and English—in February 1634. In the words of one contemporary account they 'drew him out by the heels, his head knocking upon every stair, all bloody, and threw him into a coach and carried him to the castle where the rest [of the dead] lay naked, close together . . . and there he had the superior place of them, being the right hand file, which they could not do less, being so great a general'.

The Triumph of France

The new commander of the imperial army was the Emperor's son and heir, the Archduke Ferdinand, titular King of Hungary. He was married to the Spanish Infanta and had already established friendly links with her brother, the Cardinal-Infante, who had been nominated as governor of the Spanish Netherlands. The King of Hungary and the Cardinal-Infante were young men of great ability, determined to revive the faltering alliance between the Austrian and Spanish Habsburgs and to recover for the catholic faith the ground lost to protestantism. In 1634 the Cardinal-Infante set out with a large army along the land route from Italy to take up his appointment. The King of Hungary, with the imperial army, marched to meet him, and in September of that year the two joined forces at Nordlingen. The main Swedish army, under Horn and Bernard of Weimar, moved rapidly south to assault the town and break this dangerous combination before it broke them. But in the battle that was fought just outside Nordlingen, the Swedes were annihilated and Horn himself captured. This was the catholic equivalent of Breitenfeld. It brought to an end the period of protestant ascendancy and it re-established the Emperor's supremacy within the Empire. While the Cardinal-Infante continued on his way to the Netherlands, the King of Hungary mopped up Swedish garrisons until, by the spring of 1635, the whole of southern Germany was once again under imperial control.

John George took no part in the fighting, because he was already negotiating terms with the Emperor. In May 1635 he signed the Peace of Prague, which was subsequently extended to any other state which cared to sign it and thereby became the possible basis for a general settlement. Under its provisions the Edict of Restitution was at last abandoned and the Lutherans were to have all the ecclesiastical lands they had held in 1627. Since this was the date when imperial power was at its most extensive, the catholic Church would still be a gainer, but from the Lutheran point of view (nothing was said about the Calvinists) 1627 was infinitely preferable to 1555, the date laid down in the Edict. There was to be an amnesty for all those who had fought against the Emperor, except the Bohemian exiles and the family of Frederick V, and the Emperor promised to revive the *Reichskammergericht*, the symbol of imperial (as distinct from Habsburg) justice, and to refer all disputed cases to it. The Peace of Prague marked the triumph of John George's *Politique* programme and made it possible for the princes to unite behind the Emperor on the basis of the old imperial constitution (i.e. 'German liberties'). It won widespread acceptance. Brandenburg followed Saxony's lead, and Maximilian of Bavaria, anxious to rebuild the prosperity of his ravaged lands, agreed to sign the Peace, to dissolve the Catholic League, and to place its remaining forces under the King of Hungary's command. Only a handful of princes, none of them major ones, still held out. The greater part of Germany had at last made peace with itself.

It was a tragedy for Germany that her destiny was no longer in her own hands, since the war had laid her open to the intervention of outside powers, particularly Sweden and France. The Swedes were determined to continue fighting until they received territorial 'satisfaction' for their heavy expenditure, and as for Richelieu, he was not willing to abandon the struggle until the Habsburgs had been defeated and France's claim to be 'Defender of German Liberties' acknowledged. He had so far been able to sustain the struggle against the Habsburgs without formally committing himself, but after Nordlingen he could do so no longer. In April 1635, therefore, he concluded the Treaty of Compiègne with Oxenstierna, by which France and Sweden agreed to fight on until such time as their demands were satisfied. In the following month, France declared war upon Spain.

The open commitment of France to the anti-Habsburg struggle at first made little difference, because French troops were ill-disciplined and inexperienced. Richelieu recognised this and therefore concentrated on building up alliances. In July 1635, for instance, he signed a treaty with Savoy, Mantua and Parma for joint operations in northern Italy, and sent the Huguenot general Rohan (now reconciled to Louis XIII) to lead the Swiss protestant cantons in a campaign to occupy the Valtelline. Then, in October, he took Bernard of Weimar and his entire army into French service. Nevertheless the military situation was not favourable to France. In Italy the Spaniards won over the Swiss by timely concessions and persuaded them to abandon Rohan, who had therefore to withdraw from the Valtelline. Nearer home, the Spaniards decided to try and capitalise on Richelieu's unpopularity with the French by invading France itself. In the summer of 1636 the Cardinal-Infante and his army advanced from the Netherlands into Picardy, and pushed forward as far as Compiègne. There was panic in Paris, and it was generally assumed that Richelieu would be dismissed. But the king stood firm behind his minister and called on the citizens of Paris to provide money for their own defence. 'It is not I who am speaking,' he reminded them. 'It is my state and its necessities. Those who contradict my wishes do me more harm than the Spaniards.' The unexpected stiffening of French resistance, combined with supply difficulties and the operations of Bernard's army, forced the Spaniards to withdraw. Nevertheless the prestige of France had been diminished, and this was clearly demonstrated in the autumn of 1636 when the Electors, again meeting at Regensburg, at last agreed to Ferdinand's request that his son, the victor of Nordlingen, should be elected King of the Romans. It was a timely gesture, for in February 1637 Ferdinand died and his son succeeded him as Ferdinand III.

The military balance gradually tilted against the Habsburgs. In the late summer of 1636 the Swedes defeated a combined imperial and Saxon force at Wittstock in Brandenburg and occupied much of northern Germany. They were driven back into Pomerania in 1637 but recovered in the following year, struck into the heart of Bohemia, and reached the suburbs of Prague; 1638 also saw Bernard triumphant over imperial troops at Rheinfelden, on the Rhine. From there he advanced to Breisach, a vital link in the Spanish land route from Italy, which was being besieged by the French general Turenne. By December Breisach had fallen and the Spanish lifeline had been severed. Bernard went on to occupy Alsace, but then embarrassed Richelieu, who had long coveted this strategically important area for the crown of France, by claiming it for himself. Fortunately (from the French point of view) Bernard succumbed to fever in July 1639 and died at the early age of thirty-five. His army now came under the immediate control of French generals, who were learning from experience and who included two naturally gifted commanders, Turenne and Louis II, Prince of Condé.

Soon after the capture of Breisach cut off the Spanish Netherlands from reinforcement by land, the Dutch naval victory in the Downs (in 1639) severed the sea route. The Cardinal-Infante managed to hold back the Dutch army, but the strain was enormous and contributed to his early death in November 1641. By that date disaster had struck Spain herself, for in 1640 revolts broke out in Catalonia and Portugal, and it began to seem as though the Spanish state might totally disintegrate.

The Peace of Westphalia

Throughout Europe there was general war-weariness and a longing for peace. But after twenty years of fighting none of the major parties was ready to sacrifice its gains or its still unachieved ambitions without some compensation, and the problem was one of deciding a basis for agreement. One proposal was that put forward by France and Sweden when they made the Treaty of Hamburg in March 1638. On the face of it this was simply a treaty of alliance in which France agreed to continue her subsidies to Sweden, support Swedish claims on Pomerania, and declare war on the Emperor, in return for a Swedish promise not to make a separate peace. But the treaty went further than this, for both parties agreed that although they would need 'satisfaction' in the form of territorial concessions, there should in principle be a return to the *status quo* of 1618.

The Emperor, however, was still hoping to preserve something from the years of bitter struggle, and in the summer of 1640 he proposed to a meeting of the Electors at Nuremberg that negotiations should open on the basis of the Peace of Prague. But the Electors preferred 1618 to 1627 as the *status quo* date, and were clearly more favourably inclined towards the Franco–Swedish proposals. Ferdinand, hoping for support from the smaller states, therefore summoned a Diet to Regensburg in September 1640. At first all seemed to go well, and in November the Diet decided to appoint representatives to open negotiations on the basis of the Peace of Prague. In the following month, however, the Elector of Brandenburg died and was succeeded by Frederick William, the Great Elector. The new ruler of Brandenburg lost no time in declaring that the Peace of Prague was an inadequate basis for a general settlement, and in July 1641 he proved his point by making a separate truce with Sweden. This threw the Diet into disarray and put an end to any unity of purpose. It was dissolved in October 1641, with nothing of substance accomplished.

Nevertheless the pressure for peace mounted as it became increasingly obvious that a military solution would not be forthcoming. In 1642 the Swedes swept into Moravia, and although they were forced back into Saxony by the imperial army under Piccolomini, they turned and defeated him at the second battle of Breitenfeld in November. The French were also successful, occupying Artois in the north and Roussillon in the south; and in May 1643 Condé won a resounding victory at Rocroi, near the Netherlands' frontier, in which he wiped out the flower of the Spanish infantry. In the following year the fortunes of war favoured the Emperor, but in 1645 the Swedes once again advanced into Bohemia and in March defeated an imperial army at the battle of Jankau. Meanwhile the French, under Condé, thrust towards the Danube, and in July, at the second battle of Nordlingen, routed an imperial-Bavarian force. These defeats brought home to the Habsburgs the unpalatable truth, that they could not hope to win the war; yet at the same time they demonstrated that France and Sweden were in no position to exploit their victories. The devastation of the countryside over which campaigns were repeatedly fought created wellnigh insoluble supply problems and brought successful armies to a halt. Peace would be found only at the negotiating table.

In 1644 two parallel sets of negotiations opened: with the Swedes and the German protestant states at Osnabruck, and with the French and the German catholic states at Munster. The process of peace-making had at last begun, but it was slowed down by interminable disputes over precedence and also by the fact that there was no general cease-fire. Military operations continued, and the negotiators were always looking over their shoulders at the battlefields, seeking to exploit a victory or to play for time after a reverse. It was defeat rather than diplomacy that broke up the Habsburg coalition. After a Swedish invasion in September 1645 the Saxons laid down their arms; in 1647 French and Swedish forces compelled Maximilian of Bavaria to abandon his alliance with the Emperor, and when he broke his promise in the following year his territories were again devastated and he was forced to agree to a truce. The pressure on the Habsburgs never relaxed. In August 1648 the Emperor's brother Leopold, now governor of the Netherlands and promising to be another Cardinal-Infante, was overwhelmed by Condé at the battle of Lens, while the Swedes were once again fighting their way into Bohemia and had laid siege to Prague. It was against this background of continuing defeat that the Emperor decided to cut his losses and make peace.

The treaties negotiated at Osnabruck and Munster, and known jointly as the Peace of Westphalia, were formally concluded in October 1648. In secular affairs the *status quo* of 1618 was restored, with certain significant exceptions. Charles Louis, eldest son of the unhappy Frederick V, whose intemperate haste in accepting the Bohemian crown had started the war, was restored to the Lower Palatinate and was also given a specially created electoral title—the eighth and junior one. Maximilian kept both the original electoral title and the Upper Palatinate. Saxony held on to Lusatia, while further north the Elector of Brandenburg reluctantly agreed to divide Pomerania with Sweden, leaving her the more valuable western part, in return for the cession to Brandenburg of the secularised bishoprics of Halberstadt and Minden and the reversion of Magdeburg. Sweden, in addition to western Pomerania (which included the major port of Stettin), received the secularised bishoprics of Bremen and Verden. She was now in a very strong economic position, since she controlled the estuaries of the Weser, Elbe and Oder, along which so much German trade flowed, and she was also promised a large indemnity to enable her to pay off her army. As for France, she took over from the Emperor the tangle of sovereign rights which he held in Alsace, as well as a number of key

positions, of which the most important were Breisach and Philippsburg.
The boundaries of the Empire were further restricted by the formal
admission that they no longer included the bishoprics of Metz, Toul
and Verdun, or the Netherlands and Switzerland. A further formal
acceptance of an established fact came from Spain, which at last agreed
to recognise the United Provinces as an independent sovereign state.

In religious matters the abandonment of the Edict of Restitution was
confirmed by the provision that the situation of 1624 should be
restored. This time Calvinism was explicitly recognised and given the
same protection as Lutheranism. But the old principle of *cuius regio,
eius religio* (see p. 135) was abandoned. Rulers retained the right to lay
down what the public worship of their state ought to be, but they could
no longer drag their subjects with them if they changed their religion.
In effect, the political consequences of Reformation and Counter-
Reformation were declared to have worked themselves out by 1624.
Any changes that had taken place since that date were to be annulled.
As for those people who, on grounds of conscience, could not accept
the public profession of worship of the state in which they lived, they
were to have a minimum of five years in which to put their affairs in
order and emigrate. Freedom of private belief was to be permitted
in the Empire but not in the Habsburg hereditary lands (except for
minor concessions in Silesia) and the eradication of protestantism from
Bohemia and Austria was confirmed. This was the one positive gain
for the Emperor, since the common acceptance of the Roman Catholic
faith became one of the relatively few bonds holding together the
Habsburg possessions. The Emperor thereby reinforced the structure of his family inheritance in eastern Europe at the same time as he
tacitly abandoned most of his pretensions to imperial power within
Germany. Charles V's division of his inheritance had proved to be
irreversible, and the Holy Roman Empire had been abandoned in
favour of an Austrian one.

As for the rulers of individual German states, they were recognised
as equal (the Electors were no longer to have precedence) and virtually
autonomous. They were acknowledged as sovereign over their own
subjects, and in foreign affairs they were free to make any alliances with
other powers as long as these were not directed against the Emperor.
There could be no question in future of the Emperor confiscating or
granting away German lands, nor was he permitted to bind the Empire
by any treaty obligations or to declare war or impose taxes without the
consent of the German states. Imperial institutions continued to exist,

as did the shadowy concept of the Empire itself, but in fact it was now a hotchpotch of independent principalities. Yet even in peace the Empire was not to be free from outside interference, for Sweden and France were named as guarantors of the Treaty of Westphalia, and thereby acquired the right to intervene when they thought fit.

The settlement of 1648 did not bring with it a general European peace, since the war between France and Spain continued. But it did put an end to fighting in central Europe, and gave the inhabitants of that unhappy region a breathing-space in which to rebuild their homes and re-establish a more normal pattern of living. There is no agreement among historians about the economic effects of the Thirty Years War.[1] The 'traditional' view, which still has powerful adherents, is that it brought disaster to many areas, decimating populations, destroying towns, breaking down established patterns in agriculture and commerce, and leaving a trail of desolation and despair behind it. A somewhat more 'modern' view is that the German economy was already in decline before 1618 and that the war had relatively little long-term effect upon this. It merely confirmed, and perhaps accelerated, what would have happened in any case.[2]

There are three major reasons for these differences in interpretation. The first is the lack of reliable statistics. No one can be certain what the population of Germany was in this period, and estimates are little more than inspired guesswork. It is therefore very difficult to decide whether, and to what extent, depopulation was taking place. Secondly, the area loosely referred to as 'Germany' was not an economic unity. There was a major division, for instance, between east and west, with the Elbe as the dividing line, and what was true of one side might well be false of the other. This disparity goes much further down the scale, for even within relatively small areas there were pockets of prosperity existing side-by-side with pockets of depression. And thirdly, the concepts of 'economic decline' and 'economic advance' are difficult, if not impossible, to define. A region might appear to be flourishing, for instance, but still be a long way behind the rate of growth of England and Holland, so that its 'absolute' prosperity would conceal a 'relative' decline. Conversely, an apparently backward area might be substantially better off in 1648 than it had been in 1618.

[1] The political significance of the war is considered above, in chapter 19.
[2] Cf. S. H. Steinberg: *The 'Thirty Years War' and the Conflict for European Hegemony 1600–1660*, Arnold, 1966.

There is clear evidence of depopulation in certain parts of Germany. This was most marked in the countryside, for open villages provided little protection against armed bands of soldiers or robbers, and in the disturbed conditions brought about by the war many peasants chose to abandon their landholdings and seek refuge in walled cities. Once inside, they were exposed to another enemy, for crowded and insanitary conditions promoted the spread of infection, and urban populations were consumed by epidemics. There was nothing new about this, of course, since even in peacetime some 6–7 per cent of the inhabitants of a town were killed off by disease, but under wartime conditions this figure rose to an average of 12 per cent.

While some towns were swollen with refugees, others were being deserted. Munich, for instance, which had 22,000 inhabitants in 1620, had only 17,000 thirty years later, while during the same period the population of Augsburg shrank from 48,000 to 21,000. The fortunes of a town depended very much on its geographical location. Hamburg, to take one example, was well placed to handle the heavy traffic in food, clothing and weapons generated by the presence of substantial armies in Germany, and it emerged from the war as one of the most prosperous cities in Europe. Magdeburg, on the other hand, was destroyed by fire, and many smaller towns were devastated to a greater or lesser extent.

Some of the population shifts that took place during the war were reversed in the years of peace that followed. Once the armies had been disbanded, peasants were free to leave the walled cities and go back to the countryside, and in northern and eastern Germany it was rural rather than urban areas that led the way in economic recovery. Physical destruction was also shortlived. Magdeburg had been rebuilt by the time the war ended, and Leipzig, which had suffered from repeated sieges, bombardments and occupations, nevertheless managed to establish an annual trade fair which turned it into a major centre of international commerce. In any case, the actual area of devastation caused by the passage of armies was surprisingly restricted. The fact that there were two battles of Breitenfeld and two of Nordlingen serves as a reminder that fighting tended to be concentrated round places that were strategically significant—particularly river-crossings. Those parts of Germany which had the good fortune to be strategically insignificant seldom if ever saw the armies which in other places were only too frequently and destructively apparent.

The older interpretation, then, in which the war is depicted as the scourge of God, reducing great areas of central Europe to wilderness and turning the inhabitants into savages and cannibals, can no longer be accepted as universally applicable. But there has been a tendency to go too far in the opposite direction and give the impression that the war was little more than a local irritant, leaving no lasting effects. This was certainly not the case in some regions. A recent study of the war by the Czech historian J. V. Polisensky concludes that 'Throughout much of central Europe [the war] was in fact incalculably deleterious, setting back the development of communities by nearly a century';[1] and the American historian T. K. Rabb has pointed out that while the war in some cases accelerated a decline that was already taking place, in others it put an abrupt end to a period of growth and development. 'Whatever the long-term effects of the war, therefore, its direct, immediate effects were destructive. At best, the Thirty Years War started a general decline that had not previously existed; at worst, it replaced prosperity with disaster.'[2]

[1] J. V. Polisensky. *The Thirty Years War*, Batsford, 1971. p. 262.
[2] Theodore K. Rabb. 'The effects of the Thirty Years War on the German economy'. *Journal of Modern History*, 34 (1962).

TWENTY-ONE

France 1598–1660

Administration and Finance

The French monarchy, which during the Wars of Religion had been humiliated and all but extinguished, emerged in the seventeenth century as the most powerful in Europe. There was nothing inevitable about this. It was the result of the conscious enhancement of royal authority by strong monarchs such as Henry IV and Louis XIV, and the hard work and ruthless persistence of devoted servants of the crown, most notable among them Sully, Richelieu and Mazarin.

Yet if there was nothing inevitable about the development of royal absolutism, neither was there anything particularly new about it. Ever since the French monarchy had risen triumphant from the Hundred Years War, successive kings had asserted their authority against those elements in the state which threatened it. Francis I, for example, had tamed the nobles and forced the *Parlement* to bow to his will (see p. 222), and but for the tragedy of Henry II's untimely death and the fact that his children were all minors, these achievements might have been consolidated. Yet although the kings of France frequently spoke the language of absolutism, they made little attempt to eradicate the institutions which restricted their power, and never even envisaged, the fundamental remodelling of the French state. They operated *within* the existing system—which, on the whole, worked to their advantage— and either by-passed institutions which they could not control or created new offices to duplicate their functions. The result of all this was a highly involved system of government, with overlapping jurisdictions, in which deadlock and inertia were avoided only by the forceful operation of the royal will. When this will was weakened, through incapacity or, more usually, through a minority, the balance of the constitution was upset, the various elements began struggling for supremacy, and confusion became general. This was why France appeared to fluctuate abruptly between periods of strong government and no government, absolutism and anarchy.

At the heart of French government was the royal council, but this was a body which varied in size—usually expanding under weak monarchs and contracting under strong ones—and had various names. It was sometimes referred to as the royal council, at other times as the privy council, or, more and more frequently, the council of state. Nobody had an automatic right to membership, and appointment to it was in the king's gift alone; but normally princes of the blood, magnates, the greater prelates and the holders of major offices were to be numbered among its members. It was too large and too amorphous a body to formulate policy and supervise its execution. The first of these functions—the making of policy—was concentrated in an inner ring known as the *Conseil des affaires* or *Conseil d'en haut* (because it usually met in an upstairs room). This was a small body consisting of some half dozen members, and the king was normally present at its daily meetings. The second function—execution of conciliar decisions—had originally been the concern of the great officers of state and certain committees of the council, such as those which handled finance and justice. These conciliar committees were declining in importance, however, and more and more of the actual business of administration was being carried out by departments under the charge of a minister. Oldest and greatest of these departments was that presided over by the chancellor, who was not only the head of the judiciary but also custodian of the great seal which authenticated government decrees. The complex business of managing the royal finances came within the competence of the *Surintendant's* department; while foreign affairs, local administration and later the army and navy, were dealt with by new departments growing up around the increasingly significant figures of the secretaries of state.

The royal council, taken as a whole, could claim to be a sovereign body in that it gave formal expression to the royal will, but there were other institutions which were known as 'sovereign courts' and had an important, though ill-defined, role in the government of France. Most important of these were the eight *Parlements*, and in particular the *Parlement* of Paris (often referred to, quite simply, as 'the *Parlement*'). These bodies were principally supreme courts of appeal in legal cases, but they also had the duty of registering royal edicts to make them valid for the area over which they had jurisdiction. The *Parlement* of

Paris was not content simply to register royal edicts. It had acquired the right to present a 'remonstrance' to the king before registration took place, and although these remonstrances were supposed to deal only with the appropriateness of the proposed legislation and its relationship to existing laws, the 'right to remonstrate' was the basis of the *Parlement's* claim to be a political, and not simply a legal, body.

The *Parlement* of Paris was, in fact, an offshoot of the medieval royal council and claimed to be the oldest formal expression of the king's will. Members of the *Parlement* recognised only the king and the chancellor as their superiors, and affected to despise the contemporary royal council as an upstart body which had arrogated to itself powers that belonged of right to the *Parlement*. Francis I had used his authority to check the political pretensions of the *Parlement* but he had not destroyed them. During a royal minority the authority of the *Parlement* expanded to fill the void left by the absence of the king, and at such times its self-appointed role as guardian of the established order did not seem so far-fetched. In 1610, for instance, it was the *Parlement* which formally requested the young Louis XIII to bestow the regency upon his mother, while thirty-three years later the *Parlement* set aside the will of that same Louis XIII by confirming the claim of his widow, Anne of Austria, to be sole regent.

The *Parlement* could not, of course, impede government indefinitely by refusing to register a royal edict. The king could hold a *lit de justice*—a ceremony in which he publicly imposed his will and ordered the registration of his decree. In the long struggle between Richelieu and the *Parlement* this weapon was of great value to the Cardinal. In 1632 Louis XIII had already authorised the royal council, during his absence on campaign, to annul any orders of the *Parlement* which encroached upon the authority of the crown, and in 1641 he held a *lit de justice* in which he forced the *Parlement* to register an edict severely curtailing its right to concern itself with the administration, finance and government of his kingdom. 'A monarchic state', declared this edict, 'cannot suffer anyone to lay his hand on the sceptre of the sovereign or to share his authority. The power which is concentrated in the person of the king is the source of the glory and the grandeur of monarchies and the foundation upon which their sure continuance is laid.' Yet although the *Parlement's* rights had been reduced to such an extent that it appeared to be politically impotent, the institution itself survived and so did the shadow of its claims. The moment Louis XIII was dead the *Parlement* became once more a power in the land, and both the queen regent and the magnates were anxious to have the support of its traditional authority.

There would have been no clash between the *Parlement* and the crown if the government had been content to work within the accepted framework. But under the strain of war and the urgent necessity of raising money, the crown was compelled to cut through the tangled undergrowth of bureaucracy by appointing special commissioners, most notorious of whom were the *Intendants*, to enforce its will. The *Parlement* took the view that time-honoured methods were sufficient for all purposes and that short cuts endangered the 'liberties' and property of the subject. Among those who cared most passionately for their 'liberties' and property were the great magnates, many of whom believed that the way in which royal authority was being expanded threatened their own position. During the 1620s and 1630s, therefore, the *Parlement* and the magnates drew closer together in opposition to absolutist tendencies at court, and this union led to open revolt against Mazarin. Yet the two allies were far apart in their basic assumptions. In the last resort members of the *Parlement* were upholders of the monarchical system, and, as office-holders who were doing well out of the existing order of things, they feared the radicalism that was always latent among the lower sections of society and could easily be fanned into flame by the recklessness of the magnates. Although they might use revolutionary language when defending their vested interests, they were a long way removed from the aggressive political commitment which characterised their English namesake—a far more representative body.

The tension between the *Parlement* of Paris and the royal council was often paralleled by that between the provincial *Parlements* and the royal governors. There was one governor for each province, and these offices were shared out among certain magnate families which had acquired what was virtually a hereditary right to them. The functions of the office were mainly honorific, but the fact that a magnate, as well as having substantial lands within a province, was also its official governor, gave him considerable power, particularly when the crown was weak. Henry IV began the practice of appointing lieutenant-governors, nominally to assist the governors but in fact to hold them in check. This device was not entirely satisfactory, however, since lieutenant-governors tended to become locally based and soon passed beyond the range of immediate royal control. As far as the crown was concerned, then, there was still a great need for an officer who should be at the same time responsible solely to the king and yet effective in the localities.

In certain provinces, mainly those which had not formed part of the crown's original demesne lands but had been acquired at a later stage, representative assemblies, or Estates, met annually. They discussed local affairs and sent *Cahiers* to the king listing their grievances, but their major function was to grant taxes to the crown. The amount of these taxes was a matter for negotiation between the royal government and the Estates, and the king usually managed to get about two-thirds of the sum he asked for. The most important of the provinces which had retained their own Estates and 'liberties' were Brittany, Burgundy, Provence and Languedoc. Dauphiné had kept its 'liberties' without its Estates, while Normandy had Estates that were politically impotent. The significance of these *Pays d'Etats*, as they were called, was that by voting their own 'gifts' to the crown they managed to lighten their fiscal burden.

Ninety per cent of the yield in direct taxation came from the *Pays d'Election*, which covered most of northern and central France. For these areas the *Surintendant des Finances*, in consultation with the king, decided on the total amount to be raised by the *Taille*, the major direct tax. This amount was then apportioned between the *Pays d'Election*, where it was further subdivided among the smallest administrative units, the *Elections*. There were some 150 of these *Elections*, each under the charge of an *Elu*; but these *Elus*, being local men, were notorious for their partiality and corruption when it came to apportioning the *Taille* among households. Their task was admittedly a difficult one, for not everybody was liable to tax. In general the nobility were exempt, as were clerics, and the privilege of exemption covered servants and labourers on their estates. Many towns had commuted their *Taille* for a jump sum payment, while many individuals had bought exemption from it. In short it was only the poor and those who were unable, for one reason or another, to wriggle out of the obligation, who actually paid, and not surprisingly they bitterly resented doing so.

As well as the *Taille* there were a number of indirect taxes, or *Aides*, and the tax on salt known as the *Gabelle*. The incidence of these taxes varied with the locality. Brittany, Béarn and Navarre, for example, were exempt from the *Gabelle*—and as always it was those who were least able to afford it who paid most. In theory it might have seemed desirable, following the restoration of royal authority after the Wars of Religion, to sweep away the whole unfair, unjust and unproductive system, and replace it with something more coherent and lucrative. But such a step, even had it been possible without causing a major revolt, would have been quite contrary to the assumptions of the *ancien régime*. Henry IV and his chief minister, Sully, were concerned to make the existing machinery work and not to start rebuilding the state from the foundations upwards. Taxation was always unpopular, but traditional methods were more acceptable than new ones. Sully worked on the assumption that there was nothing wrong with the existing system, provided that it was used properly, and he set out to demonstrate the truth of this contention after he became *Surintendant des Finances* in 1600.

Maximilien de Béthune, whom Henry IV created Duke of Sully, was born in 1560 of Huguenot parents, and narrowly escaped death in the Massacre of Saint Bartholomew in 1572. Four years later he joined Henry of Navarre, beginning an association that was to endure without a break until Henry's assassination in 1610. Henry was never, of course, a cipher. Although he had a kind heart and a ready wit, he was ruthless in pursuit of his major objective, the restoration and expansion of the crown's authority, and he chose his ministers from men who were similarly committed. While Henry decided on the main lines of policy he was content to leave the details of financial administration to Sully, provided the results were satisfactory. He had no cause to complain. In 1594 expenditure was twice as high as income, in 1596 it was nearly three times as high, but by 1600 Sully had balanced his budget. He was fortunate in that his period in office coincided with external peace, and he was therefore able to economise on military expenditure. As far as the collection of taxes was concerned, he handed over the *Aides* to a Parisian financier who farmed them so efficiently that the yield showed a marked increase. Encouraged by this, Sully farmed out the *Gabelle*, with the same happy result.

Sully's responsibilities were not confined to the financial sphere. In 1599 he was appointed to the new office of *Grand Voyer*, with the duty of improving communications throughout the kingdom. He was also made Superintendant of Fortifications and Grand Master of Artillery. He was actively concerned to promote French trade and commerce, spent large sums on bridges and canals, and built up a fleet. There was hardly any aspect of the French economy that did not come under Sully's enquiring eye, and his work in this field laid the foundations on which Richelieu was to build. The same is also true of his financial administration, for in an effort to cut down on corruption Sully sent royal officials into the localities to enquire into specific matters and report back to him. Sully's most recent biographer has described how 'in every region they were at work; reporting to the king on financial, military and general affairs, taking over work on roads, bridges and dykes; representing the king at meetings of provincial Estates, destroying private strongholds, controlling towns' accounts, and drawing up the first extensive statistical surveys of their regions'.[1] It may be that Sully was merely developing an administrative device that had its origin during the reign of Henry III, but he was responsible for showing how, within the existing framework of French government, the king's will could be directly enforced. In so doing he prepared the ground for the more systematic use of *Intendants* under Richelieu and Louis XIV.

The Sale of Offices

There would have been no need for the despatch of special royal commissioners to the localities if the existing officials had been doing their jobs satisfactorily. This, however, was far from being the case. The problem of exercising effective central control over the localities was not unique to France nor to the seventeenth century, but it had been made far more difficult by the growth of venality—the sale of offices. This had been systematised by Francis I in 1522, when he set up a special department to handle sales. Technically speaking the office reverted to the crown on the death of the holder, but there were a number of devices by which it could be bequeathed or transferred. Offices had in fact become pieces of property, and this was officially recognised by Henry IV in 1604, on condition that the office-holder paid an annual tax. This tax was farmed out by Charles Paulet, who inadvertently gave his name to it, and the *Paulette* became the office-holder's guarantee of security. As long as he paid it, he could sell his office for what it was worth—quite often considerably more than it had cost him. All office-holders received salaries from the crown, but this was not the reason why office was so highly prized. The main advantage of office was the prestige that went with it. Many offices conferred nobility either for one generation or in heredity, with the

---

[1] D. Buisseret; 'A phase in the development of the French *Intendants*: the reign of Henry IV', *Historical Journal*, ix (1966) p. 38.

accompanying exemption from *Taille* and other privileges. Even where this was not the case, the holding of office was a step upwards on the social ladder, and many a noble family could trace its origin, if it cared to do so (which it usually did not), to a peasant or artisan who had managed to save enough money to buy one of the lesser offices.

The possession of office was a confirmation of a newly achieved social position as well as a means to it, since purchase required a certain amount of capital. A successful merchant, for instance, would often buy up land and establish himself socially before acquiring office, so that his children would have an economic basis for their gentility as well as the outward symbol of it. The fact that social advancement could be purchased made for fluidity within the middle ranks of French society, but office-holders, whether noble or not, quickly became distinct from the bourgeoisie or tenant-farmers from whom they had emerged. They came to form a distinct class, though one that was open to constant recruitment from below.

The demand for office was so great that the crown created new offices simply in order to sell them. From time to time it also threatened to withold the regranting of the *Paulette* until the office-holders had agreed to pay a lump sum for confirmation of their position. At other times salaries would be raised, but only, once again, after a capital payment by the office-holders. This amounted to a forced loan on which the crown paid interest by way of salary, and although the office-holders provided the required sum rather than risk losing the *Paulette* and all that it implied, they increasingly resented the way in which they were treated as milch cows. Yet the sums involved were far too great for the crown to be able to dispense with this peculiar means of raising money. Under Henry IV about eight per cent of the total revenue came from the sale of offices; in the 1620s this proportion rose to 30 per cent, while by the late 1630s it was 50 per cent. Only at this stage did the market show clear signs of saturation.

The sale of offices had obviously undesirable economic effects, in that it soaked up capital which might otherwise have gone into productive investment in commerce, industry or agriculture. In this respect venality was similar to the *Rentes*—government bonds, backed by the city of Paris, which guaranteed an annual income to the purchaser (and provided an opportunity for manipulation by unscrupulous financiers). Venality also had serious political effects, in that it prevented the advancement of those who had talent but little or no money, thereby weakening the crown's control over the administration. In theory all office-holders could be dismissed by the government if they failed to carry out their duties, but they would have to be paid a lump sum equivalent to the capital value of their office, and this was something that governments shied away from. The crown could, and did, create new offices to take over the functions of existing ones, but after a brief time these in turn became part of the bureaucratic undergrowth which hindered government rather than facilitating it.

Those who, by buying office, simultaneously acquired noble status, formed a new aristocracy. This *Noblesse de robe* was made up mainly of successful lawyers and merchants, but covered a wide social and economic range. The old aristocracy, or *Noblesse d'épée*, affected to despise the upstarts of the *robe*, and there was all the difference in the world between a magnate like Condé and a recently ennobled merchant. Yet the contrast between the two aristocracies was greater in theory than in practice. Many of the *Noblesse d'épée*, despite their proud titles, were country gentlemen living in relative poverty and obscurity; while others had themselves bought offices and thereby become members of the *robe*. Old nobles were not above marrying the rich daughters of new ones, and the obsession of the *Noblesse d'épée* with birth and rank sprang from insecurity rather than confidence. In so far as the old nobility had been pushed out of office by the members of the *robe*, this was its own fault. Kings and their ministers, however wary they might be of the ambitions of a handful of magnates, had no dislike for the old nobility as such. Sully and Richelieu both came from the *Noblesse d'épée*, and Sully in particular regretted the decline of the old families. But ministers could not ignore the facts of political life, and these were that most members of the *Noblesse d'epée* were more concerned with asserting their social superiority than training themselves for the royal service. Members of the *robe*, on the other hand, frequently had some legal knowledge and a desire for self-advancement that made them useful servants of the crown.

Aristocratic Factionalism and the Huguenots

The leading members of the *Noblesse d'épée* took it for granted that they should dominate the political as well as the social life of France, and their ambitions made them a constant threat to the stability which the royal government was striving to maintain. Greatest of the magnates were the princes of the blood, members of the royal family who had all the advantages of birth without any of the responsibilities of public office. Henry IV held them in check as long as he was alive, but in February 1610 he was stabbed to death by a fanatical catholic schoolmaster, François Ravaillac. His son and successor, Louis XIII, was not yet nine years old, and after the relative peace and order of Henry IV's reign, France was faced with the alarming prospect of a royal minority.

Henry had not nominated a regent, but at the formal request of the *Parlement* this office was assumed by his widow, the thirty-seven-year-old Marie de Medici. At first she kept Henry's system of government in operation, and the old ministers, among them Sully, retained their positions. But two changes swiftly became apparent. The first was the abandonment of the anti-Habsburg policy in favour of a Spanish alliance, to be cemented by the marriage of the boy king to the Infanta of Spain. The second was the regent's increasing reliance on a court clique in which the leading figures were her childhood friend, Leonora Galigari (the daughter of Marie's former nurse), and Leonora's husband, Concino Concini, a Florentine adventurer. Concini, later created Marshal d'Ancre, regarded royal favour as an invitation to self enrichment, and set about accumulating a fortune by the speediest and most unscrupulous means possible. His triumph was symbolised by the resignation of Sully in January 1611.

Henry IV had advised his wife to keep the magnates happy, and she tried to do this by organising constant festivities at court and pouring out largesse on a generous scale. But the magnates were increasingly resentful of the new regime. They despised Concini (whose motives in fact were not so dissimilar from their own) and they whipped up popular feeling against the 'foreigners'—a term that could be applied, of course, to the queen regent herself. In February 1614 the magnates displayed their hostility by leaving court and retiring to the provinces where, by virtue of their estates and their governorships, they could raise troops. They accused Marie of wasting the royal revenues, demanded the summoning of the Estates General, and called for the postponement of the Spanish match. Marie was not prepared for a showdown, since this might have endangered her son's throne. She therefore agreed to the magnates' demands and also promised them substantial cash payments—the rewards of rebellion.

The magnates had assumed that the elections to the Estates General would produce a substantial majority in their favour, but in this they had miscalculated. Before the elections took place, Marie and her young son set out on a tour of the provinces. Everywhere Louis XIII was received with great acclamation, and Marie took advantage of this to declare him of age in October 1614. The minority was now at an end, in name at least, and the magnates could no longer use the regent as a convenient excuse for attacking the crown itself. In these circumstances it was not surprising that the Estates General, which assembled in October 1614, accomplished virtually nothing. There was deadlock between the old nobles, who wanted an end to the *Paulette* (the basis, they believed, of the predominance of the *robe*), and the Third Estate, which demanded that the government should stop subsidising the magnates by way of pensions and outright gifts. Failure to agree on anything constructive led to the dissolution of the assembly early in 1615 and the return of delegates to their localities. Among them was the Bishop of Luçon, who had created a favourable impression in certain circles by a speech in which he not only championed royal authority but also pointed out that the clergy, by virtue of their training, were well suited to the service of the crown.

Frustrated in their hopes of using the Estates General to force their way back into power, the magnates resorted to rebellion once again, and this time linked up with the Huguenots. But outbreaks of plague and a hard winter persuaded both sides to compromise. The Prince of Condé,[1] greatest of all the magnates, was appointed head of the royal council, and in spring 1616 he made a triumphal entry into Paris. Concini, however, was alarmed by the implied threat to his own position and persuaded the queen regent to strike while she was still strong enough to do so. In September 1616, therefore, Condé was arrested and sent to the Bastille. Following this the council was reconstructed and fresh blood brought in. Among the new ministers was Armand de Richelieu, Bishop of Luçon. His timely speech in the Estates General had brought its reward, and in November 1616 he was appointed Secretary of State for Foreign Affairs. The magnates had meanwhile reconstituted their party, and were recruiting mercenaries. Civil war looked inevitable, but it was averted at the last moment by an unexpected *coup de théâtre* in which the king took a leading part.

Louis XIII had hitherto been conspicuous by his insignificance. He was a sensitive boy, skilled in music and drawing, but inhibited by shyness, which led him to stammer, and by ill-health. As a child he had been starved of affection, and he found human relationships difficult to

---

[1] Henry II, Prince of Condé, grandson of Louis I, Prince of Condé,who had led the Huguenots in the early stages of the Wars of Religion, and son of Henry I, Prince of Condé, who had been forced to abjure his faith at the time of the Massacre of St Bartholomew (see family tree on p. 543).

handle. He had been obedient and respectful to his mother—whom he asked to continue as regent even after he was declared of age—and she had deliberately surrounded him with mediocrities in order to preserve her own power and that of her favourite, Concini. But among the king's attendants was his falconer, Charles, Duke of Luynes, a fine figure of a man, some twenty years Louis' senior. Louis came to trust Luynes and it was at Luynes' prompting that the king decided to assert his own authority. The rule of 'the Italians' came to a sudden and violent end in April 1617 when Concini, attempting to avoid capture, was assassinated. His wife, Leonora, was put on trial for sorcery, found guilty, and executed. As for the queen mother, she was placed under house arrest in the château of Blois. The Paris mob, which had hated the foreign favourites, showed its delight by digging up Concini's body and mutilating it. Louis, for once, was equally demonstrative. When he heard the news of Concini's death he leapt on the billiard table crying out 'Now I am king! Now I am your king!'

Luynes was the head of the new administration (from which Richelieu was excluded) and he held out an olive branch to the magnates by summoning an Assembly of Notables to Rouen. In 1618 this body drew up an edict accepting much of the magnates' programme. The authority of the *Parlements* was confirmed, and newer institutions and officers, such as the royal council and the *Intendants*, had their wings clipped. Although this edict was only partially effective, it marked an attempt to restore the traditional balance of the constitution and reverse the trend towards centralisation and absolutism. But there was no question of bringing the magnates into government, since this would have meant a dilution of royal authority. On the contrary, Luynes deliberately excluded them and filled key positions with his friends and family. Royal authority by itself, however, was not enough. Effective administration was essential and this was something which neither the king nor his favourite could readily provide. Luynes called back a number of Henry IV's former ministers, but they did little except quarrel among themselves, even in the king's presence. As one magnate cynically observed: 'The tavern is just the same. Only the inn sign has been altered.'

Disillusioned with the new administration, the magnates once again withdrew from court and joined the queen mother, who had escaped from Blois. Condé was not with them, for he had been freed from the Bastille by Luynes and was now on the side of the government. Civil war broke out in 1620, but it was a half-hearted and short-lived affair.

Luynes called on Richelieu to negotiate a settlement, and the bishop managed to reconcile the king and the queen mother. Open hostility gave way to an uneasy peace, and Luynes was now free to turn his attention to another major threat to royal authority—that which came from the Huguenots.

In the second half of the sixteenth century French protestantism had an energy and purposefulness that made it appear irresistible. By the 1620s, however, much of the fervour had gone, and aggressive expansionism had been replaced by an inward-looking, defensive mentality. This contrasted with the revival that was everywhere, and increasingly, apparent in French catholic life. In 1615 an Assembly of the Clergy formally accepted the Trent decrees, and there was a gradual improvement in the quality of the episcopate, although non-residence and lack of spirituality remained major defects. The over-riding need was for a better educated clergy, and this was met—to some extent, at any rate—by new religious orders. In 1611, for instance, Pierre Bérulle founded the Oratory, whose members were dedicated to the task of educating the clergy and placed themselves at the disposal of the bishops for this purpose. Another order, committed to the training of parish priests, was established by St Vincent de Paul. Many seminaries were founded—though not all survived, and of those which did, not all flourished—and slowly the standard of parish clergy improved.

At the same time the task of educating the laity was tackled with great enthusiasm. The Jesuits took the lead in providing humanist education firmly based on Christian doctrine, though their effort was mainly directed towards the upper classes. In 1604 the first convent of Ursulines was founded, and this order, which was dedicated to the education of women, spread rapidly. The reform movement among women was not confined to the cloister, however. Under the inspiration of St Vincent de Paul, the wives and daughters of noble French families, particularly those which were resident in Paris, began charitable work among the poor, distributing alms and visiting the sick. Although there was an element of exaggeration in all this activity—devotion to works of charity became the fashion in Paris high society—it was a reflection of an unmistakable revival of catholicism in France, just at the moment when the Huguenots were on the decline.

The legal basis for the existence of French protestantism was provided by the Edict of Nantes, but the political privileges which the

Huguenots valued so highly had been contained not in the Edict itself but in the supplementary articles, originally granted for eight years but subsequently renewed. Henry IV had not been punctilious in his observance of the terms of these supplementary articles. He witheld permission for the renovation of fortifications in Huguenot strongholds, put obstacles in the way of Huguenots who sought public office, and encouraged catholic missionary work in Huguenot regions. The Huguenots, not surprisingly, became convinced that they must look to their own defence. From the early days of the establishment of Calvinism in France the protestant nobles had played a key role, and in the opening years of the Wars of Religion there had been a danger that the whole Huguenot movement would become a tool in the hands of aristocratic faction leaders. This was what happened in the early seventeenth century. The Huguenots came together with the discontented magnates and set up a political organisation, based on a number of 'Circles', each with its own military force and commander. There was an obvious comparison with the 'Circles' of the Holy Roman Empire, and the magnates envisaged enjoying the same degree of independence as the German princely rulers. This was something which no French king could tolerate for a moment, and even if Louis XIII had not been a devout catholic it would have been in his political interest to check the separatist tendencies of aristocratic protestantism.

In the case of Louis XIII political and religious inclinations coincided, and his actions brought simmering Huguenot suspicions to boiling point. Among the problems bequeathed to Louis by his father was that of Béarn and Navarre, which formed part of Henry's patrimony and passed to the French crown on his death. In return for his acceptance into the Church of Rome, Henry had promised that all ecclesiastical properties in these regions which had been taken over by the Huguenots would be restored. He never carried out these promises, however, nor did his widow after she became regent. Louis, on the other hand, was not prepared to compromise on what he believed to be his religious duty, and in June 1617 the royal council ordered the restoration to be put into effect. Even though the crown promised compensation for those whose land was now to be taken from them, the decree caused an outcry in the whole Béarn-Navarre region, and Huguenot pastors took the lead in organising resistance. The committed catholics at court (the *Dévots*) urged Louis to go in person to Béarn and put an end to incipient revolt. This Louis did, and by the end of 1619 the resentful inhabitants had apparently been brought to heel.

Following Louis' departure, however, resistance revived and was only put down when a royal army 'occupied' the province. This acted ruthlessly in expelling Huguenot ministers, handing over their churches to the catholics, and desecrating their cemeteries. As news of these repressive and brutal actions spread throughout the rest of France, the Huguenots took fright and summoned a representative assembly to meet at La Rochelle in November 1620. The assembled delegates decided to concert defence measures and to place a magnate in charge of each of the 'Circles'. On the face of it their position was strong, for there were some eight hundred Huguenot congregations, concentrated mainly in the coastal and mountainous regions of the south and west, and they controlled about a hundred fortified places. They also had a good leader in Sully's son-in-law, Henry, Duke of Rohan, who saw the Huguenots as a foundation on which magnate power could be rebuilt.

There were some voices among the king's councillors urging moderation and compromise, on the grounds that the Huguenots were not basically disloyal but merely wanted the confirmation of their freedom to worship. Condé, however, was in favour of war, and so was Luynes, who believed, rightly, that France would not be free to pursue her own best interests abroad until she had dealt with the Huguenot problem at home. In the spring of 1621, therefore, Louis set out on his first campaign against the rebellious protestants, after issuing a decree in which he assured all his Huguenot subjects that as long as they obeyed his orders their religious freedom would be guaranteed. Louis enjoyed the campaign. He was far more at ease among soldiers than among courtiers, and he relished the open-air life and the excitement. Yet the expedition was not entirely successful. A number of Huguenot strongholds were captured, but La Rochelle was too formidable a proposition to be attemped, and Rohan beat off all attacks on Montauban. By the end of the campaign of 1622 Louis was ready for peace, and in October terms were signed at Montpellier. The Huguenots gained most of their demands. The Edict of Nantes was confirmed in all its main points; Rohan and his brother, the Duke of Soubise, were pardoned and granted pensions; and the Huguenots were allowed to retain all their old defensive positions, although new fortifications on both sides were to be demolished. The Peace of Montpellier was, in fact, no more than a truce. The king had made little obvious gain from two years of campaigning, but he had demonstrated his power sufficiently for the Huguenots to be really alarmed. Both sides now prepared for the next round.

One of the casualties of the campaign against the Huguenots was Luynes, who died of fever in 1621. The king had already tired of his favourite and suspected the ambitions of the man he called 'King Luynes'. The obvious replacement for Luynes was Richelieu, whose adherence to the queen mother's cause had hitherto kept him out of office but whose reputation had grown during his absence from power. The king was still suspicious of him, but the reconciliation between Louis and his mother, which followed Luynes' death, opened the way to Richelieu's return to favour. In September 1622 he was made a cardinal, two years later he was readmitted to the royal council, and by August of 1624 he had become head of it. From then until his death in 1642 he was the king's chief minister.

Richelieu

Armand du Plessis, Cardinal Richelieu, was born in 1585 of an old noble family. His father had served both Henry III and Henry IV, and died at the siege of Paris, leaving Armand an orphan at the age of five. Armand's mother, who came from a *robe* family (her father was a successful Paris lawyer and member of the *Parlement*) was left with a large number of children and little money, and so retired to the family property at Richelieu in Poitou. There Armand passed his youth until he was sent to Paris in order to prepare himself for a military career. As a third son he was destined for the army, but his future prospects were transformed when his elder brother decided to become a monk instead of taking the family living of Luçon, near La Rochelle—Henry III's gift to Richelieu's father. A bishopric, even as relatively poor and insignificant a one as Luçon, was far too precious to be allowed to pass out of the possession of an impoverished family, and Richelieu's mother insisted that he should prepare himself for holy orders. 'God's will be done,' he replied. 'I will accept everything for the good of the Church and the glory of our house.'

Richelieu, however, was under age and needed a papal dispensation before he could take the living. He therefore set out for Rome, where he personally persuaded the Pope to issue the necessary documents. In 1607, at the age of twenty-two, he was ordained priest and consecrated bishop on the same day. By Christmas of the following year he had taken formal possession of the bishopric of Luçon. He at once set about restoring both the material and spiritual condition of the see. He repaired and refurbished the tumbledown episcopal palace, he carried out a formal visitation of the parishes that made up his diocese, and he invited Bérulle to send some Oratorians to establish a seminary. In short, Richelieu brought to Luçon the purposeful approach of revived French catholicism, thereby establishing his links with the *Dévots* at Paris, who began to look to him as a future champion.

Richelieu was a man of intense nervous energy, occasionally prostrated by severe headaches and emotional exhaustion, but driven on by his determination to succeed. He never wavered in his adherence to the catholic Church, and detested and despised Huguenots, contrasting the petty squabbles of the various protestant sects with the majestic uniformity of Rome. And yet at the same time he was not intolerant, and was prepared to allow the Huguenots freedom of worship so long as they showed themselves to be loyal and obedient subjects. Richelieu believed that the answer to all France's problems, domestic and foreign, was to be found in elevating and enforcing the authority of the crown, and he had long wanted to use his enormous talents in the royal service. His speech at the Estates General in 1615 had been a calculated bid for power, and it was one that eventually paid off.

Shortly after Richelieu became head of the royal council, in 1624, he was faced with a Huguenot rising, for the protestants were convinced that the appointment of a cardinal to be chief minister—and one who, moreover, was linked with the *Dévots*—was the prelude to their destruction. In fact Richelieu was only concerned to curtail the Huguenots' political irresponsibility, but he could not afford to be too tolerant towards them for fear of alienating the *Dévots* at court, from whom much of his support initially derived. His position was complicated by the fact that in foreign policy he stood at the opposite extreme to the *Dévots*. They wanted peace with the Habsburgs and a catholic alliance against protestants at home and abroad. Richelieu, on the contrary, came to believe that Habsburg power was a major threat to France, and one that must be eliminated. If the Pope supported the Habsburgs then the Pope must be resisted; for as Richelieu observed, 'while religiously obeying the Pope in spiritual matters, one may justly oppose him in his temporal designs'. Richelieu, in short, was a catholic nationalist, like Philip II, and firmly believed that what was for the good of the French monarchy was for the benefit of the Church as a whole. Although in some ways a Counter-Reformation figure, he did not share the sense of the unity of Christendom which pervaded much Counter-Reformation thought. As he wrote in his *Political Testament* his aims were 'to ruin the Huguenot party, to cut down the arrogance of the magnates, to reduce all the king's subjects to their proper obedience, and to raise the king's name among foreign nations to the point where it ought to be'.

Fighting the Spaniard abroad and the Huguenots at home imposed a great strain on French resources, and more or less forced the royal government to deal with each problem consecutively rather than simultaneously. With relative peace abroad, the attack on the Huguenots could be pressed home; but if the Spanish threat suddenly took a more ominous form, then a settlement with the Huguenots became imperative. In January 1625 Soubise had seized the islands of Ré and Oléron which dominated the seaward approaches to La Rochelle, and defied the government to expel him. Richelieu had to collect a fleet and send a royal army to drive Soubise from his refuge, but the Huguenots were far from pacified. English mediation brought about a truce between the French government and the Huguenots in February 1626, yet the Rochellois remained suspicious of Richelieu's intentions, particularly after he refused to destroy a fort which had been built near the city. By the spring of 1627 they were again in open revolt, and they looked to England for assistance. In June an English force under the Duke of Buckingham landed on the island of Ré, but Louis' troops held out and in November the English were forced to withdraw. In the following year another English fleet was driven off, and the city of La Rochelle was left to fend for itself.

Richelieu directed the siege of La Rochelle in person, with a brilliance that showed how much the army lost when he was persuaded to abandon a military career. Although by this time he had a sizeable fleet available, he decided to build a great mole to cut the city off from all succour by sea, while the royal army, under the direct command of the king, blocked the landward approaches. Hunger inexorably weakened the resistance of the Rochellois. The population was said to have shrunk from twenty-five to a mere five thousand, and when at last the city capitulated and the king made his triumphant entry, on the first day of November 1628, he found the inhabitants more like scarecrows than human beings. Richelieu had insisted on unconditional surrender, but once this had been complied with he was prepared to be generous—or, rather, realistic, since he wanted to reconcile the Huguenots by showing them that they really had nothing to fear from the crown. In June 1629 the king issued the Grace of Alais, reaffirming the Edict of Nantes but not the supplementary articles. The Huguenot military organisation was to be broken up, fortresses were to be demolished, and catholic worship was to be revived wherever it had formerly existed. No more government money was to be made available for maintaining protestant garrisons or educating and supporting protestant clergy.

This was the end of the Huguenot 'state within a state', although sporadic resistance continued in the south. Yet protestantism as a faith was not proscribed, only the political privileges that had been associated with it. The campaign against the Huguenots was essentially part of Richelieu's general policy of centralising the government of France under the authority of the crown. La Rochelle, for instance, had been the urban counterpart of the turbulent magnates: quasi-independent, privileged and irresponsible. With the fall of this commercial 'republic', the coastal regions of France were once again brought under effective royal control.

In the course of the struggle against the Huguenots, Richelieu had been made aware how weak were the naval defences of France. In 1625 the crown did not have a single warship in the Channel or Atlantic, and Richelieu had to endure the humiliation of borrowing ships from the English and Dutch to deal with Soubise's revolt. In theory naval affairs were the responsibility of the two admirals, but these were great magnates who had gained their high offices by inheritance—one of them, for instance, was Soubise himself, who, although he did indeed raise naval forces, used them *against* the crown. In 1626, therefore, Richelieu had himself appointed 'Grand-master, Chief and Superintendent-general of Navigation and Commerce', and set up a commission to enquire into the administration of the coastal regions. In 1627 the office of admiral was abolished, along with that of constable, and the *Ordonnance de la Marine* later annulled all grants of land and jurisdiction in coastal districts and brought these directly under royal government. In 1629 an edict was issued laying down a programme for creating a French navy, and Richelieu encouraged shipwrights from England and the Netherlands to settle in France, bringing their skills with them. By 1636 an Atlantic fleet of nearly forty ships had been called into being, and in the following year a French naval squadron drove out the Spaniards from the Lerin Islands. This was merely a foretaste of what was to come, for in 1638 the French won their first major sea battle when they defeated a Spanish fleet coming to the relief of Fuentarrabia.

Richelieu saw the strengthening of French naval power as one part of a much larger programme to increase the wealth of the kingdom through the encouragement of overseas commerce. He was conscious of the fact that the protestant states of England and the United Provinces were growing daily richer through the enterprise of their merchants, and he assumed, like Sully before him and Colbert afterwards, that the royal government should take the initiative in promoting French trade. In 1627, therefore, it was decreed that no cargoes should be carried in foreign ships if French ones were available. Two years later an *ordonnance* encouraged nobles to engage in maritime trade by assuring them that they would not thereby suffer any loss of status, and domestic industries such as glass-making, tapestry and silk-weaving were given government protection and privileges. Overseas trade was closely connected with colonial enterprise, and in 1628 Richelieu set up the Company of New France to promote the settlement and exploitation of French Canada. Later he gave government backing to a French West India Company based on Le Havre.

All this activity was an indication of Richelieu's hopes rather than an index of actual performance. There were some encouraging results. In 1628, for example, no French ships had passed through the Sound, but in the following year Richelieu concluded a commercial treaty with Denmark which resulted in a lowering of tolls on French vessels, and in 1631 over seventy French ships were engaged in this valuable Baltic trade. As far as the colonial companies were concerned, poor organisation, Spanish hostility and rivalries among the various French ports limited their effectiveness, but Guadeloupe was settled in 1635. The major weakness of Richelieu's policy in the economic sphere was that he never had the time or the resources to devote to it. A long period of peace was needed for French trade to expand, but this was never obtained. The money and men that might have been used for overseas settlement were eaten up by the battlefields of Italy and Germany.

By 1630 Richelieu's dominance in the royal council was unchallenged, and in April of that year the king formally appointed him principal minister. This supremacy had not been achieved without considerable effort, since the old nobility resented their exclusion from government and were engaged in constant plotting. They were assisted by bad relations within the royal family itself, for the king's uncle, Gaston. Duke of Orleans, and his mother, Marie de Medici, were constantly ready to assist any conspiracy to overthrow the all-powerful favourite. So also was the queen, Anne of Austria, who blamed Richelieu for her husband's lack of affection. Princes of the blood were, to all intents and purposes, above the law, but lesser nobles who were caught up in their machinations were not so privileged, and Richelieu struck all the harder at these smaller men in order to frighten their masters. In 1626, for example, Henri de Talleyrand-Périgord, Count of Chalais and Master of the Wardrobe to the king, was involved in a plot to remove Richelieu, in which the leading figures were the queen herself and Orleans. Richelieu had Chalais arrested, tried and executed in August 1626. The queen and Orleans hastened to make their peace with Louis, who received them back into favour, but the nobles in general were deeply shocked by this brutal treatment of one of their number. They had further cause for resentment when Richelieu ordered the end of duelling, which was an integral part of the aristocratic code of honour. The young Count of Bouteville showed his contempt for all such prohibitions by fighting a duel under Richelieu's very window. Bouteville was connected by blood with some of the greatest families in the land, but this did not shield him from the long arm of the crown. Richelieu rejected all pleas for clemency, and Bouteville went to the block in 1627.

The Montmorency affair of 1632 was more serious. Henry, Duke of Montmorency and brother-in-law of Condé, was governor of Languedoc and hereditary admiral. In 1626 he lost his position of admiral for being involved in the Chalais plot, and in the following year he saw the office abolished altogether. This gave him sufficient grounds for bitterness, and his opportunity for revenge came when Richelieu, following the suppression of the Huguenot rebellion in southern France, decided to convert Languedoc from a *Pays d'Etats* into a *Pays d'Election*. The Languedoc Estates rose in protest against this threat to their existence and called on Montmorency to defend them. At the same time the duke was involved in negotiations with Orleans, now in exile, who agreed to bring mercenary troops to his aid. By June 1632 Languedoc and its governor were in open rebellion against the crown, and the rising only came to an end after a royal army had taken the field and defeated the rebels. When the king arrived in Languedoc he restored the privileges of the Estates, but there was no mercy for the captured governor. Montmorency was tried for treason, condemned and beheaded. His execution was a further reminder to the aristocracy of what they could expect if they continued to flout the will of the king and his chief minister.

Richelieu could not simply take the king's support for granted in these cases, but he knew that Louis had an unsentimental appreciation of his own best interests. When the king appeared to waver over the proposed execution of young Bouteville, Richelieu asked him whether he intended to put an end to duelling or to his own authority, and the point was taken. At the time of the Chalais case, Richelieu, convinced that he was not getting sufficient backing from his royal master, formally resigned his office in June 1626. But the king knew that Richelieu was irreplaceable, and in an uncharacteristically warm letter assured him that 'I have every confidence in you, and it is a fact that I have never found anyone who could serve me to my satisfaction as you do. I beg you to have no fear of calumnies. Be assured that I shall never change, so that whoever may attack you I shall support you.'

Louis' resolution was soon put to the test, for in late 1630 he fell seriously ill and seemed likely to die. The *Dévots* took this occasion to remind him that he had offended against God by attacking his fellow catholics abroad while he weakened his kingdom at home, and Marie de Medici urged him to rid himself of the man who was responsible for this unholy policy. By November the king had recovered, but was still weak and unable to resist the pressures put on him. A violent scene between Marie and Richelieu took place in the king's presence, and Louis, emotionally exhausted, retired to his hunting lodge at Versailles. Marie was triumphant, and the courtiers were counting the hours until Richelieu's downfall. But it never came. This was the 'Day of the Dupes', on which the king asserted himself against his family and their supporters. He confirmed Richelieu in office and ordered his mother to retire from court. For a time she was under house arrest in her château at Compiègne, but in July 1631 she escaped to the Spanish Netherlands. Never again did she set foot in France. In the following year, after the collapse of the Montmorency rising, she was joined in exile by Orleans. Richelieu was at last triumphant, and the king celebrated his minister's victory by making him a duke and peer of France. Sporadic plotting continued, but the Day of the Dupes marks the point at which Richelieu finally brought the royal family and the magnates to realise that they must either submit themselves to the king's will, as expressed by his chief minister, or face exile and death.

The 'king's will' was more than an empty phrase, for Louis was never a cipher and insisted on his right to examine all proposals and take the final decisions on policy. In general, however, he was content to leave the day-to-day business of government to the cardinal. In fact Richelieu was mainly concerned with the formulation of policy. Administration as such was largely in the hands of his 'creatures', the secretaries of state. With the exclusion from the council of the princes of the blood, the magnates and the hereditary great officers, there was no more in-fighting among rival factions. Richelieu dominated the council as he dominated France, and he would not tolerate opposition.

Richelieu's victory on the Day of the Dupes meant that France had committed herself to the policy of glory at whatever cost. So far as finance was concerned, Richelieu worked on the assumption that money must be found. Between 1626 and 1636 the *Taille* was almost doubled, while the *Gabelle* was more than doubled, yet there was never enough money to meet the demands of war. All thought of abolishing venality had to be abandoned, and the creation of offices for sale was resumed. From every part of France there came complaints about the burden of taxation. In 1633 one observer reported that 'misery is so general on all sides and among all sorts of people that unless there is some relaxation the people will be impelled by their powerlessness towards some dangerous solution', and six years later Richelieu's own *Surintendant des Finances* warned him that 'expenditure in cash is up to at least forty million livres . . . and the people will not pay either the new or the old taxes. We are now scraping the barrel and I fear that our foreign war is degenerating into a civil war.'

There was little element of exaggeration in these forebodings, since disorder was already endemic in the towns and countryside. In the spring of 1636 a peasant rising took place near Angoulême and rapidly spread until nearly a quarter of the entire kingdom was in arms against the government. This was only put down after troops had been withdrawn from the front, and it was followed in the summer of 1639 by a rising in Normandy. The leadership of this, as of a number of peasant revolts, was taken by the local gentry and clergy who resented the fact that the inordinate demands of government left tenants unable to pay dues to their parish priest and landlords. Twenty thousand rebels, calling themselves the *Va-nu-pieds*,[1] ravaged the Normandy countryside, and the citizens of Rouen joined in the revolt. Once again a royal army had to fight a prolonged campaign against the king's own subjects, and Normandy was treated like occupied enemy territory, in which martial law, with all its brutal accompaniments of summary judgments and mass executions, replaced the normal course of justice.

Richelieu must have been aware of the misery caused by his policies,

---

[1] *lit.* 'those who go bare-footed.'

but he never questioned their wisdom, nor did he relax his grip. He built up a network of informers, issued *lettres de cachet* ordering the imprisonment of suspects without trial, and employed pamphleteers and the official *Gazette*—which he founded in 1631—to try and win over public opinion. Since so many local officials were out of sympathy with the aims of the government, Richelieu resorted to the increasing use of *Intendants*. In 1629 he forced the *Parlement*, by a *lit de justice*, to admit the right of the *Intendants* to override local authorities and communicate direct with the council; in 1635 he began issuing commissions on a regular basis; and by 1637 he had dispatched *Intendants* to every province. Their competence was extended until it covered all judicial matters; and royal decrees of 1642 and 1643 also transferred fiscal functions to them.

The *Intendants* became symbols of the might of the central government, and soldiers were available to them to suppress resistance from taxpayers and other disaffected elements. Not surprisingly, they were hated by all those who found their 'liberties' threatened by this drastic extension of royal power. Yet the opposition to them must not be exaggerated. The *Intendants* were instructed to work in co-operation with local officials, such as the *Elus*, and not to sweep them to one side. They could never have accomplished what they did without the co-operation of such officials, however reluctantly this was given, for the propertied section of society recognised that in the last resort its interests were better protected by a powerful crown than by peasant revolts and anarchy. It was to preserve this identity of interests, however fragile, that the royal government refrained from wholesale abolition of smaller offices. This would no doubt have led to greater efficiency, but the office-holders would have been outraged and alienated, and in any case the *Intendants* themselves would have become so powerful in the localities as to constitute a potential threat to the authority of the crown. The old system, therefore, continued to exist alongside the new, but this did not prevent the groundswell of resentment mounting against Richelieu's authoritarian government.

Richelieu also had to face the continuing hatred of the *Noblesse d'épée*, who could count on support from Brussels for any plot they hatched. Although the cardinal was undoubted master of the kingdom as long as he retained the approbation of the king, he could never afford to relax his watch. It was in order to maintain his hold on Louis that Richelieu introduced the seventeen-year-old Marquis of Cinq Mars into the king's household. Louis was enchanted with this handsome and arrogant youth, made him Master of the Horse, and lavished affection on him. Richelieu had assumed that Cinq Mars would show his gratitude for this sudden promotion to high favour by cementing the good relations between the king and his chief minister, but in this he had calculated wrongly. Cinq Mars was convinced of his own ability and regarded the cardinal as a rival. By 1642 he was deeply involved in a plot whereby Orleans would invade the kingdom with a mercenary army, 'persuade' the king to switch to a pro-Spanish, *Dévot* policy, and have Richelieu assassinated. The cardinal's spies duly reported all this, and in 1642 Richelieu struck. He confronted Louis with a copy of the incriminating document in which Cinq Mars had allied himself with the Spaniards, and persuaded the shocked king that he must part with his favourite. Cinq Mars was arrested, and in September 1642 he met his death on the block. Richelieu profited from this incident by reinforcing his position still further. He refused to stay in office until the king gave a written assurance never to have another favourite and not to take advice from anyone except members of his council. Louis also agreed that his household should be remodelled and that a number of officers suspected of being less than fervent in their devotion to the cardinal should be dismissed.

In fact these precautions were unnecessary, for Richelieu's days as a minister were numbered. In November 1642 he fell ill, and on 4 December he died. Shortly before his death he composed his own epitaph, when he told the king, who had come to see him, that 'in taking leave of Your Majesty I have the consolation of leaving your kingdom in the highest degree of glory and of reputation which it has ever had, and all your enemies beaten and humiliated'. It was true; but he said nothing of the enormous cost in human suffering entailed in such an achievement. Perhaps Pope Urban VIII's comment was more perceptive. 'If God exists, he [Richelieu] will have to atone. If not, he was a good man.'

Louis did not long survive his minister. In March 1643 his weak lungs gave way again and he realised he was dying. He arranged that his queen, Anne of Austria, should be regent, with Orleans as Lieutenant-General of the kingdom, but bound both to work in harmony with a council of which the secretaries of state and Mazarin should be members. In other words the king wanted to ensure that the policies of Richelieu should continue to be executed by the men who had helped the cardinal to carry them out. But he could not control events from the grave, and one of the first actions of the queen after his death in

May 1643 was to compel the *Parlement*, by means of a *lit de justice, to* free her from any restraints. She now exercised the full royal authority in the name of her four-year-old son, Louis XIV.

Mazarin and the Frondes

The enemies of Richelieu—a group that at times seemed to include the majority of Frenchmen—longed for a reversal of his policies and above all for an end to the war. But there was no change, since Richelieu's successor, Mazarin, was determined to pursue the same objectives. Giulio Mazarini was an Italian by birth, though a Spanish subject, since he was born in Naples. He came to Richelieu's attention when he was serving as papal nuncio, entered the service of Louis XIII in 1630, and nine years later was naturalised. In 1641 he was created a cardinal—a sure sign of Richelieu's favour—and after Louis' death the queen regent looked to him for advice. Her affection for Mazarin extended beyond the sphere of politics, for they lived in close and intimate harmony, and may even have been secretly married. Mazarin was, in effect, another Richelieu, though devious where Richelieu would have been direct, and even more unpopular. Richelieu had at least been French, and a member of the old nobility into the bargain. Mazarin was regarded as little more than an Italian adventurer, another Concini, who was bleeding France to death for his private profit. It was this bitterness which produced the *Frondes*.

The name *Fronde* comes from the slings used by the urchins of Paris to hurl stones at the carriages of the rich, and in a sense the *Frondes* were little more than children's games. But they did have a deeper significance, for they demonstrated how the strains imposed on French society by the demands of war were leading to breakdown. The revolt began not with the masses but with the office-holders, who had long been bitter at the way in which they were mulcted. In April 1648 the government announced that the *Paulette* would be renewed in return for a 'gift' equivalent to four years' salary—in effect a forced loan. Members of the *Parlement*, who were, by virtue of their position, major office-holders, joined with representatives of the other sovereign courts in Paris, and held a protest meeting in the Chambre Saint Louis. Out of this emerged a 'charter' calling for an end of tax-farming,[1] a 25 per cent reduction in the *Taille*, the recall of the *Intendants*, the restoration

---

[1] From 1645 the *Taille* had been farmed, as well as the other major taxes.

of power to office-holders, and an end to the creation of new offices and of *lettres de cachet*. There was nothing revolutionary about this programme. It was, on the contrary, an attempt to preserve traditional 'liberties' and to make government flow once again in customary channels. In particular it was an attack on the tax farmers and financiers who seemed to embody all the worst features of the existing system. The vast sums of money extorted by way of taxation went largely to pay the tax farmers interest on their loans to the crown, and while the kingdom suffered the financiers flourished. The delegates who assembled in the Chambre Saint Louis hoped that the regent, by accepting their demands, would be able to restore stability and identify the monarchy once again with the well-being of the inhabitants of France.

The government, after some hesitation, accepted the charter. In July 1648 the *Surintendant des Finances* was dismissed and replaced by a new man, and the rate of interest paid to the financiers and tax farmers was cut from fifteen to six per cent. But Mazarin had no intention of breaking with the financiers altogether. He could not afford to do so as long as the war continued, and although the peace treaties of Westphalia were about to be signed, the struggle against Spain was to go on. He had the support of the generals—among them Louis II, Prince of Condé—who did not relish the prospect of peace, and he hoped for a victory which would give him sufficient prestige to assert himself. He provided Condé with men and money, and Condé repaid him with the victory at Lens. Encouraged by this good news, Mazarin persuaded Anne to order the arrest of three of the leaders of the *Parlement*.

This action led to open revolt in Paris in August 1648. Barricades appeared in the streets, the citizens brought out their arms, and the arrested leaders became heroes overnight. Mazarin again temporised, anxious not to expose France to the danger of civil war before the peace treaties had been signed. The leaders of the *Parlement* were released, and in October the government again affirmed its acceptance of the charter. There were to be no more new offices created for a period of four years, while some existing ones were to be abolished; and *lettres de cachet* were no longer to be used to override the normal course of justice. These concessions were, in fact, of limited significance, since they reflected the weakness of the government rather than any real change of heart, but the barricades came down, life returned to normal, and in the same month of October 1648 the peace treaties of Westphalia were at last signed.

If Mazarin had chosen to follow up the Westphalia settlement with a Spanish peace treaty, he could have abandoned the tax farmers and championed the cause of reform. But he was as convinced as Richelieu had been that the power of the Habsburgs must be humbled and that with Spain so near defeat there must be no relaxation of the French military effort. He was also influenced by events in England, where Parliament had just concluded a successful war against the king and was about to put him on trial. It seemed to Mazarin that what had happened in England could easily happen in France, and in January 1649, the month of Charles I's execution, Mazarin persuaded the queen to withdraw from Paris to Saint Germain, on the grounds that her young son's life was in danger. Now that the king could no longer be held hostage by the capital, Paris could be subdued by force, and the government ordered Condé to besiege the city and starve it into surrender. The *Parlement*, apprehensive of mob violence, was ready to compromise, but the queen refused to receive a delegation of members. This united all the various opposition elements in the city against the government. The *Parlement* took the lead in raising troops for the defence of Paris and issued a declaration in which it named Mazarin as the sole cause of all the troubles and demanded that he should be sent into exile.

At this stage a new element entered into the struggle between the *Parlement* and the royal government. Condé's brother, the Prince of Conti, and his brother-in-law the Duke of Longueville, arrived in Paris and declared their support for the *Parlement*. It looked as though aristocratic factionalism was about to resurface, but the *Parlement* was still anxious for compromise. Members had no fellow-feeling with the magnates, and were aware that as a result of bad harvests and rising prices a really radical and revolutionary movement was emerging in Paris. The government was also eager for a settlement, since Mazarin had clearly failed in his attempt to browbeat his critics and enemies into submission. In March 1649, therefore, the Peace of Rueil brought the *Fronde of the Parlement* to an end. The government once again affirmed its acceptance of the demands contained in the charter, and also agreed that the rebellious magnates should be pardoned and pensioned. The *status quo* had apparently been restored.

It was not long, however, before trouble broke out again, though this time the cause was the more or less 'traditional' one of princely ambition combined with magnate discontent. Condé expected honours and pensions for himself and his followers as a reward for his loyalty. He may also have hoped to replace Mazarin as the *de facto* head of the administration. But Mazarin was not prepared to part with power, and for fear that Condé's swelling influence should prove irresistible he persuaded the queen regent to order the arrest of Condé, Conti and Longueville in January 1650. This was the signal for revolt by many discontented elements, including a number of provincial *Parlements*. Sporadic civil war continued throughout the rest of the year, and the threat to royal government became even more acute in December, when a Spanish invasion force threatened Paris. Mazarin was so obviously the focus of discontent that he decided, with the queen's reluctant consent, to go into exile for a time and let passions subside. In February 1651 he crossed the frontier into the lands of his friend, the Archbishop of Cologne, freeing Condé *en route*: at the same time the government, in an attempt to win back public support, announced the recall of the *Intendants*.

There followed a period of considerable confusion, with various groups jockeying for power. In Paris, for instance, there were the members of the *Parlement*, who distrusted Mazarin and wanted to reverse the trend towards absolutism; there was the faction that revolved round Cardinal de Retz, co-adjutor to the Archbishop of Paris and a man of burning ambition; there was the bourgeoisie, anxious for the restoration of order; and finally there was the proletariat, driven by hunger into violent courses. In Mazarin's absence, Condé was the only person who could resolve the situation, but this intensely ambitious and gifted man never really knew what he wanted. As for the queen regent, she was concentrating on holding the tattered fabric of royal government together until such time as Louis XIV could be proclaimed of age.

In September 1651 the king celebrated his thirteenth birthday, and was now, in law, old enough to assume the responsibility of governing his kingdom. As usual the end of a royal minority clarified the situation, for the princes could no longer screen their personal ambitions behind a façade of 'constitutional' protest against the arbitrary actions of the regent. By the end of the year Condé was in open revolt against the crown in southern France, while Orleans had announced his support for the rebels and had joined the *Parlement* of Paris in blaming Mazarin for all that had occurred and calling for his execution.

In December 1651 Mazarin returned from exile, bringing with him an army of mercenaries, and military operations continued in Anjou and Guienne throughout the summer of 1652. Condé suffered a number of reverses, and moved on Paris, to link up with the disaffected elements in the capital. By this time the *Parlement*, disgusted at the return of Mazarin, had thrown in its lot with the princes and agreed to form an alternative government in which Orleans was to be Lieutenant-General of the kingdom while Condé was to command the army. Deputies assembled in the Hôtel de Ville to concert defence measures, but while they debated, Condé—erratic and short-tempered as ever—lost patience and told his soldiers to find a swifter solution. The troops ran riot, shooting and massacring at random, the Hôtel de Ville went up in flames, and Condé and the new 'government' were totally discredited. The members of the *Parlement* and bourgeoisie, appalled at the upsurge of the radical democratic movement within the city, were ready for peace; but Mazarin remained, as before, the major obstacle. In August 1652, therefore, he once again went into exile. He was followed by Condé, who, failing to find sufficient support within France, took himself and his men off to the Netherlands, to seek fame and honour in the service of the King of Spain. There could have been no clearer demonstration of the princes' ultimate commitment only to what they conceived to be their own best interests.

In October 1652 the young Louis XIV made a triumphant entry into Paris, where the inhabitants welcomed him as the guarantor of their security. He held a *lit de justice* in which Condé was declared to have shown disrespect to the crown and was condemned, in his absence, to lose his property. As for the *Parlement*, a number of its leaders were exiled, and a royal decree was registered forbidding it in future to dabble in matters of state. In February of the following year, 1653, Mazarin returned to France, never again to leave it, and although disorder continued in the provinces—particularly in Bordeaux, where the radicals had achieved their greatest success—by August the kingdom had been pacified. The royal government signalled its victory by despatching *Intendants* to the provinces once again.

The *Frondes* had demonstrated both the weakness and the strength of the French crown. Its weakness came from the existence, within a superficially unified state, of separate power centres—the magnates and *Parlements*, for instance—and from the way in which the workings of the financial system alienated the holders of office and property. Its strength lay in the disunity of its opponents and the fact that none of them was representative of more than a narrowly sectional interest or had any effective alternative to offer to royal rule. By overriding traditional 'liberties' and putting the demands of policy before the welfare of his subjects the king always risked revolt, but if he held firm he could be reasonably sure of containing it. This was the lesson which the *Frondes* taught Louis XIV.

The young king had been introduced to politics even before he attained his majority, for Mazarin took him to a meeting of the *Conseil d'en haut* in September 1649, when he was only eleven. He had a charm of manner and a natural dignity that promised well, and Mazarin acted as his father and tutor, teaching him the arts of government and instilling in him the consciousness of his own divinely ordained authority. Sully, Richelieu and Mazarin had been great servants of the crown, but what if the king should be his own chief minister? Then the theory and practice of absolutism would be fused into one, and power would be concentrated instead of dissipated. It was Mazarin's deliberate and conscious aim to bring about this fusion of authority in the person of Louis XIV, and he had the satisfaction of knowing that he had an apt pupil. 'I believe,' he said, 'that [Louis] will be a prince as accomplished as any that we have seen in several centuries.' He was to be proved right, but Louis was content to bide his time, and not until after the death of Mazarin, in March 1661, did he show how much he had profited from the cardinal's tuition.

TWENTY-TWO

Spain under the Habsburgs, 1598–1700

Sources of Weakness

When Philip III ascended the throne on the death of his father in 1598 Spain was still the greatest power in Christendom. Yet a little less than seventy years later, at the death of Philip IV, she was clearly in decline. The change from greatness to relative insignificance was not sudden, but neither was it so slow that Spaniards themselves were unaware of it. On the contrary, in governmental and intellectual circles there was constant discussion on the causes of Spanish decline and how best to reverse it, and many reform programmes were put forward. There was general agreement—in theory at any rate—that public spending should be cut, taxation reduced, and agriculture and industry protected and encouraged. Such measures would undoubtedly have been highly beneficial, yet even so they would not have affected the fundamental weaknesses in the Spanish social and economic structure.

It was no coincidence that Spain had risen to predominance following her expansion into the New World, for trade with America stimulated the Spanish economy in the short term, while in the second half of the sixteenth century the bullion shipped over from the mines of Mexico and Peru made possible the ambitious foreign policies of the Habsburg rulers. But by 1600 the colonies in the New World were coming of age and could no longer be neatly fitted into the subordinate role from which Spain profited. For one thing their own economies had developed, and what they needed from Europe was not Spanish agricultural produce but more sophisticated manufactured articles that could only be obtained outside Spain. And, for another, shortage of labour, particularly in Mexico, was leading to a cutback in mining, which was prodigal of manpower. There was also the fact that capital generated within America could now be more profitably employed there than in the mother country. For all these reasons the import of bullion into Spain sharply diminished. At Philip III's accession it was still running at the rate of two million ducats a year, but during 1619–21 the annual average was only 800,000 ducats and although there was a recovery in the next twenty years the level never rose appreciably above one and a half million and was usually nearer one million. This was particularly serious for the Spanish government since the American revenue was not committed in advance, as were so many of the other sources of income, and often made all the difference between a forward and a defensive policy. It was at the very moment when the forward party gained power and committed Spain to expensive military commitments that the flow of treasure, which alone could sustain such ventures, began to dry up. No reform programmes, however well conceived, could have affected this shift in the relationship between Spain and her colonies.

The same is true of the weakening of Castile's position as the vital part of the peninsula, whose lifeblood sustained the other kingdoms. This predominance had been based on a large and vigorous population, but in 1599 bubonic plague carried away half a million Castilians and there were repeated attacks during the seventeenth century. Had the population been well fed it might have been more resistant to disease, but in fact there had been a steady drift from the countryside to the towns, where people were herded together in conditions that encouraged the spread of infection. Rural depopulation was a direct consequence of the intolerable burden placed upon the shoulders of the small cultivator. He had to pay tithes to the Church as well as taxes to the crown, and these were in addition to rent and other dues which he owed to his landlord. At least half his income disappeared in payments to other people, and the remainder was often not sufficient to live on, particularly in times of dearth. Small landowners might have profited from rising prices, but since 1539 the crown had regularly fixed a maximum price for grain, which had the effect of diminishing the peasants' real income. It is hardly surprising that many died of hunger while others sold out to the big landowners.

The growth of large estates was one of the features of Spanish society in the late sixteenth and seventeenth centuries. Economically speaking there was no reason why this should not have been an advantage, but in fact the great landowners were more concerned with prestige than profits. They despised manual labour, they took little or no interest in increasing the yield of their estates, and after the accession of Philip

III they were frequently absentee landlords, spending their time more congenially in the hunt for pensions and places at court.

The contempt for work and the passion for titles were regarded by many observers as peculiarly Spanish. In fact much the same was true of other countries—France for instance—but in Spain the ratio of nobles to non-nobles was exceptionally high: about one-tenth of the entire population claimed noble status, and with it exemption from personal taxation. The clergy, also, were exempt, and by 1660 there were at least 200,000 clerics in Spain, while the Church owned about one-fifth of all the land. Churchmen, like lay landlords, had a conservative attitude towards their estates, and they tended to prefer pasture-farming to tillage, since wool was always in demand and the privileges of the *Mesta* (see p. 61) had given sheep-rearing advantages over other forms of agriculture. Big sheep ranches could be run with relatively few labourers, and those for whom there was no employment drifted to the towns. But there was no compensatory reduction in taxes or other burdens, and the families which remained on the land had to pay more in order to meet their obligations. As one observer commented in 1600, 'the peasant who works in the field has to support himself, his lord, the clergy, the money-lender, and all the others who batten on him'.

The drift to the towns could have been an incentive to industry, and the swelling urban population might have found employment in manufacturing. But Spanish industry was contracting rather than expanding. It suffered from the general contempt for all activities other than those connected with the army, government or the Church, and its market was limited by the fact that with such a low general standard of living there was a very small demand. The rich needed manufactures, of course, but their requirements were mainly luxury goods. It was the larger-scale industries which suffered from restricted markets, and because their volume of production was small their costs were high. This made them vulnerable to foreign competitors, especially the Dutch, who took the whole world for their market. The situation became markedly worse when, with the advent of peace in the early seventeenth century, political barriers against foreign competition were swept away.

In her economy Spain was far more like an eastern European country than a western one. There was no serfdom—though the state of the Spanish peasant was often little better than that of a serf—but there were the typical vast estates, producing raw materials which were exchanged for manufactured articles. In Eastern Europe, however, the estates were highly organised economic units concentrating on grain production; in Spain they were deadweights, often consuming most of what they produced.

Since Spain was flooded by foreign manufactures she suffered from a markedly unfavourable balance of trade, and the difference had to be made up with bullion. Thus, at a time when the supply of precious metals from the New World was shrinking, the pressure on Spain to part with her bullion was increasing. Despite the treasure fleets which made their way across the Atlantic to Seville, Spain suffered from a shortage of silver, and it was to offset this that the government introduced a copper coinage (*Vellon*) in 1599. Further issues were made over the next twenty years, with the result that price inflation, which in other European countries was slowing down, continued in Spain. No longer was it a question of steady inflation but of sudden fluctuations as the government tried to manipulate the value of *Vellon* to its own short-term advantage. Such fluctuations were a further blow to Spanish industry, which already suffered from crippling drawbacks, and Spanish traders were further damaged when the government confiscated their receipts from the New World, which were in silver, and issued *Vellon* in their place. The existence of a copper coinage did not even fulfil its primary purpose of easing the pressure on silver, since the copper itself came from Sweden and had to be bought on the Amsterdam market, where it was paid for in silver!

For the financing of its expensive foreign policy, the Spanish government looked to foreigners, as it had done since the sixteenth century. The Genoese were the leading financiers until the 1620s, when the demands of the crown became such that they could not meet them. They were also badly hit by the 'bankruptcy' of 1627, when the crown refused to meet its interest payments, and their place was gradually taken by Portuguese financiers, many of them Jewish converts. These were patronised by Olivares (see p. 411), who hoped to use their expertise not simply on the international money market but also nearer home. In 1599 the *Cortes* of Castile had approved an outline scheme for a national banking system, to direct investment into channels that were economically productive, but this had never been carried into effect. Olivares took the first steps towards putting it into practice in 1623, when banks and pawnshops were set up in over a hundred towns. But the *Cortes* refused to sanction a forced loan to establish these on a sound footing, nor did it support a proposal that the banks should be given a monopoly of lending. It showed the same hostility towards Olivares's attempt to set up a royal bank, under the management of an Italian financier, in 1627, and effectively killed all projects for modernising the financial structure of Spain.

The opposition of the *Cortes* sprang in part from the natural suspicion of men who felt that they were already paying enough and that any 'reform' was simply a device to squeeze more money from them. But they also had a vested interest in the existing system of *Juros*, or government bonds, which guaranteed the investor a regular annual rate of return. This inflow of private money to the state was, of course, very welcome to the government, but Olivares and other reformers had long recognised that funds invested in this way were essentially unproductive. Agriculture and industry were starved of capital, and the money that might have transformed the Spanish economy was consumed by the court, the administration and the military machine. By rejecting Olivares's proposals the *Cortes* was preventing Spain from breaking out of the vicious circle of low productivity, high taxation and inflation.

Lack of public interest and shortage of capital were not the only inhibitions on Spanish commercial and industrial enterprise. There were also physical impediments, such as poor communications and Customs dues. In the general climate of apathy it is not surprising that Spain fell behind the rest of western Europe in technology. In shipbuilding, for instance, the Spaniards clung to old designs at a time when the Dutch and English were experimenting with bigger and faster vessels. Spanish merchants preferred to use foreign ships, and whereas at the accession of Philip III Spanish-built vessels had dominated the Atlantic trade, by 1650 only forty per cent of the ships on this route were the products of Spanish yards. The same was true of other industries. English cloth, for instance, was driving out the native article, and even in the vital field of armaments manufacture the Spaniards were dependent on foreign suppliers.

It may be that technological backwardness was a result of Spain's increasing isolation. From Philip II's reign onwards the Spaniards had adopted a fortress mentality, deliberately cutting themselves off from protestant Europe and abandoning the international Erasmianism which had characterised them in the time of Charles V. However beneficial this isolation may have been in the sphere of religion it had stultifying effects on the intellectual climate, and fostered a narrowly nationalistic and conservative attitude that was antipathetic to innovation and experiment.

The weakness of the Spanish economic and social system, combined with the slowing down in the flow of bullion imports, affected Castile more than other parts of the peninsula, and this was particularly dangerous in that Castile was the rock upon which Spanish greatness had been built. With a population of some six millions she was still by a long way the most important of the constituent kingdoms of Spain, for Aragon and Portugal had little more than a million inhabitants each. She also contributed by far the greater part of the revenue of the Spanish crown. In 1610, for example, the total amount produced by taxation in Aragon, Catalonia and Valencia was 600,000 ducats, but in Castile the *Alcabala* and *Millones* (a new tax on foodstuffs) by themselves brought in more than five million. Castile could not hope for relief from other parts of the empire. Money raised in the Netherlands was all spent locally, and the war against the Dutch was only sustained by subsidies from Spain. The Italian possessions were heavily taxed, but by the middle of the seventeenth century plague and privateering were taking their toll and Italy was turning from a financial asset into a liability. Portugal contributed nothing to general expenditure, and the other kingdoms very little. In Philip III's reign the *Cortes* of Valencia voted only one subsidy, as did that of Catalonia: the *Cortes* of Aragon voted none at all. It is true that Castilians dominated the administration of Spain and the empire and were inclined to look down on non-Castilians as lesser breeds. Yet however great the rewards of Castilian predominance the cost was too high, and it was the increasing impoverishment of Castile and its incapacity to sustain the demands made upon it that accounts, to a large extent, for the decline of Spain.

Philip III and Lerma

The need for reform of the Spanish state was already apparent by the time Philip III came to the throne in September 1598, but he was hardly the man to inaugurate it. Short, stout and red-haired, this good-natured twenty-one-year-old was interested mainly in eating and hunting. He had no aptitude for politics and, unlike his father, was incapable of sustained hard work. One modern historian has described him as 'the laziest king in Spanish history'.[1] Philip II, perhaps recog-

---

[1] John Lynch, *Spain under the Habsburgs*, vol. ii, *Spain and America, 1598–1700*, Blackwell 1969. p.15.

nising his son's incapacity, had left a small council for his guidance, but one of Philip III's first actions was to dissolve this and to place the making of policy in the hands of his favourite, the Duke of Lerma. Unfortunately for Spain, Lerma was not much more capable than his royal master. He was a middle-aged man from a distinguished but impoverished family, and he used his natural charm of manner to stay in power and enrich himself and his relatives. He was the pawn of the magnates, the great aristocrats who had been excluded from power under Charles V and Philip II but were now determined to regain what they regarded as their rightful position. The council of state (composed almost entirely of magnates), which had played little more than a formal role under Philip II, now became the heart of the administration, and the secretaries declined in importance.

Lerma and his king inherited the war against England and the Dutch which was still dragging on, despite the conclusion of peace with France. Neither Philip nor his minister was particularly peace-loving. They both assumed that it was the duty of Spain to defend the catholic faith and the possessions of the Habsburg crown. But among their advisers there were those who recognised that however holy the Spanish cause it could not be sustained without the requisite financial resources, and that if these were not forthcoming it would be better to make peace with the heretics. Most prominent among the advocates of this realistic approach were the Archduke Albert, ruler of the Netherlands, and Spinola, the commander-in-chief of the Spanish forces. As Spinola told the king in 1607: 'If Your Majesty could assure the regular despatch, for a given time, of 300,000 ducats a month, we could continue operations with some hope of reducing the pride of the rebels. But such an effort is beyond the resources of Spain. Therefore there is only one course to take—to end this long and costly war.' In fact, the Archduke Albert, who had been responsible for initiating the discussions that led to peace with England in 1604, had already opened negotiations with the Dutch. Eventually both sides agreed to a cease-fire, on condition that the Archduke recognised the independence and sovereignty of the United Provinces, and although Philip and Lerma were furious at what they regarded as a betrayal of Spanish interests, financial stringency forced them to follow suit. In 1609, therefore, the long war between the Spaniards and the Dutch was at last brought to an end by the twelve-year truce.

Just at the moment when Spain had reluctantly made peace with the United Provinces, it looked as though she would be dragged into war with France over the Cleve–Julich question (see p. 323). Henry IV had already concerted plans with the Duke of Savoy for an attack upon the Spaniards in Milan, and it seemed certain that in a matter of months French and Spanish armies would once again be locked in conflict. But the Spaniards were saved by the miracle (from their point of view) of Henry's assassination in 1610. His forward policies were promptly abandoned by the regent, Marie de Medici, and the reassertion of Spanish influence was marked by a double marriage treaty in 1611: Louis XIII was to marry Philip III's daughter, Anne of Austria, while Louis' sister was to marry the Infante Philip, heir-presumptive to the Spanish throne.

Lerma and his royal master had been half-hearted converts to the peace policy advocated by the moderates, but they had no real choice. By 1607 the accumulated debt amounted to twenty-three million ducats, and the entire revenue was committed for several years ahead. There was simply no 'free' money available to finance forward policies, and in fact the government only relieved itself from the immediate pressure of indebtedness by suspending payments of interest in 1607—a virtual confession of bankruptcy. Peace brought with it the prospect of solving Spain's financial problems, but there was little chance of accomplishing this while Lerma was in power. Far from embracing the cause of radical reform, he spent the money saved on the war in lavish handouts to the aristocracy, hoping that this influential section of Spanish society would thereby acquire a vested interest in the continuance of his rule.

The only major 'reform' measure with which Lerma was associated was in fact not a reform at all. In April 1609 the decision was taken to expel all the Moriscos from Spain, on the grounds that they were a threat to security. It is true that the Moriscos were potentially a fifth column of the Turks and Barbary corsairs who were active in the western Mediterranean, but in fact there was little likelihood of a Turkish invasion. The real reasons for the expulsion of the Moriscos are to be found elsewhere. Because they worked hard and were moderately prosperous, they aroused the jealousy of those many Spaniards whose daily lot was unemployment and poverty. They also provoked resentment because they clung to their own way of life and refused to be assimilated into Spanish society. These, however, were long-standing grievances. The actual timing of the expulsion was probably determined by the Spanish government's need to compensate for the humiliation of being forced to make peace with rebels and heretics: it was more than mere coincidence that the decision to expel the Moriscos was taken on the same day that the truce with the Dutch was signed. The Moriscos, in short, were to be the scapegoats for Spanish military failure.

The expulsion, which Richelieu described as 'the most fantastic, the most barbarous act in the annals of mankind', was carried out with considerable efficiency. There was little resistance, and where it did occur it was suppressed by use of troops. The decree of expulsion was published in September 1609, and by 1614 about 275,000 Moriscos had been shipped across to North Africa. Only some 10,000 or so managed to remain. The loss of such a large section of the population did not have any markedly harmful effects—in the short run at any rate—but neither did it contribute in any way to the solution of Spain's fundamental problems. One of these, rural depopulation, was in fact made more acute by the removal of Morisco cultivators from the land, and the whole operation symbolised the triumph of Castilian over non-Castilian interests. The Moriscos formed only a small part of the Castilian population but they were a third of the inhabitants of Valencia, and their expulsion was a blow to the Aragonese landowners for whom they had worked. This became yet another item in the long list of Aragon's grievances against Castile.

While Lerma was in power there was little or no chance of genuine and fundamental reform of the Spanish state. He sold offices, titles and grants of jurisdiction, he debased the copper currency which he introduced, and he chose as his own favourites men whose political morality was as crudely self-interested as his own. The first of these was the Count of Villalonga, who was appointed secretary to the council of finance, with responsibility for improving the administration of the royal revenues. In the course of his operations, however, he showed such naked greed that he shocked even his contemporaries, and was made to disgorge part of his profits and retire from office. He was succeeded by Rodrigo Calderon, created Marquess of Siete Iglesias, whose main concern was likewise self-enrichment. So long as Lerma was in power Calderon prospered, but following the favourite's fall he was arrested and executed.

Even the king became aware that Lerma's administration was not above reproach and that the financial situation was getting worse rather than better. Opposition to the favourite was also growing amongst those who believed that peace was destructive to Spanish interests. They argued that the truce of 1609 had opened the way to Dutch penetration into Spanish and Portuguese territories. This was particularly alarming in that one of the main reasons for Portugal's acceptance of the Spanish takeover had been her evident inability to defend her overseas trade and possessions. If Spain now showed the same inability there would be little incentive for the Portuguese to maintain the union of crowns. As Baltasar de Zuñiga, one of the hard-liners, observed: 'If the republic of these rebels goes on as it is, we shall succeed in losing, first the two Indies, then the rest of Flanders, then the states of Italy, and finally Spain itself.'

Those who were convinced that Spain must fight her way out of decline and assert her predominance in the world had their first taste of success in 1618, when the Bohemian crisis (see p. 341) made a reappraisal of Spanish policy necessary. The council of state was divided— in itself a sign of Lerma's weakening control—and the king no longer had confidence in his favourite. Lerma tried to strengthen his position by getting a red hat from the Pope, but although this may have saved him from loss of life or imprisonment it could not prevent his fall from power. In October 1618 he was dismissed by Philip III and ordered to retire to his estates. There he lived undisturbed—after restoring to the state part of the enormous fortune he had made in its service—until his death in 1623.

Philip announced that in future he would be his own chief minister, but he simply did not have the capacity, and before long a new favourite came to the fore. This was Lerma's son, the Duke of Uceda, and although he was never granted the formal supremacy that his father had enjoyed, his power in fact was just as great. But it depended on the king's favour, and this came to an abrupt end in March 1621 when Philip III died at the early age of forty-three.

Olivares

Philip III's son now ascended the throne as Philip IV. He was a boy of sixteen, lively, quick-witted and intelligent, with an interest in literature and the fine arts as well as hunting and women. Yet he had no strength of character, and was dominated by Gaspar de Guzman, Count of Olivares, who, after his elevation to a dukedom, was usually known as the count-duke. Olivares came from a junior branch of the great aristocratic family headed by the Duke of Medina Sidonia, and had entered the household of the future Philip IV in 1615. He soon

came to control both the household and its master, and was impatient
to display his talents on a broader stage. His opportunity came, earlier
than anticipated, in 1621, for there could be little doubt that Olivares
would be the new king's chief minister. For once the man was worthy
of the responsibility. Olivares was a formidable figure, dark in complexion, heavy in build, with a personality like a battering-ram. He
enjoyed the wealth and prestige that came from high office and royal
favour, but he was not solely concerned with his own enrichment, as
Lerma and Uceda had been. He cared deeply for Spain and was
determined to restore the greatness of his royal master abroad. Since
this could not be done without radical reforms at home, he was also
determined to undertake the task of social and political reconstruction
that had been shirked by his predecessors.

There was no shortage of reform schemes. Uceda had gone so far as
to instruct the council of Castile to consider how to improve the state's
finances, and this body had drawn up a report advocating reduction in
expenditure—particularly on the royal household and aristocratic
display—a more equitable fiscal system, and a general lightening of the
burden of taxation. Olivares now put much of this programme into
effect. He persuaded Philip IV to cut his household expenses and, far
more effective, he drastically reduced the rate at which the crown's
revenues were diverted to the nobility by way of royal grants. Philip
III had been prodigally lavish in this respect, acting as paymaster to the
Castilian aristocracy. But with the arrival in power of Olivares the fat
years came to an end, to be replaced by lean ones in which the nobles
were not only cut off from royal grants but actually made to contribute
to taxation. A title became something of a financial liability, and the
nobles never forgave Olivares for this 'betrayal' of his own order.

In 1622 the Count-Duke appointed a special *Junta de Reformacion* to
investigate corruption among office-holders and suggest further reform
measures. Yet this furious activity produced only limited results, for
Olivares constantly came up against vested interests which he could not
circumvent. Sumptuary laws, for example, designed to cut down on
aristocratic extravagance, were virtually unenforceable, although he
did succeed (with some help from the vagaries of fashion) in getting
rid of the ruff, that symbol of costly uselessness. Similarly, in his
proposals to spread the load of taxation more fairly, he came up
against the *Cortes*. In 1623–24 he suggested the abolition of the *Millones*,
a tax on foodstuffs which hit the poor, but the *Cortes* would not hear of
it: members had rigged the existing system to their own advantage and

were not open to arguments based on concepts of natural justice or economic efficiency. Nevertheless Olivares went ahead with the imposition of new taxes which did mulct the rich as well as the poor. He put a duty on the first year's income from offices, he introduced a stamp tax in 1637, and he put pressure on the clergy to make increased 'voluntary offerings' to the royal treasury.

So far as central administration was concerned, Olivares bypassed the council of state, which was too exclusively aristocratic for his liking, by increasing the number of smaller committees, or *Juntas*. One of the most important of these was the *Junta de Ejecucion*, set up in 1634 to consider what extraordinary measures were necessary to stem the tide of defeats which seemed likely to overwhelm the Spanish armies. This *Junta* soon became the main policy-making body, sending its advice direct to the king, and since its members were all appointed by the Count-Duke the *Junta de Ejecucion* was, in fact, little more than the formal expression of his own will. The excluded nobles added this further item to their rapidly lengthening list of grievances against Olivares.

Although the energy of Olivares in pushing through reforms was everywhere apparent, there is a striking contrast between his majestic aims and his limited achievement. Vested interests and inertia were partly responsible for this, but even more important was the war. For Olivares came to power at a moment when Spain was just about to commit herself to military intervention in Germany, and he never had so much as a year of peace in which to concentrate on the task of reform. Always he was faced with the necessity of finding enough money to keep Spanish armies on the move, and however inadequate the existing fiscal system he did not dare scrap it at a time when every ducat was essential. He could, of course, have given domestic reforms priority by taking Spain out of the war, but this would have run counter to his own deepest beliefs, for he was convinced that if Spain did not strike against her enemies she would be bled to death by the wounds they were inflicting on her commerce. Like Richelieu he wanted to stimulate the economy and rationalise the financial structure of the state but could not do so while the demands of war were so pre-emptive. And, again like Richelieu, although he realised the long-term social and economic danger that came from such expedients as the sale of offices and titles, he had to resort to them in order to obtain ready cash. It could be said of both ministers that they were their own worst enemies in that their determination to restore national greatness blocked the fulfilment of their desire to reform the antiquated structure of their states.

Olivares did not regard his policy as aggressive. For him it was the protestants, and in particular the Dutch, who were the real aggressors, even though they operated under cover of peaceful commerce. Like Zuñiga, whose nephew he was, Olivares believed Spain must fight to *defend* her position. As he told Philip IV in 1621, 'almost all the kings and princes of Europe are jealous of your greatness. You are the main support and defence of the catholic religion. For this reason you have renewed the war with the Dutch and with the other enemies of the church who are their allies, and your principal obligation is to defend yourself and to attack them.' The big question in 1621 was whether to extend the twelve-year truce with the Dutch, which was about to expire. Archduke Albert was still in favour of doing so, but he died in July 1621 and sovereignty over the Netherlands reverted to Spain. His widow, Isabella, and the great commander, Spinola, were also advocates of peace, but Olivares overruled them. For one thing the bellicose Orange party had come to power in the United Provinces (see p. 430), and, for another, the situation seemed particularly favourable for Spain. The Emperor had put down the Bohemian revolt and was apparently well placed to dominate Germany; the Spanish 'lifeline' had been secured by occupation of the Valtelline and part of the Palatinate (see p. 345); and bullion imports from America had suddenly and unexpectedly soared. The decision was therefore taken to renew the war against the Dutch and to concentrate all available resources on defeating them.

The campaign opened promisingly in May 1625, when Spinola captured Breda, but two years later Olivares decided to give Italy priority over the Netherlands. This was partly because no major breakthrough had been achieved against the Dutch, but even more because of Spanish bitterness at the lack of assistance from the German catholic princes. There was some resentment also against the Emperor, who had eagerly accepted Spanish subsidies but had shown himself very reluctant to carry out Spanish plans for domination of the Baltic. His general, Wallenstein, was poised on the southern shores of this sea, and Habsburg control of the Baltic, which would have cut at one of the main sources of Dutch wealth, seemed a very real possibility. But the chance was lost, never to recur.

In these circumstances it seemed better to concentrate on another theatre, and the 'bankruptcy' of 1627 (by which interest payments were suspended, and the financiers forced to accept *Juros* at a lower rate) made money available for such a venture. The opportunity came in December 1627 when the Duke of Mantua died, leaving his territories to a French claimant, the Duke of Nevers. Spain had every reason to dread the presence of a French puppet state so near the Valtelline, and the decision was taken to intervene. In fact, as Olivares himself later recognised, the decision was disastrous, for the war of the Mantuan Succession involved Spain in very considerable expenditure, renewed all the old fears of Spanish aggressiveness, and provided France with an ideal excuse to reassert her interest in northern Italy. The war dragged on until 1631, when it was ended by the Treaty of Cherasco, but this left the French in possession of Pinerolo. Three years of fighting and the expenditure of ten million ducats had led to a settlement which, from the Spaniards' point of view, was far worse than that which they had fought to prevent.

Since Spain could not employ all her resources simultaneously on two fronts, bullion supplies to the army fighting in the Netherlands were cut by 60 per cent, to the detriment of military operations in that area. Yet even so there was not enough money available to meet the widespread Spanish commitments, and at this critical moment, in 1628, the Dutch captured the silver fleet. It was the first time such a disaster had befallen the Spaniards, and it meant that no 'free' money was now available for offensive operations. One consequence of this was the Spanish decision to end the war in Italy, even on the unfavourable terms of Cherasco. With the landing of Gustavus Adolphus in Pomerania in 1630, and his sweeping victory at Breitenfeld a year later, Germany had clearly become the principal theatre of war, and Spanish support for the imperial and catholic cause there was now more important than ever. It seems probable that at this stage Olivares would even have been ready to accept a truce with the Dutch, but he had to reckon with Philip IV, who regarded his inheritance as a sacred trust and would not willingly part with a single portion of it. The struggle in the Netherlands therefore continued, but resources were somehow found to raise a new army to link up with the Emperor's forces and try to stem the tide of protestant success in Germany.

The result of this new initiative was the astounding victory of Nordlingen in September 1634 (see p. 361). In a way the triumph was almost too complete, because it opened the way to Habsburg domination of Germany—something that France would never accept. In

1635, therefore, France formally declared war on Spain. After fifteen years of fighting and the consumption of enormous sums of money the Spaniards were confronted with the open hostility of the enemy they most dreaded. The war with France now took priority over everything else—much to the relief of the Dutch, who were able to renew their offensive—and even though supplies were sent to the Netherlands they were designed for operations against the French. Olivares hoped for a knockout blow before French strength could be mobilised, and he almost got this in 1636 when a combined Spanish and imperial army came within striking distance of Paris. But the French showed just how strong was their will to resist, and the offensive petered out. Olivares was left with the problem of finding yet more men and more money for a war that now looked as though it would never end.

The strain of continual fighting was making itself felt in France as well as Spain, and it was a question of which country could hold out longer. By a bitter irony it was Olivares, the symbol of Spanish strength, who sparked off the revolts that opened the way to French triumph. The count-duke had long recognised that the burden on Castile was too great for that kingdom to bear, and that the other territories of the peninsula must be made to take a larger share. He may have overrated the capacity of these other territories. Aragon, for instance, was a dry and impoverished region; Valencia was suffering from rural depopulation; Catalonia had been hit by the decline of her Mediterranean trade; while Portugal was weakened by the Dutch penetration of her overseas possessions. Yet Olivares could not just wait and hope, as Lerma had done, for the years 1625–27 saw bad harvests in Castile, and these, coming on top of acute monetary instability due to fluctuations in the value of *Vellon*, reduced the tax yield. Philip IV was nominally king of all Spain, yet in fact his rule was largely confined to Castile. Olivares saw the remedy as lying in the assertion of royal power over the whole peninsula. As he told Philip in 1625, 'The most important thing in Your Majesty's monarchy is for you to become King of Spain. By this I mean, sire, that Your Majesty should not be content with being King of Portugal, of Aragon, of Valencia, and Count of Barcelona, but should secretly plan and work to reduce these kingdoms of which Spain is composed to the style and laws of Castile, with no difference whatsoever.'

As a first step towards achieving this desired uniformity, Olivares put forward proposals, in 1626, for a 'Union of Arms'. This would have involved the creation of a reserve army, to which each region would contribute men and money. In return for the sharing of the burden, Olivares was prepared to abandon Castilian exclusiveness, for he did not share the contemptuous attitude of the Castilians towards those who were born in other regions, nor did he believe that the king should be the sole property of Castile. It was at his suggestion that in 1626 Philip IV went in person to the opening of the *Cortes* of Aragon, to demonstrate by his presence there the end of old attitudes and to encourage the Aragonese to accept the Union of Arms. In fact the Aragonese and Valencians were very reluctant to make any such concessions, for they saw what was intended, but after prolonged opposition they eventually agreed to vote substantial sums of money to the crown. The king then went on to open the *Cortes* of Catalonia, but there he met with an outright refusal to contribute.

Catalonia had long been a law unto itself. Society was dominated by the mass of small nobles whose main occupation was banditry and who clung to their 'liberties'—the *Fueros* of Catalonia—as an assurance that this state of anarchy would continue. The appointment of a strong governor in 1615 had led to some measure of order being imposed, but the Catalans deeply resented this high-handed action on the part of the government in Madrid and were simply strengthened in their determination to resist further innovations. There were, of course other reasons for discontent. French competition in the Mediterranean had crippled Catalan trade and had undermined the prosperity of Barcelona, while plague and bad harvests had affected Catalonia as elsewhere. Yet by any standards Catalonia had contributed very little to the expenses of the Spanish monarchy. No taxes had been voted since the *Cortes* of 1599 (the last to meet until that of 1626); no Catalan contingents fought in the Spanish armies, nor did the Catalans even contribute towards the upkeep of those soldiers who guarded their frontier with France. Olivares was not exaggerating when he declared that the Catalans were 'entirely separate from the rest of the monarchy, useless for service, and in a state little befitting the dignity and power of His Majesty'.

For more than a decade after the abortive attempt to persuade the Catalonians to contribute to the Union of Arms, Olivares bided his time. But in 1639, when the French invaded Roussillon, on the northeastern frontier of Catalonia, he grasped the opportunity of welding the Catalans into a unitary Spanish state. He ordered the whole population to be mobilised, and when complaints were made that he was infringing the *Fueros*, he dismissed them out of hand. 'We always have to look and see if a constitution says this or that,' he commented bitterly. 'We have to discover what the customary usage is, even when it is a question of the supreme law, of the actual preservation and defence of the province. . . . The Catalans ought to see more of the world than Catalonia.' In the winter of 1640 he ordered that the Spanish forces fighting in Roussillon should be billeted in Catalonia at the expense of the inhabitants. The billeting of ill-disciplined and rapacious troops was always something of a punishment, and constant brawls between civilians and soldiers inflamed feelings to such an extent that by May 1640 Catalonia was in open revolt. Royal officers were assaulted, and in June the viceroy himself was killed in a tussle in Barcelona.

Olivares had tried to avoid direct attack on the Catalonian *Fueros* and had been ready for concessions. But now that rebellion had come he prepared to meet it. He needed the Catalan ports for communication with Italy, and he dared not let disorder spread to such an extent that it would invite French intervention. But the rebels were already looking to France, and in return for the promise of military assistance they agreed to place themselves under the sovereignty of Louis XIII. Catalonia now became one of the French king's dominions, and Louis appointed a royal governor to exercise his authority.

Catalonia's resistance to Olivares's schemes inspired revolt in Portugal. There had already been riots in 1637 over the imposition of new taxes for defence and for the recovery of Brazil, but the Portuguese nobility had held aloof. The nobles still valued the Spanish connection and were hoping for effective support in driving out the Dutch from Brazil, though at the same time they were suspicious of Olivares and of the future of their own 'liberties' if his projects were carried through to completion. In the autumn of 1638 a joint Spanish and Portuguese naval force sailed for Brazil, but it accomplished nothing. This demonstration of the uselessness of the Spanish connection came just at the moment when the Catalans rose in revolt, and by this time the Portuguese nobles were ready to join in throwing off Spanish rule. Unlike the Catalans, they had a 'pretender' in the Duke of Braganza, descended from the former ruling house of Portugal, and in December 1640 they declared him king, as John IV. Olivares's attempt to unite all the states of the peninsula under the effective rule of Philip IV had therefore ended in disastrous failure, and to outsiders it seemed as though Spain was breaking up. As the English ambassador reported in 1641, 'concerning the state of this kingdom, I could never have imagined to have seen it as it now is, for their people begin to fail, and those that remain, by a continuance of bad successes and by their heavy burdens, are quite out of heart'.

In every way the situation was unfavourable. The flow of silver from the Indies dried up completely in 1640 and was only one million ducats in 1641. In 1637 the Dutch, profiting from the Spanish preoccupation with the French war, recaptured Breda. In the following year Bernard of Weimar captured Breisach, thereby cutting the vital lifeline from Italy to the Netherlands, and when the Spaniards tried to reopen the sea route up the Channel in 1638 they were defeated by the Dutch in the Battle of the Downs. All these disasters reflected on Olivares, and his enemies urged the king to get rid of him. Philip IV eventually succumbed to this pressure, and in January 1643 he gave the count-duke leave to retire to his estates. There Olivares died in July 1645, unsound in mind, and with him went, in the words of one historian, 'the first and last ruler of Habsburg Spain who had the breadth of vision to devise plans on a grand scale for the future of a world-wide monarchy: a statesman whose capacity for conceiving great designs was matched only by his consistent incapacity for carrying them through to a successful conclusion'.[1]

The Decline of Spain

Philip IV was determined that the powers of the crown should never again be delegated to a subject. But he was no more capable now than he had been twenty years earlier of exercising the great authority which he had inherited, and it was not long before a new favourite emerged. This was Luis de Haro, the nephew of Olivares and a man of mediocre talents, who retained power only by abandoning his uncle's domestic policies and reverting to aristocratic rule. The *Juntas* were abolished, the authority of the councils, and in particular of the council of state, was restored, and the fundamental reconstruction on which Olivares had embarked was postponed to the Greek kalends. There was no change in foreign policy, however, except in so far as shortage of money made necessary a more realistic appraisal of the situation. The rapid decline of the Atlantic trade had reduced bullion imports to a level where they could not even sustain a sufficient scale of

[1] J. H. Elliott, *Imperial Spain 1469–1716*, Arnold, 1963. p. 345.

operations on the Netherlands front. Lack of pay was one of the reasons for the Spanish defeat at Rocroi, for it was the disgruntled mercenaries who ran away while the native Spanish infantry were cut down where they stood. In 1647 the state again declared its bankruptcy by stopping interest payments, and famine and plague ravaged Andalucia, Valencia and parts of Castile, causing half a million deaths. The same year also saw outbreaks of rebellion in Sicily and Naples, though these were contained without further straining the resources of Philip IV's government. Peace with the Dutch was clearly imperative, and was at last concluded in 1648, by the Treaty of Munster. In accepting this, Philip IV had formally to acknowledge the fact that the United Provinces were an independent sovereign state. He abandoned earlier Spanish insistence on freedom of public worship for catholics in the area under Dutch control, and also agreed that the Scheldt should remain closed—thereby confirming the economic subordination of Antwerp to Amsterdam. All that the Spaniards gained in return was the recognition of their own sovereignty over the southern Netherlands, and the end of the Franco-Dutch alliance. Now they were free to concentrate on the war against France.

By this time France herself was suffering from the strain of war, and the outbreak of the *Frondes* seemed to herald much the same break-up of the state as had already occurred in the Iberian peninsula. But Spain was too exhausted to take full advantage of this sudden change in the situation. She managed to push the French out of Catalonia, and in October 1652 a Spanish army recaptured Barcelona after a siege lasting over a year. Catalonia once more became a possession of the Spanish crown, and the original causes of revolt were removed when Philip IV confirmed all the traditional *Fueros*. In the Netherlands, however, the war went badly, and the balance was tipped against Spain by the intervention of the English republic in 1656. In that year Admiral Blake intercepted one Spanish treasure fleet, and in the following year he destroyed another. Without silver the Spanish armies could not fight, and the military weakness of what had once been the most formidable power in Europe was demonstrated in June 1658, when a mixed Franco-English force defeated the Spaniards at the Battle of the Dunes and captured Dunkirk. This put the whole of the southern Netherlands in danger, and Philip IV now had to agree to make peace.

Negotiations took place with due regard to the susceptibilities of both parties, and the plenipotentiaries held their meetings on the Isle of Pheasants—in the middle of the river Bidassoa which marked the frontier between the two countries. Out of their bargaining emerged the Treaty of the Pyrenees, signed in November 1659, which brought to an end the war that had started, in effect, more than 150 years earlier, when Charles VIII of France led his army across the Alps. Its terms recalled many of the changes of fortune of that epic struggle. Spain, for instance, ceded Cerdagne and Roussillon to France, agreed to French occupation of a number of key defensive positions in the Netherlands, and formally renounced all her pretensions to Alsace. France was to retain the fortress of Pinerolo, but only on condition that she abandoned her historic claims to territorial possessions in Italy. She was also to withdraw her support from the Catalans and Portuguese who had rebelled against the authority of the Spanish crown.

The Treaty of the Pyrenees was clearly a defeat for Spain. She did not have to concede a great deal in the way of territory, but she had to acknowledge French primacy. The pill was sweetened by the provision that Philip IV's daughter, Maria Theresa, should be married to the young French king, Louis XIV. Certain conditions were attached to this, the most important being that the bride-to-be should renounce all claims to the Spanish throne. At French insistence this renunciation was made dependent on the regular payment by Spain of Maria Theresa's dowry—a condition that, given the chronic state of Spanish finances, seemed unlikely to be fulfilled. Philip IV could take comfort from the fact that his descendants through the female line would share in French greatness, while his young son would preserve Habsburg rule in Spain.

Now that Catalonia had returned to the Spanish fold only Portugal, among the kingdoms of the Iberian peninsula, remained outside. Philip IV was determined that this part of his inheritance should be reconquered, and with the French war at last brought to an end Spain could concentrate her energies and resources on the recovery of Portugal. But in the twenty years that had elapsed since her declaration of independence, Portugal had grown much stronger. An access of nationalist fervour, combined with the shaky condition of the Dutch West India Company, had enabled her to reconquer Brazil and once again to enjoy the profits of the sugar and slave trades. She had also had the invaluable support of Cromwell's England, and the Restoration, far from upsetting this alliance, confirmed and strengthened it, since Charles II married John IV's daughter, Catherine of Braganza. The Portuguese had already driven back one Spanish offensive at the battle of Elvas in 1659, and they won further victories at Ameixial in 1663 and Villaviciosa in 1665. Philip IV, however, refused to acknowledge defeat: he had already betrayed his God-given trust by parting with his Netherlands' inheritance, and he was convinced that it was his sacred duty to hold on to the rest, no matter at what cost in suffering to his Spanish subjects. His death in September 1665 removed this major obstacle to peace, but not until February 1668 did his widow, now regent, recognise Portugal as an independent and sovereign state.

The tragedy of Spanish decline was not yet over. The last act was played out in the reign of Philip's son, Charles II, who was only four years old when he became king in 1665. Charles was physically weak and mentally unstable. Despite two marriages he produced no children, and the major interest of his reign came to be speculation about when it would end. The queen regent, Philip IV's widow, took charge of the administration, and ruled through her favourite, the Austrian Jesuit John Nithard, whom she had naturalised and appointed Inquisitor-General. Opposition to Nithard's ineffectual regime centred on Philip IV's bastard son, Don John, a soldier of some reputation who had established his power and popularity in Aragon and Catalonia. In 1669 he marched on Madrid—thereby reversing the normal process whereby Castile imposed her will on the other kingdoms—and forced the queen regent to dismiss the favourite. He was unwilling to take power himself, however, and instead left the exercise of authority to a regency *Junta*, as provided for in Philip IV's will.

It was not long before a new favourite emerged, in the shape of Ferdinado Valenzuela, a man of obscure origins who by 1676 had been granted the title of Marquis of Villasierra and was to all intents and purposes chief minister. The regency *Junta* was dissolved and the queen regent and Villasierra ruled as they pleased. The nobles, who had always regarded their own interests as identical with those of the Spanish state, resented the intrusion of this upstart and looked to Don John for assistance. In 1677, therefore, Don John once again led an army into Madrid and forced the queen regent to dismiss her favourite. But this time the sequel was different, since Don John took power himself and remained Charles II's chief minister until his death two years later in 1679.

For some years after Don John's removal from the scene there was no dominant figure in Spanish government. The king was too weak to sustain one against the will of the aristocracy, and it was not until 1685 that political intrigues and faction-fighting gave way before the Count of Oropesa. He was a man more in the style of Olivares than the recent favourites, and he brought to government the same sort of energetic determination to reform. Distrusting the old-established councils, which were strongholds of aristocratic power, he set up a department of finance on the French model, and began reconstructing the fiscal system. His actual achievement was limited, but his reforming zeal threatened the vested interest of the nobility and in 1691 they persuaded the king to dismiss him. From then until the end of the reign in 1700 there was virtual stagnation so far as the central administration was concerned, but, although it was not clear at the time, the lowest point in Spain's fortunes had been passed. In some areas, particularly Catalonia, the economy was slowly beginning to revive; the savage deflation carried through by the government in 1680 began to have benefical effects after some years of wildly fluctuating prices; and the reforms of Oropesa, although most of them remained projects, had stimulated discussion about the nature of the changes needed to transform Spain into a modern state. All that was needed was firm direction from the top, but this could not come so long as the neurasthenic and melancholy Charles II remained on the throne. His death in 1700, and the accession of a Bourbon king, bringing with him French experts, opened the way to a reinvigoration of Spanish government in which the native reform movement as well as outside influences played their part.

TWENTY-THREE

The Netherlands, 1609–72

Oldenbarneveld

In the first half of the seventeenth century the independent United Provinces reached the summit of their power and became for a short time one of the major states in Europe. The southern Netherlands, meanwhile, remained under Spanish rule, despite the nominal independence granted to the Archdukes. Yet in many ways the south seemed to be the more stable, more assured and even more successful society—the living embodiment of the old Burgundian traditions. The court at Brussels carefully cultivated its magnificence, employing the services of no less a painter than Rubens, and to it flocked the nobility who were still predominant in local life, unchallenged by any burgher oligarchs. The south was not without its towns of course, but generally speaking these were in decline. Ghent and Bruges had faded with the Middle Ages, and as for Antwerp, the commercial capital of Europe in the sixteenth century, it had been crippled by war, the emigration of many of its leading citizens, and the Dutch blockade of the River Scheldt. But while the towns decayed the countryside prospered, and the existing social system was buttressed rather than weakened by economic developments. Another powerful force working towards the consolidation of society was the Church. Under the impetus of the Jesuits, and with the active encouragement of the government, the decrees of the Council of Trent were put into effect, and reformed catholicism permeated every aspect of life. Heresy was virtually eradicated by the expulsion of all protestants who refused to accept conversion, and deep devotion to the catholic faith became one of the strongest bonds linking the inhabitants of the Spanish Netherlands to each other and to the court at Brussels.

This outward appearance of grandeur and tranquillity was not, however, the whole truth. The civilisation of the south was cosmopolitan, a resplendent facet of the international catholic world, but for this reason it could not satisfy such nationalist sentiment as existed. Nor could this find an outlet in administration, for although local law and provincial assemblies were preserved, the central government was firmly in the hands of Spanish advisers. The native nobility were represented on the council of state, but, as in Spain under Philip II, this was a largely formal body with no real power. The inhabitants of the south could take comfort from the fact that in the Archduke Albert they had a ruler of their own, but he died in 1621, and the Netherlands reverted to direct Spanish rule. Albert's widow, the Archduchess Isabella, remained as governor, but her chief adviser was the Spanish Cardinal de la Cueva, who became the object of intense hostility because of his arrogant assertion of the primacy of Spanish interests. It was well known that the Archduke had been in favour of extending the twelve-year truce with the Dutch, which was due to expire in 1621, but the decision to renew the war was taken in Madrid, not Brussels. This high-handed action aroused such intense feeling in the Netherlands that one observer gave it as his opinion that the southern provinces had never been 'more bitter in their enmity towards Spain. If the Prince of Orange and the rebels were not kept by their fanatical intolerance from granting liberty of worship . . . then a union of the loyal provinces with those of the north could not be prevented.' The Archduchess showed herself to be aware of the danger, for in 1629 she dismissed Cueva and gave the council of state a more important role in government. This removed the immediate grievance but did nothing to solve the basic problem—which indeed could not be solved so long as Spain was determined to exercise its sovereignty over the Netherlands.

Yet however much the inhabitants of the south might detest the Spaniards, they recognised the advantages of catholic, monarchical rule, particularly when contrasted with the situation in the north. The government of the United Provinces was in the hands of merchant oligarchs—the 'regents'—who kept alive the tolerant Erasmian tradition of the early sixteenth century. But they had to move cautiously in order to avoid alienating the hard-line Calvinist ministers and their devotees among the artisans and urban proletariat. They were also inhibited by the fact that they were not a homogeneous group. While most of the regents were unfanatical, middle-of-the-road Calvinists, there were hard-liners among them; and since the number of offices in central and local administration was limited, some members of the regent class were unable to gratify their desire for power. Such 'outsiders' reverted to the Sea Beggars' tradition and gave themselves a mass following by embracing Calvinism in its most extreme and uncompromising form. They were then in a position to challenge the 'established' regents, whom they accused of being lukewarm in their adherence to the Calvinist faith and ready to compromise with the catholic Spanish enemy.

The contrast between south and north, between Counter-Reformation homogeneity and Calvinist factionalism, had its parallel in the institutions of government. The Archdukes and their successors were all-powerful in the Spanish Netherlands, but in the north authority was divided among the seven constituent provinces of the Union, with the additional complication of the quasi-monarchical element of the Stadtholderate. The provinces were sovereign, and although they sent delegates to the Estates General, which was in permanent session, they could refuse to be bound by decisions taken at the Hague. There were times when it seemed as though the ramshackle constitution of the so-called 'United' Provinces would give way completely, but the fledgling state was held together by the province of Holland, which contributed well over fifty per cent of the national revenue and had a correspondingly predominant influence on national policy. The chief officer, or 'Advocate', of Holland was Jan van Oldenbarneveld, and it was on the basis of this provincial authority that he made himself the most important man in the Dutch state in the years following the truce of 1609. In so far as the United Provinces had a prime minister, it was Oldenbarneveld.

The two biggest problems confronting him were those of foreign policy and religion. Although he had been in favour of peace with Spain he was not blind to the threat that Spanish Habsburg power presented to the protestant republic. With England more or less impotent under its first Stuart monarch, Oldenbarneveld was the leading protestant statesman of his day, and worked in close co-operation with Henry IV of France to build up an anti-Habsburg coalition. This collapsed in May 1610, when Henry was assassinated, but the United Provinces did not retreat into neutrality. It was a Dutch army, under Maurice, which intervened in Cleve and Julich to put the claimants into possession (see p. 323), and some years later, in 1614, the Dutch joined with Brandenburg to occupy the fortress of Julich. This prompted a counter move from Spain, when Spinola was sent to occupy the Rhine town of Wesel, in the Duchy of Cleve. Wesel was close to the Dutch frontier, and the forward party in the United Provinces was in favour of forcibly expelling the Spanish troops. Oldenbarneveld resisted this on the grounds that the republic would be endangered if it acted alone, and that no effective support would be forthcoming. The Spanish occupation of Wesel was therefore accepted as a *fait accompli*, but the hard-liners in the United Provinces, who now included Stadtholder Maurice, were convinced that Oldenbarneveld was guilty at best of weakness and at worst of treason.

The second major problem was that of religion. The dispute between the 'Libertinists' and the 'Precisians' had never been healed (see p. 250), and was revived in the early seventeenth century by the controversy between two Leyden theologians, Jacob Arminius and Francis Gomarus. Arminius and his followers—the Arminians—wanted to modify the rigid interpretation of the doctrine of predestination, which emphasised the inflexible justice of God rather than His mercy, and left sinful man apparently without hope. The Gomarists, on the other hand, adhered to the strict Calvinist position and bitterly attacked the Arminians for opening the gate to heresy. The Arminians were only a minority among the clergy and had virtually no influence outside Holland. They there-fore sought the assistance of Oldenbarneveld, and with his tacit approval sent a 'Remonstrance' to the Estates of Holland, in 1610, setting out their views and appealing for protection. The Estates could hardly refuse this request. The regents of Holland were far closer in temperament to the Arminian position than the Gomarist one, and in any case they were determined to assert the right of the civil govern-ment to decide on the religious settlement. They therefore ordered that all ministers should refrain from theological controversy—which amounted to a defence of the Arminians (or 'Remonstrants', as they were now often called), since it was the Gomarists who were on the attack.

In 1614 the Gomarists presented a 'Counter-Remonstrance' and called for a national synod to decide all matters in dispute. Olden-barneveld opposed this. A national synod would almost certainly come down against the Remonstrants and would try to impose religious uniformity on the strict Calvinist model. This was contrary not only to his private beliefs but also to the principle that each pro-vince should make its own decisions on matters of religion. There was the further consideration that the Counter-Remonstrants had close links with Stadtholder Maurice and the war party. If they gained power they might well destroy the fragile peace from which the United Provinces, and particularly the merchants of Amsterdam, were profiting.

In normal circumstances Oldenbarneveld could have looked for support from the magistrates of Amsterdam, but his very success had created him enemies, and these had already come together in support of proposals to establish a West India Company. Oldenbarneveld had led the opposition to this scheme. He had been responsible for the formation of the East India Company in 1602 and believed, rightly, that the proposed new body would be more concerned with privateering than with trade. The war party was in favour of it, of course, and so were the religious radicals, but Oldenbarneveld had cut the ground from under their feet by negotiating the truce of 1609. This opened the Spanish empire to peaceful penetration, and plans for a West India Company committed to aggressive and piratical activities had therefore to be put into cold storage. This did not please those members of the Amsterdam merchant community who had looked forward to profiting from the new venture. They blamed Oldenbarneveld for their rebuff and joined with the opponents of his foreign and religious policies, despite their general sympathy for his liberal outlook in religion.

Oldenbarneveld's critics had the powerful support of Stadtholder Maurice. The office of Stadtholder was a survival from the days of the united Netherlands, and the limited powers it conferred—such as choosing magistrates from a short-list drawn up by the provincial Estates—were as nothing compared with the prestige and influence it afforded. William the Silent had bound the Stadtholderate to the Orange family, and it formed a monarchical element in a nominally republican state. The regents looked with some suspicion on the princely Stadtholder, for they had everything to gain from the existing constitution of the merchant republic and feared absolutism as much as democracy. But the House of Orange was popular among the artisans and urban proletariat, and in the six provinces other than Holland the regents were not so numerous or so well established that they could afford to ignore such elements. The threat of popular unrest was ever present, and for them the Stadtholder represented not so much a challenge as a guarantee of stability. They were usually prepared to follow Holland's lead, but when, as over the question of Oldenbarneveld, the rulers of Holland were divided among themselves, these regents of the other provinces began to fear for their safety, and looked to the Stadtholder for protection.

Maurice had not been in favour of making peace with Spain in 1609 and was eager to renew the struggle. In particular he called for aid to the French Huguenots—among whose leaders was his brother-in-law, the Duke of Bouillon—and rejected Oldenbarneveld's view that the French monarchy was in the last resort a bulwark against Spain. So far Maurice had not openly comitted himself in the Dutch religious conflict, but in 1617 he refused a request from the Estates of Holland to put down an illegal Counter-Remonstrant congregation at the Hague, and later joined in open worship with it. Maurice, as Captain-General, was commander of the army, but the individual regiments were maintained by the separate provinces, and over half of them were on the pay-roll of Holland. In August, therefore, Oldenbarneveld persuaded the Holland Estates, in which his supporters were still in the majority, to order all regiments to obey the municipal authorities even if this meant defying the orders of the Captain-General.

Maurice regarded this, rightly, as a challenge to his authority, and one that he could not ignore. Oldenbarneveld and his followers were already the targets of a powerful propaganda campaign, and Maurice could count on the support not only of a majority of the Estates General but also of a minority within Holland itself. Early in 1618 he acted in his capacity as Stadtholder of Gelderland and Overijssel by dismissing all Remonstrant magistrates within these provinces. He then forced Utrecht to take the same course, thereby leaving Holland isolated. In August, provided with a warrant by the Estates General, he arrested Oldenbarneveld, along with a number of his leading supporters, and then 'progressed' with his army from town to town within Holland, dismissing Remonstrant magistrates as he went. The new town councils appointed fresh delegates to the provincial Estates, and Oldenbarneveld's majority there was gradually eroded. His downfall was confirmed when the Holland Estates agreed to set up a special court to try him. It was made up of his enemies and in May 1619 it sentenced him to death. A few days later he was executed.

Frederick Henry and the Defeat of Spain

With the overthrow of Oldenbarneveld the balance of the constitution in the United Provinces swung in favour of the Stadtholder and against the regents. Maurice's triumph was a victory for the war party, just at the moment when the question of renewing the twelve-year truce was coming to the fore. It was also a victory for the religious radicals, whose predominance was confirmed by the national synod which assembled at Dordrecht in November 1618. To it came representatives of protestant churches from many parts of Europe, and debates concentrated on the thorny problems of predestination and salvation. The Arminians were hopelessly outnumbered and given no adequate opportunity to state their case. The Synod of Dort, as it came to be known, affirmed the strict Calvinist position and was a triumph for the Counter-Remonstrants. Its decisions were adopted by the Estates of all seven provinces, and so, for the first time, the republic had a single religious settlement. The Remonstrants were forbidden to worship, their churches were closed and congregations dissolved, they were dismissed from public office and often forced into exile.

The success of the Counter-Remonstrants and the war party meant that national interests had apparently prevailed over provincial ones. Oldenbarneveld and the regents in general clung to provincial liberties as the surest safeguard of their own position, but the Stadtholder stood for central control over domestic and foreign policy. Such was the extent of Maurice's victory that he might well have turned the United Provinces into a monarchy under the hereditary kingship of the house of Orange, but in fact he never did so. His main concern was with the Spanish war, which broke out again in 1621, and his reputation suffered from military defeats. In outward appearance, therefore, the Dutch constitution was unchanged at the time of his death in April 1625.

He was succeeded by his younger brother, Frederick Henry, who was much closer in temperament to the liberal Erasmianism that had been characteristic of his father, William the Silent, and was prevalent among the regent class. He put an end to persecution of the Remonstrants and allowed them gradually to resume their place in public life. This was made easier by the fact that the 'outside' regents who had come in to power with the Counter-Remonstrants in 1619 were swift to recognise the dangers of theocracy and asserted their right to a decisive voice in questions of public worship just as firmly as their moderate predecessors had done. With the fall of Oldenbarneveld, the renewal of war, and the subsequent setting-up of a thrustful West India Company, the political temperature had been lowered, and this was reflected in an increasingly tolerant attitude in religious matters. By

1627 Remonstrants were once again to be found among the magistrates of Amsterdam, and four years later the town council formally suspended the Estates General's edict against them. Religious uniformity on a national scale had been abandoned, and the supremacy of provincial rights, with all that this entailed, had been reasserted.

The Counter-Remonstrant victory of 1619 had been in some ways more important for its effect on foreign policy than for its shortlived impact at home. As the end of the twelve-year truce came nearer, voices were raised on both sides calling for its renewal. Oldenbarneveld and the peace party in the United Provinces were not blind to the drawbacks inherent in any permanent peace settlement. They knew that this would almost certainly have to include the opening of the Scheldt—which would threaten the commercial supremacy of Amsterdam—as well as an end to the forcible Dutch penetration of the Spanish and Portuguese empires. But they were also aware that in the years of peace Dutch merchants had flourished as never before, and they could hope for a compromise solution on disputed questions so long as feelings were not hardened by religious intolerance. The Spaniards were insistent on some measure of freedom of worship for Roman Catholics in the United Provinces, and such a concession was not entirely out of the question so long as the moderate regents were in power. The triumph of the Counter-Remonstrants, however, put an end to all this. They preferred a holy war to a compromise peace, and far from attempting to damp down religious controversy they inflamed it. By giving the war with Spain something of the character of a protestant crusade they emphasised the differences between the two parts of the Netherlands and made reconciliation and reunion less likely.

Although Maurice was the hero of the Counter-Remonstrants, he had a sound appreciation of military realities and recognised the weaknesses of the Dutch position. He shocked his co-religionists by bringing about an alliance with catholic France in 1624, and he dismayed them by failing to drive back the enemy. The truth was, of course, that Spain was still very powerful and possessed, in Spinola, a commander of genius. In 1622 Spinola laid siege to the important fortress of Bergen-op-Zoom, which was only saved by the unanticipated appearance of Mansfeld's mercenary army, and three years later he captured Breda, which Maurice himself had taken from the Spaniards in 1590. All Maurice's efforts to drive out Spinola failed, and he died in the attempt, leaving the future conduct of the war in the hands of Frederick Henry.

For some years Frederick Henry had to fight hard simply to hold his own, but in 1628 he was strengthened (and the Spaniards correspondingly weakened) by the Dutch capture of the Plate fleet. At last he could go over to the offensive, at the very moment when the Spaniards had decided to give priority to Italy and were becoming involved in the war of the Mantuan Succession. Frederick Henry laid siege to Bois-le-Duc (Hertogenbosch), the major town of Brabant, and captured it in September 1629. This was a major victory, for it brought Dutch forces beyond the line of the great rivers and opened the way to the reconquest of the southern Netherlands. But any such reconquest would necessitate the co-operation of the local population, since the Dutch did not have the military strength to occupy and hold down the entire area. It was at this point that the fervour of the Counter-Remonstrants worked against the ideal of reunion, for they insisted that liberty of worship should not be permitted in any newly conquered territories, and in Bois le Duc they excluded the Roman Catholics from office, even though there were virtually no protestants among the inhabitants. In these circumstances it was hardly surprising that no mass rising took place in the south in favour of the 'liberators' from the north.

The Archduchess Isabella took advantage of this evidence of northern intolerance to emphasise the positive advantages of Spanish rule, which included the preservation not simply of the true faith but also of the established social order. Yet she was well aware of the widespread dissatisfaction with Spanish policy, especially now that it had led to invasion of the south, and of the desire for some peaceful settlement. In 1632, therefore, on her own initiative and against the wishes of Philip IV, she summoned a meeting of the Estates General—the first since 1600. Secret negotiations were already under way between Frederick Henry and the southern nobles, and for a time there seemed to be a very real chance of a peace settlement. The northern Estates General issued a call for a mass rising in the south and promised freedom of worship and the preservation of existing political liberties. Meanwhile Dutch troops continued their advance, occupying Venloe and Roermond, and in August took possession of Maastricht. If Frederick Henry had made a dash for Brussels he might have sparked off a general rebellion against Spanish rule, but he was by temperament a cautious man in military matters, and with Gustavus Adolphus continuing his triumphal progress through Germany there seemed no need for haste.

By 1633, however, the death of Gustavus Adolphus had radically altered the situation, and negotiations between south and north had reached deadlock. Mutual suspicion was reinforced by the fear of the Dutch regents that peace would mean the end of their profitable expansion into the Spanish and Portuguese empires. The West India Company, founded in 1621, had achieved its first major success in 1628, with the capture of the Plate fleet, and had used the profits to mount an attack upon the Portuguese colony of Brazil. In 1630 the Dutch captured Recife, the capital of the province of Pernambuco, and seemed well set to take over the entire country in due course. The Spaniards, anxious to retain Portuguese goodwill and thereby preserve the union of crowns, insisted that one of the terms of any peace settlement should be the return of Pernambuco, but this was a condition which the Dutch were unwilling to accept. The southern Netherlands had no interest in Pernambuco, but they were pawns in a power game that was directed from Madrid. Separated from the Dutch by religion, and from the Spaniards by politics, they were not free to work out their own salvation.

After the death of Archduchess Isabella in December 1633, administration of the Netherlands passed into the hands of a council in which the Spaniards were predominant, and in June 1634 Philip IV ordered that the Estates General at Brussels should be dissolved. He had already appointed his brother, the Cardinal-Infante, as governor of the Netherlands, and in September 1634, while on his way to take up his new post, the young man won the battle at Nordlingen which seemed to herald the revival of the Habsburg cause. There was no more talk of peace at Brussels, only of resistance, and the city decorated itself magnificently, under the artistic direction of Rubens, to greet the new governor. Nationalist feeling in the south had once again found a focus, and a separate identity under Spanish sovereignty seemed preferable to absorption by the northern provinces.

As it became clear to the Dutch that the southern Netherlands were not going to respond to their appeal, they determined on a renewal of the war of conquest. Under the terms of a treaty of alliance made with the French in 1635 a joint invasion was to take place, leading to a partition in which the Walloon provinces and Flanders would go to France while Brabant would become part of the United Provinces. The territory had first to be conquered, however, and this was easier said than done. Although a combined force invaded Brabant in 1635 and captured Tirlemont, the ruthless treatment of the town shocked public opinion in the south and encouraged other places to hold out. Louvain was besieged but refused to surrender, and its resistance gave the Cardinal-Infante time to gather his forces and launch a successful diversionary attack.

The entry of France into the war meant that the Netherlands had to take second place in the Spanish list of priorities. Men and money that would otherwise have been used against the Dutch were consumed in operations on or across the French frontier. Yet the southern Netherlands continued to hold out against Dutch attacks. In 1637 Frederick Henry recaptured Breda, but in the same year the Cardinal-Infante won back Venloe and Roermond and in 1638 he repulsed a Dutch assault on Antwerp. The Spanish capacity to resist was weakened in 1639 when the Dutch admiral, van Tromp, attacked a fleet carrying reinforcements to the Netherlands, drove it into the Downs, off Dover, and there destroyed it. A year later came the revolts in Catalonia and Portugal which seemed to announce the break-up of Spain, and in 1641 the Spaniards in the Netherlands suffered a severe blow in the early death of the Cardinal-Infante. He had been a soldier of genius, the embodiment of the will to resist, and a symbol round which the inhabitants of the south could rally. There was no one to take his place.

If the Dutch had committed themselves wholeheartedly to the offensive they might well have conquered Brabant while the French occupied Flanders. But despite the renewal of the French alliance in 1644 and a formal commitment to make no separate peace, the Dutch were increasingly lukewarm in their attitude towards the war. Part of the explanation for this lies in the fact that Frederick Henry was sixty in 1644, gout-ridden and more cautious than ever. But more important was the financial strain, which the Dutch could no longer bear, and the quarrel among the regents between those who wanted to press on with the war until Spain was completely defeated and those who favoured an early peace in order to leave a barrier between the United Provinces and an expanding and aggressive France. The war party would normally have been pro-French, but they were upset by Mazarin's insistence on a more tolerant attitude towards Roman Catholics, and were coming to recognise the danger of replacing one catholic power in the Netherlands by another. The consequent lack of enthusiasm was largely responsible for the collapse of the 'great design' to capture Antwerp in 1645, and in the following year Dutch suspicions were apparently confirmed when the Spaniards revealed Mazarin's offer to exchange Catalonia (now under French occupation) for the Netherlands. The peace party could no longer be restrained, and Dutch negotiators were despatched to Munster in 1646. In January 1648 they signed the Treaty of Munster, and agreed to stop fighting. In return, Philip IV abandoned his claim to the rebel provinces (including the territory they had acquired since 1609), and recognised them as 'free and sovereign states ... unto which ... he makes no pretensions, nor shall his heirs and successors'.

Frederick Henry, who had led the Dutch to victory, did not live to see the peace. By the time he died, in March 1647, his popularity was already on the wane, largely because of his dynastic ambitions. As elected Stadtholder of five out of the seven provinces, and also Admiral-General and Captain-General, he was clearly the most important man in the republic, and his 'creatures' were in the majority on the council of state. He could claim to embody the national interest in a way that the regents, with their commitment to provincial particularism, never could, and on this basis he might well have erected a monarchy. He already had his court at the Hague—French in language and manners, and far removed in appearance and moral tone from the regent-dominated Estates General—and was treated as a *de facto* sovereign by representatives of foreign powers. In 1641 he had the opportunity to link himself to a major royal house when Charles I of England put forward his daughter, Mary, as a bride for Frederick Henry's son, William. The Stadtholder was quick to accept this offer, and thereby became committed to supporting the House of Stuart in the English civil war. This was hardly in the interests of the Dutch people, who would be the first to suffer from any retaliatory action taken by the English Parliament against Dutch trade. The Estates General therefore adopted an ostentatiously neutral attitude towards the civil war—which, in fact, was a tacit acknowledgement of their sympathy with Parliament—and Holland instructed its deputies to keep a close watch upon the actions of the council of state and make sure it was not used simply as an instrument of the Stadtholder's dynastic policy.

Frederick Henry's commitment to the Stuart cause had repercussions beyond the immediate sphere of Anglo-Dutch relations. In 1644, for instance, when war broke out between Denmark and Sweden, the regents of Amsterdam seized the chance of ending Danish tolls on their ships passing through the Sound. An Amsterdam merchant, Louis de

Geer, who had already acquired a monopoly of trade in Swedish minerals, fitted out a Dutch fleet for service against Denmark, and the Estates of Holland insisted on open co-operation with the Swedes. Frederick Henry was reluctant to agree, since the English royalists were hoping for support from Denmark and were anxious to avoid any action which might prejudice this. As suspicion mounted between the Stadtholder and the regents, Holland threatened to cut off her subsidies for the army. This persuaded Frederick Henry to give way. The Dutch navy was sent to convoy a large merchant fleet through the Sound without paying Danish tolls, and in the subsequent Treaty of Christianople between the United Provinces and Denmark the dues were reduced to an acceptable level.

Regent suspicion of Frederick Henry and his ambitions was intensified when the Spaniards revealed that he had been party to the French proposal to exchange the Netherlands for Catalonia. An open quarrel was averted by Frederick Henry's death, but the dispute continued with his son, William II, who was determined to pursue the same dynastic policy. William, however, had the advantage of greater popular support, for the course of events in England had led to the overthrow of the Presbyterians and the triumph of the Independents, who were far less acceptable to hard-line Calvinist opinion in the United Provinces. The old alliance between the house of Orange and the religious radicals was now re-formed, and as public opinion swung behind the Stadtholder the regents outside Holland, exposed and apprehensive, began to follow. The Prince of Wales took up residence at The Hague, where he was welcomed by William, and the execution of Charles I evoked outbursts of public anger against the English republicans.

Holland, however, insisted on the need to preserve peace, and when the Estates General refused to recognise the republican regime in England, the province sent its own 'ambassadors'. Holland had also taken the lead in reducing the Dutch army, following the peace treaty of 1648, and had disbanded the regiments for which she was responsible. By doing so she was not simply easing the very real financial strain upon herself; she was also depriving the Stadtholder of his most powerful weapon. William protested, on the grounds that by taking unilateral action Holland was in effect breaking up the Union, and in June 1650 the Estates General authorised him to use whatever measures he thought necessary. William, following the example of Maurice in 1618, made a formal progress to each of the eighteen towns in Holland which sent representatives to the provincial Estates, hoping to win them over and thereby change the official attitude of the province.

He was given a far from friendly reception, however, and therefore decided on firmer measures. In July 1650 he arrested six members of the Holland Estates, imprisoned them in his castle at Loevenstein, and ordered an army under the command of his cousin, the Stadtholder of Friesland, to overawe Amsterdam. But the magistrates of Amsterdam refused to be overawed and made it clear that they would fight rather than surrender. William himself assumed the direction of operations and prepared to lay formal siege to the city. At this juncture, when civil war seemed certain, the magistrates at last gave way and agreed to conform to the wishes of the Estates General on condition that 'Loevensteiners' were released. This eased the immediate tension, but did nothing to solve the long-term problem, since William was engaged in secret negotiations with France for a renewal of the war against Spain. Holland was determined to oppose him on this, and another clash of wills seemed inevitable. It was averted only by a sudden stroke of fate. In November 1650 William II was struck down by smallpox and died at the age of twenty-four.

De Witt and the Regent Republic

The Orange party was now in disarray, for William's heir was his posthumous son, also named William. A newborn baby could hardly lead resistance against the regents of Holland, whose wealth was the lifeblood of the whole country, and for the next twenty years the United Provinces were a republic in fact as well as name, for the first time in their history. Since the Estates General was still dominated by supporters of the Orange party, Holland invited the other provinces to send their Estates to a 'Grand Assembly' at The Hague. This would be a truly sovereign body—unlike the Estates General, which was theoretically subordinate to the individual provinces—and Holland was clearly hoping to establish the republican regime on a new constitutional basis. In fact the Grand Assembly turned out to be just as divided and given to bickering as the Estates General, and simply reinforced the tendency towards particularism that seemed to be inseparable from regent rule. Yet although the Assembly broke up with no major achievements to its credit, Holland had secured acceptance of the principle that there should be no more quasi-monarchs. Only two provinces elected Stadtholders (from the Nassau branch of the Orange family); the other five remained formally republican. Nor was anyone appointed to take William's place as Captain-General; the army was to be without a single head and under the direct command of the separate provinces.

The regent republic was faced with an immediate challenge to its authority when worsening relations with England culminated in the outbreak of war in July 1652. Defeat at sea led to shortage of grain, food riots, and the revival of Orangist sentiment. But a new figure was emerging in the person of John de Witt, the son of a 'Loevensteiner', who was appointed 'Grand Pensionary'[1] of Holland in 1653. He was totally committed to the ideal of republican rule, and came to personify its virtues. It seemed as though, after a long period of Stadtholder pre-dominance, the days of Oldenbarneveld had come again. Negotiations had already opened with England, where Cromwell was now in power, and de Witt brought these to a conclusion by the Treaty of West-minster in May 1654. Cromwell had insisted on a guarantee that the House of Orange—the ally of the House of Stuart—should not be restored. The negotiators from Holland were only too happy to agree to this, but recognised that the landward provinces, with their more rural, aristocratic society, were unlikely to approve. They therefore made a secret declaration that Holland, at any rate, would never elect a member of the Orange family as Stadtholder and would oppose any move on the part of the Estates General to appoint anyone from the proscribed house as Captain-General. In a secret meeting the Estates of Holland formally accepted this 'Act of Seclusion' and although there was strong criticism from Orange supporters in the other provinces when the news leaked out, nobody was willing to upset the settlement for fear of reopening the war with England.

Meanwhile the struggle between France and Spain was still going on, and the Spaniards, profiting from French weakness at the time of the *Frondes*, had recaptured a number of key towns in Flanders. In 1657, however, the tide turned against them, for Cromwell allied with France and sent an English army to join in offensive operations along the Flanders coast. In 1657 Mardyck was taken and handed over to England (in accordance with the terms of the treaty of alliance). A year later Dunkirk was besieged, a Spanish relief force was beaten back at the Battle of the Dunes, and the town itself was captured and passed

---

[1] The office of 'Advocate' had been changed to that of 'Grand Pensionary' in 1618.

into English possession. France had now occupied a considerable part of western Flanders and seemed well set to conquer the rest. Dutch fears of a too powerful neighbour were rapidly reviving, and De Witt therefore welcomed Mazarin's proposal that after the expulsion of the Spaniards the southern Netherlands should be turned into an independent republic, a buffer state between France and the United Provinces. In fact the proposal came to nothing, for the political situation changed very rapidly with the death of Cromwell and the ending of the Franco–Spanish war. By the Peace of the Pyrenees in 1659 Spain ceded to France the province of Artois and a number of places in Flanders, Hainault and Luxembourg, but kept the rest. Although the Dutch had not been responsible for the terms of this agreement, in fact it suited them well.

The United Provinces were by now a major European power, but the great age of Dutch commerical supremacy was over. English and French competition, both in Europe and overseas, was cutting Dutch profits, and Dutch merchants were now more concerned with keeping what they had than with opening and exploiting new markets. This defensive attitude was reflected in their desire to avoid foreign entanglements, yet the government of the United Provinces could not remain completely neutral in European affairs, particularly when major Dutch commercial interests were involved. This was especially true of the Baltic region, since the north–south trade was still the foundation of Dutch wealth. With the emergence of Sweden as a great power, the Dutch switched their support to Denmark, for their consistent aim was to prevent domination of the Baltic by any one state. In 1658, therefore, when the Swedes launched a surprise attack upon Copenhagen and looked as though they might finally overwhelm Denmark (see p. 447), De Witt decided to intervene. A Dutch fleet was sent to drive off the Swedish navy and in May 1659 De Witt secured the co-operation of England and France in the 'Hague Concert' to restore peace in the Baltic and keep the Sound open. The instrument of this policy was the Dutch fleet, and its triumph was a demonstration of the power of the United Provinces.

De Witt was justifiably praised for the success of his foreign policy, but he knew that the Dutch were not strong enough to act alone. He would have been happy to maintain good relations with England as well as France, but the situation was complicated by the connection between the Stuarts—now restored in the person of Charles II—and the House of Orange. The Act of Seclusion had been repealed in 1660, partly as a friendly gesture and partly because it had been imposed on the Dutch at the dictate of a foreign power, but Holland remained opposed to all suggestions that William III should be restored to some of the offices traditionally associated with his family. Charles II, on the other hand, would have welcomed the end of the republican regime, and his ambassador at the Hague, Sir George Downing, was in close contact with the leaders of the Orange party. De Witt therefore turned to France, and in 1662 persuaded the Estates General to accept both a commercial agreement and a treaty of alliance with Louis XIV.

The value of this alliance was tested in 1665, when colonial disputes between England and the United Provinces, as well as the hostility engendered by Downing's activities, led to open war. The republican regime, built as it was on the defence of particularism, had neglected the army, and no troops were available to deal with an invasion of the eastern provinces by the Bishop of Munster. Here the intervention of France was decisive, and the bishop was forced to pull back. At sea, however, the French gave no support (despite a formal declaration of war on England in January 1666) and the Dutch were defeated off Lowestoft in 1665. In the following year, however, they took their revenge in the Four Days Battle fought in the Channel, and shortage of money, combined with the diminishing prospect of victory, persuaded Charles II to open peace negotiations in 1667. When these threatened to drag out indefinitely, De Witt ordered the Dutch fleet to carry out a most audacious operation. It sailed up the Medway, attacked the English fleet which was lying at anchor there, and towed away the flagship. The Peace of Breda followed almost immediately, in July 1667.

Charles II's reluctance to conclude negotiations had been due to the fact that war had reopened in the Spanish Netherlands. In September 1665 Philip IV of Spain had died, leaving his territories to his young son Charles, the child of his second marriage. In certain regions of the southern Netherlands, however, the prevailing custom of inheritance was that of 'devolution', whereby all the children of the first marriage took precedence over those of the second. Philip IV's daughter by his first wife was Maria Theresa, who had been married to Louis XIV of France in 1660. Louis now professed to believe that by right of devolution the whole of the southern Netherlands should pass to Maria Theresa—which meant, in effect, to himself and to France. When, in 1667, Spain refused to surrender the Netherlands which she had struggled so long and so hard to keep, Louis sent Turenne, with an army of 50,000 men, to take them by force.

The Dutch were alarmed by the French advance, and so were a number of influential English politicians, including Sir William Temple, who was a personal friend of De Witt. It was through Temple's mediation that in January 1668 England and the United Provinces made a formal agreement to act together to check French aggression. They were later joined by Sweden in what became known as the Triple Alliance. Louis had earlier suggested to the Dutch that they should divide the Netherlands with him, and what was now proposed was that France should be 'compensated' by certain limited territorial gains. If Louis refused to accept these terms then England and the United Provinces would compel him to return to the original frontier. This potentially dangerous alliance of protestant powers was a shock, as well as an affront, to Louis, but rather than cement it by hostile action he decided to make peace. He therefore agreed to the Treaty of Aix-la-Chapelle in 1668, by which the greater part of the southern Netherlands remained intact under Spanish rule.

De Witt and the regents who supported him had been given a breathing space, but opposition to them at home was increasing and found a focus in William III. In order to stave off demands that the prince should be restored to his family's traditional offices, De Witt persuaded Holland to make William a 'child of state' for whose upbringing the province would be responsible. But the basic attitude of suspicion towards the Orange family had not changed, and in 1667 the Estates of Holland passed the 'Perpetual Edict', reaffirming the terms of the Act of Seclusion. The other provinces accepted this by the Act of Harmony of 1670.

To outward appearances De Witt had strengthened his own position, but the republican regime was under increasing strain. The regents no longer had the intimate links with commercial life that had enabled them, with some justification, to identify their own interests with those of the country as a whole. Profits from foreign trade now had to be fought for, and many regents preferred to diversify their interests, investing in stocks and shares and land. They became much more of a closed caste, and resentment at their exclusiveness as well as envy of their enormous wealth added to their unpopularity. Their generally moderate attitude towards religion had never been acceptable to the hard-line Calvinists, nor could they look for support among the artisans and urban proletariat. As long as William was a minor, there was no one to challenge their authority, but in 1671 the Prince of Orange came of age. He had already shown himself to be a man of strong character and ambitions.

In the last resort the survival of the regent regime depended on the maintenance of peace, but this was something over which De Witt had no control. Peace could only be preserved if Louis XIV agreed to moderate his ambitions, but among the French king's close advisers were some who believed that the Dutch republic must be taught a lesson and deprived of the wealth that she took from the rest of Europe. The leading spokesman of this group was Colbert, who commented bitterly: 'as we have crushed Spain on land so we must crush Holland at sea. . . . So long as they are the masters of trade, their naval forces will continue to grow and to render them so powerful that they will be able to assume the role of arbiters of peace and war in Europe, and to set limits to the king's plans.' It was at Colbert's suggestion that in 1667 a punitive tariff was imposed upon Dutch imports, and when the Estates General riposted with duties on French goods, this was regarded as an unfriendly act. Louis in any case had not forgiven the Dutch for their 'betrayal' in allying with England in 1668. His diplomats had been hard at work isolating the United Provinces and preparing the way for war. This was declared, by France and England, in the spring of 1672.

The Dutch army, sapped by provincial particularism and the generally pacific attitude of the regents, was in no state to offer effective resistance. French troops swiftly occupied Utrecht and Gelderland, while in the east the Bishops of Munster and Cologne took possession of Overijjsel, Drente and part of Gröningen. It seemed as though the days of the United Provinces were numbered, and the Estates General called for peace. Holland, however, was determined to hold out, and De Witt had ordered the flooding of large tracts of land so as to slow up the French advance. But at this critical moment, when De Witt's leadership was more necessary than ever, he was attacked and badly wounded by a band of Orange supporters in June 1672.

The regents were by now openly defeatist and asked Louis for terms. But among the people as a whole the will to resist was mounting, and they called for William to take command. The regents—who found Louis' conditions unacceptably high, and feared rebellion if they did not appease public opinion—gave in to the clamour. In July 1672 Holland and Zeeland elected William as Stadtholder and the Estates General appointed him Captain-General and Admiral-General. Shortly afterwards De Witt resigned as Grand Pensionary, but William's supporters blamed him for all the misfortunes that had fallen upon their country, and on 20 August he was assassinated by an Orangist mob at The Hague.

In this abrupt and violent manner twenty-two years of regent republicanism came to an end. The monarchical element had once again asserted its pre-eminence in the political life of the United Provinces, and the embodiment of the state was now to be found in the Stadtholder Prince of Orange. Yet William's victory, though decisive, did not bring about any fundamental social changes. In the heady days of 1672, when the enemy were at the gates, there had been some revival of democratic feeling. Rioters called for the restoration of the people's rights in the election of magistrates, and if William had chosen to make himself the champion of the masses he might have swept away the foundations of existing Dutch society. But although he made use of popular support to gain power, William was no more a lover of democracy than the regents themselves. A section of the regents—those who had been excluded from office under De Witt—appreciated this and were willing to work with the new Stadtholder. The 'outs' now came 'in', but they were members of the same regent class, which held the Dutch economy in so firm a grip that no regime could hope to survive withouts its co-operation.

Although the uneasy combination of Stadtholder and regents, monarchy and republicanism, seemed to offer only the worst of both worlds, it was a true reflection of social and political realities in the Dutch state. The regents stood, as always, for the rights of the provinces, the preservation of their own commercial and financial interests, and moderation in religious matters. The Stadtholder, on the other hand, represented the people as a whole rather than any sectional interest, and embodied the sovereignty of the state as distinct from that of its constituent provinces. In an age when absolutism was the fashion, the Dutch system of government seemed cumbrous and ill-defined, but it had its roots deep in the past, in the old Duchy of Burgundy where the authority of the prince had coexisted with that of self-governing cities, and it worked. In the last resort this was all that mattered.

TWENTY-FOUR

The Baltic Powers in the Seventeenth Century

Sweden

Gustavus Adolphus was only a boy when he became ruler of Sweden in 1611, but he was well grounded in both the theory and practice of kingcraft. He had studied the classical writers; he had a good knowledge of history, theology and law; he was fluent in German and a number of other modern languages; and since the age of ten he had been a frequent attender at council meetings, so that he knew from first-hand experience how the state worked. Perhaps the most important among his many qualities was his natural aptitude for soldiering. He enjoyed leading an army and he had made a close study not only of mathematics, mechanics and optics, which were of crucial importance in the development and deployment of artillery, but also of military organisation and strategy. He had learnt much from the innovations pioneered by Maurice of Nassau, the hero of Dutch resistance, but he was himself an originator of genius when it came to fighting a battle.

There could be no question of an adventurous foreign policy in the opening years of Gustavus Adolphus's reign since the treasury was empty. Sweden had a population of less than a million, mainly engaged in agriculture, and the tax revenue was not sufficient for maintaining a large army. In any case the first call on the resources of the state was the ransom of Alvsborg (see p. 305), which was not accomplished until 1619, and only then by a heroic effort. The Dutch played a major part in this, for they provided large sums of money against the security of Swedish copper, which was sold to the rest of Europe through the market at Amsterdam. Without Swedish mineral wealth and Dutch mercantile and financial expertise, Gustavus Adolphus's reign would have taken a very different course, and he recognised this by encouraging Dutch investment and employing individual Dutchmen in the service of the crown. He and his chancellor, Oxenstierna, also used Dutch methods when they remodelled the machinery of Swedish government. Control over each of the major departments of state was vested in a council, or 'college', and by the time this collegiate system was fully operational it had given Sweden 'one of the best-developed, most efficient, and most modern administrations in Europe'.[1]

By 1621 Gustavus had sufficient money and men to be able to intervene in the European power struggle. He would have welcomed an alliance with the protestant states, not simply on religious grounds but also because he numbered among his greatest enemies the Roman Catholic King of Poland. But the German protestants were anxious to limit the area of conflict rather than encourage outside intervention, and they had no reason to believe that Gustavus's assistance would be of any great value. As for England and the United Provinces, they looked to Denmark rather than Sweden. Christian IV offered cheaper terms, he had an established reputation, and he brought no commitments with him. Gustavus, on the other hand, insisted that Poland was as much a threat to protestant Europe as to Sweden, and saw the two struggles—in northern and central Europe—as essentially one.

It was fear of Poland rather than the search for glory or profit that drove Gustavus to launch an attack on Polish Livonia in 1621. His aim was to secure Sweden against Polish invasion by gaining control of the southern shores of the Baltic; only at a later stage did the acquisition of territory become an end in itself. Gustavus's short campaign achieved its immediate objective, the capture of the major port of Riga. A few years later he renewed the war and rapidly occupied the greater part of Livonia. He was now free to take over another stretch of coast, and in 1626 he landed at Pillau, in ducal Prussia, and occupied Elbing. In August of that year, however, Tilly won the battle of Lutter and Habsburg power moved dangerously close to the Baltic (see p. 350). Wallenstein's siege of Stralsund in 1628 was an implied threat to Sweden, and Gustavus made his first move towards intervention in Germany by arranging for a permanent Swedish garrison to be stationed in that city. In 1629 he took advantage of Richelieu's mediation to accept the truce of Altmark with Poland, which left Sweden in possession of most of her gains, and in the following year he made his historic and fateful landing in Pomerania.

---

[1] Michael Roberts, *Gustavus Adolphus: a history of Sweden 1611–32*, Longman, 1953. Vol. i, 278.

By successfully intervening in the Thirty Years War, Gustavus turned Sweden into a major European power, and this was acknowledged in the considerable territorial gains she made by the Treaty of Westphalia, particularly the acquisition of western Pomerania. Gustavus had also established Swedish supremacy in the Baltic region by launching a lightning attack upon the Danes in 1643 and forcing them to accept the Peace of Bromsebro two years later. Denmark had to abandon the Norwegian provinces of Jamtland and Harjedalen, the islands of Gotland (off the east coast of Sweden) and Osel (guarding the entrance to the Gulf of Riga), and also the secularised bishoprics of Bremen and Verden. In addition she had to grant the Swedes freedom from tolls on trade passing through the Sound. Swedish success, however, aroused the jealousy of other powers. The Elector of Brandenburg, for instance, regarded all Pomerania as rightfully his, and was determined, in due course, to drive out the Swedish interlopers. Sweden had little cause to fear her enemies while she was rich and powerful, but it was in these years of triumph that the seeds of future anti-Swedish coalitions were sown.

The policies of Gustavus were continued by Chancellor Oxenstierna, but by the time he died in 1654 the period of Swedish expansion was drawing to a close. One reason for this was shortage of money. Despite Swedish mineral wealth and the dues levied on Baltic trade the royal revenue was insufficient to meet the cost of defence. Crown lands, rights and revenues were sold off to raise capital, but this merely diminished the royal income. The gap could be closed only by increased taxation, but since the nobles were exempt the main burden fell upon the three other estates represented in the *Riksdag*: the clergy, the burghers and the peasants. They protested with increasing vehemence against the way in which one section of the population was profiting at the expense of the crown and the rest. As one member asked, rhetorically in 1650, 'What honour, what glory, has Your Majesty by the subjection of foreign lands, when some few only are allowed to possess them? . . . or what have we gained beyond the seas if we lose our liberty at home?'

The alienation of royal estates had started early in the reign of Gustavus Adolphus, but the rate increased rapidly under his daughter Queen Christina, who was not content simply to sell her patrimony but made lavish gifts as well. She also distributed titles with an open hand, thereby unintentionally creating a new aristocracy and weakening the crown's traditional links with the old. Among the royal rights transferred to private hands were those of taxation, and many free peasants found that they were now obliged to pay their taxes not to the crown but to a noble landowner. They feared that, should they fall into debt, the landowner would foreclose and put an end to their liberty. This would also mean the end of the fourth estate, since only free peasants were eligible for membership of the *Riksdag*. Fearful for their own status and security, the non-noble classes therefore demanded a 'Reduction', i.e. a resumption by the crown of the lands, rights and revenues with which it had parted. Christina made use of this class hostility for her own ends. She had been converted to Roman Catholicism and was determined to abdicate in favour of her cousin Charles. There was opposition to her choice among the nobles, some of whom perhaps hoped to restore the elective monarchy and with it their own predominance in political as well as social life. Christina threatened them with a 'Reduction', and when the *Riksdag* met in 1650 encouraged members of the three lower houses to voice their anger. The nobles capitulated and accepted Charles, whereupon Christina dropped her support of the reform programme. The lesser Estates could not hope to press their campaign against the combined strength of monarch and nobles, so had to swallow their anger. But the problem of how to augment the crown's revenues remained acute, and Christina had merely postponed the day of reckoning.

Charles X, whose reign began with Christina's formal abdication in 1654, in fact accepted the principles of the reformers and, with the support of the *Riksdag*, began a partial 'Reduction'. But in 1655 he launched into war with Poland, and from then on reform had to give way to the overriding need to get enough money to keep the Swedish armies moving. Charles could, of course, have held aloof from the struggle for power in northern Europe, but with Poland under heavy Russian attack the situation in the eastern Baltic area was changing rapidly and in a way that might well be detrimental to Sweden. If Russia were successful she would almost certainly try to break Sweden's stranglehold on the Gulf of Riga and to free her trade from Swedish tolls. To prevent this Charles would have been prepared to aid Poland against the invader, but long-standing differences, including the Polish claim to the Swedish throne, stood in the way of agreement. He therefore decided to attack Poland himself, on the assumption that if this vast region were going to be dismembered it would be in Sweden's interest to take over a substantial portion. It was a fundamental weakness of Sweden's strategic position that if she kept out of all military entanglements she risked losing control of the south Baltic coast, thereby opening the way to a future invader; yet if she intervened she was dragged further and further into campaigns that sapped her strength.

In 1655 Charles delivered a two-pronged assault on Poland. From Pomerania one Swedish army moved through Brandenburg (without the Elector's permission) into western Poland, while another struck south from Riga. The campaign was highly successful. Warsaw and Cracow were both occupied, and by the end of the year the Swedes were already in control of the greater part of Poland and Lithuania. When the Poles attempted a counter-attack in the summer of 1656 they were beaten back by the Swedes in the battle of Warsaw. Yet in a sense the Swedes were too successful, for they encouraged their enemies to combine against them. The Elector of Brandenburg, who had made an alliance with Charles in January 1656 in return for Swedish recognition of his sovereignty over Prussia, now offered his aid to Poland on the same terms. The Emperor, who did not want another Gustavus Adolphus rampaging through the Empire, negotiated a truce between the Poles and Russians which left the latter free to attack Sweden's Baltic provinces. And in 1657 the Danes, who had long been thirsting for revenge, declared war, hoping to win a swift victory while the Swedes were still entangled in Poland.

Charles was more than equal to the situation. Abandoning the Polish threatre of war, he invaded Jutland and took his army across the ice to the island of Zeeland on which Copenhagen stands. The Danes thereupon sued for peace, and accepted the terms drawn up at Roskilde in 1658. Sweden now gained recognition of her sovereignty over the peninsular territories of Bohuslan, Halland, Blekinge and Skane, which gave her control of one side of the Sound and meant that she was no longer dependent on Danish goodwill for the free passage of her ships. When the Danes showed some unwillingness to ratify this treaty, Charles laid siege to Copenhagen. But the citizens put up a spirited defence while they waited for help. This was not long in coming, for the Dutch were appalled at the possibility that Sweden might close the Sound to their warships and levy tolls on their merchant vessels. By way of asserting their right to a naval presence in the Baltic they sent a squadron which wiped out the Swedish fleet and left Charles virtually marooned in Zeeland. This military initiative was followed up by a diplomatic one when the Dutch brought into being the Concert of the Hague and imposed a settlement. The Treaty of Copenhagen of

1660, which brought the war between Denmark and Sweden to an end, confirmed the terms of Roskilde, but only on the understanding that the Sound should remain an open waterway, not subject to closure or control by either of the two states which now bordered it.

In 1660 Charles X died and was succeeded by his four-year-old son, Charles XI. Power was formally vested in the hands of the queen mother, but in fact it was the aristocratic council, under the leadership of chancellor de la Gardie, which came to control policy. The opening of the new reign coincided with the restoration of peace to the troubled Baltic area, for Sweden, Poland and Brandenburg concluded the Treaty of Oliva, in 1660, which brought the First Northern War to an end. This treaty restored the *status quo* but removed one important cause of friction, in that the Polish king now formally renounced any claim to the Swedish throne. As for the struggle against Russia, this was ended by the Peace of Kardis in 1661, also on the basis of the *status quo*.

The oligarchs who now ruled Sweden were faced with a difficult problem. Sweden was apparently at the height of her power, the northern equivalent of Louis XIV's France, yet in fact she did not have the financial resources necessary to maintain her greatness. Charles X had hoped to take over the Sound tolls, but Dutch intervention had put an end to this and the problem of finding enough money to meet the demands made upon the Swedish government remained acute. There could be no question of a 'Reduction', now that the aristocrats were in power, for they were the main beneficiaries from the alienation of crown lands and revenues. The only alternative was foreign subsidies, but in accepting money from another power Sweden might well be dragged into a war from which she had nothing to gain. This in fact happened in the late-1670s. By a treaty of alliance made with France in 1672, Sweden, in return for French subsidies, was bound to give military assistance when called upon. The call came in 1675, when Brandenburg joined the coalition against Louis XIV (see p. 457). Swedish troops attacked Brandenburg from the rear, but in 1675 they were defeated by the Great Elector at Fehrbellin—a comparatively minor encounter, but one which shattered the myth of Swedish invincibility. Worse was to follow, for the Swedes were gradually forced out of the whole of western Pomerania, including Stettin (which fell in 1677), and from Bremen and Verden. They were saved from the humiliating consequences of defeat only by the success of their French ally, for it was Louis' intervention which secured the restoration of the *status quo* by the treaty of Fontainebleau in 1679.

Sweden's failure in the war of 1675–79 brought the aristocratic regime to an abrupt end. In 1672 Charles XI had come of age, and two years later he began freeing himself from the grip of his uncle, de la Gardie. Charles was not personally impressive, and observers commented unfavourably on his hot temper and stubbornness, but he was devoted to the army and his headquarters in the field became an alternative power centre to the aristocratic council. All the discontented elements in the state now looked to the king, and the demand for a 'Reduction' made itself heard with increasing insistence.

Charles recognised that a 'Reduction' would be the only way in which he could maintain a large standing army without being dependent upon foreign subsidies. He therefore embraced the cause of reform, not, as Christian had done, for the sake of short-term advantage, but because he saw in it the only effective solution to the problems of the Swedish state. In 1680, with his encouragement, the *Riksdag* declared that all major grants made by the crown should be resumed, and Charles set up a 'Great Commission' to investigate the actions of the magnates and compel them to repay to the state the profits they had made from it. A number of magnate families were ruined, and the social pre-eminence which had been one of the foundations of their power was undermined by the Order of Precedence of 1680, by which rank was in future to be based not upon birth but solely on service to the state. This attack on aristocratic privilege, in which the king worked in close co-operation with the *Riksdag*, could have opened the way to some sort of democratic rule, but in fact it led to royal absolutism. Now that the non-noble Estates had achieved their aim they were content to leave government in the king's hands. By the end of the reign Charles had acquired virtually unlimited control over foreign policy and taxation, and by the Declaration of Sovereignty of 1693 the *Riksdag* recognised him as 'an absolute sovereign king, whose commands are binding upon all, and who is responsible to no one on earth for his actions'.

The absolutist regime was remarkably efficient. The state's debts were eliminated, salaries were regularly paid, and the army was kept at a high pitch of readiness. Since Sweden could not afford foreign entanglements, Charles did his best to keep out of them, for, as he once observed, 'a war is soon begun, but as to its ending—that is in God's hands'. As the nature of Louis XIV's aggressive policies became increasingly obvious, Charles abandoned the French alliance and in 1681 concluded the Treaty of the Hague with the United Provinces. He could now be sure of Dutch naval assistance in the event of another attack by Denmark. War between the two Scandinavian states seemed likely in 1684, when Denmark drove out the Duke of Holstein–Gottorp from his lands, which were intermingled with those of the Danish crown along the border between Denmark and Germany. The dukes of Holstein–Gottorp were related by marriage to the kings of Sweden, and Charles, like his father, recognised the value of keeping open this back door into Denmark. But although he was prepared to use force as a last resort, he preferred diplomatic pressure, and this in the end was successful. In 1689 the Duke of Holstein–Gottorp was restored without the loss of any Swedish blood or treasure.

Although Sweden joined the League of Augsburg in 1686, she took no active part in the wars against Louis XIV, and as the allies became increasingly successful Charles trimmed his sails and veered towards France. It was in Sweden's interest to maintain a balance of power in Europe, and it was only by navigating skilfully between one bloc and another that she could hope to retain her freedom of action and preserve at least the outward appearance of a great power. Charles XI's success in executing these tricky manoeuvres was demonstrated shortly before his death in 1697, when Sweden was invited to act as mediator in the negotiations leading up to the Treaty of Ryswick. She had a great reputation and had managed to avoid putting it to the test. Only in the reign of Charles's son did it become clear to the rest of Europe that Sweden was no longer mistress of the Baltic, no longer predominant among the states which bordered it.

Denmark

Denmark was an elective monarchy, and every Danish king, at his accession, agreed to a 'capitulation' confirming the privileges of the nobles, who were, in effect, partners in his rule. Such a sharing of power did not make for efficient government, but Christian IV's attempts to increase his authority were not very effective. His intervention in the Thirty Years War, which might have given him the necessary prestige, led only to his defeat at Lutter in 1626 and the abandonment of his territorial ambitions in Germany. He was equally unsuccessful in his struggle against the rising power of Sweden, and in 1645 had to accept the harsh terms of the Peace of Bromsebro. When his long reign came to an end in 1648, therefore, the crown was still held in check by the nobility, and the new king, Frederick III, had to make the usual capitulations.

This situation was transformed by the war with Sweden of 1657–60. The Danes had hoped that while Sweden was fully committed in Poland they would be able to recover some of the territory they had lost at Bromsebro, but the Swedish response was much faster and fiercer than they had anticipated. In the closing stages of the war, with the Swedes besieging Copenhagen, the very existence of Denmark seemed at stake, and there was mounting criticism of the aristocracy, who were blamed for Danish defeats. The king took over the leadership of this opposition movement, and the clergy and burghers—who formed the lower house of the Danish Diet—rallied behind him. The nobles feared that the entire basis of their highly privileged social and economic position would be swept away, and rather than risk this they accepted the king's proposal that all reform measures should be consolidated into one—namely the establishment of royal absolutism. The other Estates gave their enthusiastic approval, and at a ceremony held in October 1660 the king was formally recognised as hereditary absolute sovereign.

In Sweden the creation of absolutism was accompanied by a resumption of crown lands and revenues, but in Denmark the reverse was the case. Crown lands, which were often poor in quality, were forced on unwilling creditors in satisfaction of their demands, and royal finances were reconstructed on the foundations of a new land tax and a Dutch-style excise. These brought in far more than the old crown lands had ever done, and the absolute monarchy therefore became solvent by the somewhat unorthodox method of parting with its major territorial assets. The old aristocratic council was replaced by a council of state, appointed by and responsible to the king, and a new nobility gradually emerged, based upon service to the state as well as landholding. This was of no benefit to the peasants, who were hard hit by heavy taxation and did not have the capital resources available to big landowners. While the establishment of absolutism in Sweden was a guarantee of security for the free peasants, in Denmark they virtually disappeared.

The dominant figure in the new regime was Frederick III's brother-in-law, Hannibal Sehested, who was appointed treasurer of the kingdom. He hoped to cut expenditure on the army by bringing about a reconciliation with Sweden, and for some years he tried to resolve the outstanding differences between the two states. But this policy had only limited success, and the accession of Christian V in 1670 marked a return to the more traditional posture of enmity towards Sweden. Following the Swedish defeat at Fehrbellin in 1675, Christian arrested the Duke of Holstein–Gottorp, whose lands straddled the frontier region between Denmark and Germany, and forced him to abandon not simply his Swedish alliance but also any claims to be an independent ruler. In the following year the Danes invaded Skane, on the southern end of the Swedish peninsula, but were beaten back in a savage battle at Lund. It was at this point that Louis XIV intervened and imposed the Peace of Fontainebleau by which the *status quo* was restored (see p. 457). Despite her victories Denmark had gained nothing.

Peace was followed by another attempt to reach an understanding with Sweden, but it broke down on the question of Holstein–Gottorp, since neither side was prepared to give up its ambitions in this strategically important region. Denmark therefore looked for allies and as Sweden moved towards the Dutch she came to terms with the French, in 1682. It was with the assurance of French support that in 1682 Christian V invaded Holstein–Gottorp, drove out its ruler and incorporated the ducal lands into the possessions of the Danish crown. But Louis XIV, despite his great power, could no longer intervene directly in northern Germany. He relied upon Brandenburg to do this for him, and when the Great Elector abandoned the French alliance Denmark was in fact isolated. The extent to which her power had declined in comparison with that of Sweden was symbolised by the restoration of the Duke of Holstein–Gottorp to all his territories. Denmark had been forcibly reminded of one of the cardinal truths about her situation: that without effective allies she was at the mercy of her stronger neighbour.

Brandenburg–Prussia

Brandenburg was one of the largest of the German princely states, and its ruler was one of the seven Electors, yet until the second half of the seventeenth century it was not of major importance. Its soil was poor (mainly sand and swamps), its towns were in decay, and its political and social life was dominated by the aristocracy. The Electors of Brandenburg, right up to the Thirty Years War, were crippled by shortage of money and at the mercy of their noble-dominated Estates. Their salvation came not through war but through marriage, for in the late sixteenth century John Sigismund, heir to the then Elector, married the eldest daughter of the Duke of Prussia, who also happened to be the niece and residuary legatee of the last Duke of Cleve–Julich. It had long been agreed that if the Prussian line of the Hohenzollern family were to die out, the territory would revert to the senior, Brandenburg branch, and John Sigismund's marriage merely reinforced his claims. In 1618, on the death of the second and last Duke of Prussia, his title and estates passed to John Sigismund, who held them as a fief of the crown of Poland. This union between Brandenburg and Prussia was the germ of future greatness.

Cleve–Julich was a more disputed inheritance, but by the Xanten agreement of 1614 John Sigismund (who had shocked his Lutheran Brandenburg subjects by embracing Calvinism) gained possession of the mainly protestant regions of Cleve, Mark and Ravensburg. The possibility of further territorial expansion for Brandenburg opened up in 1637, when the last Duke of Pomerania died. This duchy, like Prussia, had been in the hands of a junior branch of the Hohenzollerns, and Brandenburg now claimed its reversion. She had to reckon with *de facto* Swedish occupation, however, and by the Treaty of Westphalia in 1648 Sweden was confirmed in her possession of the western (and richer) section of Pomerania. Brandenburg was compensated with possession of the secularised bishoprics of Kammin (in the middle of eastern Pomerania), Minden and Halberstadt. The Elector now held more territory in Germany than any other prince except the Emperor himself.

John Sigismund, who became Elector in 1608, ruled for eleven years, and on his death in 1619 was succeeded by his son, George William. This unfortunate prince had to concentrate on preserving his inheritance from the various armies which roamed over northern Germany in the course of the Thirty Years War, and his efforts to secure Pomerania only opened the way to Swedish invasion of his electorate. By 1637 the Swedes were in possession of the greater part of Brandenburg, and had so wasted it that the Elector could no longer sustain himself and his household. He had to move to Königsberg in Prussia, and it was there that he died in 1640. He left as heir his twenty-year-old son Frederick William, a heavily built, muscular man, with a large hooked nose and piercing blue eyes; but although the new Elector was nominal ruler over some half dozen states, in fact he inherited little more than his titles.

Even within Brandenburg itself the Elector's authority was restricted

George William's chief minister had been the Rhinelander, Count Schwarzenberg, who had little patience with the Brandenburg nobility or respect for the privileges of the Estates which they dominated. Following the example of the Swedish army of occupation, he collected taxes without waiting for authorisation by the Estates, and when the latter protested, in 1636, he simply dismissed them. The nobles looked to Frederick William to change this situation, and were in no mood for compromise. In particular they wanted to see the end of the war council, set up by Schwarzenberg in 1630 to supersede the old privy council on which they were strongly represented. Frederick William, who had been on bad terms with his father, had no great desire to keep his father's minister, but Schwarzenberg was a major prop of the electoral regime and his dismissal might well have led to the collapse of the whole edifice. Fortunately for Frederick William the problem was solved for him by Schwarzenberg's death in 1641. The Elector now became his own chief minister, and made peace with the nobles by abolishing the war council, reviving the privy council, and restoring control over taxation to the Estates.

Frederick William had much in common with the nobles, of whose way of life he approved, and whom he regarded as the backbone of his state. Yet there was a fundamental divergence of interests in that the nobles desired nothing so much as peace and total demobilisation, so that they could restore their ravaged estates, produce more grain for export, and so increase their income, while the Elector had interests that extended beyond the boundaries of Brandenburg and wanted at least the nucleus of a standing army. In 1652 he summoned a full Diet, instead of the usual representative body, and demanded the grant of a permanent excise, to be paid by all his subjects, noble and non-noble, and to be used for the maintenance of an army. The Diet refused, and Frederick William therefore dismissed the greater part of them and tried his luck with the smaller representative body. This was not quite so intractable. The nobles refused to accept the excise, but in return for confirmation of their privileges—which meant, in effect, the imposition of serfdom upon the peasantry—they granted a substantial subsidy. This was not meant to be a permanent tax, but it did give the Elector enough to raise a small army, and once this had been called into existence it became a political fact of life with which the Estates had to reckon.

The new army was soon blooded, for in 1655 Swedish forces moved through Brandenburg to attack Poland, and early in the following year they virtually forced the Elector to make a treaty of alliance. His troops now joined the victorious Swedes and shared the honours of the great victory outside Warsaw in July 1656. Frederick William's reward came in November of that year, when the King of Sweden formally recognised him as sovereign independent ruler of the duchy of Prussia. But with the entry of Denmark into the war, and the shift of Swedish attention from Germany to the Jutland pensinula, Frederick William changed sides and agreed to support the Poles. They in turn recognised his sovereignty in Prussia, and this was confirmed by both Sweden and Poland in the Treaty of Oliva, which brought the first Northern War to an end in 1660.

The inhabitants of Prussia, however, were not so eager to recognise their duke as sovereign. They had little love for Poland, but it was to their advantage to have a right of appeal to his feudal overlord against the often arbitrary actions of the Elector-Duke. Prussia had suffered heavily from Swedish occupation during the recent war, and following the peace there was a widespread refusal to pay taxes. In 1661 this flared into open revolt in Königsberg, the major city of Prussia, where a radical lawyer, Hieronymous Roth, put himself at the head of a popular movement whose demands included respect for the constitution and an end to arbitrary taxation. The rising was not put down until Frederick William himself arrived at the head of an army and surrounded the rebellious city. Roth surrendered and spent the rest of his days in a Brandenburg prison. Following this demonstration of ducal power the Prussian Estates voted a three-year excise, but only in return for a promise that they would be regularly summoned. The struggle between the Estates and their ruler continued throughout Frederick William's reign, yet the odds were heavily stacked in his favour, for he had an army behind him while they did not. Konigsberg remained a major centre of resistance until its independence was crushed by a military occupation in 1674. As for the Estates, their authority was eroded by the war council, which was set up in 1669 and gradually took over the administration of taxation.

The Elector was equally triumphant in Brandenburg, where, despite opposition from the Estates, an excise was introduced in the years following 1667. By 1682 this was levied on all towns, and when the municipal authorities proved ineffective or half-hearted, their place was taken by government agents. In this way urban independence was brought to an end, and a sharp line was drawn between the towns, whose gates were guarded by the hated excise collectors, and the countryside, with its great estates under the control of noble land-owners exempt from taxation. In 1680 the war council, which had been allowed to lapse, was revived, and, as in Prussia, gradually extended its scope until it had replaced both the privy council and the Estates so far as fiscal administration was concerned. The war council also assumed responsibility for the encouragement of trade and industry, and after 1685 it took a leading part in settling immigrant Huguenots in the towns and countryside of Brandenburg, where their skills were not only of intrinsic value but ultimately of great profit to the state. The war council was staffed by civilians—much to the chagrin of the generals—but the very fact that the economy of the state was geared to the needs of the army meant that military considerations outweighed all others. The state was the army, the army the state, and the consequences of this—not only for Brandenburg–Prussia but for the rest of Europe—were to become increasingly apparent.

When Frederick William succeeded his father in 1640, he had a force of some 4,500 mercenaries available to him, but during the Swedish–Polish war of 1655–60 the army increased in size until it numbered 20,000 men. In the 1670s, when Brandenburg was committed to the anti-French alliance, Dutch subsidies made it possible to expand the army to more than 45,000, and even though this number declined with the coming of peace, it never dropped below 30,000. The maintenance of such a large force was an enormous strain upon the Elector's territories, particularly Brandenburg itself, which provided the greater part of the revenue from taxation. Yet without this army Brandenburg would not have been a state to reckon with, nor would the Elector's authority have been so firmly established. The nobles in both Brandenburg and Prussia had fought tenaciously to preserve their political privileges, but they eventually abandoned these and acquiesced in absolutism because the rewards it offered were so great. The Elector guaranteed their social and economic position and gave them the opportunity of profitable service in either the army or the civil administration. In this way the aristocracy became committed to the absolutist military state.

Despite the considerable sums raised by taxation, Frederick William could not do without foreign subsidies, and these limited his freedom of action in much the same way as they did that of Sweden. In 1672 he joined the coalition against Louis XIV by allying with the United Provinces, who agreed to pay half the costs of his army. A Brandenburg force based on Cleve undertook operations against the French, but these were singularly unsuccessful and in the summer of 1673 Frederick William had to make peace. In the following year, however, he again committed himself to the anti-French alliance and was preparing to reopen his campaign along the Rhine when the Swedes, in fulfilment of their treaty obligations to Louis XIV, invaded Brandenburg. The Elector was bitter in his condemnation of this stab in the back. 'I am resolved to revenge myself on the Swedes', he declared. 'Now that they have left me no more than my life, I shall persist, come what may, in ridding myself of them.' He was as good as his word. In 1675 he defeated them at Fehrbellin in an engagement that won him the unofficial title of 'the Great Elector', and he went on to drive them out of Pomerania altogether. When France made peace with her enemies at Nymegen, however, she insisted on the restoration of Swedish Pomerania. Frederick William, having achieved his lifelong ambition of uniting the whole duchy under his rule, refused to accept such an unpalatable decision. Louis XIV, only too pleased to demonstrate the value of a French alliance to those who embraced it, therefore sent an army into Germany. As it moved towards Berlin, Frederick William, aware that he could not expect help from any quarter, capitulated. Electoral troops were withdrawn from western Pomerania, and the great port of Stettin, which he had taken only after a long siege, was returned to the Swedes.

Disillusioned and embittered by what he regarded as an act of betrayal on the part of his allies, Frederick William made an abrupt change of course and in 1679 allied with France. He had hopes of replacing Sweden as Louis XIV's major client in the north and he was granted a substantial French subsidy. Yet the alliance brought him little else. France would not abandon Sweden, nor would she support Frederick William's claims to Pomerania. The Great Elector also became alarmed by the implications of Louis XIV's religious policy. As Calvinist ruler of a mainly Lutheran state he was conscious of the political advantages of toleration, and when Louis formally revoked the Edict of Nantes, Frederick William issued the Potsdam Declaration, inviting Huguenot refugees to settle in his territories. In the same year he made a defensive alliance with the United Provinces, and he followed this up, in 1686, by coming to terms with the Emperor. Brandenburg was clearly moving towards the anti-French coalition, but Frederick William died in May 1688, a few months before the actual outbreak of war.

The Great Elector's achievement was considerable, for he inherited a ramshackle collection of territories, mostly under enemy occupation, and seemed doomed to play the part of an insignificant pawn in the European power game. Yet by seizing his opportunities and selling his alliance first to one side and then the other, he made himself a figure of consequence among the rulers of Europe. At the same time he established his authority within Brandenburg–Prussia by concentrating his limited resources of men and money upon the army and the civil administration, thereby circumventing the older power centres, such as the Estates and the nobility. By the end of his reign he could have boasted, with far more justification than Louis XIV, that in Brandenburg–Prussia the Elector *was* the state.

Poland

Poland–Lithuania had a population of some ten millions in the seventeenth century, and was one of the richest agricultural regions in Europe. Yet her size and wealth were not reflected in her power, since they could not be adequately focused by the elective monarchy. The kings of Poland had an unenviable task, for they were at the mercy of the nobles who dominated the Diet, their military and financial resources were strictly limited, and their subjects were divided in language and religion. The wealth and the weakness of Poland made her a prey to aggressive neighbours, and the task of defending the enormously long frontiers was too much for any ruler, however talented. The astonishing fact about Poland–Lithuania is not that it declined but that it survived at all.

A major change in the relative position of Poland was brought about by the emergence of Russia as a great power, but this did not happen until the second half of the seventeenth century. In the opening decades of the century it was Poland which seemed all set to dominate Russia, and by the Truce of Deulino, which brought the Russo–Polish war to an end in 1618, the Tsar had to abandon a large area on his western frontier including Smolensk, Starodub, Novgorod–Seversk and Chernigov. Although, in the 1630s, the Russians took advantage of Poland's troubles on her southern borders to try and recapture this region they were unsuccessful, and the Peace of Polyanov of 1634 confirmed Polish sovereignty over the disputed territory.

In the south, Poland came up against the Turks, but both sides were anxious to avoid open war and preferred to conduct their hostilities through intermediaries. In the case of the Turks these were the Crimean Tatars, who raided deep into Poland and Russia. The Poles made use of the Cossacks, who occupied the area on either side of the Dnieper River, maintained a quasi-autonomous position, and looked with suspicion not only on the Turks but also on the Polish landowners who were colonising the region. They were prepared to defend Poland against the Turks, but only as long as this was to their advantage. Further west the Poles had not given up hope of reasserting their control over Moldavia and Wallachia, Christian states under the rule of *Voivodes* who were in fact vassals of the Sultan, and despite the Peace of Buzsa of 1617, by which Poland promised not to interfere in Moldavian affairs, skirmishes continued. This led to open war in 1620. The Polish magnates were, as always, reluctant to vote sufficient supplies for a royal army that they feared might later be used against them, but they were shaken out of their complacency by the big Turkish victory at Jassy in 1620. Troops were raised, the Turkish advance was stemmed, and in 1621 the *status quo* was restored by the Truce of Chotim. The uneasy peace that ensued was frequently fractured by Tatar raids and occasionally open Turkish intervention, but the Turks had their own troubles and were content simply to maintain their overlordship in this troubled area.

In some ways the Cossacks were more of a threat to Poland than were the Turks or Tatars. The Cossacks were the descendants of people who had fled from Russia and Poland in order to find freedom, and they had hopes of eventually creating an independent state in the Ukraine. They distrusted the Polish landowners who were colonising the Dnieper region, particularly since these were Roman Catholics while they were staunch adherents of the Orthodox faith. Their suspicion led to open rebellion in 1636–38, but this was suppressed by the Polish government and the process of colonisation continued. Ten years later, in 1648, a far more serious revolt broke out. This was led by Bogdan Chelmintsky, who became a great popular hero and succeeded in establishing an independent Cossack Ukraine. John Casimir, who had been elected to the Polish throne in 1648 on the death of his brother, Ladislaw IV, simply did not have the resources to suppress this rising. In 1649 he signed a peace treaty with the Cossacks, accepting most of their demands, but he intended this only as a breathing-space while he marshalled Polish strength. Fighting continued and Chelmintsky called on the Tsar to protect the new state. Russian armies now invaded Poland and occupied the greater part of the country. This was the signal for Sweden to attack, and in 1655 John Casimir had to flee from his war-ravaged kingdom and take refuge in Habsburg Silesia. Chelmintsky, who had opened the way to this disastrous reversal of Polish fortunes, remained at the head of the independent Ukrainian state until his death in 1657, but Cossack unity did not long survive him. Civil war broke out among the various factions and by calling in foreign aid they effectively put an end to their own independence.

On the northern frontier the main threat to Poland came from Sweden. By 1625 Gustavus Adolphus had conquered Livonia, and in the Truce of Altmark of 1629 Poland had to recognise Swedish sovereignty in this area. Following the death in 1632 of both Gustavus Adolphus and King Sigismund of Poland, there was a move towards settling outstanding differences between the two powers. This culminated in the twenty-year Truce of Stuhmsdorf, signed in 1635, in which Poland—now ruled by Sigismund's son, Ladislaw IV—confirmed her acceptance of Swedish sovereignty over Livonia. The signing of a treaty could not, however, eradicate the basic enmity between Sweden and Poland. Sweden was, among other things, the protestant champion and declared enemy of the Habsburgs, whereas Poland was catholic, and her king, Ladislaw, was not simply an ally of the Emperor but also his son-in-law. It was the fundamental clash of interests which led to renewed war with Sweden in 1655 and the near-dissolution of the Polish state. Only the intervention of the major European powers made possible the restoration of the *status quo* by the Peace of Oliva in 1660, and Poland managed to escape with nothing more damaging than a formal recognition of what had long been an established fact—namely the sovereign independence of ducal Prussia.

Ladislaw IV, who ruled from 1632 to 1648, tried among other things to solve the problems arising out of the diversity of religious beliefs among his subjects. Except in the German-speaking areas protestantism was on the decline, and had never really taken a firm hold on the mass of the population. The Orthodox, however, were more strongly entrenched. In 1596 the leaders of the Orthodox Church in Poland had agreed to unite with the Roman Catholics, but they were not followed by all their flock. The Cossacks, in particular, clung to Orthodox purity, and an underground hierarchy was soon established to replace the 'Uniates', who were accused of betraying the sacred cause. Ladislaw, who was personally tolerant and hoped to see the reunion of Christendom, recognised this unofficial hierarchy in 1633 and granted full freedom of worship to the adherents of Orthodoxy. He also summoned a meeting of representatives of all the main religious groups to a conference at Thorn (Torun) in 1644, hoping to establish some sort of common ground between the warring parties. In this, however, he was disappointed, for religious passions were intense and the conference served merely to show how wide a gap separated one branch of the Christian faith from another.

Ladislaw's brother, John Casimir, who ruled from 1648 to 1668, was more concerned with constitutional than religious problems—though as a former Jesuit and a cardinal his own religious commitment was clear. In particular he hoped to gain acceptance of the principle that the heir to the throne should be nominated during the reigning monarch's lifetime. This would make possible a smooth succession instead of the usual period of interregnum that weakened and endangered the Polish state. It would also put an end to the degrading spectacle of the election Diets, in which foreign powers distributed largesse and threats on behalf of their favoured candidates. In this aim, however, John Casimir was not successful, for the Polish nobles feared that any reform would open the way to the establishment of a hereditary monarchy and ultimately absolutism. It was this same insistence on the preservation of their own 'liberties' even to the detriment of the security of the kingdom, that established the right of any member of the Diet to bring a session to an end. The use of this *Liberum Veto* became increasingly frequent in the second half of the seventeenth century and made effective government all but impossible. The weakness of the Polish crown was strikingly demonstrated in 1663, when John Casimir attempted to regain control over the Ukrainian Cossacks and their Russian protectors. He received so little co-operation from the nobles that in 1667 he was compelled to accept the Truce of Andrusovo, by which Poland abandoned all the gains she had made in 1618 and returned Smolensk, Starodub, Novgorod–Seversk and Chernigov to Russian ownership.

John Casimir's disillusionment with the Polish nobles led him to abdicate in 1668. In the ensuing election the French and Habsburgs each pushed their own candidate, but the Diet defied tradition by choosing one of its own number, Michael Wisnwiecki. King Michael was an undistinguished figure, however, and although he was a Polish magnate he could get no more co-operation from his fellow nobles than the Vasa kings had done. He was faced with the resurgence of trouble in the Ukraine, for the Cossacks had called on the Sultan for aid, and the Turks struck north from Moldavia towards Lvov (see p. 526). The

Poles had a good general in the person of John Sobieski, but he was hindered by the Diet's unwillingness to provide sufficient men or money. By 1672 King Michael had come to the conclusion that further resistance was pointless, and in that year he accepted the treaty of Bucac, which bound Poland to cede Podolia (the large area between the Dnieper and Dniester rivers) and to acknowledge the Sultan as over-lord of the Ukrainian Cossacks. A 'Patriot Party' in the Diet was opposed to this humiliating treaty and refused to allow its ratification. Their hero was Sobieski, and as bitterness between them and the supporters of Michael increased, civil war seemed inevitable. It was only averted by the sudden death of Michael in 1673, leaving the Polish throne once again vacant.

On the day after Michael's death, Sobieski won a great victory over the Turks at Chotim, and such was his prestige that when the Diet assembled to elect a new sovereign, Sobieski was the man they chose. The new king made peace with the Turks in 1679 on terms that were only marginally more favourable than those secured by Michael, but a few years later he allied with the Emperor in a crusade against the common enemy and played a vital part in defeating the Turkish army outside Vienna in September 1683. He tried to follow up his success by recovering Podolia and conquering Moldavia and Wallachia, but Turkish resistance stiffened and the Diet, as usual, was tardy in voting supplies. This was due partly to traditional reluctance to pay for royal policy, but also to increasing suspicion about Sobieski's dynastic ambitions. In fact he hoped to gain Moldavia for his own family, thereby leaving his heir strategically well placed to claim the Polish throne. These ambitions came to nothing because Moldavia could not be conquered, and the Diet proved to be unmanageable as more and more sessions were brought to a premature close by the use of the *Liberum Veto*. Although Sobieski had made a great name for himself by the time he died in 1696, he had not succeeded in strengthening the authority of the Polish crown, nor had he given Poland security on her frontiers. Failing any sense of national commitment on the part of the Polish nobles, it seemed unlikely that any of his successors would be able to do better.

Russia

With the election of Michael Romanov as Tsar in 1613 the 'Time of Troubles' drew to a close and Russia set out along the road of recovery.

Her frontiers were defined by the Peace of Stolbovo with Sweden in 1617, and the Truce of Deulino with Poland in the following year. At Stolbovo the Swedes returned Novgorod but held on to Ingria, thereby denying Russia any outlet to the Baltic. At Deulino the Russians had to part with a long strip of territory running from Smolensk in the north to Chernigov in the south. In 1633, following the death of Sigismund of Poland, the Russians tried to recapture this huge area, and in fact occupied most if it with the exception of Smolensk. But the Poles rallied, the Crimean Tatars attacked from the south, and the rate of desertion from the Russian armies increased at an alarming rate. In 1634, therefore, the terms of Deulino were again confirmed, but with the significant addition that Michael was now formally recognised by the Poles as lawful ruler of Russia.

For defence against the Turks and Tatars the Russian government looked to the semi-independent refugee communities of Cossacks, settled along the Lower Don. But by supporting and encouraging the Cossacks, the Russians risked being drawn into open war with the Turks. This nearly happened in 1637, when the Cossacks seized the Turkish fortress of Azov and offered it to the Tsar. Michael recognised the strategic importance of Azov, but he also knew that Russia was not ready for war. With the agreement of the *Zemski Sobor* he therefore declined the offer and in 1642 persuaded the Cossacks to return the fortress to the Sultan.

In the reign of Michael's son, Alexis (1645–76), the Russian government was again in difficulties with the Cossacks, but this time there was a direct confrontation. The leader of the Don Cossacks, Stenka Razin, made a plundering expedition into the Persian territories on the Caspian, and captured Astrakhan in 1670. He then turned north, towards Russia proper, and what had started out as a raid turned into a rebellion. Razin declared war on landlords and officials, on all those whose arbitrariness and brutality were corrupting Russian society, and thousands of the oppressed flocked to join him. For a time it looked as though Razin might overthrow the Tsarist regime, but he was captured and killed in 1671 and the revolt collapsed. Nevertheless it had shown how much resentment lay scarcely concealed beneath the surface of Russian life.

The causes of this resentment were to be found not simply in the wide gulf between the landowners on the one hand and the peasants, mainly serfs, on the other. There was also the physical problem of ruling such an immense area, poorly provided with communications.

Confronted with the inertia or deliberate opposition of the localities, the central government would impose its will by brute force, and its arbitrary and often violent actions were repeated on a lower scale at all levels of Russian life. Another source of resentment was the tension between those who clung to old customs, beliefs and attitudes, particularly in religious matters, and the advocates of change. The nature of Russian society made compromise and coexistence all but impossible, and here again violence bred violence.

After the accession of Tsar Alexis in 1645, an attempt was made to remove some of the worst features of despotic rule by drawing up a code of law, and the *Zemski Sobor* formally approved this in 1649. Composed of a thousand separate articles, based on custom and royal decrees, it brought order out of chaos, but only at the cost of further rigidifying Russian society and completing the process of subordinating the individual to the state.

Among the provisions of the new Code was one which forbade the Church to acquire any more land. There was much to be said for this inhibition, since the Church was suffering from affluence rather than poverty. Complaints were frequent about the poor moral and intellectual condition of the Orthodox clergy, but reform projects had made little progress. In 1618 Tsar Michael's father, Filaret, returned from captivity in Poland and was appointed patriarch. For the next fifteen years, until his death in 1633, he was the virtual ruler of the Russian state as well as Church, but he was no reformer. Faced with the challenge from reviving Roman Catholicism in the west, he turned towards the east, stressed the historic links of the Russian church with Byzantium, and gloried in its unique traditions.

This nationalist attitude towards religion aroused widespread support among the masses, but in the upper social levels, particularly at court, there were those who realised that many of the traditions of the Russian church were in fact corruptions of the Greek originals, and that the conservatives' opposition to change was holding up spiritual regeneration. These advocates of reform looked to Kiev, where the Orthodox church, in the front line of defence against Polish catholicism, had purified itself and returned to the uncorrupted texts and practices of Greek Orthodoxy. They had the support of Tsar Alexis, who chose a famous Kiev preacher to be tutor to his children, and also of Nikon, who was appointed patriarch in 1652. The 'Old Believers', who were the embodiment of conservatism in every sphere, protested against changes imposed by Nikon, but he was a man of forceful character who brooked no opposition to his rule. The Old Believers were expelled from the Church and ruthlessly persecuted. Many of them fled to the Cossack refugee communities in the south, and added religious grievances to the already long Cossack list of charges against the Tsarist regime.

Nikon at first worked closely with the Tsar, but he came to resent the way in which the Church in Russia was surbordinated to the state. This had been demonstrated by the setting-up of a 'Monasteries Office', staffed by laymen and given responsibility for the administration of the Church and its finances. Nikon wanted to free the Russian church from this stranglehold at the same time as he reformed it, and from 1654 he became openly critical of the Tsar and asserted the superiority of the spiritual over the secular. This high-sounding claim had been acceptable when it was made by Filaret, who was the father of the Tsar, but from Nikon it seemed like a challenge to royal authority, and Alexis eventually resolved to deal with it. In 1666, therefore, he summoned an oecumenical council, including the patriarchs of Alexandria and Antioch, which formally deposed Nikon and confirmed the Tsar's supremacy over the Russian Church.

Nikon's defeat did not mean the end of the reform movement. This went ahead not only in the Church but also in the state, for there was increasing consciousness of the fact that western European countries were developing their economies at a very rapid rate, and that if Russia were to hold her place among the major powers she also would have to modernise. The task was enormous, but several important steps had already been taken. In 1628, for instance, an attempt had been made to carry out a census of the population as a prelude to tax reform, and the 1630s saw the introduction of foreign mercenaries and advisers to train the Tsar's army. Alexis continued the practice of sending Russians abroad to study advanced techniques; and Dutch, English and German artisans were encouraged to settle in the Tsar's dominions, where they could not only practise their crafts but also teach them to the Russians.

The modernisation of Russia was clearly a long-term task and one that needed peace. For this reason both Michael and Alexis did their best to keep out of military adventures, but there were some situations that they could not ignore. One of these occurred in 1653, when the leader of the Ukrainian Cossacks, Chelmintsky, appealed to the Tsar for protection. Alexis summoned a *Zemski Sobor* (the last of such assemblies to play more than a formal part in government) which recommended that he should take the Cossacks under his protection. In fact he had little choice, for failing the Tsar the Cossacks would turn to the Sultan, and the Turks were already enough of a threat to Russia's southern borders. In 1654, therefore, Russian troops advanced into Poland and captured Smolensk. This expansion of the western frontier was confirmed by the Truce of Andrusovo in 1667, by which Russia kept Smolensk and also that part of the Ukraine which lay to the east of the Dnieper. The west bank, with the exception of Kiev, was to go to Poland. In this way the once independent Cossack state of the Ukraine was partitioned between two of its major adversaries, but there was a third party—the Turks—which was not content simply to accept this *fait accompli*. The collapse of Polish resistance in the 1670s led to the Turkish occupation of Podolia, and Russian troops were once more in action on the west bank of the Dnieper. In 1672 they took the Cossack capital of Chigirin, but the Turks fought back and four years later recaptured it. The sultan was no longer strong enough, however, to maintain a puppet Cossack state, however much he would have liked to do so. By the Treaty of Adrianople of 1682 both sides agreed to accept the Dnieper as the frontier between them (with the exception of Kiev) and the fighting came to an end.

Tsar Alexis died in 1676 and was succeeded by his eldest son, Theodore (Fedor), who reigned until 1682. By the time Theodore died Russia had more or less fully recovered from the 'Time of Troubles' and was beginning to assert herself as a major power. She still had to contend with the Swedes in the Baltic, the Poles in the west and the Turks in the south, and had only just embarked upon the task of domestic reform. But there were obvious signs of change, both at home and abroad, and after nearly a century of inactivity the Russian colossus was beginning to stretch itself.

PART FIVE

Bourbon Europe

TWENTY-FIVE

The Habsburg Inheritance and the Triumph of Absolutism

The epic struggle between the Habsburg family and the kings of France, which had been the major theme of European political history in the sixteenth and early seventeenth centuries, took a different form after 1648. Ever since Charles V split his vast empire, Spain, with the treasure of the New World behind her, had been the major Habsburg protagonist, but by the time the Thirty Years War came to an end she was clearly in decline. Now it was the turn of the Austrian branch of the family to assert its pre-eminence, and Vienna replaced Madrid as the major centre of Habsburg power.

In many ways the situation in the 1680s resembled that of the 1520s, with the Emperor fighting hard to fend off a Turkish threat to his hereditary lands at the same time as he tried to contain France within her established frontiers. Louis XIV was, as it were, another Francis I, deeply suspicious of the Habsburg bid for mastery in Europe, and adopting an aggressive posture as the best means of defence. Yet here the resemblance between the two periods stops, because the collapse of Spain had created a new and more complex picture. This is shown most clearly by analysing the position of Louis XIV, for he was not simply another king of France taking up the age-old struggle against Habsburg power. He was also, in his own right, heir to the Spanish Habsburgs, through his direct descent from Philip III and his marriage to Philip IV's daughter, and, although he never formulated it in this way, he symbolised the traditional Spanish Habsburg assumption that the interests of western Europe must take precedence over those of the centre and east. To the extent that he succeeded in imposing his attitude, Paris—or rather Versailles—was the new Madrid; and Charles II, the last Habsburg ruler of Spain, was not simply being perverse when he left his great inheritance to his French, rather than his Austrian, kinsmen.

Louis' own bid for dominance derived support from the fact that western Europe was economically far stronger than the east, which it used as one vast granary created for its own benefit. The Emperor, whose authority had contracted until it was virtually confined to this underdeveloped, eastern part of the continent, seemed doomed to become a satellite of his powerful western challenger, particularly since, during the first twenty-five years of Louis' personal rule, the Austrian Habsburgs were preoccupied with the Turkish menace, which had become more acute than at any time since the days of Charles V. The declining importance of the Emperor in central Europe was dramatically demonstrated in 1678, after the conclusion of the peace of Nymegen. The Elector of Brandenburg refused to accept the provision requiring him to give back Pomerania to France's ally, Sweden, no doubt assuming that French power could not reach so far into the heart of Germany. But Louis promptly ordered his generals to march on Berlin, and as it became clear that no one and nothing could stop them, the Elector capitulated.

There now seemed no bounds to the extent of Louis' influence, but in fact it had reached its limit. France's neighbours were so alarmed by his vigorous assertion of French interests that they united in defence of their own, and after the repulse of the Turkish attack upon Vienna in 1683 the Emperor was free to join them. Leopold's success in driving back the Turks and recovering Hungary for the Christian faith gave him a reputation that equalled and in some places eclipsed that of Louis XIV. Even the German princes looked to him as a friend and possible saviour after French armies devastated the Palatinate in 1689. The clock could not be turned back completely, of course, and the Emperor never became ruler of the Holy Roman Empire in more than name, but the revival of Habsburg power in the east created a balance of political forces in Europe as a whole, and left the states of the centre more or less free to work out their own destinies.

Louis could hardly have made a bid for supremacy in Europe unless he had first established his mastery at home. In this he was so successful that he provided a 'model' which other rulers were swift to copy. One of the major problems confronting European states in the early-modern period was that of harnessing their various resources and co-ordinating them so as to produce the maximum effect. A country could have great potential but be unable to realise it. England, under the early Stuarts was the most obvious example of this failure to focus, but the United

Provinces, despite their emergence as a major power, were also lacking in political concentration, and to a greater or lesser extent this was true of all other countries. Louis XIV's achievement consisted in the fact that he consciously made himself the embodiment of the French state, the sole channel through which the desires, the ambitions and the achievements of its inhabitants could find expression on a wider stage. It was a narrow channel, but for this very reason the water flowed through it at a great rate and threatened to inundate the rest of Europe.

The absolutism of the French monarchy was given formal expression at Versailles—that fairy-tale world in which every detail, no matter how insignificant, had its place in the worship of the Sun King. In real life, however, the royal authority was not unchallenged. It was held in check by its own history, for successive reigns had seen the creation of overlapping institutions that clogged the governmental machine. To be truly absolute a ruler would have to clear away much of this lumber, and in the opening years of Louis' personal rule this was apparently what Colbert had in mind. He was restrained, however, by Louis' reluctance to allow fundamental reform for fear that it might disturb the foundations of the monarchy, and by his own appreciation of the difficulties involved in abolishing existing institutions without creating new ones that might be even more resistant to central control.

Greatest of all restraints, however, on Colbert's freedom of action, was the pressure of war. There could be no radical reconstruction of the finances and administration of the French state while the overriding need was for hard cash in great quantities, and Colbert's misfortune, like that of Richelieu before him, was that France was almost perpetually at war. To wait for a long period of peace was, in effect, to postpone reform indefinitely. Colbert therefore squeezed all he could out of existing resources, and was, on the face of it, remarkably successful. But quite apart from the fact that this process built up enormous resentment in the middle and lower reaches of French society, such an achievement was possible solely because of the unremitting labour of the king as well as his ministers. Absolutism was an efficient method of government only when the monarch was hard-working and capable, like Louis XIV. Under a *roi fainéant* its weaknesses quickly became apparent.

There was, however, no very appealing alternative to absolutism in the late seventeenth century. England provided its own parliamentary 'model' after 1689, but for many years its deficiencies were more obvious than its inherent strength. Much the same was true of the

Dutch 'model', since the uneasy yoking of the quasi-monarchical Stadtholder and the theoretically sovereign Estates only too often produced deadlock. Absolutism, on the other hand, seemed synonymous with efficiency, even when the absolute ruler was hundreds of miles from his state, as was the case with Charles XII of Sweden during his years of enforced exile. The invigorating effect of absolutism was shown in Spain, where the accession of the Bourbon Philip V brought a new energy to the administration and set the country firmly on the road to recovery. The Habsburg rulers of Spain had been nominally absolute, but not until Philip V was the royal authority made effective in all the constituent kingdoms of the Spanish crown by the abolition of those 'liberties' which had long stood in its way. Russia provided an even more convincing demonstration of the potentiality of absolutism, for Peter the Great compelled his state to fit the mould he designed for it, and by so doing assured it a place among the major powers of Europe.

Both Peter and Louis had to overcome opposition from those who had a vested interest in the *status quo*. At the bottom end of the scale were the serfs and peasants who had been taught by bitter experience that any change would simply increase the burden of taxation which they already found intolerable. Because their protests went unheeded, their despair and anger found its outlet in rebellion; but the absolute monarchs met violence with violence. It was a major part of their strength that they disposed of large and powerful armies, and they employed these as much against their domestic enemies as their foreign ones. Peter and Louis, in fact, were at perpetual war with their poorer subjects, and whatever the philosophical justification of absolutism, at this lowest of all levels it was based on brute force.

At the other end of the scale, Louis tamed the magnates by domesticating them at Versailles, and continued his predecessors' practice of creating a new aristocracy to counterbalance the old. Peter was more ruthless—in keeping with the traditions of Russian life—and destroyed the status of the old boyar nobility by decreeing that in future a man's rank in society should depend solely on the degree of service which he rendered to the state. He applied much the same criterion to the Church, which he brought under the control of a specially created government department. Peter, like Louis, acknowledged (in practice) no higher good than that of the state, and he would not tolerate opposition from the Old Believers, who valued tradition more than novelty, and put their devotion to God and the Russian church above all secular loyalties. In France the 'Old Believers' were the Jansenists, who regarded all earthly authority—even that of the Sun King—as of no significance compared with the majesty of the Almighty, and stubbornly refused to bend their consciences to the royal will. They did not go so far as the Old Believers—who practised mass suicide rather than submit to Peter —nor were they persecuted in the same savage manner, but they served as a reminder that in France, as in Russia, there were thousands of men and women for whom obedience to the absolute ruler, even when he claimed divine sanction, was conditional and secondary.

This 'protestant' attitude had earlier found expression among the Huguenots, but they were quiescent by the time Louis began his personal rule. Had he been content to emulate Richelieu's *Politique* approach, Louis would almost certainly have had no trouble from them; but French absolutism post-1660 harked back to the days before the Wars of Religion, and Louis XIV showed his Habsburg ancestry in nothing so much as his intolerance of religious dissent. Like Philip II he equated the catholic cause with that of himself and his dynasty, and was prepared to risk economic and political upheaval for the sake of religious uniformity. By identifying French absolutism with bigoted and uncompromising catholicism, however, Louis recreated the old Habsburg menace in a Bourbon form, and thereby added a new element to the European opposition to him.

TWENTY-SIX

France under Louis XIV

Louis XIV and his Ministers

'God has given you all the qualities for greatness. Your Majesty must put them to use, and that you can easily do ... acquiring by the application that you give to affairs the necessary knowledge and experience.' The author of these words was Mazarin, and the young man to whom they were addressed was Louis XIV. Mazarin died before he could see whether Louis had taken his advice to heart, but his confidence proved well founded. Louis was a natural king. He had a fine presence, he inspired respect, and above all he had an unshakeable belief in his own greatness and a total commitment to the task which— he never doubted—God had given him. His devotion to duty had been shown early on, when despite his passionate attachment to one of Mazarin's pretty nieces he agreed to marry the far less attractive Maria Theresa, who, as daughter of the King of Spain, was politically the ideal match. This marriage did not bring Louis much emotional satisfaction, and for the next twenty years he lived the life of a libertine, openly parading his mistresses; but it symbolised the subordination of his private interests to those of the state. Throughout his reign he cultivated his public image, turning the routine of everyday life into a solemn ritual in which he, the Sun King, was worshipped and glorified. It was not without significance that in the royal chapel at Versailles the courtiers sat facing the king, with their backs to the altar; the intrusion of God into what was only nominally a Christian ceremony would have savoured of blasphemy.

The success of Louis XIV is demonstrated by the contrast between his reign and that of his father. Louis XIII had never really tamed the aristocracy, and the *Frondes* showed how near the surface were the forces of disorder in French life. But under Louis XIV the aristocracy

were brought to heel, the princes of the blood were sent to fight the
enemy abroad, and the royal authority was extended into every corner
of the kingdom. All this was Louis' personal achievement, for although
he had capable ministers they were his servants, not his masters. He
demonstrated this most spectacularly at the very outset of his personal
rule, after the death of Mazarin. It was widely assumed that a new
favourite would in due course take over the administration, and the
obvious candidate for such a post was Nicholas Fouquet, the enormously wealthy *Surintendant des Finances*. But Fouquet had prepared
the ground too well. In order to secure his own position he had, with
Mazarin's consent, obtained professions of loyalty from certain army
and navy officers, infiltrated his 'creatures' into a number of key
positions, and bought and fortified the island of Belle-Ile as a possible
refuge. Fouquet had a great deal to lose and he was merely taking what
seemed to him to be wise precautions in case Mazarin's death should be
followed by a struggle for power. But to Louis such measures were a
personal affront. He was determined that those who felt in need of
protection should look to the crown and not take the initiative themselves. It was this reasoning, rather than envy of the *Surintendant's*
wealth or desire to possess his exquisite chateau at Vaux-le-Vicomte,
that prompted Louis to act. Without a word of warning, Fouquet was
arrested in September 1661, accused of treason, and tried by a specially
constituted chamber of justice. Louis anticipated a death sentence, but
the evidence was too flimsy even for these handpicked judges, and
instead they sentenced Fouquet to exile. This did not suit the king's
purposes, and he changed the penalty to one of perpetual imprisonment. Fouquet spent the rest of his years a close prisoner in the fortress
of Pignerol, and his fate was a warning to all those who had doubted
the king's firmness of purpose. In the France of Louis XIV there was
no room for a favourite.

Although Louis kept the reins of policy firmly in his own hands he
needed ministers to carry out his decisions, and he selected these with
great care. 'I wished to divide the execution of my orders among
several people', he wrote at a later date, 'the better to bring them under
my authority. It was with this in mind that I chose men of diverse
talents and professions . . . and I distributed my time and my confidence
according to the understanding that I had of their virtues and the
importance of the affairs that I gave over to them.' Great nobles were
conspicuously absent from the small *Conseil d'en haut* in which the
really important decisions were taken. Instead Louis turned to men

who came mainly from the *Noblesse de robe*, from families that had already distinguished themselves by service to the crown. As the Duke of Saint Simon—that most disdainful of aristocrats—acidly commented, 'the one essential qualification without which no man was ever admitted into the council during the entire reign of Louis XIV [was] a complete absence of any claim to good birth'.

Among the ministers whom Louis inherited from Mazarin were Michel Le Tellier and Jean Baptiste Colbert. Le Tellier came from a family which had close connections with Paris and the *Parlement*. He served as a master of requests and *Intendant* of the army under Richelieu, and was appointed by Mazarin as secretary of state in charge of military affairs. At that time the army was a mixture of mercenaries and semi-independent units under noble commanders. It was lacking in discipline, in organisation, and above all in co-ordination. Over the course of the next twenty years Le Tellier changed all this. He issued detailed regulations on recruiting, training and discipline, adjusting them where necessary in the light of experience; he brought the aristocratic commanders under the sway of the civilian administration which he created; and he waged unremitting war against corruption and extravagance. His work was brought to culmination by his son and successor, the famous Louvois, who made himself a master of logistics and ensured that by the time the soldiers began their march, supplies were already awaiting them. Although Louis came to dislike Louvois, whose harsh, bullying manner seemed intolerable—especially in a subject—it was Louvois' meticulous attention to detail that made possible the victories of Louis' marshals, and his death in 1691 left a gap that could not be filled. To the Le Telliers, father and son, belongs the credit for forging an army that in size[1] and efficiency was to be for many decades unparalleled in Europe; and since the glory of Louis XIV was based in large part upon the success of his arms, their achievement was crucial.

Colbert

Louis neutralised his great servants, and preserved his own independence, by pitting one faction against another, and it was in pursuit of this strategy that he advanced the Colberts as a counterweight to the Le Telliers. The first Colbert to make his career in the royal service was Jean Baptiste, the son of a merchant draper of Rheims. He was trained

---

[1] The size of the army increased throughout the reign. 1667: 72,000 men. 1672: 120,000. 1688: 290,000. 1703: nearly 400,000.

in law and also had some experience of banking before he entered the administration. He began his official career as a clerk in the war department, since he was distantly related to the Le Telliers, but later he entered Mazarin's household and became the cardinal's financial adviser. Colbert was a cold man (known, appropriately, as 'the North'), but like Louvois he had an enormous capacity for work and was prepared to devote his life to serving the crown. He recognised the need to bring order into the chaos of the state's financial system, and was convinced that the first step must be to eradicate the speculators who drained into their own coffers the greater part of the money raised by taxation. If these unproductive middlemen could be removed the rate of taxation could be cut, at the same time as the royal revenue was increased.

Colbert's chance came with the fall of Fouquet, for the *Surintendant* had established very close ties with the leading speculators, believing—with some reason—that only through them could he find sufficient money to meet the demands of royal policy. Colbert took a leading part in the attack on Fouquet, and it was at his insistence that the specially created chamber of justice was kept in being and had its competence extended. The speculators were brought before it and made to disgorge. Colbert regained the equivalent of one year's entire income, and with this windfall he began buying back offices and *Rentes* (see p. 377) in order to release that part of the crown's revenues which was committed in advance. He did not attempt any fundamental changes in the tax system, but he did succeed in eliminating some of its worst features. The burden of the *Taille* was lightened, the number of exemptions was cut down, and yet at the same time the flow of money into the royal treasury was increased. In some ways Colbert was too successful, for Louis drew the conclusion that money would always be forthcoming and that policies could be formulated without any consideration of financial limitations. Colbert himself knew that this was not so, and in a remarkable outburst in 1680 he tried to bring Louis to reason: 'With regard to expenditure,' he wrote, 'although this does not concern me in any way, I beseech Your Majesty to allow me to point out that in war and peace Your Majesty has never considered his finances when resolving on his expenditure—a thing so extraordinary that there are assuredly no other examples.' But such remonstrances were of little effect, for Louis regarded it as his ministers' function to find the means for executing his policies, and was convinced that they could do so.

After Fouquet, the office of *Surintendant des Finances* was abolished, but Colbert's functions were virtually the same as his predecessor's and in 1665 he was given the title of *Contrôleur-Genéral*. He would have liked to rationalise the tax system, stop the sale of offices, and get rid of the *Rentes*, but such fundamental reforms could have been carried through only with the wholehearted support of the king, and this was not forthcoming. Louis feared that any attempt to remodel the existing system might result in a decline of revenue, and Colbert had therefore to operate within it. He did what he could, by insisting on accurate book-keeping, driving hard bargains with the tax farmers, keeping up the attack upon corrupt practices, and reducing the rate of interest on *Rentes*. But the fundamental weaknesses of the financial machinery could not be eliminated. Even internal Customs duties, which had long been criticised as an unjustifiable anachronism, survived. The central region of the 'Five Great Farms', which corresponded with the old Capetian kingdom of France, remained in effect a fortress protected by tariff walls; and as far as newly acquired regions were concerned— Alsace, for instance—they could trade more easily with Germany than with the rest of France.

As a merchant's son Colbert recognised the need to increase the wealth of the kingdom by stimulating industry. Since private capital consumed itself unproductively, in the purchase of *Rentes* and offices, the state would have to provide the necessary money and encouragement. But this was not to be done in a haphazard fashion. Colbert had a passion for order, and he determined to bring the entire manufacturing capacity of the kingdom under the closest possible supervision. He graded about a hundred of the leading industrial processes in an elaborate hierarchy—beginning with the Gobelins manufactory, which produced tapestries and other works of art for the royal household, and going down the scale to basic industries such as cloth, silk, linen and lace manufacture, as well as iron foundries, arsenals and dockyards. All these were allowed to use the prefix 'Royal' and were assured of the king's protection and support: workmen employed by them were given exemption from the *Taille*, and nobles who took part in their activities were allowed to retain their status. Foreign craftsmen were encouraged to settle in France, and foreign capital was welcome: at Abbeville, for instance, Netherlands entrepreneurs set up a cloth manufactory that was designed to decrease the dependence of France on Dutch and English goods.

As for lesser trades and industries, these were not allowed to go unregulated. An edict of 1673 required them all to be organised in gilds, and Colbert appointed inspectors of manufactures who were sent round the country to enforce detailed regulations. This 'economic absolutism' had its adverse effects, of course. The degree of regulation tended to stifle initiative, and the order of priorities laid down by the state was not necessarily that which would most have benefited the economy. But without government intervention French industry might well have remained stagnant, and, in the economic sphere at any rate, France would have become a satellite of the maritime powers, England and the United Provinces. It was Colbert who took the initiative in forcing France to meet the industrial challenge from her protestant rivals.

As part and parcel of the same process, Colbert fostered the development of overseas trade. In 1664 he founded the East India and West India Companies, and later formed the Levant Company and the Northern Company (for trade with the Baltic). Most of these were dissolved in Colbert's lifetime, but they succeeded in their primary objective of opening up new trade routes and increasing the French share of overseas markets. A flourishing traffic in sugar was built up with the West Indies, and the number of French ships on this route increased from less than half a dozen in the early 1660s to more than two hundred by the mid-1680s. The west coast ports prospered as a result of all this activity, and Bordeaux, La Rochelle and Nantes became major centres of international commerce. By the time Colbert died, France was taking her place among the great trading powers, and the impetus which he had given lasted long after his death. In 1698, for example, a company was set up for trade with China, while in 1701 the Guinea Company was formed to take over the slave trade with the Spanish colonies. The French obsession with the Spanish inheritance was not prompted merely by politics or personal glory: mercantile interests saw in it the chance of outstripping their Dutch and English rivals, and they were now equipped for the attempt. Much of this development would have taken place, of course, whether or not Colbert had given the lead, but he undoubtedly provided the initial stimulus and accelerated the rate of advance.

The expansion of overseas trade was accompanied by an increase in the size of the French navy, for Colbert recognised that the two were inextricably linked. Shipbuilding was subsidised, the Ordinance of Water and Forests of 1669 laid down a long-term strategy for the conservation of timber supplies, and Toulon and Brest were developed as major dockyards. Maritime conscription was enforced in the ports and a reserve of trained men was thereby built up for the fleet. By 1677 the French navy was the largest in the Mediterranean, and in the Atlantic could compare in size with those of the United Provinces and England. French interests could no longer be ignored by the maritime powers, nor could French merchants be excluded from overseas markets. Colbert's attitude to foreign trade, in short, was aggressive. He believed that France must force her way into international commerce and compel other nations to recognise her claim to a share of what he assumed to be a limited amount of wealth. This mercantilist attitude achieved his aim of expanding French trade, but at the same time it impeded his policy of rationalising the French fiscal system, for it led him to advocate war against the United Provinces in 1672, a war which led to a big increase in state expenditure and put an end to all Colbert's hopes of fundamental reform.

The range of Colbert's activity was enormous. His determination to create order out of chaos led him to support proposals for the rationalisation of the law, and it was as a result of his initiative that a number of codes were promulgated in the years 1667–85, among them the Code Louis (civil), the criminal code of 1670 and the maritime and commercial codes of 1672 and 1673. It was also Colbert who saw the need to concentrate the various police functions in Paris into the hands of one official. At his suggestion Louis created the new post of Lieutenant-General of the Paris Police, with responsibility for imposing order and maintaining the rule of law in the notoriously disordered and lawless capital.

So far as the provinces were concerned, the enforcement of the royal will was often blocked by the vested interest of office-holders who, having purchased their position, were irremovable. For Colbert, whose belief in royal absolutism was as deep as Louis', such a situation was intolerable, especially when it deprived the crown of much-needed revenue. In 1663 he drew up a memorandum defining the duties of certain masters of requests whom he planned to send into the provinces to gather information and statistics about the effectiveness of the fiscal system, with a view to reforming it. These officials were given the title of *Intendants* of Justice, Police and Finance, and were instructed to enquire into the functioning not simply of the tax mechanism but of local government in general. It was not Colbert's intention that they should supersede local officials, but they were given authority to override such officers and to hold special courts if the need arose. Colbert was thinking in terms of a brief but concentrated enquiry, with each *Intendant* dealing with a number of localities before returning to Paris to give an account of his actions. So complex was their task, however, that they stayed in the provinces, sending back regular written reports, and by 1680 they were virtually resident administrators. The presence of the *Intendants* in the localities considerably improved the effectiveness of royal government, for they were appointed by the crown and could be removed at will. There was nothing predetermined about this systematisation of *Intendant* rule, nor did it take place all at once— Brittany, for instance, received its first *Intendant* only in 1689—but it transformed the administration of France by removing power from the localities and concentrating it at the centre. In this way the work of Sully and Richelieu was brought to completion.

Traditional rights and vested interests suffered from this extension of royal authority. Towns, which had long maintained a degree of independence under elected officers, were brought under the control of crown-appointed mayors by an edict of 1692. Higher up the social scale the *Parlement* of Paris also had its wings clipped. In 1673 letters patent confined its right of making representations about proposed legislation to the period immediately *following* the registration of edicts: there was to be no question of bargaining where the king's will was involved. The changing role of the *Parlements* and other sovereign courts was symbolised by Louis's order, in 1665, that they should change their name to 'superior courts', and three years later he instructed the chancellor to destroy the record of the *Parlements'* activities at the time of the *Frondes*. All sovereignty was henceforth to be concentrated in the person of the king, not dispersed by a time-honoured system of checks and balances.

Nevertheless there were limits on absolutism. Despite Colbert's attempts at codification there was still a wide gap between the civil law of the south and the great variety of customary laws in the north, and regional differences were emphasised not only by natural factors but also by poor communications and the survival of internal Customs. The royal government had constantly to negotiate with separate bodies, such as the Assembly of Clergy or the provincial Estates in the *Pays d'Etats*. The king's commissioners could usually be sure of getting their way, but this was only because they operated within the existing framework. By creating new officers to operate alongside old ones, Louis made the pattern yet more complex. If he could have started with a clean slate he and his servants might well have produced something far more rational, ordered and efficient. But such a new beginning was out of the question. The old order had to be modified and adapted by men who were, to a large extent, prisoners of it, and in the process much that was inimical to the crown's interests survived.

Great ministers like Louvois and Colbert would have dominated a weak king, but in Louis' case there was never any doubt who was the master. He encouraged his advisers to speak their minds in the *Conseil d'en haut*, but once he had decided on his course of action he would brook no criticism. When Colbert broke this unwritten rule in 1671 the king sent him a letter that forcibly reminded him of it: 'Do not risk annoying me again', he wrote, 'because after I have heard your arguments and those of your colleagues and have given my opinion on all your views, I never wish to hear more about it.' However arrogant such an attitude may seem, at least it made clear where authority lay. Much of the harm from which France had suffered during the previous century had been caused by *rois fainéants*, kings who were too young or too irresolute to play the forceful role in government which birth had assigned them. Louis had been brought up to despise such weaklings. As a boy he was encouraged to model himself on Henry IV, and even his writing exercises were on the theme of the obedience that is owed to kings. Little wonder that he expected to be obeyed: but more than this, he had the strength of character to take responsibility for his failures as well as his successes.

The Le Telliers and Colbert were not the only members of the *Conseil d'en haut*. The diplomatist Hugues de Lionne, who was in charge of foreign affairs long before he purchased the appropriate secretaryship of state in 1668, was also to be found there until his death in 1671. He was succeeded by Arnauld de Pomponne, who served as foreign minister from 1672 to 1679 and again from 1691 until his death in 1699. Pomponne was a moderate, who distrusted the increasingly aggressive policies advocated by Louvois and Colbert, particularly towards the Dutch. In 1679 his two powerful colleagues combined against him, and Pomponne, whose position had also been weakened by his Jansenist connections, was dismissed. Yet he was not disgraced, and the very fact that the king had made use of his services and was prepared to employ him again shows that Louis could appreciate quality even in men whose views on policy did not entirely coincide with his own, and never allowed himself to be totally identified with one or other faction.

Jansenism and Relations with Rome

The Jansenist controversy, which was among the factors leading to Pomponne's dismissal in 1672, had its origins in the *Augustinus* of Cornelis Jansen, Bishop of Ypres, published in Paris in 1641. Jansen, reacting against what he regarded as the lax theology of the Jesuits, put great emphasis upon the omnipotence of God. Conversion, he believed—and in this he was close to Luther—was not achieved by man's merits but by the apparently arbitrary action of the Almighty, and those to whom grace was not granted were destined for damnation. Jansen's teachings made a great impact in France, and his austere attitude was adopted wholeheartedly by—among others—the nuns of the Cistercian convent of Port-Royal in Paris and its sister house of Port-Royal-des-Champs near Versailles. The abbess of Port-Royal, until her death in 1661, was Angélique Arnauld, *Mère Angélique*, and one of the most famous defenders of the Jansenist cause was her brother, Antoine Arnauld, who in 1643 published a work entitled *De la Fréquente Communion*, which the anti-Jansenists found offensive and unacceptable. Pomponne was Antoine's nephew and therefore closely associated, by birth if not by inclination, with the Jansenist movement.

Mazarin had detested the Jansenists, because of their close links with members of the *Parlement* and the fact that they counted among their adherents a number of princely families implicated in the *Frondes*: Cardinal de Retz, for instance, was sympathetic to the Jansenists, and so were the Prince of Conti and his sister, the Duchess of Longueville. Louis inherited this detestation, and in any case would have been out of sympathy with an attitude that exalted God to such a height that it left even Kings of France looking insignificant. In 1653 and 1656 papal bulls had condemned as heretical five propositions said to be taken from the *Augustinus*, and an assembly of the French clergy, held in 1656, declared its opposition to Jansenist doctrines. Antoine Arnauld was expelled from the Sorbonne, and when Pascal, who had lived in the lay community attached to Port-Royal-des-Champs, published his *Lettres Provinciales* in support of Arnauld, these too were denounced by the government.

Louis needed papal support for his campaign against the Jansenists, but relations with Rome in the early years of the reign were far from good. In 1662 a clash had occurred between the Pope's Corsican guards and the attendants of the French ambassador, and Louis took this opportunity to assert his own supremacy in the most public manner. He refused to accept the Pope's regrets, threatened to invade the papal territory of Avignon, and only moderated his wrath after the Pope had agreed to dismiss the Corsicans and make an abject apology. However, when Louis asked for papal support against the Jansenists he received it, and in 1665 Alexander VII issued a bull requiring all clergy to accept a formulary condemning the five propositions. Many clerics, including the nuns of Port-Royal, either refused their assent or made the proviso that while the five propositions were indeed heretical they were not to be found in the *Augustinus*. Such hair-splitting was not to Louis' liking, and he insisted that the formulary should be accepted without any reservations. The result was a split in the French church, which was not papered over until after the election of a new Pope, Clement IX, in 1667. Clement was prepared to accept the view that as long as the five propositions were condemned there was no need to assert that they were actually contained in the *Augustinus*, and this was the basis of the 'Peace of the Church' in 1668, which opened the way to reconciliation between the Jansenists and their critics.

The position of the Jansenists was enormously strengthened by the election of Innocent XI in 1676, for he was a man of great strength of character, determined to recover for the papacy the prestige which it had lost. He approved of the Jansenists' strict morality and disapproved of the worldliness of Louis: no longer would the authority of the papacy be used to buttress the glory of the King of France. A new subject of dispute was by now affecting relations between Paris and Rome. The crown had long claimed the *Régale*—the right to the revenues of vacant sees—but it had also long been recognised that certain sees were exempt from this. In 1673 and 1675 Louis issued decrees applying the *Régale* to all bishoprics, without exception, and this led to immediate protests. Among the leaders of opposition were two bishops who had earlier refused to accept the anti-Jansenist formulary, and in this way the Jansenist controversy was revived. Antoine Arnauld was sent into exile, the nuns of Port Royal were forbidden to accept any novices, and Pomponne was dismissed.

Since Innocent refused to accept Louis' ruling on the *Régale*, the king summoned a general assembly of the French church in 1681, and presented four articles for consideration. These laid down the principles that lay rulers were not subject to ecclesiastical authority in

secular matters and could not therefore be deposed or excommunicated; that the authority of the Pope was inferior to that of councils of
the Church; that this authority was limited within France by the
traditional 'liberties' of the French ('gallican') church;[1] and that any
papal judgments on disputed matters were invalid if they ran counter
to ecclesiastical opinion as a whole. The French clergy were not
enthusiastic about these articles, but under pressure from the crown the
assembly accepted them in 1682. Louis then promulgated an edict
requiring the four articles to be acknowledged and taught throughout
his kingdom.

Innocent XI refused to recognise the validity of this edict and
declined to institute to benefices any clergy who had taken part in the
assembly. Louis, on the other hand, refused to present any clergy for
institution except those who had taken part. The result was stalemate.
By 1688 thirty-five sees were without a bishop, and the bitterness
between crown and papacy had been increased by further trouble over
the French ambassador in Rome. All the other diplomatic representatives there had agreed to waive their right of granting immunity to
wanted men, on the grounds that such immunities had long been
abused. The French ambassador, however, refused to follow suit, and
on his death in 1687 Innocent announced that he would accept no replacement. Louis ignored this and sent a coarse-grained bully of a man
who made it clear that he would take orders from no one but the King
of France. When Innocent excommunicated the ambassador the latter
ignored it, on the grounds that spiritual penalties were of no validity
when directed against servants of the French crown. Innocent therefore went to the extreme stage of privately excommunicating Louis
himself, in 1688. The king riposted with an invasion of Avignon and
a propaganda campaign designed to whip up gallican sentiment.

By this stage there seemed to be a real possibility that the French
church would secede from Rome, but schism was averted by the death
of Innocent XI in 1689 and Louis' simultaneous involvement in a
major European war. The king was now ready to draw back from the
extreme position he had taken up, though not to abandon the substance of his claim. In 1692 Innocent XII confirmed in the possession
of their sees all French bishops who had not taken part in the assembly,

[1] Those who upheld the 'liberties' of the national church were known as
'gallicans'. Their opponents, who gave priority to papal supremacy, were sometimes called 'ultra montanists', because their principal loyalty was to the Pope,
who lived 'beyond the mountains', in Rome.

and a year later he did the same for those who had taken part—but only after he had received from each of them a letter of apology. Louis, in return, withdrew official recognition of the four articles and announced that the edict of 1682 would no longer be enforced. The basic question of the *Régale* remained unsettled, but in fact Louis kept it. He had won a sort of victory, but only at the cost of inflaming anti-papal sentiment to such a point that it was now difficult to control.

Once harmony had been restored between king and Pope, the two co-operated to suppress Jansenism. In 1705 Clement XI issued the bull *Vineam Domini*, which forbade any reservations when accepting the formulary, and thereby put an end to the 'Peace of the Church'. The nuns of Port-Royal, who still insisted on making reservations, were expelled in 1709, Port-Royal-des-Champs was demolished in the following year, and the remains of the dead were exhumed and scattered. In 1713 came the bull *Unigenitus* condemning a number of Jansenist propositions. The *Parlement* and the Sorbonne, nourished on gallicanism, were reluctant to accept this, but Louis insisted. When the Archbishop of Paris and some other bishops drew up a protestation declaring that the Pope should not be allowed to treat French bishops as mere executants of his orders, they were exiled to their sees by royal warrant. In this extraordinary manner Louis XIV, who had been an uncompromising upholder of the liberties of the French church against what he declared to be unjustified papal claims, transformed himself into the adovocate of ultramontanism. It was now the Jansenists who were gallicans, and in the struggle with the crown, which continued long after Louis' death, they had the support of the Sorbonne, the *Parlements*, and all those elements in French life which, while they had been swept aside by the imperious gestures of royal absolutism, had not been destroyed.

The Huguenots

It was at the height of his struggle with Innocent XI, and in order to demonstrate his unimpeachable orthodoxy, that Louis XIV took action against the Huguenots. There were about a million of these still left in France and still enjoying the liberties granted them by the Edict of Nantes. Louis had no hatred for the Huguenots—who had demon-strated their loyalty at the time of the *Frondes*—but he feared that disunity in the Church might encourage divisions within the state and thereby undermine the foundations of his monarchy. By about 1680 he was, in any case, becoming more conventional in his attitudes. His salad days were nearly over and he was increasingly attached to the devout Madame de Maintenon (whom he may indeed have married after the death of Maria Theresa in 1683). She recorded in 1679 that 'the king is full of excellent sentiments and often reads the Holy Scripture, which he finds the finest of all books. He confesses his weaknesses and recognises his faults. We must now wait for the spirit of grace to reveal itself. He is thinking seriously about the conversion of heretics and in a little while he will work on this matter to some purpose.'

Following the Peace of Nymegen in 1678 the Edict of Nantes was enforced with increasing strictness. A number of Huguenot schools were closed, as were many Huguenot churches (*temples*), and more and more trades and professions were barred to non-catholics. The rate of conversion was already increasing, especially after the establishment of a special bureau in 1676, to which part of the revenue from vacant sees was transferred. This money was used to 'compensate' converts who had suffered financially by changing their faith, and further inducements were held out in the way of pensions and exemption from taxation. Among the major advantages of conversion was freedom from billeting, for in 1681 the *Intendant* of Poitou had begun burdening Huguenot households with the maintenance of royal dragoons. These soldiers, drawn from the lower depths of French society, had the habits of hardened criminals and were encouraged to make life difficult for their unwilling hosts.

As a result of these *dragonnades* the number of 'conversions' rose dramatically, and Louis was persuaded that with so few Huguenots left the Edict of Nantes was now an anachronism. The foreign situation seemed highly favourable, in view of the accession of the catholic James II to the English throne, so in 1685 Louis issued the Edict of Fontainebleau, which formally annulled and replaced that of Nantes. Under its terms Huguenot ministers were required to accept conversion or go into exile; all remaining Huguenot schools and churches were to close; and protestant worship, both private and public, was to cease. Huguenot laymen were given no choice at all, for they were now declared to be catholic whether they liked it or not. After more than a century of existence there was no longer—in law at any rate—a protestant church in France. The 'Most Christian King' had shown the world how unity and orthodoxy could be restored.

In fact a number of protestant communities did survive within the kingdom; and while ex-Huguenots were officially forbidden to emigrate, some 200,000 managed to do so. They found refuge in the United Provinces, England and Brandenburg, where their skills were very much appreciated, but the effect of their departure upon the French economy is hard to determine. A number of trades and crafts were depressed, but the reasons for this were to be found in the strain of war and the inequities of the fiscal system as much as in emigration. Although about a fifth of all the Huguenots went into exile they were less than one-hundredth of the population of France as a whole, and in many places their departure made little obvious difference. So far as the richer ones were concerned, they settled in places like Geneva, where they built up banking organisations, maintained their contacts in France, and provided much of the capital that financed Louis' war effort. It was the Huguenots who stayed at home who became a thorn in Louis' flesh, for in 1702 a protestant revolt—'the War of the Camisards'—broke out in the Cevennes, and a royal army under the command of Marshal Villars had to be sent to suppress it. Even so the leaders held out until 1710, and French protestantism, although it went underground, survived.

Poverty and Riches

Religion was not the only cause of unrest in Louis XIV's France. Poverty was even more potent in driving people to rebellion. In 1674, for example, there was a major outbreak in Bordeaux, while in the following year trouble occurred in Brittany on so large a scale that the government had to recall troops from the front. In fact the king's soldiers were almost as active against his subjects at home as against his enemies abroad, and Colbert informed the *Intendant* at Limoges that 'you can be reassured, and may make the fact public, that the king keeps prepared twenty leagues from Paris an army of 20,000 men ready to march into any province where there is suspicion of a rising, in order to inflict exemplary punishment and to illustrate to all the people the obedience they owe to His Majesty'.

The glory of Louis' reign was bought at an appalling cost, for the peasants, from whose unremitting labour the wealth of France and the French king was mainly derived, were crippled by heavy taxation. Although there were wide fluctuations between one region and another, bad harvests could lead to death by starvation, and in such circumstances revolt, however hopeless, seemed preferable to extinction. In the closing years of the reign, when poor harvests coincided with very severe taxation and defeat abroad, revolt became endemic, and in 1709 the *Controleur-Général* reported to the king that 'for four months now not a week has passed without there being some seditious outbreak. Troops have been needed in nearly every province to keep them under control'. It was largely to deal with the problem of internal order that the Militia was established in 1688. This force, drawn from the dregs of the population, was responsible for guarding grain convoys, rounding-up bands of salt smugglers trying to evade the hated *Gabelle*, and holding disaffection in check until such time as firstline troops could arrive. Its savage methods made it hated, but the royal government, committed to ambitious and expensive policies, saw in popular revolts little more than treasonable activities that must be ruthlessly suppressed. Those who blamed the unjust fiscal system and urged reform ran the risk of falling into disfavour.

Colbert's successors, called on to find money for a war that seemed never likely to end, had recourse to all the old methods, such as sale of titles and offices, manipulation of the currency, and borrowing on the security of future revenue. They also introduced new taxes which, for the first time, affected the hitherto privileged classes. In 1695, for example, Louis de Pontchartrain (*Controleur-Général* from 1689–99) imposed a poll tax, known as the *Capitation*, which was applied to all except the clergy. Protests from the nobles led to its abandonment after the signing of the Peace of Ryswick, but it was reimposed in 1701 and became a permanent feature of the tax system. Pontchartrain, who was well-intentioned but something of a mediocrity, was succeeded by the equally mediocre Michel Chamillart. Not until the appointment of Colbert's newphew, Nicholas Desmarets, in 1708, were French finances again in the hands of a man of real ability. In 1710 he introduced the *Dixième* (a sort of income tax), and although the nobles managed to reduce their share of this, as of the *Capitation*, they were being forced to contribute at least something towards the heavy expenditure of the French state. But it was still the poor—by far the greater part of the population of France—who paid most, and for them the royal government and its policies were objects of hatred and ridicule. Their attitude is reflected in a parody of the Lord's Prayer, current in the closing years of Louis' reign. 'Our Father, which art at Versailles, thy name is no longer hallowed, thy will is no longer done either in earth or sea. Give us this day our daily bread. Forgive our enemies, who have beaten us so many times, but not our generals, who have allowed them to do it. Do not be led any more into the temptations of La Maintenon, and deliver us from Chamillart. Amen!'

War, and the heavy taxation which accompanied it, was for some people the opportunity for enrichment on a princely scale. These were the financiers who farmed the taxes, made loans to the crown at a high rate of interest, and took a substantial commission from all the many deals in which they engaged. Such men, mainly of humble birth, constituted what was virtually a new class, and although the established aristocracy affected to despise them, many an impoverished nobleman was happy to marry himself or his son to a financier's daughter. Antoine Crozart, for example, was the son of a lackey, but he became enormously rich, patronised Watteau and other artists, and married his daughter to the grandson of the Duke of Bouillon. Even the Duke of Saint Simon, for all his aristocratic hauteur, married the daughter of a tax farmer, and his example was widely copied. The established aristocracy was in any case frequently of bourgeois origin, for French society, despite its outward rigidity, was remarkably fluid in its upper levels. Buying an office could often be the first step along the road to ennoblement: the ancestor of the Marshal Duke of Villeroy, for instance, was a porter in the Paris hay market who saved enough to purchase an office of no great significance, and from that moment the family rose rapidly. Service to the crown was another means of social advancement, and alongside the old families, and frequently intermarried with them, were new dynasties such as the Le Telliers and the Colberts. Among Colbert's sons-in-law were three dukes, and although Colbert himself died in 1683 his family remained ensconced in the highest levels of government: his son, the Marquis of Seignelay, succeeded him as secretary of the Navy, while his young brother, the Marquis of Croissy, and his nephew, the Marquis of Torcy, both served as minister of foreign affairs.

The focus of this aristocratic world, to which the opening was given by birth, talent and worldly success, was the court. In the early years of Louis' personal rule the court was centred at the Louvre, but Louis had no love for Paris, from which, as a small boy, he had been forced to flee. He preferred the hunting lodge at Versailles, where he had passed many pleasant hours during his youth, and following the Peace of Aix-la-Chapelle in 1668 he set on foot building operations which swiftly transformed this comparatively modest residence into the largest and most magnificent palace in Europe. By 1682 the court was installed there, and the ritual worship of the Sun King was carried on in richly gilded apartments decorated and furnished with all the skill of which French craftsmanship was capable. Versailles was a temple of the arts, but the arts themselves were strictly subordinated to the needs of the monarchy. Colbert founded academies for this purpose, and in return for royal patronage writers, musicians, painters and architects were expected to place their talents at the king's disposal. The result was a display of brilliance that dazzled the whole western world, and the fame of France spread through her arts as much as her arms. In many parts of Europe French became the language of polite society, and it replaced Latin as the medium for diplomacy. French fashions set the tone even in states that were hostile to Louis' policy, and Versailles became a magnet that drew crowds of sightseers—curious, envious and adulatory—from far and wide.

In Louis XIII's reign the magnates had signalled their dissatisfaction by 'leaving court'—in other words retiring to the provinces in order to prepare for armed revolt. This potent symbol of discontent was effectively removed by Versailles and the king-worship which Louis fostered there. To leave court was to absent oneself from the source of all delight as well as from all hope of place and profit. Nobles vied with each other to catch the king's eye, to bask in the sunshine of a royal smile, or—summit of all happiness—to be invited to take part in the intimate assemblies at the château of Marly. Versailles was a whole world, and to leave it was virtually to go into exile. One nobleman, recalled to court after a long period of disgrace, told the king that 'far from Your Majesty one is not only unhappy; one is ridiculous', and the Duke of Richelieu declared that he 'would rather die than spend two or three months out of the king's sight'.

Versailles, then, was more than a folly, more than a preposterous and extravagant display of personal glory. It was consciously designed to dazzle Europe and to tame the French aristocracy. As such it succeeded, beyond all doubt. At the same time it cut off the leaders of French society, including the king himself, from the people they ruled. The court became something extraneous, almost a foreign element, and bore little relation to the world of ordinary men and women except in so far as they were taxed, sometimes beyond endurance, to maintain it. All this glory was built on the backs of the peasants, and no account of Louis XIV's achievement would be complete that put in Versailles but left out this other France in which incessant toil, poverty and starvation were daily realities. In the words of La Bruyère, 'one sees certain savage animals in the countryside, blackened, livid and burned by the sun. They seem to be able to articulate, and when they stand on their feet they show human faces: and in effect they are indeed men. They retire at night into caves, where they live on black bread, water and roots.'

TWENTY-SEVEN

France and Europe, 1660–1720

The Struggle for the Netherlands

For more than a century after the election of Charles V as Holy
Roman Emperor, Europe had been dominated by the Habsburg family
from its twin centres in Spain and Austria. By 1648 this was no longer
the case. Spanish power was visibly declining, the Emperor was preoccupied with the Turks, and relations between the two branches of
the Habsburg house, previously so close, were becoming more distant.
The Austrian Habsburgs had clung to the family alliance so long as it
suited their own interests, but as Spain became more of an encum-
brance than a buttress there were those among the Emperor's advisers
who urged him to cut loose. Their views carried greater weight after
the accession of Leopold I in 1657.

Into the European arena vacated—for a time at least—by the Habsburgs strode Louis XIV. As a great king personifying a great state he
was determined to increase the glory of his name, for, in his own
words, a monarch who 'is the admiration of his own subjects soon
arouses the amazement of neighbouring nations. And if he makes use
of this advantage there will be nothing either inside or outside his
empire which he cannot obtain in course of time.' Louis' main aim was
to close those 'gates' on the French frontiers through which an enemy
might be able to force his way, and in particular to strengthen the
French defensive position on the border with Germany and the
Netherlands. The Treaty of Westphalia had confirmed France in
possession of the bishoprics of Metz, Toul and Verdun, and had
transferred to her a complex of rights in Alsace, but there was no
certainty that the Emperor was prepared to accept such a settlement as
permanent. Vienna had its long-term objectives as well as Paris, and
among them was the reincorporation within the Empire of those

territories taken from it at the sword's point. Louis's aggressive stance was, in one sense at any rate, a defensive posture, and in the long run he was successful in preserving the 1648 settlement.

The opening years of Louis' personal rule did not offer much opportunity for a forward policy, but the king's determination to assert himself was shown in a number of minor incidents. In 1661, for example, there was a dispute over precedence between the French and Spanish ambassadors in London, which led to a major diplomatic confrontation. Louis threatened war, and Philip IV had to give way and agree that in future Spanish ambassadors would allow the French precedence everywhere, except in Vienna. This apparently trivial dispute showed that the Peace of the Pyrenees had not put an end to Franco–Spanish hostility. France still coveted part at least of the Spanish Netherlands, in order to strengthen her north-western frontier, and also Franche-Comté in the east. Louis had bought Dunkirk from Charles II of England in 1662, thereby extending French sovereignty along the coast of Flanders; he had also cultivated good relations with the United Provinces, whose assistance, or at least benevolent neutrality, would be desirable in the event of open war with Spain. It was in fulfilment of his treaty obligations to the Dutch that Louis declared war on England in 1666, hoping not only to demonstrate that the French always kept their word but also to make the Dutch feel so grateful that they would overlook the threat implicit in a French invasion of the southern Netherlands.

Such an invasion was already being planned, for in September 1665 Philip IV of Spain had died, leaving all his territories to the five-year-old son of his second marriage, Charles II. Even at this early stage three was clearly a possibility that Charles might die without heirs, in which case the great Spanish inheritance would pass to the ruler who was best placed to claim it. Louis himself was a claimant, by virtue of his descent from Philip II and his marriage to Philip IV's daughter. His lawyers advised him that in certain parts of the Netherlands the children of a first marriage took precedence over those of a second in matters of inheritance, and Louis chose to apply this right of 'devolution' to the entire Spanish Netherlands. These, he asserted, belonged not to the new King of Spain but to Maria Theresa, Queen of France. To drive his point home he ordered Le Tellier and Louvois to assemble a large army, and in 1669 he sent this into the Spanish Netherlands in the opening stages of the War of Devolution.

The Dutch were alarmed by the French advance towards their own border, and in January 1668 allied with England in what became known, after the addition of Sweden, as the Triple Alliance. Nevertheless there was virtually no opposition to the French thrust, and if it had been pressed home the Netherlands might well have passed under Louis' rule. But Louis, possibly in reaction to the Anglo–Dutch insistence on a negotiated settlement, checked the campaign in the Netherlands and recalled Condé to take charge of an army designed for operations in Franche-Comté. In a brief campaign Condé occupied the whole of Franche-Comté, thereby extending French frontiers to the Swiss border. By this time Louis had achieved one of his principal objectives— the recognition of his claim to part at least of the Spanish inheritance— for in January 1668 he and the Emperor had signed a secret partition treaty, under which France was to have the Spanish Netherlands, Franche-Comté and Spanish Navarre, as well as Naples and Sicily, should Charles II die without heirs. It was with this guarantee behind him that Louis opened peace negotiations, for he was anxious to put an end to the war before the ominous Anglo–Dutch alliance developed into a real threat. In May 1668 peace was concluded at Aix-la-Chapelle. Louis had hoped to hold on to Franche-Comté, abandoning his gains in the Netherlands in return, but the Spaniards preferred to sacrifice their possessions in Flanders, knowing full well that by doing so they would increase Dutch suspicion of the French. France therefore returned Franche-Comté but kept the areas around Dunkirk and Lille, as well as a number of isolated fortresses, including Tournai, Ath and Oudenarde. The new frontier in Flanders was not much of an improvement on the old, but at least it gave Louis a number of bargaining counters for possible future use and made it marginally more difficult for an enemy to attack from that quarter.

Louis had been shocked by what he regarded as Dutch ingratitude in allying with England and Sweden to impose peace terms upon him. 'Rather than being interested in my good fortune', he declared, they 'wished to impose their law upon me and oblige me to make peace. They even dared threaten me in case I should refuse to accept their mediation.' But there was more to his change of attitude than mere personal pique. Louis believed that possession of the Spanish Netherlands was essential to French security, and if the Dutch would not agree to his plans to take over this vital area he was prepared to use force against them. In this he was encouraged not simply by the war party associated with the Le Telliers but also by Colbert, who was convinced that only by war could Dutch commercial domination be broken. In

1664 Colbert had imposed a moderate tariff on imports into France in order to stimulate French industry, and when this was shown to be ineffective he increased it to prohibitive heights in 1667. Refined sugar from the United Provinces was virtually excluded from the French market; the Dutch, angry and alarmed, riposted with a counter-tariff and in 1672 imposed a year's ban on all French imports. In that same year Louis ordered his armies to strike at the republic.

Before the troops moved, Louis had isolated the Dutch diplomatically and secured English support. He had also persuaded the Rhine bishoprics to allow their territories to be used not only for the passage of French armies but also for the concentration of supplies at key points. Some 100,000 men were massed against the Dutch in an awesome display of military might. Moving north from Liège, the French armies crossed the Rhine in June 1672, under the personal supervision of the king, and captured Arnhem, the southern pivot of the Dutch line of defence. The Dutch retreated to Utrecht, but Condé, following hard on their heels, captured it. The way now lay open to Amsterdam, and Condé was eager to press forward. He was restrained, however, by Louis and Louvois, who were afraid that the army might outrun its supplies. Meanwhile the Dutch regents, seeing no possibility of resistance, offered to surrender Maastricht and also the Generality lands taken from the Spaniards in the closing stages of the War of Independence.[1] This would have made it possible for the French to attack the Spanish Netherlands simultaneously from south and north, but Louis rejected the proposals. The success of his arms had been so complete that the prospect of annexing the United Provinces as well as the Netherlands had now opened up, and even if the republic was permitted to survive, Colbert was insistent that it should surrender Nymegen and put an end to all restrictions on French trade. The war therefore continued, the Dutch spirit of resistance was revived by William of Orange, who seized power after the overthrow of De Witt and the regent regime (see p. 441).

By pausing after the capture of Utrecht, the French had given the Dutch time to flood the area round Amsterdam. This put an end to the prospect of a lightning French victory and also to the diplomatic isolation of the Dutch. In 1672 the Emperor and the Elector of Brandenburg came to their assistance, and although their combined forces were defeated by Turenne in 1673 they had at least enabled William of

---

[1] So called because they were under the direct control of the Estates General.

Orange to launch a successful operation against Louis' ally, the Archbishop Elector of Cologne. Spain had also declared war on France, although this did not materially affect the military situation. The struggle continued for several more years, but although the French pushed forward into Flanders and captured Valenciennes, Cambrai and St Omer, the cost in men and money was heavy and the strain was beginning to tell. Peace negotiations opened in 1676 but two more years of fighting were necessary before terms were finally agreed at Nymegen in August 1678. The French restored a number of gains they had made at the earlier peace of Aix-la-Chapelle, including Ath and Oudenarde, but they were confirmed in possession of St Omer, Aire, Ypres, Valenciennes, Cambrai and Mauberge. This represented a very considerable strengthening of their Netherlands border, and in addition Spain ceded the whole of Franche-Comté in the east. Louis was pleased with his success, and later boasted that 'I was able to profit from every opportunity I found to extend the boundaries of my kingdom at the expense of my enemies'. But the acquisition of territory had been only one of the original French objectives in making war. Among the others was the destruction of Dutch commercial supremacy, and in this the French were not successful. Louis even agreed to abandon the 1667 tariff, much to the chagrin of Colbert, who recognised that from his point of view the war had been a failure. Anger and disappointment at this may have been among the contributory causes of his death, which took place in 1683.

The Nine Years War

Superficially at any rate the forward policy pursued by Louis had paid handsome dividends, and the declining influence of the moderates was shown by the dismissal of Pomponne in 1679. Now that the Netherlands frontier had been strengthened, Louis turned his attention towards his eastern borders, and in December 1679 ordered the setting-up of a special chamber within the *Parlement* of Metz to investigate and enforce his rights in the bishoprics of Metz, Toul and Verdun. The example of this *Chambre de Réunion* was followed by similar bodies at Breisach (for Alsace), Tournai (for Flanders) and Besançon (for Franche-Comté). The chamber at Breisach was particularly effective, and by August 1680 had brought the whole of Alsace under effective royal control, with the exception of the city of Strasburg, which was therefore occupied by French troops in 1681. Meanwhile the chamber at Metz had 'reunited' to the French crown a number of areas in

Germany, including most of Luxembourg, but not the fortress which gave its name to the region. In 1684 Louis ordered Vauban, the master of siege warfare, to take this stronghold, and Luxembourg duly fell. This 'gnawing peace'—which seemed to give Louis all the advantages of war without the formality of declaring it—was possible only because of the disarray of his enemies. Charles II of England was determined to keep free from all foreign entanglements; William of Orange could not persuade the Dutch regents to risk open conflict with France; and as for the Emperor, he was so heavily committed to the struggle against the Turks that in 1684 he signed the Truce of Ratisbon with Louis.

Nevertheless it had become apparent to a number of German princes that unless they took steps to concert their defence they would simply fall prey to French ambitions. In 1686, therefore, the rulers of Saxony and the Palatinate joined with Spain and the Emperor in the League of Augsburg, which had as its objective the maintenance of the territorial settlements agreed at Westphalia and Nymegen. This amounted to formal warning to Louis that he would have to stop nibbling away at the frontier regions. But Louis was not disposed to take such threats seriously, for he was convinced that the unity among his enemies was more apparent than real, and he was confident of the supremacy of French arms. By 1688 he was deeply involved in the problem of the Cologne succession, following the death of the Archbishop Elector in June. The episcopal territories were strategically of great importance, and the Archbishop was ruler of Liège, which had served as a French base in the war against the Dutch and was also the centre of the coal and iron industries upon which the supply of arms and munitions depended. Even before the Archbishop died, Louis had persuaded the chapter to elect as his coadjutor and presumed successor the francophil William von Furstemburg, but the Pope, whose relations with Louis were at their nadir, had refused to confirm this. In July 1688 Furstemburg was duly elected as archbishop, but not by a sufficient majority, so once again the decision reverted to Rome. It was certain that the Pope would not uphold Furstemburg's election, and Louis therefore decided upon a *coup de main*. In September 1688 French troops moved into the episcopal territories, while another force struck into Germany and captured the Rhine fortress of Philippsburg.

The campaign against Phillipsburg (near the border of the Palatinate) was intended mainly as a warning to the German princes not to interfere—though there was a subsidiary purpose in that Louis' sister-in-law, the Duchess of Orleans, had some claim to the Palatinate, following the death of her brother, the Elector Palatine, in 1685. But Louis' hopes of limited military action leading to a speedy settlement were not fulfilled. His enemies were prepared to fight rather than allow the continued extension of French power, and the operation against Philippsburg signalled the opening of what was to become known as the Nine Years War. While Louis' attention was concentrated on the Rhine, William of Orange had successfully invaded England and brought that state into the anti-French orbit. By 1689, therefore, Louis was at war with a formidable coalition of European powers, including the Emperor, England and the United Provinces, who had joined together in the League of Augsburg. It was clear that the major theatre of war would be the Netherlands, and Louis decided to withdraw from the Palatinate, which his troops had occupied. Before leaving, however, they devastated the countryside and sacked a number of towns, among them Mannheim. Louis' purpose was to make it impossible for his enemies to use the Palatinate as a base for the invasion of France; he also meant to show the German princes what they might expect if they dared oppose him. In this he miscalculated, for the devastation of the Palatinate aroused German patriotic sentiment and stiffened the resolve of the princes to stand firm.

In the Netherlands the war at first went well for France. Mons was captured, so was Namur, and a counter-attack by William was beaten off at Steinkirke in August 1692. But earlier in that year the allies had gained mastery at sea by defeating the French off La Hogue, and from then onwards they kept up a blockade which gradually began to make its effect felt. The situation was aggravated by poor harvests which brought famine to some parts of France. Even Louis felt the strain and recorded that he was 'inconsolable at finding everywhere difficulties and obstacles that I cannot overcome'. The first big blow to French prestige came in 1695, when William recaptured Namur, and shortly after this peace negotiations were set on foot. Both sides were nearing exhaustion, and there was the further consideration that the death of Charles II of Spain seemed likely at any moment and that France must therefore be well placed to claim at least a share of the Spanish inheritance. It was probably to create a favourable climate of opinion that in the Peace of Ryswick of 1697 Louis agreed to give up all his conquests, with the exception of Strasburg, and to accept Dutch military occupation of a row of barrier fortresses in the southern Netherlands—including Courtrai, Oudenarde, Mons, Charleroi, Namur and Luxembourg.

The Spanish Succession

If this was indeed Louis' purpose it seemed to have succeeded, for in 1698 William of Orange suggested that the Emperor, France and England should agree to partition the Spanish empire, following Charles II's death. Under the terms of this first partition treaty, Spain, the Netherlands, Sardinia and America were to go to the young Prince Joseph Ferdinand of Bavaria, grandson of the Emperor and his Spanish wife. The dauphin was to have all the rest, except Milan, which was to go to the Emperor's second son, the Archduke Charles. When the news of this partition treaty leaked out it caused great offence in Spain, which had not been consulted about the future disposition of these territories to which it had, at present, sole right. Charles II was determined that the great Spanish empire should not be split up, and decided to leave all his possessions to Prince Joseph Ferdinand. This might have been acceptable as a solution, but was never given a chance, for in 1699 Joseph Ferdinand died at the age of seven, leaving the question of the Spanish inheritance wide open once again.

In 1700 Louis put forward proposals for a second partition treaty under which the Archduke Charles was to have Spain, America and the Netherlands and the dauphin Naples, Sicily and Lorraine, while the Duke of Lorraine was to be compensated with Milan. William accepted these terms, although he had considerable reservations about Louis' good faith; but the Emperor refused to do so. Leopold was enjoying the prestige that came from the success of his campaign against the Turks and his identification with the 'German interest'. As a grandson of Philip III he was now ready to claim the entire Spanish inheritance and to bring Europe once more under Habsburg domination—though this time from Vienna and not Madrid. For more than a hundred years the two branches of the Habsburg house had intermarried in order to keep their possessions within the family, and there was more than a touch of irony about the fact that when at last the critical moment came relations between Madrid and Vienna were so bad that Charles II preferred to bequeath his territories to Louis' younger grandson, Philip of Anjou. Under the terms of his will the Archduke Charles was to inherit only if France refused the bequest.

Charles II of Spain died, at last, in November 1700 and Louis was faced with the dilemma of whether to accept his will or stand by the second partition treaty. In fact he had little choice, for if he rejected the proffered inheritance it would pass to the Emperor, who would most certainly accept it. There was little likelihood that England would join France in forcing the Emperor to accept the terms of the partition treaty. Since France would have to fight alone in any case, Louis decided to gain the maximum advantage, and therefore accepted the will. His action did not immediately lead to hostilities, and England and the United Provinces both recognised his grandson as Philip V of Spain. It was Louis' subsequent proceedings that virtually drove the maritime powers to fight, for he registered a document with the *Parlement* of Paris affirming the hereditary order of succession to the French crown—in other words refusing to exclude the possibility that Philip V might one day be ruler of both France and Spain.

Furthermore, Louis accepted his grandson's request that he should act as regent of the Netherlands, and immediately ordered the Dutch to withdraw their garrisons from the barrier fortresses. The Dutch had long feared a French presence on their southern frontier—an attitude that was summed up in De Witt's pregnant phrase *Gallicus amicus non vicinus*[1]—and now that this had become a reality the war party triumphed. In September 1701, therefore, the Dutch joined the English and the Emperor in the Grand Alliance against France. After four brief years of peace, Europe was about to be plunged into the War of the Spanish Succession. Louis was fighting as the upholder of Charles II's will. His opponents were agreed only on a few basic principles: that the French and Spanish crowns should never be united (they were quite content to leave Philip V with his Spanish throne so long as this condition was observed); that the Dutch should have a barrier in the southern Netherlands; and that the Emperor should be given a 'satisfaction' in Italy and the Netherlands.

The allies formally declared war on France in May 1702—although imperial troops under Prince Eugene had been campaigning in Italy since the previous year—and Louis despatched a force to the assistance of his sole German ally, the Elector of Bavaria. In fact the Elector and the French commander, Villars, disagreed so fundamentally about strategy that the latter had to be recalled (to take charge of operations against the Huguenots in the Cévennes) while the Elector went off to attack the Habsburg homelands in the Tyrol. Now it was the Emperor's turn to call for assistance, and in 1704 the Duke of Marlborough, commander of the Anglo-Dutch forces, was given permission to leave the Netherlands and strike into the heart of Bavaria. A French army

---

[1] 'Let the French be friends but not neighbours'.

under Tallard was hastily despatched to the Elector's aid, but although the two forces united they were crushingly defeated at the battle of Blenheim (on the Danube, north-west of Augsburg) in August 1702. Tallard was captured, the Elector retired to the Netherlands, of which he was nominally the governor, and for the rest of the war Bavaria was occupied by imperial troops. France was now without allies in Germany.

Blenheim was the first major defeat suffered by the armies of Louis XIV, and Marlborough wanted to follow it up by invading France along the line of the Moselle. But French defensive positions in this region were too strong and he therefore shifted his attention to the Netherlands front. In 1705 he broke through the defensive lines of Brabant, and would have pressed on to Brussels had it not been for the timidity of the Dutch political commissioners—who accompanied Marlborough's army as they did all Dutch forces. But Marlborough fortunately could count on the full support of Anthony Heinsius, who had emerged as the leader of the United Provinces after the death of William in 1702, and it was Heinsius who persuaded the Estates General to recall their commissioners and replace them by men of bolder temperament. This gave Marlborough the opportunity to strike a major blow against the French in the Netherlands, and in 1706 he won the second of his great victories, at Ramillies.

The French could no longer hold on to Brabant and Flanders, which they had occupied for the previous five years. Louvain, Brussels, Ghent and Antwerp all fell to the victorious allies, and in June 1706 the Estates of Brabant and Flanders formally recognised the Archduke Charles ('Charles III') as their sovereign. Their change of heart and allegiance was not prompted entirely by idealism. When the Elector of Bavaria had first been appointed governor of the Netherlands, in 1691, he had entrusted the administration to Count Bergeyck, who had begun to centralise the administration and whittle away local and personal 'liberties'. The French had intensified this reform programme, mainly for military purposes. They created a standing army based on conscription, appointed Bergeyck as *Surintendant des Finances*, and gave him their full backing in his attempt to improve the collection of existing taxes as well as raise new ones. Such activity was most unwelcome to all those who felt their privileges threatened, particularly the nobles, who had hitherto been exempt from taxation, and there was a widespread sense of relief when the French were driven out by the advancing allied armies.

After Ramillies, the Netherlands—all except for the Walloon provinces of Hainault, Namur and Luxembourg—were brought under an Anglo–Dutch condominium. The Dutch were mainly concerned to extend their influence and establish themselves so strongly that they could be sure of retaining a barrier once the war was over. The intervention of these northern 'tradesmen' was resented by the Flemish nobility, but generally speaking Anglo–Dutch rule was less effective and therefore more acceptable than that of Bergeyck and the French. For Flanders and Brabant, then, Ramillies was a victory for particularism.

Although the Netherlands were once again united there was no question of putting the clock back and recreating the old Burgundian state. The differences between north and south had become too marked, not only in religion but also socially, and southerners resented the obvious Dutch determination to exploit the commercial opportunities opened up by victory. The Dutch obsession with a barrier came to be as much economic as defensive, since control of these key fortresses carried with it domination of the main river routes along which trade flowed. Yet it was not simply avarice which drove the United Provinces to exploit this new market. The expansion of English and French seaborne trade had slashed Dutch profits at a time when the United Provinces were hard hit by the demands of war. The Dutch raised an army of some 150,000 men, half of whom were mercenaries, and the cost was a great strain on their economy. Occupation of the southern Netherlands offered some hope of relieving this burden and not surprisingly they grasped it with both hands.

Although Ramillies was the principal defeat suffered by French arms in 1706 it was not the only one, for in Italy Eugene routed a French force which was besieging Turin, and began advancing south, down the peninsula. In the following year the French were more successful, beating off an allied attack upon Toulon and sending troops once again into southern Germany and the Netherlands. In the spring of 1708 they captured Brussels and Ghent, but in May of that year Marlborough and Eugene caught them at Oudenarde and once again routed them. Northwestern France now lay open to allied invasion, and Marlborough wanted to push forward to Paris, as the Cardinal-Infante had done seventy years earlier. But the Dutch, who had no Channel to protect them in a case of defeat, were afraid of leaving great fortresses untaken in their rear, and allied troops were therefore committed to the siege of Lille, Vauban's masterpiece. The town held out until December 1708, and by that time it was too late to launch an invasion of France.

In the spring of 1709, follownig a very severe winter, the allied advance was renewed. Tournai was captured, Mons was besieged, and Paris was clearly threatened. But the French were far from crushed, and the invasion of their own land brought out reserves of patriotism and a will to resist that materially affected the course of the war. Louis recalled Villars, who told his troops that 'the only hope of the king for an honourable peace rests with your bayonets. . . . We shall give no quarter and ask for none.' He was as good as his word, for when the French and allied armies clashed at Malplaquet in July 1709 it was the allies who suffered most heavily. The French had to withdraw from the field and abandon Mons, but the allies were left licking their wounds and were in no shape to renew their thrust towards the French capital.

Louis, however, was under no illusions about the probable outcome of the war. The bitter winter had caused famine in some parts of his kingdom and grain was in such short supply that there was barely enough for the troops. Money was also difficult to come by, and although he set an example by having much of his plate melted down, such measures were little more than short-term palliatives. For any long-term solution peace was essential, and secret negotiations had already been opened. Louis was prepared to abandon all his conquests, including Strasburg, and to withdraw his troops from Spain. But the allies, and in particular the English, did not trust him. They therefore insisted that Philip V should give up the Spanish throne within two months, and that if he refused to do so, French troops should be used to expel him. The allies never believed that such an eventuality would arise, for they assumed that Spain was a French satellite and that Philip would obey all orders sent him from Paris. But Louis knew that this was not the case, and that his grandson, far from being a puppet, had identified himself with Spain and Spanish interests.

Philip was only a timid seventeen-year-old when he arrived in Spain in 1701, but he had good advisers, particularly the French financier, John Orry. It was these advisers who began translating into practice the reform programme sketched out by the Spaniards themselves in the reign of Charles II but never executed because of the lack of a strong monarch. The political power of the aristocrats was broken, departments of state were established to bypass the old councils on which the nobles were predominant, the financial administration was overhauled, and a special committee, the *Junta de Incorporacion*, was set up in 1707 to recover for the crown some of the property and rights granted away in the half century since Olivares. Phiip V became the symbol of this revival of the Spanish state, and when, in 1702, an Anglo-Dutch force landed near Cadiz, it found no support from the population. Two years later, however, another expedition was despatched, this time to Portugal, which had been sufficiently impressed by the evidence of allied naval power to abandon its former alliance with France. This led to the opening of a new front, in western Spain, and was followed in 1705 by a renewal of the war in Catalonia, where the Archduke Charles captured Barcelona. The latent hostility between Catalonia and Castile came into the open once more. Catalonia declared for 'Charles III', civil war broke out in Aragon and Valencia, and in 1706 allied troops, advancing from the west, forced Philip to evacuate Madrid.

This allied victory, coming as it did in the year of Ramillies, seemed to presage the collapse of the French cause in Spain as in the Netherlands, and among the Castilian aristocrats, resentful at French innovations, there was a pro-Austrian reaction. But public opinion was increasingly behind Philip, and the Spanish army, under the command of the Duke of Berwick (natural son of James II of England), was becoming an efficient fighting force. In 1707 Berwick defeated the allies in the battle of Almanza and Philip was able not only to put out the embers of revolt in Aragon and Valencia but also to do what none of his predecessors had been able to achieve, namely bring these areas under the direct rule of the Spanish crown by abolishing their traditional '*Fueros*, laws, and customs'. Catalonia still held out against him, however, and in 1710, following the withdrawal of all French troops from Spain, the allies again took possession of Madrid, and 'Charles III' made a formal entry into 'his' capital. But Castile was by now firmly committed to the cause of Philip V, and a small French force, sent back to restore the balance, defeated Charles's troops at Villa Viciosa in December 1710. Philip was once again unchallenged master of all Spain except Catalonia, and in the following year 'Charles III' left the peninsula, never to return.

It was against this background of increasing Spanish support for Philip V that Louis had to embark upon his delicate and unrewarding task of persuading his grandson to abdicate. 'I cannot hide from you the fact that peace becomes more necessary every day', he wrote to him, 'and you must not be surprised if I accept the offers that my enemies seem about to make'. When Philip replied that he could not abandon his people, Louis reminded him that 'should gratitude and affection for your subjects be strong inducements with you to adhere to them, I can tell you that you owe the same sentiments to me, to your family, and to your country, in preference to Spain'. But despite this heavy pressure Philip clung to his adopted country and refused to budge. Louis was therefore forced to continue a war which he seemed certain to lose and which was exacting a heavy toll in death, poverty and starvation.

In 1710 the allies, who had learnt their lesson at Malplaquet and now avoided pitched battles, captured Douai and Béthune, two of the fortresses which guarded the French frontier, while Villars drew back behind the defensive positions which he had hurriedly constructed —the Ne Plus Ultra lines. In 1711 Marlborough broke through these, and although French resistance continued to be stubborn it seemed as though nothing, in the long run, could prevent the allies from taking Paris. Fortunately for Louis such decisions were no longer to be made on the battlefield, for a change of government had occurred in England, and the new Tory administration was intent on peace.

The allies had themselves been feeling the strain of war, and the Dutch would have been prepared to accept Louis' concessions in 1709 had it not been for the English insistence that 'Charles III' should have Spain. This had not been one of the original aims of the Grand Alliance, and it seemed all the more pointless when, in 1711, following the death of the Emperor Joseph I, Charles was elected to take his place. The allies were now apparently committed to a never-ending war which had as its main objective the establishment of Habsburg predominance in Europe, and the futility as well as the absurdity of this was fully appreciated by the new Tory ministers in England. They were determined to make peace, and set about this with a ruth-lessness that took no account of the susceptibilities of their allies. Marl-borough was dismissed, the English army was ordered to refrain from any offensive operations, and secret negotiations were opened with Louis XIV.

One of the conditions on which the English insisted was that Philip must either leave Spain immediately, or, if he wished to remain as king, formally renounce all claim to the French throne. Philip opted for the second alternative, and with this major difficulty out of the way terms agreeable to both sides were rapidly concluded. France was to keep Alsace, including Strasburg, and also most of her gains in Flanders. The Emperor was to have the Spanish Netherlands, Naples and Sardinia, while the Duke of Savoy was to have Sicily. As for the Dutch, they were to have their barrier, though nothing like so strong a one as they had been promised by the English in 1709 in return for their continued support of the war. Nor were they to enjoy any of the commercial advantages of trade with Spanish America, which the English pre-empted for themselves. The Dutch were understandably bitter at this betrayal, and reluctant to accept the terms more or less dictated to them. However they were in no position to keep fighting on their own, and in April 1713 they signed the Treaty of Utrecht. A few months later Spain also made peace, ceding Gibraltar and Minorca to England, but not until March 1714 did the Peace of Rastatt formally put an end to the war between Louis and the Emperor.

The peace treaties of 1713 and 1714 did not solve all the problems connected with the Spanish succession. 'Charles III', who was now the Emperor Charles VI, refused to renounce his claim to the Spanish throne, and further fighting took place before the resolution of all outstanding differences by the Treaties of Madrid and the Hague in 1720. Charles at last recognised Philip V as the legitimate ruler of the Spanish kingdom, while Philip acknowledged Austrian sovereignty over Habsburg Italy—including Sicily, which the Duke of Savoy was persuaded to exchange for Sardinia. As for the Dutch determination to have a barrier in the southern Netherlands, now Austrian, this was satisfied by the Barrier Treaty of 1715, although the actual provisions did not come into effect until the following year. The barrier was to consist of the fortresses of Furnes and Ypres (held by France since 1678, but given up at Utrecht), Warneton, Menin, Tournai and Namur. These were to be garrisoned by some 30,000 men, most of whom were to be provided by the Emperor and maintained out of the revenues of the Netherlands. In this way the southern provinces were to be made to pay for the defence of their northern neighbours and one time brothers.

The long war of the Spanish Succession had lowered Louis XIV's reputation at home and abroad and left the royal finances in a far worse state than they had been at his accession. He died in September 1715 at the age of seventy-seven, after advising his five-year-old great-grandson and successor to 'try to remain at peace with your neighbours. I loved war too much. Do not follow me in that or in over-spending.' It is not possible, of course, to strike a balance between

French expenditure in men and money on the one hand and French gains in territory and general security on the other. Yet Louis' achievement was considerable. He gave France much stronger frontiers in the north and east; he secured part of the great Spanish inheritance for his own Bourbon family; and he held the reviving power of the Austrian Habsburgs in check. He also prevented the modification of the treaty settlement of Westphalia in ways that might have been detrimental to French interests, and by constantly claiming more than he needed he retained more than might otherwise have been the case. There was an element of the confidence-trickster about Louis, and he frequently overplayed his hand, but he left France firmly established among the great powers of Europe and French culture predominant throughout the entire continent. The price paid for this was high, perhaps too high, but Louis shared the prevailing assumption that money must serve the demands of policy, not dictate it. Oblivious to the sufferings of his subjects, he made *La Gloire* his objective and pursued it with such determination that he dazzled his contemporaries and established at least a claim to greatness.

TWENTY-EIGHT

Charles XII, Peter the Great, and the Great Northern War 1700–21

Charles XII

In 1697 Charles XI of Sweden died at the early age of forty-two, leaving as heir his fourteen-year-old son, also named Charles. For a few months there was a regency, but the longer this continued the more likely it seemed that the magnates who had suffered from the 'Reduction' would lead a counter-attack against the absolutist regime. In order to prevent this, Charles XII was declared of age, thereby re-establishing in all its fulness the authority of the crown. The new king was tall, slim and fair-haired, with brilliant eyes and a jutting nose—not a handsome man but a striking one. He had a keen intelligence, loved music, and when he had time read widely, but his main interest was war. He positively enjoyed fighting, and this was just as well since the expansion of Sweden had aroused the envy of her neighbours, and they were hoping to take advantage of what they assumed would be the weak rule of a boy king.

Charles and his advisers knew that they must look to their own defence, and in 1699 they increased the size of the army to 75,000 men and also expanded the navy. They were anticipating an attack from Denmark, the traditional enemy of Sweden, but they did not realise that the key figure in the anti-Swedish coalition was in fact the King of Poland.

Following the death of John Sobieski in 1696 the Polish crown was offered to Frederick Augustus, Elector of Saxony, who accepted it and took the title of Augustus II. There was no common frontier between Saxony and Poland—which were divided by the Habsburg Silesian lands and the Oder provinces of Brandenburg–Prussia—nor was there any religious bond, since Saxony was Lutheran while Poland was mainly Roman Catholic. But Poland was rich in raw materials, while Saxony was industrially advanced, so the prospects for fruitful collaboration in the economic sphere were good.

Any expansion of Polish–Saxon trade would, however, be limited by Swedish control of the Baltic, and the same limitation applied to Russia, whose outlet to the west was confined to ports under Swedish domination. The only way in which this stranglehold could be broken was by force, and in 1698 Augustus and Peter of Russia met secretly to plan a joint attack on the Swedish empire. In the following year the coalition was joined by the new King of Denmark, Frederick IV, and it was agreed that while Augustus struck into Swedish Livonia, Frederick would attack Sweden's ally, the Duke of Holstein-Gottorp, and then launch an invasion of the southern provinces of Sweden itself. Peter's share in these combined operations was to be a thrust into Ingria, on the eastern shore of the Gulf of Finland, but it was understood that his campaign could not get under way before peace had been concluded with the Turks. This failure to synchronise operations was to prove the undoing of the entire allied strategy.

Augustus had the tacit support of the ruler of Brandenburg–Prussia —who was still hoping to gain possession of Swedish Pomerania—and Saxon troops were allowed to pass through the Oder provinces *en route* to Livonia. When Charles XII made a request for similar transit rights, this was rejected, thereby freeing Augustus from the fear of a Swedish attack on his rear. In February 1700, therefore, Augustus's troops crossed the border into Swedish Livonia, while in the following month the Danes thrust into Holstein. The Great Northern War had begun.

The Swedes had a great advantage in the support of England and the United Provinces, with whom she had signed an alliance in 1700. They sent a fleet to the Baltic, and it was under the cover of this formidable protection that the Swedes launched an attack on Zeeland. Copenhagen was besieged and Frederick was confronted with the unpalatable choice of total defeat or surrender. He chose surrender and in August 1700 signed the Peace of Travendal, which restored the *status quo* and took Denmark out of the anti-Swedish coalition. The Swedes would have liked to follow up this success with a direct attack upon Saxony, via Brandenburg–Prussia, but the maritime powers, afraid that a general war might break out in northern Europe at a time when the question of the Spanish Succession was coming to a head, made clear their opposition to such a venture. The Swedes therefore reinforced their troops in Estonia, and Charles led his army eastwards in a winter campaign against the Russians, who were besieging Narva. In a sharp and successful engagement, in November 1700, the besiegers were routed and Narva was saved. The Swedes had once again demonstrated their military superiority.

Augustus was afraid that Russia would follow Denmark's example and pull out of the war, leaving him isolated. It was to prevent this that he made a secret agreement with Peter, promising Polish recognition of the Russian claim to Estonia and Livonia so long as the Tsar kept on fighting. This agreement was far from pleasing to the Poles, and in 1701 the Diet insisted that Poland should remain formally neutral in the war. Already a 'patriot party' was forming, which saw Russia as the greatest menace to Polish independence and wanted alliance with the Swedes. There were also the neutralists, who feared that if Augustus were successful in the war he would establish monarchical absolutism in Poland and trample underfoot the 'liberties' which the Polish aristocracy and gentry valued as guarantees of their own privileges.

Although the Poles were theoretically neutral, their ruler, with the support of Saxon troops, was engaged in open war with Sweden, and it was for this reason that in January 1702 Charles XII launched a full scale invasion of Poland and occupied Warsaw. This action rallied some sections of Polish opinion behind Augustus, who was now formally authorised to use native troops against the invader. The Polish army hoped to link up with the Saxons, but before it could do so Charles crushed it at the battle of Kliszow in July 1702. Following his victory Charles would have been ready to sign a peace treaty, but Augustus was determined to keep fighting and was heartened by the news that Russian troops were flooding into Lithuania. He could not break the Swedish hold on the western part of his kingdom, however, nor could he prevent the neutralists from summoning an assembly to Warsaw in January 1704, which declared him deposed and offered the throne to one of their own number, Stanislas Leszczynski. Yet this action in some ways strengthened Augustus's position, for the majority of the Polish gentry were shocked by the election of a man whom they regarded, with some justification, as a Swedish puppet, and in May 1704 they came in great numbers to the General Assembly of Sandomierz, where they pledged their loyalty to Augustus and voted in favour of a declaration of war against Sweden.

In 1705 Stanislas, crowned king at Warsaw, signed a treaty with the Swedes, giving them a highly favoured position in commercial relations with Poland and authorising them to garrison key Polish towns. But Stanislas's authority extended only so far as the Swedish military presence could be made effective, and this was bound to be limited while Augustus stayed in the war. It was to put an end to this intolerable situation that in 1706 Charles decided to invade Saxony, The maritime powers were no longer concerned to restrain him, since they were clearly winning their war against France, and in August, therefore, Charles took his troops across Silesia to the Saxon frontier. This gesture sufficed. The Saxons had no intention of suffering invasion simply for the sake of their Elector's monarchical entanglements, and they forced Augustus to accept the Peace of Altranstadt, by which he recognised Stanislas as King of Poland and agreed to end hostilities against Sweden.

The formidable alliance which had confronted Sweden in 1700 had now been broken, and only Russia remained in the field. Denmark and Saxony had both been knocked out of the war by attacks upon their homeland, and Charles decided to take the same action against Russia. He prepared for a major campaign which would, he hoped, lead to the capture of Moscow and bring about peace on terms favourable to Sweden. Since he knew that the Russians would retreat, scorching the earth before them, Charles took great care over arrangements for the maintenance of his army. He reckoned that as he struck eastwards, towards Smolensk, the Russians would pull back from the Baltic provinces. This would be the opportunity for Lewenhaupt, his commander there, to assemble a massive supply train and take it, with a substantial body of reinforcements, to Charles's aid.

At first all went well, and by the summer of 1708 Charles had reached Mohilev, within striking distance of the Russian border. The way to Smolensk lay open, but he did not dare advance until his supply train had reached him, and Lewenhaupt was held up by heavy rains. The campaigning season was drawing to a close, and if Charles was to prevent his army from starving during the winter he would have to turn south, to regions which had not been devastated. A further incentive to this course of action was given by the news that the Cossacks were in revolt against the Tsar. From Mohilev, therefore, Charles turned south-east into the Ukraine, where he was welcomed by the Cossack leader, Mazeppa, who hoped for Swedish assistance in re-establishing an independent state. Lewenhaupt, following in the wake of Charles's army, was defeated in September and lost most of his supply train, but by this time it was no longer essential to Charles. More important were the men whom Lowenhaupt brought with him when at last he linked up with the main Swedish force.

The winter of 1708–09 was exceptionally severe in the Ukraine, as in the rest of Europe, and the Swedes suffered great hardship. But by the spring of 1709 Charles was ready to continue his advance on Moscow, taking the southern route. The key to this was the town of Poltava (on a tributary of the lower Dnieper) which was defended by a Russian army ensconced in a strongly fortified position. Charles could not lead the attack on this in person, since he had been wounded in the foot some weeks earlier, but he directed operations from his stretcher. The assault was launched in June 1709 but was beaten back with heavy losses. Seven thousand Swedish troops were killed, another 2,000 were taken prisoner, and Charles had to flee south with the remaining 16,000. There could be no question now of an advance on Moscow. Charles hoped to make his return home through Poland, but this meant moving south-west to a point where the Dnieper could be crossed. Charles, with a strong bodyguard, went ahead, accompanied by Mazeppa and the other Cossack leaders, for whom capture by the Russians would have meant death. He assumed that the main body of the army, commanded in his absence by Lewenhaupt, would stand and fight, but the Swedes were dispirited and saw no chance of surviving unless they capitulated. In July 1709, therefore, Lewenhaupt surrendered to the Russians at Perevelojtna, and the Swedish campaign, which had opened with such high hopes, came to an inglorious end.

Charles and Mazeppa were given refuge on Turkish soil, and the king established his 'court' at Bender, waiting for an opportunity to return to his native land. He could, of course, have gone by sea, but he was not at home in this element, and feared that he would be captured or, if he was given a safe conduct, be compelled to accept conditions that might limit his future freedom of action. The only possible land routes were through Poland or Hungary, but the Hungarian border was closed because of the outbreak of plague, while southern Poland was in the hands of his enemies. For the time being he had therefore no altern-ative to staying at Bender, from where he established close links with the war party among the Turks and whipped up feeling against Tsar Peter. It was partly as a result of his efforts that the Sultan made repeated declarations of war against Russia. In 1711 Ottoman forces surrounded Peter and his army near the Pruth river and forced them to capitulate, but this victory was not exploited in the way that Charles would have hoped. Although Peter promised to recall his troops from Poland and to put no impediment in the way of the king's return to Sweden, there was still no certainty that Charles, if he once set out on the long and hazardous journey, would ever arrive. He therefore stayed on at Bender, making use of his enforced leisure by reading widely and reflecting on the nature and problems of government and administration. It was during this period of involuntary exile that he worked out the basis of the reform plan which he put into operation after his return home.

Although Charles was many hundreds of miles away from Sweden, he kept in regular contact with his ministers and sent them directives. In particular he ordered them to raise an expeditionary force which should fight its way from Pomerania through Poland and provide an armed escort for his return. In fact the Swedish army was fully occupied in resisting another Danish invasion of the southern Swedish peninsula, but in February 1710 the Danes were defeated and forced to withdraw. The Swedish force now crossed to Pomerania, where it was again victorious, but the fleet which had convoyed it was wiped out by a Danish squadron. In an attempt to repeat the brilliant manoeuvre of 1700 the Swedish force struck west towards Holstein, determined to invade the Danish heartland. But in early 1713 it was surrounded in the Holstein fortress of Tonning by Saxon, Danish and Russian troops, and had to surrender.

This blow to Charles's hopes was softened by the news that the Turks had made peace with the Russians at Adrianople in 1713 and secured a further promise from Peter that he would put no obstacles in the way of Charles's return home via Poland. But the Tsar could not bind Augustus, who had reclaimed the Polish throne following Charles's defeat at Poltava and was convinced, with good reason, that his occupancy of it would be threatened the moment Charles arrived in northern Europe. However, the consent of his enemies was no longer essential to the king's plans, for with the ending of the plague epidemic the frontiers between the Ottoman empire and Hungary were again opened. In September 1714, therefore, Charles set out on his journey, travelling incognito, and by November he was in Stralsund. There he stayed for some months, organising the defence of the city in readiness for the anticipated Danish attack, and returned to Sweden only in 1715.

The military situation, from the Swedish point of view, was bleak. Brandenburg–Prussia and Hanover—whose ruler was now King of Great Britain—had joined the anti-Swedish coalition, and little remained of the overseas empire that Sweden had built up during the course of the seventeenth century. But Charles, who at thirty-six was still a comparatively young man, saw no reason to despair. He planned to destroy his enemies piecemeal, starting, as usual, with the Danes, and in 1718 he opened a campaign against them in Norway. What might have happened afterwards must remain for ever unknown, for in December Charles was killed by a stray bullet while directing siege operations, and the campaign was called off.

Charles had never married, so the throne passed to his sister, Ulrica Eleanor, and her husband Frederick of Hesse. This marked the end not only of the Swedish empire but also of absolute monarchy in Sweden, for Frederick, in return for the support of the nobles, allowed them to establish what was virtually an oligarchy. During the course of the next few years peace terms were negotiated which brought the long and exhausting war to a close. By the Treaty of Stockholm in 1719 Hanover purchased Bremen and Verden from Sweden, while Prussia at long last acquired the greater part of Swedish Pomerania. Two years later the Treaty of Nystad gave Russia sovereignty over the Baltic provinces of Livonia, Estonia, Ingria and eastern Karelia, while Denmark took over the disputed Holstein–Gottorp lands. Sweden was left with only a small portion of Pomerania (including Stralsund), the island of Rugen and the port of Wismar. If this was little to show for a century of conflict, Sweden had at least gained control of her own peninsula, having driven the Danes out of the southern provinces once and for all. She had also broken the Danish stranglehold on the Sound. It was her attempt to control the overseas trade of Russia that had signally failed, and in a sense the rise of Sweden had only been possible because of the long period of domestic upheaval and isolation into which Russia had been thrown by the 'Time of Troubles'. As soon as the sleeping giant began to awake, as it did under Peter the Great, the days of Swedish greatness were bound to be numbered, for in natural resources, population and wealth Russia was incomparably stronger. After Charles XII's sudden death it became increasingly obvious that a fundamental shift of power had taken place in northern Europe.

Peter the Great

Peter was born in 1672, the first child of Tsar Alexis and his second wife. Alexis died when Peter was only four years old, and the throne was claimed by Theodore (Fedor), one of the two sons of Alexis's first marriage. On Theodore's death, in 1682, Peter was proclaimed Tsar, as Theodore's brother Ivan was feeble in mind and body. But the rivalry between the families of the first and second marriages was so acute that a revolt took place, sparked off by the Moscow *Streltsy*. For three days the soldiers ran riot, pillaging the Kremlin and massacring all the boyars they could lay hands on. Peter's supporters had to flee, and order was only restored when Peter and Ivan were proclaimed joint Tsars, under the regency of Ivan's elder sister, Sophia.

Peter's hatred of the *Streltsy* and of the Kremlin dates from this time. During Sophia's rule, Peter and his mother lived outside Moscow, and the young boy spent much of his time in the German settlement, a township occupied mainly by ex-soldiers from all over Europe. It was from these men that he learned the rudiments of warfare, and from an early age he showed his delight in acquiring technical knowledge and mastering practical skills. He engaged a Dutch tutor to teach him mathematics, and he also studied the theory of ballistics and fortification. Not content simply to learn about military matters at second hand, Peter formed a small army out of his household servants and trained them in war games. This force was to come in useful in 1689, when Sophia attempted a coup against Peter's mother. In the first moment of alarm Peter fled to a monastery, but he soon rallied his supporters and regained control of Moscow. Now it was Sophia's turn to flee to a convent, while Peter's mother took over the direction of government in the name of her son.

Peter was a huge man, nearly seven feet tall and bursting with energy. He was never still for a moment, and the strain of holding his violent temperament in check showed in nervous movements such as the twitching of his head and constant gesturing with his arms. His wild appearance could frighten people, and his enemies believed he was the devil incarnate. Peter's passion was to change Russia, to turn it from a backward and isolated state into a great European power. To do this he needed two things: first, western technical knowledge, and second, a change of attitude on the part of his people. The first was relatively simple to acquire, although the application of it might take many years. As for a change of attitude, this might also have taken years, but Peter was in a hurry and tried to bludgeon his subjects into new and un-congenial ways. For instance, since the wearing of beards was a long-established custom he ordered all his subjects (except the peasants and clergy) to shave theirs off and took the razor himself to some of his more refractory courtiers. He even proscribed traditional Russian costume and ordered his officials to set an example by wearing western-style garments.

In 1697 Peter set out on a tour of western Europe. His object was not pleasure, nor was it primarily diplomacy, though he hoped to build up an anti-Turkish coalition. He was going to see western techniques at first hand and to recruit foreign artisans and experts for Russia. In Holland he worked as a shipbuilder in the East India Company yards, and from there, in January 1698, he went to England, where he spent his days working in the dockyard at Deptford and his nights in drunken carousals—much to the horror of John Evelyn, who had placed his Deptford house at the Tsar's disposal, only to find that it was treated like a pigsty. Peter intended to go on across Europe to Venice, but news reached him that the *Streltsy* were again in revolt and that there was talk of deposing him and getting rid of the hated foreigners and their newfangled ways. Peter therefore sped back to Moscow, put down the revolt, arrested, tortured and executed the *Streltsy* ringleaders, and disbanded the remainder of the regiments. Now he really was master of his state and could set about the task of reform in earnest.

Before embarking on his 'Great Embassy' to the west, Peter had directed operations against the Turkish fort of Azov, which controlled the mouth of the river Don. His first attempt to take the town, in 1695, was a failure, because of Turkish mastery of the sea, but Peter ordered ships to be built on the Don and in the following year his troops assaulted and captured Azov. He hoped to push the Russian frontier further south, towards the Black Sea, and was encouraged by the fact that the main Turkish forces were fully engaged in war against the Emperor. In January 1699, however, the Emperor made peace at Carlowitz, in a settlement that took no notice of Russian claims. Peter was bitter at what he regarded as a betrayal, but he could not fight on alone. In any case he had already been invited to join the anti-Swedish coalition that Augustus of Poland was forming. He therefore turned his attention away from the problems of his southern frontier towards the Baltic regions in the north.

In July 1700 a peace treaty was signed between the Russians and the

Turks, leaving Peter as ruler of Azov, and on the day he received the news of the signing Peter declared war against Sweden. By this time Denmark had been forced to capitulate and withdraw from the coalition, and in November 1700 the Russians themselves were badly mauled by Charles XII at Narva. Peter kept up the pressure in the Baltic provinces, however, and his troops captured Narva in 1704. He also sent men and money to the aid of Augustus of Poland, not simply to keep Charles away from Russian soil but to stake out a claim to Livonia as well. On the eastern shores of the Gulf of Finland Russian forces occupied the greater part of Ingria, and to show that Russia was now laying perm-anent claim to a share in Baltic trade Peter founded a new city, St Petersburg, in the region from which the Swedes had only just been expelled. With the same relentless determination that had produced a fleet out of nothing on the Don, Peter mobilised resources on a huge scale and at a great cost in lives and suffering, to create out of the marshes of Ingria the beautiful city which he later made the capital of Russia.

Resentment at the Tsar's ruthless methods led to revolt among the Don Cossacks in the south in 1707, and Peter had only just brought this under control by the time Charles XII invaded Russia. The defeat of the Swedish king at Poltava showed that the new army created by Peter was far superior in equipment, organisation and fighting capacity to anything his predecessors had known. Yet two years later, while engaged in war against the Turks, Peter's troops were surrounded on the banks of the river Pruth and forced to capitulate. Peter himself only just avoided capture, and following this disaster he had to restore Azov to the Turks—which meant the end of the Black Sea fleet—and to promise that Russian forces would evacuate Poland.

These checks in the south did not affect the progress of Russian arms in the north, now that Charles XII was out of the way. In 1714 the Russians occupied Finland, and by the Treaty of Nystad, which ended the war in 1721, Peter was confirmed in possession of Livonia, Estonia, Ingria and eastern Karelia—territories that had previously cut Russia off from access to the Baltic. Up to this time direct Russian trade with the west had been confined to Archangel on the White Sea, which was not easily accessible; now, however, the whole Baltic coast from Riga to Viborg was in Russian hands.

Following the defeat of Russian forces at Narva in 1700, Peter set about creating a modern army. Conscription was introduced, foreign officers were brought in to train Russian commanders, and heavy industry was encouraged to produce the necessary weapons. Since access to the Baltic meant that Russia was now a sea power, Peter also created a Baltic fleet, set up a navigation school at Moscow in 1701, and established a naval academy at St Petersburg in 1715. This expansion of the armed forces was very expensive, but the finances of the Russian state were in a poor way. Shortly before Peter's accession there had been an attempt to streamline them by replacing the complex tax based on land with a general levy on households, but this cumbersome system led to a fall in revenue. After many experiments and false starts, Peter introduced a poll tax in 1717 and to ensure its efficient functioning he ordered a census to be carried out. This aroused enormous opposition and was only effected through the use of troops, but its success was shown by the fact that the new poll tax, which came into full operation only in 1724, produced far greater sums than anything known before. Although Russian military expenditure was high, and constantly growing, Peter did not have to burden himself and his successors with debts. The cost was met out of direct taxation—though the advantages of this were not, of course, apparent to the bulk of the population, who were aware simply of the enormous demands made upon them.

The improvement of Russian financial administration was only part of a general restructuring of government. There had been some development along bureaucratic lines prior to Peter, and forty or so *Prikazes* had been set up to control various state departments. These were remodelled in 1699–1701, but their functioning was still impeded by lack of definition and overlapping. Peter therefore decided to do away with the *Prikazes*, or at any rate subordinate them to 'colleges', on the Swedish model. An official was sent to study the actual working of the Swedish system, and in 1718 the first Russian colleges were set up. By the end of the reign there were ten of these departments, each with a nationwide jurisdiction—unlike the old *Prikazes*. The colleges were responsible to the Senate, a small executive council established by Peter in 1711 to take the place of the boyar *Duma*. Regional government also was reformed on the Swedish model. In 1708 the whole of Russia had been broken up into eight huge provinces, but the governors of these miniature states soon became notorious for their corruption and inefficiency. In 1718, therefore, Peter increased the number of provinces to eleven and divided each one into smaller administrative units called counties. These were only subordinate to the governor in military matters: for everything else, except justice, the *Voivode* of the county was responsible, and he dealt directly with the central government. From 1719 onwards judicial matters came under the aegis of the newly established College of Justice, and eleven judicial districts were created, parallel to the provinces but theoretically distinct from them. The idea was to separate justice from administration, but in fact the local courts soon fell under the influence of the local nobility, and as with so many of Peter's reforms the reality was a long way from the ideal. Urban government was also remodelled. It had previously been the responsibility of elected councils, but in 1721 the right of election was confined to the wealthier town dwellers, organised in two gilds, and a new college was set up at St Petersburg to supervise the municipalities. This rapidly expanded its activities to such a degree that it effectively stifled urban independence.

Peter's reforming zeal was not confined to the sphere of administration. Like Colbert he used the resources of the state to regulate and foster industrial development. Nearly a hundred factories were set up at the government's expense and leased out to entrepreneurs on favourable terms. Heavy industry, so essential to the army, was stimulated by the building of ironworks, particularly in the Urals—a region that had hitherto been neglected. In 1719 a College of Manufactures was created with the specific function of making capital grants to assist the development of industry, and Peter pursued a protectionist policy, imposing heavy duties on foreign products where they competed with Russian ones. He ordered the merchants to organise themselves into trading companies on the western model, he made commercial treaties with a number of foreign states, and by opening up the Baltic he stimulated the growth of Russian trade and shipping. All that one man could do, he did, and the results were impressive, particularly in heavy industry. But exhortation, even when accompanied by force and threats of force, could not create a highly developed economy overnight. Government regulation could be a hindrance as well as a stimulus, and the sharp division of Russian society into rulers and ruled opened the way to petty oppression and maladministration, inefficiency and downright corruption.

In Peter's eyes, every one of his subjects was a servant of the state. The nobles served it directly, either in the armed forces or the civil administration; the peasants indirectly, by providing the labour and the rents without which the nobles would not have been free to devote themselves to government. The vast majority of peasants were serfs, and Peter clamped the burden even more heavily on them by tying

them to their master's land and subjecting them to heavy taxation as
well as forced labour. Even a French peasant might have felt highly
favoured compared to a Russian one. But although the nobles, unlike
their serfs, were free to move from their estates, they might do so only
in order to serve the Tsar. In 1714 nobles were instructed to send their
children to schools which were to be established in every province, but
this scheme was stillborn and two years later Peter decreed that sons of
nobles were to be educated at St Petersburg in one of the specialist
institutions—the naval academy, for instance. Those who eventually
opted for the army would have to spend some time in the ranks of a
guards regiment before receiving their commission. In this and similar
ways the nobles were given a sense of corporate identity and linked
very closely with the Tsarist regime. Even before the beginning of
Peter's reign the old rigid hierarchy of Russian ranks, based on birth,
had been breaking down. Peter brought this process to culmination in
1722 by decreeing that henceforth social status was to depend solely
upon service to the state. A table of ranks was published, setting out
the various stages in parallel military and civil careers, and the upper
grades automatically entitled a man to noble status. In this way the old
boyars were replaced by an aristocracy of service.

There were many people for whom Peter's ambition to modernise
Russia by importing western ideas and techniques was anathema, and
they had the support of many others who, while they might have been
prepared to accept the long-term objectives, bitterly resented the
arbitrary way in which Peter was trying to achieve them. From time
to time this opposition came into the open, as with the revolt of the
Don Cossacks in 1706–08, but even when a state of peace nominally
prevailed throughout the country a continuous war was going on
between the reforming Tsar and those of his subjects who preferred the
old ways.

The conservatives were particularly strong in the Church, the
embodiment of the traditions of 'Holy Russia', but Peter firmly
asserted his control over this institution. In 1701 he revived the Monasteries Office, which took over monastic lands and diverted a great part
of their revenues to the royal treasury. Smaller monasteries were closed,
discipline was enforced, and an upper limit was set for the number of
novices allowed to enter the monastic life. Peter was determined that
the Church as a whole should look to him and to no one else as its
leader; he did not wish to suffer from any repetition of the challenges

made by the patriarchs Filaret and Nikon. In 1721, therefore, he abolished the patriarchate and set up a 'Holy Governing Synod' to rule the Church. This was in effect a department of state, like the other colleges, and although it was superior to them in status there could be no doubt about its subordination to the Tsar.

The Church was divided in its attitude towards Peter. His drunken revels, during which he indulged in crude parodies of religious services, caused great offence; yet, on the other hand, the patriarchs had made themselves unpopular by their arrogance and extravagant claims. There was a big gap between the rich higher clergy and the great mass of poverty-stricken priests. There was also a divergence between those who wanted to see the Church purged of the superstitious accretions of past centuries and those for whom change was betrayal. The diehard conservatives refused to have anything to do with the official Church and proudly proclaimed themselves to be the 'Old Believers'. They were subjected to harsh treatment, ranging from minor harassment— such as paying fines in order to retain their beards—to persecution, exile and death. Peter might have been content to let the Old Believers worship as they pleased if only they had declared their loyalty to him, but this they would not do. The forces of tradition were hostile to the Tsar, and they found a focus in Peter's own son, Alexis. In 1716 Alexis, who was frightened of his formidable father and opposed to the policies with which Peter was identified, fled to Habsburg territory. Two years later he returned, publicly apologised for his flight and accepted his exclusion from the succession. But this was not enough for Peter, who feared that so long as Alexis lived he would be a source of hope and encouragement to the conservative opposition. Alexis was therefore arrested and tortured to death. Peter thereby demonstrated that even the closest ties of blood would not be allowed to stand in the way of his determination to drag Russia into the modern world.

By the time Peter died, in February 1725, Russia had emerged from isolation and taken her place in the ranks of the major European powers. The Tsar's ambassadors were to be found in all the principal capitals, and outside Russia there was considerable admiration for this dynamic ruler who had, as it seemed, imposed order on a people hitherto renowned only for their lawlessness and savage habits. Yet at the heart of Peter's reforms there was a paradox. He tried to change the lives, thoughts and habits of his subjects without changing their hearts. Because he was a pessimist where human nature (or Russian nature, at any rate) was concerned, he used fear instead of persuasion. By so doing he built up a barrier of hatred to the fulfilment of his wishes, and identified the cause of reform with the methods of brutality.

Peter himself never seems to have been aware of this paradox in his own policy. 'Was not everything done by force,' he asked in 1723, 'and are not the people grateful for what has resulted?' His people might have been genuinely grateful if only everything had not been done by force. And yet the need to move fast and to goad a sleeping giant into life before he was dismembered by his enemies goes far to explain Peter's attitude. In so far as he carried to conclusion changes that had been taking place before he ascended the throne, he built on firm foundations. Much of the rest of his work was transformed in the reigns of his successors or swept aside. But his success in turning Russia away from introspection towards contact with the more advanced world of western Europe was undeniable. As his chancellor rightly declared in a speech in 1721: 'By your tireless labour, and under your guidance, we have been led from the shades of ignorance to the stage of glory before the world. We have been, so to speak, led from nothing to life, and we have rejoined the company of political nations.'

TWENTY-NINE

The Ottoman Turks, and Central and Eastern Europe, in the Seventeenth Century

The Ottoman Turks

Turkish power seemed to be declining in the first thirty years of the seventeenth century. The death of Ahmed I in 1617 was followed by a disputed succession, and although his eldest son was proclaimed Sultan, as Osman II, intrigues continued unabated. In 1622 a Janissary revolt led to the deposition and murder of Osman and a further succession struggle. In 1623 Osman's brother was proclaimed Sultan, with the title of Murad IV, but for ten more years the situation remained confused, with the Janissaries in a rebellious mood and various elements at court struggling for power. In 1632, however, Murad emerged from the shadows and asserted his authority. From that moment onwards a new vigour showed itself in Turkish policy at home and abroad, and European powers had to take cognisance of the unpalatable fact that the Ottoman menace was once again a reality.

At first the revival of Turkish power made itself apparent in the east. War between Turkey and Persia had broken out in 1623, and the Persians had captured Baghdad. After a number of preliminary campaigns, Murad eventually recaptured the city in 1638, and in the following year Ottoman sovereignty over Iraq was confirmed by the Peace of Zuhab. He then returned in triumph to Constantinople, where he died early in 1640. Murad's successor, Ibrahim I, was a weak character who could not hold the competing factions in check. In 1644 he assented to the dismissal and execution of his highly capable vizier and took over direct responsibility for policy. This proved to be his undoing, for a Turkish onslaught against the Venetians in Crete bogged down before the fortress of Candia, and the blame for this reverse was laid on Ibrahim. In 1648 the Janissaries again revolted, deposed the Sultan, and replaced him by his young son, Mohamed IV.

Factions truggles continued until 1656, when the seventy-one-year-old Mohamed Koprulu was appointed grand vizier on terms that made him virtual dictator. He purged the administration in a merciless manner, executing thousands of his opponents and establishing a reign of terror. By clamping down on corruption, raising compulsory loans, squeezing more out of the holders of fiefs, and increasing the tribute paid by the principalities of Moldavia and Wallachia—now once again brought under effective Turkish control—he transformed the financial situation and made possible the continued expansion of Ottoman power. His major achievement in this field was the take-over of Transylvania, whose ruler, George Racoksky II, had been trying to assert his independence (see p. 533). By the time Koprulu died in 1661 Transylvania was once again an obedient puppet state.

The death of Koprulu did not mean a relapse into faction politics and endless plotting. One reason for this was Mohamed IV's decision to remove his court to Adrianople, where it was free from the dangerous combination of Janissary discontent and palace intrigues that made life at Constantinople so dangerous. Another and even more important reason was the appointment of Koprulu's son, Ahmed Koprulu, as grand vizier. Ahmed Koprulu had all his father's administrative ability without any of his more ferocious characteristics. He also had the advantage of being able to base his own work on his father's achievements. His immediate objective was to confirm the takeover ot Transylvania, and in 1664 he was apparently successful, since the Emperor signed the Peace of Vasvar, by which he promised to recognise the Turkish puppet ruler as legitimate head of this small but strategically significant state. Fighting continued, however, and in August ot that same year the Turks were heavily defeated at St Gotthard. They had to pull back to the Danube, and if the Emperor had followed up his victory Ahmed Koprulu might well have been disgraced and executed. But the imperial troops were exhausted after the hard-fought battle, and the Emperor needed peace in the east so that he could turn his attention to the problem of the Spanish Succession. He therefore confirmed the terms of Vasvar, and Ahmed Koprulu was able to make a triumphal return to Constantinople. Four years later his prestige was further increased when the Venetian fortress of Candia at last surrendered, after a siege lasting nearly a quarter of a century. The Turks were once again masters of the eastern Mediterranean.

In 1670 the Hungarian rebels appealed for Turkish aid (see p. 533), and had Ahmed Koprulu gone to their assistance he might seriously have weakened Habsburg control over Royal Hungary. Instead he chose to renew the struggle against Poland. Throughout the sixteenth and seventeenth centuries the Poles and Turks had been engaged in a running battle over Moldavia, to which the Polish crown had historic claims, but Ahmed Koprulu was now thinking in terms of a new puppet state, a Cossack Ukraine under the Sultan's sovereignty, straddling the Dnieper. The Poles, exhausted by their long conflict with Russia, were too weak to impose their will in the Ukraine, and the Cossacks now accepted the Sultan as their overlord. A joint force of Turks, Cossacks and Crimean Tatars struck into Podolia in 1672 and pushed west as far as Lvov. This revived the crusading spirit in Poland, and John Sobieski, blessed by papal prayers and supplied with papal money, took the offensive in the name of Christendom. In 1673 he defeated the invaders at Chotim, thereby adding greatly to his own reputation and strengthening his claim to the Polish throne. Yet after he had been elected King of Poland, he came to terms with the Turks and in 1676 recognised the Sultan as ruler of Podolia.

The Turkish empire was at its maximum extent in western Europe by the time Ahmed Koprulu died, in 1676. He was succeeded by his brother-in-law, Kara Mustafa, who planned to turn Royal Hungary into a vassal state and push beyond it to Vienna. A large army was assembled and Sultan Mohamed in person led it as far as Belgrade, where Kara Mustafa took over. By July 1683 it had reached Vienna, and the Habsburg capital was once again in grave danger. But the Turks were short of siege guns and they were overconfident. Sobieski, with 20,000 men, joined up with the imperial forces under Duke Charles of Lorraine, and in September 1683 they attacked and routed the Turkish army. Kara Mustafa sped back to Belgrade to organise a line of defence against the advancing imperial troops, but in December he was strangled, by the Sultan's orders.

Mohamed IV soon found that it was easier to get rid of grand viziers than to find adequate replacements for them. Intrigues and in-fighting among factions once again became the order of the day, and in the nineteen years from 1683 to 1702 there were no less than twelve grand viziers. Meanwhile the Pope had proclaimed a crusade to drive the infidel out of Christendom, and the Emperor, nothing loth to do his religious duty at the same time as he extended his own power, responded to the call. While imperial armies pushed steadily south, capturing Buda in 1686, the Venetians, who were also members of this

Holy League, invaded the Morea and in 1687 took possession of Athens. In August of that year a Turkish counter-attack against the imperial forces was heavily defeated at Nagyharsany, not far from Mohacs, and in September 1688 the Emperor's troops entered Belgrade. By this time Mohamed IV was no longer ruler of the Turks. While his soldiers suffered and died he had devoted himself to the pleasures of the chase—an attitude which savoured of irresponsibility and drove the army to revolt. In November 1687, therefore, he was deposed and replaced by his half-brother, Suleiman II. The change of ruler seemed to presage a change of fortune, particularly after the appointment of Mustafa Pasha as grand vizier in 1689. He was the youngest son of Mohamed Koprulu and had inerited a good share of the military and administrative ability with which that formidable family was endowed. In 1690 Mustafa Pasha recaptured Belgrade, but in the following year he was killed in battle. 1691 also saw the death of Suleiman II, who was succeeded by his half-brother Ahmed II.

Although the Turks fought hard to defend their position in Europe they were unable to stem the advance of the Christian forces. In 1696 a new enemy appeared on the scene in the shape of Peter the Great of Russia, who directed the operations leading to the capture of the Turkish fortress of Azov. Meanwhile, in the Balkans, Prince Eugene commanded an imperial army which, in 1697, routed the Turks in the battle of Zenta. By this time morale in the Turkish army was at a low ebb, money was in short supply, and the Sultan—Mustafa II, who came to the throne in 1695—was ready for peace. The maritime powers, England and the United Provinces, had offered to act as mediators, since they were anxious to release imperial troops for operations against Louis XIV, and Mustafa accepted their services. The outcome of these negotiations was the Peace of Carlowitz of 1699. The Sultan recognised the Emperor as sovereign over Hungary and Transylvania; he also agreed that Podolia should be returned to Poland and that Venice should have Dalmatia, the Morea and the island of Aegina. The Russians were not included in this settlement, but in 1700 the Treaty of Constantinople confirmed them in possession of Azov.

Despite a succession of defeats, the Turks were still far from beaten. In 1703 a military rising led to the deposition of Mustafa II and his replacement by Ahmed III, a ruler of some ability who in 1706 appointed the very capable Chorlolu Ali Pasha to be his grand vizier. Unfortunately for Chorlolu, however, he became entangled in the complicated web of intrigue and counter-intrigue which resulted from the arrival of Charles XII on Turkish territory. Chorlolu hoped to use Charles as a pawn in his power-game with the Russians, and exchange him in return for a settlement of outstanding questions. But Charles found support among the advocates of an agressively anti-Russian policy, and succeeded in securing Chorlolu's dismissal in 1710. This was immediately followed by a declaration of war against Russia. Peter led an army into Moldavia, calling upon the Christian inhabitants to rise against their infidel masters, but he was surprised by a rapid Turkish advance and his army was surrounded near the Pruth river in 1711. Peter surrendered without fighting and had no alternative but to accept whatever terms the Turks chose to impose upon him. These turned out to be remarkably mild. Peter had to agree to the restoration of Azov to Turkish rule; he also had to promise to withdraw his troops from Poland and allow safe passage home to Charles XII; but there was no question of surrendering all the conquests that Russia had made in the Great Northern War. The grand vizier who dictated these terms preferred a swift and peaceful settlement to the continual war that was being advocated by the circle around Charles XII. He also knew that the Turkish army was tired of fighting. In fact war was declared again in the following year because Peter had been slow to honour his promise to withdraw Russian troops from Poland, but the original peace terms were ratified by the Treaty of Adrianople in 1713.

Having dealt with the Russians, the Turks turned their attention to the Venetians. In 1715 the Turkish fleet captured the islands of Aegina and Tinos, while the Turkish army gradually squeezed the Venetians out of the Morea. But at this stage the Emperor joined in the war, and Eugene was appointed to command the army which thrust south-east towards Belgrade. In 1716 the Turkish defending forces were put to flight at the battle of Peterwardein, and in the following year Belgrade was once again occupied by imperial troops. The Turks sued for peace, and terms were agreed at Passarowitz in 1718. The Emperor now took possession of the Banat—the territory lying between Hungary and Transylvania—and the regions of Serbia and Wallachia adjoining it on the south and west. The great days of the Koprulus were now clearly over, and never again would Turkish armies thrust up into central Europe and besiege the Habsburg capital. For two centuries they had dominated the Balkans, occupied the greater part of Hungary, and threatened the south-east frontier of Christian Europe. Their retreat was one of the signs that a new power pattern was emerging.

Germany

The Holy Roman Empire had never had much more than a shadowy existence in the early-modern period, and the Peace of Westphalia confirmed its political insignificance. Its institutions continued to function, after a fashion, and the fiction of 'electing' an Emperor was maintained. In 1653, for instance, the Electors assembled to choose a new King of the Romans, and four years later they formally offered the imperial crown to Leopold I. Yet despite the hopes of Louis XIV there was never much chance that the choice of the Electors would fall on anyone other than the son and heir of the reigning Emperor. The Habsburgs had established a prescriptive, if not a hereditary, right to the imperial throne, and since they accepted the *de facto* limitations on their power there seemed no reason for the Electors to break with tradition.

In 1692 the Emperor granted the electoral title and privileges to the ruler of Hanover, much to the annoyance of the other Electors, who had not been consulted. Yet the electoral dignity, although coveted as a mark of honour, had little significance after 1648. The Electors, it is true, formed the upper house of the Diet, but although this body continued to meet, its discussions rarely produced effective action. In 1653 Ferdinand III tried to persuade the Diet that taxes should be voted for defence—a proposal which, if carried out, might have turned the Empire into a political force even at that late hour. But the Diet decided that in fiscal matters unanimity should be the rule, which was merely a polite way of rejecting the suggestion altogether. Nearly twenty years later, in 1674, the Diet actually brought itself to the point of declaring war on Louis XIV, but not until 1681 was the decision taken to form an imperial army. Some 60,000 men were raised and placed under the Emperor's command, but the larger of the German princes, who had sizeable armies of their own, preferred to hire these out to the Emperor rather than commit them to a combined force. Although the creation of a standing army showed that there was still a flicker of life in the imperial instructions, this was the result of special circumstances—the aggression of Louis XIV, which clearly threatened the states of Germany—rather than of any intrinsic vitality.

The half century following the Peace of Westphalia witnessed a number of shifts in the power pattern of the German principalities. In the Palatinate, Charles Louis, eldest son of the luckless Frederick, was restored in 1649 and took up residence in the beautiful capital at Heidelberg. He no longer ruled over the Upper Palatinate, which had been transferred to Bavaria, but the Rhine territories were potentially rich. Economic recovery from the effects of the war was slow, however, and successive devastations of the region by the armies of Louis XIV were a further setback. So, too, was the expulsion of many Calvinists after the Palatinate passed into possession of a junior, Roman Catholic branch of the ruling family in 1685. As a consequence the Palatinate had ceased to be one of the principal states of Germany by the end of the seventeenth century.

In Bavaria, Maximilian and his son and successor Ferdinand Maria, who reigned from 1651 until 1679, enjoyed the prestige that came from the acquisition of the Upper Palatinate and the grant of the electoral dignity. They were absolute rulers, and the representative element was confined to a small 'Council of Estates' which voted taxes. The period of greatest peril for Bavaria came during the war of the Spanish Succession, when the Elector Max Emmanuel sided with Louis XIV and was expelled from his country by the victorious imperial troops. At French insistence he was restored at the end of the war, however, and ruled Bavaria until his death in 1726. Fighting and military occupation had much the same effect on Bavaria as on the Palatinate—though to a markedly lesser extent—in that they slowed down the rate of recovery from the devastation caused by the Thirty Years War.

Saxony was another state which emerged with more territory and greater prestige after the peace settlement of Westphalia. In 1697, however, the Elector Frederick Augustus turned Roman Catholic in order to obtain the Polish crown, and his fortunes became bound up with those of Peter the Great and Charles XII. There was little enthusiasm in Saxony for the Elector's Polish ambitions, and the Saxon Estates only agreed to support him after he had promised not to attempt in any way to subvert the Lutheran church settlement. Their increasing prestige and influence was in marked contrast to the subordination of the Estates in Bavaria. This was part of the price paid by Augustus for the crown of Poland.

The position of Saxony was affected by the rise to power of Brandenburg and Hanover, as well as the increasing influence of Russia in the Baltic region. The emergence of Hanover really started in 1683, when the ruler introduced primogeniture in order to put an end to the repeated fragmentation of the state. By 1705 all the bits and pieces had been joined together under George Louis, a distinguished soldier whose commitment to the imperial cause had been rewarded by the grant of the electoral dignity to Hanover in 1692. Elector George, as he became at his accession in 1698, had to contend with powerful Estates, dominated by the aristocracy, but his prestige was considerably augmented when, in 1714, he inherited the crown of Great Britain. There were now two kings among the German princes—the Elector of Brandenburg, recognised by the Emperor as King of Prussia in 1700, and the Elector of Hanover, King of Great Britain—and the glory of these titles cast its shadow over the other principalities which had earlier been of greater importance.

The Habsburg Lands

None of the German princes could compare, in dignity, prestige and international significance, with the Emperor, for although 1648 marked another stage in the decline of the Empire it left the imperial title and dignity intact and strengthened the foundations of Habsburg power in the hereditary lands. The Emperor Ferdinand III, worn out by the strain of war, died in 1657 before reaching the age of fifty. He was succeeded by his son Leopold I, on whose death in 1705 the imperial crown passed, in successive elections, to his two sons Joseph I (1705-11) and Charles VI (1711-40). The administration of the Empire was in theory distinct from that of the hereditary Habsburg lands, but in fact there was a great deal of overlapping, and the government at Vienna suffered from the clash of interests between various departments. Administrative reform only began to make headway during the reign of Joseph I, and there was no 'cabinet' until 1709.

In the hereditary territories—Austria, Bohemia and Hungary— economic, religious and linguistic differences were only too apparent. Protestantism in these regions had been closely linked with the power of the Estates, and the defeat of one usually meant the decline of the other. In the negotiations at Westphalia Ferdinand III had agreed that Sweden should have Pomerania in return for a Swedish promise not to insist on freedom of worship for the protestants in Austria, and throughout the hereditary lands the strengthening of Habsburg authority went hand-in-hand with the advance of the Counter-Reformation.

The success of this policy was demonstrated in Bohemia, where a country that had a long tradition of unorthodoxy in religion was completely reclaimed for the Roman Catholic Church at the same time as it was turned from an elective into a hereditary monarchy. In 1627 a royal edict ordered all protestants to accept conversion or go into exile, and in the same year the Emperor paid a formal visit to Prague, declared the Bohemian crown to be hereditary in the Habsburg family, and demonstrated the reality of this by having his son crowned King of Bohemia. The university of Prague was handed over to the Jesuits, and, with the active encouragement of the state, a missionary campaign was set on foot. Preaching and education were its main instruments, and with the fervour of the catholic revival behind them the Jesuits were astonishingly effective in winning back people to the old faith. Protestantism lingered on to some extent among the aristocracy, but the nobles in general appreciated the advantages of an imperial connection that preserved their social privileges at the same time as it strengthened their stranglehold over their peasants. In Bohemia, as in the rest of eastern Europe, the growing foreign market for agricultural products led to the extension of serfdom, and the Emperor was content to uphold landlord power in return for loyalty. Bohemia therefore became fully integrated into the Habsburg hereditary lands, and although its Estates continued to meet they played little more than a formal role in the government of their country. All the major decisions were taken in Vienna.

The situation was very different in Hungary, where Habsburg rule had been confined to 'Royal Hungary,' a small strip of Croatia with its capital at Pressburg. Just under half of the former kingdom of Hungary was now the autonomous principality of Transylvania, ruled over by the Calvinist Bethlen Gabor from 1613 to 1629, while the rest was under Turkish occupation. The presence of a protestant prince just across the frontier was a great advantage to the protestant nobles of Royal Hungary, and they jealously preserved the considerable measure of liberty granted to the Estates in the period 1606–18 (see p. 329). The Counter-Reformation was making its effect felt, and a number of significant conversions took place among the Hungarian aristocracy, but at the Diet of Pressburg in 1647 religious freedom was confirmed and guaranteed.

George Racoksky I, who followed Bethlen Gabor as ruler of Transylvania, died in 1648 and was succeeded by his son, George Racoksky II. This vain and ambitious young man hoped to carve out a kingdom for himself by taking over Poland and uniting it first with Transylvania and ultimately with the whole of Hungary. In 1657 he invaded Poland and linked up with Charles X of Sweden, who had agreed to partition the kingdom with him (see p. 447). But shortly afterwards Charles was compelled to withdraw his troops in order to meet the Danish threat, and George Racoksky was left high and dry. It was only by paying a large indemnity to his enemies that he was able to return safely to his principality. His actions, however, had alarmed the Turks, who regarded Transylvania as a puppet state and had no wish to see its ruler establish himself as an independent sovereign prince. In 1658 they launched an invasion of Transylvania; in 1660 they defeated George Racoksky II, who died shortly afterwards; and in 1662 they defeated and killed his successor. Transylvania now became part of the Ottoman empire, and there was no longer a puppet state to act as a barrier between Turkish and imperial lands.

From Transylvania the Turks thrust towards Pressburg and Vienna, but their defeat at St Gotthard in 1664 put an end to their advance, and by the Peace of Vasvar they had to agree that Transylvania should once again be nominally independent, though acknowledging Turkish overlordship. This did not satisfy the Hungarian nobles, who longed for the freeing of all Hungary, including Transylvania, and the re-creation of the former kingdom. They blamed the Emperor for not following up his victory at St Gotthard, and their anger led to an uprising in 1670. If the Turks had chosen to invade at this stage they might have detached Royal Hungary from the Habsburg empire, but Ahmed Koprulu turned against Poland instead, and imperial troops were able to suppress the Hungarian revolt. The ringleaders either fled into exile or were arrested and executed. Martial law was proclaimed in Hungary, and under the protection of military occupation the campaign for conversion to Roman Catholicism was stepped up.

The Hungarian exiles bound together and with the help of French money fomented a new uprising against Habsburg rule. This broke out in 1678, at a time when the Emperor, increasingly alarmed by Louis XIV's forward policy in western Europe, wanted to be free from entanglements in the east. In 1681, therefore, Leopold summoned the Hungarian Estates to meet at Pressburg and formally confirmed their 'liberties'. There was to be no taxation without the consent of the Estates; the Hungarian administration was to be staffed only by natives; and protestant churches and schools were to be allowed to remain in all those areas which had not declared for catholicism.

At this stage Leopold was negotiating from weakness, but following the imperial victory outside Vienna in 1683 the situation was gradually transformed. In 1686 Buda was captured, and a year later the imperial commander, Charles of Lorraine, smashed the Turkish army at Nagyharsany. The fact that this battle took place almost on the site of Mohacs was more than a historical curiosity. The verdict of Mohacs had in fact been reversed, and for the first time in a hundred and fifty years the old kingdom of Hungary was a free and united country. The Estates were once again summoned to Pressburg, this time to declare the Hungarian crown to be hereditary in the house of Habsburg, and in December 1687 the Archduke Joseph was crowned king.

Despite occasional setbacks to imperial armies, and the constant drain on Habsburg resources caused by the struggle against Louis XIV, the Turks were steadily driven further and further back. After Eugene's defeat of the last effective Ottoman army at Zenta in 1697 the Turks made peace at Carlowitz, recognising the Emperor as ruler of Hungary, though they still clung on to Belgrade. Transylvania preserved its separate identity and its long-established toleration of religious diversity, but to all intents and purposes it was now ruled from Vienna. As for Hungary proper, the nobles were far from happy about the presence of large numbers of imperial troops and officials in their country, and resented the subordination of Hungarian to Habsburg interests. In 1700 they again broke out in revolt, under the leadership of Francis Racoksky and with financial support from France. Fortune at first favoured them and they established their control over substantial areas of Hungary. However, their eventual success or failure depended on the outcome of the war in the west. Following the crushing defeat of the French at Blenheim in 1704, imperial troops were transferred to the Hungarian front, Racoksky was defeated, and the areas under rebel control were gradually reconquered. By 1712 the imperial position had been restored to such an extent that Charles VI went in person to Pressburg to be crowned King of Hungary; but in the Diet which assembled for this purpose he made it clear that his policy would be one of reconciliation. Protestant rights and the 'liberties' of the landowners were confirmed, and the Emperor promised to summon the Hungarian Estates regularly and to consult with them on all matters affecting the kingdom. The long struggle of the Hungarian nobles had therefore been successful, and Hungary, alone among the hereditary Habsburg lands, retained its 'liberties'.

Charles VI could afford to be generous, for by the time of the Peace of Passarowitz in 1718 he had extended his rule not only into the Balkans but also into Italy. With the extinction of the Spanish Habsburg line the Emperor was now the unchallenged guardian of his family's great inheritance, and Habsburg power, which in the darkest years of the Thirty Years War had seemed likely to disappear from Europe, had re-emerged in an unexpectedly triumphant form. While the Bourbon rulers of France might dazzle western Europe, the dominant figure in the cast was the Habsburg Emperor.

TABLES OF RULERS

Popes

NICHOLAS V 1447–55
CALIXTUS III 1455–58
PIUS II 1458–64
PAUL II 1464–71
SIXTUS IV 1471–84
INNOCENT VIII 1484–92
ALEXANDER VI 1492–1503
PIUS III 1503
JULIUS II 1503–13
LEO X 1513–21
ADRIAN VI 1522–23
CLEMENT VII 1523–34
PAUL III 1534–49
JULIUS III 1550–55
MARCELLUS II 1555
PAUL IV 1555–59
PIUS IV 1559–65
PIUS V 1566–72

GREGORY XIII 1572–85
SIXTUS V 1585–90
URBAN VII 1590
GREGORY XIV 1590–91
INNOCENT IX 1591
CLEMENT VIII 1592–1605
LEO XI 1605
PAUL V 1605–21
GREGORY XV 1621–23
URBAN VIII 1623–44
INNOCENT X 1644–55
ALEXANDER VII 1655–67
CLEMENT IX 1667–69
CLEMENT X 1670–76
INNOCENT XI 1676–89
ALEXANDER VIII 1689–91
INNOCENT XII 1691–1700
CLEMENT XI 1700–21

Holy Roman Emperors

FREDERICK III 1448–93
MAXIMILIAN I 1493–1519
CHARLES V 1519–56
FERDINAND I 1556–64
MAXIMILIAN II 1564–76
RUDOLF II 1576–1612

MATTHIAS 1612–19
FERDINAND II 1619–37
FERDINAND III 1637–57
LEOPOLD I 1657–1705
JOSEPH I 1705–11
CHARLES VI 1711–40

Rulers of Spain

FERDINAND of Aragon 1479–1516 ⎤
ISABELLA of Castile 1474–1504 ⎦
CHARLES I (Emperor Charles V)
   1516–56
PHILIP II 1556–98

PHILIP III 1598–1621
PHILIP IV 1621–65
CHARLES II 1665–1700
PHILIP V 1700–46

Kings of Portugal

ALFONSO V 1438–81
JOHN II 1481–95
MANOEL I 1495–1521
JOHN III 1521–57
SEBASTIAN 1557–78
HENRY 1578–80

PHILIP II of Spain 1580–98
PHILIP III of Spain 1598–1621
PHILIP IV of Spain 1621–40
JOHN IV 1640–56
ALFONSO VI 1656–83
PETER II 1683–1706

Kings of France

LOUIS XI 1461–83
CHARLES VIII 1483–98
LOUIS XII 1498–1515
FRANCIS I 1515–47
HENRY II 1547–59
FRANCIS II 1559–60

CHARLES IX 1560–74
HENRY III 1574–89
HENRY IV 1589–1610
LOUIS XIII 1610–43
LOUIS XIV 1643–1715 (personal rule
   began in 1660)

The House of Orange

WILLIAM the Silent. d.1584
MAURICE d.1625
FREDERICK HENRY d.1647

WILLIAM II d.1650
WILLIAM III (King of England from
   1689) d.1702

Kings of Denmark

CHRISTIAN II 1513–23
FREDERICK I 1523–33
CHRISTIAN III 1533–59
FREDERICK II 1559–88

CHRISTIAN IV 1588–1648
FREDERICK III 1648–70
CHRISTIAN V 1670–99
FREDERICK IV 1699–1730

Rulers of Sweden

GUSTAVUS I 1523–60

ERIC XIV 1560–68

CHARLES IX 1604–11 (*de facto* ruler from 1598)

GUSTAVUS ADOLPHUS 1611–32

CHRISTINA 1632–54

JOHN III 1568–92

SIGISMUND 1592–99

CHARLES X 1654–60

CHARLES XI 1660–97

CHARLES XII 1697–1718

Kings of Poland

CASIMIR IV 1447–92

JOHN ALBERT 1492–1501

ALEXANDER 1501–06

SIGISMUND I 1506–48

SIGISMUND II 1548–72

HENRY (Henry III of France) 1573–1574

STEPHEN BATHORY 1575–86

SIGISMUND III (King of Sweden 1592–99) 1587–1632

LADISLAW IV 1632–48

JOHN CASIMIR 1648–68

MICHAEL 1669–73

JOHN SOBIESKI 1674–96

AUGUSTUS II (Elector of Saxony) 1697–1704

STANISLAS LESZCZYNSKI 1704–09

AUGUSTUS II 1709–33

Tsars of Russia

IVAN III, the Great 1462–1505

BASIL (Vasili) II 1505–33

IVAN IV, the Terrible 1533–84

THEODORE (Fedor) I 1584–98

BORIS GODUNOV 1598–1605

THEODORE (Fedor) II 1605

Pseudo–DMITRI 1605–06

BASIL (Vasili) SHUISKI 1606–10

LADISLAW 1610

MICHAEL 1613–45

ALEXIS 1645–76

THEODORE (Fedor) III 1676–82

IVAN V, co-Tsar 1682–96

PETER I, the Great 1682–1725 (personal rule began in 1694)

Ottoman Sultans

MOHAMED II 1451–81

BAYEZID II 1481–1512

SELIM I 1512–20

SULEIMAN I 1520–66

SELIM II 1566–74

MURAD III 1574–95

MOHAMED III 1595–1603

AHMED I 1603–17

MUSTAFA I 1617–18

OSMAN II 1618–22

MUSTAFA I 1622–23

MURAD IV 1623–40

IBRAHIM I 1640–48

MOHAMED IV 1648–87

SULEIMAN II 1687–91

AHMED II 1691–95

MUSTAFA II 1695–1703

AHMED III 1703–30

FAMILY TREES

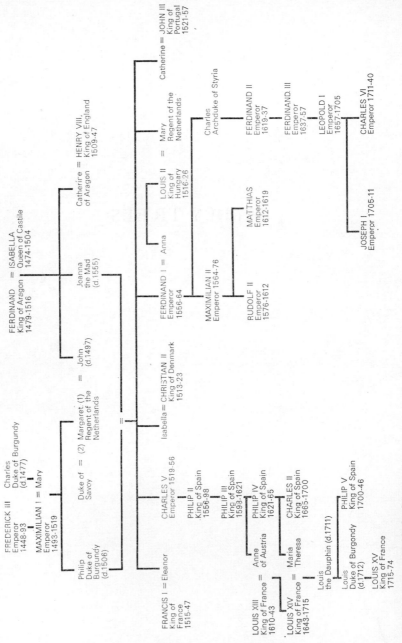

The House of Habsburg

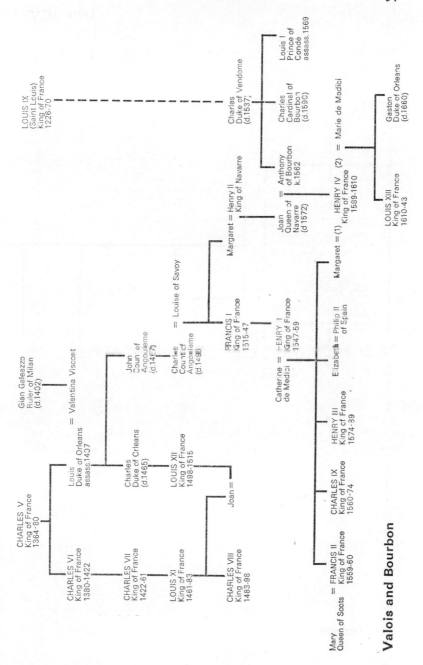

Valois and Bourbon

GUISE   LONGUEVILLE

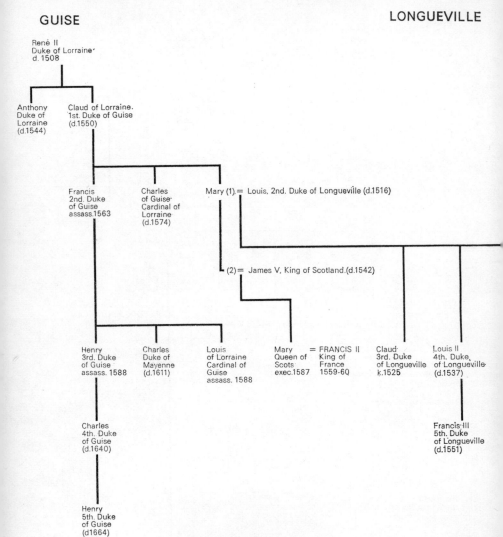

French Noble Houses

MONTMORENCY

CONDÉ

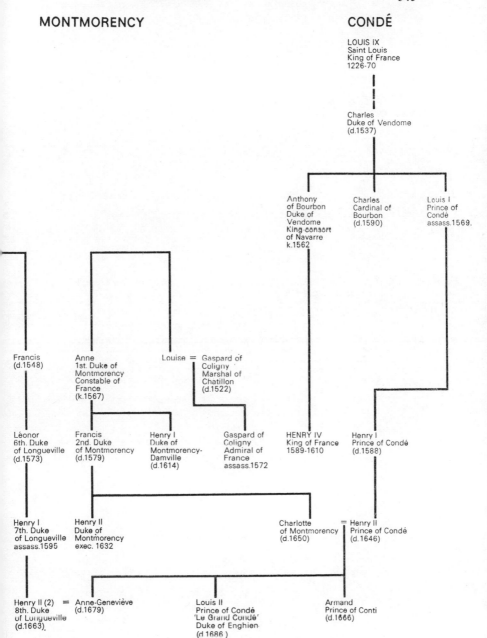

LOUIS IX
Saint Louis
King of France
1226-70

Charles
Duke of Vendome
(d.1537)

Anthony
of Bourbon
Duke of
Vendome
King consort
of Navarre
k.1562

Charles
Cardinal of
Bourbon
(d.1590)

Louis I
Prince of
Condé
assass.1569.

Francis
(d.1548)

Anne
1st. Duke of
Montmorency
Constable of
France
(k.1567)

Louise = Gaspard of
Coligny
Marshal of
Chatillon
(d.1522)

Léonor
6th. Duke
of Longueville
(d.1573)

Francis
2nd. Duke
of Montmorency
(d.1579)

Henry I
Duke of
Montmorency-
Damville
(d.1614)

Gaspard of
Coligny
Admiral of
France
assass.1572

HENRY IV
King of France
1589-1610

Henry I
Prince of Condé
(d.1588)

Henry I
7th. Duke
of Longueville
assass.1595

Henry II
Duke of
Montmorency
exec. 1632

Charlotte
of Montmorency
(d.1650)

= Henry II
Prince of Condé
(d.1646)

Henry II (2)
8th. Duke
of Longueville
(d.1663).

= Anne-Geneviève
(d.1679)

Louis II
Prince of Condé
'Le Grand Condé'
Duke of Enghien
(d.1686)

Armand
Prince of Conti
(d.1666)

MAPS

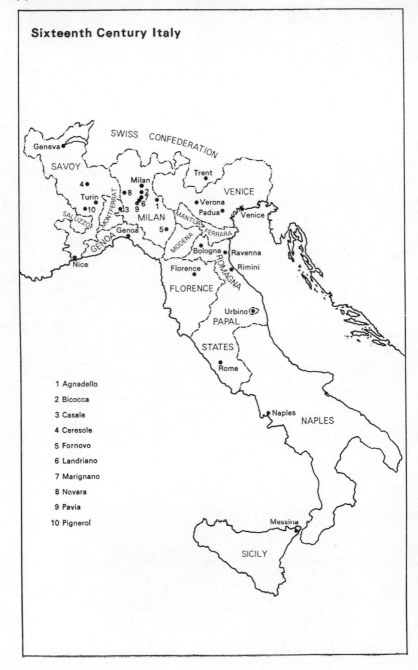

Sixteenth Century Italy

SWISS CONFEDERATION

Geneva

SAVOY

Trent

Milan

VENICE

4 Turin

8

2

Verona

10

6 1

Padua

Venice

3 9

MILAN

MANTUA

SALUZZO

MONTFERRAT

Genoa

5

FERRARA

GENOA

MODENA

Bologna

Ravenna

Nice

Florence

Rimini

ROMAGNA

FLORENCE

Urbino

PAPAL

STATES

Rome

1 Agnadello

2 Bicocca

3 Casale

4 Ceresole

5 Fornovo

6 Landriano

7 Marignano

8 Novara

9 Pavia

10 Pignerol

Naples

NAPLES

Messina

SICILY

The Netherlands in the seventeenth century

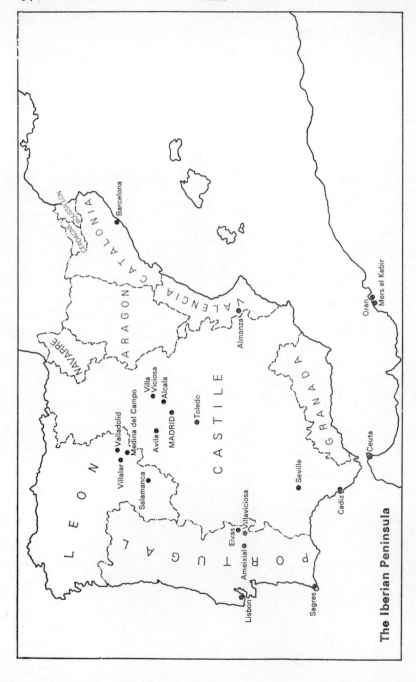

The Iberian Peninsula

Barcelona

Mers el Kebir
Oran

Almanza

Villa
Viciosa
Alcala

Toledo

MADRID

Avila

Medina del Campo

Valladolid

Villalar

Salamanca

Ceuta

Seville

Cadiz

Elvas
Villaviciosa

Amexial

Lisbon

Sagres

CERDAGNE
ROUSSILLON

CATALONIA

VALENCIA

ARAGON

NAVARRE

LEON

CASTILE

GRANADA

PORTUGAL

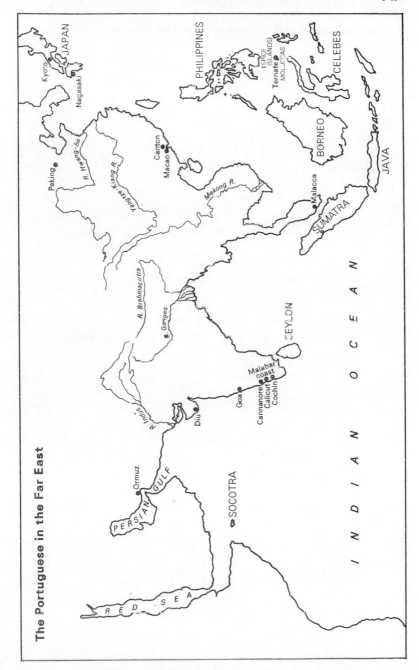

The Portuguese in the Far East

JAPAN

Kyoto

Nagasaki

Peking

R. Hwang-Ho

Yangtze-Kiang R.

Canton

Macao

Mekong R.

PHILIPPINES

(SPICE ISLANDS)
Ternate
MOLUCCAS

CELEBES

BORNEO

JAVA

Malacca

SUMATRA

R. Brahmaputra

R. Ganges

CEYLON

Malabar coast

Goa

Cannanore
Calicut
Cochin

R. Indus

Diu

Ormuz

PERSIAN GULF

SOCOTRA

INDIAN OCEAN

RED SEA

The Spaniards and Portuguese in the New World

MEXICO

Mexico City
(Tenochtitlan)

Vera Cruz

Acapulco

Havana

BAHAMAS

CUBA

GREATER

JAMAICA

HISPANIOLA

PUERTO RICO

ANTILLES

VICE-ROYALTY OF NEW SPAIN

Nombre
de Dios

DARIEN

Panama

Orinoco delta

VICE-ROYALTY

Lima

OF

Potosí

PARAGUAY

Recife

B R A Z I L

Bahia

PERU

Rio de Janeiro

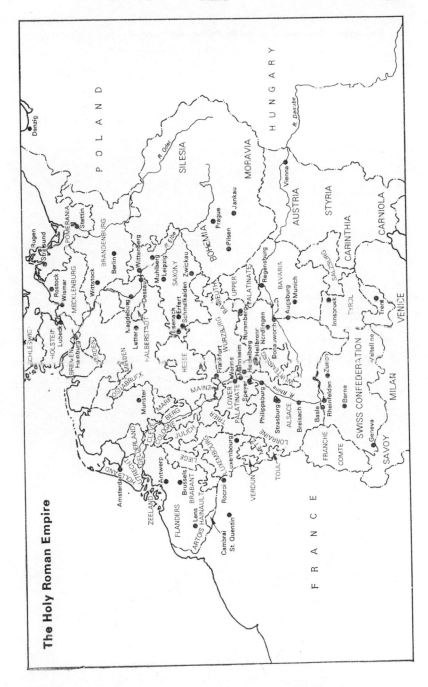

The Holy Roman Empire

Sweden, Denmark and Brandenburg-Prussia

R. Torne

White Sea

Archangel

R U S S I A

N O R W A Y

R. Ume

JAMTLAND

HARJEDALEN

S W E D E N

KARELIA

Kexholm

Lake Ladoga

Stolbovo

St. Petersburg

Bergen

Oslo

Gulf of Finland

INGRIA

Reval

Narva

Novgorod

Vasteras

Stockholm

ESTONIA

OSEL

Dorpat

Pskov

BOHUSLAN

Gulf of Riga

LIVONIA

Alvsborg

GOTLAND

Riga

HALLAND

Kalmar

Bromsebro

P O L A N D -

Knared

BLEKINGE

The Sound

SKANE

R. Niemen

JUTLAND

Roskilde

Lund

Pillau

Konigsberg

Odense

Copenhagen

DENMARK

Oliva

ZEELAND

Schleswig

Rugen

Danzig

Elbing

PRUSSIA

Tonning

Travendal

Stralsund

Kammin

Wismar

Stettin

L I T H U A N I A

HOLSTEIN

Lubeck

R. Vistula

BREMEN

VERDEN

Fehrbellin

Berlin

MINDEN

BRANDENBURG

HALBERTSTADT

R. Elbe

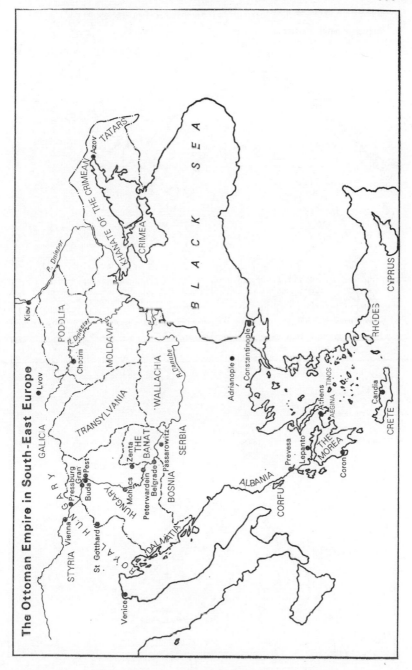

The Ottoman Empire in South-East Europe

Russia and Poland

BIBLIOGRAPHY

The best short guide to the enormous volume of writings on this period is Alun Davies, *Modern European History 1494–1788* (Historical Association 1966).

The following selective list consists mainly of books and articles which have appeared within the last twenty-five years.

General

THE NEW CAMBRIDGE MODERN HISTORY, Cambridge University Press.
I. ed. G. R. POTTER, *The Renaissance 1493–1520* (1961)
II. ed. G. R. ELTON, *The Reformation 1520–59* (1958)
III. ed. R. B. WERNHAM, *The Counter-Reformation and the Price Revolution 1559–1610* (1968)
IV. ed. J. P. COOPER, *The Decline of Spain and the Thirty Years War 1609–48/59* (1970)
V. ed. F. L. CARSTEN, *The Ascendancy of France 1648–88* (1961)
VI. ed. J. S. BROMLEY, *The Rise of Great Britain and Russia 1688–1715/25* (1970)
XIV. ed. H. C. DARBY and HAROLD FULLARD, *Atlas* (1970)

THE FONTANA HISTORY OF EUROPE, Collins, Fontana Books.
J. R. HALE, *Renaissance Europe 1480–1520* (1971)
G. R. ELTON, *Reformation Europe 1517–59* (1963)
J. H. ELLIOTT, *Europe Divided 1559–98* (1968)
JOHN STOYE, *Europe Unfolding 1648–88* (1969)

THE RISE OF MODERN EUROPE, Harper Torchbooks.
MYRON P. GILMORE, *The World of Humanism 1453–1517* (1952)

CARL J. FRIEDRICH, *The Age of the Baroque 1610–60* (1952)
F. L. NUSSBAUM, *The Triumph of Science and Reason 1660–85* (1953)
J. B. WOLF, *The Emergence of the Great Powers 1685–1715* (1951)

HISTORY OF MODERN EUROPE, Weidenfeld & Nicolson 1971.
   EUGENE F. RICE JNR., *The Foundations of Early Modern Europe 1460–1559*
   RICHARD S. DUNN, *The Age of Religious Wars 1559–1689*
   LEONARD KRIEGER, *Kings and Philosophers 1689–1789*

PEUPLES ET CIVILISATIONS (Paris).
   H. HAUSER and A. RENAUDET, *Les Débuts de l'Age moderne* (1956)
   H. HAUSER, *La Préponderance espagnole 1559–1660* (1948)
   P. SAGNAC and A. DE ST LEGER, *La Préponderance française: Louis XIV 1661–1715* (1949)

GENERAL HISTORY OF EUROPE, Longman.
   H. G. KOENIGSBERGER and G. L. MOSSE, *Europe in the Sixteenth Century* (1968)
   D. H. PENNINGTON, *Seventeenth Century Europe* (1970)

ASHLEY, MAURICE, *The Golden Century: Europe 1598–1715* Weidenfeld & Nicolson, 1969.
ASTON, MARGARET, *The Fifteenth Century: the Prospect of Europe*. Thames & Hudson, 1968.
ASTON, TREVOR, ed., *Crisis in Europe 1560–1660* [essays from *Past & Present*]. Routledge & Kegan Paul, 1965.
BRAUDEL, FERNAND, *The Mediterranean and the Mediterranean World in the Age of Philip II*. Collins, 1972.
CARTER, CHARLES H., *The Western European Powers 1500–1700* (The Sources of History: Studies in the Use of Historical Evidence). Hodder & Stoughton, 1971.
CHAUNU, PIERRE, *La Civilisation de l'Europe classique*. Paris, 1966.
CLARK, G. N., *War and Society in the Seventeenth Century*. Cambridge University Press, 1958.
COHN, HENRY J., ed., *Government in Reformation Europe* (Stratum Series). Macmillan, 1971.
ELTON, G. R., *Renaissance and Reformation 1300–1648* [extracts and documents] Collier–Macmillan, 1968.

HATTON, R., *Europe in the Age of Louis XIV*. Thames & Hudson, 1969.

KAMEN, HENRY, *The Iron Century: social change in Europe 1550–1660*. Weidenfeld & Nicolson, 1971.

KOENIGSBERGER, H. G., *Estates and Revolutions: essays in early modern European history*. Cornell University Press, 1971.

KOENIGSBERGER, H. G., *The Habsburgs and Europe, 1516–1660*. Cornell University Press, 1971.

LAPEYRE, H., *Les Monarchies européennes du XVIe Siècle* (Nouvelle Clio). Paris, 1967.

MALAND, DAVID, *Europe in the Seventeenth Century*. Macmillan, 1966.

MATTINGLY, GARRETT, *Renaissance Diplomacy*. Cape, 1955.

MOUSNIER, R., *Les XVIe et XVIIe Siècles, 1492–1715*. Paris, 1961.

RICH, E. E. and WILSON, C. H., eds., *The Cambridge Economic History of Europe*. Vol. IV. *The Economy of Expanding Europe in the Sixteenth and Seventeenth Centuries*. Cambridge University Press, 1967.

ROUTH, C. R. N., *They Saw it Happen in Europe 1450–1600*. Blackwell. 1965.

ROWEN, HERBERT H., *From Absolutism to Revolution, 1648–1848* [Documents] Collier–Macmillan. 1968.

SWART, K. W., *The Sale of Offices in the Seventeenth Century*. The Hague. 1949.

TREVOR-ROPER, H. R., ed., *The Age of Expansion: Europe and the World, 1559–1660*. Thames & Hudson. 1968.

TREVOR-ROPER, H. R., *Religion, the Reformation, and Social Change*. Macmillan. 1967.

WILLIAMS, E. N., *The Ancien Regime in Europe: Government and Society in the Major States, 1648–1789*. Bodley Head, 1970.

WILLIAMS, NEVILLE, *Chronology of the Expanding World, 1492–1762*. Barrie & Jenkins, 1971.

The Renaissance and Christian Humanism

The Renaissance

BOLGAR, R. R., *The Classical Inheritance*. Cambridge University Press, 1952.

BREISACH, E., *Renaissance Europe, 1300–1517*. Collier-Macmillan, 1973.

BURKE, PETER, *The Renaissance* (Problems and Perspectives). Longman, 1964.

BURKE, PETER, *The Renaissance Sense of the Past* (Documents of Modern History). Edward Arnold, 1969.

DANNENFELDT, KARL H., ed., *The Renaissance: medieval or modern?* (Problems in European Civilisation). Heath, 1959.

EISENSTEIN, ELIZABETH L., 'The advent of printing and the problem of the Renaissance'. *Past & Present* 45 (1969). See also *Past & Present* 52 (1971).

FAURE, PAUL, *La Renaissance* (Que Sais-Je?). Paris, 1965.

FERGUSON, WALLACE K., *Europe in Transition, 1300–1520*. Allen & Unwin, 1962.

GADOL, JOAN, 'The unity of the Renaissance: humanism, natural science and art', in Charles H. Carter: *From the Renaissance to the Counter-Reformation*. Cape, 1966.

HALE, JOHN; HIGHFIELD, ROGER; and SMALLEY, BERYL, eds., *Europe in the Later Middle Ages*. Faber, 1965.

HAY, DENYS, *The Renaissance*. BBC, 1963.

HAY, DENYS, *Europe in the Fourteenth & Fifteenth Centuries*. Longman, 1966.

HAY, DENYS, ed., *The Renaissance Debate* (European Problem Studies) Holt, Rinehart & Winston, 1965.

HAY, DENYS, ed., *The Age of the Renaissance*. Thames & Hudson, 1967.

KRISTELLER, P. O., *The Classics and Renaissance Thought*. Harvard University Press, 1955.

SINGLETON, CHARLES S., ed., *Art, Science and History in the Renaissance*. Johns Hopkins Press, 1967.

WEISS, R., *The Renaissance Discovery of Classical Antiquity*. Blackwell, 1969.

WIGHTMAN, W. P. D., *Science and the Renaissance Vol. I*. Oliver & Boyd, 1962.

YATES, F. A., *Giordano Bruno and the Hermetic Tradition*. Routledge & Kegan Paul, 1964.

Italy

ADY, C. M., *Lorenzo dei Medici & Renaissance Italy*. English Universities Press, 1970.

BURKE, PETER, *Culture and Society in Renaissance Italy 1420–1540*. Batsford, 1972.

CHAMBERS, D. S., ed., *Patrons and Artists in the Italian Renaissance*. Macmillan, 1971.

CHAMBERS, D. S., *The Imperial Age of Venice, 1380–1580*. Thames & Hudson, 1970.

COCHRANE, ERIC, ed., *The Late Italian Renaissance, 1527–1633* (Stratum Series). Macmillan, 1970.

HALE, J. R., *Machiavelli and Renaissance Italy*. English Universities Press, 1961.

HAY, DENYS, *The Italian Renaissance in its Historical Background*. Cambridge University Press, 1961.

LAVEN, PETER, *Renaissance Italy*. Methuen, 1966.

LOGAN, OLIVER, *Culture and Society in Venice, 1470–1790* (Studies in Cultural History), Batsford, 1972.

PULLAN, BRIAN, *A History of early Renaissance Italy, from the mid-Thirteenth to the mid-Fifteenth Century*. Allen Lane, 1973.

ROBEY, DAVID, 'P. P. Vergerio the Elder: republicanism and civic values in the work of an early humanist', *Past & Present* 58 (1973).

SIMONE, FRANCO, ed., *The French Renaissance: medieval tradition and Italian influence in shaping the Renaissance in France*. Macmillan, 1970.

STEPHENS, JOHN N., 'Heresy in medieval and Renaissance Florence', *Past & Present* 54 (1972).

WEINSTEIN, DONALD, *Savonarola and Florence: Prophecy and Patriotism in the Renaissance*. Princeton University Press, 1970.

WEISS, R., 'The dawn of Humanism in Italy', *Bulletin of the Institute of Historical Research* 42 (1969).

Erasmus

BAINTON, ROLAND H., *Erasmus of Christendom*. Collins, Fontana, 1972.

DEMOLEN, RICHARD L., *Erasmus* (Documents of Modern History). Edward Arnold, 1973.

DOREY, T. A., ed., *Erasmus*. Routledge & Kegan Paul, 1970.

HUIZINGA, J., *Erasmus of Rotterdam*. Phaidon Press, 1952.

PHILLIPS, M. M., *Erasmus and the Northern Renaissance*. English Universities Press, 1970.

Reformation and Counter-reformation

The Reformation

The best general guide is HAROLD J. GRIMM, *The Reformation in Recent Historical Thought*, American Historical Association Publication No. 54, Macmillan Company of New York, 1964.

BAINTON, ROLAND H., *The Reformation of the Sixteenth Century*. Hodder & Stoughton, 1953.

BAINTON, ROLAND H., 'Interpretations of the Reformation', *American Historical Review* 66 (1960).

CHADWICK, OWEN, *Pelican History of the Church*. Vol. III. *The Reformation*. Penguin Books, 1964.

CLASEN, C.-P., *Anabaptism: a social history, 1525–1618*. Cornell Universities Press, 1972.

COHN, NORMAN, *The Pursuit of the Millenium*. Temple Smith, 1970.

DICKENS, A. G., *Reformation and Society in Sixteenth Century Europe*. Thames & Hudson, 1966.

GRIMM, HAROLD J., 'Social forces in the German Reformation', *Church History* 31 (1962).

GRIMM, HAROLD J., *The Reformation Era, 1500–1650*. Collier-Macmillan, 2nd ed., 1973.

HILLERBRAND, H. J., *The Protestant Reformation* [Extracts]. Harper Torchbooks, 1968.

LÉONARD, E. G., *A History of Protestantism: the Reformation*. Nelson, 1965.

MALLETT, M. E., *The Borgias*. Bodley Head, 1969.

REID, E. W. STANFORD, ed., *The Reformation: revival or revolution?* (European Problem Studies). Holt, Rinehart & Winston, 1968.

RITTER, GERHARD, 'Why the Reformation occurred in Germany', *Church History* 27 (1958).

SMITH, L. B., 'The Reformation and the decay of medieval ideas', *Church History* 24 (1955).

SPITZ, L. W., *The Religious Renaissance of the German Humanists*. Harvard University Press, 1963.

SPITZ, L. W., ed., *The Reformation: material or spiritual?* Problems in European Civilisation). Heath, 1962.

STRAUSS, GERALD, 'Protestant dogma and city government. The case of Nuremburg', *Past & Present* 36 (1967).

WILLIAMS, GEORGE H., *The Radical Reformation*. Wiedenfeld & Nicolson, 1962.

Luther

ATKINSON, JAMES, *Martin Luther and the Birth of Protestantism*. Penguin Books, 1968.

ATKINSON, JAMES, *The Trial of Luther*. Batsford, 1971.

BAINTON, ROLAND H., *Here I S and. A life of Martin Luther*. Hodder & Stoughton, 1950.

DICKENS, A. G., *Martin Luther and the Reformation*. English Universities Press, 1967.

DICKENS, A. G., *The German Nation and Martin Luther*. Edward Arnold, 1973.

EBELING, GERHARD, *Luther: an introduction to his thought*. Collins, Fontana, 1970.

GREEN, V. H. H., *Luther and the Reformation*. Edward Arnold, 1964.

RUPP, E. G., *Luther's Progress to the Diet of Worms*. S.C.M. Press, 1951.

RUPP, E. G., *The Righteousness of God*. Hodder & Stoughton, 1953.

RUPP, E. G. and DREWERY, BENJAMIN, *Martin Luther* (Documents of Modern History). Edward Arnold, 1970.

SIGGINS, IAN D. KINGSTON, ed., *Luther* (Evidence and Commentary). Oliver & Boyd, 1973.

Calvin

BARON, HANS, 'Calvinist Republicanism and its historical roots', *Church History* 8 (1939).

BIÉLER, ANDRÉ, *La Pensée économique et sociale de Calvin*. Geneva, 1959.

CLARK, FRANCIS, ed., *Calvin and other Reformers*. Open University, 1972.

HALL, BASIL, *John Calvin*. Historical Association, 1956.

KINGDON, R. M., *Geneva and the Coming of the Wars of Religion in France, 1555–63*. Geneva, 1956.

KINGDON, R. M., *Geneva and the Consolidation of the French Protestant Movement, 1564–72*. University of Wisconsin Press, 1968.

MCNEILL, J. T., *The History and Character of Calvinism*. Oxford University Press, 1967.

PARKER, T. H. L., *The Doctrine of the Knowledge of God*. Oliver & Boyd, 1969.

WALZER, MICHAEL, *The Revolution of the Saints: a study in the origins of radical politics*. Weidenfeld & Nicolson, 1966.

WENDEL, FRANÇOIS, *Calvin: the Origins and Development of his Religious Thought*. Collins, Fontana, 1963.

Zwingli and other reformers

BIRNBAUM, N., 'The Zwinglian Reformation in Zurich', *Past & Present* 15 (1959).

HILLERBRAND, H. J., 'Menno Simmons—sixteenth-century reformer', *Church History* 31 (1962).

MANSCHREK, CLYDE, *Melanchthon, the Quiet Reformer*. New York, Abingdon Press, 1958.

MCNAIR, PHILIP, *Peter Martyr in Italy: an anatomy of apostasy*. Oxford, Clarendon Press, 1967.

RILLIET, JEAN, *Zwingli, Third Man of the Reformation.* Lutterworth Press, 1964.

The Counter-Reformation

BOSSY, JOHN, 'The Counter-Reformation and the people of Catholic Europe', *Past & Present* 47 (1970).

BURNS, E. M., *The Counter-Reformation.* Princeton University Press, 1964.

CLARK, FRANCIS, ed., *The Catholic Reformation.* Open University, 1972.

DAGENS, J., *Bérulle et les origines de la Restauration catholique, 1575–1611.* Bruges, 1952.

DELUMEAU, JEAN, *Le Catholicisme entre Luther et Voltaire* (Nouvelle Clio). Paris, 1971.

DICKENS, A. G., *The Counter-Reformation.* Thames & Hudson, 1968.

EVENNETT, H. O., *The Spirit of the Counter-Reformation.* Cambridge University Press, 1968.

FENLON, DERMOT, *Heresy and Obedience in Tridentine Italy: Cardinal Pole and the Counter-Reformation.* Cambridge University Press, 1972.

JANELLE, PIERRE, *The Counter-Reformation.* Milwaukee, Bruce Publishing Co., 1963.

JEDIN, H., *History of the Council of Trent,* 2 vols. Nelson, 1957, 1961.

MATHESON, PETER, *Cardinal Contarini at Regensburg.* Oxford, Clarendon Press, 1972.

The Empire, Germany, and the Thirty Years War

The Empire

BRANDI, KARL, *The Emperor Charles V.* Cape, 1939.

Charles Quint et son Temps. Paris, 1959.

CRANKSHAW, EDWARD, *The Habsburgs.* Weidenfeld & Nicolson, 1971.

HALKIN, L. E., *La Réforme en Belgique sous Charles Quint.* Brussels, 1957.

MACARTNEY, C. A., ed., *The Habsburg and Hohenzollern Dynasties in the Seventeenth and Eighteenth Centuries* (Documentary History of Western Civilisation). Macmillan, 1970.

STOYE, J. H., *The Siege of Vienna, 1683.* Collins, 1964.

STOYE, J. H., 'Emperor Charles VI: the early years of the reign', *Transactions of the Royal Historical Society* (1962).

WIMES, ROGER, 'The Imperial Circles: princely diplomacy and imperial reform 1681–1714, *Journal of Modern History* 39 (1967).

Germany

CARSTEN, F. L., *The Origins of Prussia*. Oxford, Clarendon Press, 1954.

CARSTEN, F. L., *Princes and Parliaments in Germany from the Fifteenth to the Eighteenth Century*. Oxford University Press, 1959.

CLASEN, C.-P., *The Palatinate in European History 1555–1618*. Blackwell, 1963.

FAY, S. B., *The Rise of Brandenburg-Prussia to 1786*. Holt, Rinehart & Winston, 1965.

HOLBORN, HAJO, *A History of Modern Germany*, 2 vols. I. *The Reformation*. II. *1648–1840*. Eyre & Spottiswoode, 1965.

LAU, FRANZ and BIZER, ERNST, *A History of the Reformation in Germany in 1555*. A. & C. Black, 1969.

ROSENBERG, HANS, 'The rise of the Junkers in Brandenburg-Prussia, 1410–1653', *American Historical Review* 49 (1943).

SCHEVILL, FERDINAND, *The Great Elector*. University of Chicago Press, 1947.

The Thirty Years War

KAMEN, HENRY, 'The economic and social consequences of the Thirty Years War', *Past & Present* 39 (1968).

LIVET, G., *La Guerre de Trente Ans* (Que Sais-Je?). Paris, 1965.

PAGÈS, G., *The Thirty Years War*. A. & C. Black, 1971.

POLISENSKY, J. V., *The Thirty Years War*. Batsford, 1971.

RABB, T. K., 'The effects of the Thirty Years War on the German economy', *Journal of Modern History* 34 (1962).

RABB, T. K., ed., *The Thirty Years War: Problems of motive, extent and effect* (Problems in European Civilisation). Heath, 1964.

STEINBERG, S. H., *The Thirty Years War and the Conflict for European Hegemony 1600–60* (Foundations of Modern History). Edward Arnold, 1966.

WEDGWOOD, C. V., *The Thirty Years War*. Cape, 1938.

Spain

CASEY, JAMES, 'Moriscos and the Depopulation of Valencia', *Past & Present* 50 (1971).

CHUDOBA, B., *Spain and the Empire 1519–1643*. Chicago University Press, 1952.

ELLIOTT, J. H., *The Revolt of the Catalans*. Cambridge University Press, 1963.

ELLIOTT, J. H., *Imperial Spain 1469–1716*. Edward Arnold, 1963.

ELLIOTT, J. H., 'Revolts in the Spanish monarchy', in Robert Forster and Jack P. Greene, eds., *Preconditions of Revolution in Early Modern Europe*. Johns Hopkins Press, 1972.

HARGREAVES-MAWDSLEY, W. N., ed., *Spain under the Bourbons, 1700–1833* (History in Depth). Macmillan, 1973.

HESS, ANDREW C., 'The Moriscos: an Ottoman fifth column in sixteenth-century Spain, *American Historical Review* 74 (1968).

HESS, ANDREW C., 'The evolution of the Ottoman seaborne empire in the age of the oceanic discoveries, 1453–1525', *American Historical Review* 75 (1970).

KAMEN, HENRY, *The Spanish Inquisition*. Mentor Books, 1968.

KAMEN, HENRY, *The War of Succession in Spain, 1700–1715*. Wiedenfeld & Nicolson, 1969.

LIVERMORE, H. V., *A New History of Portugal*. Cambridge University Press, 1966.

LYNCH, J., 'Philip II and the Papacy'. *Transactions of the Royal Historical Society* (1961).

LYNCH, J., *Spain under the Habsburgs*, 2 vols. I. *Empire and Absolutism 1516–98*. II. *Spain and America 1598–1700*. Blackwell, 1965, 1969.

MARQUES, A. H. DE OLIVEIRA, *History of Portugal*. 2 vols. Columbia University Press, 1973.

MATTINGLY, GARRETT, *The Defeat of the Spanish Armada*. Cape, 1959.

ORTIZ, A. D., *The Golden Age of Spain, 1516–1659*. Weidenfeld & Nicolson, 1971.

PARKER, GEOFFREY, 'Spain, her enemies and the revolt of the Nether-lands, 1559–1648', *Past & Present* 49 (1970).

PARKER, GEOFFREY, *The Army of Flanders and the Spanish Road 1567–1659*. Cambridge University Press, 1972.

PARKER, GEOFFREY, 'Mutiny and discontent in the Spanish army of Flanders, 1572–1607', *Past & Present* 58 (1973).

PIERSON, PETER O'MALLEY, 'A Commander for the Armada,' *Mariner's Mirror* 55 (1969).

THOMPSON, I. A. A., 'The Armada and administrative reform: the Spanish council of war in the reign of Philip II', *English Historical Review* 82 (1967).

The Netherlands

BARBOUR, VIOLET, *Capitalism in Amsterdam in the Seventeenth Century*. University of Michigan Press, 1963.

CARR, RAYMOND, 'Two Swedish financiers', in H. E. Bell and R. L. Ollard, *Historical Essays 1600–1750*. A. & C. Black, 1963.

DILLEN, J. G. VAN, 'Amsterdam's role in seventeenth-century Dutch politics and its economic background', in J. S. Bromley and E. H. Kossmann eds., *Britain and the Netherlands*, vol. II. Gröningen, J. B. Wolters, 1964.

GEYL, P., *The Revolt of the Netherlands*. Benn, 1932.

GEYL, P., *The Netherlands in the Seventeenth Century*. Part 1: *1609–48*. Part 2: *1648–1715*. Benn, 1961, 1964.

GEYL, P., *Orange and Stuart 1641–72*. Weidenfeld & Nicolson, 1969.

HALEY, K. H. D., *The Dutch in the Seventeenth Century*. Thames & Hudson, 1972.

HOBOKEN, W. J. VAN, 'The Dutch West India Company: the political background of its rise and decline', in J. S. Bromley and E. H. Kossmann, eds., *Britain and the Netherlands*, vol. I. Chatto & Windus, 1960.

HUIZINGA, J. H., *Dutch Civilisation in the Seventeenth Century*. Collins, Fontana, 1968.

KOENIGSBERGER, H. G., 'The organisation of revolutionary parties in France and the Netherlands during the sixteenth century', *Journal of Modern History* 27 (1955).

PARKER, GEOFFREY, 'Spain, her enemies and the revolt of the Netherlands 1559–1648', *Past & Present* 49 (1970).

ROORDA, D. J., 'The ruling classes in Holland in the seventeenth century', in *Britain and the Netherlands*, vol. II (see above).

SCHOFFER, I., 'Protestantism in flux during the revolt of the Netherlands', in *Britain and the Netherlands*, vol. II (see above).

SMIT, J. W., *The Present Position of Studies regarding the Revolt of the Netherlands*, in *Britain and the Netherlands*, vol. I (see above).

SMIT, J. W., 'The Netherlands Revolution', in Robert Forster and Jack P. Greene, eds., *Preconditions of Revolution in Early Modern Europe*. Johns Hopkins Press, 1972.

TEX, JAN DEN, *Oldenbarnevelt*. 2 vols. Cambridge University Press, 1973.

WEDGWOOD, C. V., *William the Silent*. Cape, 1944.

WILSON, CHARLES, *The Dutch Republic*. Weidenfeld & Nicolson, 1968.

France

General

BOSHER, J. F., ed., *French Government and Society, 1500–1850*. Athlone Press, 1973.

COGNET, L., *Le Jansénisme* (Que Sais-Je?). Paris, 1961.

GOUBERT, P., *The Ancien Régime*. Weidenfeld & Nicolson, 1972.

LOUGH, J. W., *Introduction to Seventeenth-century France*. Longman, 1970.

MALAND, DAVID, *Culture and Society in Seventeenth-century France*. Batsford, 1970.

MANDROU, R., *Introduction à la France moderne, 1500–1640*. Paris, 1961.

MANDROU, R., *Classes et luttes de classes en France au début du XVIIᵉ siècle*. Messina, 1965.

MANDROU, R., *La France aux XVIIᵉ et XVIIIᵉ Siècles* (Nouvelle Clio). Paris, 1967.

PAGÈS, G., *La Naissance du Grand Siècle*. Paris, 1948.

PORCHNEV, E., 'The legend of the seventeenth century in French history', *Past & Present* 8 (1955).

SHENNAN, J. H., *The Parlement of Paris*. Eyre & Spottiswoode, 1968.

SHENNAN, J. H., *Government and Society in France, 1461–1661* (Historical Problems: Studies & Documents). Allen & Unwin, 1969.

TREASURE, G. R. R., *Seventeenth-Century France*. Rivingtons, 1966.

WALLACE-HADRILL, J. M. and MCMANNERS, JOHN, *France: government and society*. Methuen, 1957.

Sixteenth Century

DOUCET, R., *Les Institutions de la France au XVIᵉ siècle*. Paris, 1948.

GUNDERSHEIMER, WERNER L., ed., *French Humanism, 4170–1600* (Stratum Series). Macmillan, 1969.

KNECHT, R. J., 'The Concordat of 1516', *University of Birmingham Historical Journal* (1963).

KNECHT, R. J., *Francis I and Absolute Monarchy*. Historical Association, 1969.

KOENIGSBERGER, H. G., 'The organisation of revolutionary parties in France and the Netherlands during the sixteenth century', *Journal of Modern History* 27 (1955).

LIVET, G., *Les Guerres de Religion 1559–98* (Que Sais-Je?). Paris, 1966.

MAJOR J. RUSSELL, *Representative Institutions in Renaissance France, 1421–1559*. University of Wisconsin Press, 1960.

SALMON, J. H. M., ed., *The French Wars of Religion: how important were religious factors?* (Problems in European Civilisation). Heath, 1968.

SUTHERLAND, N. M., *The French Secretaries of State in the Age of Catherine de Medici*. Athlone Press, 1962.

SUTHERLAND, N. M., *Catherine de Medici and the Ancien Regime*. Historical Association, 1966.

SUTHERLAND, N. M., *The Massacre of St Bartholomew and the European Conflict 1559–1572*. Macmillan, 1973.

WOLFE, MARTIN, *The Fiscal System of Renaissance France*. Yale University Press, 1973.

Henry IV and Louis XIII

BUISSERET, D., 'The legend of Sully', *Historical Journal* 5 (1962).

BUISSERET, D., 'A stage in the development of the French Intendants: the reign of Henri IV', *Historical Journal* 9 (1966).

BUISSERET, D., *Sully and the Growth of Centralised Government in France*. Eyre & Spottiswoode, 1968.

BURCKHARDT, C. J., *Richelieu and his Age*, 3 vols. Allen & Unwin, 1967, 1970, 1972.

CHURCH, WILLIAM F., *Richelieu and Reason of State*. Princeton University Press, 1973.

HAUSER, H., *La Pensée et l'action économique du Cardinal de Richelieu*. Paris, 1944.

HUXLEY, ALDOUS, *Grey Eminence* [Father Joseph]. Chatto & Windus, 1941.

KOSSMANN, E. H., *La Fronde*. Leiden, 1954.
See the critical article by P. Goubert, 'Kossmann et le Fronde', *Annales* 13 (1958).

LUBLINSKAYA, A. D., *French Absolutism: the Crucial Phase 1620–29*, Cambridge University Press, 1968.
See the critical article by David Parker, 'The social foundations of French Absolutism 1610–30', *Past & Present* 53 (1971).

MOOTE, A. LLOYD, 'The French crown versus its judicial and financial officials, 1615–83', *Journal of Modern History* 34 (1962).

MOOTE, A. LLOYD, *The Revolt of the Judges: the Parlement of Paris and the Fronde 1643–52*. Princeton University Press, 1971.

MOUSNIER, R., *La Venalité des Offices sous Henri IV et Louis XIII*. Rouen, 1946.

MOUSNIER, R., *The Assassination of Henry IV: the Tyrannicide Problem and the Consolidation of the French Monarchy in the early Seventeenth Century*. Faber & Faber, 1973.

MOUSNIER, R., 'The Fronde' in Robert Forster and Jack P. Greene, eds., *Preconditions of Revolution in Early Modern Europe*. Johns Hopkins Press, 1972.

RANUM, OREST A., *Richelieu and the Councillors of Louis XIII*. Oxford University Press, 1963.

TAPIÉ, V. L., *La France de Louis XIII et de Richelieu*. Paris, 1967.

TREASURE, G. R. R., *Cardinal Richelieu and the Development of Absolutism*. A. & C. Black, 1972.

WEDGWOOD, C. V., *Richelieu and the French Monarchy*. English Universities Press, 1949.

Louis XIV

ANDRÉ, L., *Michel Le Tellier et Louvois*. Paris, 1942.

ASHLEY, MAURICE, *Louis XIV and the Greatness of France*. English Universities Press, 1946.

CHURCH, WILLIAM F., ed., *The Greatness of Louis XIV: myth or reality?* (Problems in European Civilisation). Heath, 1959.

COLE, C. W., *Colbert and a Century of French Mercantilism*, 2 vols. Cass, 1965.

GOUBERT, P., *Louis XIV and Twenty Million Frenchmen*. Allen Lane: the Penguin Press, 1966.

HATTON, R., *Louis XIV and his World*. Thames & Hudson, 1972.

HATTON, R. and BROMLEY, J. S., eds., *William III and Louis XIV 1680–1720*. Liverpool University Press, 1968.

JUDGE, H. G., 'Church and State under Louis XIV', *History* 45 (1960).

JUDGE, H. G., *Louis XIV* (Problems & Perspectives). Longmans, 1965.

MANDROU, ROBERT, *Louis XIV en son Temps*. Paris, 1972.

MÉTHIVIER, HUBERT, *Le Siècle de Louis XIV* (Que Sais-Je?). Paris, 1968.

OGG, DAVID, *Louis XIV*. (Home University Library.) Oxford University Press, 1933.

ORCIBAL, J., *Louis XIV et les Protestants*. Paris, 1951.

RANUM, OREST A., *Paris in the Age of Absolutism*. Wiley, 1969.

RANUM, OREST and PATRICIA, *The Century of Louis XIV* (Documentary History of Western Civilization). Macmillan, 1973.

ROWEN, HERBERT H., 'Arnauld de Pomponne: Louis XIV's moderate minister', *American Historical Review* 61 (1956).

RULE, JOHN C., ed., *Louis XIV and the Craft of Kingship*. Ohio State University Press, 1969.

SAGNAC, P., *La Formation de la Société française moderne*: vol. I. *La Société et la Monarchie absolue, 1661–1715*. Paris, 1945.

WOLF, JOHN B., *Louis XIV*. Gollancz, 1968.

WOLF, JOHN B., ed., *Louis XIV* (World Profiles). Macmillan, 1973.

ZELLER, G., *Les Temps modernes: de Louis XIV à 1789* (Histoire des relations internationales). Paris, 1955.

ZIEGLER, G., *The Court of Versailles in the Reign of Louis XIV*. Allen & Unwin, 1966.

Scandinavia

DUNKLEY, E. H., *The Reformation in Denmark*. S.P.C.K., 1949.

HATTON, R., *Charles XII of Sweden*. Weidenfeld & Nicolson, 1968.

JEANNIN, PIERRE, *L'Europe du Nord-Ouest du Nord aux XVIIe et XVIIIe Siècles* (Nouvelle Clio). Paris, 1969.

KRABBE, L., *Histoire du Danemark*. Paris, 1950.

ROBERTS, MICHAEL, *Gustavus Adolphus: a history of Sweden 1611–32*. Longmans, 1953.

ROBERTS, MICHAEL, 'Queen Christina and the "General Crisis" ', *Past & Present* 22 (1962).

ROBERTS, MICHAEL, 'Charles XI', *History* 50 (1965).

ROBERTS, MICHAEL, *Essays in Swedish History*. Weidenfeld & Nicolson, 1967.

ROBERTS, MICHAEL, *Sweden as a Great Power, 1611–97* (Documents of Modern History). Edward Arnold, 1968.

ROBERTS, MICHAEL, *The Early Vasas: a history of Sweden, 1523–1611*. Cambridge University Press, 1968.

ROBERTS, MICHAEL, *Gustavus Adolphus and the Rise of Sweden*. English Universities Press, 1973.

Russia, Eastern Europe, and the Turks

Russia

BLUM, J., *Lord and Peasant in Russia*. Princeton University Press, 1961.

CLARKSON, J. D., *A History of Russia from the Ninth Century*. Longmans, 1962.

CRACRAFT, JAMES, *The Church Reform of Peter the Great*. Macmillan, 1971.

FENNELL, J. L. I., *Ivan the Great of Moscow*. Macmillan, 1961.

KLYUCHEVSKY, VASILI, *Peter the Great*. Macmillan, 1958.

LEWITTER, L. R., 'Russia, Poland and the Baltic 1692–1721', *Historical Journal* 11 (1968).

RIASANOVSKY, N. V., *A History of Russia*. Oxford Unviersity Press, 1963.

SUMNER, B. H., *Peter the Great and the Ottoman Empire*. Blackwell, 1950.

SUMNER, B. H., *Peter the Great and the Emergence of Russia*. English Universities Press, 1970.

VERNADSKY, G., *The Tsardom of Moscow 1547–1682*, 2 vols. Yale University Press, 1969.

Eastern Europe

ALLEN, W. E. D., *The Ukraine*. Cambridge University Press, 1940.

BLUM, J., 'The rise of serfdom in Eastern Europe', *American Historical Review* 62 (1957).

HALECKI, O., *Borderlands of Western Civilisation: A history of east central Europe*. Ronald Press Co. (New York), 1952.

MACARTNEY, C. A., *Hungary: a short history*. Edinburgh University Press, 1966.

MCNEILL, W. H., *Europe's Steppe Frontier 1500–1800*. University of Chicago Press, 1964.

REDDAWAY, W. F., ed., *Cambridge History of Poland*; I. *From the Origins to 1696*: II. *1697–1933*. Cambridge University Press, 1950, 1941.

STAVRIANOS, L., *The Balkans since 1453*. Holt, Rinehart & Winston, 1958.

The Turks

ANDERSON, M. S., *The Eastern Question, 1423–1774*. Macmillan, 1966.

COLES, P. H., *The Ottoman Impact on Europe*. Thames & Hudson, 1968.

INALKIK, HALIL, *The Ottoman Empire: the Classical Age, 1300–1600*. Weidenfeld & Nicolson, 1973.

KORTEPETER, C. MAX, *Ottoman Imperialism during the Reformation*. University of London Press, 1973.

LEWIS, B., *The Emergence of Modern Turkey*. Oxford University Press, 1968.

LEWIS, B., ed., *The Encyclopedia of Islam* (new edn in progress). Luzac, 1970.

MERRIMAN, R. B., *Suleiman the Magnificent, 1520–66*. Harvard University Press, 1944.

PALLIS, A., *In the Days of the Janissaries*. Hutchinson, 1951.

RUNCIMAN, S., *The Fall of Constantinople*. Cambridge University Press, 1961.

VAUGHAN, D. M., *Europe and the Turk: a pattern of alliances, 1350–1700*. Liverpool University Press, 1954.

WITTEK, P., *The Rise of the Ottoman Empire*. Royal Asiatic Society Monographs XXIII, 1938; new edn, Luzac, 1965.

New Worlds

BOXER, C. R., *The Portuguese Seaborne Empire, 1415–1825*. Penguin Books, 1973.

BOXER, C. R., *The Dutch Seaborne Empire*. Penguin Books, 1973.

CHAUNU, PIERRE, *Conquête et Exploitation des nouveaux Mondes, XVIe Siècle* (Nouvelle Clio). Paris, 1970.

CIPOLLA, CARLO M., *European Culture and Overseas Expansion*. Penguin Books, 1970.

CORTES, HERNAN, *Letters from Mexico* [Correspondence between Cortes and Charles V, 1519–26]. Oxford University Press, 1973.

CRONE, G. R., *The Discovery of America*. Hamish Hamilton, 1969.

ELLIOTT, J. H., *The Old World and the New, 1492–1650*. Cambridge University Press, 1970.

HALE, J. R., *Renaissance Exploration*. BBC, 1968.

HANKE, LEWIS, *The Spanish Struggle for Justice in the Conquest of America*. University of Pennsylvania Press, for American Historical Association, 1949.

HEMMING, JOHN, *The Conquest of the Incas*. Macmillan, 1970.

INNES, HAMMOND, *The Conquistadors*. Collins, 1970.

JENSEN, DE LAMAR, ed., *The Expansion of Europe* (Problems in European Civilisation). Heath, 1967.

JOHNSON, DOUGLAS, ed., *The Making of the Modern World: I. Europe discovers the World*. Benn, 1971.

MAURO, F., *L'Expansion européenne 1600–1870* (Nouvelle Clio). Paris, 1964.

MORISON, S. E., *The European Discovery of America: the northern voyages A.D. 500–1600*. Oxford University Press, 1971.

PARRY, J. H., *The Age of Reconnaissance*. Weidenfeld & Nicolson, 1963.

PARRY, J. H., *The Spanish Seaborne Empire*. Penguin Books, 1973.

PARRY, J. H., ed., *The European Reconnaissance* [Documents]. Macmillan, 1968.

SCAMMELL, G. V., 'The new worlds and Europe in the sixteenth century', *Historical Journal* 12 (1969).

Thought, Society, and the Economy

Thought

ALLEN, J. W., *Political Thought in the Sixteenth Century*. Methuen, 1928.

CHURCH, W. F., *Constitutional Thought in Sixteenth Century France*. Harvard University Press, 1941.

EVANS, R. J. W., *Rudolf II and his World: a study in intellectual history, 1576–1612*. Oxford University Press, 1973.

FRANKLIN, JULIAN H., *Jean Bodin and the Rise of Aboslutist Theory*. Cambridge University Press, 1973.

HAZARD, PAUL, *The European Mind 1680–1715*. Penguin Books, 1964.

KAMEN, HENRY, *The Rise of Toleration*. Weidenfeld & Nicolson, 1967.

MAZZEO, J. A., *Renaissance and Revolution: the remaking of European thought*. Methuen, 1969.

WALKER, D. P., *The Ancient Theology: studies in Christian Platonism from the fifteenth to the eighteenth Century*. Duckworth, 1973.

YATES, FRANCES A., *The Rosicrucian Enlightenment*. Routledge & Kegan Paul, 1973.

Society

ANDERSON, ROBERT T., *Traditional Europe: a study in anthropology and history*. Prentice-Hall International, 1971.

GATELY, M. O.; MOOTE, A. LLOYD; and WILLS, J. E. jnr., 'Seventeenth Century peasant "Furies": some problems of comparative history', *Past & Present* 51 (1971).

GLASS, D. V. and REVELLE, ROGER, eds., *Population and Social Change*. Edward Arnold, 1972.

MOUSNIER, R., *Problèmes de stratification sociale*. Paris, 1968.

The Economy

BURKE, PETER, ed., *Economy and Society in Early Modern Europe* [Essays from *Annales*]. Routledge & Kegan Paul, 1972.

CARUS-WILSON, E. M., *Essays in Economic History*. I. [Articles from the *Economic History Review*]. Edward Arnold, 1954.

COLEMAN, D. C., ed., *Revisions in Mercantilism* (Debates in Economic History). Methuen, 1969.

DOLLINGER, PHILIPPE, *The German Hansa*. Macmillan, 1970.

GREEN, ROBERT W., ed., *Protestantism and Capitalism: the Weber thesis and its critics* (Problems in European Civilisation). Heath, 1959.

MAURO, F., *Le XVIᵉ Siècle européen: aspects économiques* (Nouvelle Clio). Paris, 1966.

PULLAN, BRIAN, ed., *Crisis and Change in the Venetian Economy* (Debates in Economic History). Macmillan, 1958.

Science and the Arts

Science

BOAS, MARIE, *The Scientific Renaissance, 1450–1630*. Collins, 1962.

BULLOUGH, V. L., ed., *The Scientific Revolution* (European Problem Studies). Holt, Rinehart & Winston, 1970.

BUTTERFIELD, HERBERT, *The Origins of Modern Science, 1300–1800*. Bell, 1949.

CROMBIE, A. C., *Augustine to Galileo:* II. *Science in the late Middle Ages and early Modern Times, 13th to 17th Centuries*. Penguin Books, 1969.

DIJKSTERHUIS, E. J., *The Mechanisation of the World Picture*. Oxford University Press, 1961.

HALL, A. R., *The Scientific Revolution, 1500–1800*. Longman, 1954.

HALL, A. R., *From Galileo to Newton, 1630–1720*. Collins, 1963.

KEARNEY, H., *Origins of the Scientific Revolution* (Problems & Perspectives). Longmans, 1964.

KEARNEY, H., *Science and Change, 1500–1700*. Wiedenfeld & Nicolson, 1971.

KOESTLER, A., *The Sleepwalkers*. Penguin Books, 1970.

KOYRÉ, ALEXANDRE, *From the Closed World to the Infinite Universe*. Johns Hopkins Press, 1957.

SMITH, A. G. R., *Science and Society in the Sixteenth and Seventeenth Centuries* (Library of European Civilisation). Thames & Hudson, 1972.

WIGHTMAN, W. P. D., *Science in a Renaissance Society*. Hutchinson, 1972.

The Arts

THE PELICAN HISTORY OF ART. Penguin Books.

BLUNT, A., *Art and Architecture in France, 1500–1700* (1953)

FREEDBERG, S. J., *Painting in Italy 1500–1600* (1971)

GERSON, HORST and KUILE, E. H. TER, *Art and Architecture in Belgium 1600–1800* (1960)

HEMPEL, E., *Baroque Art and Architecture in Central Europe: Germany, Austria, Switzerland, Hungary, Czechoslovakia and Poland* (1965)

KUBLER, G. and SORIA, P., *Art and Architecture in Spain and Portugal and their American Dominions 1500–1800* (1959)

OSTEN, G. VON DER and VEY, H., *Painting and Sculpture in Germany and the Netherlands 1500–1600* (1969)

ROSENBERG, J.; SLIVE, S.; and KUILE, E. H. TER, *Dutch Art and Architecture 1600–1800* (1966)

WITTKOWER, R., *Art and Architecture in Italy 1600–1750* (1958)

BERENSON, BERNARD, *Italian Painters of the Renaissance*. Collins, Fontana, 1969.

CHASTEL, ANDRÉ, *The Golden Age of the Renaissance: Italy 1460–1500*. Thames & Hudson, 1965.

CHASTEL, ANDRÉ, *Crisis of the Renaissance, 1520–1600*. Zwemmer, 1968.

HASKELL, F., *Patrons and Painters*. Chatto & Windus, 1963.

KITSON, MICHAEL, *The Age of Baroque*. Hamlyn, 1967.

LEVEY, M., *Early Renaissance*. Penguin Books, 1970.

PORTOGHESI, PAOLO, *Rome of the Renaissance*. Phaidon, 1972.

TAPIÉ, V. L., *The Age of Grandeur: Baroque and Classicism in Europe*. Weidenfeld & Nicolson, 1960.

TREVO-RROPER, H. R., *The Plunder of the Arts in the Seventeenth Century*. Thames & Hudson, 1970.

WOLFFLIN, HEINRICH, *Renaissance and Baroque*. Collins, Fontana, 1964.

Index

THE LIBRARY
ST. MARY'S COLLEGE OF MARYLAND
ST. MARY'S CITY, MARYLAND 20686

079138